# A Mind-blowing Birding Trip to a Planet called Earth

NIGEL WHEATLEY

Copyright © 2021 Nigel Wheatley

All rights reserved.

ISBN: 9798684185144

# DEDICATION

This book is dedicated to Planet Earth

This book is for my boys, Ned and Tom

# CONTENTS

Acknowledgements

| | | |
|---|---|---|
| 1 | Early Days | 1 |
| 2 | Twitching | 25 |
| 3 | Camargue and Pyrenees | 94 |
| 4 | Pakistan, India and Nepal | 102 |
| 5 | Texas | 166 |
| 6 | Kenya | 195 |
| 7 | Malaya, Borneo, Sulawesi and Java | 264 |
| 8 | Venezuela and Chile | 300 |
| 9 | Hong Kong | 354 |
| 10 | Australia | 377 |
| 11 | The Gambia | 416 |
| 12 | California and The Grand Canyon | 424 |
| 13 | Cuba | 437 |
| 14 | Malawi and Zambia | 452 |
| 15 | Peru | 478 |
| 16 | Gabon, São Tomé and Príncipe | 506 |
| 17 | Mexico | 537 |

| 18 | Kenya, Uganda and Tanzania | 563 |
|---|---|---|
| 19 | The Falkland Islands, South Georgia and Antarctica | 609 |
| 20 | New Guinea | 644 |
| 21 | The Local Patch | 716 |
|    | St Agnes, Isles of Scilly | 727 |
|    | St Mary's, Isles of Scilly | 755 |
|    | St Just, Cornwall | 773 |

| Bibliography | 810 |
|---|---|

# EDITOR'S NOTE

## Capitalizing of birds' and other animals' names

Since so many kinds of birds and other animals are mentioned in this book I have followed standard scientific practice of capitalizing the names of species. There are over 10,000 species of birds on Earth and capitalizing their names, as well as those of other animals, brings clarity to the text. For example, there are many black birds but the (Eurasian) Blackbird is a particular species, and most sunbirds could be described as beautiful but there is one species which is actually named Beautiful Sunbird. Readers who are unfamiliar with birds and other animals may find all the capital letters distracting at first but I hope they will soon become accustomed to them.

## ACKNOWLEDGEMENTS

I would like to thank the many birders who have travelled the world and recorded and published their experiences for the benefit of others, usually in the form of fascinating trip reports, and all the people who have accompanied me on my own trips, helped me to see so many great birds and other wildlife, and made those trips so enjoyable and exciting.

*Blackcap, Robinswood Hill, Gloucester, England, 12th April 1976*

# 1

# EARLY DAYS

I arrived on this blue dot in space in the year '1960'. The planet was renowned for its beautiful oceans, landscapes, birds and other wildlife but there did not seem to be anything amazing in or around my parents' garden in Gloucester, England or around the nearby school which I attended. Perhaps I was too young and too busy playing to notice. Certainly, when I was old enough to roam the meadows and woods on Robinswood Hill, a small outlier of the Cotswolds at the end of our road, on my own, I started noticing colourful flowers, butterflies and birds.

My friends and I used to make dens and defend them against imaginary enemies with spears made from the straight stems of elderberry bushes. We climbed trees, played in farmers' haystacks, scrumped their apples, caught frogs and toads and newts, and ripped our clothes and skins in the great thickets of bramble and hawthorn trying to get to birds' nests and eggs. I think it was the tantalizing glimpses of colourful mysteries seen flying off that got me all excited about birds; blue-winged Jays, red-breasted Bullfinches and Yellowhammers perhaps, or it might have been the exquisite Blue Tits looking for caterpillars on Dad's cabbages. Whatever it was, I soon realized that taking the eggs of such beautiful birds was a terrible thing to do and that I would much rather look at the birds than their eggs in my old cooking tin of sawdust.

I am glad to say that my egg collection never reached twenty. At the age of fourteen with some pocket money from my parents and the rest saved from my paper round I bought a pair of cheap *Prinz* binoculars and instead of hanging about outside the youth club with the friends who used to play with me on the hill I strode there alone. On my first bird watching trip with binoculars and notebook one day in late March I could not find many birds but I did see my first Goldcrest, a tiny green delight with big dark eyes. A few days later I was back, climbing up through the oak trees rising from the steep slope of Matson Wood, lured by the loud, laughing song of what turned out to be a 'Yaffle', a big, colourful Green Woodpecker which looked so colourful through binoculars. As I scrambled through the undergrowth a pigeon-sized rich brown bird burst softly from my feet and with deep down-strokes of its broad wings zigzagged away through the maze of tree trunks. Whump, whump, whump went the rounded wings, just like my heart. I had no idea what it was. With my mind whirling with the possibilities I walked on, stopping to look at a Great Spotted Woodpecker, a shocking black, white and red bird. I forgot how cold it was until I reached the top of the slope and the bitter breeze hit me. Snow began to fall; beautiful thick snow, in enormous flakes. It settled quickly. Mother would be worried. I thought I had better head for home, where I discovered I had been very fortunate to have seen a Woodcock, which my new *Observer's Book of BIRDS* described as 'secretive and usually remains under cover'. To me it was something rare, beautiful and mysterious, and I thought to myself, if bird watching was always going to be so exciting then that was how I was going to live my life.

Many more wanders and wonders followed. At the age of 16 I had an unbelievable amount of energy, burnt up bird watching, playing every sport available at school, and yearning for a girlfriend, not that I could look a girl in the eye let alone speak to one. While my friends rarely left their bedrooms I was out before first light in time to experience the incredible volume and variety of sound called the dawn chorus. 'Cuck-oo, cuck-oo' carried across the slopes with the scent of May blossom. Warblers called Chiffchaffs 'chiff-chaffed'. Woodpeckers drummed and Nuthatches whistled in the woods. Wrens blasted out their trills in the scrub where Whitethroats sang their scratchy warbles again and again, and the sweet, wavering whistles of Willow Warblers seemed to rise from the top of every tree. More than once I carefully stalked, by moving closer while the bird sang, a Grasshopper Warbler, until I was close enough to look down the red gape as it reeled away.

*Nuthatch, Robinswood Hill, Gloucester, England, 16th April 1977*

My parents were shocked when I pleaded to be allowed to get up at three in the morning so I could be in my favourite place on the hill at dawn. When I returned mid-morning with all my incredible news they were not interested. I felt crushed, but not for long. I might have been an odd boy but I was happy. I felt so alive, roaming those woods and meadows. Sometimes I would get home and head straight for the library with my Dad. I read every book about birds and other wildlife at least once, some many times. The one I had out on virtually permanent loan was *The Way to an Island* by R. M. Lockley, probably because he too was considered to be a 'strange boy ... going after birds'. He found his way on what he named 'Moorhen Island', in a swamp near Southerndown in South Wales. I found my way on Robinswood Hill. He dreamed of living on a bigger island when he was older and he did, that wild one off Pembrokeshire called Skokholm. I dreamed of seeing the birds, animals and wild places in the pictures plastered across my bedroom wall.

Some birds I dreamed of turned up on the hill, mostly on their way north in spring; sparkling Redstarts, shy Ring Ouzels, and once, two new birds in two minutes; a stunning male Pied Flycatcher and a Tree Pipit. I saw those two with Roy Hunter, the man who walked the other side of the hill, and who helped me to identify birds, especially their songs. The bird I loved the most was the Blackcap, a summer visitor to the hill. The first time I saw one was an April morning in Matson Wood. The clouds were dispersing. Rays of warm sunshine broke through the canopy. I was propped up against an old oak at the edge of a brambly glade where a lovely melodious warble was being belted out again and again, with barely a pause, from deep inside the thickest tangle. The bird, whatever bird it was for I did not know at the time, was singing its head off. I gripped my binoculars tightly and held them on the tip of my nose, peering over the top in readiness for a movement, ready to lock on to the bird as quickly as possible, waiting with incredible excitement to catch sight of something I had never seen before. The pure, clear, fluty whistles continued to pour forth. I saw nothing. My mind was empty of everything except the hope of seeing the songster. I raised my binoculars once more, aimed them at the sound and focused on the front then the middle then the back of the tangle, scanning left and right and up and down, again and again. At long last I saw a flicker. I tucked my binoculars tightly into my eye sockets and focused and refocused until ... there it was. The bird was side-on and the whole of its head seemed to be open, pointing to the treetops. Its throat throbbed with every note, its whole body was all of a quiver, and the raised black feathers on the top of its head were vibrating in high excitement. 'A Blackcap', I said in my head, 'It must be a Blackcap!' It was a moving experience being with that wild bird in that wood, a primordial one in which I felt part of nature, and I was totally absorbed until the bird suddenly stopped singing. The silence that hit the wood was shocking. The Blackcap shook its soft grey feathers back into place and looked immaculate, as if it had just been created, there and then, in that glade, not as if it had just flown from Africa. Then it was gone, like something too good to be true.

Then half the wood was gone too. At that time in my life there was no place I would rather have been than in that wood. It was such a happy and peaceful place for me but others thought they could make some money chopping half of it down and replacing it with a dry ski-slope, and some other people thought they could make even more money by ripping out the meadows surrounding the wood and building a golf course and housing estates. Where once birds sang and butterflies flew, where I felt truly alive, where I learnt to love beauty, where I found my way, there was now a plastic ski-slope, and barren fairways and little red-brick boxes people are supposed to be happy living in. They call this progress.

The hill was my local patch, the place I could walk to from my front door and went a wandering in search of birds, although I did see some very exciting birds elsewhere, mainly thanks to my driver, my Dad. We had some fun jumping muddy creeks at Frampton-on-Severn, not always successfully in dad's case, just to see some distant dots on the miles of mud out on the Severn Estuary. He was with me for the highlight of my life up to that point, the day shortly before my sixteenth birthday, when an Osprey soared over that mud. Dad liked a walk so he didn't stay with me at Slimbridge he just dropped me off because I used to sit for hours in the bone-chilling Holden Tower, a house-sized, two-storey wooden hide overlooking the grass fields and saltmarsh known as The Dumbles. While I was there great flocks of Curlews, Lapwings, Wigeon, White-fronted Geese and Bewick's Swans were disturbed by Merlins and Peregrines, and I loved every minute of it. A few times, Mr Lowis, my A Level Biology teacher, would decide a trip to Slimbridge was as good a lesson as any so we raced down there in his Citroën 2CV, on two wheels around the roundabouts.

He was a great teacher and an A level in Biology meant I could take a degree in Biology down at Portsmouth Polytechnic in Hampshire. There my local patch became the gravel seafront from Southsea, where I lived, to Eastney, at the entrance to Langstone Harbour, perhaps better described as a giant, almost square-shaped, estuary, and best viewed from Farlington Marshes, a bus ride away, where I spent most of my time what I now called birding.

On a form for first-year students I stated that I would prefer to share a room, preferably with someone interested in birds. That someone was Paul Anderson, a strapping lad in *Green Flash* tennis shoes, jeans and T-shirt from Sunderland, known to his friends as Ando. Over a few pints the first evening we met I discovered he was madder about birds than me, had seen loads more and knew a lot more about them. Once I had tuned in to his strong accent and adjusted to the high speed at which he talked and the even faster rate at which he drank I started learning a lot about birds. We visited Farlington for the first time a couple of days later, seeing my first Ruff amongst the spectacular selection of shorebirds which graced the rough pasture, lagoons and surrounding mudflats almost all year round. We had many fine times there out on the marshes, especially on crisp, sunny, winter days. One shorebird not at Farlington was the Purple Sandpiper, a small flock of which spend the winters along the Southsea shoreline. At high tide in my day they roosted on the rusty steps at the very tip of the pier where it was possible to watch them snooze, almost at touching distance, by laying down on the boards above and looking through a gap.

A week or so after Ando and I settled into our small room there was a knock on the door. It was another tall lad called Rob and he wanted to know if he could sleep on our floor for a few nights because he had just got back to his room along the corridor and the art student he had been paired with was standing in front of a mirror painting a picture of himself in the nude. Rob, who was studying chartered surveying, slept on our floor and in our beds, sometimes all day, sometimes with girls, for the rest of the term and the next term and the term after that, the whole of the first year in fact. We didn't mind. He had a cassette tape player which although it worked only with a knife stuck down the side of the play button, provided us with some music, and sometimes he would go poaching and return with a few trout. He was interested in all wildlife and had a Badger's skull on his bedside table when I shared a room with him in the second year. When I visited his home in Chesham his mum frequently reminded him, with a shriek, that there was a cow's skull in a bucket in the garage, waiting to be cleaned up. He even liked rats and on one occasion, while birding with me and Ando, he ran across the black mud of a rubbish tip after a rat and sank up to his waist and we had to sit with him on the bus home. Another time he spotted the outline of a flatfish in a ditch at Farlington. After taking off his *Doc Martens* boots and socks he eased down into the water and crept carefully up to the fish, grabbing it quickly, only to find the stinking, long dead creature falling apart in his hands.

Rob was also learning karate and was almost obsessed with keeping fit for that. After acquiring a metre long stray concrete kerbstone he liked to lie on his back on the floor of our room and lift it up and down, not a good idea after a heavy drinking session in the *India Arms*, our local, and so it proved one late night when he dropped it on his chin and sported a deep gash for a while. 'Tombstoning', leaping off the Round Tower into the shallow channel at the entrance to Portsmouth Harbour, was one of several favourite dangerous pursuits he introduced to me, and that was fun until a friend emerged from the water with blood pouring from wounds to his face. Rob liked the water and once while swimming off Southsea Beach with Rodney, another friend, we were approached by the local lifeguard boat and told to turn back because we were in the shipping lane. Robert Roberts, that was his full name, was one of those people that something extraordinary seemed to happen to everyday, good or bad, and he was excellent company for it.

One dull January Sunday Rob and I wandered down to Eastney and saw a very confiding little grey and white bird spinning in the channel. We never had a clue what it was until we got back to our room and grilled our field guide and an envious Ando who reluctantly agreed it could only be a Grey Phalarope. Poor Ando, he had to wait almost two years to see one. It was an early October day at Farlington. On arrival we stopped as usual to talk to David Billet, famous for identifying the first Franklin's Gull, an American bird, to be seen in Europe, at Farlington, and for being notoriously difficult to get any information out of about rare or unusual birds on the marshes. He was fiercely protective of the reserve he had almost single-handedly set up and successfully managed for many years. Long ago, while protecting the marshes and the birds, he received a blast of shotgun pellets in his chest from what he described as a 'marsh cowboy'. As usual, that day Ando and I turned up he somewhat reluctantly told us about the best birds about and we were off, walking rapidly around the sea wall to a small lagoon known as The Deeps.

Snuggled down tight in the grassy bank below the horizon we watched in amazement as two dainty Grey Phalaropes, foraging frenetically with turning bodies, bobbing heads and darting bills, and seemingly oblivious to our presence (had they ever seen a human before?), drifted closer and closer until they were virtually within arm's length of us. It was a brilliant moment, another one of those all too rare times spent so close to something wild, and for so long.

*Grey Phalaropes, Farlington, Hampshire, England, 5th October 1981*

During our first winter in Southsea Rob persuaded me to join him on a trip to the north Norfolk coast where we hoped to see a few new birds such as Shore Larks, Twites, and Lapland and Snow Buntings. Hitchhiking was hard and we ended up walking most of the way between Cley and Snettisham, and having to retrace our steps when we reached wide, muddy creeks. On the last night it was so cold in the tent, pitched at the top of Hunstanton beach, that Rob decided to light the gas stove for a bit and if he had not noticed his sleeping bag was about to set alight we may never have seen our first Snow Buntings the next day, a superb flock of them along the strandline of said beach. We never saw any Shore Larks, Twites or Lapland Buntings.

In the meantime Ando had tested out the train service from Portsmouth to the New Forest and discovered a wonderful new place for birds. So I joined him on his second visit to the Bishop's Dyke area around Beaulieu Road railway station, our dropping off point. Within ten minutes I was listening to the lovely 'lu-lu-lu' of a Woodlark in high songflight. Shortly after, in the heather outside Denny Wood, I saw two singing male Dartford Warblers. Still in shock we then came across the wintering Great Grey Shrike, a frosty, prince of a bird perched atop a lone birch tree, to complete a hat-trick of new birds for me, all the better for being in a beautiful expanse of bogs, heather and woods. Many more visits followed, when any three of Great Grey Shrike, Dartford Warbler, Woodlark, Hen Harrier, Hawfinch and Lesser Spotted Woodpecker were sure to make a great day, and where one early May a male Montagu's Harrier flew low and slow across the heath. We walked on air for the rest of that day and the next day we celebrated with roast Pheasant, fresh roadkill found by our friend Tig, a fellow biology student who bore an uncanny resemblance to Tigger. Without a mark on it and still warm Tig plucked it and spit-roasted it over a great fire in a quiet glade and we ate it with our bare hands with great delight. We pitched the tent later and fell into contented sleep listening to Nightingales.

At the end of the same month Ando and I got a train to the other side of London then hitchhiked to East Anglia, and it was mostly hitching and not much hiking, for a change. "The thing I like most about this neck of the woods," a U.S. airman who dropped us off near the Suffolk coast said to us, "is the beautiful women." We didn't notice, we were birding hard from dawn to dusk, enjoying over a hundred different species of birds at the wonderful Minsmere, all celebrated in *The Eels Foot Inn*. Late on the second day, it was with some reluctance that we accepted a lift from Ando's friend Mickey Watson, to Potter Heigham in the Norfolk Broads where there was still time to have a few pints before pitching the tent on the soft grass outside the church.

We walked out to Hickling Broad at dawn the following morning and were very happy to find the Black-winged Stilt still present. The bird stepped delicately through the shallows on its ridiculously long red legs, picking insects off the surface with its needle of a bill, and it looked very exotic to our poorly travelled eyes. Neither of us had left the British mainland yet. Less exciting was our first Savi's Warbler shuffling up and down a reed stem while singing its buzzy reel. Near Weeting in The Brecks we got lost. Walking up a long track, we came across a Mole waddling across the ground in front of us in broad daylight. It was bald apart from a few stubborn black hairs at its rear end. Shortly afterwards, a police van came along. We knew not where we were but the policeman asked several questions about what we were doing there. Once he was convinced we were not egg collectors his tone changed dramatically and we were invited to clamber into the back of his van for a lift to the heath we were looking for, thee place to see thee Breckland bird. Our first Stone Curlews were like no bird we had seen before; sandy and streaked, with large yellow eyes evolved for nocturnal foraging over bare, stony ground.

The sign to our next destination read, 'Lakenheath 3½ miles' but they must have been East Anglian miles not normal miles because it took so long to reach the *Half Moon* the pub was no longer serving food. Fortunately the landlord could see our sorry state and made us some cheese rolls which went down very well with a couple of pints. We pitched our tent on a wide verge next to the quiet road out of the village.

Early the next morning, after a long walk, we entered a large poplar plantation. Apart from Garden Warblers singing here and there the 'wood' appeared to be lifeless. Farther in however, we thought we could hear, drifting eerily through the tall yellowy trees, the mellow, fluty whistles of the birds we had travelled so far to try and see. However, we had never heard them before and we could not be sure that the distant notes were not those of Blackbirds. As the mysterious, magical music drew us deeper into the trees we eventually agreed they must be 'the birds'. Clouds were drifting apart, warm, welcome sunlight was firing through the gaps in the canopy, and suddenly the wood was a spellbinding, exotic place which resounded with the sounds of Garden Warblers, Cuckoos, and the yodelling 'Weelo-Wee Weeo's of invisible orioles. Hearing them was easy, seeing them we had been warned, would be much, much harder. The birds were so perfectly camouflaged in the canopy of the yellow-leaved poplars hours went by without so much as a glimpse so we abandoned random wandering in favour of sitting still at the edge of a glade and very soon we were treated to a spectacle we have never forgotten. Four jet black and deep yellow male Golden Orioles chased two apple green females just a few paces in front of us, low down, their colours flashing only in flight, so perfectly matched were they to their secret home there in East Anglia.

# A MIND-BLOWING BIRDING TRIP TO A PLANET CALLED EARTH

*Golden Orioles, Lakenheath, Suffolk, England, 27th of May 1980*

Half way through our degree course Ando and I bumped into Nick Cobb, another chartered surveyor, who went by the name of Chief because he called everyone Chief. His interest in birds collapsed during his late teens but we soon unleashed a remarkable renewed enthusiasm with our birding tales, told numerous times. In late August he joined Ando, Steve Howat, Ando's friend from Sunderland and me on a long weekend at Minsmere, where we hoped to see some shorebirds and scarce landbird migrants. We saw at least 35 Spotted Redshanks, some Curlew Sandpipers and Little Stints, and best of all, my first

Wryneck, not quite what we had imagined, but still exciting, and we had a great time. On the way up we stayed at the famous disc jockey John Peel's house near Stowmarket. We were invited to do so by Ando's not quite girlfriend Lois, who had got the job as the Peel's nanny partly because her name was the same as that of *Superman's* girlfriend, *Superman* being a great favourite of the Peel's children. We thought we were in for a touch of luxury only Mr Peel thought otherwise and insisted we sleep in his barn not his farmhouse, where we were woken up the following morning by his large dog licking our faces.

The next night we decided the nearest place to Minsmere where we could get food and drink was a village called Yoxford which we reached via train, bus and a twelve mile walk to Minsmere and back, a tiring, thirsty day. By putting up tents late at night and packing up and leaving early in the morning we found we could camp almost anywhere on our birding adventures but we came unstuck in Yoxford. At the crack of dawn we were woken up by a tirade of abuse from a very irate man dressed in what one would expect for a wealthy landowner, an image completed with a dog and a walking stick. It appeared that the people in the pub the previous evening had given us directions to a luxuriant grassy mattress in the grounds of a country estate and the owner was very upset when he discovered two tents on his lawn. "Actually, I don't mind so much but whatever you do, do not shit on my property!" was the gist of his disgust.

We decided to stay in the public hide by the beach at Minsmere after that. The only trouble was it was two miles to the nearest pub *The Eels Foot Inn* which also did not sell food. One dark night we got so drunk on empty stomachs that on the long walk 'home' Chief got lost having a pee in a tall corn field, Steve gouged a chunk out of his shin when he stumbled into a fence, Ando fell over a stile which he claimed was a foot high on one side and three feet high on the other, and I decided to do 'An Alan Pascoe', a famous hurdler in the 1970s, sailing beautifully over a five-bar gate before landing in a wet ditch where Steve nearly killed me when he threw a large, pointed fence post in my direction to help me get out which landed very close to the side of my stomach. The other three laughed so much they collapsed on the ground. After rescuing me, we wobbled on until less than a hundred paces from 'home' Chief, who was the wobbliest when we left *The Eels Foot*, decided he could continue no more and lay down in a puddle to go to sleep. We managed to get him back to the hide where we were rudely awoken at dawn by a reserve warden who, as we scrambled into sitting upright birding positions at the hide windows, was given short shrift when he wondered aloud if we had been sleeping in the hide. Once he had moved on it was time for breakfast. A bar of chocolate and a packet of crisps for me, seven *Mars* bars for Ando.

Some migrating landbirds stopped off at Farlington during the spring and autumn but we heard Portland was much better, so, Chief and I decided to give the place a go on a September weekend. The moment we got off the bus we were told an Alpine Swift had just flown over. After an hour of hard walking in the direction it had flown, with our eyes skyward, we calmed down a bit and agreed that the bird was probably a long way away by then, so we turned around and began the long trudge back toward the southern end of the island. We had not got very far when a car pulled up beside us and the unknown driver said, "Get in. It's at Easton!", and it was still there when we arrived, swooping spectacularly along the rooftops of the only street, and we were able to watch our first Alpine Swift, a fantastic sight, for hours. The next morning we saw our first two Melodious Warblers and the next afternoon our first Aquatic Warbler. The latter was at Lodmoor where after three hours waiting we saw the bright buff and chocolate-striped bird materialize from a clump of hand-high *Juncus* for ten seconds then merge back into it and to our utter disbelief, despite the clump being surrounded by birders, disappear altogether. 'Maybe,' we thought, 'Aquatic Warblers are aquatic.' We slept in the Garden Hide at Portland. Well, Chief, who once fell asleep in a speeding Tuk Tuk in Delhi, did. I managed a couple of fitful hours.

On our next trip to Portland we decided we would be better off trying to sleep in the barn in the top fields. It was early October and Ando was with us and, as hoped, we saw a lingering juvenile Sabine's Gull. During long weekends at Portland from then on it was a stroll down from the barn to the Bill for a dawn seawatch, bread, biscuits, crisps and milk for brunch, miles of walking in search of migrant birds, pasty, chips and beans washed down with plenty of pints in the *Eight Kings* and a great night's sleep on the soft, warm straw in the barn. Nige Crook, a fanatical birder masquerading as a window cleaner from Havant near Farlington where we met him joined us on some weekends. He was poor but he had a car, a clapped-out old *Cortina*, and he would often switch the engine off on long downhill stretches of road to save fuel and money. He did not like sleeping in the barn because of the rats and we would often doze off laughing as he complained about them. Chief hid his rucksack with his sleeping bag in, under the bales in the barn one morning, so he didn't have to carry it around all day but when we got back late that night, a little worse for the drink, he couldn't find it because the farmer had added a couple of hundred more bales. We were in hysterics watching his cursing silhouette slowly disappearing into a giant hole, made by him flinging bale after bale out of it into the moonlit night in a desperate search for his sleeping bag. The tramp I jumped down on to from our lofty bed one morning was not so amused.

Two years after Rob and I visited the North Norfolk coast Ando and Chief joined me for a second attempt at seeing some Shore Larks, Twites and Lapland Buntings. It was even colder than the last time and we got so drunk one night we somehow managed to walk past the huge hides at Titchwell where we intended to sleep and ended up in the dunes where we put up the two-man tent. The next morning we woke up half-in and half-out of the tent, and I raised my heavy head and saw some Snow Buntings a few paces away, from us and the incoming tide. I saw my first Twites, at Cley, but once again Norfolk's now mythical Shore Larks and Lapland Buntings eluded us.

One early May, Chief decided to hitchhike to Kent for a weekend's birding, sure he was going to see lots of rare spring migrants Ando and I would be very jealous of. We were supposed to be revising for our finals but while Chief was away we discovered there was a Franklin's Gull at Radipole in Weymouth near Portland, only the seventh to be seen in Britain, so Ando and I got the train there on the

Monday and saw the bird with striking white 'spectacles' before returning home the next day and meeting up with Chief who regaled us with tales of the amazing birds he had seen. Only he hadn't. A few hours later he revealed that he had in fact spent most of his time waiting for buses and trains, his restless nature not being suited to hitchhiking, and he had seen very few birds and certainly nothing rare or even unusual. Worse still he would dearly have loved to have seen a Franklin's Gull and it wasn't long before he was on another train, this time to Radipole where the lucky so and so saw the Franklin's Gull stood next to a Ring-billed Gull, a bird Ando and I had yet to see, or so he said.

Student life was brilliant. We had plenty of time to go birding, spent as much time playing pool in the pub, and partied when there was a party, but because I loved the course I was on I still made most of my early morning lectures and practicals. We did some stupid things of course, mainly under the influence of alcohol and other drugs, and there were plenty of hangovers. When we lived in shared houses the first person up in the morning would usually ask if anyone else wanted anything from the shop, the best reply to which was Ando's, "Aye, a new head."

When we couldn't face writing up practicals, or we were unable to get into the field to watch birds, or we were waiting for the pub to open, we spent a lot of time playing *The Field Guide Game*. This involved one person reading out parts of the descriptions of the birds in *The Hamlyn Guide to Birds of Britain and Europe*, those parts which were least likely to give away the species, and the other person or persons in the room hazarding a guess as to which species it was. Thanks to that game I know when I see a bird with a 'prominent ochreous stripe over eye' it will be a Siberian Accentor. Ando won most of the time. He was more interested in birding and drinking than he was in revising and so when the final exams came along he achieved an 'Unclassified Degree', one that has not even been given a grade it is of such a low standard. Rob never lasted the course; he was no quantity surveyor although he did end up in the building trade. Chief passed, Tig passed and I passed, somehow. I was green when I went away to do a degree. I learnt a lot about biology, a lot more about birds and an awful lot about life during those three years, and then I found out what it felt like when a group of friends who get on so well together are not slowly but suddenly shorn apart by the march of time and scattered to the four winds. Fortunately the desolate wasteland that seemed to be left behind soon came to life. The bonds were strong and so, although we took our separate paths they were to cross frequently in the future.

While becoming a Bachelor of Science I also met a girl. I was sitting in the common room at the beginning of my second year when she, in her first term of her first year, walked in and I lost track of what my friend Paul Southgate was saying while desperately trying not to give him any idea that I was unable to take my eyes off her. I spent a lot more time in the common room after that, in an effort to see her, and I invented ways to bump into her, to have a chat, as she walked to and from the common room but never acted on them. Sometimes I saw her out at night and some months later I finally gathered myself together, mustered all the courage I had, mostly Dutch, and spoke to her. We struggled to get off the ground, went months apart at times, but when all was well we soared to great heights and we were still flying high when I finished my degree so I stayed on in Southsea while she completed her final year.

That was one reason for not going home. The other was I did not know what to do next in life. So I took some time out, rented a bedsit, signed on the dole, went birding and sat in an old, deep chair by the window where the sun came in and read a book called *Walden* by Henry David Thoreau, a Harvard graduate 'with hair which looked as if it had been dressed with a pine-cone.' Published in 1854 it is about the two years he took out, in a hut he built next to Walden Pond near the village of Concord in Massachusetts. I was electrified by almost every page of the book. Thoreau seemed to be saying what I was thinking, only in the language of a poet and the perception of a philosopher. 'I went to the woods because I wished to live deliberately ... and not, when I came to die, discover that I had not lived', 'If a man does not keep pace with his companions, perhaps it is because he hears a different drummer', 'What a man thinks of himself, that is what determines, or rather indicates, his fate', 'I desire that there may be as many different persons in the world as possible; but I would have each one be very careful to find out and pursue *his own* way ...', 'I have spent many an hour ... having paddled my boat to the middle [of Walden Pond] ... lying on my back across the seats ... dreaming awake ... days when idleness was the most attractive and productive industry ... for I was rich, if not in money, in sunny hours and summer days, and spent them lavishly ...', 'If one advances confidently in the directions of his dreams, and endeavors [*sic*] to live the life he has imagined, he will meet with a success unexpected in common hours', 'If the day and the night are such that you greet them with joy, and life emits a fragrance like flowers and sweet-scented herbs, is more elastic, more starry, more immortal, - that is your success', and, nothing was truer to me than, 'There can be no very black melancholy to him who lives in the midst of Nature ...' for however low I felt at times, having no job, no money, no home and no future, I had birding and that soon lifted me up again.

Thoreau also wrote, 'Be rather the [explorer] of your own streams and oceans; explore your own higher latitudes ... it is easier to sail many thousand miles through cold and storm and cannibals ... than it is to explore the private sea, the Atlantic and Pacific Ocean of one's being alone.' I resolved to travel my mind *and* the world. How else was I going to see the birds, animals and wild places in the pictures on my wall when I was a boy?

I needed money to travel but I worked in a bank for six months when I left school and that was more than enough time to work out that a career, a car, a suit, a savings account, a pension, a mortgage, a flat, a house, routine, security, ambition, admiration, wealth, status, fame, what society calls 'success', none of these were for me.

We all need a hut in the woods but I couldn't build one on a friend's land like Thoreau or any other land because it all belongs to someone. For more than the beans given to me by the government because I was unemployed, for enough to feed myself properly and to see the world, I needed a job but I was careful not to get sucked into something I didn't want to do, something I didn't like at all, something that would bore me senseless for eight hours a day five or six days a week for at least the next forty years, the healthiest, most energetic, best years of my life, so that I could earn an employer far more money than I would ever earn and pay a bank or building society far more money for a box than it was worth, for as Thoreau wrote, 'And when the farmer has got his house, he may not be the richer but the poorer for it, and it be the house that has got him.' I didn't want a job so I could pay the mortgage on a box full of stuff and perhaps have enough left over to 'get away from it all', from the daily drudgery, for a few weeks a year, and to pay for the final escape from it all, the final box, the one they would bury me in, along with my dreams. I wanted a job I could use my passion for.

*Needle-tailed Swift, Hoy, Orkney Islands, Scotland, 3rd June 1988*

# 2

# TWITCHING

**Twitching** – *travelling to see a rare bird, sometimes at the drop of a hat, often on long, overnight drives, sometimes to distant, out-of-the-way places, and usually as quickly as possible in case the bird flies away. Most rare birds are relatively common in other parts of the world and normally undergo long migrations on which they lose their way or are blown off course. For example, some birds which spend the northern summer in northern North America and migrate south to spend the northern winter in Central and South America during the* *autumn may be blown across the Atlantic by low pressure systems, and reach Britain and Ireland where they are 'rare'.*

*The origins of the term 'twitcher' are uncertain. Some think a 'twitcher' is a person who twitches with excitement and nervousness when the weather forecast looks good for rare birds, or they hear about a rare bird and twitch with anticipation, of seeing it, or trepidation, of not seeing it, or they actually twitch with excitement when they see such a bird. Another possibility is that the word was coined by Bob Emmett and John Izzard in the 1950s to describe their friend Howard Medhurst who on getting off the back of Bob's Matchless 350 motorcycle after long journeys to look for rare birds would twitch from being so cold. This happened so regularly that Bob and John referred to the journeys as 'being on a twitch'.*

*Twitching in Britain really got going in the 1970s, took off in the 1980s and by the 1990s there were hundreds if not thousands of twitchers, although most were only able to twitch at weekends. At first, evenings, especially Fridays, were spent on the landline telephone, swopping information on the grapevine and discussing logistics before a weekend in a car traversing the length and breadth of Britain, usually sleeping rough in lay-bys, barns and places such as the 'Beach Hotel', a weather shelter in a car-park at the seaward end of Beach Road next to Cley Marshes on the north Norfolk coast. During the 1970s and 1980s in the nearby village of Cley-next-to-the-sea there was a small cafe called Nancy's, which occupied no more than the dining room of an end-of-terrace flint cottage. The openhearted owners were Jack and Nancy Gull. They sold simple, cheap food, especially for birders it seemed, and perhaps more importantly they helped keep an up-to-date notebook with the all the latest bird sightings in. This was placed next to a landline telephone that people could ring to find out the news, and that telephone rarely stopped ringing, until Nancy's closed in December 1988. By then Birdline, a telephone news service, had been up and running for two years, providing national as well as regional and county bird news. In 1991 the birding scene changed dramatically with the arrival of pagers, providing instant news of rare birds, then came mobile phones, the use of which took off in the 2000s, and smart phones, on which it was possible by 2019 to receive alerts of the latest birdnews, touch the map provided and get directions to the site the bird was at, all via something called an 'app' (an application, or computer program).*

*If a twitcher does not see a rare bird they have travelled to see then they have 'dipped'. To dip is deeply depressing. When someone sees a rare bird and a friend of theirs does not see it that friend is said to have been 'gripped off'. This is also deeply depressing, although some enjoy gripping others off, usually just for the fun of it. Most twitchers (or 'listers' as they are called in America) keep lists of the birds they see for one or all of the following; garden, house, local patch, parish, county, state, country, group of countries (such as Britain, sometimes including Ireland) and world, and many also keep these lists as year lists. When a twitcher sees a new bird that bird may be added to a personal list or ticked off on a prepared list and it is often referred to as a tick so that seeing a new bird in Britain constitutes a British tick and seeing a new bird abroad is a World tick or Life tick or Lifer. Some might say a birder is very keen on birds and a twitcher (or a ticker) is obsessed with birds, and some twitchers are more obsessed with their lists than the birds, to the point, in some cases, where a few twitchers have very little if any interest in the aesthetic qualities of the birds; they are merely interested in adding birds to their lists.*

*A twitcher, or anyone for that matter, who has a reputation for unreliable or unverified sightings of rare birds, or any birds, may, usually behind their back, be called a 'stringer'.*

Although we had seen a few rare birds we started twitching for real when Chief got a job and a car. He was living in London so in late February 1983 I hitchhiked up from Southsea and in the early hours we set off for the Isle of Sheppey in Kent where just after dawn we saw a Rock Thrush. The speckled grey and orange bird looked like a big, plump Wheatear bounding with giant, springy hops, making its way from garden to garden and pouncing on insects along Minster seafront. We dipped a Rough-legged Buzzard at Capel Fleet but the dinky, dumpy female Kentish Plover was still present at Cliffe, its pale body shining brightly amongst the larger Ringed Plovers it was roosting with. Back on Sheppey, this time at Elmley, we failed to see the Rough-leg' again. We fared better at Stodmarsh where the two Glossy Ibises came into roost at dusk looking like small pterosaurs, all dark against the cloudy evening sky with long legs, long, outstretched necks and long, downcurved bills.

Chief then drove to Eastbourne on the Sussex coast with us in great spirits, having seen three new birds. It was late by the time we arrived at Hampden Park Industrial Estate, the unlikely setting for a Lesser Yellowlegs which had been present since early February. Since we intended to sleep in the car we had little choice but to pull up next to a massive warehouse. After an early start and a long day we were looking forward to pushing the seats back, lying as flat as possible and closing our eyes, and we were just about to enter longed for sleep when the alarms went off on the warehouse. We were parked right next to one alarm and it was so loud there was no chance of sleeping until someone turned the damned thing off. Ten minutes later we were glad to see a police car turn up. The two officers got out and walked over to us. We wound down the windows and asked them how long it would be before they could turn the alarms off. They said they had no idea and asked what we were doing in a car parked next to a warehouse. Then they asked if they could look in the boot of the car and then they arrested us.

In a state of utter disbelief we were taken to the local police station, charged with attempted burglary and put in separate cells. I was told to remove the laces from my trainers (should I decide to hang myself?) and strip to my underwear which, it being February, consisted of a thick red t-shirt and blue long-johns. "Bloody hell it's Clark Kent!" one of the policemen present announced to the other, hoping for and getting a muffled laugh. I was left alone for a while before being taken to an interview room where I was grilled by a detective who insisted I had made up the scribbled note with directions to the industrial estate on, to use as an alibi. It may have looked like I had made it up - 'Lesser Yellowlegs at ...' but he must have known about a bird which had been present on his beat for a few weeks and visited by hundreds of other twitchers. He could have thought, I suppose, that we were either very cunning or incredibly stupid burglars, choosing to pretend to sleep in our 'getaway car', a *Renault 5*, not the fastest vehicle on the roads, next to the warehouse we had just tried to burgle.

Whatever he was thinking he interrogated me like I was a hardened criminal and I actually started to think he was going to make the charge stick, a rather frightening experience. Until that is, I heard Chief laughing in his cell down the corridor. Another policeman came into the room I was in shortly afterwards and he and my aggressive inquisitor departed swiftly.

Fifteen minutes later Chief came in shaking his head, followed by the station sergeant who was carrying a tray with tea and biscuits on. "There seems to have been a mistake," he said, with total disregard for the gravity of the 'crime' committed by them. Their crime was thinking they could have some fun at our expense on a quiet night and they did until Chief, who took his time but on realizing how serious they seemed to be about proceeding with their ridiculous game, casually informed them who his father was; the Detective Chief Inspector of another, nearby police force. So, it was not long before they were escorting us to a seafront car-park where they said we would be free to sleep the rest of the night. I don't remember sleeping much but I do remember the Lesser Yellowlegs stepping delicately around the edge of a very big puddle. It was one of the most elegant birds I had ever seen and more than worth a sleepless night dealing with the local constabulary.

We headed back to Kent mid-morning and spent an hour or so scanning Chislet Marshes for a Crane, without success. At Stodmarsh we were hoping for better views of the Glossy Ibises and we were not disappointed. The bronzy birds walked slowly across a wet, rough grass field, probing the ground regularly with their bills. On the way to Capel Fleet for our third attempt at the Rough-leg' a very tired Chief drove straight into the back of another car at some traffic lights. Fortunately the damage was not enough to end our trip and our determination to carry on was rewarded, not with the Rough-leg', but with Chief's first Peregrine which powered across the marshes into the westerly breeze. We finished up at Elmley where once again we could not find the Rough-leg' but it didn't matter, it had been a very memorable weekend.

Living in Southsea I had mostly been birding alone during the eight months since we all finished our degrees, at Farlington and Eastney where I saw a Red-necked Grebe before the trip to Kent and a superb summer-plumaged Black-throated Diver in April, enough to keep me going until the next big weekend birding with Chief at the end of May 1983, the first of some great spring weekends based on the North Norfolk coast. On the way we saw three Golden Orioles, including two singing males, at Lakenheath, two Woodlarks, including a singing male, at Santon Downham, and two Stone Curlews at Weeting Heath. At Cley our first Terek Sandpiper was dashing around the mud picking up insects with its very long, thin and extraordinary upturned bill, and also on the reserve were two Bitterns, two Garganeys and lots of Avocets. We finished a top day on Salthouse Heath where a Nightjar flew past while we listened to Nightingales.

Stirring slowly from our poor slumbers in the cramped car, a keener birder than us came running into the car-park at Cley shouting, "A Cattle Egret's just flown into Eye Field!" Chief sat upright, rolled his seat up, opened his eyes, turned the engine on and drove as fast as he could to the Beach car-park. There it was, our first Cattle Egret, our first egret of any kind, standing amongst a small herd of cattle. It looked very small and compact to our inexperienced eyes and was white with a buffy beak and buffier, shaggy crown. When it flew it was mobbed by Black-headed Gulls and we could hardly believe that they were almost as big as the poor egret. With it lost we headed to Hickling Broad where a Savi's Warbler remained silent and hidden in the reeds so we moved on to Minsmere where we also saw nothing out of the ordinary and our frustration was compounded when we got back to Cley after dark and found out that we had missed a Red-necked Phalarope and a Night Heron.

We were in the hide overlooking the pool the phalarope was last seen on as the first chink of light glowed on the eastern horizon but it was gone ... or so we thought. I had noticed a couple of wet flashes at Salthouse just along the coast a couple of days before and mumbled grumpily to Chief that perhaps we should go and see if it was on one of them. When we arrived we were surprised to discover that no one else had had the same idea and even more surprised to see the Red-necked Phalarope on the first flash we scanned. It was a smashing little bird, barely bigger than a sparrow, a lead-grey 'sparrow' that could swim and had a red neck and a beak like a needle. He didn't want to leave it but Chief got in the car and drove to Cley to let everyone else know where the beauty was and within an hour a crowd of nearly a hundred had gathered.

We moved on, to Titchwell where we saw a superb summer-plumaged Black Tern but not the Spoonbill known to be present. Back at Salthouse the phalarope was still delighting a constant stream of visitors, many of whom made up the two hundred or so lining the top of the West Bank toward dusk, hoping the Night Heron would do exactly the same as it did the night before. Two Bitterns boomed as a Short-eared Owl rowed buoyantly over the rough fields and reed beds. A Barn Owl came out and I watched it through my telescope pounce on three voles in thirty minutes, taking them back one by one to its youngsters in the windmill. There were less than fifty twitchers left by ten minutes past nine, the time the Night Heron appeared. The broad-winged, short-billed, chunky black, grey and white bird flew right over our heads on its way to the reserve for a night's fishing, leaving us to celebrate yet another great day in our lives.

We did not see the Marsh Sandpiper that dropped into Cley for two hours the next day, but an absolutely stunning male Red-backed Shrike singing its scratchy warble from the top of a flowering hawthorn bush the following morning was a fine end to a fantastic long weekend.

I was still writing up my notes and trying to absorb it all when, a week later, I telephoned *Nancy's*. A couple of hours later I was in position at the southern end of the M27 in Portsmouth with my thumb high in the air and a few hours later I was at Chief's place in London. We were at Minsmere in Suffolk at dawn the next day watching our third and last member of the phalarope family, a gorgeous female Wilson's Phalarope which was a little larger than the Red-necked we had seen ten days ago and a little more attractive thanks to the black mask on its snow white face merging into claret-coloured neck sides, set off against the blue-grey back. I could have watched that phalarope all day but we had to leave at half past five in the morning so Chief could get to work on time. A few swift lifts for me hitchhiking and just twenty-four hours after hearing about the bird I was sitting in my favourite chair in my bedsit, the phalarope plate in the field guide open on my lap, letting the beauty and excitement sink in.

In late July Chief drove us up to Sunderland where with Ando and Steve Howat I saw my first Roseate Terns at Whitburn. The next morning the four of us headed north on my first trip to Scotland where during two days in some beautiful country I saw my first Capercaillies, Crested Tits, Red Grouse, Ptarmigans, Arctic Terns and Golden Eagle, a young bird with a white base to the tail, white wing flashes and a golden hood, gliding back and forth over a high ridge at Ruthven. Back in northeast England we visited Langdon Beck in the Pennines and watched six male Black Grouse, yet another new bird, and the next day Chief and I took a left on our way back to London and twitched another member of what was fast becoming my favourite family of birds, the shorebirds; a long-legged, long-necked and long-billed Marsh Sandpiper which graced a lagoon at Holme on the north Norfolk coast. It foraged, often in water up to its belly, right in front of the hide and the bird's delicate elegance was stunning.

When my girlfriend Carolyn moved back home to Surrey after finishing her degree I returned to Gloucester where my Dad had a day to go birding and at Frampton-on-Severn we came across a Purple Heron standing in the reeds at the edge of a mere. After a slow stalk and a couple of darts into the water with its spear-like bill it suddenly took flight and headed off toward Slimbridge leaving me to glow with good fortune, although I discovered months later that the bird had been present for three days already. I was still not on the local grapevine but I could find out the national 'gen' (general information) via *Nancy's* or my slowly growing number of twitching friends, and I was just starting to love life as a twitcher when I went and got a bloody job, just before Ando, Chief and I were due to go to the Isles of Scilly for our first autumn trip. It was a great job, one I had held out for, although I was only eligible for it because I had been unemployed for twelve months.

My main task was to promote awareness of birds and other wildlife in Gloucester, and it being my first job a year after graduating I was not prepared to risk it by dashing off to Scilly or for a bird on the mainland. So, come October 1983 I had to grin and bear almost nightly phone calls from Chief and Ando with tales of birds I had hardly heard of but would very much loved to have seen; Bobolink, Grey-cheeked and Swainson's Thrushes, Sora Rail, Red-eyed Vireo, Rose-breasted Grosbeak, Upland Sandpiper, Parula Warbler (only the sixth ever seen in Britain), and Cliff Swallow (the first one ever seen in Europe), all very rare birds from America, and, almost as if to rub salt into my multiple wounds, they even stopped off to see an American Redstart in Kenidjack Valley, far west Cornwall, on their way home.

However, by 1984, I had some money, for the first time in my life, and I was determined to use some of it to see as many birds as possible on weekends and holidays. Late in January I could hardly eat a meal out after being told there was a White-tailed Eagle near Brill in Buckinghamshire. The next day Gordon Avery, who I met while trespassing on his local patch around Gloucester's rubbish tip, picked me up and we headed east. The biggest bird I had ever seen sailed on its massive fingered wings into the north wind, causing a great stir amongst the masses of twitchers lining the country lanes. Everything about the bird was big - its wings, body, beak, claws, everything, and it made every other bird look tiny.

About a month later I was off to the north Norfolk coast for my third winter visit. The previous two had been great adventures but I saw very few of the birds the beaches, dunes, pine woods and marshes were famous for. This time Chief and I had much more gen, and a car. It may not have been so bold and adventurous but our chances of seeing some great birds were much higher. We arrived at Wells Woods on a beautiful cold, clear, sunny, almost still, mid-February day and we were soon watching our first Parrot Crossbills, two males, which dropped down from a pine top to drink from a puddle in the car-park. About an hour later we saw our second new bird and the best of the day, eleven Shore Larks, foraging tight to the sand in the dunes at Holme, their pastel black and yellow faces and sandy upperparts a perfect match for the wild scene. I may have been a twitcher but the combination of a wild place and one of the birds that completed it was fast becoming something special to me. Less stirring but new bird of the day number three was Lapland Bunting, two of which flicked up from some rough grass at Burnham Norton. After a chilly night in the car we scoured the Norfolk Broads for Cranes. We couldn't find any but Chief came up with a handsome Great Grey Shrike.

In late February Gordon Avery and I headed east again to Bracknell in Berkshire where there was a very neat and boldly streaked Olive-backed Pipit wandering about a lawn under the pine trees in Dave Parker's strange back garden, the first ever to be seen during the winter in Britain. My next big day out was in early March. It was planned and executed with great enthusiasm and precision by Trevor Williams who I had met at Portland. We were at Tregaron Bog in west Wales just after ten in the morning and within seconds my first Red Kite flapped lazily into view, fanning and twisting its rich ruddy tail as it flew slowly across the wonderfully wild terrain looking so much better than I had imagined, as did all the others we saw that day. Trevor knew Wales well and thanks to him I also saw a male Hen Harrier, a male Merlin, a male Peregrine, and four Choughs and four Bottlenose Dolphins at Llangranog on the coast, all celebrated with a fine meal back at Trevor's house.

A Penduline Tit had been seen on and off at Stodmarsh in Kent since the first day of March but the news on Saturday the 17th was that it had been seen very well so I jumped on the first train to Chief's; there was no need to hitchhike now I had some money. By dawn the next day we were standing on the Lampen Wall, an embankment providing excellent views across extensive reed-beds. However, it was rather exposed to a bitter easterly wind. After three hours almost frozen to the spot there were just a few of us left, not including Chief who was asleep in the relative warmth of the car a long way back along the trail. Then a tiny bird flew over our heads calling 'zeeeu' and landed on a bulrush head. It was instantly identifiable thanks the bold black mask, blue-grey crown and rufous back, making it look like a miniature Red-backed Shrike. In action the tit resembled a woodpecker as it tore tiny seeds out of the sausage-shaped spike of flowers with tremendous gusto. News reached the car-park rapidly and Chief was soon enjoying the beauty too, along with over two hundred happy twitchers who then headed somewhere warmer.

A planned long weekend with Chief based at Portland in mid-April got off to a brilliant start when we saw our first ever Hoopoe, at Honington in Warwickshire. The crazy exotic-looking bird was probing a roadside verge for ages before it flew up to a gate with its broad black and white wings widespread. As it landed it raised its tall crest then it flew off across a field looking like a giant butterfly as it wavered from side to side with extravagant flicks of its fanned wings. After many hours trying we finally saw our first Goshawks in the New Forest but when we got to Portland Nige Crook gripped us off with news of a Serin.

*Hoopoe, Honington, Warwickshire, England,*
*20th April 1984*

As we contemplated where to look for the Serin, Lee Evans burst out of the telephone box in Southwell complaining hysterically about a Stilt Sandpiper which he said had been flushed off a lagoon at Frodsham in Cheshire. By the time we sat down with our first pint of the evening in the *Eight Kings* everything had fallen into place. We had seen the singing male Serin, not far from the pub, and after pasty, chips and beans, Chief, Nige Crook, Trevor Codlin and I were off to Frodsham because the sandpiper was back.

If it stayed more than a day it would be the first Stilt Sandpiper to do so on the British mainland since one at Minsmere in 1969 hence there were already about fifty cars in the car-park when we pulled in to it during the early hours, some with steamed-up windows some with twitchers too twitchy to sleep, while others paced up and down outside, chatting, smoking and twitching while waiting for the first chink of light. By dawn a few hundred of us were in position overlooking a shallow lagoon, checking the murky silhouettes of shorebirds to see if any of them could possibly be the bird. It was impossible to identify anything for certain until the sunny day dawned proper though, and there it was; to tell the truth a rather drab grey, albeit long-billed, long-necked and long-legged, shorebird with a limp. For once, a bird, a shorebird even, did not turn out to be better than expected, its gammy leg preventing it from foraging the way only such elegant shorebirds can.

On Wednesday the 9th of May a summer-plumaged Ross's Gull turned up at Cley. Three tense days later I was in the North Hide at dawn. Nine hours later, at two o'clock in

*Ross's Gull, Cley, Norfolk, England, 12th May 1984*

the afternoon, I was opposite the hide on the southern side of the reserve when I saw what looked like ants converging on the North Hide. The sight could mean only one thing. I had a difficult choice. Head west to Beach Road then north or go east then north along the East Bank. I decided the latter was the shortest way and ran. I couldn't run the whole way, about a mile, so I trotted a bit and walked a bit, and I got there pretty quickly. However, I was sweating and shaking so much I could hardly hold my binoculars or telescope steady, and I was desperately trying to stay calm because I wanted to enjoy the small, delicate gull with black underwings, a snow white wedge-shaped tail and an absolutely gorgeous pink flush below. The truly beautiful bird was hanging in the north wind, as light as a feather, occasionally dipping down gracefully to pluck food from the surface, and it was a wonderful, soothing sight.

When the telephone in the hall in the house I shared with three other people, none of whom had the slightest interest in birds, rang at eight o'clock on a Sunday morning I had a feeling it was someone trying to get hold of me. None of their friends would ring them at that time. Reluctantly I fell out of bed and climbed carefully down the stairs. It was Nige Crook. He had just nailed the 'funny little bird' that had been present at Church Norton in Sussex for a few days. It was a Trumpeter Finch, only the fourth ever recorded in Britain and the first twitchable one since 1971. I was awake by the time I put the telephone down. I picked it up again and rang Chief. I was at the train station shortly afterwards but it being a Sunday it took hours to get to Reading where Chief now lived. He, Mike Crosby and John Lucas were anxiously waiting for me and none too happy it had taken so long for me to get there. We did not get to Church Norton until nearly five o'clock in the afternoon and it took me just as long to get home. So, it was a hell of a day and I wish I could say for a hell of a bird but that would be lying because the grey-brown Trumpeter Finch was no Ross's Gull.

A week later, Chief, Steve Howat and I set out to record as many birds as possible in a day in Norfolk, each one sponsored to raise money for the Gloucestershire Trust for Nature Conservation (GTNC), for which I was working at the time. Despite a late night in the *White Horse* in Blakeney we were on Salthouse Heath at dawn, listening to Nightingales, and by the time we headed for breakfast we were on an almighty 90 species; a final total of well over a hundred, which would easily be our best ever, was a certainty, disasters permitting. Then, while standing in the corridor at *Nancy's* waiting for a table to become available the telephone rang yet again. This time it was not a twitcher after news it was someone at Spurn on the east coast of Yorkshire with some sensational news; the first ever twitchable Blyth's Reed Warbler in Britain. *Nancy's* emptied quickly, a table became available and over breakfast we tried to resist going but when we took into account that there was also a Sprosser (Thrush Nightingale) at Spurn and a Great Reed Warbler nearby, both of which would be new birds for Chief and I, we buckled.

We arrived at Spurn at two-thirty in the afternoon and I soon saw my first Long-eared Owl, perched out in the open. It was difficult to know which way to turn after that, as the Sprosser was showing then the Blyth's and *vice versa*, and people were running between the two, *and* between them and a grey eastern Willow Warbler which kept being shouted out as the Blyth's, but over the course of a few hours we managed to see first the Sprosser, which was singing from the base of a thick hedge, then the Blyth's, which was trying to sing from the top of the same hedge but was prevented from doing so by idiots getting too close. We also saw the Willow Warbler, a Savi's Warbler and a female Red-backed Shrike before leaving Spurn to go to Saltmarshe Delph, not far inland along the Humber. We could hear the loud 'kara kara's and 'g-urk's of the Great Reed Warbler before we got out of the car. It was a huge warbler and bold to boot, a real tonic after the skulkers of Spurn. We ended the day at Blacktoft Sands where a Reedling was the twelfth species we saw after leaving Norfolk and therefore number 102 for the day on the list we presented to the GTNC. They may have been rather surprised by the birds on it, and they ended up with less money than if we had stayed in Norfolk but it would not have amounted to much anyway because I have never been very good at confronting people with sponsor forms.

Before the Norfolk weekend Chief and I had failed to even glimpse a highly elusive Collared Flycatcher in Margate, Kent. We should have gone to Shetland instead, where a Needle-tailed Swift was zooming around Quendale, but Shetland was like a different country to us then so we returned to Margate and after a further eleven and a half hours, fifteen in total, I finally locked on to the little tinker, seeing a very neat black-and-white bird with a jet black hood and broad white collar. Its appearance was all too brief though and Chief, who was carrying out Plan B, 'Random Wandering', instead of sticking to the area where it made occasional appearances, never did see it.

The next day Chief, Nige Crook, Pete Gamage, John Walters and I headed to the Hebrides in a hired car. As dawn broke we were still motoring, alongside Loch Lomond, then Loch Tulla where a handsome Black-throated Diver swam. By the side of a rocky river we stopped to watch a Dipper walking underwater. Near Loch Garry we saw two Black Grouse. When we reached Kyle of Lochalsh Nige eased the car on to the early morning ferry to Skye, a half-hour crossing during which I saw my first Black Guillemots, better known in Scotland by their Norse name, Tysties. They were brilliant, their bright red feet flashing as they dived into the azure sea. Skye's mountain slopes were awash with sunlight but their peaks were mostly hidden by gloomy clouds. They looked immense to our inexperienced eyes. We wanted to climb them and look for Golden Eagles but we had another ferry to catch, from Uig across the Little Minch to Lochmaddy on North Uist, one of the Outer Hebrides. This crossing took much longer, nearly five hours, and we saw a lot more birds; more Tysties, a few Puffins, at least a hundred Manx Shearwaters and a surprise Pomarine Skua.

The first person we met on North Uist was an Australian. He was tall and thin and looked like a tramp but he had an expensive-looking rucksack on his back and binoculars around his neck so we stopped to ask him if he had seen any birds. "Heaps!" he said and reeled off a long list but he had not been where we were going. We drove south, across North Uist then Benbecula, more loch than rock, to South Uist and past yet more lochs, and big beds of yellow irises and wind-blown shell-sand grassland called machair, white with cotton grass heads. To the east rose the mountains of Hecla then Beinn Mhor. To the west was our first stop, Verran Island, a rocky outcrop, where we sat on the soft grass between the rocks with our telescopes and began scanning the sea for a very rare bird. It was not long before the shout went up, shattering the soothing background sound of 'cooing', courting Eider ducks. Among them was a very different kind of eider; a Steller's Eider, a striking black and white drake with a rich orange breast. Through our telescopes we could make out the curious, single, bold black spots on each side of the breast, just above the waterline, and even stranger, the four tufts of tiny feathers on its head, two in front of its eyes and two on the back of its head that looked like round, lime-green pin-cushions. The bird had been present on South

Uist since 1972 but two months later it disappeared and was never seen again. It sure picked a wonderful place to live all those years; Atlantic rollers crashing and splashing softly into and over the offshore rocks, a white, shell-sand beach running as far as we could see to the north, the sun shining in a clear sky, barely a breeze off the sea, not another human being in sight, and no sign of any person ever having been there at all, at least to destroy anything. I was where I loved to be; in a wild place, watching birds.

There was no time to truly absorb it though. We moved on, to Peninerine, in search of the Corn Crake. There is a yarn about a twitcher who was so desperate to see the elusive Corn Crake that, after many years trying but failing to see one, he travelled over to Ireland to a bog which, it was claimed, was crawling with Corn Crakes. At dusk a Corn Crake uttered its Latin name; a rasping 'crex crex'. It rasped, as they do, for a while, so the man rubbed a stick along his comb to mimic the bird's call and hopefully trick it into moving closer to what it might assume was a rival male trespassing into its territory. The calling Corn Crake never budged so the man began making his way into the bog, rubbing his comb and trying to make sure the black ooze didn't flow over the top of his wellington boots. An hour or so later he had given up hope of staying dry and was now on his hands and knees crawling slowly through the muck toward the calling Corn Crake, which was still going strong. When he was within what seemed like several paces of his first *Crex crex* he got down on his belly and as quietly as he could shuffled very slowly forward on his elbows to where he thought the bird must be and there almost in his face it seemed but hidden by the thick clumps of rushes he heard a loud and clear 'crex crex'.

'The bastard must be behind that clump there' he convinced himself and so he moved forward again, even more quietly and slowly than before, closer and closer, until he thought he was close enough to rise up and peer over the rushes and see his first Corn Crake, the bird he had spent years looking for. So, he got up on to his knees in the stinking black mud and water, and peered over the rushes, and there it was, another desperate birder with a comb and a stick.

There was no mud where we were. We were stood in sunshine at the side of a quiet road listening to a Corn Crake in a meadow, hoping its head would pop up, just for a second. Just a head; that is all we dared hope for, preferably for more than a second though, but it was not to be. We gave up near midnight and led down in our sleeping bags on the soft machair at the top of the beach. There, on nature's springs, Dunlins rippled all around us, and fresh air wafted across my face, and after delighting in the sensation of being overcome by satisfactory slumber, knowing it had been a great day's birding and that I would be doing what I loved all day again tomorrow, I slept like a log, where man was meant to sleep, outdoors.

The next day dawned as bright as the last, with a light, cooling northeasterly breeze. Lochs sparkled. Corn Crakes called. Mid-morning, we were listening to one when a second bird began calling. This rival male stimulated the bird in front of us to produce its loudest call yet and in so doing it stretched up just enough for us to see its head rise above the grass with its gape pointing skywards. We could hardly believe it. We had seen a Corn Crake, well a bit of a Corn Crake, on only our second day.

## A MIND-BLOWING BIRDING TRIP TO A PLANET CALLED EARTH

It was nearly noon when we pulled up alongside the minor road between Ben Aulasary and Ben Ernakater on North Uist and sprawled on the soft turf in the sunshine and scanned the mountain tops for Golden Eagles. For a few hours we were in a magical place; just us, the meadows, the mountains, the sky and the birds. A pair of Ravens rocked and rolled during some synchronised flying over the crest of Ben Ernakater, their deep 'korrp' calls breaking the brilliant silence. Below, a male Hen Harrier and several Common Gulls were quartering. Their soft whites and greys, and jet black wing tips, looked very striking against the rich brown peat bog where, bouncing buoyantly on long, stiff wings, there was a golden Short-eared Owl. We watched it hunt, wavering on rowing wing beats, this way and that, head down, eyes scanning the ground. When it landed we focused our telescopes on its yellow eyes, staring straight back at us. After a few minutes the owl turned its head almost all the way around and looked up at the mountain top. Ravens were sounding the alarm with loud 'krack-krack-krack' calls and powering toward a massive raptor, a magnificent Golden Eagle, with long, dark brown wings and a golden shawl. It glided along the south ridge of Ernakater to the summit where it wheeled higher and higher in small circles as the Ravens gave up their pursuit. Then the eagle plunged strongly down on half-closed wings behind the Ben and out of sight, leaving us elated.

Back in the Paible area on the west coast of North Uist we heard a *Crex crex* as soon as we got out of the car. It sounded like it was in the middle of a small iris bed but it wasn't, it was standing at the edge, rasping loudly with its head thrown back, right out in the open, for the whole world to see. We could not believe our binoculars. There, through the glass, was a Corn Crake, a whole Corn Crake. Through telescopes we could see the black speckles on its brown neck, the black chevron-shaped centres to the rich buff back feathers, even the narrow white bars across the rufous flanks. We could marvel at the detail of every neatly marked feather of the supposed crepuscular skulker. The bird then began to preen, taking on all manner of contortions, stretching and shortening its neck, fanning its rich red-brown wings, and puffing out its body feathers then flattening them again. We moved to an old hay cart nearby to lean our telescopes on without the bird taking any notice. We were even able to tell each other how amazed we were but we were soon silent again because a second bird emerged cautiously from the irises. It was just ten paces away and once out in the open it began creeping very slowly toward us along the road, with its neck and head held out low in front of its body. It kept going, right past our astonished eyes, and then it crept under the car! After crouching there for a while it walked down the bank behind the car, into the grass and away, leaving us all wondering if that timeless hour on the Hebrides had really happened.

It was midnight by the time we hit the machair and we were up four hours later in order to catch the ferry back to Skye, where a Golden Eagle rode the wind over a roadside ridge. Back on mainland Scotland the road through the highlands of Ross and Cromarty ran alongside Loch Carron before, at the head of the flat river valley, the mountains suddenly closed in on us, so tightly it seemed that the road must come to an end but it squeezed through somehow and we left the steep slopes for rolling hills and then the flood plain of the River Bran before we arrived at the Cairngorms. These mountains, in the words of Nan Shepherd in *The Living Mountain*, are 'a mass of granite thrust up through the schists and gneiss that form the lower surrounding hills, planed down by the ice cap, and split, shattered and scooped by frost, glaciers and the strength of running water'.

We were soon up top, wandering across the wildest land in Britain, in search of our first Dotterels, across treeless whale-backs, around corrie lakes and past small summer snowfields, while the sun shone on a perfect afternoon for a walk of steep ascents and awkward descents across sharp and slippery terrain. There were few birds; a Peregrine and a couple of Ptarmigans, and another, last, scan revealed no Dotterels once again. There was no need to scan though. Our first Dotterel seemed to materialise before us. It was just twenty paces away. We stood stock still and raised our binoculars very slowly but there was no need to worry about a famously tame bird flying or running away. When we sat down it walked toward us. The normal parental roles are reversed in Dotterels and while the male incubated the eggs in a nest farther away it was the much more brightly coloured female that was foraging a few paces in front of us and what a beautiful sight she was with her black cap, snow white stripes on the sides of her head, black and white necklace and deep rufous underparts, and what a wonderful wild place in which to watch her. Gloriously happy, Chief and I danced down the mountain, leaping from rock to rock.

We spent most of the next day searching for Capercaillies, seeing a female late on, then drove hundreds of miles south overnight to Rutland Water where Chief, who did most of the driving, got out of the car and into his sleeping bag by the side of the road, while the rest of us scanned the vast reservoir in vain, for the first twitchable Bridled Tern in Britain. The rumour was it had been 'booted', flushed by a selfish idiot of a twitcher desperate to get the bird on his list. It had certainly moved on but it didn't matter; it had been an epic trip to Scotland.

The summer of '84 was far from dull thanks to a Little Bittern (one of a pair that raised three young in Yorkshire), a Forster's Tern at Point of Air in Wales, a Great White Egret at Minsmere and a Least Sandpiper at Dungeness in Kent but all I could think about was my first trip to the Isles of Scilly in the autumn. First of all though there was the small matter of a Cream-coloured Courser at Hadleigh Marsh, Essex, the first twitchable one since a bird in Norfolk in 1969 which stayed so long virtually every twitcher, birder, birdwatcher and anyone with the slightest interest in birds saw it. I begged Chief and his friend Martin Hallam not to go for the latest one on Sunday the 30th of September, the day after it turned up, and to wait for the first day of my long holiday, Wednesday the 3rd of October. They kindly waited but the bird didn't. I was stunned by my first major dip and felt terrible for Chief and Martin, and I had plenty of time to dwell on it on what was the quietest overnight drive I've ever been on. Paul Sampson, one of the keenest twitchers in the country, cheered us up when we arrived at *Sullivan's Cafe* in Penzance at six the following morning. He told us that there was a Yellowthroat on Scilly, on the island of Bryher, only the third time ever one had been seen in Britain. He was not very happy about it, because he was trying to win the race to see the most birds in Britain during 1984 and was one of the few who had already seen a Yellowthroat, a stunning male on the island of Fetlar in Shetland back in early June, the first since one on Lundy in 1954.

When we arrived on the Isles of Scilly the Yellowthroat had gone missing so my first afternoon was a bit of an anticlimax, the best bird being a Pectoral Sandpiper at Porth Hellick Pool. My first full day was more like I imagined. It began with a Rough-legged Buzzard, possibly of North American origin, roosting on a rock at Porthloo Beach on St Mary's. On the island of St Agnes my first Blackpoll Warbler, which had not been seen for a while, popped up in front of me and Paul Sampson outside the post office. It was from America but the third new bird of the day was a Yellow-browed Warbler from Siberia. This was normal on Scilly; birds from 3000 miles (4800 km) away to the west met birds from 3000 miles away to the east, and that is why many twitchers thought it was the best place to see rare birds in Britain. It also happens to be one of the most beautiful corners of the British Isles, a small archipelago with white sand beaches in a shallow sea 28 miles (45 km) off Land's End.

It seemed the Yellowthroat had gone so we got the tripper boat to the island of Tresco the next day. We were following up rumours of an odd 'peep' (a small shorebird) and thanks to Peter Grant, friendly Chairman of the *British Birds Rarities Committee*, we saw our first Semi-palmated Sandpiper. A Barred Warbler on St Mary's the next day was number 299 on my British List and that evening when I entered my now favourite pub, the *Bishop and Wolf*, I heard about the best possible 300th.

We left our rented house in Hugh Town well before dawn. Groups of other twitchers were already walking along the main street and others were appearing from every side-street and alleyway, marching to the harbor, hoping to be on the first boat to Bryher. There were already a lot of people lined up at the top of the steps on the quay but I was the last one on the first boat and consequently the first off it, jumping down on to the white beach then walking as fast as possible in order to be in prime position, looking directly at the wind-cropped apple tree at the base of the bracken-covered Samson Hill. It was half past seven. Thirty minutes later there was a Yellowthroat in that tree. Even in the dull conditions I could see that its throat was quite bright yellow and its mask blackish but in a matter of seconds it was gone and despite hundreds of eyes staring at that tree it was not seen again all day.

The next day I saw three new birds again. A Solitary Sandpiper on St Mary's, a Swainson's Thrush under the apple trees in the parsonage on St Agnes, now my favourite place in the world, where we also saw the Blackpoll Warbler and a Melodious Warbler, and a Common Rosefinch back on St Mary's, but none were as good as the Yellowthroat which I was able to watch through my telescope on Bryher the next day, noting especially its gorgeous lime-green undertail. After seeing nine new birds on my first five full days, including at least five from North America, three days without much action were actually very welcome. There was time to appreciate the beautiful setting I was seeing the birds in, to absorb the brilliant atmosphere, the buzz of being with so many fellow bird fanatics, and to enjoy the excitement of the dawn, of what might turn up, the long days in the field, and the sheer energy of the evenings in the *Bishop and Wolf*. It was like the best days as a student day after day; a two-week long party and I loved it.

It was back to normal on the 13th: three new birds in a day, all on St Mary's; Short-toed Lark, Red-rumped Swallow and Tawny Pipit. In between we dipped two Little Buntings on St Agnes. No matter, we saw them the next day, along with our first Woodchat Shrike, and the next morning added our first Ortolan Buntings on St Mary's. We then got the boat to Tresco to look for a Dusky Warbler but despite staying until dark and hearing its distinctive snappy 'tskakk' call several times the brief views we had were not good enough to say we had actually seen a Dusky Warbler so we returned the following morning and there it was hopping about in the middle of a field, not what 'Duskies' normally do. Shortly afterwards we were enjoying watching a Tawny Pipit catching sand flies on the beach near New Grimsby when Chris Gibbins ran past calling out, "Olivaceous Warbler on St Mary's!" We ran after him and his crew but just missed the first boat and had to watch in agony as the passengers landed commando-style at Bar Point, the closest spot to Watermill where the bird was. By the time our boat got over from St Mary's the tide had come up so we had to get off in Hugh Town and spend beer money on the first taxi with room. The Olivaceous Warbler was leaping about the top of a bramble bush plucking insects from the branches with its long pointy beak, dipping its tail downwards and calling all the time; a short, sharp 'chack'. Deliriously happy, having seen Dusky *and* Olivaceous Warblers in the same day, I headed toward Porth Hellick Pool where there was a Bluethroat, yet another new bird for me in what was fast becoming a blur of them, but before I got there Lee Evans ran past me shouting, "Rock Thrush on Penninis!" and so I ran after him and joined the crowd there, seeing the small grey-brown thrush with dark bars just before dark to complete yet another incredible day. I saw the Bluethroat before breakfast the next morning and a Rustic Bunting before the '*Bishop*'. The Bluethroat was foraging at the edge of the reeds at close enough range to see a few blue dazzles on its upper breast, the Rustic, on Tresco, was a bit more distant but close enough to see its lovely orangey upper breast. It was my tenth new bird in five days and my nineteenth since arriving on Scilly. I had to wait two days for my twentieth, a Red-throated Pipit, in the same field as the Dusky Warbler was, on Tresco.

I must have been in love by the end of my first trip to Scilly because when the end was near I felt like I was about to leave a lover and didn't know when I was going to see her again. I was so glad to have met the islands and their birds, but very, very sad to have to leave them. A delayed sailing of the *Scillonian III* created time for a last pint or two in the *Bishop* which Chief, several old and new friends, and I relished but our last-minute celebrations were blown to bits when Keith 'Dipper' Lyon burst in to tell us that there was an, "Eye-browed Thrush at Salakee!" Beer was spilt, pool balls and cues went flying and tables were nearly toppled as we squeezed out of the narrow doorway into the road desperately flagging down vehicles for a lift. It was the first ever twitchable Eye-browed Thrush in Britain and the boat was leaving shortly. We had to get there fast and we did. In fact we were the first there, in time to see a beautiful rarity with striking white 'eyebrows' above its blue-grey face and lovely orange flanks.

We were on our way out of the area of fields with tree-lined lanes when many more were on their way in, plodging through shin-high mud. At least one person went over face first into the muck. Others, on seeing the bird, were swearing loudly, voicing their joy and ruining a *BBC Radio* programme about twitching. Well, at least they knew what it was all about now. They couldn't get any sense out of people who had not even dared to dream of seeing such a bird, something so rare and unexpected, something mystical, and something worthy of excess celebrations. A great life, that's what I was celebrating, the life of a twitcher who dreams of seeing rare birds in wild places and sometimes sees them, and so much more. I didn't want the dream to end but we had a boat to catch.

It wasn't time to go home quite yet though. The agony of the comedown was delayed by news of a Sociable Plover at the mouth of the River Neath in south Wales so after the ship had docked in Penzance a convoy of several cars formed and by dawn the next morning we were in position for the fly past of the black, white and brown wings. The plover was followed by my first Surf Scoter, a distant dark blob at nearby Burry Port, and a Long-billed Dowitcher at my occasional stomping ground, Frampton-on-Severn. That was the 290th species I had seen during the year, making the amazing total of 300, something I had been thinking about for a while, a definite possibility with two months of the year to go, although it would never be easy for a twitcher with a full-time job and no driver's license.

Fortunately I had a great friend in Chief who was happy to pick me up and take me to Berry Head in Devon to watch an Isabelline Shrike catching bees on the cliff-top. Two

Cirl Buntings were also my first of the year. The two Pallid Swifts, the third and fourth for Britain, at Portland, were gone when Trevor Williams and I got there and I could not persuade anyone to drive nor did I have time to hitchhike to Porthgwarra near Land's End for the Desert Wheatear. So, I was glad Chief was up for a trip to Ringstead Gravel Pits in Northamptonshire for a drake American Wigeon, and Snettisham in Norfolk for two Little Auks, on another hastily arranged day off, leaving me just six short of the 300.

Two days later Ando and Steve met me off the train in Newcastle and took me to the hospital, not for a check up from the neck up, for the long-staying Laughing Gull. It was on some nearby football pitches. When I met Ando back in 1979 my British and Life List was on 157 and his was on 218. With the Laughing Gull he moved on to 295, the same total as my list for 1984. After a good look at the gull we jumped on the metro to Jarrow to watch a Lesser Grey Shrike dice with death on a dual-carriageway, flying low in pursuit of prey from one side to the other. We then adjourned to the nearest hostelry to celebrate, in my case, two new birds in two hours, and two more toward the magic 300, now just four away, and a disturbing obsession.

In early December Ando visited me and helped to pin down two Hawfinches at Nagshead in the Forest of Dean, one of which sat out in the open long enough for our best ever views. I turned to Robinswood Hill, where all this malarkey started, for Lesser Spotted Woodpecker but could not find one. Chief and Martin Hallam were keen to try for the Pied-billed Grebe and Black Duck in North Wales and although we only saw the latter I was happy because I was just two short now and Barnacle Goose at Caerlaverock on the Solway Firth was a certainty for the 299 on a trip planned for the 22nd of December. From there Dave, a colleague at work interested in seeing what twitching was like, drove across the Pennines to Guisborough where I dearly wished my 300th bird of 1984 would be the Waxwings which had been seen there but they had moved on and I had to endure a long, long drive back to Gloucester with someone who never wanted to go twitching again, one short of the now seemingly unreachable target.

I used the time to hatch a plan and so Christmas was spent persuading Dad to go on a little adventure down to Devon where at Lopwell Dam on the River Tavy a Spotted Sandpiper marked the milestone, which, I have to say, came more as a relief than anything else. The roads were a bit icy and Dad was even more perturbed when he saw a sign saying 'Welcome to Cornwall' as I navigated him to the Upper Tamar Lakes where the female Ring-necked Duck was still present and number 301 for the year. Yet another attempt to winkle out a Lesser Spotted Woodpecker on Robinswood Hill on the last day only confirmed it to be the bogey bird of the year, a year which was tremendously exciting and often uplifting, if a little frustrating, even traumatic at times once I had decided to go for the 300. The best thing about twitching for me by far though was seeing great birds in great places, places I may never have seen were I not a twitcher, and when I laid my head on my pillow at the end it wasn't the 300 that mattered it was that if I wasn't a twitcher I probably would never have seen a Ross's Gull, a Steller's Eider, an Eye-browed Thrush and so on.

I tried to get my breath back at the beginning of 1985, resisting the temptation to dash after a Little Crake at Cuckmere Haven in Sussex, and a Pine Bunting followed by a Calandra Lark on the Isles of Scilly, even though I was out of work again, my eighteen-month contract having come to an end. I didn't get really excited about a bird until Mark Golley, a new friend who lived in Devon, called me at the end of April. I was on the road at dawn the next morning. It took me six hours to hitchhike to the beautiful deep, wooded Erme Valley and on looking up there was a magnificent creature soaring high above. After circling it floated down like a giant feather and my first Black Stork landed half-way up a huge dead tree so close I could see the red skin around its eye and the big black ruff on its neck. It was one of the most extraordinary sights my poorly travelled eyes had ever seen and although it took even longer to hitchhike home I didn't mind. I was elated.

A month later I saw my first stunning male Bluethroat at Blakeney Point and a fine female Red-footed Falcon near Cromer on the now annual late May long weekend in Norfolk. However, Chief and I got to Fairburn Ings in Yorkshire two hours too late to see a Needle-tailed Swift. Like many of the other 500 or so twitchers who turned up we were devastated but at least we could still dream about seeing the ultimate bird to see in Britain. Two days later it took me seven hours to hitchhike to Portland and eight to get back and I dipped a Black-eared Wheatear.

A planned trip to Shetland in July could not come soon enough. It started well. Chief and I could not find what would have been our first King Eider at the mouth of the Ythan, north of Aberdeen, but up river near Straduff Burn we saw our first Otter. The surprisingly large and fish-like mammal merged into the river and emerged a few minutes later with a flatfish. When it had finished eating the Otter oozed back into the water before bounding off across a mudbank with its back arched and tail raised, leaving us wondering if an Otter was better than a King Eider. On the ferry to Shetland we met up with Bryan, a friend from Sunderland, and enjoyed a North Sea full of birds; numerous auks with chicks, Gannets, Great Skuas, some Arctic Skuas and even a couple of European Storm Petrels but once again it was a mammal that was more exciting, this time in the form of three Pilot Whales, close enough to the ship to appreciate their impressive bulk.

Lerwick, the capital of the Shetland Islands, looked bleak at six o'clock in the morning, like a little fishing village which had become a large town overnight, with small fishing boats next to huge, cold, grey warehouses, the rooftops of which were sprinkled with Great Skuas, reminding us that we had never been so far north, and that out there beyond the town lay adventures with new birds in new terrain, the best any birder can hope for, and we couldn't wait. We picked up a hire-car and Chief drove north across the rolling, tree-less, moorlands of the long islands of Yell and Unst, stopping now and again so we could watch Red-throated Divers and Whimbrels on and around the numerous lochs. Eventually, we reached the end of the road at Stackhoull. The walk across Mill Fiel to Bluescudda Kame was hazardous. The Great Skuas, or Bonxies as they are known in Shetland, had young hiding amongst the tussocks and they warned us to keep away by dive-bombing us. It was no use hoping they would sweep away at the last moment. One struck me and from then on we had to watch them very closely as they came steaming in at speed looking fearless and powerful. Ducking once was not enough. The attacker just turned and came in again, with even more gusto, determined to strike. Only when we reached an unknown distance from the fluffy white chicks did the attacks become less venomous.

The scene from the top of Bluescudda Kame was magnificent. Great clouds of auks, Kittiwakes and Gannets swirled below, across the face of the mighty grey cliffs, rising over 600 feet (180 metres) from the sea. Every ledge, every horizontal bit of rock, every nook and cranny, it seemed, was packed solid with birds and on the swinging sea far below were rafts of auks as far as our eyes could see. I felt a little giddy looking down, past my red Dr. Martens, at the sea splashing, crashing and exploding against the rock face in a great roar of sound that was actually barely audible amongst the screeching and screaming of the seabird metropolis. I stepped back from the edge and immediately a few Puffins came whirling down with their webbed orange feet outspread and landed a few paces away. I had an image in my mind of what Hermaness might be like, having visited the seabird cities of Skomer and, only the morning before, the Bullers of Buchan, but my image was nothing like the magnitude of the massive cliffs I could see and the immense population of birds that lived there.

To our left was the main part of the gannetry and we settled down to search through the white-backed Gannets for a dark-backed bird which was one of the reasons why we were there. It was a southern hemisphere bird which had somehow crossed the equator and flown to

Hermaness every summer since 1972, even building a nest, and there it was, sat on its egg-less nest, spending yet another summer all alone. There are probably other Black-browed Albatrosses in the North Atlantic but the chances of a male and a female meeting, getting together, producing fertile eggs, and raising young are very remote, so our excitement at seeing our first albatross, the size of the surrounding Gannets and with handsome black eyebrows, was tinged with sadness. It was also laced with frustration for there was little chance of seeing an albatross as one should see an albatross, riding the air above the waves. 'Albert Ross' as the bird was affectionately known did stretch out one of its long, narrow wings briefly but it spent most of its time sleeping and my attention soon turned to the Puffins nearby.

They were so close and so tame I got down on my stomach to look them in the eye, and to examine the odd, ornamental, blue patches of skin above and below the red eye-rings, and their extraordinary, triangular, blue, yellow and red bills, and then I sat up, stood up and took a few steps back and tried to take in the whole scene before me; a group of five Puffins resting on the roof of the huge, precipitous, seabird city of Hermaness.

Nearly six hours had flown by and it was time to head for the island of Fetlar where we soon located three fabulous Red-necked Phalaropes, floating on a tiny, well-vegetated lochan near Muckle Wirawil, another wonderful wild place alive with Bonxies, Arctic Skuas, Whimbrels, Golden Plovers, Redshanks, Lapwings and Snipes. The petite phalaropes walked out of the water to preen before moving off into the luxuriant bog, leaving us to enjoy all the other birds. The warden said we could stay in a tiny caravan next to the reserve. There were two short and narrow beds and just enough floor space for a third person but we were not bothered, we didn't want to sleep we wanted to stay in the field.

So, in the half light of nearly midnight we braved some more Bonxies and walked to the cliff tops of Grunnigeo where we sat and waited for some European Storm Petrels to come in to their nesting burrows. The few we saw looked like bats tumbling into the cliff face although two were close enough for us to notice their white rumps. The Bonxies took to the air again on the walk back and they were even more menacing in the dark but on breaching the brow of the Scord of Grunnigeo they were forgotten in an instant as we were greeted by a monstrous moon rising over the moorland, a moon so big we could see the craters with our naked eyes. It lit up the whole island as it rose and was a fitting end to a fantastic day and unforgettable night. There is so much more to birding than the birds. Finally it was time to sleep, and to drift off while thinking about how fortunate I was to have discovered birds and birding and all the wonders that go with it.

A beautiful night became a bleak, cold, misty and wet morning so we stayed in our sleeping bags until midday. The warden warned us we were unlikely to see a Snowy Owl, the bird we hoped to see more than any other on Fetlar. Snowy Owls nested on the island from 1967 to 1975 and females had been present, more or less, ever since, but they moved between Fetlar and Unst and the only recent sightings were from Unst. We were not willing to risk that one had returned to Fetlar though, so inspite of the grim conditions we trudged across the rocky moors through the wet air and sweeping rain for nine hours. We saw no owls but a pair of Red-throated Divers with a chick materialising out of the mist billowing over Skutes Water was a memorable moment, and when the sun did break through for a while during the evening the three islands of Sound Gruney, Urie Lingey and Daaey shone like emeralds in the flat, grey sea off Vord Hill. They were some sight but we were soaked through and glad to get inside the caravan and lie down somewhere dry.

The gentle slopes of Unst were liberally sprinkled with snowy owl-like white rocks and after three hours checking and double-checking a million of them the thought entered my head that I might not actually see a real Snowy Owl. We were convinced there wasn't an owl on those rock-strewn hills but all we could do was scan and scan until the time came to leave. We changed position yet again, scanned lower down and looked at a million more rocks. Left to right, right to left, we swept with our binoculars, across the rocky slope, until one of those rocks looked a bit different to a rock, a bit like a bird, a lot like a bird actually, and what's more, once we had got our telescopes lined up on it that rock was glaring at us with two big, bright yellow eyes. Our first Snowy Owl, our first magnificent Snowy Owl, was richly barred grey and black, and almost perfectly matched the landscape but not quite, thank goodness. The bird knew we could see it and suddenly it sprung off the ground, spread its beautiful broad, black-and-white wings and flew up the slope low over the ground with stiff, powerful wing-beats and landed next to another rock. It was three very happy birders who boarded the ferry home.

The next morning we headed for the Ythan again and we could hardly believe it when after just ten minutes Chief spotted the sky-blue head of the drake King Eider sleeping on a sandbar with about two hundred everyday Eiders. We sat down on the beach and waited for the bird to wake up. This it did about an hour later and then flew into the channel where it bobbed up and down on the cool blue waters of the North Sea river mouth, near enough to clearly see its bright red and orange bill, greenish face, and two 'Killer Whale fins' on its back, formed by the elongated scapular feathers.

*Snowy Owl, Gallow Hill, Unst, Shetland, 11th July 1985*

## A MIND-BLOWING BIRDING TRIP TO A PLANET CALLED EARTH

A week after getting home, Nick Wall, who lived in Bristol, gave me a lift to Dawlish Warren in Devon where we saw a Lesser Crested Tern. He then drove across country overnight to Minsmere in Suffolk. Nick once trained to be a fighter pilot and he drove a car like one. When he reached a vehicle in front of the car he was piloting he positioned half of the car in the lane it was supposed to be in and the other half in the other lane so he could assess if it was safe, in his view, to overtake the annoying obstacle. When he decided it was safe he slammed his foot down and it was full speed ahead. I took a while to adjust to this exciting driving technique but it never became conducive to sleep so I was somewhat bedraggled by the time we entered the hide at Minsmere.

We soon saw the Greater Yellowlegs we were hoping to see but not for long and when Chief and Martin Hallam arrived after the bird had flown we took great delight in greeting them with, "Oh, you should've seen it! The legs were the same colour as the tern's beak!" They had not seen the tern either but instead of moaning about it Martin suggested we go see his friend Cliff Waller, the warden at the nearby Walberswick National Nature Reserve. The Greater Yellowlegs was seen at Minsmere from the 4th of July to the 14th of August 1985 but its appearances were very erratic and many a twitcher dipped it at least once. We were about to find out why. Cliff led us through what seemed like miles of head-high reeds to a screen, made out of reeds of course, from behind which the five of us were privileged to watch the Greater Yellowlegs chasing sticklebacks around a secret shallow lagoon deep in the heart of the vast reedbeds of Walberswick, home, Cliff told us, to 3000 Reedlings.

After another rigid night in Nick's passenger seat to see a Greater Sand Plover at Cley we were off to the Camargue and Pyrenees. The day we drove down through France a Little Whimbrel landed on the north Norfolk coast and stayed eleven days, more than long enough for 3000 twitchers apart from us to see it. This was the price to pay for foreign birding, a tiny one I concluded after fulfilling long-standing dreams of seeing my first Bee-eaters, Rollers, Lammergeiers, Wallcreepers, and so on. I was only back in Britain for a short time before four months in Pakistan, India and Nepal. When I was at Corbett National Park in December I met Martin Goodey and Nick Hunt from the Isles of Scilly, the latter on the trail of his dead father David Hunt who was killed by a Tiger in that very park only ten months before. They gave me a day-by-day account of October 1985 on Scilly, concentrating on the 12th when it was possible to see an unprecedented seven American landbirds, all on St Mary's; Black-billed and Yellow-billed Cuckoos, Myrtle and Parula Warblers, Rose-breasted Grosbeak, Bobolink and Red-eyed Vireo. I missed one of the most incredible autumns for rare birds on Scilly and the best October for rare birds ever in Britain and Ireland, and more woe was to follow. Five days later, at Bharatpur, I met Elizabeth Forster, a lively 70 year old on her seventh visit to India. She lived in Wiveton, near Cley, in Norfolk and she had the very latest news from home, including that of a Sora Rail at Pagham in Sussex, a Nutcracker near Westleton in Suffolk, and, the black-and-white bombshell for me, my all-time dream British rarity, a Black-and-white Warbler, had turned up in a wood in Norfolk, of all places, and stayed for nearly two weeks in December. It was all hard to believe, too much to take in and rather depressing until I thought about the mind-blowing birds and places I had seen instead.

After just a couple of weeks back in Britain my Himalayan dreams came true when I saw my first Waxwings *and* an Ivory Gull on the same day in early February. The black-faced and black-speckled gull seemed like it was still in the high Arctic, standing over a Guillemot carcass on Saltburn beach in Cleveland in a raging blizzard blowing in off the dark grey almost black North Sea. About five miles inland at Guisborough, after an agonising wait, the Waxwings came in and nature sprinkled them across the top of a hawthorn hedge. I counted 27, gracing the bare branches with the most beautiful colours. Not the gaudy reds and blues of some tropical species but exquisite touches of buffs and pinks. Sleek and immaculate one moment, big and fluffy the next, as their gorgeous soft feathering was raised against the cold, my first Waxwings were some of the most beautiful and confiding birds I had ever come across. We plodged through the snow to within a few paces, close enough to see their long crests, black masks and bibs, the intense salmon-pink colouring in the feathers on their foreheads and cheeks, the incredibly deep yellow tips to the primary flight feathers and tails of the adults, and even on some the narrow red waxy spikes sticking out from the secondary flight feathers which gives these phenomenal birds their name. Never before had I been so engrossed by birds and I had seen quite a few now.

It was a long time before I experienced such a meeting with nature again. Work for graduates was still hard to come by in the mid-eighties and someone with a Biology degree who was not prepared to work in a laboratory or be a medical representative, a fancy word for a salesman, found it especially difficult to find meaningful employment. I resorted to applying for a job with the London Wildlife Trust and was astonished to be offered the post of Field Officer for the London Borough of Camden. Moving to London for a job in nature conservation seemed perverse but I thought that I could help those who cared about what wildlife was left to try and save it. So, in late March 1986 I landed on a sofa in Shepherd's Bush, in a flat rented by several people, one of whom was a good friend of Chief's called Rodney. Having seen so many amazing birds abroad twitching was not as attractive as it once was but I was still very disappointed to miss out on a white Gyr in Devon that turned up when I turned up in London. Working alternate weekends did not help allay a little twitching apathy either.

However, by October I was looking forward to returning to Scilly, for a break from London as well as some proper day-to-day birding in a great place for scarce and rare birds. I never expected the two weeks to be as exciting as 1983, 1984 or 1985, and they were not. However, I still saw my first Bonelli's, Pallas's and Radde's Warblers, Red-eyed Vireo and Rose-breasted Grosbeak, and I got some intimate time with some of nature's wonder which it seemed I was really after, when I spent ages on Porthloo Beach watching a beautifully crisp, intricately marked, grey, black and buff juvenile Semi-palmated Sandpiper. It was foraging amongst the bundles of bladderwrack, the light bouncing off the white sand up on to its frosty belly, on a day when the air was clean and the light sparkling, as it often is on those brilliant islands.

When I got back I was appointed manager of Camley Street Natural Park, a tiny, innovative, urban nature reserve near King's Cross in central London. I also got to leave the sofa I had been sleeping on for so long. I swopped it for a futon in my own room in a flat in Tottenham which a couple who had lived with me in Shepherd's Bush had taken out a mortgage on. I became their lodger, mainly because the flat was within walking distance of Walthamstow Reservoirs, a large green space good for birds, few and far between in the sprawling capital. Wintering Long-eared Owls, and Goldeneyes and Goosanders, made for a happy start to 1987.

One Friday in February, the day before my alternate weekend off work, three Great Bustards finally looked like they had settled down in some fields at Theberton near Minsmere in Suffolk. It was all arranged; Gordon Avery was going to drive from Gloucester with Nick Wall and pick me up in Tottenham in time to get us to Theberton by dawn the next day, only Mr Avery failed to get out of bed when his alarm went off and we didn't make it until the next day, which of course was a day too late.

On Scilly I met Tony Clarke, a twitcher who in 1977 hitchhiked from Fair Isle to the Isles of Scilly to see the Black-and-white Warbler at Lower Moors. He put me in touch with Alun Hatfield who lived 'down the road' from me in Islington and was a new, raw, keen twitching machine. After our first telephone conversation that was it, he called me about every rare bird, the instant he heard about it, and if he needed it for his British List he would find a way of going for it, and he would go out of his way to try and take me with him, usually picking me up at home or work. This was a new experience for me and a very pleasant change from having to walk or hitchhike or get a bus or a train to a main road where a pick-up had been arranged, *and* I always went along free of charge in his company car.

Al worked in the murky world of finance, earned a fortune and had more suits in his wardrobe than some clothes shops. Before donning a suit he was a Royal Marine, a career derailed by a leg broken in several places. Having completed one of the most demanding training regimes possible, including the infamous commando course, arguably the toughest mental and physical test there is he was not one for giving up on a rare bird easily. He was also highly trained in not eating, at least between huge meals, sleeping much and doing all the driving without getting tired. All this together with his infectious energy and the arrival of numerous rare birds made 1987 a very special year indeed.

It didn't begin until May however, Monday the 11th to be precise, when Al picked me up mid-afternoon and drove like the wind to Cley where we saw a Wilson's Phalarope before moving on to Minsmere where we somehow arrived before dark but still dipped a Caspian Tern. The next evening we were at Chichester Gravel Pits watching a Little Bittern followed by a Black-winged Stilt on a familiar lagoon from my past at Farlington Marshes. I got back home at 11 p.m. and could not believe the message by the telephone, especially since I had just finished my two days off work. Al then called, of course, and promised we would be back in time for work, so three hours after getting home we set off again, back to Cley for dawn. We were joined by about 300 other twitchers who were as glad as we were when the birds materialised on the mud in front of the North Hide shortly after 4.30 a.m., leaving plenty of time for us to get back to that time-consuming sideline of life that pays for what really counts; birding, twitching and the birds. We were in London at 9 a.m. as Al predicted, in plenty of time to wallow in the almost unbelievable sight of two Slender-billed Gulls in Britain, the first record of the species since 1971. Probably a pair, they were in the full flush of breeding plumage, both with lovely pink blushes on their white bellies.

A dashing male Red-footed Falcon in Dorset was next up then on the 30th of May I heard the great news that there was a Roller near my old favourite the Beaulieu Road Station area of the New Forest. It would make a wonderful birthday present the next day and since it was my birthday, Carolyn, back in my life again, came along on her first twitch, with me, Al and Chief. She wasn't too happy about having to get up at two in the morning so we could be there at first light and was even less impressed after two hours passed by without a sign of the promised big bright blue bird. I think she liked the Barn Owl, a nice diversion for the rest of us, but that was soon forgotten when the shout went up and there it was, a beautiful Roller perched half way up a pine tree. Carolyn got to see twitchers running from every direction and setting up their telescopes as fast as they could, and after feeling the excitement and seeing the bird I think she had a little bit more of an idea as to why we twitchers twitch.

During the summer Al and I seemed to spend most of the time we were not working, in Norfolk. An attempt to see a

Caspian Tern, visiting Hickling Broad on and off, was a failure but we did see the family of Black-winged Stilts at Holme, including the three juveniles which looked like big bumblebees on stilts. A few days later we were back, for a Whiskered Tern at Pentney Gravel Pits. We then dipped, for the second time, what would have been Al's first Purple Heron at Welney before finally catching up with not one but two Caspian Terns as the carmine sun dropped below Breydon Water. After a fly past the huge but elegant terns settled on the mud next to a Shelduck and to our surprise were almost the same size. Persistence eventually paid off with the Purple Heron as well when, at the third attempt, we were able to look at the beauty through our telescopes, seeing the bright yellow spear of a beak, crimson neck and breast stripes, purple shoulders and thighs, and silvery scapulars elongated to form lovely plumes.

The next crazy fast drive north after finishing work was to the beach car-park at Cley in late August. We didn't get there until gone six p.m. so we had to yomp along Blakeney Point. Halfway to Halfway House we came across a small group of twitchers next to a large area of sodden *suaeda*, knee-high plants that tired birds blown across the North Sea from Scandinavia take cover in, in this case a superb, bright green and silky white Greenish Warbler, with a line of lime-green secondary feathers in its wing. There was no time to get to know it; we had to get to Halfway House. When we got there the Great Snipe, a great rarity, flew right past us and landed on the shingle, standing erect with its legs flexed and neck outstretched in an extraordinary pose, the boldly barred breast and flanks clearly visible. It didn't like being in the open so it wasn't there long, and soon we were on our way back. There wasn't much time, the light was fading, but we still managed to see an Icterine Warbler, a Wood Warbler, four Wrynecks, at least ten Garden Warblers and a Pied Flycatcher to complete a brilliant couple of hours and leave us wondering what else we might have seen given better weather and more time. There lies the rub with the twitching business; it's incredibly exciting but there never seems to be time to actually find any birds.

Eleven days later, in early September, the new shorebird was a rufous-capped adult Sharp-tailed Sandpiper at Sandwich Bay in Kent, and the new warbler a very confiding Booted Warbler with bluish 'boots' in the observatory moat at Dungeness, Kent.

October 1987 began with a brilliant full summer-plumaged White-billed, or rather yellow-billed, Diver off Flamborough Head in Yorkshire. Then I really did twitch. On the memo-pad at work a colleague wrote, 'Nigel won't be in today. There's a Black-and-white Warbler in Devon.' They knew all about Black-and-white Warblers at work. I never stopped going on about them, for although I had seen many of the cracking little things in Texas I still dreamed of seeing one in Britain. So, on hearing the news there was not much chance of me concentrating on work or anything else to do with normal life like eating, drinking and sleeping, until I got to Prawle in Devon. With a Wood Thrush, the first for Britain, on St Agnes in the Isles of Scilly and the potential for so much more we were off. Al, Martin Hallam, Robin Chittenden and I picked up Mark Golley in Okehampton on the way to East Prawle Woods where we arrived not long after 7 a.m. The bird had

*Black-and-white Warbler, Prawle, Devon, England,
9th October 1987*

already been seen but lost and during the next couple of hours it gave everyone, especially me it seemed, the run around, roaming the woods with a tit flock, but, with the clock ticking down to the time we had to leave to make our flight to Scilly I finally arrived at the corner of the woods where it had been seen again in time to lock on to the brilliant bird. It was shuffling along a lichen-covered horizontal hawthorn branch as only a Black-and-white Warbler can do, like a dainty Nuthatch but all striking black and white streaks and stripes, and then it was gone, with the fast-moving tit flock, and yet another dream had come true.

After only an afternoon's birding on St Mary's the following day, due to an excessive celebration of the warbler, I was celebrating life I love you again in the *Bishop and Wolf* when new news spread like wildfire through the crowded pub. There was a Philadelphia Vireo on Tresco, another first for Britain, following one in Ireland two years before. Well before dawn the narrow gap alongside those of us sleeping in the corridor of the house in Springfield Court, where we had been allowed to crash, was busy with excited birders and we soon joined them. The fifteen or so of us in that tiny house were out in no time, even though most of us had only been in a few hours, having celebrated the news of the vireo late into the night in the Porthcressa. We joined hundreds of others in the streets on the quick march down through town to the quay.

The boatmen were fully aware of the unfolding event and they and their boats were bobbing up and down just off the steps ready to come in and take us across to Tresco as soon as there was light enough to see. It was pandemonium along Borough Farm Lane as every bird which appeared in the hedge the vireo was seen in the day before caused an almighty panic, and yet there was no need to panic because the bird appeared in the sycamores lining the lane itself, and what a little beauty it was, with a blue cap, white eyebrows flaring behind its eyes, a green back and a bright yellow throat. It made several hundred people very happy, even the Scilly veterans around the dinner table in Springfield Court, including Bryan Bland, Peter Grant and Pete Milford.

The Isles of Scilly are an incredible place for rare birds. The next day an Eye-browed Thrush from Siberia turned up and the day after that a Blackpoll Warbler from America, and Al was very happy, number one because he had never seen either of them before, and number two because I had and he had now gripped both of them back. He also got to see his first Swainson's Thrush, another grip back, in the beautiful Cot Valley in far west Cornwall, on the way home. That was Tuesday the 13th. Overnight on the 15th-16th of October 1987 southern England was battered by a big storm but we managed to make it to Nanquidno, the valley a mile south of Cot, on the 17th, in time to see our first fabulous Parula Warbler in Britain. The brightly-coloured ball of energy foraged so close to us we could marvel at its blue-grey head, shining green back and bright yellow throat with a splash of orange.

There was nowhere near enough time to spend with the Parula. Much to our girlfriends' disgust we were on our way to Scilly again. Steve Howat had come across a Hermit Thrush on St Agnes, only the third ever seen in Britain. Alas, it was gone by the time we got there. Chief was in town though so there was nothing for it but to party. No more rarities turned up on the islands but we got back to London in time to see two Sabine's Gulls, stragglers from the storm, foraging over a field a couple of miles from home in Tottenham. It was still October and the way the month was going we felt sure there were more rare birds to come and we didn't have to wait long for the next, a handsome male Desert Wheatear at Landguard in Suffolk. Two days later we heard there was a Veery on the island of Lundy off Devon, the second and first twitchable one in Britain. Another overnight drive began and the next day we were watching a lovely warm brown and smoky grey thrush, all the way from America.

I was happy twitching, I was happy birding, I was not happy at work. I wanted to be involved in nature conservation outdoors not indoors. I was spending far too much time at a desk, often dealing with matters that had nothing to do with birds and other wildlife at all, and almost every day at work seemed to involve my name being called out a million times, to sort this and that out. I thought long and hard about it, and decided, while I was still young and healthy, and I had enough money in the bank, to fulfill my long-held dream of travelling to Africa. When I returned I would look for another, more appropriate, job. So, in late December 1987 I got on a plane to Kenya where I spent a month touring the country with three friends, and another two months on my own.

I didn't get back from Africa until late March, when Chief let me move into a room in his house in Reading, the ideal location from which to twitch from, and yet there was nothing to twitch until mid-May when the first Caspian Plover in Britain since 1890 landed on my favourite place in the world, the island of St Agnes. The news broke late afternoon. The next day was a Sunday so there were no flights or sailings to Scilly. However, so many twitchers bombarded the *Isles of Scilly Steamship Company* with telephone calls the company decided to put on a special sailing of the *Scillonian III*. Al and Chief dared not cancel arrangements with their girlfriends. I was not seeing Carolyn that weekend. It took me until nearly midnight to secure a lift, thanks to Tony Clarke, and boy was I glad when my name was called out on the quay along with nearly 300 others, to board the boat. I was off, back to Scilly yet again, only to face the worst dip ever. It was hard to believe but the bird was gone.

A week later another great rarity turned up although the news did not reach the twitching scene until Thursday morning the 2nd of June. Once again Chief was unable to go. Al was and he spent the whole day (at work) on the telephone making sure the team he was also putting together had places on the ferry to the island of Hoy in Orkney, the next morning. Well behind schedule, Al drove over from London and picked me up gone 10 p.m. with Tony Clarke and Robin Chittenden already in the car, and we headed north, picking up Ian Ricketts on the M6. Worried about the time it would take to reach John O'Groats we stopped only for fuel and zapped along at a steady ton, so when we came to a surprise roundabout near Inverness the car went straight on instead of to the left, thanks to some oil on the road according to Al who was driving. The rest of us, half asleep, were woken up by two big bumps as the front then back wheels rose over a high kerb, and then we came to a shuddering halt in the middle of the roundabout. Still shaken, we nearly came to a worse end farther north, when the car refused to round a hairpin bend. Al, who had passed an advanced driving test, just about managed to stop the car two feet short of a barrier that overlooked a steep cliff by turning the steering wheel and therefore the front wheels wildly from side to side. It was therefore with some relief that we got out of the car at John O'Groats, only to be presented with news of a Pallas's Rosefinch, a potential first for Britain, on a different Orkney island, North Ronaldsay. There was pandemonium, as people discussed which bird to go for first. I had no problem deciding and was very relieved when, after a lengthy delay, the 50 or so twitchers on the quay agreed to go for the bird on Hoy first.

We were taken to Melsetter House at the southern end of Hoy in a fleet of rusty cars and minibuses. After an hour watching the empty sky over the large garden and surrounding area the time came for everyone to make a big decision. People ummed and aahed for ages. Having no money and no job since I got back from Kenya I could barely afford the cost of getting to Hoy let alone an extra ferry trip on top and I wasn't bothered about the rosefinch anyway since it could easily be dismissed as an escaped cage bird, and even though a few people offered to lend me the money I decided to stay put on Hoy. I wanted to see what promised to be one of the best birds in the world and I didn't care if it took one or two days.

In the end about half stayed and half left. A few hours later I was scanning from a lane when I saw a tiny black-and-white rocket come bombing in over the fields. "There it is!" I shouted to no one and ran back to the garden to relay the news only to find the bird already there, swooping in low and back out again. We all moved out on to the lane and there it was, working the flies along the edge of the sycamore stand at the bottom of the garden with unbelievable speed and agility. One slight movement of its wings acted like a turbo switch as it shot up high before arcing back around and down low over a grass field giving supreme views of its coppery-edged silver mantle in the sunlight. Then it would make a turn, head toward us again and shoot past just above our heads with a whoosh and its beak open and ready to gobble up the bluebottles gathered in the sun and out of the breeze at the edge of the trees. Time and again it did this until near dark when, after three unsuccessful attempts to land on the house to roost, the bird disappeared.

The five of us left retired to the local hostelry for some much-needed food and a celebratory drink or two before returning to Melsetter where the very friendly owners let us sleep in their summer house. The Liverpool crew departed early the next morning, leaving me alone with a Needle-tailed Swift. I could not take my eyes off the ultimate flying bird, even when I was tucking into some surprise sandwiches and coffee brought out to me by the residents of the house. I was still enjoying the treat when I heard a minibus pull up out front. The first couple of crews who had been for the rosefinch scrambled out of it and after assuring them that the bird was still present I said, "Follow me" and they strode quickly down the lane behind me to the sycamores where they let out a great roar of delight as the bird made its first pass over their heads. A few minutes later most were agreeing with me that it was by far the best bird and most amazing thing they had ever seen.

A Black-winged Pratincole in Clevedon a week later and a Bridled Tern on Anglesey in early July were impressive but they were nowhere near as good as the Needle-tailed Swift. In mid-July another Caspian Plover turned up at Aberlady Bay in Scotland but it was mid-week and it didn't stay until the weekend. I then got a job with the London Wildlife Trust again, helping to save and manage as much habitat as possible left in Thamesmead, a new town being built on the south bank of the river east of Woolwich. Twitching became less important for a while but it was *Jean Michel Jarre in Docklands* with Carolyn that did for a bright young male Baltimore Oriole on St Agnes. A two-week trip to Scilly in October was also impossible and I had to settle for a long weekend. It began well when Chief, Mark

Golley and I watched a Parula Warbler in Cot Valley as it foraged at speed along eye-level branches, hanging upside-down and performing all manner of contortions to catch insects hiding on the undersides of the remaining leaves. On Scilly we saw the first twitchable Buff-bellied Pipit for Britain on St Mary's, and better still, a bright, beaky, active Arctic Warbler, busy chasing flies in the lighthouse garden on St Agnes.

A breakdown in communications caused me to miss the American Robin at Inverbervie in Scotland over the Christmas period and I wouldn't cross the road to look at a Double-crested Cormorant let alone go all the way to Billingham in the north-east of England for one, even if it was the first for Britain. No, I was becoming more discerning about what I twitched now. I was only going to go for what I considered to be good-looking birds, and they don't come much better looking than Golden-winged Warblers. No one could believe it when one was seen by a birder on his way to post a letter on a housing estate in Kent in February 1989. There had never been one in Europe let alone Britain and it had never even been predicted to turn up and yet there was one an hour down the road from where I lived. Al and I were there by one o'clock in the afternoon. We saw a lovely Waxwing but dipped the warbler, not surprising considering most of the thirty or so twitchers present including Al were in suits and spent more time avoiding the television cameras than looking for the bird, not wishing to be seen by their fellow employees and employers on the news that evening. Al, Chief, Ando, who happened to be in London for the weekend, and I returned two days later. It was a Saturday and there were hundreds of twitchers dashing around that housing estate. The scenes were unbelievable as they blocked roads and crowded around tiny walled gardens, as they tried to lock eyes on the very mobile bird. It was a stunner but it was most certainly not a beautiful wild bird in a beautiful wild place. It was a lost bird, who knows maybe not even a wild bird, an escape perhaps, and it was being chased around by a mob. Had it been on St Agnes in the presence of a few hundred it might have been a more wholesome and enjoyable experience but I was determined to be *even* more careful about which birds to twitch now.

My reservations didn't stop me from travelling with Chief to Roch in west Wales to see a Baltimore Oriole which had been visiting a sheltered garden on the shores of St Bride's Bay since the beginning of the year. The blood was then stirred by news of a male Desert Wheatear at Barn Elms Reservoirs in London and so work came to an abrupt halt and I dashed across the city on the tube to lie down on the ground and watch the beauty with a jet black throat, wings and tail. Continued ruminations about twitching did cost me a Baillon's Crake. I turned down Al's offer of a lift to see the one which walked by people's feet in Mowbray Park, Sunderland, in mid-May, partly because I was birding like mad locally, in preparation for the Big Bird Race, the national event to raise money for conservation, in which I thought our team could see a hundred species within the Greater London boundary. Unfortunately our sponsored four-wheel-drive got stuck in a lagoon outfall at Rainham Marshes and we fell five short. I have still not seen a Baillon's Crake, anywhere in the world.

I had no problem dropping everything when I heard there was a Blue-cheeked Bee-eater at Great Cowden in

Humberside. It was the sixth for Britain, but if it stayed one more day it would be the first twitchable one. I had dreamed of seeing the beauty in Britain ever since reading Hilda Quick's gripping account of the one on St Agnes in 1951. I had seen many in Kenya but never looked one in the eye so it was one of the tensest twitches ever. I could not get to sleep all the way there and was out of the car as soon as the dawn rain stopped. Not long after, I saw a long-looking green bird a long way off on a low barbed wire fence. It had to be it - even in the dull, cloudy conditions it was unbelievably bright green - unless it was a parakeet. When I moved a little closer it was obviously a bee-eater, a beautiful bee-eater with turquoise eyebrows and cheeks, a yellow forehead and chin, and a deep red throat. The dazzler made frequent sallies from its favourite fence, dashing out low over a field of barley where with a quick hover and a twist it plucked a bee out of the air then swept high up in an arc and swooped gracefully back down to the fence, flashing its brilliant coppery underwings and occasionally letting out a lovely 'turturula' call or two. I watched it with a flood of joy, marvelling at the colours and particularly its bold flights. After a fly-past, overhead, when it just looked absolutely fantastic, the bird moved off to some high, inaccessible, telegraph wires in the distance, and so we left, glowing with satisfaction.

The next day Al drove north again, to Boughton Fen in Norfolk where we watched a River Warbler singing its rolling metallic rattle from the top of a hawthorn bush in the middle of a reed-bed. Good numbers of Cory's and Great Shearwaters had been seen flying past Porthgwarra so Al, Chief, Martin Hallam and I decided we would head down there for Saturday the 12th of August but that didn't happen. The prospect of an overnight drive from London to the far southwest corner of the land for what we assumed would be distant views of our first Cory's Shearwaters was not a thrilling one, especially to Al. When we did get our act together the following night he dropped out at the last minute, a decision he was to regret for ever.

We were in position at 7 a.m. in surprisingly benign conditions for a seawatch; a lot of sunshine and a light westerly breeze, and yet from the moment we started scanning the sea there was a more or less constant stream of large shearwaters going by. The broad wings and languid flight of my first Cory's looked very different from the narrower wings and slightly more dashing passing of the Greats, only one of which had I seen before. We saw 60 Cory's and 20 Greats during the morning, as well as 19 Sooty Shearwaters and five Balearic Shearwaters but they were all blown out of the water when a man yelled out, "Soft-plumaged Petrel!" The bird was halfway to the Runnel Stone Buoy apparently, "flying with a Sooty!" Fifty or so birders looked around in shock then looked back at the sea with their telescopes and desperately tried to locate the fastest flying seabird out there. It was a frantic few seconds but the man's directions were spot on and virtually everybody including us three managed to get on it in time to see a dark 'M' across its grey wings. Then it was gone and a great roar spread through the fortunate crowd of ecstatic birders who could not believe they had just seen the first *pterodroma* petrel, probably a Fea's, to fly past a British or Irish headland since the only other one off Cape Clear Island in 1974! We did not know at the time but what was probably the same bird had flown past the day before, and it, or another, flew past the day after.

The man who got us on that bird was Peter Harrison, who wrote and illustrated *Seabirds*, one the classic bird books. We had a chat with him on our way to the car to return home. He was on his way back to seawatch after a short break and said we should stay on because he was sure that there was going to be a Little Shearwater past that afternoon, but Chief had to be back for some do with his girlfriend and so we missed not one but two Little Shearwaters. They didn't matter though; thanks to the *pterodroma* we were buzzing for weeks.

Four days later I was enjoying another seabird feast, with Ando at North Gare, Teesmouth, on yet another quest for Long-tailed Skua. A wreck of sprats in the estuary mouth had attracted around three thousand Kittiwakes and about a hundred Arctic Skuas, and we spent seven hours watching them and working through them for a Long-tail, alas to no avail. It was pulsating birding though. The skuas were sweeping through the Kittiwakes and a hundred Sandwich Terns, and not long before we had to leave, four 'Poms' came powering in from the North Sea and immediately pounced on the backs of Kittiwakes.

A Nighthawk, yet another dream bird to see in Britain, was found on Tresco in mid-September and it was still present on a Friday when Al and Chief decided to go for it but I bottled, partly because I thought it had been there so long the chances of it staying any longer were slim, and partly because I was not willing to risk the cost, especially considering I would be heading to the islands for a fortnight in a week's time. They dipped, saw nothing else, got stuck on the islands due to bad weather and didn't get back to work until the Wednesday. On the Saturday I got groggily off the overnight bus from London to Penzance, wobbled the short distance to the quay and boarded the *Scillonian III* at the start of a long-awaited birding sojourn on Scilly.

A stunning stripey Aquatic Warbler popped up in front of me in Lower Moors and I learnt an awful lot about how to identify a fine range of other scarce birds in Britain but never saw anything in the same league as a Nighthawk. By the end of the trip Chief had joined me and Al arrived on Friday the 13th. He went straight to the *Bishop and Wolf*, got so drunk he was unable to join Chief and I for a Melodious Warbler on Tresco the next day and, having not seen a bird since landing on Scilly, took my seat on the first plane off the islands when news broke of a Red-breasted Nuthatch in Norfolk because I could not get back to St Mary's in time.

Chief and I had to get the boat like many others and drive overnight to Holkham where we arrived at dawn. The nuthatch, the first of its kind to be seen in Britain, was in a massive pine forest and all the talk amongst the hundreds of twitchers present was about its call which, apparently, sounded like a toy trumpet and was touted as the best way to locate it. All very well except when someone shouts out they've just heard it at one end of the forest while another is claiming they can hear at the opposite end. To be fair, the bird was very mobile, which meant the three times we managed to get to where it had been seen fairly quickly the views were brief, and we had to wait until mid-afternoon, when we just happened to be in the right place at the right time, to see the bird in all its glory. Normal Nuthatches are great birds. They are energetic, they climb up and down trunks, and along the tops and bottoms of branches, vigorously searching for food, and they are blue and red with black masks, but the dinkier Red-breasted Nuthatch is something else thanks to its striking black and white face that contrasts with the brighter blue upperparts and deeper red underparts, so it was with considerable relief that we finally got to grips with the very smart bird that had somehow made it from North America to Norfolk.

The first bird I twitched in 1990 was a Naumann's Thrush a tube ride away in London. Driving overnight to see a Pine Bunting at Big Waters Nature Reserve in Northumberland I nearly killed the crew of Chief, John Archer, Tony Morris and myself when I lost control of Tony's car on a patch of sheet ice while overtaking a long lorry on the A1 in the middle of the freezing night. Fortunately we arrived at Ando's in Sunderland in good time to be served up bacon rolls before he navigated us to Big Waters where the feeding station afforded stunning views of rarely seen, at least in my case, Tree Sparrows and Yellowhammers, which were far more enjoyable than the dowdy bunting. A week later a male Sardinian Warbler reached Stratton in Cornwall the day before a planned long weekend there with friends. Chief and I were prepared for a long wait to see what is a well-known skulker but it flew out and landed on the handle of the garden owners' spade not long after we arrived before dropping to the ground to forage in full view amongst the early flowers a few paces away. Al, Chief and I were back in the southwest on the first day of spring to watch a Great Spotted Cuckoo catching caterpillars in the Dawlish Warren dunes in Devon and Ando, Chief and I went to Shoreham in Sussex to see another in April.

## A MIND-BLOWING BIRDING TRIP TO A PLANET CALLED EARTH

The stunning news in mid-May was of a Pallas's Sandgrouse on Shetland, a bird few dared to even dream of seeing in Britain. Al, Chief and I spent hours discussing the possibility of breaking our law not to get on the slippery and expensive slope of twitching Shetland, and the bird was still present and we were still talking about it on Sunday the 27th when we heard there was an Alpine Accentor on the Isle of Wight, the first in Britain for twelve years. I was glad I always took the last week of May off work, just in case there was a mega or two, as there often was, because the first Monday morning ferry to the island was no problem for me, although I did have to put up with just two hours with the confiding bird so that Al and Chief could get back to work. Not that they got much work done, for plans then had to be put in place to rush to Lundy, from where there was even more shocking news than the sandgrouse. The first Ancient Murrelet to be seen away from the Pacific turned up there the same day as the Alpine Accentor and the second White-throated Robin in the British Isles which landed on Skokholm, a site too sensitive to host a massive twitch what with all those Manx Shearwater nesting burrows. So, two days after visiting The Needles on the Isle of Wight we were sat at the top of Jenny's Cove on Lundy watching the extraordinary auk from Alaska as it flew out from the cliff and landed on the sea where it loafed about with the local Guillemots and Razorbills for over an hour.

Chief had the twitching fever back now and wangled the next day off so we could twitch a male Black-headed Bunting at Marloes in far west Wales but the bird did not become a birthday present for me. In the meantime Al was busy sorting out Shetland. Yep, what with the Black-browed Albatross being seen recently, two Snowy Owls on Fetlar and other migrants turning up, we cracked. After the overnight drive to Aberdeen there was enough time on the Saturday morning to see the sleepy King Eider and eight far more handsome Black-throated Divers on the Ythan Estuary before our flight. It was wet and windy on Shetland and it was a shaky landing. We were glad to get in the hire car and speed to the Loch of Hillwell but it took a while to find the sandgrouse which was a bit bedraggled to be honest, sheltering from the driving rain behind a tussock of grass, and something of an anticlimax. It was a dapper but damp dove-like bird with an orange face, sky-blue eye-rings and sandy upperparts with wavy black bars.

Leaving it to dry off in peace as the weather improved we moved on to Scalloway where there had been a Barred Warbler earlier in the week, a very rare bird in Britain during the spring. We were pessimistic. We didn't know if it was still present and we didn't know where to look for it so we just stopped at the first area of scrub and out popped a first-summer male Barred Warbler, which started singing, a short song which sounded like a cross between a Blackcap and a Whitethroat, and it showed so well we were able to see its yellow eyes, the pale grey crescent-shaped bars along its breast sides and flanks, darker on its vent, and the lovely soft blue-grey upperparts with two narrow white wing bars. It was such a rare and unusual bird we thought it was better than the sandgrouse.

Until the next day that is, when grim weather forced us to abandon the long slog north to look for the albatross and owls, and return to the sandgrouse. The low cloud and rain had cleared when we arrived back at the Loch of Hillwell in the early afternoon and the bird was foraging at close range in a large bare field, the nearest thing to the Asian steppes, where it was from, it could find. It was a lovely, very neat and compact, delicately marked bird, foraging across the ground with the sandgrouse shuffle on its short, feathered legs, and I was very happy watching it. On turning to go I saw an odd bird on a fence which turned out to be a Red-backed Shrike and the next day we added an Icterine Warbler which was singing in the Sumburgh Hotel garden, before dashing to Loch of Spiggie where once again I heard but did not see a certain bird and so we left Shetland with me having seen a Pallas's Sandgrouse in Britain but never a Quail.

We thought that was it, the remarkable late spring surge of rarities was over, but after being home for three days we were on the road again, overnight again, to Penzance and the *Scillonian III* again, to St Mary's where the first Tree Swallow ever seen this side of the Atlantic was sweeping low across Porth Hellick beach, its lovely blue-green back shimmering in the sunlight. It was great to be on our fifth major twitch in twelve days, watching yet another incredible rarity in yet another wonderful setting, with so many familiar faces, many of whom had become even more familiar during the crazy days of late May-early June 1990, but the boat beckoned and another long drive home was ahead of us, presenting plenty of time for the satisfaction to sink in.

Then it was time to face the comedown as normal life resumed. Another extended week off work was gone in a flash, though not for Carolyn. Time, precious time, and money; several hundred pounds that could have been spent on a holiday for us, had slipped away. Even I was upset by how much I had spent. It seemed to me that after several years twitching there were not so many new birds to see and those that were new tended to turn up on offshore islands which were expensive to get to, and though the drug that twitching is was still a powerful attraction I couldn't help feeling that the money would be much better spent in foreign lands where so many more new birds could be seen in even more wonderful places. And Carolyn was distraught.

I resolved to be more considerate. The list of birds I had seen in Britain was about 390. The 400 barrier was in sight. I promised to come up with a list of five birds I would drop everything for. The rest could be got by just the odd twitch on weekends. There was no hurry but if any of the five turned up, on the mainland or on an easily accessible and cheap-to-get-to island, I would be off. The big five were; Bee-eater, Wallcreeper, Hawk Owl, Red-flanked Bluetail and Rüppell's Warbler. I stuck to my guns and none of them turned up in the next couple of months - even an irresistible second ever spring male Pied Wheatear turned up on a weekend - but the years of scribbled messages by the telephone, plans changed at the last minute, cancelled weekends together, complete and utter selfishness, an obsession almost out of control, a life revolving around birds, had taken their toll, the damage was done and irreparable, and Carolyn was gone.

One bird not on my list was Yellow-throated Vireo. It had not even been predicted to turn up by Chandler Robbins in his paper *Predictions of future Nearctic landbird vagrants to Europe* in *British Birds* magazine in 1980 and his list included virtually every other bird from North America that had turned up. Yet one reached Kenidjack in Cornwall in September and Al and I were there at dawn the day after the news broke, a Thursday, along with several hundred others who didn't dare wait for the weekend. Although the bird was very active I was able to latch on to it for long periods, even with the telescope, staring in amazement at how bright its yellow spectacles and throat were, how neat the white trims to its black wing feathers looked, and how lovely the soft blue-grey wing-coverts looked, the colours and patterns combining perfectly to make one very smart very rare bird.

There was nothing else to get the juices flowing before Al, Chief and I headed to Malaya, Borneo, Sulawesi and Java in mid-December, and it was not until October the following year when the next major twitch took place. Al and I headed north, for a dainty, yellow-eyed Desert Warbler at Flamborough Head in Yorkshire. A week later I was back, with Chief, for another look, because he was also going for a Nutcracker in Staffordshire, a bird the like of which I had never seen before, a flamboyant character of a bird, like an agile, giant Starling, chocolate-coloured with bold white streaks and teardrops, and instantly a very memorable bird. December came around and I was off abroad again, with Al and two other friends, this time to Venezuela and Chile.

I had to wait two years after coming up with that list for Carolyn, until September 1992, to reach a total of 400 birds seen in Britain. I had seen a few 'Rüpe's' along with 'Krüpe's', 'Cretzsch' and 'Scops' on a trip to Turkey that summer, as well as some lovely Masked Shrikes, so I was very happy for Britain's fourth Rüppell's Warbler, at Holme in Norfolk, to bring up the milestone, and I did a little dance of delight in celebration.

Another year and a bit passed, part of which was spent in Australia, before the next one on the list came along. When the news broke I was literally twitching; there was a Red-flanked Bluetail on the British mainland and not only that it was at Winspit in Dorset, 'down the road' as far as twitching was concerned. Al and I got in from a party at 4 a.m. but were on the road at nine and the little gem appeared almost at arm's length, showing a surprisingly bright blue upper tail and orange flanks. I had seen another of Britain's mystical rarities but I had to wait another six years for the third one of the five on the list. It was not such a rarity but it *was* a Bee-eater, on St Mary's in the Isles of Scilly in September 1999, the forerunner in the first fantastic run of birds since 1990, some of which turned up where I happened to live at the time, on my local patch, the island of St Agnes.

*Bee-eaters, Mas D'Agon, Camargue, France, 25th August 1985*

## 3

# CAMARGUE and PYRENEES

Nick Wall almost casually mentioned he was driving down to the Camargue and Pyrenees with two friends for a couple of weeks and sort of asked if I would like to join them. Since I was unemployed again, this time with money in the bank, and had dreamed of Bee-eaters, Rollers and especially Wallcreepers since buying *The Hamlyn Guide to Birds of Britain and Europe* years ago, I did not take long to answer in the affirmative. Arthur Singer's striking paintings to illustrate Wallcreeper take up half a page and made it look like the most exotic bird in Europe to me. I also longed to go birding abroad. My only experience of foreign fields had been during my first summer holiday as a student when I hitchhiked to Germany to spend a hot summer living with Ando, Rob, Tig and a lot of cockroaches in a tiny flat in Munich where I earnt enough money labouring to buy a motorbike. Rob and Tig did the same. Ando spent most of his money on drink although there was enough left for a new telescope. We did not have much time to go birding, saw very little apart from our first Honey Buzzards, when we did, and found it a bit disappointing so I was incredibly excited about going to the Camargue and Pyrenees, which I knew were two of the best places for birds in Europe.

So, one August night, we boarded the ferry to France; me, Nick and his two friends, Ian and Neil, who were not interested in birds but were keen to travel around southern France sampling the food and wine, so during the trip Nick and I were often left to get on with the more serious business of birding after we dropped them off in some town or village. We slept under the stars in the Massif Central the first night and awoke to sunny skies full of raptors. Virtually the first bird I saw was my first Booted Eagle and a little farther along the D12 my first Short-toed Eagle flew over. Red Kites were followed by Black Kites and the third eagle of the day, a Golden, soared above the spectacular Gorges du Tarn. By dusk we had reached the quiet Pont de Crau campsite just outside Arles, our base for five days birding the Camargue.

It rained for most of the first day but that was a minor inconvenience as we looked for new birds in new terrain, the way to live life. The rain was very heavy first thing and Nick thought it might be best to head for the semi-arid stony plains of La Crau first, where the weather might be better. It was, a bit, and I was soon watching my first Rollers, spectacular birds with blue wings flashing as five of them flew between fence posts and dropped to the ground to pounce on big beetles, just a few paces away.

My first taste of the Camargue was nothing like I had imagined. Rain poured from a gloomy grey thundery sky on to the large lakes known as *etangs* that were full of drenched flamingos. My first Bee-eater was not dazzling in foreign sunshine it was perched on a telegraph wire with its bill pointing skywards and raindrops running down it. Despite the dull conditions its exotic colours glowed in the gloom and the combination of black mask, deep yellow throat, sky blue undersides, coppery crown and mane, golden back, and long blue-green wings was brilliant. I had never seen a bird with such rich and colourful plumage and it was the first of many, for during the following days we frequently encountered flocks of up to 42 and stopped to watch them every time. The birds were never still, always dashing from bushes, trees and wires, flying fast in pursuit of bees and dragonflies then sweeping back to their perch on stiff wings, calling constantly, and what beautiful calls they were; rolling purrs something like their French name *Guepier*. The strong, cold and dry wind called the mistral blew from the northwest for a couple of days, clearing the sky, and in the sunshine which flooded the Camargue the ever-hunting, constantly calling Bee-eaters, their glorious but not gaudy colours flashing, were the highlight of every day. They were the highlight of my life so far. Bee-eaters were quite simply, the best birds I had ever seen.

The Camargue was a dream world to me, a paradise where birds abounded. On the marshes at Mas D'Agon there were always over a hundred Whiskered Terns, lots of Little Egrets, smaller numbers of Night, Purple and Squacco Herons, a few Black-winged Stilts, and Marsh Harriers everywhere. Some of the large *etangs* were full of flamingos and on one occasion on *Etang du Lion* three Caspian Terns patrolled and plunged just offshore. A few Slender-billed Gulls were seen on the huge saltpans, along with hundreds of Kentish Plovers, and it wasn't all waterbirds. Perched on top of the waist-high *salicornia* scrub near Saintes-Maries-de-la-Mer we saw some very small and very smart Spectacled Warblers, although to my eyes they were not as good-looking as the Sardinian Warblers at *Les Baux* in the limestone hills inland called *Les Alpilles*. Patience and persistence, two essential qualities in a birder, produced brilliant views of two male 'silverbacks' with jet black hoods and red eye-rings. We heard the deep, far-carrying 'buu-uu' calls of an Eagle Owl in those convoluted hills one evening but could not locate it and we failed to find any Blue Rock Thrushes but it didn't matter, I had seen twenty new birds, and any day with Bee-eaters, Rollers and Hoopoes is a great day.

After two days trying to find a tiny Wallcreeper in the immensity of the high Pyrenees without so much as a flicker of those fabulous wings there was just one day left. Above the mountain village of Gavarnie the early morning mist dispersed to reveal a warm, sunny day and the sun lit a magnificent amphitheatre of precipitous grey rock, snow and ice, a cirque to be exact, 5000 feet (1500 metres) deep in places. We were heading for the distant summits of its crest, rising over 10,000 feet (3000 metres). The road flirted with a deep valley to our left and as Nick's car with the four of us and all our gear in it struggled with the steep ascent we were going slowly enough for me to notice a strange falcon. It was all dark, with extremely long, slim wings and a long, narrow tail, and it flew with astonishing agility, mostly with its wings sharply angled back, dashing from one side of the valley to the other before finally plunging out of sight. I shouted at Nick, sitting next to me in the driving seat, to have a look. He pulled over and saw it and when it had gone I turned to look him in the eye and he was looking me in the eye when I said, "That had to be an Eleonora's!" He agreed. He had seen some before. I hadn't. The nearest breeding colonies were a long way away in the Mediterranean but that is what it had to be and as it sank in I felt more and more of a glow because it was a terrific bird.

Finally we arrived in the small car-park at the base of *Pic du Taillon*, a 10,000 foot (3000 metre) peak. Four scruffy Alpine Accentors pecked at crumbs, virtually at our feet, but our attention soon turned to three Snowfinches which dropped down on to the adjacent grassy slope already adorned by black and white, orange-spotted Apollo butterflies. A flock of Alpine Choughs wheeled overhead and looking up at them two Griffon Vultures sailed out from the mountainside where Marmots whistled from rock tops. The huge vultures drifted by as we began the ascent, skirting slopes of scree, leaping across cascades of meltwater, and traversing a small glacier before reaching

*La Brèche de Roland*, a natural rectangular gap in the crest of the cirque, fifty paces across and a hundred high. There we took a breather while Alpine Swifts lashed through the rock window, crossing the border between France and Spain. Through the gap and right we walked, along the dusty, rocky top of a gigantic slope of scree at the base of a virtually vertical rock face. I was never more alert. This was as far as we could go on this trip. This was my last chance to see a Wallcreeper.

I wanted to keep stopping to scan the rock face in the hope of a flash of red but the more ground we covered the better chance we had of just coming across one so we pushed on. As we approached *Le Doigt*, 'The Finger', an odd rocky outcrop sticking up from the Pyrenean spine, something caught my eye to the left. There it was, flying, below me, along the top of the scree slope, my first Wallcreeper, looking for all the world like some giant butterfly, the crimson-carmine wings with bright white drop-shaped spots at the tips flashing as it fluttered erratically across the front of us and on to the rock face. I rushed forward and the bird took no notice of me as it crept across the bare rock, flicking its gorgeous wings as it probed tiny crevices with its long needle of a bill, just a few paces away. As I watched it with wild eyes another one appeared then another and another and another. I could not believe it. There were five Wallcreepers on the cliff in front of us.

A glorious hour then passed in what seemed like seconds, in the company of those fantastic birds in that fantastic place.Then, it was getting late and we had to leave, and the others had to almost drag me away from what was yet

*Wallcreeper, Pic du Taillon, Pyrenees, 3rd September 1985*

another dream come true. To cap the incredible day, back at the bottom of *Pic du Taillon* a magnificent adult Lammergeier drifted out from behind a slope and to our disbelief proceeded to drop a bone on to the rocks below. The massive bird then dropped to the ground rose into the air and dropped the bone again and again before sweeping down behind a ridge to presumably eat the contents of the now smashed bone. The sun then disappeared below the high ridges, the sky turned pink and the cold night came quickly as we pitched our tents on a nearly flat shelf below a giant slope of grass and rocks. In a matter of minutes the inviting mountain tops of the high Pyrenees where Wallcreepers live were transformed into a forbidding landscape. It felt like we were much farther from the comforts of the world below than we actually were, that we were in a place far removed from the one we were used to, far enough to feel a little frightened and yet to be even more excited by the wildness of it all. I put on my coat for the first time since the beginning of the trip, shook myself into it, wrapped it tightly round me and sat on a rock by the gas burners cooking our 'hoosh' with a glass of wine to reflect on a phenomenal time.

While making morning coffee, thinking 'life I love you', a Beech Marten came bounding into camp from the slope above, rose up on its hind legs to have a look around and see what was going on, then wandered on as if we were not there. A sea of cloud drifted steadily up from the valley below and engulfed us so we drove down through it to the *Vallee d'Ossoue* for a last wander around the mountains, fording rocky streams, walking slowly through bushy boulder fields, scanning the sheer rock faces, keeping an eye on the sky, watching Lammergeiers. I was having the time of my life and that was it now, all I wanted to do was wander around wild places looking for the birds and other wildlife which completed them.

*Ibisbills, Chutran, Shigar Valley, near Skardu, Baltistan,
Pakistan, 10th January 1986*

# 4

# PAKISTAN, INDIA and NEPAL

Half an hour after checking in at London Heathrow, the first time I had checked in at an airport in my life, I was summoned on the intercom. I was taken quickly to a small office where I was grilled about the contents of my rucksack. I listed what I had put in it and was then informed that the camping stove, which I had taken great care to clean the previous day, still had traces of petrol in it and was therefore a potential bomb in the hold of the plane. After a telling-off the stove was removed for collection on my return home and I was allowed to continue my journey. This all took a long time so I was fortunate the flight on *Tarom Romanian Air Transport* to Karachi via Bucharest was delayed. A fellow passenger told me this was because the airline had run out of fuel and did not have a credit account at Heathrow to pay for enough fuel to fly to Bucharest, so the aircraft staff had to use all their money to get the plane as far as Zurich where the airline did have an account.

My first view from 33,000 feet (10,000 metres) was of a wonderful cloudscape over England. The next morning I saw a glowing sunrise over an Asian desert. Having never been past the Pyrenees stepping outside the airport in Karachi was a disconcerting experience. I had never seen anything like it. The place was crazy with people. I got into a taxi and suddenly the car was weaving through a madness of other taxis, cars, motorcycles, tuk-tuks, brightly-coloured buses and plainly-dressed people; a bustling, noisy mass of humanity in a strange place.

I must admit the excitement of being in a new land to look for new birds was in danger of being crushed by fear. When I then emerged out of the taxi into the maelstrom of mankind at Karachi Cant railway station I seriously began to wonder what the hell I was doing but my fears subsided as I was almost overwhelmed by local people willing to guide me to the right ticket office and advise me which ticket to buy. There was a choice of two; first-class passengers got a seat, second-class didn't. When I was informed I was going to be spending about 34 hours on the Awam Express as it travelled the one thousand miles

(1600 km) north to Rawalpindi I quickly decided it was worth 200 rupees (£12 sterling) for a seat. It may have been a tiny seat with no room to stretch my legs amongst the luggage which covered virtually every square inch of the floor of the whole train, in places up to the ceiling, but at least it was a 'window seat', albeit an iron-barred glassless window. It was not long before the dust from the Thar Desert the train trundled almost gracefully through at a snail's pace covered me and lay in a thick layer in my ears, eyes, nose and mouth.

Throughout the day and the night and the next day multitudes of people got on and off, and walked up and down that train, many of them with something to sell, from samosas to scissors, or a sad story to tell, or a sad song to sing, with their hands held out and cupped in the hope of a few rupees, and some beggars, including children, were grotesquely deformed and disfigured, and a few didn't even have any limbs, just heads and torsos, and they lived on a rubber mat.

I found it all hard to comprehend but I spent most of my time looking out of the 'window'. On a train travelling at rarely more than thirty miles per hour (50 km/h) it was like being in a mobile hide. Wires were adorned with colourful and striking birds including my first Little Green Bee-eaters, Indian Rollers, Smyrna Kingfishers and Long-tailed Shrikes, and every marsh, pool or stretch of river was full of waterbirds like egrets, Black-winged Stilts and Red-wattled Lapwings. Over one large pool I saw my first Pied Kingfishers, striking black and white birds with black spears for beaks, pointing to the water below as the birds hovered high above. What with parties of Rose-coloured

Starlings and lots of Hoopoes it was an exotic, incredibly exciting introduction to the birdlife of a new continent.

When the red sun dropped below the parched plains of central Pakistan I was so tired I had no trouble sleeping on my seat and when the sun came up again I was ready to look even harder for birds. It was almost a shame to reach Rawalpindi. There to meet me was my old friend Rob Roberts. His father, who worked at a phosphate mine, had use of a house near Abbottabad, and Rob was using it as a base to visit the nearby Karakoram, the mountain range northwest of the Himalaya proper, where there is the highest concentration of peaks over 26,000 feet (8000 metres) anywhere on Earth, including K2, the second highest peak on the planet at 28,251 feet (8611 metres), and where Rob dreamed it might be possible to see a Snow Leopard and perhaps even photograph one and maybe even publish the photographs in *National Geographic* magazine. Months before, I was invited to tag along and took about ten seconds to accept the invitation.

Between many meetings in Abbottabad where much good advice was received, introductory letters penned and permits organised there was a bit of time to look for some birds, at nearby Thandiani where we leapt from boulder to boulder down a narrow rocky river through a beautiful deep forested valley seeing a Wallcreeper, Brown Dippers, two exquisite, black and white Little Forktails, Plumbeous Redstarts and startling, snowy-capped, black-backed and rusty-bellied River Chats, while in the forested Murree Hills we added black and red Long-tailed Minivets and two spectacular Yellow-billed Blue Magpies with very long, drooping sky blue tails.

*Little Forktail, Thandiani, Pakistan, 10th October 1985*

We were advised to head for Skardu, a town in the remote district of Baltistan, bordering Kashmir in India. About 25,000 people lived there, mostly Shiite Muslims whose language is an unwritten archaic form of Tibetan but there were plenty of people used to dealing with westerners, mainly mountaineers, because, during the summer months, Skardu is the gateway to the Baltoro Glacier and K2. It is not easy to get to though. Some said we should take the one-hour flight from Islamabad because it was the most spectacular flight on Earth. Others insisted it was the most dangerous flight in the world, although not as dangerous, statistically, as travelling there by bus, a 420 mile (675 km) journey that takes at least 36 hours, almost a third of it along the Indus Gorge on a track hewn from the side of the Karakoram known as 'the road that eats jeeps'. We decided to try the flight. On the first day it was cancelled, due to cloud preventing the pilot from flying the plane safely through the narrow valleys of the high Karakoram. On the second day we were in the air for 45 minutes before the pilot decided there was too much cloud again and turned back. On the third day, after a night on the floor at the airport, we made it all the way, so, in the end, it took a lot longer to reach Skardu than it would have by bus, over 50 hours, but it was worth it.

Not long after leaving Islamabad the view from the twin-engine *727 Fokker Friendship* was fantastic; high snowy mountains as far as my eyes could see and rising majestically above them was a huge pyramid of rock known as Nanga Parbat, at 26,660 feet (8126 metres) the ninth highest mountain on Earth. The plane was so close, the mountain so massive and the top of it so far above that it was difficult to get the peak in a photograph. Faced with a wall of rock the pilot swung the *Fokker* eastwards around its flanks and after skimming a ridged plateau at nearly 20,000 feet (6000 metres), dropped into the Indus Gorge, now too narrow to turn the plane around in and too high at the sides to cross, the plane's flight ceiling being about 21,000 feet (6400 metres). With no radar or computer the pilot was flying on sight alone and we could see there was very little margin for error, for it looked like the wing tips might scrape the snow off the sides of the mountains. After several S-turns the valley opened up and before us was a magnificent broad alluvial plain at the junction of the Indus and Shigar Rivers. Then we descended to the town of Skardu where we headed straight for the K2 Motel and there outside was the Tourism Officer.

He was shocked to see two westerners. "No one comes up here in the winter," he said, "The motel is closed."

We explained that we did not want to stay *in* the motel, it was way beyond our budget, we wanted to camp in the garden, although looking at it we were not so sure because it was just a small patch of rough grass. He said, "No problem." then took us to meet Shah, a local mountaineer and general fixer, who took us to talk to the District Commissioner, the Police Superintendent and the District Forest Officer (D.F.O.), all sat behind big desks in bare rooms in different buildings. After numerous cups of green tea called chai and endless chit-chat we were granted permission to visit the Narh Valley, so called because it is the place where the male (Narh) Ibex gather to rut and the D.F.O. said there were usually many Ibex there and that Snow Leopards prey mainly on Ibex in the mountains around Skardu.

The small town of Skardu lies in an arena rather than a valley, a stupendous cold desert of grey sand, boulders and scree at 7500 feet (2286 metres), about twenty miles (32 km) long and eight miles (13 km) wide, and surrounded by rocky mountains that rise to jagged snowy crests and peaks above 17,000 feet (5000 metres), although it is difficult to appreciate the scale because the air is so clear everything seems close. The scene looks desolate at first but when we began walking we found some poplars here and there, and farther afield there were apricot groves and corn fields on the fertile floodplain of the Indus River, flowing slowly through the middle of it all. Pakistan's 2000 mile (3200 km) long lifeline flows down almost the entire length of the country, carrying meltwater from glaciers in Tibet through Ladakh, Jammu, Kashmir and Baltistan then south through the arid middle of Pakistan to the Arabian Sea near Karachi. Even at Skardu, over a thousand miles (1600 km) from the sea, the river may be up to five miles (eight km) wide with meltwater during the summer, but in the freezing winter the flow is much reduced and vast banks of grey sand and fields covered in deep snow lie either side of it, above which rise the immense snowy mountains of the Karakoram. Add two Wallcreepers and the scene was complete.

On the way to Narh we picked up our guide Ghulam-Hadar, a happy man who we guessed was about 50 years old. Many of the people who live in Baltistan are indifferent to time and most, like Hadar, have no idea how old they are. He was stocky with a dark, sun-burnt face, light black beard, honest eyes and a flat, off-white woollen cap, circular with a rolled-up tubular rim, called a pakol, worn by man and boy throughout the region. Fifteen miles 24 km) east of Skardu we got out of the jeep and walked down to the river bank to catch the 'ferry' to Narh. There are few bridges in Baltistan; the locals use pulley-ropes, some with seats some without, suspended high above the rivers, to pull themselves from one side of a gorge to the other, or rafts known as zakhs made out of air-filled goat skins topped with thin planks of wood tied together. It was one of these we stepped carefully on to and watched Hadar and a very old man paddle the surprisingly stable craft slowly across the Indus.

The village of Narh was magical; an intricate hamlet of tiny stone, straw and wicker houses set in the base of a precipitous mountainside surrounded by small fields, where corn is grown, and orchards, irrigated via meltwater collected and distributed by a labyrinth of stone aqueducts. Most of the men and children came out to greet us but the women are subject to purdah, seclusion from the eyes of unrelated men, and watched us from gaps in wooden doors and walls. We were led to an empty house with a large room with a stove in the middle and another room with two charpoys, wooden beds with ropes tied between the frames, acting as mattresses. Chai and greasy paratha, a flaky flatbread, were soon served then we had time for a walk during which we saw lots of Rock Buntings, several Blue Whistling Thrushes and two striking male Güldenstädt's Redstarts, black above and red below with snow white caps and big white flashes in the wings.

The next morning we were introduced to Hussein, our second guide, and cook, for the trip. We thought he was older than Hadar, possibly over sixty, but, up there, where life is tough, he could have been in his forties. He was thinner than Hadar and he wore his pakol rolled down low over his small head, almost as far as the top of his sharp nose. His face was grubby and had seen much sun but his eyes were as bright as diamonds. He was certainly poor. His off-white cotton tunic and loose trousers were faded from long use and his feet were bare. Neither he nor Hadar spoke a word of English and we had only picked up a few words of Balti so all we managed to find out, or should I say presume, mostly from gestures and grunts, was that, like Hadar, Hussein was a veteran of many trips to K2 as a cook and porter.

It was with great anticipation and excitement that we waved goodbye to the happy people of Narh early the next morning and headed off, rucksacks on backs, along the edge of the small fields at the dusty base of the Masherbrum Range. The small, narrow Narh River ran fast and strong down the valley, splashing around rocks adorned by River Chats and Little Forktails. Alongside, on the bushy, rocky slopes were lots of Brown Accentors, a few Rufous-breasted Accentors and some dinky Red-fronted Serins with fiery foreheads. The going was easy at first, along a narrow trail well-trodden by shepherds and firewood collectors. We then crossed the river and the trail suddenly steepened and we climbed higher and higher along the base of gargantuan slopes of scree, frequently looking up the valley to the magnificent pyramid of rock dead ahead but far in the distance, a massive mountain with no name. A Lammergeier drifted by high overhead, a Golden Eagle much lower. Hadar, used to the thinning mountain air, set a fast pace but I found the landscape, the birds and the air exhilarating and even with a heavy rucksack managed to keep him in sight. Rob, with all the camera gear, was struggling, and often I stopped to wait for him and Hussein, and when they caught up Hussein would produce a welcome handful of dried apricots.

Rob spotted our first pikas, small, pale, sand-coloured mammals like large mice with no tails, standing on the tops of rocks in the warming sun. We climbed until the early afternoon when we came to where the valley levelled out a little and widened a lot, forming a beautiful giant meadow in the mountains, made up of steep grey peaks rising above sharp snowy ridges to over 18,000 feet (5500 metres). There were three Ibex on one of the vast slopes but I was more interested in the bird in the tall juniper thicket, one of the most beautiful birds I had ever seen. It looked like a delicate tit with a rufous crown, white eyebrows, olive-brown back, bluish rump and tail, and the most exquisite fluffed-up pastel blue and purple flanks. I had no idea what it was called and I didn't care; not everything has to have a name, and I didn't find out for a month because the only bird book I had with me was *A Field Guide to the Birds of South-East Asia* by Ben King with sketches and notes on other birds I had added and it was not in there. I found out when I saw the cover of *A Guide to the Birds of Nepal* by Carol and Tim Inskipp in a bookshop in Kathmandu. On that cover was a painting of a Stoliczka's Tit Warbler, a species which, according to that book, 'haunts scrub above the treeline in semi-desert areas [on the] Tibetan facies north of the Himalayas in Baltistan, Gilgit and Ladakh east to Nepal'. It was a bird befitting such wild and beautiful country.

Fitting too I thought that the bird should be named after Ferdinand Stoliczka, a Moravian palaeontologist who died during his third and last expedition which set out from Rawalpindi in 1873. On the return journey in June 1874 after crossing the high Karakoram and suffering severe headaches for three days his condition deteriorated and he died. His death was put down to, 'spinal meningitis deteriorated by over-exertion in strenuous endeavours after information, and the great height'. Today a doctor would probably call it Altitude or Acute Mountain Sickness which leads to fluid on the lungs and/or swelling of the brain and death in a third of people who suffer it.

We had climbed about 4000 feet (1200 metres), to about 11,500 feet (3500 metres), during the morning so that may explain why, after almost gliding up that fantastic valley

*Stoliczka's Tit Warbler, Narh Valley, Pakistan,
18th October 1985*

with my big rucksack on, I turned to look back down the trail and saw Rob face down, prostrate on a rock. He was struggling with, 'over-exertion in strenuous endeavours' and we were already in trouble.

A few dried apricots and a bun washed down with mountain water were all I had eaten all day and yet I felt great to be alive. The mountain air was invigorating but having stopped climbing I felt a severe chill as soon as the sun dropped below the wall of rock and so it was with great satisfaction that I sat down on the straw floor of the warm stone hut Hadar had chosen for us to stay in. It was warm because he and Hussein had a fire going. In a pot hanging over it was Chukar stew. The Chukar is a kind of partridge and I was already looking forward to a tasty meal to end a great day. The last of the light filtered through gaps in the walls and the shafts faded out in the thick smoke. Hussein warmed his bare feet on the embers of the fire as Rob and I listened to him and Hadar talking in low, rumbling voices. As the stew cooked we tried to talk with them but it was very difficult. However, after a mighty effort before and after eating the delicious Chukar we were almost sure that Hadar had two wives and ten children, that the rudimentary hut we were in was used by shepherds during the summer when they took their goats up high to the rich grazing, and that soon the vast meadow we were about to sleep in would be covered in snow.

The next morning Rob woke up feeling exhausted and with a bad head so instead of hiking farther up the valley in search of Snow Leopard he stayed put and I hunted down Stoliczka's Tit Warblers in the mountain arena under a blue sky, finding a small party of the gorgeous things as well as a few new birds, notably Robin Accentors, a Black-throated Thrush and a Pied Flycatcher-like flycatcher, blackish above with a silvery crown, and white below. It was another mystery to me which I identified later as a mis-named male Blue-headed Redstart. The next day Rob who did not feel much better insisted on climbing as high as possible up the slopes of the Shimshak side of the valley so that we could scan for Snow Leopards. Hadar indicated that Hussein would guide us while he went off higher up the Narh with his gun in search of supper. Barefoot Hussein left us in his wake as we scrambled up the scree in our big boots, sending stones cascading down, while he seemed to flow upwards, stepping nimbly across the loose rocks with the minimum of effort. There was not a cloud in the huge sky. Lovely warm sunshine washed over us. Flocks of Alpine Choughs flew around, swooping so close at times that we could hear the whoosh of their wings. Looking up and twisting to get the best views made us wobble on the edge of some colossal precipices. A Wallcreeper whistled softly as it flapped haphazardly by. An Alpine Accentor scampered between some rocks and when I stopped to try and get a better view of it a party of Himalayan Snowcocks burst out from one side of a ravine and shot across it on stiff wings before dropping down and out of sight amongst the boulders on the other side.

At the top of the ravine we sat down on a narrow shelf, propped ourselves up against the mountain, and while Hussein made chai from snow, Rob and I scanned the slopes below. We saw nothing but after climbing higher Hussein and Rob found a short stretch of Snow Leopard tracks. Rob was ecstatic and as we examined them carefully it dawned on him that those pugmarks meant there could be a Snow Leopard watching us at that very moment. The tremendously exciting discovery spurred us on upwards and upwards until Rob could take the pain in his head no more. Near the top of Shimshak, 18,403 feet (5609 metres) high, we reached a ridge with the greatest view I had ever seen. We were surrounded by the innumerable unclimbable pyramidal peaks of the Karakoram, to K2 and beyond, above the beautiful Narh Valley. The mountain tops were too sheer for snow to settle on but there was deep snow on their shoulders and so broad were the shoulders that much of the scene surrounding us was almost blinding white, beneath a bright blue sky. A Lammergeier glided over and, like a Snow Leopard perhaps, we watched three Ibex grazing a grassy whaleback way below us for ages.

After a few hours a cold wind picked up so we reluctantly agreed to Hussein's gestures that we really ought to be starting down the mountain. Long after the sun had disappeared behind the walls of rock and snow we reached the stream at the base, a tumbling torrent when we set out, frozen now. We headed as quickly as we could toward the smoke puffing out of our stone hut in the distance, looking forward to a spicy meal around a warm fire. Rob's headache continued to get worse and he was in a state of near-collapse as Hadar and I helped him over the final few paces and into the hut. Hadar was very concerned and while we sat around the fire smoking and drinking chai he took his time trying to explain that he had seen no sign of Snow Leopards at the top of Narh and that Rob was too ill to go there, as planned. He made it pretty clear that it was best that Rob went down the mountains not up them. He also managed to get across that it was better for us to return to Narh in the middle of the winter when the snowline, the Ibex and '*Chitah*', the local name for Snow Leopard, would be lower.

"Then Chitah come closer," he said, showing off his new English.

By now the stew was almost ready. When I tried to find out what was in it Hadar got up and gestured for me to step outside. There he showed me a bird's head hanging from the roof. It was metallic green with a strange long crest like a tassel and I thought it must be some kind of pheasant. Hadar was even happier than usual because he had secured a bird big enough to feed four of us for two nights. I was not happy. The bird was delicious but I would rather have seen it alive because it *was* a 'pheasant', an exceptionally beautiful one called a Himalayan Monal. After eating it, while Hadar and Hussein broke into song, all I could think about was getting up to the top of Narh where there must have been more iridescent blue, copper and green monals. I calmed down a little listening to their wailing melodies, which seemed to be an expression of their delight of life in the snowy mountains of Baltistan, and apart from the monal in the pot in front of me I could see why people would be so happy living in such a beautiful part of the planet.

Knowing how much he and I wanted to see a monal Rob persuaded me to wait another day before heading up the valley, while he hopefully acclimatized to the altitude. If he felt better at the end of the day we would explore the top of Narh, if not, we would retreat and return in the winter, and that is what we had to do, and it very nearly broke my heart to leave, not because of the monal because for a few days in Narh life had been simple, and full of peace and beauty.

We were joined by a couple of hill men on our way down. They were carrying bundles of hay on their backs, so huge and heavy that the men were bent double. They looked and sounded like two apes as they half-walked, half-skipped down the valley, communicating with each other in a guttural tongue. About half way down we all stopped for a rest and they insisted we had a smoke from an Ibex horn they carried with them. Whatever was in there, mostly hashish we suspected, it was not pleasant and I was glad I had some *Gauloises* with me to take the taste away. I handed them around and the hill men, Hadar and Hussein all took one and after a couple of deep drags Hadar pretended to swoon, intimating that they were also laced with hashish, and we all laughed. Once across the Indus we had to wait on the dusty trackside for a vehicle to come along and hope we could hitch a ride into Skardu. Rob, feeling better now he was lower down, placed a large stone on top of a big boulder and as he did so Hadar immediately armed himself with some small stones. He was always happy, always ready for some fun, so full of energy, and of course the first to hit the stone. In Skardu we said, "Goodbye, see you in the winter!" and shook the man's hand and looked him in the eyes and smiled. He said, "Salaam Alaikum." (Peace be upon you) and smiled back.

We missed the bus to Gilgit. Fortunately we met Zeb, who offered us a lift in his jeep. It took six hours to traverse a hundred miles (160 km) through the narrow crack carved by the Indus between the Haramosh and Deosai mountain ranges, with three stops; one to replace a punctured tyre, one to drink chai and one to smoke hashish. Travelling by jeep is much scarier than flying. Hashish is used as a sedative, to help keep drivers (and some passengers) calm as the vehicles hurtle along a dusty, grey track covered in loose rocks that is little more than a narrow shelf really, hewn out of the mountain sides. It snakes through the mass of rock across shattered, near-vertical slopes of scree, and is so narrow that when two vehicles meet the passengers by the outside windows in the vehicle on the outside of the track face looking down terrifying drop-offs. Sometimes I felt relaxed and brave enough to look down at the wheels of the jeep, spinning round and throwing up dust and stones at the edge of sheer drops hundreds of feet and metres above the Indus rushing along its rocky path down in the chasm below. There were hundreds of bodies down there, too far away to see, and too frightening to think about. Once a vehicle goes over no one has a chance of surviving, the gorge is just so deep.

Zeb invited us to stay at his rented house just outside Gilgit for the night, and treated us like kings, serving up mulberry vodka from Hunza followed by grilled chicken with naan bread. Next morning we went to see Mr Iftikharuddin, the District Commissioner, who talked a lot about 'east is east and west is west' but knew of nowhere in particular to look for Snow Leopards, so we carried on the track, on the extravagantly decorated overnight bus to Abbottabad, a riot of colour between silver trims. It left Gilgit when twice the number of passengers the bus was designed to carry had been crammed in, plus what appeared to be most of their life's belongings. With no room to stretch our long legs *rigor mortis* had nearly set in by the end of the fourteen hours. The first part of the journey was along a rough track, the second part on the Karakoram Highway which runs 800 miles (1300 km) from Kashgar in western China to Islamabad. When we reached tarmac the driver suddenly turned into a maniac, driving as fast as possible down the mountains, throwing the vehicle and us around the bends high above the Indus, never braking, horn blaring but barely audible above the din of the music, with absolutely no regard for the certain death a slight error in judgement would result in. Every bone in my body, all 206, ached at the end, and yet there was still so much beauty in the snowy mountains, floodlit by a red full moon in a total lunar eclipse.

While waiting for the snow and Snow Leopards to descend the Karakoram we decided to spend a couple of months in India and Nepal. First stop was Delhi but we were not allowed to travel there cheaply by road or train from Pakistan because it was too dangerous for foreigners to pass through Amritsar where there was some tension between Sikh separatists holed up in the 'Golden Temple', their spiritual centre, and the Indian Government. So, we had to fly and use up much more of our funds than we would have liked. However, the lure of famous bird and wildlife reserves such as Bharatpur and Ranthambore in India, and Chitwan in Nepal, was irresistible, so we boarded the 'Flying Coach' from Abbottabad to Lahore. At one o'clock in the morning we came to an abrupt halt and two hours later we were in the same place, stuck in a crazy traffic jam.

On the subcontinent as many people travel at night as during the day, if not more, because it is much cooler. On this particular night two trucks collided and the front wheels of both were badly damaged. As a result the two-lane highway became five lanes of chaos as everyone tried to squeeze past. Our bus got by just after 4 a.m. but it was 6:30 a.m. when we got to the bus station in Lahore and our flight was at 7 a.m. We hailed a three-wheeler scooter taxi. The driver seemed to understand our urgency or he drove full throttle all the time. We ran to the check-in desk. It had a 'closed' sign on it but they opened it up for us. Then we faced customs where, despite the imminent departure of our flight, our rucksacks were ransacked. Stuffing our stuff hurriedly back in as we ran to the departure area we reached it ten minutes before the flight was due to leave, a forty-minute flight which was then delayed, because of fog, for eight hours.

During the long wait we met Remi, a Frenchman who on hearing that we had not arranged anywhere to stay in Delhi said he had a friend who might be happy to put us up for the night. Christiane, a beautiful, charming Frenchwoman with two children who worked at the French Embassy and lived in a large, bright and spacious house along one of the wide tree-lined avenues of New Delhi was very happy to put us up for the night. Her Tibetan cook served up a delicious risotto before she and Remi took us out on the town, to the Hyatt Hotel where the staff didn't like our shorts but lit our cigarettes, the even more lavish Orient Express Bar in the Taj Palace and the ridiculously opulent Sheraton Hotel which served ice-cream sandwiches at two o'clock in the morning. We all got on so well Rob and I indulged in another day and did the same the next night. It was not the introduction to India we were expecting. That which we had read about and prepared ourselves for was just outside the places we went to and far, far removed from the world Christiane and Remi inhabited. Away from the fancy bars, restaurants and hotels, round the corners, in the dark, the poor people dressed in rags were somehow eking out an existence under corrugated iron, ripped tarpaulins and ragged hessian sacking, next to open sewers.

After jasmine tea and croissants Rob and I shook Remi's hand, kissed Christiane goodbye and boarded the Bombay Express to Bharatpur, seeing our first Painted and Woolly-necked Storks, and nine tall Sarus Cranes during the very exciting three hour train ride. The name 'Bharatpur' rolled longingly off my tongue. I knew all about the waterbird spectacle the site is world famous for and had dreamed about seeing it for years but could it be as good as everyone said it was?

At the entrance, a bearded man with a big smile approached us and told us that his name was Dinesh. Talking to him we soon realized that he knew Bharatpur like the back of his hand. He promised to show us roosting owls and nightjars, and all sorts of other wonders, and after some protracted negotiations we agreed to a fee of 20 rupees per hour. We were with him for eleven hours, from dawn to dusk, but the expense was nothing when taking into account the experience. In what seemed like seconds we saw thousands of birds of 135 different species including fifty I had never seen before, the most birds and the most new birds I had ever seen in a day.

As soon as we entered the reserve Dinesh led us off the main track into an area of low scrub where during the first few minutes of the day we saw a brilliant Black-rumped Goldenback, a medium-sized black and white woodpecker with a truly golden back, Brahminy Mynas, dark pink and silvery starlings with what looked like shiny black wigs, Stone Curlews, stood stock still in the shade under small thorny trees, Indian Rollers sat on snags, and White-browed Fantails in almost every bush. At the end of an avenue of trees in a quiet corner a friend of Dinesh's made chai while we scanned the floods called *jheels*. The seemingly endless shallow waters with thick mats of floating vegetation, interspersed with flooded woodland, were literally covered in birds. Spoonbills, storks, ibises, egrets, pond herons, Purple Herons, Purple Swamphens, cormorants and darters, numerous species of numerous ducks, Bronze-winged and elegant chocolate and white Pheasant-tailed Jacanas liberally sprinkled across the lily pads, Sarus Cranes here and there, and eagles above; Crested Serpent, Greater Spotted, Lesser Spotted, Imperial, Steppe and Tawny, and above them, circling, were White-rumped Vultures and a Red-headed Vulture. There was no time to drink chai; we could not keep our eyes off the masses of birds before us.

We walked around some *jheels* to watch the birds close up until noon when the blazing sun was high in the cloudless sky of Rajasthan. After more chai we hired bicycles and glad of a breeze cycled to the outer reaches of the reserve where Dinesh showed us an Indian Nightjar and a Mottled Wood Owl, both at roost. At the edge of the wood the owl was in there was a giant *jheel* with two large dead trees in the middle. In one, a Pallas's Fish Eagle was sat in a nest made out of a platform of sticks. Only its pale buff head and neck were visible but after a few minutes its mate swooped in, showing its very long wings and black and white tail. In the other tree a Black-necked Stork stood on its nest, a crazy, tall, black and white bird with a very long black beak, glossy dark blue neck and bright red legs.

When we moved on we came across three bee-eaters swooping out to catch dragonflies. There was a party of Little Green Bee-eaters nearby but the ones we were watching looked slightly larger and stockier. They had pale chestnut hindcrowns and no tail streamers, and we all thought they were Chestnut-headed Bee-eaters, out of range but as Dr Hilary Fry states in his fine *Poyser* monograph *The Bee-eaters*, the species is 'in places strongly migratory' and 'Tends to occur unexpectedly in forested areas far from known breeding areas.'

In another wood we saw a roosting Collared Scops Owl, before gliding on our bicycles through some mostly dry, open country full of Peacocks, Purple Sunbirds, Coppersmith Barbets, Smyrna Kingfishers, tiny, white-spangled, Red Avadavats and, on a quiet, almost dry pool, a long-legged White-tailed Plover with some Red-wattled Lapwings. A short trip in a punt took us out to some flooded Babul trees full of nesting ibises, spoonbills and storks including some beautiful Painted Storks in the flush of breeding plumage complete with big pink tertial feathers hanging over their tails. Experienced guide that he was, Dinesh saved the best till last. We cycled down a smooth track to another *jheel*, the largest we had seen so far, and immediately saw three huge white birds out in the middle. Through my telescope, resting on Rob's shoulder, I watched a family of Siberian Cranes, two adults and their youngster, foraging knee-deep in water. They were Bharatpur's star birds and there were plenty of contenders.

That first day was overwhelming so I was glad of a second to watch some birds for longer, but there were so many birds at Bharatpur weeks would not have been enough to absorb them all. Just a couple of more days would have been appreciated but Rob, who had another big cat on his mind, was very keen to move on so off we went, to Ranthambore, India's premier Tiger Reserve. We walked in to a chorus of weird and wonderful bird calls and songs including the incredibly loud 'pee-ow, pee-ow, pee-ow' of

Peacocks in the massive Banyan trees where silky, long-haired, long-tailed Langur Monkeys loafed.

We were not allowed to walk around the reserve though, for obvious reasons, and we could not afford to hire a vehicle or pay for any jeep rides, so we sat down next to the beautiful Lake Padam Talao and waited for a vehicle to come along so that we could try and hitch a lift and this is what we did for the next four days. It was the longest time I had ever been held up anywhere while hitchhiking but it was also the best place in the world to be stuck. Little Grebes and Pied Kingfishers dived after fish, Purple Herons tried to spear fish from the lakeshore, the beautiful lily-trotters, Bronze-winged and Pheasant-tailed, trotted across islands of lilies, Crested Serpent Eagles soared overhead and Mugger Crocodile heads floated on the surface. In the trees lining the lake a brilliant shiny blue, fiery red and white Tickell's Blue Flycatcher hunted flies above our heads. Later in the day the shy Stork-billed Kingfisher would usually perch right out in the open for a while. Langur Monkeys often foraged in the trees across the water and at dusk each night giant bats called Indian Flying Foxes left their daytime roosts and took to the air, flying high across the lake.

On the three lifts we managed to secure, with Indian families, we saw lots more birds, as well as plenty of Sambar and Spotted Deers, a few small gazelles called Chinkaras, and large blue-grey antelopes known as Nilgais or Blue Bulls, but the Indians drove so fast there was more chance of them running over a Tiger than seeing one. We scanned the low woodland and scrub as best we could of course but by the end of each ride I was actually glad I didn't see a Tiger because I didn't want to see one like that. On the first night we joined one of the families by their barbecue, sipping rum and enjoying the atmosphere, until the park manager, a vociferous buffoon, arrived. Rob put up with his extraordinary arrogance as long as he thought there was a chance of getting a free lift in search of Tigers with him, not that there was. Then we made our excuses and went off to bed down in our sleeping bags. The park manager, now full of rum, then insisted on us moving from where we were about to sleep because we were on a Tigress's regular nightly route. He showed us the pugmarks and said we would be safe twenty paces away from where we were, under one of the biggest Banyan trees in India. It was a fine spot.

The trouble was when I was asleep the next night Rob, who could not stand the mosquitoes and had moved to the breezy lakeside, heard a terrifying roar nearby and woke me up to tell me I should probably move as well. I was reluctant, because I was tired and I had to make a choice, between sleeping by the trail of a Tigress that was not a man-eater but might become one overnight, or bedding down right next to a lake full of crocodiles. Once I had decided on the latter and got used to the frequent splashes, presumably of fish, possibly trying to escape crocodiles, I enjoyed sleeping on the ground-floor veranda of the Jogi Mahal, the unoccupied lavish hunting lodge built for the members of the royal family of Jaipur. We were told that Mick Jagger and his family had stayed there a couple of weeks before we arrived. Rob and I were sure they would have given us a few lifts to look for Tigers, at a more leisurely pace, and that we would have seen one, and that they probably would have fed and watered us as well, and presumably with better food than we were served up. I was not impressed with the cook, especially on our last morning when the closest we got to seeing *Shere Khan* was when he saw a Tiger, with my binoculars. It was across the other side of the lake and gone by the time he handed them to me, so we spent four days at the best place in the world to see Tigers and never saw one.

It felt good to be back on the move again, even though we had ten rupees between us and had to try and sleep with a mass of Indian travellers, beggars, hawkers and wallahs selling chai, samosas, parathas and curry, in the incredible din of Delhi railway station. I couldn't sleep so I walked outside and tried to take in the mass of humanity, keeping warm by kerosene stoves outside small, shabby wooden stalls and open 'shops' with crumbling mortar, and workshops where carpenters and welders worked all day and all night. I had just enough rupees for a street omelette - I don't think I would have survived a trip to India were it not for omelettes - cooked on a burner on a pram and I ate it looking around at the scene lit by bare light bulbs hanging from a labyrinth of cables and wires.

When I did almost get to sleep at the end of the night the station sweepers came along and moved us on. The Tourist Officer at the station told us that the train to Gorakhpur was fully booked for the next three days. We decided he must mean 'Tourist Class' so we joined the mile-long queue at Counter 31 for second-class tickets and we were swiftly invited to go straight to the front where we bought two tickets without so much as a raised eyebrow. The Tourist Officer was right about one thing; the train was fully booked, so that in a compartment for eight people there were nearer twenty, *and* all their gear, not just bags but huge metal cases, tyres, everything imaginable, stacked up to the ceiling in the corridors as well. People were standing on the luggage because there was nowhere else to stand. It looked like and felt like half the population of Delhi was moving to Gorakhpur, by train. Even the floor below our seats was covered in luggage and we had no choice but to rest our booted feet on bags and cases, despite discouraging looks from the owners. But at least we had a seat, until the ticket inspector arrived and insisted that our seats had been reserved for the two people standing behind him. We put up a fight but it was no good, we had to move.

"Where to?" we kept asking.

There was nowhere to stand let alone sit on the whole train, which must have been half a mile long. The ticket inspector just shrugged. Somehow, we managed to manoeuvre ourselves and our giant rucksacks out of the compartment and along the corridor to the end of the carriage and there we spent the following twelve hours, next to a stinking toilet on the sliding metal plates between carriages. Rob was so tired he laid down on them for a while and tried to sleep. I attempted to sleep standing up, in my two square feet of space, but all I could do was stare enviously at the far more accomplished Indians, dozing contentedly in tiny spaces, on and between the piles of luggage.

The bus to Sunauli wasn't much more comfortable. True, we had seats, but they were bone-hard, there was nowhere to put our long legs, the road was badly corrugated, pot-holed or just bumpy and the temperature was shocking. We were so beat when we arrived we couldn't face the last 100 miles (160 km) to Chitwan National Park so we booked into a guesthouse and luxuriated in lying down flat.

At dawn we boarded a colourful bus to Narayangat and travelled in the breeze on top of the heap of luggage on the roof, north along a good road through a great wide valley of fields and forests, the low-lying land known as the *Terai* which lies at the foot of the distant snowy mountains of the Himalaya. We were in Nepal and it was a beautiful part of the world. At Narayangat we switched to a minibus which took us to Tandi Bazaar where we were crammed into an old jeep with several other tourists for the remaining few miles to Suaraha. Above us, several locals clung to the roof as we bobbled along a rough track at a ridiculous speed and into a thigh-deep wide river where we came to an abrupt halt. The locals jumped off the roof and began pushing and soon we were on our way again. At Sauraha, a Tharu village of mud and daub huts with thatched roofs and gardens of banana trees just across the Rapti River from Chitwan National Park we moved into a hut at Wendy's Lodge. While eating divine spring rolls and drinking chai we had a long chat with Giri, the owner. He seemed very knowledgeable about rhinos and the local birdlife and was happy to let us know the best places to look for them, and we were soon thinking about what our first day birding in Nepal might be like.

After exchanging many "Hello"s and "Bye-Bye"s with the children in the village we followed Giri's directions to a creek adorned by some very smart black, grey and sandy River Lapwings. We waded across and entered the 'jungle', broadleaf subtropical *Sal* forest, where a very surprising frustrating couple of hours followed, for there seemed to be very few birds in a largely silent world, although we did see a superb Velvet-fronted Nuthatch, violet-blue above with a velvety black forehead and bright red beak. Outside the forest we scanned the wide Rapti River, which was more sand than water, over which a flock of about twenty dainty grey birds with striking black and white underwings were flying around quickly but gracefully hawking flying insects and catching them with a quiver of wings; they were our first Small Pratincoles. It was so hot Rob got in the water and an Osprey dived for a fish about twenty strokes from him.

Back in the jungle early the next morning it was alive with birds. In a sunlit glade a strange greenish bird with a glistening blue beard of feathers turned out to be a Blue-bearded Bee-eater, a solitary hunter nothing like the gregarious bee-eaters I had seen before. In the next glade was a Himalayan Goldenback, a woodpecker with a big red crest, black and white striped face, and deep golden back and wings. As we tried to keep up with the busy bird two tiny, barred, Jungle Owlets appeared. They were being mobbed by a mixed flock of birds containing three absolutely gorgeous Golden-fronted Leafbirds, bright and shiny green with golden foreheads, and throats which were black from one angle blue from another, according to how the light caught the feathers.

Six cups of sweet chai in an hour out of the sun was sufficiently reviving to see us marching off in the opposite direction from Wendy's in the afternoon, into thicker riverside forest where a stunning Verditer Flycatcher was followed by a pair of deep dark blue and glowing red White-rumped Shamas. After watching a small flock of Pied Hornbills which Giri had said were feasting in a big fig tree about halfway along a narrow, little-used trail, we turned to go and around the next corner, in the luxuriant undergrowth, we almost bumped into two Indian Rhinos. They turned their heads and looked back over their shoulders at us. We stared back, at their huge one-horned heads, then they shuffled and looked almost as alarmed as us so we turned on our heels and walked away, quickly but quietly, looking back over our shoulders to make sure the Rhinos were not following us.

Giri laughed when we told him about the Rhinos and said we did the right thing and that it would be fine to retrace our steps, albeit carefully, the following afternoon, in order to watch the hornbills again, which we did. The white-beaked mainly black birds with long tails plucked fruit from the outer branches of the big fig tree with great agility and precision for such large birds. The next morning Rob was throwing up so I ventured out alone, slowly along the riverbank, watching the Small Pratincoles. Then I walked along the creek and into the jungle where a fabulous golden yellow male Black-hooded Oriole was in full yodelling song and flying from tree to tree with fanciful exuberance, presumably trying to impress a female which I could not find. Rob just about managed to make it into the field the next day when we saw our first Lesser Yellownape, another colourful Asian woodpecker, with a deep yellow tufted nape and golden green upperparts.

On our last day at Chitwan, just after crossing the creek, we watched a small brownish bird turn its head toward us and its throat shone like a ruby, like a Siberian Rubythroat, which it was, a bird I had dreamed of seeing for many a year and one of the birds I most hoped to see on the trip. It stayed still long enough to see the black and white border to the glowing throat as well but the shy skulker dropped down after that and we could not relocate it despite a prolonged search, during which a flock of Plum-headed Parakeets landed in a tall tree at the edge of the forest. There was no time to wallow in the wonder of the rubythroat; here were more beautiful birds, tropical birds with deep purple heads, deep green bodies and long blue-green tails.

The scene from the roof of the bus as it climbed steadily through the magnificent Narayani then Trisuli River Gorges was glorious. Through the deep gorges flowed greenish rivers, tumbling and cascading down lush wooded slopes and occasionally spilling over waterfalls adorned by the greenest ferns and mosses. Then it all changed; we were approaching Kathmandu. All the glory was being stripped away by the rising human population. Just the odd clump of shade trees dotted the Himalayan slopes where beautiful forests once grew. They had been bulldozed and replaced with terraces to grow food for the rising numbers of people, whose children lived in hovels, wore rags and ran across the mud to wave at the tourists who had come to see their beautiful country.

After a chilly night in the *Monumental Lodge* in 'Freak Street' I woke up with a cold and joined the throng of other people with runny noses and tickly coughs in Kathmandu's chilly, foggy streets. It seemed almost everyone, locals as well as tourists, had a cold. Dodging bicycles, rickshaws, starving cows and people asking us if we wanted to change money or fly to the sky with some hash we made our way through the narrow streets past open-fronted butchers' shops with skinned, yellow goats' heads hanging outside and floors littered with bits of buffalo, and numerous other stalls selling cakes, carpets, chess sets, gems, puppets, silver dragons and grotesque models of Buddha, in search of the National Parks and Wildlife Conservation Office where Rob wished to discuss the possibility of looking for Snow Leopards.

We did not track down the office until the next day when we were told to visit Karan Shah, a biologist and lecturer at the Tribhuvan University who had spent four years studying Snow Leopards near Jumla in the remote high Himalaya and probably knew more about Snow Leopards than anyone else. He had bad news. Yes there were ten Snow Leopards in 150 square miles (400 sq km) about 50 miles (80 km) north of Jumla but it was a restricted area as far as foreigners were concerned and His Majesty's Government of Nepal was highly unlikely to grant us permission to go there. One good thing did come out of the meeting; Karan was interested in buying my Hertel & Reuss *Televari* telescope. I had worked out that I had £2.30 a day to last me until the end of January when I was due to fly home, nowhere near enough to be able to relax and enjoy my travels, so another £100, which I hoped Karan would buy my 'scope for, would be extremely welcome.

The next afternoon Karan looked over my 'scope very carefully for a long time before apparently forgetting about it altogether and taking us off to his house to look at some slides of Snow Leopards. While we looked at them my health worsened and when the subject of the 'scope came up again my defences were weakened and I buckled at 1240 Indian rupees, a paltry £70 or so. It was virtually the same amount we had paid to fly from Lahore to Delhi so it was good to recoup that, and it was a massive weight off my mind to have some more money for the rest of the trip but there was no time to relish the renewed freedom. Back in our room my stomach went crazy and I ended the day throwing up. The next day I had to lie on a thin mattress all day wishing my stomach would calm down while Rob and Scott, an American friend we had met on the road, went birding in a rare patch of remnant forest at Nagarjung, and when they returned, endure their tales of a forest alive with birds, not the best nighttime story. I forced myself out of bed in order to join Rob the next day on the long cycle ride up to the forest and was very glad I did for I saw my first White's Thrush, another rare vagrant to my home country I dearly wished to see on the trip, a strange, skulking bird suited to life in the shadows with its dappled black, white and golden plumage. A celebratory bowl of Tibetan mushroom soup went down very well, and stayed down.

I was well enough to attend the local bird club's field outing the next morning, led by Mr Hari Saran 'Kazi' Nepali, the foremost authority on birds in Nepal. We joined ten or so young birders on a walk around the fields at the confluence of the muddy Monohara and Hanumanti Rivers southeast of the city, during which we saw just a few species in thick fog, including three Yellow-breasted Buntings and about 30 Grey-headed Lapwings. In the afternoon Kazi kindly lent his forty years of experience to another visit to Nagarjung, helping us to marvel at three exotic Red-billed Blue Magpies perched side by side preening on a branch, and a male Rufous-bellied Niltava, a dark blue flycatcher. The bird I hoped to see more than any other on our travels was the Ibisbill, a unique mainly grey and white shorebird perfectly camouflaged for the stony rivers it lives on in and around the Himalaya. Kazi told us to try a stretch of the Bagmati River south of Kathmandu where we came across a Long-billed Plover, as rare as Ibisbills in Nepal but not as exciting, for us, as an Ibisbill would have been, although I was quite glad we didn't see one because it would have looked out of place in a river full of litter and sewage. We rushed to Kazi's to tell him about the plover and spent another interesting evening in his small apartment in Chhetrapati, drinking homemade firewater in a den of bird books, notebooks, papers, posters and other memories. One night he carefully scooped the skin of a bird out of his collection of over 500 specimens, telling us it was one of the few ever found in Nepal, and looked impressed when I identified it as a Dusky Thrush.

Early one morning we met Aneil, Keran and Raje, three young birders, at Godaveri Botanical Gardens and climbed the slope of Phulchowki up to the best remaining stand of damp, verdant, evergreen subtropical forest in the Kathmandu Valley, full of fabulous birds, and yet as we listened to the multitude of wonderful unknown calls and songs we also heard the local women breaking branches as they collected firewood, and the local men firing up chainsaws and blowing up quarries of marble that were eating away at the hillside. It is hard to enjoy the birds in such circumstances, knowing they will not be there much longer, and especially heartbreaking when the birdlife is so rich. We only saw a few species but they included dazzling Green-tailed Sunbirds, black-masked Yellow-bellied Fantails, an extraordinary orange-yellow ball shooting from bush to bush which we were told was a Golden Bush Robin, and a pair of Orange-bellied Leafbirds, also with an appropriate name, describing the beauty of what look like the freshest, shiniest, greenest leaves from above and the most beautiful autumn leaves from below. Best of all though was a bird that should have the word fantastic in its name, a bird actually called White-crested Laughingthrush. Our young guides told us that the people of Nepal don't believe such a creature exists, since it is beyond belief. We could understand such reverence because the birds do seemingly belong to another world, thanks to the loud, almost maniacal laughter of a fast-moving foraging flock of them hyperactively bouncing and jumping through the undergrowth, and because of their stunning looks, being big bold birds with neat, chestnut brown bodies, and black masks across white heads with wild, fluffy, snow white crests flashing in the forest gloom.

Shonshun, the happy ten-year-old boy with a twinkle in his eye charged with 'manning' the desk at the entrance to *Monumental Lodge* overnight, woke us up on time to catch the bus to Pokhara and away we went on the roof, westward through the middle of Nepal up and down river valleys and across hills dotted with villages and small, surviving forest patches. At the sprawled-out town of Pokhara we moved into a small, basic private house catering for guests. There was no water but we liked the view from the garden. To the north the magnificent thirty-mile (50 km) long Annapurna Massif rose like a giant wave of rock and snow from behind partially forested hills, the lower slopes hidden by cloud, the peaks shining in sunlight and rising to 26,795 feet (8000 metres) at the top of the snowy pyramid of Dhaulagiri, the seventh highest mountain on Earth.

We were keen to get into the field and look for birds. There did not seem to be any on Phewa Tal Lake but the forest on the slope on the far side looked promising. However, we could not find an easy way to get there before dark and we were both feeling ill so we gave up. The now regular stomach cramps and long, foul-smelling belches suggested the protozoan *Giardia lamblia* had infected us but that was not the reason Rob started throwing up. He was too weak to join me when I searched out a way to that forest the next day. There were many birds in it but most were very difficult to see as I scrambled up the steep slopes through the lush undergrowth, and it took me a particularly long time to get a decent view of a very furtive flock of flame-throated gems called Pekin Robins, small birds that are actually babblers and also known as Red-billed Leiothrixes. Encouraged by that success I worked hard for the next one too, an expert skulker keeping to thick ferns which turned out to be a Grey-bellied Tesia, a tiny forest-floor bird with long legs, a teeny tail, green upperparts and grey underparts.

Rob was with me the next day when a proposed casual post-illness stroll in search of the Pekin Robins turned into a six hour assault on the forested slope, mostly clambering down into and up out of deep, dank ravines full of ferns. We saw the robins, and the tesia, and Beautiful Niltavas and White's Thrushes and White-crested Laughingthrushes but even they struggled to compete with a Brown Fish Owl which we accidentally flushed on to an open branch by the lakeside, as well as a very striking White-browed Scimitar Babbler with a black and white head, deep brown upperparts and snow-white underparts with chestnut flanks, and, most amazing of all, a Green Magpie, a brilliant green vision with flashing crimson wings.

Kazi told us about a site near Pokhara where we might see Ibisbills so we headed to the bus station early one morning. Rob was not up to it but he didn't want to miss seeing an Ibisbill, and he threw up before we got on the bus, much to the delight of some pigs. We got off the bus after about 30 miles (50 km) at Damauli and after crossing a swing-rope bridge over the River Seti headed south along the bank of the sparkling rocky waterway below ferny forest in a deep, dark gorge. The beautiful setting was the ideal place to see an Ibisbill but once again we had to settle for less, although not much, it being a Wallcreeper.

With the Ibisbill giving us grief we decided to return to Chitwan. Back there, we walked to the luxurious lodge called Gaida Wildlife Camp where Raje, who we met in Kathmandu, worked. He treated us, with coffee, a roosting Brown Fish Owl, a large lunch, a roosting Brown Hawk Owl, a trip into the National Park during which we saw a mother Rhino with a youngster, and a glass of rum in front of an open fire at the end of a very fine day. With the help of Giri we saw another Rhino the next afternoon. He climbed a tree and spotted one heading for its evening wallow. After a short walk there it was, lying in a small patch of wet mud with an Indian Pond Heron on its back. Unfortunately Giri, anxious to please, let us walk too close and after the Rhino had seen him off it swung round and headed for me, at speed. I turned and ran along a narrow trail into the jungle hoping it wouldn't catch up with me. I never saw it but when I got back to Giri and Rob they told me it had rolled in right after me. It was a good job I took a right fork and it presumably a left.

After taking in a last Chitwan sunset, another one in which the crimson sun set in pink dust behind the elephant grass across the Rapti River, we took an ox-cart to Tandi Bazaar and rode a bus roof back to India, arriving in Lucknow at four in the morning. No one would give us a room so, very tired, we just laid down on the drive of one place and someone soon appeared and since the next leg of our journey was another overnight one Rob negotiated a room for the day for 15 rupees. It was the cheapest room in town, overlooking an oil-stained bus repair yard and a festering pool of slime inhabited by four pigs. We spent most of the day in it, the room not the pool, writing and dozing, rather than walking the streets of the sticky hot hovel that was Lucknow, where black smoke billowed from buses, the stench of sewage rose from street-side gutters, the streets were littered with dead dogs, and men were pissing and spitting everywhere.

After twelve hours on a train we got to Kathgodam, Uttar Pradesh, where we transferred to a bus to Nainital, a two hour long trip back up into the Himalayan foothills where we hoped to see flocks of new birds in beautiful forests surrounding a picturesque hill resort. That's what the books and tour reports suggested. In the event Nainital consisted of a bird-less lake with monstrous hotels along one side and forests full of shit on the others; human shit.

The birds don't mind though and during an afternoon walk we saw our first Lanceolated Jays, White-tailed Nuthatches and some very handsome Red-headed Tits with reddish crowns, white eyebrows and broad black masks. We were still not tempted to stay another day, not when Corbett National Park beckoned, so we were off again, down through a thick layer of cloud to Ramnagar where we had to wait four hours for a bus to Dhikala. That would not have been so bad *if* we had known at the time that the Kosi River above Ramnagar was a great place for Ibisbills.

At Dhikala we soon sorted out a bunk each in the park dormitory, where, early the next morning, we awoke to a sickening soft thump on the concrete floor. A girl from New Zealand had fallen out of her bunk. She was out cold and all of us in the dormitory waited anxiously for what seemed like an age for her to come around. She was terribly shaken and had at the least a badly bruised cheekbone. The doctor said she would have to go to hospital immediately, in Delhi, a day away, adding that she may have suffered a fit in reaction to the pills she was taking to keep malaria at bay, although that sounded like idle speculation to us.

Once the poor lass was on her way we were on ours. Six Great Stone Plovers or Thick-knees were loafing on a spit out on the Ramganga Reservoir, next to River Lapwings and two crocodiles, not Mugger Crocodiles, Gharials, crocodilians with long, very thin snouts. A strange-looking raptor in the sky was a Brahminy Kite, a deep chestnut bird with a bold white head. It landed in a dead tree already occupied by an Osprey. A couple of Black-necked

Storks were stalking some shallows, completing a marvellous scene. Off we went then with Howard from England, Kim from Denmark, and Martin Goodey and Nick Hunt from the Isles of Scilly in England who had been around a few days and wanted to show us a pair of Tawny Fish Owls. The massive boldly streaked, orangey owls were still present at their daytime roost. Perched atop a dead snag nearby was a Collared Falconet, barely bigger than a sparrow with a stunning white head with a black crown and mask, shiny black upperparts and rich rufous-orange flanks. During an evening vigil from the watchtower overlooking forest canopy on three sides and the shallow Ramganga River on the other, a huge Crested Kingfisher, beautifully vermiculated with fine silver-grey, perched briefly above the river, and near dusk a small herd of Elephants emerged from elephant grass and crossed the river slowly, in a line.

Nick Hunt was retracing his father's footsteps. David Hunt, who was leading a bird tour in Corbett earlier in the year, was killed by a Tigress protecting her cubs. Apparently, he had left his group and its armed guard on a main trail in order to investigate an owl that he had heard or saw some distance off the trail, and he stumbled across the Tiger family. As a result, visitors to Corbett were forbidden from walking outside the compound without an armed guard making it very difficult to see many birds so being young and foolish we and a few others ignored the warnings and ventured into Tiger territory, diving for cover whenever we heard a jeep, possibly with park guards in it, approaching. We were very lucky not to meet a Tiger or worst still a Tigress with cubs and to meet some stunning birds including Slaty-headed Parakeets, Black-crested Bulbuls, Scarlet Minivets, White's Thrushes, two Himalayan Rubythroats, their jewelled throats surrounded with black, and, best of all, a gorgeous Chestnut-headed Tesia, a tiny, long-legged, upright, yellow-bellied grounddweller which ventured out into the open just long enough for a great view.

It turned out that Tigers were as difficult to see in Corbett as they were in Chitwan. Our only chance was to return to Ranthambore. The trouble was we had all but promised Christiane we would visit her for Christmas and we were extremely tempted to spend a few more days living it up there. However, when it came to the crunch, Rob was so keen to photograph Tigers we decided to use the little time and money we had left to go back to Ranthambore, a plan which was soon in tatters because the vice-president of India decided to spend Christmas there and tourists would not be allowed in. Rob was devastated. I was disappointed but not for long; Rob's mind turned to photographing Siberian Cranes and I was very happy to be heading back to Bharatpur.

Howard joined us and we arrived at Bharatpur railway station at 2 a.m. and got in three separate cycle rickshaws. It was a chilly night, the riders were cold and glad of the surprise custom so we found ourselves in a fiercely competitive race to *Sarus Lodge*, the three pedalling in a cartoon blur as we sped along the pot-holed road at breakneck speed, being thrown violently from side to side while holding our rucksacks with one hand and the side of the seat with the other, and wincing with pain and laughing with joy. The miserable young night watchman at the lodge brought us back down to Earth, insisting every bunk was taken, a response we were used to when turning up in the middle of the night so Rob pleaded with him and the poor kid eventually let us bed down in the bar for a few hours, once Rob had checked the dormitory was full of course - it was.

At dawn the party staying overnight departed, we threw our rucksacks on a bunk each and dashed to the reserve. Howard had been at Bharatpur more recently than us and took us straight to a small pool where our first three Painted Snipes were snoozing in some sedges. They were all males, which are, unusually, duller than females in this species, and yet still intricately marked with a snakeskin of greys and browns. Soon after, we were on a bicycle each in the warm sunshine, cruising through masses of waterbirds and raptors, and life was great. We even located the lone Falcated Duck among the many thousands of ducks and later on saw our first Bar-headed Geese, over a hundred of them, birds that had flown over the Himalayas from their breeding grounds in Central Asia since our last visit. Two Siberian Cranes, a Dusky Horned Owl on its nest and three Bimaculated Larks followed before we took chai at *Bharatpur Forest Lodge*.

After another day amongst a grand parade of beautiful birds we decided to try and see as many species as possible on Christmas Day, although not until we had cycled way out into the arid, open bush to successfully track down a very handsome male Blackbuck, a black and white antelope with long spiral horns. While looking for Blackbucks we came across the carcass of a cow that was attended by a seething mass of nearly a hundred screaming, squealing, hissing Griffon, Long-billed and

White-rumped Vultures. The ugly, hungry, vicious birds were striking out with their snake-like necks and pecking any bird in their way with shocking ferocity. The most aggressive were even climbing over others to get into the open belly of the cow where they tore strips of flesh and organs off and gobbled them down as fast as they could. They were so focused on the foul-smelling rotten meat that we could almost touch them. Those that had filled their bellies emerged from the cow with their heads dripping with blood and half walked, half flew away from the scene before flapping madly to get airborne and join the fifty or so that had already managed to haul their distended bodies off the ground and up into nearby trees. One bird slid its head and neck into the cow's mouth and throat in an attempt to yank the tongue out. When it succeeded after several minutes, the vultures standing by and watching immediately rushed forward and tussled with each other in order to pounce on the thick flesh first. Others were viciously attacking the rear end of the dead animal, ripping out the bowels and squabbling over shreds of them in tug-of-wars. It was exciting but gruesome and a relief to back away a little, from the melee, and the smell, before moving on.

With an hour or so of light left the day-list was impressive and included Siberian and Sarus Cranes, Black-necked and Painted Storks, Falcated Duck, Bar-headed Goose, Bronze-winged and Pheasant-tailed Jacanas, Painted Snipe, six eagles, three owls, Little Green Bee-eater and Indian Roller. We headed back toward town gloriously happy, freewheeling along the road on our bicycles before sweeping off the tarmac on to a sandy playing field where we hoped to see some pipits but to our shock and delight found five Yellow-wattled Lapwings instead. The long, yellow-legged, sandy-brown birds with yellow wattles at the base of their beaks were so confiding I was able to circle one bird and almost look straight down at its mottled grey crown from the saddle of my bicycle. Back in town the last bird of a long, hot day, was a Brown Rock Chat, the 160th species, a remarkable total for such a tiny part of the planet.

I was more than happy to spend the next day taking my time to watch some of those birds at length, especially seven Painted Snipes venturing out furtively from cover to begin their nocturnal foraging, although the most stirring sight was of a species not seen the day before, a flock of about forty Common Cranes gliding gracefully overhead in V-formation, their wild, deep trumpeting calls carrying far across the marshes over which they wheeled before landing.

"Where going?" every other person yelled as we left Delhi railway station.

We spoke to a tall turbaned man with a greying beard.

"We're looking for a place to sleep for the night, somewhere cheap!" Rob said.

"Come with me," the man said.

He led us through an increasingly intricate maze of alleyways to one guesthouse after another but they didn't look like guesthouses to us and we managed to escape and find a slightly less suspicious-looking character who led us to the *Navasha Hotel*. Pleading poverty - we had 30 rupees between us - we were given a room next to the kitchen overlooking a block of flats and went to sleep with five rupees left.

After two months in India and Nepal it was so good to return to the 'House of Elrond' in Abbottabad where Rob's dad had arranged for the old cook, nicknamed Buckshee, to pamper us and this he did with steaks and apple fritters which we ate by candlelight because there was no electricity on what was a very cold mid-winter night. The next night we were on a bus to Gilgit although we had been warned that we may not make it beyond there, all the way to Skardu, because the road had been closed for two weeks due to snow and landslides in what was already, in late December, the worst winter in Baltistan for 37 years. The overnight bus headed up the Karakoram Highway through Besham, Dasu and Chilas, and fourteen hours later we were in Gilgit, a long, straggling cultivated strip of land in a barren valley with bare mountains rising steeply on both sides and with a long, straight street forming the bazaar where we were told that, despite the way now being open, the only vehicle travelling to Skardu that day was an old and already overloaded *Ford Transit* pickup. Our insistence on being allowed to travel on it was met with equal resistance. The Baltis did not want to let the only two foreign travellers in town board an overcrowded vehicle, especially a month after two Japanese tourists were among 50 people killed when a bus left the road and plunged hundreds of feet down a sheer cliff into the Indus. Rob was having none of it; we squeezed in behind the driver, anticipating all too good a view of what promised to be a scenic but frightening journey.

The dusty, stony way weaved through magnificent mountain scenery. Frozen waterfalls and huge icicles lined trackside cliffs and overhangs, and above them rose great barren slopes of loose rock and scree, up to snow, huge swathes of snow across the slopes, everywhere except for on the steep pyramidal peaks, and below us more grey-brown scree fell almost straight down the Indus Gorge to the rocky, glacial, grey-green river hundreds sometimes thousands of feet below, where now and again we saw amazing green oases of fertile land on riverside terraces, emerald jewels in a desert of grey dust and sand, but for the most part the scene was of bleak cold desolation and what a fantastic sight it was. The hazards were many; gangs of men with shovels and little else, clearing avalanches, landslides, huge boulders, and snow drifts, were a frequent sight. We slowed down and squeezed past, always on the outside, above nauseating drop-offs. All the while I kept my eyes peeled for Wallcreepers and I saw six. At 10 p.m. on New Year's Eve we finally hurtled into Skardu, shaking from the journey and shivering from the cold.

Shah Jehan, the owner of the *Shangri La*, Skardu's busy inn where we had spent many a happy hour a few months before, greeted us like long lost friends. He made room for us in the middle of the huddle of equally friendly customers around the stove where we ate Dhal Chapati and drank many cups of chai before I buried myself under a pile of blankets provided in the room we lavishly booked for the night. It was so cold I felt like hibernating and may well have done so had I not heard Shah Jehan shouting, "Utho! Utho!" which Rob and I assumed meant, "Get up! Get up!" and actually means "Rise! Rise!"

It was 1 p.m. and still freezing but we got up and dressed, in record time. After some warming chai and Dhal Chapati we headed out to see the District Forest Officer (D.F.O.). The scene stopped us in our tracks; Skardu was surrounded by a magnificent arena of snowy mountains set against a blue sky. The air was bitingly cold but there was no wind and the sunshine was pleasantly quite warm.

Rob's first question to the D.F.O. was, "When can we go to Narh?"

"You cannot go to Narh," the D.F.O. replied, "there is too much snow."

We tried to convince him that we were willing to put up with that but he was adamant that there really was too much snow and that we would not see a Snow Leopard there because of that, and because there were no Ibex. We were devastated, but not for long.

"I do have some good news," he said. "Two days ago one or maybe two Snow Leopards were seen on Khardrong, the mountain just here, next to Skardu."

This was so exciting that at first we did not believe him. Khardrong is an isolated mountain that rises over 1100 feet (350 metres) above the town of Skardu, which lies at 8200 feet (2500 metres). It would be the easiest place in the world to see a Snow Leopard if it were true. The D.F.O. then told us that a flock of nineteen wild sheep called Urial had found their way to the mountain and the Snow Leopard or Leopards were assumed to be hunting them. The news seemed more plausible by the minute and by the end of the meeting we were even more excited.

"When can we go?"

"Tomorrow, I will arrange it for tomorrow."

The D.F.O. then spoke to his two assistants one of which went away and came back some time later, and then the D.F.O. said, "It is done. You will come here at 9 a.m. tomorrow morning and the guide will take you."

We thanked him many times and shook his hand firmly then walked to the K2 Motel to ask Habib the caretaker if it was ok to sleep on the floor there. He said, "No ... you sleep in my room!" His room had two charpoys and an electric fire no less.

It was a long, hard climb, across scree, up steep slopes covered in a foot of beautiful snow and along narrow, icy ridges, to the summit of Khardrong. The view was phenomenal. We looked at it with open-mouthed awe. There were snowy mountains all around, with sharp peaks pointing into the oh so pure, deep blue sky. Below them were vast snowy slopes and grey cliffs. The sheer brilliance of it all was completed by the great swathes of snow far below; snowfields, snow dunes, a desert of snow, through which flowed the icy, grey-green water and icebergs of the Indus.

We saw three female Urials with pale brown coats. We didn't see a Snow Leopard but Rob was sure some of the tracks we found in the snow were those of *Chitah*, and they were fresh. We stayed until the warming sun fell below the peaks and turned the horizon deep pink beyond the rugged crest of the Deosai Range, the colour intensifying by the minute, almost to a glow. The descent, down the other side of the mountain, was easier than expected although without torches we may have had to try and survive the night on the mountain, listening to the Wolves across the valley while shivering in icy socks and soggy boots. Moving kept us warm; when we stopped to work out the way down the air bit hard. Eventually the few lights of town appeared in the distance and then we could look forward to the lovely warm lamplight atmosphere of the *Shangri La* where the Dhal Chapati tasted better than ever. Then we joined the other customers, wrapped in grey blankets, around the stove, had a smoke with our chai and felt great to be alive.

We didn't need a guide now; we set off on our own the next day and saw a small flock of Urial including a fine male stood atop a prominent rock above us, his thick, ribbed horns curving back to a sharp point behind his head. A Wallcreeper crept up a cliff close by and down below, way down below, we could see ten Goosanders, including two resplendent drakes, looking very much at home amongst the ice floes of the Indus. The next day we walked around the whole base of Khardrong, beginning in an apricot grove where the treecreeper was a Wallcreeper, flicking its wings half-open, flashing the black, white and red in them, while probing the cracks in the bark at the base of the trunks with its long, slender beak, hoping to find spiders and other invertebrates hiding from the cold. Nearby, two real treecreepers, Himalayan to be exact, the ones with barred tails, were doing exactly the same, only less flamboyantly. Other hardy birds were Great Tits, Wrens, Brown Dunnocks, Streaked Laughingthrushes and a small flock of Black-throated Thrushes.

Beyond the trees we had to plough through half a mile or so of deep snow to reach the bare rock and scree at the base of the mountain. We crossed the precipitous eastern face to the northern side which lies in almost permanent, mind-numbing cold shade during the long winter, and while shuffling our way through over a foot of fortunately light and fluffy snow we were amazed to come across a hoary hamlet called Nansok. It looked like something out of a fairy-tale: about ten flat-roofed stone and wicker huts on a small shelf above the Indus surrounded by deep, untrodden snow and apricot trees entirely encrusted with thick frost, and yet there were birds about; the usual Great Tits, Brown Dunnocks and Streaked Laughingthrushes, and, most incredible of all, a big snipe which we flushed from the side of a tiny rivulet of running water. Its wings were broad and rounded, and we thought it was a Wood Snipe when we looked it up weeks later but it was probably a Solitary Snipe. It dropped down about ten paces on, we approached it very carefully, the sudden surge of adrenalin warming our shivering bodies, but just as I focused on its heavily barred flanks it took to the air again and flew off toward the other side of the summer settlement where we looked for it in vain.

Beyond Nansok the deep snow was heavy going so we climbed out and up a steep rock face above and made our way along a ridge where, in some snow, Rob found what appeared to be fresh *Chitah* tracks. We proceeded very slowly and with great caution hoping more than anything else in the whole world that we would see a Snow Leopard over the next ridge and every ridge from then on but it was not to be. Before beginning our descent a huge owl sailed along the slope above us and we soon realised that up there it could only be a Eurasian Eagle Owl, a great end to the day, as far as birds were concerned. Back in the *Shangri La* we heard that the temperature in Skardu the night before fell to minus 22°C. It was time to keep my thermals on, step into my thermal sleeping bag liner, shuffle into my sleeping bag designed to withstand minus 20°C and think about what had been another wonderful day in the mountains of the Karakoram, and those to come.

We got up very late after a restless night during which the temperature fell to minus 27°C, although when we set off for the D.F.O.'s office mid-morning it was only minus 16°C. After three days scouring Khardrong for Snow Leopard without seeing one Rob wanted to know if there was another good place to look. The D.F.O. did know a place; it was called Botlaw Nullah, in the Haramosh Range at the head of the Shigar Valley, about 20 miles (32 km) from Skardu, and he promised to arrange for us to go there the next day. The following morning we were at his office on time. Four hours later we were told that we had missed all jeeps to Shigar.

Frustrated, we retired to the *Shangri La* to simmer down then headed up Khardrong once again. Just as we were about to climb the last stretch to our favourite lookout point, a high ridge with a view of a large part of the mountain, Rob spotted a pair of furry ears poking above another ridge, seemingly hiding from a Urial that was approaching from below. We threw ourselves to the ground and crawled behind a large rock. Peering very carefully over the rock, we looked at the ears then the Urial then the ears, again and again, with our hearts pounding like never before. Whispering to each other, we discussed what it could be, desperately trying to suppress any thoughts of it being a Snow Leopard but unable to, especially after the mysterious beast moved a little and showed a tiny bit of the grey fur on its body. The minutes passed by in what seemed like hours and it may well have been an hour we spent staring at the Urial and the ears hoping a *Chitah* would leap up and reveal itself. By now we were almost convinced. 'This is it,' I thought, 'we're actually going to see a Snow Leopard!' Then the beast rose to its feet, shook its furry grey coat and trotted off. It was a fox, a Red Fox, a common-or-garden Red Fox, just like the ones at home except it was rather grey. We could not believe it.

We had never seen a fox on Khardrong. We could not understand why some of its fur looked grey and why a fox was stalking an animal twice its size.

"Not all Red Foxes are red," Rob said dejectedly, "and it probably wasn't after the Urial, it was probably just sunning itself and watching the Urial at the same time."

Whatever was going on it still didn't make sense to me. Nor did what happened when it was dark and we were descending a huge scree slope. A flock of Urial suddenly bolted, not because of us we were sure, and not long afterwards we heard what sounded like very heavy breathing and the tumbling of scree down the slope. It was a very exciting and scary moment and on full alert again, adrenalin pumping into our bloodstreams, we looked around feverishly, desperately trying to see what it was breathing so loudly. We were certain it must be some kind of large mammal and considered Urial, Snow Leopard,

Wolf, even Yeti, but we will never know what it was because as quick as the action took place all went quiet again. Then the eagle owl began calling a deep 'boo-bu' and a meteor shot across the starry sky, then another, then another. It was all too much to take in but when we calmed down a little we searched the scree in the star light, checking behind big rocks and the entrance to a cave which we found at the top of the slope. Whatever we had heard was probably in there but we decided it was too dangerous to go in and we never saw nor heard it again.

After the previous night's events we forgot about Shigar and returned to Khardrong to investigate. We climbed ever so slowly up the scree to where there had been so much commotion the night before, searching and scanning very carefully, and we checked the cave but there was nothing to see or any sign of any large mammal having ever been there. Rolling stones whizzed past us but we thought they had been released by freeze-thaw not something living, so we climbed higher, to our lookout ridge with a view of the scree slopes and cliffs above the snow dunes, the ice desert and the Indus far below. Where there had been one there were now three foxes, all curled up in the warm rays of the sun, and they sunbathed all afternoon. At dusk we returned to the slope where we were shaken up the night before and waited until our hands turned purple and our toes started to hurt but there was no sign of life and it became so, so cold after dark we could resist the warming walk back to chai and Dhal Chapati no longer. Whatever it was up there we would never know.

The next day we travelled to Shigar in a jeep, east at first then north across the Indus on a swaying wooden suspension bridge then we continued north through a wide, flat valley on a rough track past poplars and willows, and orchards where carefully maintained meltwater channels helped grow the best nectarines in the world. Few villages have such stunning views as Shigar where the single-storey, flat-roofed, stone dwellings sit between the immense mountain ranges of Masherbrum and Haramosh, both looking all the more impressive in their winter snow cover. The sheer scale of the visual brilliance of the sparkling scenery was mind-blowing. I suddenly felt exhilarated; so happy to be there, to be alive in such a place.

We were fortunate one man aboard the jeep spoke a bit of English. He helped us find our guide, Hadar Joo, who led us to a stone house where we dumped our rucksacks in time for a short walk around the now bare barley, corn and wheat fields during which we saw a flock of Shore Larks, and a few Wrens, Great Tits, Rock Buntings and Brown Dunnocks. The night must have been the coldest of the trip so far, about minus 30°C, because it was almost impossible to sleep. Waves of cold air rose from beneath the bare concrete floor through my sleeping mat, sleeping bag, thermal sleeping bag liner, thermal underwear and clothes. The stove was lit before we got up and chai and paratha warmed us up ready for the next leg of our journey. A new guide turned up, a young Forest Officer called Ehsan and he soon flagged down a passing jeep and we were off, up the Shigar Valley, walking the last few miles to the tiny hamlet of Yuno through snowy boulder fields on the eastern plain of the wide, shallow, rocky Shigar River flowing through a wild and rugged valley. Intoxicated by the scenery and the mountain air I walked merrily along stopping now and again to look at more wonder, in the form of Stoliczka's Tit Warblers, Güldenstädt's Redstarts and Wallcreepers. Then, when the sun went down behind those colossal mountains I got cold, very cold, teeth-chattering cold, even though I was walking, and I couldn't shake the shivering off, and very suddenly I felt very low, the lowest I had felt on the trip, and I dearly wished I was at home, in the warm. I often looked forward to going home but I had never been so down as to want to end the trip before the money ran out and there was still a chance of seeing a Snow Leopard.

I headed straight for the stove when we were shown to a stone hut and stood next to it for an hour before I felt better and another hour before I felt human but I never felt truly warm until after we had eaten a healthy portion of rice and potatoes, three hours later. Rob and I were both more than ready to go to sleep then, but we had to wait until all the men of the hamlet had settled down in the same room. Apparently the male folk of Yuno don't sleep with their wives at night. We were glad. We slept much better than the night before presumably because the place was so much warmer with so many bodies in it.

A quick egg with paratha and we boarded a tractor to Tisar, trundling very slowly along the rough track. At one steep icy incline the tractor slid repeatedly toward the cliff edge and we had to help cover the ice with soil and gravel in order to give the tyres something to grip. After that the tractor speeded up and the two very old firewood gatherers who we picked up earlier were now hanging on for their lives at the back. We were dropped off at a long wooden suspension bridge over the Shigar River. Here, mountaineers heading for K2 during the summer carry straight on. We turned left and walked carefully across the bridge, watching our feet so as not to step in the large holes where planks were missing. At Tisar Police Post we had to register our presence in the area before being allowed to continue. The two policemen were shocked to see two foreigners in the middle of winter and they looked like they were going to take an age to process the necessary papers so we sat outside and watched six Himalayan Griffons and a Golden Eagle soaring above the slopes of the magnificent mountains.

After about an hour we were allowed to carry on, along a narrow trail by the small, shallow Basna River flowing along the base of the unbelievably high slopes of the Haramosh. After a while we came across a short stretch of river which for a reason as yet unknown to us was lined with green banks and buckthorn bushes, not the ice and snow we were now used to, and it was alive with birds including about ten Güldenstädt's Redstarts and almost as many Stoliczka's Tit Warblers, providing a welcome splash of colour in the otherwise bleak, grey and white terrain. Ehsan was anxious to carry on but we took our rucksacks off and while Rob tried to photograph the birds I propped myself up against the Haramosh and focused my binoculars on the gorgeous Stoliczka's, one of which was working its way through a bush overhanging the river. It was a fabulous specimen with gorgeous pastel purple flanks. I watched it until the cold air began to bite and Rob and I slung our rucksacks back on and returned to the trail, through snow and over ice, a little above the river now.

The reason, Ehsan explained as we walked, why the stretch of river where we had seen so many birds, was not half frozen was because there were some hot springs not far up ahead. We then had to cross the shallow river on slippery stones, while trying not to look, in some disbelief, at the amount of steam rising from the gently flowing waters surrounded by snow and ice and rock and glorious mountains. As we tred carefully from stone to stone two birds rose from the river calling something like 'tklee-lee-tklee-lee', loud and fast. On hearing the calls and looking up and seeing two quite large shorebirds with long, down-curved bills, Rob instinctively shouted, "Curlews!" but I, on seeing that their beaks were *very* down-curved and dark red, their faces black and their wings plain grey-brown above, yelled out, much louder than Rob, "Ibisbills!"

The two birds flew upstream and we headed after them with our rucksacks bouncing on our backs and still shaking our heads in disbelief that we had, when we least expected it, come across the birds I most wanted to see on the whole trip, the one I thought I would never see, having missed them in Nepal, and it was especially unbelievable because we were now high up the mountains during the winter when they usually migrate to the foothills. Soon, we caught up with them and watched them wading through the water and steam, and it was a truly wonderful sight. The striking black, white and grey birds, the same colours as the shallow, rocky, river, had black faces and black bands across their white breasts, and they swept their blood-red bills from side to side through the water in search of food. I was shaking so much it was hard to enjoy the scene at first but after a while I calmed down, took my rucksack off and tried to take it all in; the birds, the river, the rocks, the steam, the snow, the mountains, the blue sky, the blue that was fading fast. Ehsan wanted us to move on but we were having none of it. We thought our chance had gone. Then, completely out of the blue, with just ten days of the trip to go, two Ibisbills fly up from our very feet high in the Karakoram where they would not normally be at that time of the year were it not for those hot springs which we had no idea existed. Ibisbills were not even on my mind at the time and they were all the better for that.

Eventually Ehsan persuaded us to leave them and we walked the last few hundred paces into the remote mountain hamlet of Chutran, the name of which literally translated from the Balti means 'hot water'. Ehsan showed us to the rest house, a splendid bungalow with a stove in the middle of the main room as usual and better still the river almost on the doorstep, so instead of firing up the stove and staying warm in the rapidly decreasing temperature we rushed back to the river to make sure it wasn't all a dream. A quick look and there, wading through the water and wafts of steam next to the ice-encrusted banks and fields of snow were five Ibisbills.

Over thirty years later, when I could afford to buy, second-hand, *The Birds of Pakistan* by Tom Roberts, I was shocked and excited to read that we had stumbled across the only place in Pakistan where Ibisbills are known to occur, astonishing for a mountain river bird in a land of many mountains and rivers. Up until January 1986 when we discovered them just two birds had been recorded in the country; both of them shot, near Gilgit in 1880 and near Islamabad in 1931. Since 1986 it has been established that, thanks to the hot springs, there is a tiny resident population of Ibisbills living and breeding at Chutran.

A Wallcreeper completed one of the greatest days, before we quickly retired to the rest house and got the stove on. The wood wasn't burning very well so Rob decided to give it a boost with some petrol that he kept in a canister for emergencies. As he poured too much fuel into the stove flames ran up his arm. It looked like his arm was on fire but he still had the sense not to drop the canister and burn the place to the ground, and while I tackled the stove he ran outside and threw the canister as far as he could. We thought the villagers would come running when they heard the massive bang it made when it landed but we saw no one until Ehsan brought us some rice.

An Ibisbill after breakfast was a great start to another precious day in the Karakoram. Our time in the mountains was running out. We had one day left to see a Snow Leopard. We thought the chance of seeing one was extremely slim because everyone we had spoken to since we arrived in Shigar, apart from Ehsan, indicated that there were no *Chitahs* at Chutran. I had long suspected the D.F.O. was perhaps a little too desperate to please but there we were in that beautiful mountain terrain and we had him to thank because we had seen the Ibisbill! Ehsan came to the rest house with Nisar, the local Forest Officer, and we followed them up the valley to Hemasil, an extraordinary hamlet, the centre of which was a maze of joined-up flat-roofed stone and wicker huts constructed around sound wooden beams and posts where we climbed a small ladder to drink chai with the head men of the village in a dark, cosy room too low to stand up in. Bright eyes in dirty, smoke-stained faces stared at us through the wicker work, mostly young boys, while we were given a shepherd's staff each to assist us in our ascent of the narrowing valley beyond. We needed them, to help us through the knee-high snow and up the steep slopes to Botlaw Nullah, according to the D.F.O. and Ehsan, but nobody else, a good place to see a Snow Leopard. We paused to watch a Lammergeier soar with a pair of Golden Eagles, the mighty eagles dwarfed by the monstrous 'geier. Eight Himalayan Snowcocks flew rapidly across the upper valley, their wings a blur then stiff as they approached their landing site. There were a few Stoliczka's too, and a handsome Rufous-naped Tit with a short black crest.

When we reached a narrow gap in the sharp ridge at the top of the valley wall where we were going to scan for Snow Leopards we came across two men with binoculars and guns. They were hunters and promptly arrested by Ehsan and Nisar. The prolonged, loud palaver meant scanning for Snow Leopards was pointless. We tried of course but not for long and reluctantly agreed to help escort the prisoners back to Hemasil, all hopes of seeing a Snow Leopard now gone. When we reached Hemasil we suddenly felt exhausted, as though all the energy had been sucked out of us. Our lethargy may have been due to the high-altitude climb or the massive anticlimax; probably a combination of both, and maybe, given the hunters argument that they were after wild sheep to boost their meagre winter diet, the nagging thought that if there were wild sheep up there then there may well have been a Snow Leopard as well, or perhaps it was just the terrible feeling that the trip was effectively over now.

Ehsan told us that the hunters faced a 2000 rupee fine and years in prison if found guilty of shooting more wild sheep than allowed, far worse if they were hunting Snow

Leopards, the pelts of which would be worth a small fortune. If that is what they were after then there must have been Snow Leopards there but whatever was really happening we would never know, we could not speak the language, so we had to face the truth; we had neither the time nor the money to stay a while and we had to make it back to Shigar then Skardu then Abbottabad before the weather closed in and the winter got even worse.

After giving our thanks to the head men of Hemasil we returned to the rest house and while the captives gave their statements to Ehsan and several villagers in the main room we trundled down to the river. We couldn't see any Ibisbills, then or the next morning when we set off down the mountains with Ehsan, a couple of villagers and the prisoners. Two sparkling Wallcreepers were flicking from rock to rock in the middle of the river and along a warm stretch of water there were several Stoliczka's, Güldenstädt's, Brown Dunnocks and a Wren. Across the Shigar River at Tandara we were given a lift on a tractor. I would rather have walked. It was warmer to walk. It was freezing sitting on a tractor and the weather was looking grim. We had grown accustomed to cold but sunny days with crisp, blue skies but dark low cloud was descending the mountain sides now and suddenly the Karakoram looked very inhospitable. For the first time in the mountains I felt anxious. It looked like we could get snowed in, stuck in the Shigar Valley or Skardu if we were lucky, for days, weeks maybe. The weather was definitely deteriorating and Ehsan said that we had better get as far as we could down the Shigar Valley that day so when the tractor stopped we carried on walking and we reached Alchori for the night, where we nearly nodded off waiting for a very nice Dhal Chapati. After a pretty good sleep despite what must have been another night near minus 30°C we were up early and ready to board the Toyota Express to Skardu.

The cloud was thick in Skardu and it was so cold we spent seven hours in the *Shangri La* drinking cup after cup of chai and talking to Shah Jehan who announced proudly that he had fathered nine children and gesticulated that he was still going strong. He was a clown in a long duvet coat which he seemed to wear just to show off. At Kharpocho Fort on the eastern flank of Khardrong the next day we met Kazmi, a Forest Officer who had some slides he had taken of a Snow Leopard while Rob and I were away in India and Nepal. It had broken into an outhouse near Skardu where goats were kept and it had eaten two of them, and then been unable to move because it was so full. Looking at the beautiful creature lying on a bed of straw Rob nearly broke down in tears. We climbed up to lookout ridge from where I was amazed to see a Great Black-headed Gull flying up the Indus. It was one of ten bird species seen that day, a high total for Skardu in winter, and one which also included our first Rock Sparrow, that was in amongst a small flock of Shore Larks. On our last day we climbed to the top of Khardrong where a Golden Eagle soared, the first one we had ever seen on the mountain. At dusk, rainbow-coloured wisps of cloud glowed above the glistening grey and snowy peaks of the Deosai, formed by the last rays of sunlight shooting through the ice crystals in the clouds.

The mini-bus to Gilgit was crammed full of people and their luggage and a mass of more bags were tied to the roof. "Chalo! Chalo!" someone shouted, which we had always assumed meant something like 'Let's go', and we were off. The mini-bus hurtled along at a breathtaking speed despite the head-shaking drop-offs down to the rock-strewn, ice-encrusted Indus, a great plume of dust off the stone and dirt road exploding in the bus's wake as it zoomed around numerous tight bends, over patches of thick ice, and around fallen rocks and boulders, at the base of towering slopes and cliffs, through the sometimes narrow sometimes wide always spectacular Indus Gorge. Chai stops were a welcome respite and on one, at a tiny hamlet called Biacha, we saw our last Stoliczka's. I was looking out for Wallcreepers all the way of course and I saw nine, taking my total for the whole trip to 32, and the total for my life to 37.

In Gilgit we switched to a customised multi-coloured *Bedford* bus driven by a chain-smoking maniac who drove as fast as he possible could down the Karakoram Highway. We were glad it was dark and we could not see the full terror of the drop-offs but we did see a fox run out into the road then sprint for its life as the driver sped even faster downhill after it, swerving violently from side to side with an almost unbelievable determination to flatten the unfortunate fox. After a minute or so the terrified animal leapt over the edge of the road into the abyss, much to the amusement of the driver and passengers whose laughter could just about be heard over the chanting, wailing songs coming out of the speakers at full blast.

At half past four in the morning, after 250 miles (400 km) and twenty hours trying to stay on our seats, we wobbled down the steps of the bus to terra firma in Abbottabad and let out the usual exaggerated sigh of delight at still being alive after a bus journey on the Indian Subcontinent.

Thirty hours and a thousand miles (1600 km) on a train rolling slowly south through Pakistan was much more enjoyable, even pleasurable, thanks partly to the trackside birdlife which included the now very familiar but no less spectacular Indian Pond Herons, Indian Rollers, Smyrna Kingfishers, Long-tailed Shrikes and so on. In the darkness I was alone amongst many but sleep was a fanciful idea amidst the mayhem of vociferous passengers, shrill salesmen and weeping beggars. On hearing, "Chai chai chai" once more, I bought another cup, lit a cigarette and thought about where I was and what I was doing and a flood of joy rushed up inside of me because I had not only somehow managed to stumble across the wonder of birds and birding, which made me so happy, but I was now travelling around planet Earth in search of the birds I dreamed of, and that made me happier than I had ever imagined.

Near Khanpur at 6 a.m. the sun rose into the red dust of the Cholistan Desert. At 6.30 p.m. I arrived at Karachi Cant railway station. By midnight I was in the sky above the vast city of lights next to the Arabian Sea. I woke up as we descended to Bucharest in misty Romania and I got off the plane in London where the rain was a novelty. It was a dry morning on Robinswood Hill though, where the vibrant green landscape and Blue Tits and Bullfinches, Jays and Fieldfares, were an invigorating contrast to the Ibisbills and Wallcreepers, Güldenstädt's and Stoliczka's, in the grey and white mountains of Baltistan.

*Roadrunner, Laguna Atascosa, Texas, 7th of April 1987*

# 5

# TEXAS

It was early April and the ice along the New Brunswick coast of Canada was breaking up. We could see it 30,000 feet (9000 metres) below the jet we were on, flying from London, England to Houston, Texas, the 'we' being me, Mark Golley, Nick Wall, Chris 'Gibb' Gibbins and Barry 'The Stid' Stidolph. When it landed there was about an hour of light left and we didn't want to waste it so we set up our telescopes at passport control and watched our first Killdeers foraging on a lawn outside the huge airport windows. After dark the floodlit concrete, steel and glass skyscrapers of Houston rose out of the flat terrain of

Texas like a city on a desert planet in a science fiction movie. We cruised past in our hire car, on our way to High Island near Galveston on the coast of the Gulf of Mexico, where we booked into the *Gulfway Motel* and tried to get some sleep but it was impossible; the next day we would be looking for new birds on a new continent, one of the best experiences there is in a birder's life.

We were all twitchers who chased across Britain to see rare birds. Some of the most exciting are those which are blown across the Atlantic Ocean from North America, especially the New World warblers. However, most of the birds that reach Britain are young birds, quite colourful but not a patch on the dazzling adults. These along with many more warblers that never reach Britain, as well as a wealth of other amazing birds, millions of them, migrate from South and Central America through Texas during the spring and that is why we were there.

Warblers and other small birds on their way north take off from places such as the Yucatan Peninsula in Mexico at sunset and fly 450 to 600 miles (725 to 965 km) to the Texas coast in 11 to 18 hours, with favourable tailwinds. In good weather many continue inland until they feel the need to rest, drink and feed but in bad weather, especially northerly winds with a cold front and rain, the flight takes much longer and the exhausted birds dive into the first bushes and trees they can find. Much of the Texas coastal plain is flat, marshy and treeless, and there is little cover but there are two groves of live oaks called Boy Scout Woods and Smith Oaks at High Island, a tiny bump of land 34 feet (10 metres) above sea-level. When the weather isn't too bad there are usually a lot of birds in these woods and the surrounding area, more than enough to keep a keen birder happy. When the weather is terrible there is what is known as a fall or a fallout of birds from the sky, sometimes involving tens of thousands, and then the trees and bushes are literally alive with warblers, buntings, tanagers, thrushes, orioles and vireos, all in stunning spring plumage, and they can make a staggering sight.

"Hey, there's a bunch'a birders if ever I saw one!" an American birder said aloud as he entered the *Gulfway Cafe* where we were eating a fast breakfast.

He had just arrived at High Island and he was after some information about what birds were about. We had nothing to tell him because we had not got into the field yet but not long after we were in Boy Scout Woods and from then on we had a whole 'bunch'a stuff' to tell him about. It was a fine, sunny morning, there had not been a fall, but we still saw at least ten black and yellow Hooded Warblers and three black-capped grey Catbirds before moving on to Smith Oaks just up the road where we stood in front of a line of live oaks mesmerised by our first flock of new birds. They were foraging frantically low down just a few paces away; mostly Red-eyed Vireos but also some White-eyed Vireos, a Solitary 'Blue-headed' Vireo, yellow-rumped Myrtle Warblers and three Black-and-white Warblers, the least colourful but most striking birds in the flock which looked like they had been painted by hand, the artist having swept neat white stripes across the jet black upperparts and delicately dabbed black streaks on the white underparts. There was no time to grill them. There were new birds all around, not least some shocking male Scarlet Tanagers, a few slightly more sombre but still bright red male Summer Tanagers, true Blue Jays, Indigo Buntings and brilliant red Northern Cardinals. It was almost too much to take in. We didn't know where to look. Every movement had the potential to be a new bird and it usually was. Our heads were spinning when someone ran past saying the Black-whiskered Vireo, seen first thing in the morning, had been relocated and we dashed after him, and after several 'Red-eyes' there it was, basically another 'Red-eye' with dark whiskers and not very exciting when compared with the other birds we had just seen but only, we were told, the second ever to reach Texas from the species' usual haunts in Florida and the Caribbean, way to the east.

Still reeling from the rush we drove down to Rollover Pass and set up our telescopes overlooking the eastern end of Galveston Bay. The tide was low and before us on the mudflats and in the shallow channels of brackish water there was an astounding selection of waterbirds. From left to right; a flock of over 750 red-necked American Avocets, a lone Brown Pelican, a few Willets, loads of Snowy Egrets, a few Great Blue Herons, about ten Marbled Godwits, a summer-plumaged Western Sandpiper amongst a lot of other tiny shorebirds called peeps in this neck of the woods, a few Piping and Wilson's Plovers, a huge flock of gulls and terns out in the middle within which there were masses of Laughing and Ring-billed Gulls, and lots of Bonaparte's Gulls, and what must have been 500 Forster's Terns, 300 Royal Terns and 50 Least Terns, and standing head and shoulders above them all, two Caspian Terns. I caught my breath and continued; a flock of about 300 Black Skimmers, a hundred or so White Pelicans, a tight group of 40 Roseate Spoonbills in the same channel as a

Reddish Egret and on a wooden jetty two Belted Kingfishers. I stood there lost in wonder for hours and when the tide rose quickly in the late afternoon and the water filled the channel in front of us some skimmers took to the air and flew over on long wings. They came elegantly in from the left, dropped to near the surface and skimmed the water with their extraordinary black and red bills, hoping to connect with some small fish, before rising into the air again, all with effortless grace.

When it was too dark to see any more we drove south to Tivoli and while eating and drinking we tried to help each other remember all the birds we had seen so we could write them down in our notebooks. Then we attempted to grab a few hours sleep in the car, in a *Dairy Queen* parking lot. Early the next morning we saw two fantasy birds one after the other. A Scissor-tailed Flycatcher foraging from a roadside fence had a round-headed, soft grey look with contrasting black wing feathers neatly trimmed with white, a very long and stiff black and white tail, and peachy flanks intensifying to a deep salmon pink under the wings, richest around the shoulders, while a Swallow-tailed Kite is a long white bird with slate-grey and black wings, and a very long deeply forked black tail which seemed to float along behind it.

The raptor, a rare sight in Texas, was heading steadily north, along with flock after flock of Franklin's Gulls, flying to their breeding grounds on the Great Plains. We were heading slowly south, along the coast of the Gulf of Mexico, to Aransas National Wildlife Refuge where a big-eyed, friendly-looking Upland Sandpiper graced the lawn of the visitor centre.

*Scissor-tailed Flycatcher, Aransas, Texas, 6th of April 1987*

Aransas is the only wintering ground of wild Whooping Cranes on Earth. The birds, which nest during the summer at Wood Buffalo National Park, 2400 miles (3860 km) to the north in northwest Canada, are usually present in Texas from late October to mid-April although only a few remain until the end of the winter season and that was confirmed by the refuge staff who also told us that the birds still present were very difficult to see, so it was with some concern that we began a thorough search of the vast marshes the cranes wade through in search of crabs, crayfish and frogs, their main prey. Even through our telescopes from the top of the high observation tower we could not see any so when the afternoon was coming to an end we returned to the visitor centre for some help. The Head Ranger saved the day, giving us permission to drive along a little-used track where after another hour of relentless scanning three magnificent white cranes appeared in flight and through our telescopes we could see their scarlet crowns and black faces as they flapped majestically in our direction, low over the marshes, before dropping down out of sight and out of reach.

We were not totally consumed by the quest for cranes. The many distractions included our first Anhinga, a black and glossy green bird with silver speckles and streaks, and a neck like a snake, blue-grey and pale purple Louisiana Herons, more like egrets with their long slim necks and long spear-like beaks, Wild Turkeys and Groove-billed Anis, very strange, slow-moving, ponderous black birds with drooping wings, as well as lots of Belted Kingfishers and Black-and-white Warblers, and, at dusk, the appearance of two Nine-banded Armadillos, off out on their nightly search for ants, beetles and other invertebrates.

Another action-packed day full of wonder began when a pair of Ruby-throated Hummingbirds appeared with a whirr at the flowering bushes outside our motel in Rockport. The first hummingbirds we had seen in action for more than a few seconds were completely oblivious to our presence, allowing us to stand just a couple of paces away as we watched them sipping nectar from the knee-high flowers while flying forwards, backwards, up, down and sideways with incredible speed, agility and precision. I couldn't believe what I was seeing; the things, the creatures, were they even birds? They just seemed too incredible, even for evolution on Earth to come up with, but there they were, large as life, right in front of me, for a while anyway, because as suddenly as they had appeared they departed, in a blur, leaving me totally stunned by their brilliance.

South of Corpus Christi, about two thirds of the way down the Texas coast, the landscape changed. It was drier, flatter and scrubbier as we pushed on through the tough mesquite shrubland to Kingsville. A sprinkling of Scissor-tailed Flycatchers lit up the world and at least 70 Swainson's Hawks were resting in roadside fields waiting for the first thermals of the day to ride high into the sky and continue their journey north. At Kingsville we turned west on to a dead straight road into King Ranch, at over 1200 square miles (3340 sq km) the largest ranch in the United States. Beef is the main business, in the form of heat-resistant and tick-resistant Santa Gertrudis cattle. Birds were our business, the best of which was an aptly-named Golden-fronted Woodpecker.

Back on Highway 77 we turned south and not long after pulled into Sarita rest area where there was a small copse famous for its nesting Tropical Parulas, another fabulous member of the warbler family. We looked long and hard but could not find any of the colourful birds. However, it was still an exciting time because new birds appeared thick and fast. Firstly, a pair of spectacular Great Kiskadees, massive stocky flycatchers with broad black masks across their white heads, reddish-brown backs, wings and tails, and stunning lemon yellow underparts, then black-crested Tufted Titmice, a pair of Eastern Bluebirds, a tiny Common Ground Dove, the size of a sparrow, a massive Great Crested Flycatcher, the size of a starling, and a splendid Couch's Kingbird. Back on 'Hawk Alley', as Highway 77 is known to birders, we saw, in quick succession, a Crested Caracara, a White-tailed Hawk and a Harris's Hawk, all worthy of screeching halts and prolonged stops.

It was day three but the intense excitement I felt at the beginning of the latest foreign adventure was still with me and I think the same could be said for the others. We braced ourselves for the fall and it seemed imminent when the *only* new birds we saw during the next hour were two Plain Chachalacas and a Roadrunner, both dashing across the road to Laguna Atascosa National Wildlife Refuge, but the fall never came. In the trees around a small, shaded pond the seemingly eternal stream of brilliant new birds continued to flow with five new warblers in what seemed like five minutes, in what was the proverbial 'flock of ticks'. With a bright Black-throated Green Warbler were three Tennessee Warblers, a Nashville Warbler and two Prothonotary Warblers, the latter living up to their nickname of 'light-bulb birds' they were so yellow.

Noting the now 'usual' Black-and-white and Hooded Warblers we then focused on the wet, muddy edge of the pond where there was a Louisiana Waterthrush. Gibb, a quiet young man from Sunderland who I had met on the Isles of Scilly, settled down to sketch the strange 'warbler'. Nick and The Stid, a ship's engineer from South Shields, who was older and more fanatical than the rest of us, and who I also met on Scilly, tried to photograph the warblers. Mark, our young friend from Devon, and I just admired the beauty of all the birds before us, the birds we had dreamed of seeing for so long.

Still glowing from the latest warblers, we then saw some lovely Green Jays, with bright blue and black heads, deep green upperparts, pale green underparts, flashing green and yellow tails, and such soft, clean plumage. Moving on, we counted at least 50 Eastern Kingbirds, fresh in from South America, before spending the evening overlooking the Laguna Madre, a 130 mile (200 km) long, shallow saline lagoon, between the mainland and Padre Island, the longest barrier island on Earth. There were plenty of birds as usual but I concentrated on watching a Reddish Egret spear-fishing in the sparkling shallows, its purple-blue body shining in the low sunlight, its shaggy rufous neck plumes raised and ruffled by the breeze drifting in off the Gulf of Mexico, as it pranced about with high steps and wings arched in a canopy that was folded one minute open the next, while the bird dashed left and right stabbing at fishes with its spear of a beak, in what looked like sheer exuberance.

It was dark by the time we left Laguna Atascosa. On our way out, with the help of The Stid's one-million-candle-power halogen spotlight, we saw a Chuck-will's-widow, a large, rounded-winged nightjar, and a Pauraque, pronounced 'pow-rock-ay', a long-tailed nightjar. Laguna Atascosa was so good we returned at dawn, seeing two more specialities called Long-billed Thrasher and Botteri's Sparrow, but enjoying our first Yellow-throated Vireos and a male Painted Bunting much more, especially the vividly coloured bunting with a blue head, glowing yellow back, green wing panels and red underparts.

The vast expanse of breeze-blown rubbish at Brownsville Dump was something of a contrast. Obnoxious wafts of decaying, putrid food enveloped us as we scanned the clouds of Laughing Gulls for Mexican Crows, the only place in the United States where it was possible to see them. As soon as The Stid had ticked one off we drove into the city of Brownsville to a stake-out for Clay-coloured Robin, another bird that only just makes it to the States. While waiting for one to appear in the large, leafy gardens of Coria Street we compiled an impressive list of birds for a city suburb next to a *resaca*, a former channel of the nearby Rio Grande. They included Black-bellied Whistling Ducks, White Ibises, Plain Chachalacas, Inca Doves, Great Kiskadees, Tufted Tits and our first Altamira Orioles, big, gaudy, bright orange and black birds. Near dusk, a bird began singing behind us; a slow but long series of low rolling whistles, surely a thrush we thought, and we quickly pinned the bird down and were delighted to see that it was a Clay-coloured Robin, an appropriate name for a bird with a much better song than a suit.

Much of the mesquite scrub, thorn woods and lush subtropical forest which lined the Lower Rio Grande River which separates the United States from Mexico had been bulldozed to make way for vegetable fields and suburbia. The Jaguars were long gone and bird numbers much reduced but one tiny remnant of riparian forest where native hardwoods such as Texas Ebony were still draped with Spanish Moss and full of birds, survived at Santa Ana National Wildlife Refuge where we clambered out of the car, not long after dawn. A ranger told us that about 3000 Broad-winged Hawks had dropped in to roost the night before. We knew that virtually the entire North American population of Broad-winged Hawks, *and* Swainson's Hawks, migrated through Texas each spring but we still could not help thinking that the estimate must have been a gross exaggeration, until, that is, hundreds of hawks began rising from the woods, flying to the first thermals of the day and forming wheeling flocks known as kettles. They were gaining height so that they could glide north, more and more of them, at least two perhaps three thousand we reckoned, and while marvelling at the scene of so many birds in the air at the same time a very different raptor came flapping heavily toward us and straight over our heads. It was one of the United States' very few Hook-billed Kites, an odd-looking creature with a strongly hooked bill, very broad wings pinched in near the body, and a big tail. We could not track down a Tropical Parula which had been reported in the forest but we did find a Buff-bellied Hummingbird in the parking lot, its wings a blur, its body mainly green and its tail rufous.

During the northern winter many folk from the north of the United States and Canada relocate to the Sun Belt of the southern states where the warm winter climate is much more agreeable and a lot of these so-called 'snowbirds' drive their massive RVs (recreational vehicles such as campers, trailers and motorhomes) down to the Lower Rio Grande Valley and some of them set up in Bentsen State Park where many like to feed the birds. We toured their feeders in search of White-tipped Doves, another rather dull Texas speciality which was completely overshadowed by the much more eye-catching and confiding Green Jays and Altamira Orioles. At an old ox-bow lake of the Rio Grande our first Ringed Kingfisher, a giant among the family, flew by to a chorus of "Wow!"'s and at dusk the awe was repeated while a Lesser Nighthawk twisted and turned low over the water.

Unable to find space in the dense, thorny, desert scrub to pitch our tents we simply lay down in the gaps between the spiky bushes in our sleeping bags and were enjoying a sound night's sleep in a very pleasant temperature before waving flashlights woke us up. Two police officers thought we were 'wetbacks'. When they realized that we were merely poor, innocent, filthy British birders they warned us about the Mexicans who cross the Rio Grande at night to rob and murder, and then they got our full attention when they told us the place we were happily sleeping in was crawling with 'rattlers', highly aggressive and venomous Western Diamondback Rattlesnakes which hunt at night and are probably responsible for the second highest number of deaths from snakebite in the United States, after their eastern counterpart, as well as the majority of fatalities in northern Mexico.

"If they bite ya, ya'r dead," were the parting words of one officer.

We were momentarily troubled but too tired to care for long. We zipped our bags up as tight as they would go and closed our eyes. On a heavy birding trip every minute's sleep is precious.

At dawn we headed off to Santa Margarita Ranch where more new birds swiftly came our way, in the shape of four surprisingly smart Black-throated Sparrows, a Bullock's

Oriole, a singing male, Sardinian Warbler-like Black-tailed Gnatcatcher, three Brown Jays, the species we were particularly hoping to see, and several Pyrrhuloxias, strange, crested, parrot-billed, long-tailed, brown-grey birds with seemingly random areas of red feathers on them. Down at the Rio Grande there was a pair of Audubon's Orioles, the fifth oriole of the trip. Fishing the river was a Belted Kingfisher and two Ringed Kingfishers but the kingfisher we were looking for in particular, the smaller Green, eluded us, as it did later at Falcon Dam, along with Red-billed Pigeon and Hooded Oriole. Before pitching the tents we scanned the huge reservoir one last time while listening to the animals of the night; buzzing cicadas, other clicking and trilling insects, croaking and tinkling frogs and toads, the low purr of Lesser Nighthawks, and the occasional wild whiplashing 'whizeeeeer' of a Pauraque. There was no last-minute Green Kingfisher but a Ringed Kingfisher flew across the setting sun.

A fellow camper told us the temperature during the day had reached nearly ninety fahrenheit and we frazzled again standing at the dam most of the next day hoping a Red-billed Pigeon would fly across, a Hooded Oriole would appear or better still, much better still, a Green Kingfisher would shoot into view and perch up so we could look at it through our telescopes. A pigeon did fly across and a male Hooded Oriole appeared but the kingfisher remained a dream. Maybe it flew by while we were cooling down with a paddle in the Rio Grande, almost as far as Mexico.

When it was dark we drove to Big Bend National Park in far west Texas, a long haul, about 500 miles (800 km), which took all night. The long desert highway south from Marathon sliced through the cacti, creosote bushes, spindly ocotillos and spiny yuccas of the baking Chihuahuan Desert but the campground at the end was in a beautiful spot, shaded by big Cottonwoods next to the cooling presence of the slow-moving Rio Grande. While pitching the tents a flash of intense red gave away our first Vermilion Flycatcher. The telescopes were deployed rapidly and soon the stunning bird was filling the view, the silky feathers shining in the sun. Closer still, in the tree next to us, our first Townsend's Solitaire appeared, a weird, long, slender bird like a cross between a flycatcher and a thrush. Verdins are odd birds too, also grey but tiny, with matt yellow heads. It was 97°F, too hot to bird but we strolled around the campground and saw some more Vermilion Flycatchers, and Roadrunners.

It was crazy hot, we were sick of fruit juice and we had not had a beer for quite a while so Nick, needing a beer more than the rest of us, went off in search of some and when he returned triumphantly we all luxuriated in cold beers before joining several other birders at a stake-out for Elf Owl. Five minutes after sundown one flew out of its nest-hole in a telegraph pole and landed in a Cottonwood tree where we were able to see that it was as small as a sparrow and yet, with its yellow-eyed stare, as fierce as a falcon.

The jagged, shattered Chisos Mountains rise 7825 feet (2385 metres) out of the Chihuahuan Desert where the Rio Grande flows around a 'Big Bend'. Between the sparsely vegetated spurs of rock, forests of cypresses, junipers, maples and oaks grow in deep gullies. The Mescalero Apaches lived happily in this beautiful place until the white man came. He destroyed their peace but he did not lay waste to where they lived, as he has done so in many other places, and a superb selection of birds survives in the mountains. One of the best ways to see them is to walk the Boot Spring Trail so with rucksacks full of water bottles – people have died of dehydration in Big Bend – we set off. It wasn't long before we bumped into lots of blue and grey Mexican Jays and plenty of 'Woody' Acorn Woodpeckers with their comical creamy eyes. Like the jays they go around in noisy gangs, shouting 'whack-up whack-up'.

After a few miles we reached the wide expanse of Laguna Meadows and just above there a woman on a horse came up the slope behind us.

"You guys looking for the Colima Warblers?"

"Yeah"

"This is the place," she said as she passed by, "Plen'y of 'em here! You'll have no trouble seeing 'em. Only place in the states!"

We never even heard one but there was little time to dwell on the brown but rare bird because we came across two superb Violet-green Swallows perched on a dead branch sticking out of a rock outcrop. Not long after, the shout of "Hummer!" went up, as it did when a tiny, speedy bird zoomed past us in a blur. Nine times out of ten that would be it; "Another hummingbird sp." someone would say as the mystery bird flew away. This was the one time out of ten though. The loud metallic trill that went with the blur was characteristic of Broad-tailed Hummingbird and we were surprised and delighted to watch it land with aplomb on a branch overhanging the trail, its glistening crimson throat feathers confirming it as a male. A little higher up, Nick flushed "a bundle of grey feathers" from the side of the trail and after a scramble down a steep slope we relocated what turned out to be a tiny owl. It was perched tight against a tree trunk but it was no Elf Owl because it had black eyes and the only small owl in Big Bend with black eyes was a Flammulated Owl. To come across an owl during daylight is rare enough but to see one in the day that is rarely seen even at night was unbelievably fortunate. We were on a roll and next up was a Wilson's Warbler which Mark pulled out of the bag. Then it was my turn. A nuthatch flew past me and landed halfway up a trailside tree. Nuthatches are unusual in Big Bend and those that do occur are usually White-breasted so I was amazed to see a bird with a deep red breast and belly. Thinking it must be a Red-breasted Nuthatch I then saw a striking white eyebrow across the bird's black head and that was what it was so I whistled to the boys and one by one they arrived at my side and soon we were all admiring another stunning bird we never expected to see at Big Bend or anywhere else on that trip to Texas.

We had a spring in our step and suddenly the trail seemed less steep, even in the debilitating heat. Near the top there was even time to take in the view; the rich green, wooded gorges, and the red mountain slopes of the Chisos foothills with masses of eroded and fallen red rocks at their base. The Apache believed that after the making of the Earth the Great Spirit dumped all the left-over rocks here. Beyond the mountains lay the scorched plain of the Chihuahuan Desert, broken up here and there by vertical-sided monoliths of yet more red rock called buttes.

Strolling back down the trail in the stunning heat of the afternoon, happy as could be, Gibb, alert as ever, whistled us up to watch a Zone-tailed Hawk, a black bird-of-prey with barred underwings and a white band on its black tail, sweeping around above a ridge with stiff, slightly up-tilted wings, and as we admired it two black and white swifts hurtled past at a tremendous speed, close enough to see that they were White-throated Swifts, superb birds to end nine miles and nine hours of brilliant birding in a brilliant setting.

The only person who had not turned up one of the exceptional birds all day was The Stid which was unusual for him and he was not very happy about it but at Panther Junction on the drive back to base-camp he spotted one, as we were sure he would. It was a superb male Scott's Oriole, bright lemon yellow with a black head and black wings with white bars and feather edges.

The best bird in the curvaceous Boquillas Canyon on our last morning in Big Bend was a Canyon Wren, a big, jaunty wren with a very long bill and a fine combination of grey crown, white throat and deep rufous body, watched while standing in the cool water of the Rio Grande. Big Bend had been good to us but the Davis Mountains a hundred miles (160 km) away were mean with their Montezuma Quails so we moved on to Lake Balmorhea, a private impoundment where elegant black and white Western Grebes with red eyes and long, slim, slightly upturned bills rode the waters in perfect early evening light.

After dark we drove east to the Edwards Plateau, about 250 miles (400 km) away. On the journey to Big Bend I nodded off a few times and missed both Burrowing and Great Horned Owls so I was determined to stay awake on the next overnighter. Four hours into the drive at about half two in the morning The Stid slammed on the brakes and the rest of us were thrown into the air just in time to see a Great Horned Owl rise off its kill in the middle of the road and swoop up and over the bonnet of the car, brushing the windscreen with its huge broad wings. The kill, on inspection, turned out to be a Black-tailed Jackrabbit or Desert Hare. The owl had struck it on the back of the neck; we could see two neat bloody holes left by its talons. I was wide awake now and glad to be for not long after we came across a Striped Skunk shuffling through the roadside undergrowth. We had driven over a couple of dead skunks earlier and their foul stench filtered through the car for much of the journey but after seeing one alive I didn't mind, quite so much.

The rugged, wooded, limestone hills with gorges and canyons gouged out by rocky, clear-water streams and rivers on the Edwards Plateau in central Texas, also known as Hill Country, is virtually the only place in the world where two beautiful rare birds nest and one of the places they spend the summer in is Lost Maples State Natural Area, named after the Bigtooth Maples which grow in the sheltered canyons. That is where we arrived in time for a couple of hours sleep before there was enough light to look for them. Dawn in the deeply incised canyon was surprisingly chilly so it was a pleasure to stand in the first welcome rays of warm sunshine listening to the squeaky chattering song of one of the birds and then watch, for ages, three of the terrific tiny mites with glossy black heads, white 'spectacles' surrounding their red eyes, bright green backs and white underparts with a flush of yellow along the flanks. If we had crossed the Atlantic just to see those Black-capped Vireos it would have been worth it but while we were there we thought we might as well climb the canyon and listen out for the 'lazy dazy' song of the other bird and it was not long before we heard one. It took a lot longer to see one, in the big oaks, but it was worth the wait for such a cracking little bird with a deep yellow face, jet black bib and neat black streaks along the flanks, called a Golden-cheeked Warbler.

It was nine a.m., the sun was already hammering down and we were tired, hungry and thirsty. We had seen the 'big two' so we were ready to retreat, find a diner and coffee and food and get back to the beat but Nick saw a Green Kingfisher flash past up river so, on we went in one last almighty effort to see the bird that had eluded us down the Rio Grande. Walking uphill, alongside the River Sabinal, in the heat, we checked every overhanging branch. The sun was almost overhead when we reached the head of the valley and after a sleepless night on the road, yet another dawn start and a hard climb we finally came to our senses and flopped down to the ground. We were all exhausted, all of us except The indefatigable Stid, the one who drove overnight, the one who unbeknown to the rest of us, lying half asleep on the ground, carried on checking shaded branches over the river with his telescope.

After a welcome while The Stid said, in shock and disbelief, "Lads, look through my 'scope!"

We stood up rapidly and one by one, like The Stid, we could not believe what we saw through the telescope; the big golden eye in an emerald head, dark spear beak, white collar, rufous breast and white belly with big black droplets, of a male Green Kingfisher sitting quietly under a shady bank on a branch hanging low over the river. We danced down that valley and after a long late brunch went for a cooling swim in the Rio Frio, where a Green Kingfisher flew over our heads.

We got to Attwater Prairie Chicken National Wildlife Refuge in time for a couple of hours sleep by the roadside again, before we saw two male chickens, not my favourite type of bird and easily forgotten when there are Scissor-tailed Flycatchers around. Nuthatches *are* a great favourite of mine and during the afternoon in the Big Thicket I saw a new one, the Brown-headed Nuthatch, which like all nuthatches is a terrific, lively little bird which forages with great gusto, amongst pine cones for seeds and pine needles for insects.

We arrived near Bonanza, north of Houston, in time for another couple of hours roadside. Some winters Evening Grosbeaks irrupt from their northern breeding ranges as far south as Texas and one place where there was a chance of seeing some was in Diane Cabiness's Garden where we sat on her veranda emptying pot after pot of fine coffee watching a Ruby-throated Hummingbird, a Red-bellied Woodpecker, a Brown Thrasher, Blue Jays, Chipping Sparrows, Tufted Tits and Northern Cardinals. There were no grosbeaks but Diane's outstanding hospitality stretched to cakes and we were enjoying some relaxing birding so we found it very difficult to leave but yet more new birds beckoned at Jones State Forest where we saw five species of woodpecker in an area of pines the size of a football pitch, four of them new; Downy, Pileated, the rare Red-cockaded and the fabulous Red-headed, an extraordinary black and ivory white bird with a startling red hood. Mississippi Kites were moving north overhead and with the Pine Warblers was our first stunning Yellow-throated Warbler, the best warbler I had seen on the trip so far.

We arrived back at Boy Scout Woods, High Island, with an hour or so of light left. There was a crowd of birders in front of the puddle, kept topped up to provide water for thirsty newly-arrived birds, and the atmosphere was electric. There had been a big fall. In fifteen minutes looking at the tiny puddle we saw several now familiar and a lot of new birds, in the following order; five Hooded Warblers, a male Cerulean Warbler, two Wood Thrushes, a Swainson's Thrush, a Swainson's Warbler, a Kentucky Warbler, an Ovenbird, a couple of Northern Waterthrushes, a Louisiana Waterthrush, a Worm-eating Warbler, lots of Tennessee Warblers, a Yellow-breasted Chat, a Parula Warbler, a Blue-winged Warbler, a few Orchard Orioles, White-eyed Vireos, Scarlet Tanagers and Black-and-white Warblers, a dazzling male Golden-winged Warbler, a Prothonotary Warbler, and several male Rose-breasted Grosbeaks.

A bird would appear out of the undergrowth on a branch by the water or on the ground at the edge of the puddle, sometimes two together, sometimes three, four, five even, then it or they would drink and/or bathe and move off, to be replaced by another wave of one, two, three, four, five different birds, often new ones to us, or seconds and thirds, all delicately marked and/or brightly coloured beauties, all just a few paces away with two maybe three new birds in view through our binoculars at the same time. It was fantasy birding, the most pulsating birding of our lives. My binoculars never left my eyes for those first glorious fifteen minutes and so it went on except we managed to find a few seconds to set up our tripods and for the remaining forty-five minutes we were able to watch the birds through our telescopes as well. The time flashed by then slowly, one by one, the avian lights went out and after our first Nighthawk flew over at dusk, when all seemed quiet, we finally stood down and looked at each other and asked in silence, with our eyes only, 'Have you ever seen anything as fantastic as that in your life?', to which the answers were emphatic, 'No's.

We celebrated in *Tim's Saloon* before almost literally collapsing in our sleeping bags by the roadside at Rollover Pass. We were still up in time to drive fast to the paddy fields to see a flock of 25 Hudsonian Godwits we had been told about. I love New World warblers but I also love shorebirds and the males in that flock were superb in the full flush of their breeding plumage with pale heads, dark buff-spangled backs and deep chestnut bellies. Back in Boy Scout Woods small birds were arriving from Mexico and we soon saw a male American Redstart waving its black and orange tail, a Veery, a Blue Grosbeak and a Dickcissel, all new but all blown away by other warblers, even though we had seen them before, including Blue-winged, Golden-winged, Cerulean, Parula and Prothonotary, all good enough reasons to return to *Tim's Saloon* until midnight. It was a bar full of old fishermen, including poor old George who got up every time someone shouted over to one of us because we told everyone to call us all George since they couldn't remember our names.

Sleeping out in the High Island Post Office yard was not a good idea. We were attacked by millions of mosquitoes so at six a.m. we were waiting for the *Gulfway Cafe* to open its doors. During breakfast we held a committee meeting and decided to splash out on a room for the night in the adjacent *Gulfway Motel*. The long, tortuous night we had just endured was soon forgotten as yet another wonderful birding day unfurled. The shallow Shoveler Pond at Anahuac National Wildlife Refuge was a delight. On view were lots of alligators basking in the sunshine, lots of herons, three American Bitterns, King, Sora and Virginia Rails, Purple Gallinules, Greater and Lesser Yellowlegs, Blue-winged Teals, a Belted Kingfisher and best of all a fantastic Least Bittern which flew into a reedy channel and perched up so close we could see through its translucent orange beak before it dropped down into the base of the reeds out of sight. In Smith Oaks there were eight species of warbler in one small grove of trees; Northern Waterthrush, Black-and-white, Kentucky, Palm, Parula, Swainson's, Yellow and a stunning Yellow-throated, and in Boy Scout Woods there were even more birds including our first Chestnut-sided Warbler and at least twenty Orchard Orioles but we had to return to Smith Oaks for our first Blackburnian Warbler, another dream bird, like a Black-and-white Warbler with an orange-sorbet throat. We didn't see the Cape May Warbler also reported there but we did connect with a flock of over a hundred Eastern Kingbirds. None of us had experienced anything like this before. Birding at High Island was dream birding and we could hardly wait for the next day to come along.

It was so good to sleep in beds that over a leisurely breakfast we voted unanimously to book the room for the rest of the week and so off we went merrily to Bolivar Flats, beginning the birding day in the best possible way with a Scissor-tailed Flycatcher. We didn't see any new birds on the tidal mudflats, which made a change, and that didn't matter because there were so many great birds to watch not least Reddish Egrets and Black Skimmers. At High Island Oilfield we saw some crazy Louisiana Herons and Black-necked Stilts on the pools between the nodding donkeys. The usual array of avian delights lit up Boy Scout Woods, in the forms of warblers, vireos, orioles, thrushes, tanagers and buntings, the highlight for me being six Yellow Warblers together at the puddle. Come the evening, our table was ready for us when we arrived at the *Gulfway Cafe*. We could tell by the sign on it, written by, "I ain't from Texas! I'm from Tennessee!" Milly, the manageress, saying, 'Reserved for English Creeps'. Since Milly seemed to like us we did not complain about it since in the States the word 'creep' can mean 'deviant, disturbingly eccentric, obnoxious or weird. We were certain none of us fitted the other interpretation of 'painfully introverted'.

The next morning Mark, Nick and The Stid sped off north to Beaumont on a successful international twitch for Fish Crow, Prairie Warbler and Bachmann's Sparrow while Gibb and I went our separate ways at High Island, pottering happily around the woods in search of better, longer views of our favourite warblers, and I particularly enjoyed some close encounters with the likes of a male Cerulean Warbler, and a stunning male Blackburnian Warbler which spent a long time in one tree at the entrance to Boy Scouts Wood.

The next day we were booked on a morning 'buggy' ride at Anahuac, organised to count the wintering population of Yellow Rails. This involved standing on the back of a tractor with giant wheels as it traversed a marsh then getting off and trudging through rank wet grass in an attempt to flush the secretive birds. We were amazed to see eleven of the tiny, tawny rather than yellow, rails, in flight only of course when it was possible to see the white patches at the base of the wings. Four Virginia Rails also leapt out of our way and there were lots of Seaside Sparrows. Birding at Shoveler Pond was much more my cup of tea even though we had to sprawl face down on the boardwalk and look through the gaps to see a Marsh Wren. The exquisite little black and rufous bird with a white throat and white streaks on its black back was singing its head off in the reeds an arm's length away. We had seen so many birds at Anahuac that we decided to try and see as many species as possible in a day in the High Island area. New birds like Bay-breasted Warbler helped but there had not been a fall and we saw just 13 warbler species. However, Bolivar Flats and Rollover Pass were so bountiful we still managed to amass 127 species including 25 shorebirds, seven terns, four rails, Black Skimmers and a Scissor-tailed Flycatcher.

The woods were relatively quiet again on our penultimate day but at the oilfield pools there were three Nighthawks flying around in broad daylight, including two males, their striking white wing and tail spots flashing as they flew up high with deep, almost lazy flaps of their long, narrow wings, dived down, looped around, and flapped and glided as if floating weightless on the warm air, with wings raised, all with such light and easy grace.

On our last day the Live Oaks came alive. While standing in the big glade known as The Grove in Boy Scout Woods watching two Chestnut-sided Warblers, a Black-and-white Warbler, a Cerulean Warbler and an Ovenbird we got talking to an American who, on hearing that it was our last day and that we had still not seen Canada and Magnolia Warblers, casually mentioned that both had been seen at Smith Oaks earlier on. It didn't take us long to get there but after an hour of frantic searching we had seen neither. The binoculars were busy though and amongst the 14 warbler species present was our first Blackpoll Warbler, with three Blackburnians, a Black-throated Green, single Blue-winged and Golden-winged, a few Tennessees, a Parula, a Worm-eating, both waterthrushes and an American Redstart.

Halfway through a delicious mid-day milkshake at the *Gulfway Cafe* a Californian we had met the day before came dashing in to tell us that a Magnolia Warbler had just been seen in Boy Scout Woods. He said something about where it was but we didn't need to listen because we were right behind him, milkshakes in hands, as he entered The Grove and there was our first Magnolia Warbler, a cracking black-masked, black-backed, white-winged male with big black streaks on its bright yellow underparts. With it in the sunlit lower canopy was another and they were in the same small tree as Black-and-white, Blackburnian, Cerulean and Chestnut-sided Warblers. It was the perfect way to wrap up the trip, or so we thought.

We had given up on the one other warbler possible at that time of the spring and we were watching two very handsome Wilson's Phalaropes on a roadside paddy field when a car pulled up alongside. An American got out and said, "The word is out you guys need Canada Warbler."

"YES!" we replied in unison.

"Well, there's one in 'The Willows' at Anahuac now."

We arrived a few minutes later. 'The Willows', a small pond surrounded by about twenty big willows, were jumping with birds and the male Canada Warbler, a bright grey-green and yellow beauty with a necklace of black streaks, was with ones and twos of twelve other warbler species and three vireo species including our first Philadelphia Vireo.

The possible set of warblers complete we returned to Boy Scout Woods for the final time. Knowing that birds had been falling from the sky since mid-morning I thought it was possible to add to the total of 22 species of warbler we had seen since dawn and maybe, just maybe, make 25 in a day. Hooded Warblers had become much scarcer during the course of the week but I managed to find one skulking low down under a thick patch of shrubs in The Grove and with it was a Kentucky, another first for the day. Now all I needed to find was a Swainson's Warbler, the hardest of the lot, so I joined the rest of the crew at the evening stake-out at the puddle. More stunning warbler montages were presented to us there with one more mega 'in-the-'scope-at-the-same-time' moment involving a Northern Waterthrush with Cerulean, Kentucky, Hooded, Magnolia and Worm-eating Warblers.

News of an *empidonax*, a flycatcher species belonging to the eponymous genus, filtered back to the crowd at the puddle and someone wandered back from The Grove and wondered 'would the Brits mind having a look at it' so off we went, rather reluctantly, 'Empid' flycatchers being notoriously difficult to identify. Two American birders were watching the bird and discussing the fine details of its plumage, and we agreed with them that it looked most like an Acadian Flycatcher and we were all happy to leave it at that. I didn't care to be honest. I was soon looking elsewhere and as I hoped, an olive-brown bird with very pale eyebrows and a long, spiky bill walked out of a dark tangle under a bush, and that Swainson's Warbler became the 25th warbler species of the day, the 29th of the week, the 33rd of the trip, and the perfect end to another brilliant day on a trip full of brilliant days.

*Lilac-breasted Roller, Naivasha, Kenya, 28th December 1987*

6

# KENYA

My first view of Africa was of night time Cairo from the airplane window. After a brief stop at Khartoum airport in Sudan the old *Boeing 707* cruised at 500 mph 37,000 feet over a giant patchwork of small, square and rectangular fields alongside the mighty White Nile. Beyond the green either side of the wide river, flat sandy desert stretched all the way to the horizon. A couple of hours later I saw a Jade Sea, another name for Lake Turkana in northern Kenya, and not long after, through snowballs of cloud, there was Lake Naivasha, the place I had dreamed of visiting for so many years.

All my travels up to now had been tremendously exciting but the picture above my desk I looked at the most was of a spectacular bird called a Lilac-breasted Roller, perched on a dead snag on the African plains. It might have been that photograph I cut out of *The Dictionary of Birds in Colour* that set fire to my interest in Africa, perhaps kindled by David Shepherd's 'Wise Old Elephant' print that was hanging on the wall in the house I grew up in, I don't know for sure. What I did know, twelve years after I started looking at birds, was that I had long wanted to be in Africa more than anywhere else in the world. At the time, I was working in nature conservation and education, and seemed to have an ideal career lined up, but I was spending far more time at a desk than in the field, dealing with people more than nature, and I was crazy busy, busy enough to have a suspected stomach ulcer. I didn't know what to do. I did know that if I decided to go to Africa I wanted to be there for as long as possible, not on a short birding trip like the last one to Texas. I also knew, in my heart, that I didn't want to be busy keeping up with my career I wanted to be busy keeping up with my dreams. After I made up my mind to go to Africa I got scared but it's good to be scared once in a while, it keeps the feelings alive. My girlfriend Carolyn, my other friends, my family and my work colleagues didn't like it but I packed it all in and got on a plane to Africa.

My next view of Lake Naivasha was from the rim of the Great Rift Valley. There before me was a fantastic panorama of a hazy African plain dotted with acacias and lakes where lay so many dreams hopefully to be fulfilled. By the lake I was soon watching the first, a Lilac-breasted Roller, a glorious blue and tan bird almost the size of a crow with long tail streamers, so close I could see frosty bristle-like feathers at the base of its bill, neat silvery streaks in its deep lilac breast and brilliant ultramarine wing feathers which hinted at what the bird might look like in flight. After several minutes it did fly, diving down to the ground with shocking light blue and dark blue wings outspread to snatch and devour a large insect before returning to its lookout. It was hard to take my eyes off something I had dreamed of seeing for so long, something so much better in real life, but on the ground nearby were some Superb Starlings, iridescent red, blue and green marvels, and with a flock of Spur-winged Plovers under a stand of acacias another dream, the first of many Blacksmith Plovers, delicate black, white and grey works of art on stilts.

There were birds everywhere. Sky-blue cordon-bleus, red firefinches, bright green and orange lovebirds, and so on, and it took a long, long time to reach the lake where Goliath Herons towered over avocets and stilts and plovers, just some of the numerous shorebirds which virtually covered the narrow shoreline of mud. African Fish Eagles yodelled in the background and one glided over on huge, broad wings, its white head and chest shining in the sunshine and contrasting strongly with its chestnut body. In the lake there were Hippos. The long held dream of Africa was coming true.

I was bursting at the seams to get out there on my first full day in Africa. As the light flooded the plain around Lake

Naivasha Lilac-breasted Rollers shared the shoreline acacias with White-fronted Bee-eaters, and babblers, batises, boubous, bulbuls, weavers, shrikes and shiny sunbirds, while doves cooed and wooed from the shade. On the dusty ground below with Superb Starlings were tiny cobalt-blue gems called Purple Grenadiers, and African Hoopoes, flocks of them, the same colour as the deep buff dust until they flicked from spot to spot on shocking, broad, black-and-white wings. Perched on a reed, bent over the water, was an apple-sized ball of brilliance, deep orange below and metallic blue above with long, slightly raised crown feathers spangled with black and malachite. Sticking abruptly out of its hunched head was a long, almost translucent, scarlet dagger of a beak, belonging to a dazzling Malachite Kingfisher. Striking Pied Kingfishers flew from the reeds to hover over the lake in search of fish. African Fish Eagles glided by majestically and soared high over the grand parade of shorebirds. Stalking the shallows were egrets, herons, ibises and storks, and scattered flocks of spoonbills, flamingos and pelicans. Dinky Black Crakes with bright yellow beaks, and bronzed lily-trotters trotted across islands of water lilies, disturbed occasionally by great grey lumps of Hippopotamuses breaking the surface to take in gulps of air before rolling over and disappearing with lazy swooshes. Between the islands of flowers were islands of birds; huge rafts of coots and ducks, and above them flew countless thousands of swallows, swifts, martins, gulls and terns. It was all so unbelievable; the numbers of birds, the diversity, the fecundity, the sheer profusion and exuberance of life.

Enjoying the spectacle with me were The Stid, my old friend Chief, now a chartered surveyor of some repute, mainly for selling the most number of houses while doing the least amount of work, and his friend Tim, a quiet chap, at least compared to the rest of us, along for the mammals rather than the birds. We set up our two tents at *Fisherman's Camp* on the Lake Naivasha shoreline, on green grass under a beautiful stand of tall, yellow-barked Fever Trees.

We fell asleep listening to snorting Hippos and woke up to yodelling fish eagles. After some coffee around our campfire and a last look at some of the gorgeous birds around us, we drove to Hell's Gate, the arid Ol Njorowa Gorge where the heat was almost unbearable by mid-morning. Herds of Thomson's Gazelles, Hartebeests and Zebras grazed the coarse grasses growing on the flat floor of the gorge and on top of the high wall of reddish rock were two Giraffes peering down at us over the edge. Below them, roosting on ledges, were Rüppell's Vultures and nearby, perched on a rock, there was a huge Verreaux's Eagle, looking all black apart from a bright yellow eye-ring and cere at the base of the bill.

From a distance Lake Nakuru appeared to be encircled by a shimmering pink mirage but it was real and made up of hundreds of thousands of flamingos. With them were many other waterbirds and nearby we saw Baboons, Impalas and Defassa Waterbucks. Once again the end of the day came too soon. Grey Vervet Monkeys climbed the big Fever Trees as we entered the campsite, not to avoid us but because there was a Crowned Eagle eyeing them from its perch high on one side of the glade. We watched the dark brown, rough-crested raptor for a while then got the camp fire going and dined on sardine sandwiches.

We saw our first pair of Secretary Birds the next morning, astonishing creatures with beaks like eagles, legs like storks and long, thin, black-tipped tails like nothing else. The grey and black birds-of-prey were walking sedately across the short grass plain by Lake Nakuru, eyeing the ground, looking for insects, lizards, snakes and small mammals. Nearby was a Long-crested Eagle and on the cliffs a pair of very smart black and red Cliff Chats. The temperature rose steadily through the morning and we used the fierce heat of midday to drive north, across the equator, to Lake Baringo, through increasingly arid bush. It was by far the best road we had been on so far, a lovely, smooth strip of tarmac running through the dust in the middle of nowhere and later we found out why it was so much better than the cracked and pot-holed routes between Nairobi, Naivasha and Nakuru. The B4 to Baringo was the best road in Kenya because it led straight to President Daniel Toroitich Arap Moi's home village of Kurieng'wo. There the Kalenjin people lived basic lives in huts, a far cry from the lavish lodge for tourists on the shore of Lake Baringo. We were not staying there of course, we drove into the adjacent campsite, more rock and dust than grass, and where every bush and tree was a mass of thorns. Some trees even had thorny trunks, which we discovered when we leaned against them to steady our binoculars to look at the numerous birds. We only had time for a quick look but the hot and dry dustbowl our tents were in appeared to be the birdiest place we had been so far.

Life was great and we drank too many cold *Tuskers*, rather strong lagers, late into the last night of the year. Hangovers did not stop us seeing, with the considerable help of the lodge's resident naturalist the British ex-patriot Terry

Stevenson, sixteen new birds the next morning, all of them in the thick acacia woodland at the base of the steep escarpment a few miles west of the lake. They included Jackson's Hornbills, Bristle-crowned Starlings and, best of all, a pair of White-faced Scops Owls which were hiding from the burning ball in the top of the thickest tree in the wood. Back in the lodge grounds we saw two Spotted Eagle Owls in the tree Terry told us we would see them in. We were dehydrated and drained by the early afternoon but, by following Terry's directions very carefully, we were able to watch a pair of Black-headed Plovers, bills agape, panting in the heat under an acacia. Much more time was spent, in the high heat of mid-afternoon, failing to find the much more secretive Heuglin's Courser, another 'shorebird' which keeps to the shade during the day and hunts at night. There was no time to dwell on not seeing one bird though, not when new, fabulous birds popped up one after the other in an almost constant stream of wonder. Even covering the same old ground in the campsite, trying to get better views of the Blue-cheeked Bee-eaters, we saw three more new birds in rapid succession; a big, bright, orange and yellow Grey-headed Bushshrike and two dinky and delightful Pygmy Batises which were mobbing a massive Verreaux's Eagle Owl, a finely barred, grey brute with rather effeminate and incongruous pink eyelids. Also about were Lilac-breasted Rollers, Chestnut-bellied Kingfishers, Paradise Flycatchers, Superb Starlings and a small party of Green Woodhoopoes, their broad white-banded wings and long, tapering, white-spotted tails flashing exotically as they fluttered by. All these birds were seen in about fifteen minutes and not long after, in the same tiny patch of acacia scrub, up popped a Sulphur-breasted Bushshrike, with a deep yellow forehead and breast, glowing sulphur. Once again we lay down in our tents at the end of the day frazzled and stunned and awed by the heat, the incredible diversity of birds, and Africa.

"What's that, outside the tents!?!" Chief said.

"Dunno mun, 'av' a look," The Stid replied.

It was getting light. It was me who looked out of the flap of the tent I was in with The Stid and I saw a Hippo walk slowly past, still searching for some grass to eat in the campsite with very little.

"Hippos!" I said as quietly as possible. "We'll have to wait until they get back in the lake for the day."

"How many?" Chief asked.

"Five!"

Once the most dangerous animals in Africa had returned to the lake and we had addressed the low levels of caffeine in our bloodstreams we saw yet more new birds beginning with a Hemprich's Hornbill and a Red-and-yellow Barbet, another beauty, yellow with a red face and dark upperparts with what looked like a hundred delicately dabbed white spots. The next new bird we came across was like nothing any of us had ever seen before.

"Must be a weaver, it's that bright!" Chief reckoned, having already seen several astonishing weavers.

"No way, it's too big ... and skulkin'," I replied.

Then all the hours swotting at home helped and I added, "I think I know what plate that's on," referring to the bird paintings in my copy of *A Field Guide to the Birds of East Africa* by John Williams and Norman Arlott.

There in the middle of Plate 32 in my now rather dusty book was the stunning bird we were looking at, a jet black and scarlet Black-headed Gonolek, yet another sort of bushshrike and one of five new birds seen during the morning in exactly the same scrub we had been camped next to and looking for birds in for three days already.

It seemed crazy to leave but we had to if we were to get round Kenya in a month as planned. We drove west, over the Tugen Hills and into the Kerio Valley where we pulled over to look for White-crested Turacos at one of the few places in Kenya where they had been recorded. We could not find any but we did see our first Little Bee-eaters, green above, cinnamon below and with bright yellow throats. They were dashing out from their low perches to snatch passing bees and other flying insects with what looked like nonchalant ease.

Rain, glorious cool rain; no wonder there is a swamp alongside the Sawai River in west Kenya. Tim was hoping to see the semi-aquatic antelope called Sitatunga and it was not long before we saw a female with vertical white stripes on her brownish back and sides. We saw two more but soon turned our attention to the riverine woodland where our first Black-and-white-casqued Hornbills flapped lazily along the edge of the trees where a bright blue Woodland Kingfisher was perched. In the woods were purple Ross's Turacos with broad, flashing crimson wings, an amazing dark iridescent green Klaas's Cuckoo, white Paradise Flycatchers, big, black-and-red Double-toothed Barbets, so-called because of the two 'teeth' on their massive white beaks, and four delightful African Blue Flycatchers with very long cerulean blue tails.

From the Kongelai Escarpment we could see Uganda. It looked dark, rugged and grim, like Mordor in Tolkien's *The Lord of the Rings*. There was no time to dwell on Sauron's armies of orcs and trolls though. We were in Kenya's 'Shire' and looking for White-crested Turacos. We saw none, there or at Kitale Forest, where Chief and Tim came running out of the trees.

"We nearly got bit by a bloody Black Mamba!" a flustered-for-once Chief shouted over to The Stid and me. "Bloody thing reared up just in front of us and looked like it was going to strike!"

If it had struck Chief or Tim either could have been dead within a few hours. The local man who had agreed to guide us refused to go back into the forest, repeating the words, "Very harsh!" several times, in reference to the mamba, so we scanned the forest from the edge and watched five Black-and-white Colobus Monkeys swing swiftly yet smoothly through the trees before sitting down half way up one of the forest giants. With their loose, silky white shawls over their black bodies and their long black tails with fluffy white ends hanging down they looked like something out of a fantasy forest not a real one.

"Who cares if we don't see a White-crested Turaco?' I said. "Look at those beauties!"

That was our last chance to see the turacos because we we're moving on, south out of the species' range. A storm broke as we departed and it was in the heaviest rain we had ever seen that The Stid had to swerve around the pot holes on the last stretch of track into Kakamega Forest. All four double rooms in the basic *Forest Rest House* at Isecheno were empty but we pitched our tents outside.

We had barely crawled out of our tents when two of the loveliest birds I had ever seen glided across the forest clearing to one of the tall trees surrounding us. They were extremely long-tailed, soft apple-green birds with black and white striped heads that go by the name of White-throated Bee-eaters. Below them was a Blackcap, as dull as dishwater compared to the elegant birds above but special to me because it was one of the first birds I saw when I started out on this birding business.

A large troop of about twenty Black-and-white Colobus Monkeys moved into the trees around our campfire while we made morning coffee and planned the day ahead. Kakamega is the only surviving area of lowland rainforest in Kenya, an outlier of the Congo, and lots of birds whose ranges are mainly West African live in it and nowhere else in the country. They were the birds we were going to concentrate on looking for, and to stand a chance of some of them we needed to 'go in'. The forest edge is a much more pleasant and usually more productive place to look for birds but some birds do not venture to the edge they stay deep within the forest.

Immediately on breaching the wall of wood and leaves at the rainforest edge we entered a different world, a damp, gloomy labyrinth of massive tree trunks, branches and leaves, mostly leaves, deep and brown on the ground, every shade of green above. It is a world of wet leaves, wet branches, wet tree trunks, and damp and mossy and spongy and crumbly fallen logs, and the air is warm and humid and thick with the sweetish smell of rotting vegetation. Towering black, brown, grey and red trunks of trees rose straight and branchless for a long, long way before sprouting giant leafy canopies which intermingled to form a green and yellow ceiling above our heads. Not much light made it through to the forest floor where the narrow rarely-trodden trail we made our way along was a soggy mixture of deep leaf litter and mud. Apart from the odd dazzling flashes of butterfly wings jinking quickly by we could not see any animal life but we could hear it; the crescendo of cicadas and other insects, the scuttle of lizards, the wild barks of monkeys, the calls and songs of birds. Now and again the almost hypnotic background din made by the insects stopped dead for no apparent reason and a sudden, shocking silence hit the eerie forest, only for the barrage of sound to start up again with renewed violence a few seconds later. Even the birds seemed to fall silent during the lull. We heard some at other times, we even glimpsed a couple but that was it, there seemed to be little birdlife inside the forest. That was not true of course, it was full of birds; we just could not see them in the jungle of green. We could have 'taped them out'; played a recording of the call or song of the bird we wanted to see and hoped it would respond by thinking a rival male had entered its territory in which case it would probably fly toward the machine playing the call or song and, hopefully, land where we could see it, but I am not a fan of that. It is not only bad for the birds, wasting their valuable energy which could be used for foraging, feeding young, displaying, singing and so on instead of chasing non-existent intruders, it also makes the 'hunt' too easy for my liking. It doesn't involve much if any fieldcraft; the skills needed to track down, approach and watch birds without disturbing them. It's a lazy way to see birds, "Cheating in fact!" I stated to The Stid, not averse to a bit of 'playback' himself, as we pondered how to see the damned things. I was sure that with patience and persistence we would see at least some of the birds in that forest and they would be all the more enjoyable for the 'hunt'.

Rainforest soil is so thin and the wind so strong during almost daily thundery downpours that many of the trees cling to the ground with massive buttresses which act as anchors. Some are over head-height, much higher than the Chimpanzees and Pygmies which use them as drums to beat out messages which carry far through the forests of West Africa. Looking up we could make out the 'rigging'; the great long lianas, some as straight as plumb lines, some coiled, some twisted, some intertwined, some looped between trees. Even together with the buttresses though this superstructure sometimes buckles under the strain of the squally thunderstorms and a forest giant is felled by a gust or lightning. Part of the ceiling down, a flood of light reaches the forest floor and the rush is on. Seeds and saplings, some of which may have been lying dormant for hundreds of years awaiting their chance, shoot up toward the sky with no discernible thickening nor a branch in sight, all their energy being directed toward the light, for the first there, to that gap in the canopy, will spread its leafy limbs and shut out the light once more. It was such a sunlit glade we were hoping to come across because birding in the heart of Kakamega, the first lowland rainforest we had ever been in, was the toughest we had ever experienced.

In the forest that first morning there were gorgeous butterflies galore but nearly an hour passed before we saw a bird, a few actually, in a flock of greenish-yellow Joyful Greenbuls. After that rush of excitement there was not a movement, not a sign of a single bird, for a long, long time, only the odd call, until, finally, we reached a small clearing. A quick scan with renewed hope and there at the edge of the trees were two of the birds I hoped to see more than any other at Kakamega, a pair of Blue-headed Bee-eaters, and they were close enough for us to admire their shiny cerulean crowns, black faces, red eyes, dark chestnut backs and deep blue underparts. They looked brilliant, their tails wagging gently as they eyed the glade for bees and flies, and their scarlet bibs catching the sunlight and glowing.

After another couple of hours back inside the forest seeing very little it was a relief to get outside. We headed for the Ikuywa River where we saw another Blue-headed Bee-eater and The Stid had his *Nikon* 'Technicolor Dreamscope' with him so we could see every feather of the gorgeous thing. On the river were two relatively sombre and yet almost as beautiful Mountain Wagtails, glacial grey above and silky white below with grey necklaces, and longer tails than even the Grey Wagtails, familiar from home, which shared the rocks with them. A disturbing rumbling in my bowels sent me scurrying for cover and while squatting over the leaf litter four Crested Guineafowls walked past me, very hard birds to see in Kakamega. At dusk a White-tailed Ant Thrush ventured cautiously out of the forest on to the track we were staking out and we retired happily to the campsite where we cooked potatoes in the embers of the fire and ate the blackened vegetables with corned beef and onions, our first 'meal' for two days. It felt great sitting in a rainforest clearing full of fireflies at beer o'clock, with a full stomach for once, a *Tusker* and a smoke, reflecting on another day full of wonder with friends.

Although birding inside the forest was hot, sweaty, hard work, with very long quiet spells, interspersed with rare, short bursts of activity, the rewards for our prolonged efforts were fantastic. One such was back at the Ikuywa River where four Great Blue Turacos flew into the biggest tree around and ran along the huge almost horizontal branches before bouncing around the enormous open canopy with great grace. They were extraordinary creatures with verditer blue heads and upperparts, short, stout, red-tipped yellow beaks, crests which looked like short, stiff brushes, and long, broad tails with yellow flashes. In the trees below there was a dapper Jameson's Wattle-eye, about the size of the turacos' crests, being a stumpy little bird, glossy green-black above and silky white below with a very short tail and flamboyant turquoise wattles around its eyes. White-throated Bee-eaters, African Broadbills, Broad-billed Rollers, Black-and-white-casqued Hornbills, Grey Parrots, a fabulous array of tropical butterflies, and Black-and-white Colobus Monkeys followed.

A year or so before the trip to Kenya the brilliant book on *Shorebirds* by John Marchant, Tony Prater and Peter Hayman was published and I got hold of a copy as soon as

I could. Turning to Rock Pratincole I was very pleased to see that it was, 'Apparently sedentary at breeding sites in Kenya ...' with the map of the species' range showing that it occurred in the far west of the country north of Lake Victoria. There was nothing about them in the few trip reports I had covering other birders' visits to the country, even Steve Whitehouse's monumental effort, so when we were at Lake Baringo we asked Terry Stevenson if he knew where we might see one. He was careful not to give too much away, the information we did manage to winkle out of him was scanty and we were the worse for drink when he relayed it so when we discussed the conversation around our campfire at Kakamega all we could remember was that the name of the town ended in 'ias', it was '40 to 60 k' west of Kakamega and the birds roosted on rocks in a big river behind a sugar factory.

The only town on the map we had that ended in 'ias' was 50 or so k to the west *and* it was on a major river so we headed for a place called Mumias. The other side of there we came to a bridge over a wide, rocky, river which looked very good for pratincoles indeed but there were none there. The heat under the cloudless sky was almost unbearable but we could see what looked like a sugar factory in the hazy distance so we were off, walking as close to the river as possible although we rarely saw it through the thick stands of papyrus and reeds. The heat trapped in the rides between the head-high sugar cane was shocking. Huge Monitor Lizards scampered across in front of us. It was a long haul but eventually, near the factory, we came to an opening in the reeds and the river was strewn with grey rocks and on the rocks were 26 Rock Pratincoles. Through the telescope lugged there by The

Stid we could examine their salmon-pink beaks with neat inky black tips, the black stripes in front of their eyes and the white stripes behind, flaring on to the back of their necks. They were mainly grey but very handsome shorebirds and well worth the effort involved in getting to see them although we were not looking forward to the walk back. It was midday and the sun was blasting down but we soon forgot about the heat when a flock of seven bee-eaters swooped down around us and landed atop a low bush. Among six European Bee-eaters was our first stunning Carmine Bee-eater, a long-tailed, bright carmine-red bird with a glistening emerald-green head and an icy cobalt-blue rump. Such words can do no justice to such a fantastic creature; it has to be seen to be believed, and even then one may still have doubts about their sanity. The sun was certainly cooking our brains so maybe we imagined it. Back at the car we sliced up a pineapple and sucked the juice out of the chunks and it was the best drink we had ever had.

Back at Kakamega Wilberforce the rest house caretaker come birding guide said he had time to accompany us to the Ikuywa River where he wished to show us a Harrier-Hawk's nest. We sat on the sunny hillside overlooking the narrow strip of forest running along the river below and watched the pair of grey and black birds swop places on their eggs. A perfectly compact, lilac, orange and deep blue ball called a Pygmy Kingfisher sat still long enough for us to wonder at its brilliance before eagle-eyed Wilberforce helped us find a Turner's Eremomela, a dinky little grey and white 'warbler' with a black collar and chestnut forehead, and one of Kakamega's megas.

In *The Bee-eaters*, another great book in the refined *Poyser* series, the author Hilary Fry states that the range of Blue-breasted Bee-eater reaches Kisumu in Kenya, on the northeastern shore of Lake Victoria. Again, it was a bird not mentioned in any trip reports I had so it was a long shot but after the Rock Pratincole success we thought we would give it a go. So, we headed west out of Kisumu toward Siaport and Port Bunyala on the border with Uganda, also hoping to find some pools where Pygmy Geese and some other localised waterbirds might be present. The local police presumably did not see *wazungu* (white men) very often because their eyes lit up on spotting us and they waved us over to the side of the road where a full inspection of the car took place while we were questioned. Then we questioned them but they had never seen the bee-eaters. Reluctantly, they agreed we were not journalists and allowed us to continue, to a tiny, lily-covered pond which was almost covered with birds; Black Crakes, Lesser Moorhens, 'normal' Moorhens, Allen's Gallinule's, Purple Gallinules, African Jacanas, Fulvous Whistling Ducks and Squacco Herons, while perched on the surrounding reeds and overhead were Malachite, Pied and Striped Kingfishers, Blue-cheeked and European Bee-eaters, and Long-crested Eagles. It was a wonderful scene, despite the growing number of spectators. No matter where we stopped in Kenya kids appeared as if from nowhere. They were curious and when we explained to them what we were doing they laughed, presumably because it seemed so silly to them to watch birds, especially when their main interest was where their next meal was coming from. Watching birds may seem daft to many people but for me it is about hours like that, spent in a tiny paradise, marvelling at the multitude of colours and forms of the birds, and enjoying the astonishing diversity and flamboyance of nature. There were no Pygmy Geese on that pond or any of the others we found, and there were no Blue-breasted Bee-eaters but once again it didn't matter because, like so many days, we had seen so many amazing birds.

A storm was moving in over Lake Victoria and the night sky was almost constantly ablaze the whole way south to Kisii where we stayed the night. We got lost the next morning but kept turning south and eventually reached Migori where we turned east on to a murrum road to Lolgorien. After there, the rusty-red, gravelly soil used to surface many minor roads in Kenya was badly eroded and more damaging rain came and the track turned into a quagmire so it was not long before we were stuck. Getting out of the car to assess the situation it didn't look good. We could hardly see the wheels of our overloaded two-wheel drive car, under the mud and water. There were Zebras about and presumably Lions and, keeping their distance, some Maasai, tall and thin people dressed in wrap-around scarlet shukas and leaning on their spears. We joked that they were probably laughing at the crazy wazungu on their hands and knees digging around the wheels of their car. After a while another vehicle appeared, the only one we saw all day. 'Perfect timing' we all thought but the ex-patriot from Holland heading to his farm just slowed down a little and shouted out of his window, "You will have to wait for the track to dry," as he sped off in his high wheelbase, four-wheel drive which, with a winch, would have had us up and running in no time.

"You lot push, I'll drive," The Stid said, and after a lot of pushing, wheel spinning and sliding he got us out and on our way, which was a relief because we were trying to get to the Maasai Mara the back way and time was against us because we had to get to the gate before it closed at dusk. We didn't mind being covered in mud as long as we made that gate.

A few minutes later we heard a tyre go 'Poof!' which meant only one thing; a bloody puncture. We replaced the wheel in the rain and moved on, gingerly, in silence, worried about making it. Then we reached the edge of the Siria Escarpment and saw the Maasai Mara. There was little time but we had to get out and look at the incredible scene spread out before us. The vast African plain stretched from one end of the horizon to the other. It was mostly grass generously sprinkled with animals but there were stands of flat-topped acacias here and there, and a strip of thick woodland bordering the Mara River which ran across the panorama in a lush line, all below a sky that spanned the world, or so it seemed, for none of us had ever seen such an awesome world.

There was no time though. We had to make the gate by nightfall and it was down there somewhere in that endlessness. The steep track down the escarpment resembled a dry river bed but expert driving by The Stid ensured we made it to Oloololo Gate with minutes to spare. Once through, we immediately found ourselves on a very welcome, hard, flat track through light grassland grazed by large herds of Zebras and Thomson's Gazelles, with Buffalos and tall, handsome, purplish brown antelopes called Topis here and there, and Ostriches,

Secretary Birds and White Storks. Our first herd of Elephants was on the move and they made a magnificent sight, walking quickly but gracefully for such large animals. Watching them, and the other animals and birds, I finally felt like I was in the Africa I had dreamed of for so long.

It was dark by the time we reached *Mara Serena Safari Lodge*, from where we were escorted by an armed guard to the top of a rocky hillock, out of sight of the lavish lodge. I hesitate to describe it as a campsite for there were no facilities apart from a bit of bare, almost level ground. All we could see by torchlight beyond our tents, the only ones there, was a Spotted Hyaena biting a large bone in half. There were Buffalo about too. It was not easy getting to sleep listening to their hooves clipping the rocky ground nearby, and the laughing and whooping of the hyaenas closer still, even though we kept repeating, "There's no way they would let us camp here if it wasn't safe!" We were scared to death but it had been a long day and we were beat and eventually we nodded off, one by one.

It was worth the nerves to see the view from the hillock at dawn. Sipping coffee, sitting on rocks, we looked out over the plain, lit brilliantly by the low sun. Above us, black-and-white, seemingly tail-less, oddly elegant Bateleur Eagles pierced the sky and wheeled over a wondrous scene full of herds of Hippos, Buffalos, Elephants, Zebras, Wildebeests, Impalas and Topis, and large troops wandering Baboons, and here and there some Giraffes, standing stock still, and next to a waterhole our first Saddle-billed Stork, so tall it was an impressive sight even from so far away. A flood of joy came over me. That scene, of Africa, was what I gave up my job, my security, my future, for. It was everything I had dreamed of and more. I was scared, of the consequences of my actions, of the animals around us, of what might become of us, but after a while I felt strangely safe and comfortable, perhaps because the African plain is where man was born and our natural home. I thought I felt at home there, that I belonged there. I was certainly tremendously happy and incredibly excited, and like the others I could not wait any longer to get down there.

It took all day to drive thirty miles (50 km) through the southern Maasai Mara, because life abounds on the African plain and there was so much to watch and enjoy. Four Lionesses padded their way to shade after a night hunting, four more snoozed under an acacia, one on its back with its sore paws in the air, Elephants, Giraffes, Buffalos, Hippos, Hyaenas, Hartebeests, Wildebeests, Topis, Zebras, Impalas, Grant's and Thomson's Gazelles, Warthogs and Baboons were everywhere, with Ostriches, Secretary Birds, Crowned Cranes, Caspian and Crowned Plovers, and exquisite Temminck's Coursers in the tawny grass, and Long-crested Eagles, Lilac-breasted Rollers, Little Bee-eaters and Woodland Kingfishers adorning the acacias.

The campsite at Keekorok was in the middle of the plain, well away from another luxurious lodge. We were told to beware of the Baboons and we soon found out why. After washing up our dishes we returned to the tents and a big male Baboon was sat on the bonnet of the car finishing off our bread. Chief ran at him but the Baboon rose up and turned into a massive muscular beast baring fangs. Chief ran back past us as we watched the Baboon jump down from the bonnet and calmly climb into the back of the car to steal our last pineapple. All we could do was laugh, before we turned into our tents for the long, frightening African night.

We spent much of the next morning lost along wet tracks, pushing the car out of muddy hollows in Lion country and nearly getting crushed by Elephants, all in an unsuccessful attempt to find a Black Rhino. Dark clouds loomed over the Mara, more rain looked imminent, our tents and sleeping bags were already wet, and our vehicle was not suitable for cruising the areas favoured by Rhinos, so we decided to move out.

The track north from Keekorok was poor. We had to get out of the car regularly to push it through the mud and water. It was slow-going but the hassle was surpassed by the spectacle surrounding us. Giraffes on the run, seemingly gliding by in slow-motion, our first White-headed Vultures, easily the smartest of their clan, some might even say handsome, and, eyeing us warily from the ground, tiny Two-banded Coursers and giant Kori Bustards. Then we lost the track altogether and we had to take to the bush and navigate by the sun, north across the stony, short-grass and scrubby Loita Plains dotted with large puddles and muddy wallows. Zigzagging slowly around them and the bushes we saw more Koris, coursers and Caspian Plovers and they kept us going, because we were all a little concerned that it would soon be dark and we would be lost somewhere in the northern Mara and nowhere near the road to Narok, the nearest town, which we were aiming for. Then, not long before dusk there it was, tarmac, a wonderful sight for once. A minute or so of gloriously smooth road later, just as we thought the day's birding was probably over, two more massive bustards appeared to our left. The orange stripes running down the back of their long necks were immediately obvious and we were out of the car and looking at our first Denham's Bustards in seconds. Not long after, we were enjoying a cold beer and a meal in the *Narok Inn*, before moving on to Thika, north of Nairobi, ready for another new day.

In the steep forested ravines of the mountains known as the Aberdares we came across a flock of Golden-winged Sunbirds, a fitting fantastical name for resplendent birds, especially the males which are burnished bronze and fiery copper above, and deep black below with rich yellow wings, and glowing golden tails and tail streamers. With more sombre but still mainly flashing, yellow-winged females and younger birds, they darted from flower to flower in search of nectar with their short, slim, hooked beaks, flashing black and gold and bronze and fire like miniature fireworks. I could have watched that flock of at least ten Golden-winged Sunbirds for the rest of the day but the boys wanted to move on and so with great reluctance I walked away and off we went.

At dawn the next day, overlooking another ravine, this time at the base of Mount Kenya, another golden beauty emerged from a patch luxuriant montane forest. It goes by the lovely name of White-starred Robin because the green and bright yellow bird has a tiny, shiny, silvery spot at the base of its blue-black throat. It is a shy bird and it quickly retreated to its preferred shady haunts under the thick shrubs and trees which were busy with other birds, including green Red-fronted Parrots, green and purple

Hartlaub's Turacos, Green Pigeons and green Cinnamon-chested Bee-eaters, all very prominent, even in a world of green. The car with us and all our gear in it could not cope with the slope up to the meteorological station on Mount Kenya so we had to walk most of the way. We still got to the station, at over 10,000 feet (3000 metres), in time to try to find another dazzling sunbird, the Scarlet-tufted Malachite Sunbird, a bird of the alpine moorland above the forest, so off we trod, higher up the mountain, ascending through dwarf forest with dense bamboo thickets, ferny forest and head-high heather before we reached the open boggy moorland of great tussocks of grass, giant groundsels and lofty lobelias, the giant flowers the sunbirds favour. Except few were *in flower* so there were no sunbirds and as in the Aberdares we could not find any Moorland Francolins either, and we were wondering if the effort had been worthwhile when a pair of equally localised and nearly endemic rufous-brown Jackson's Francolins walked out from between two tussocks.

The Stid served up the luxury of a fried egg each with our usual beans and sardines in the evening, cooked to perfection on our camping stove inside our log cabin because it was so cold outside. We ate while it was still light, because we wanted to be out at dusk looking for Montane Nightjars. There were none but while we listened for their haunting whistles we heard loud, honking calls coming from the slope above us. We ran, through the trees, to the rim of the nearby ravine, and there they were, though we could hardly believe it, the birds we knew were there but were so rare and shy we never expected to see them; three Green Ibises, gliding down the ravine, their loud honks carrying far across the forest.

In the cold dawn a very shy orangey-rufous Abyssinian Ground Thrush hopped into the open between two bamboo stands and the morning coffee tasted all the better for it. After watching a small troop of white-bearded Sykes's Monkeys we drove slowly down Mount Kenya and north through arid but arable fields before descending again into increasingly arid bush where the tarmac ran out, pot holes increased in frequency and the temperature rose rapidly. It was a bumpy ride from then on, to the frontier town of Isiolo and on to the Ngare Mara Gate of Samburu National Reserve.

As soon as we entered Samburu, as if by magic, but in reality because the local tribes were not allowed to graze their excessive number of cattle inside the reserve, we saw a great variety of animals and birds, in splendid, flat, arid country with termite mounds between thorny bushes, and low, hazy, blue-grey mountains in the distance. Most of the wildlife was new to us. Blue-necked and blue-legged Somali Ostriches, not pink-necked and legged Common Ostriches, towered over spectacular Golden-breasted Starlings with breasts more deep golden than anything we had seen before, in Africa or elsewhere, and upperparts a glorious glossy palette of iridescent blues, greens and purples, and eyes pale in a black mask. A large herd of Giraffes ran gracefully past us, no ordinary Giraffes but 'Reticulated' Giraffes with crazy-paving pelts. The Zebras were different too. They were Grévy's Zebras with narrower stripes than the more familiar Plains Zebras. And there were some superb, sleek antelopes with extraordinarily long necks called Gerenuks standing on their very long back legs and reaching up with their front legs and long necks to get to the freshest foliage. Pygmy

Falcons, more shrikes than falcons, perched on short bushes. Three pastel perfect pallid green and orange Somali Bee-eaters, arid country specialists very different to the other much more vividly coloured bee-eaters we had seen, hunted from thorny saplings near the ground where a flock of Golden Pipits, almost all brilliant yellow, took to the air like a bundle of windblown autumn leaves. It seemed that everywhere we went in Kenya, places not that far apart, there was a explosion of new wonder.

The temptation to celebrate life with an slap-up meal and some cold beers in the splendid, round, open-air, thatched restaurant of *Samburu Lodge* was too much, especially after several days of meagre rations, not that we had much choice, being without supplies and new residents of the facility-less campsite, so we splashed out on sirloin steaks and devoured them accompanied by two Common Genets sitting on the beams above and Slender-tailed Nightjars flying through the restaurant and picking off the moths attracted to the lights.

Our bellies full, we ordered four more *Tuskers* and plonked ourselves down in the comfortable chairs - oh, what luxury - of the lounge and, with diaries updated and satisfied and content, we prepared ourselves for a long night-time vigil, hoping a Leopard would come in to the leg of meat tied to a tree across the Ewaso Nyiro River. A few beers later all we had seen were some Nile Crocodiles and Green Sandpipers. There was no sign of a Leopard and we felt ragged so we got up and found the guard who had told us he must accompany us on the long walk to the campsite in case we should meet said Leopard. We could not help but laugh at the big stick he carried to see off the big cat. We were not worried about the Leopard once we got to the campsite we were worried about sleeping in our tents on the bank of a river full of the biggest crocodiles we had ever seen.

"There's no way they would let us camp here if it wasn't safe!" I said, in an attempt to reassure Chief in the other tent, adding quietly to myself and The Stid, "Would they?", as we listened to the crocodiles snorting and splashing.

It was a long, hot, sweaty night, more memorable for the mosquitoes than the crocodiles, but all was forgotten once we got into the field and fell in love with Samburu. The open, seemingly endless, arid terrain, bushy in places with thickets of flat-topped acacias, and the narrow strip of tall, shady, acacias, fig trees and doum palms along the river, were all bursting with life. What fixes to be in, trying to decide whether to watch a Somali Bee-eater or a Beisa Oryx, a beautiful grey-brown antelope with a black and white face and long, straight, pointed horns, a Martial Eagle, perched on top of an acacia, or a Somali Courser, Little Bee-eaters or Lilac-breasted Rollers and so on. There was such variety of life the morning shake, rattle and roll cruise in the battered car around bumpy and dusty Samburu lasted over seven hours.

After a break to take on liquid in the middle we were out there again and managed to track down, amongst the multitude of other birds, two handsome Buff-crested Bustards, four Pink-breasted Larks which were, to our surprise, actually a very delicate shade of pink, a rare colour in the natural world, and a large flock of 35 Vulturine Guineafowl, bald-headed but very finely feathered birds, especially around the neck where a cape of very long, lanceolate cobalt-blue, black and white plumes flows down over the birds' beautiful cobalt-blue breasts.

The Leopard turned up the second night but not until we were asleep in our tents. The Baboons let out such a horrific racket that, having been awoken, we all froze rigid with fear. Now wide awake we could hear some of the other sounds of the African night. The soothing low clicking of frogs and toads, and the terrible grunts, snorts and roars of crocodiles, but it was the Baboons which were going absolutely crazy; baying, screeching and screaming so loudly we could only assume something terrible was about to happen, only there was little we could do about it lying there in the pitch black of our flimsy tents.

*Beisa Oryx, Samburu, Kenya, 14th January 1988*

"Must be a bloody Leopard," Tim said, rueing the fact that we had yet to see one.

There was certainly something scaring the hell out of the Baboons and it was a long time before the crescendo peaked and began to wane. Then our fear finally began to fade but just as we were about to think about the possibility of a little more sleep there was a tremendous rush of animals outside. We could hear hooves thumping the ground rapidly and assumed a herd of what must have been gazelles ran and sprang through the campsite, presumably pursued by a Leopard. The stampede was over in a minute or so but had the gazelles (and the Leopard?) not dodged our tents we may have had a more terrible tale to tell.

"How can they let us camp here?" Chief squealed.

I nearly repeated the old mantra, 'They wouldn't let us camp here if it wasn't safe' but I resisted.

At dawn it was a relief to get up, even though we had not had much sleep, get in the car and cruise the sandy tracks of Samburu again, looking at the now familiar and yet still fantastic wildlife. When we began making our way out of the reserve we got stuck in deep sand, in a dry creek, in Lion country. The track we were on appeared to be rarely used and we didn't expect any other vehicles to come along anytime soon so we had three choices: walk to the gate at Archer's Post, several miles ahead; walk back to the lodge, several miles behind; or dig out the wheels and collect sticks and stones to place under them for some grip. Otherwise we could be stuck for the night, or even longer, and we certainly didn't relish the thought of that.

Chief took the opportunity to remind us what we had been told in the bar the night before, about two tourists who had camped out in the bush a week or so ago. They had been robbed at spear-point and had their faces slashed, probably by Somali bandits known as Shifta. We decided to dig ourselves out and someone kept watch while another foraged for sticks and stones. After a worrying hour or so we yelled with delight when The Stid reversed the damned car out of the sand and on to harder ground. This happened in the mad midday heat so that by the time we reached Archer's Post the red sand and dust had settled in our eyes, ears, noses and mouths, as well as on the sheet of sweat covering our bodies, and congealed in the dirt of five days without water to wash. So, it was four men dressed only in shorts, hair matted with dust, faces and bodies streaked with red, who got out of the car and walked up to the office at the park gate.

The gatekeepers looked aghast. They were not expecting to see anyone all day. They didn't know what to do. So, in a fluster, they began by questioning whether we were allowed to enter Samburu by one gate and leave by another, and while a lengthy palaver took place in their hut our front right tyre went flat. By the time we had replaced it someone emerged from the hut and told us that a few more shillings were required to make our permits valid for departure from a different gate so we paid the bribe and were on our way.

Archer's Post was a one-dusty-street-town where the tall, thin Samburu people looked friendly but to the north was bandit country and we had already decided against travelling that way, not least because the car was not up to tackling the track to Marsabit and the Dida Galgalu Desert beyond where the good birds were. The tyres had at least one repaired puncture each and/or were about to blow, including the spare, the back axle was loose, the suspension knackered after two and a half weeks on mostly rough corrugated murrum tracks and pot-holed roads, and the frame of the car was so buckled the doors no longer closed properly, so we drove quickly south to Isiolo and on to Meru.

The decision to miss out on Marsabit seemed meant to be when, just inside the Murera Gate of Meru National Park, good old Stid spotted not one but two Scissor-tailed Kites, the bird we dreamed of seeing up north. The elegant grey and white raptors looked more like terrestrial terns than birds of prey as they flapped lazily and buoyantly high over the savanna, stopping occasionally to hover with their long, deeply forked tails spread. They made a wonderful sight, hunting the tawny plain, a sight we did not expect to see since they were thought to be rare and nomadic migrants in Kenya, and so it was with considerable elation that we continued along the red dust track into a land of palms, dense acacia woods and swampy grasslands alive with life.

As well as lots of Lilac-breasted Rollers we saw 26 European Rollers, and with a couple of hundred White Storks there were two Saddle-billed Storks. Montagu's and Pallid Harriers sailed over the grass where there were nearly a hundred Elephants, a lot of Beisa Oryx and Reticulated Giraffes. We spent some time watching five White Rhinos that were accompanied by armed guards to protect them from poachers. In the late afternoon we made camp near Leopard Rock Lodge, ate the usual sardines, beans and bread by the campfire and with a cold beer to hand I counted up the bird list for the trip.

"We've now seen over 500 species!" I announced. "In twenty days! And that's including over 400 new ones for me!"

"Are you sure?" Chief said in shock.

"Yep, it's incredible isn't it?"

"Phenomenal!"

"Especially when you add on the mammals as well," Tim added. "We've seen 35 of them."

"But not Leopard and Cheetah!" Chief pointed out. "And what about Black Rhino?"

"Tomorrow hopefully," Tim said, "but if not, then in Nairobi National Park."

Too much time looking for Black Rhino meant we arrived at the site for the endemic Hinde's Babbler near Embu with ten minutes of light left. The Stid was not happy.

"Another tick gone," he complained as he contemplated another blank tick box on his list.

"Question is, are we gonna look for 'em tomorra'?" Chief asked.

A long debate ensued about how much time we had left on the trip and how best to use it to try and see certain species of bird and mammal and the result was that the poor Stid was outvoted three to one, the three against looking for the babbler deciding that there were just too many amazing birds and mammals still possible to see to waste time on one, albeit endemic, bird. So, we moved on and spent another night in the *December Hotel* in Thika.

The next day was a disaster. We spent a fruitless morning looking for Giant Kingfisher, a muddy river rushing over the road instead of under it blocked our way to Lake Magadi, and our attempt to salvage something from the day looking for Purple-crested Turaco at one of the few known sites in Kenya east of the Athi River ended in failure. To cap it all, in order to be the first vehicle into Nairobi National Park the next morning and therefore maximise our chances of seeing Black Rhino and African Finfoot we had little choice but to stay the night in the capital. We had heard a lot about 'Nairobbery' but were pleasantly surprised to feel perfectly safe walking to a nice place to eat while it was still light. However, we became acutely aware of the city's problems after dark when we passed numerous shop entrances with large night watchmen dressed in big black overcoats and armed with clubs, settling in for the night.

The *Terminal Hotel* had no water and a disco so loud there was no need to set the alarm; all of us apart from Chief were still awake when we had to get up. At least we were at Cheetah Gate at the opening time of 6 a.m., not that it did us much good because we were soon stuck in mud. We had to take all of our stuff out of the car to get the damned thing out. There was another car in the middle of the next area of mud. The Kenyan driver had been there all night and was very happy to see us. We tried hard to get his car out but it was impossible so we offered him a lift back to the gate. He just managed to squeeze into the back of our car between two of us and a load of luggage. Now the car was even more overloaded and heavy so our new friend suggested taking the long way back, avoiding the worst of the mud and despite his very limited view he was the one who casually informed us, not many minutes later, that there was a Black Rhino on the left-hand side. Our friend nearly ended up in the front of the car The Stid slammed on the brakes so hard. As quietly as possible we all twisted and turned to get in a position from where we could have a good look at the rhino which was standing by a clump of bushes in tawny, belly-high grass. It has a massive bulk of a body with a long, heavy head on which there were two horns, the front one very long and tapering to a sharp point. It didn't appear to know we were watching it but of course it did and it suddenly decided it was not happy about it so it turned and broke into a nimble trot as it quickly disappeared between the bushes.

We thanked our friend with firm handshakes, dropped him off with more handshakes and headed for Hippo Pools where, at the start of the trail to the pools, there was a sign warning visitors to 'Beware of Lions whilst walking'. It wasn't the pools we were heading for it was downstream along the Mbagathi River, 'out of bounds' but our only chance of seeing African Finfoot. We made our way very slowly through the thick gallery forest alongside the river being extra careful not to startle any birds out on the muddy water and scanning constantly from every possible angle hoping to see a finfoot, a secretive, grebe-like bird likely to swim into dense overhanging cover at the slightest disturbance. The Stid was up front, I was some way behind him and Chief and Tim were way back when I heard Chief yell, "I've got one!" I made my way back to him as quickly and as quietly as I could and saw my first African Finfoot swimming very low in the water toward cover on the far bank, its dark grey head with bright red beak working back and forth. By the time The Stid arrived the bird was hidden so we left him there, thinking there was more chance of it coming back out with just one person trying to hide instead of four and because we were not supposed to be where we were. Back at the car a park ranger arrived and without even a word to us headed straight into the trees where The Stid was hiding. About forty minutes later The Stid emerged. He was dejected. He had not seen the finfoot. Nor the ranger as it turned out but because the ranger was about The Stid could not risk going back in. We waited a long time for that ranger to come out and drive off but he never did and as usual time was against us and we had to leave, with a very unhappy Stid at the wheel.

Our only chance of seeing Chestnut-banded Plover in Kenya was at Lake Magadi so we were determined to get there on our second attempt. It did not begin well but after another puncture we were very happy to see the road open where there had been water the day before and in no time at all we were at the lake, where it took exactly five seconds to locate a plover, the first of over twenty. The plump, long-legged, grey-brown and white birds with narrow, deep chestnut bands across their upper breasts ran with impressive speed across the blinding salt flats of Magadi, a surprisingly birdy place considering it was a hot and burning soda lake, caustic enough in places to strip flesh off human bones. Thousands of Lesser Flamingos with extra tough scales and skin on their legs to protect them shimmered pink in the distance, towering above what looked like mirages of Blacksmith Plovers, Black-winged Stilts and Avocets in the searing heat. The flamingos were the most numerous birds by far because they are able to eat the blue-green algae that thrives in the shallow alkaline waters, and which also contains the carotenoid pigments which makes them pink. Buoyed by the success with the plovers and befuddled by the sun we continued gung-ho past the lake south through spiky grasses and low thorny scrub toward a distant swamp drawn on a treasure map where there were reputed to be Black Herons, Dwarf Bitterns and lots of other rare waterbirds, only coming to our senses and turning around when the track started to peter out, along with the light.

We fed and watered in Nairobi before the overnight drive to Amboseli National Park. We had not been going long before the person with the spotlight relayed the often repeated instructions to The Stid at the wheel.

"Steady," if the person thought he might be on to something, which meant slow down.

"Hold it," if that person was almost sure they were on to something, which meant slow right down.

"Stop!" if that person *was* on to something.

"Stop!" Chief said, without bothering with the rest.

He was ecstatic. The bird in the spotlight perched on a roadsign, a rarity itself in Kenya, was an African Marsh Owl, a very special bird to someone whose favourite bird family is the owls.

The sight of pairs of white or yellow dots shining in the spotlight beam and car headlights increased steadily as we cruised along. They were eyes, mostly belonging to Thomson's Gazelles, Zebras, Hartebeests and Wildebeests. Then The Stid braked hard and stopped and we all stared at the road ahead while the spotlight was swung around to point at the strangest creature we had ever seen. It looked like a miniature kangaroo because it was a rabbit-sized rodent with large ears, huge back legs and feet, and a long, bushy tail, and it bounded across the road with giant hops. Tim said it was called a Spring Hare and that seemed fitting. It was the first of several and we also saw a Bat-eared Fox with three cubs, the mother a small but tall, grey animal with a dark face and enormous ears.

Namanga, the border crossing with Tanzania, was a busy place in the middle of the night. Big trucks and trailers were lined up on both sides of the road and it was a bit of a squeeze to get through and find the track east to Amboseli. Sure we were a long way out of Namanga we pulled over to grab an hour or so of sleep before dawn. We awoke to Kilimanjaro. Africa's highest mountain at nearly 20,000 feet (6000 metres) was distant but the huge flat-topped volcanic dome dominated the landscape and did so for the next few days. Not long after reaching Amboseli a medium-sized, muscular, golden-brown cat with a black-and-white face and big ears with tassels on trotted slowly alongside the dusty track. It was a Caracal, a cat Chief and Tim, the two of us most interested in mammals, did not expect to see. The beauty sauntered off into what was great country for bustards. We soon saw Buff-cresteds, Koris and White-bellieds. They liked the dry, open bush but the land turned wetter after a while and we came to a massive swamp which was alive with birds and mammals; over fifty African Jacanas lit up the scene with Black Crakes, Crowned Cranes, Blacksmith, Long-toed and Spur-winged Plovers, Squacco Herons, and Malachite and Pied Kingfishers, all constantly on the move as they were flushed by Buffalos, Hippos and Elephants. We parked well back, scared of getting stuck, and out of the car window, so close we could almost touch them, were some Collared Pratincoles, exquisite, long-winged brown birds with short, red-based bills. We wanted to stay but we had at least fifty miles (80 km) to cover before dark, a long haul, as it turned out, of uninterrupted dust, sand, rocks, ridges, bumps, pot-holes and craters. It was more like being on a boat on a rough sea than in a vehicle on a rough track as the car seemed to bend from side to side *and* front to back as The Stid negotiated the worst stretches which sometimes merged into one, long, rocky corrugation, sending shock waves up our spines and making every bone and muscle in our bodies ache.

There was little to relieve the trauma except regular Lilac-breasted Rollers, each one still greeted with a reverential call of its name. Then I spotted an unusual-looking bee-eater, a large, long, elegant and green one.

"Steady ... hold it ... stop!" I yelled and leapt out of the car.

Lining up the bird in my binoculars I then announced, "Madagascar!"

It was our tenth and last possible bee-eater species of the trip and I was very happy, although not a little worried about reaching Tsavo West National Park before nightfall when the entrance gate would be closed. Even when we got to see the large gate, in the far distance, it seemed beyond us as we progressed very slowly over the sharp edges of a lava flow. Chyulu Gate was actually being closed as we pulled up but the gatekeepers opened it again and let us in and got a firm handshake from the lot of us. Soon we were having some cold beers and a fine meal overlooking the floodlit watering hole at *Kilaguni Lodge* where a Striped Hyaena, another unexpected mammal, strolled back and forth along the high, far bank. On the way to our bandas at Kitani for the night tiny Donaldson-Smith's Nightjars flitted up from the middle of the track, alongside which strolled a gorgeous, long-legged cat called a Serval. Not long after that feline bonus we laid down horizontal on a bed each, with full stomachs, after sixty-six hours without sleep, and it felt so good and we were so tired even a manic, screaming troop of Baboons, spooked by a Leopard, was very unlikely to wake us.

As usual Chief was up and about as soon as there was a hint of light, pacing up and down and saying, "Haway, let's get in the field!" and so we were back to the bone-shaking journey through Africa. At the oasis in the rolling grasslands, low bush and barren hills of Tsavo known as Mzima Springs we were allowed to get out of our damned metal cage and walk around a beautiful azure pool where a female Giant Kingfisher was perched on a dead snag high above the water. It was our first proper view of what is a huge bird, for a kingfisher, a bird as big as a Striated Heron that is barred and speckled steel-grey and white with a chestnut belly and massive dark dagger of a beak.

Back in the car we began the long drive south through Tsavo West to Lake Jipe. Alongside the track there were numerous birds including Golden Pipits and Golden-breasted Starlings so all was well with the world. Then, suddenly, we reached the Tsavo River and The Stid slammed on the brakes. Deep muddy water was rushing along and dropping down over a 'waterfall' created by a collapsed ford. To get to Lake Jipe where we hoped to see Pygmy Goose and Black Heron would involve a detour of well over a hundred miles, much of it on rough roads and tracks. We waded in to our knees, the water rushing around our legs, to assess the possibility of the car getting across. What remained of the battered ford was broken and uneven but The Stid decided to go for it, with me in the passenger seat looking out of the open window making sure he didn't get too close to the edge of the 'waterfall'. As The Stid eased the poor, filthy, once white *Mazda 323* hatchback into the river the brown water poured in through the buckled doors. 'At least we're moving' I thought then we stopped, right in the middle of the river. There was a massive piece of ripped-up stone in the way of one of the front wheels, preventing the car from going forward. It was no time for faffing, and The Stid is not a faffer. He whipped the gear into reverse, drove back a little, put the car back in first and put his foot down. We bumped over the obstacle, bumped across the rest of the river and shot up the far bank. Water poured out of the car doors as Chief and Tim got in and since the engine was still running The Stid pulled away and we were off again, on a wonderfully smooth, dry, hard and level sandy track, without doubt the best track we had been on during the trip, and, still elated, we rounded a bend and there stood right in the middle of the track was a Cheetah. The big cat surpassed all our expectations. It was surprisingly small-headed, slender, long-legged and long-tailed but big-shouldered and it had a rich orange coat, spotted with black, which perfectly matched the scorched earth of Tsavo. After a minute or so the most beautiful cat we had ever seen walked off the track and melted into the bush, leaving us smiling, for a long, long time.

Continuing south we seemed to suddenly enter very birdy country. Ostriches, Pygmy Falcons, and, best of all, Carmine Bee-eaters were all seen before we reached Lake Jipe where in the shallow pools around its edge we found lots of plovers, sandpipers, stilts, jacanas, egrets, and herons, including the one we hoped for. There were five Black Herons, looking more like slaty egrets, and two of them were in active fishing mode, bent forward with their wings spread in a circle around their heads, to create an 'umbrella' over the water, presumably to help them catch fish, although no one really seems sure why the hunting technique works. They were certainly great to watch as they stalked the shallows, folding and unfolding their 'umbrellas', and we would have carried on doing so if we didn't think we had a chance of seeing Pygmy Geese as well. So, we wandered over to the lakeside and asked a couple of fishermen if they would take us out on to the lake in their dugout to look for the geese. They said that they would but first of all they had to go off for a few minutes and do something, so we retired to the shade of a nearby acacia and waited for Africa time to pass. After a couple of hours or so we were off, sliding silently through the reeds in an almost idyllic backwater of Lake Jipe. I say 'almost' because there were no water lilies, the best habitat for Pygmy Geese, and no geese. It was impossible to feel down though, surrounded as we were by Little Grebes,

Malachite and Pied Kingfishers, and Blue-cheeked and Carmine Bee-eaters, with fish eagles overhead.

It was a long drive east to Voi and had been dark for some time when we arrived. The owners of a very friendly guesthouse seemed pleased to see us and immediately set about grilling four massive steaks and frying a heap of chips as we enjoyed a beer and reflected on another incredible day in Africa. When the two giant beetles which sounded like tiny helicopters finally bashed themselves unconscious against the walls of the corridor outside our rooms we slept like babies.

Just inside Tsavo East National Park we soon found what we were looking for, an Upcher's Warbler, but the rather drab grey thing was completely overshadowed of course by the usual array of colourful wonders not least a metallic green and bronze Diederik Cuckoo. Birds were plentiful alongside the track east and we also saw lots of Buffalos, several Giraffes and a few Gerenuks before we came across four Belgians standing next to their vehicle with two punctures. The Stid took one of them and the two flats back to Voi, returning a couple of hours later, while the rest of us watched Blue-cheeked Bee-eaters. It was not long after The Stid returned that we saw our fourth species of bee-eater of the day; a Carmine, having already seen Little and White-throated as well.

Our next stop was Aruba Dam where we were hoping to see our first African Darter. We were disappointed but yet again there was more than enough compensation in the form of a flock of about 500 Caspian Plovers. Beyond Aruba, Tsavo was a solemn sight; flat and dry and dusty with patches of dry grass and small bushes, and dead trees for miles and miles, killed by the huge number of starving Elephants fenced into the park to protect farmers' crops outside. One of our guide books stated that there were 14,000 Elephants in Tsavo East but we did not see a single one because they were all crammed into a tiny area by a river at the northern end, the only place where there was sufficient water to sustain so many animals. We were glad to reach Sala Gate and crack on to the coast, although the car brakes then failed and The Stid had to take it very easy as we hobbled into Malindi in the dark.

It was wonderful to hear the hushed roar of the Indian Ocean, to smell it, and to feel the cool breeze coming off it, after four hot, dusty weeks in the interior, and even better to wake up the next morning, sit on the side of a bed, pick up my binoculars, look out of the window, and see my first new bird at the coast. The others had yet to stir but I woke them up with a cry of, "Sooty Gull on the beach!"

Just a few miles north of Malindi one of the longest rivers in Kenya, the Athi-Galana-Sabaki, reaches the Indian Ocean, and the long, thin estuary is one of the few places in the country where African Skimmers occur, albeit irregularly. We pulled over at the tiny village of Sabaki, gave a few shillings to a few boys to watch the car, and headed off along the north shore. It was a joy to leave the car behind and set out on foot even though the sun was already warm and it was obviously going to be very hot very soon. As well as African Fish Eagles and Pied Kingfishers there was an impressive selection of shorebirds foraging on the mudflats including Black-winged Stilts, Curlews, Marsh, Terek and Wood Sandpipers, Grey Plovers and at least 50 Spur-winged Plovers. Near the estuary mouth there was a flock of about 3000 Lesser Flamingos, and roosting on several sandbars hundreds of terns which included at least thirty Caspian Terns and our first Greater Crested Terns. It was 9 a.m. by the time we reached the ocean and the sun was already scorching hot so once we had agreed there were no skimmers out there in the shimmer we retraced our steps and drove back to Malindi to take on liquid and get the car brakes fixed. It was so hot that while waiting for the car we indulged in three cold and sweet strawberry milkshakes each, and while cooling down we talked excitedly about our next destination, Mida Creek, and our next dream, the unique Crab Plover.

In the meantime we strolled along the seafront enjoying the shorebirds and terns. There we met three English birders who said they had been to Mida Creek that morning and not seen a single Crab Plover, very alarming news considering the creek was the best site in Kenya and one of the best in the world for the species. So, having got the car back and driven south, it was with some trepidation that we got out of the car and clambered through the narrow belt of mangroves bordering the wide creek beyond. Standing free of the tangled branches and spiky roots we raised our binoculars and we all saw a Crab Plover straight away.

We all started laughing and we laughed even more a few minutes later when Chief announced in his inimitable exaggerated style, "No Crab Plovers! ... There are three hundred and five of 'em!"

It must have been a very high tide when the other birders were there. When we broke through the mangroves there was a blinding expanse of white sand, glistening mud and shallow channels generously sprinkled with birds, mostly Crab Plovers. It was little wonder they were so common; there were millions of crabs, more than enough to sustain hundreds of the very handsome birds with long legs and huge black beaks evolved to stab and crush the crustaceans. It was hard to avoid crushing a few with each step we took, as we walked carefully alongside the mangroves to get better views of the perfectly pied crab-eaters. After watching the plovers for a while I turned my attention to trying to find a Western Reef Egret, a rare bird on the Kenyan coast, but a possibility. Scan after scan and all I could see were some much larger Grey Herons and I was looking at one of them when an African Fish Eagle leapt from a nearby post at the end of a fisherman's net and dropped on to the heron's neck, killing it almost instantly. I called the others over and we watched the eagle drag the heron out of a shallow channel on to the sand and begin to tear into it and, still amazed by the eagle's fearlessness, we then spotted a medium-sized all dark heron with a yellow bill flying past; a Western Reef Egret.

Finding birds in Sokoke Forest was much harder. Even though we were in position on a trail at dawn we failed to find the 'big three' birds which occur only in the narrow strip of coastal forest which extends from Kenya south into Tanzania; Sokoke Pipit, Amani Sunbird and Clarke's Weaver. However, we did bump into a 'wave', a fast-moving foraging flock of small birds, and saw six new species in as many minutes; Tiny Greenbuls, an Eastern Nicator, a Little Yellow Flycatcher, a Blue-mantled Crested

Flycatcher, several Black-headed Apalises and four Chestnut-fronted Helmet Shrikes. By mid-morning avian activity had all but ceased in the relentless heat so we headed back to *The Baobab* in Malindi, a raised beachside café where we could eat and drink and watch the birdies at the same time. It was a splendid way to have lunch ... until The Stid jumped up with a start, began sweating even more and rapidly searched his many pockets. He then announced, several times, that he had lost about 500 British pounds worth of traveller's cheques and a thousand Kenyan shillings.

He had no idea where he had lost them and assumed they had been stolen but there was nothing we could do about it, it being a Sunday, so we headed north up the coast road to Gongoni Saltworks in search of Malindi Pipit. The men at the gate refused to let us in so we decided to try along a track to the nearby peninsula known as Ras Ngomeni, where we also hoped to see White-fronted Plover, only to sink exhaust-deep in sand. It was immediately obvious we were going to be in that sand for some time and there did not appear to be any people for miles, just saltpans in every direction. However, almost everywhere we had stopped for a while to look for birds in Kenya people had appeared, as if from nowhere, and we were only surprised it took half an hour for the first to appear. Soon there were about ten men and boys helping us to dig out the wheels but even when a few more turned up the car would not budge. We were well and truly stuck and on the hottest afternoon of the trip so far.

The only way out was with a tow and for that we needed another vehicle. One of the locals must have realized this early on and gone to get help because *bwana*, Swahili for master, an ex-patriot English owner of the adjacent farm, trundled up in a tractor with a face like thunder, and with great difficulty pulled us out. We tried to thank him but the miserable bastard just drove off. Following the tracks we were advised to we managed to get out of the hottest place on Earth and back to Sabaki where with our mashed up brains we decided to try to get along the south side of the estuary for closer views of the roosting terns, within which there might be hiding a skimmer or two. We ended up abandoning the car and fighting our way through head-high thorn-scrub in the crazy heat before coming to our senses and turning back, having seen neither the estuary nor any terns.

The next morning, while The Stid visited the police station, Chief and I reconnoitred the area around the golf course for pools which might hold Pygmy Geese. We could not find any but we did see a flock of seven fabulous Carmine Bee-eaters. We then picked up The Stid who was angry and upset because the Malindi police accused us of stealing his money. He had to return shortly afterwards so Chief, Tim and I wandered along Malindi seafront which was alive with shorebirds and terns, and right at the top of the wide beach was our first White-fronted Plover. We picked up The Stid again and took him to see the plover, which cheered him up.

Since we had now seen 600 species of bird and over 60 species of mammal during the last month, Chief, Tim and I felt we deserved a break from birding, so we, as well as a slightly reluctant Stid, took a short boat ride out to the coral reef just offshore, donned masks and snorkels and dived into another world, a world even more beautiful than the one above, where we glided and soared like eagles over the coral forest below before diving down and flying through a psychedelic paradise where the 'trees' were green *and* blue *and* red *and* every other colour and living amongst them was an unbelievable number and variety of fish, in a diversity of form, assortment of patterns and explosion of brilliant colours impossible to comprehend. From 'simple' deep blue mites called demoiselles through multicoloured spotted and striped and stippled angelfish and butterflyfish, and luminescent blue, green and purple spotted and striped parrotfish and triggerfish, to the most striking of all, the gorgeous, golden-yellow finned, Powder-blue Surgeonfish, it was a fantasy of shapes and colours, completed by crazy sea cucumbers, sea urchins, starfish and so on, the whole lot together making a staggering spectacle just a few feet below the surface of the warmest, clearest water imaginable.

It was hard to admit afterwards, when we were drying off and warming up on a sandbar with twenty Crab Plovers, but snorkelling over a coral reef as rich as that seemed at that moment in time to be even better than birding, for not only was the variety of fish so astonishing, they were almost all easy to see, and they were all living in such a small area of the warm Indian Ocean.

It was certainly a hell of a lot easier than birding Sokoke Forest which returned to for the final time, because we had an appointment with David Ngala, a forest officer based at Gedi Forest Station, who said he would show us the star bird of the forest, the Sokoke Scops Owl. We were not as confident as he was, especially when he turned up with what looked like a toy torch. As the black night got blacker we drove slowly inland, on a maze of tracks, deep into the dense forest. As well as the four of us there was David and his assistant squeezed into the car. When David asked us to stop we all clambered out of the car and listened carefully for a whistle but there was no whistle. Only cicadas, the ceaseless trills of cicadas, broke the silence. David walked on a bit then stopped and began whistling. His short series of 'too' whistles repeated every two seconds was a virtuoso rendition of the song of the Sokoke Scops Owl and a few minutes later a distant owl responded. David tried to entice the bird closer with more whistles but it was having none of it and eventually he said it was too far into the thick forest to try reaching it so we moved on.

The next owl we heard was singing closer to the track. We walked along until we were level with the bird and David told us he would try to lure it closer, perhaps to the edge of the forest where we might be fortunate enough to see it but after a lengthy duet between him and the owl the bird did not budge.

David then turned to address us and said, "Now we must enter the forest," adding after a pause, "Most visitors refuse to do this but if you want to see the owl you must."

"Why?" Chief said. "Why do they refuse?"

"Because there are Elephants and they are very dangerous if disturbed, especially at night, and there are Black Mambas ..."

"We've already seen one of them!" Chief interrupted.

"And Spitting Cobras," David continued, "But you should not be afraid because these dangerous animals feed on what nature provides, not us."

He was right. There was very little chance of bumping into Elephants and snakes, because they were bound to hear or smell us first, and absolutely no chance of seeing the owl unless we went in, so in we went. David and his assistant moved steadily and silently through the thorny undergrowth while we tried desperately to do the same but failed miserably, getting badly scratched and making a terrible racket as we crouched and scrambled with our backs bent through the tangle, in the sticky heat of a dark, dark night. When we reached David we were sweating profusely, feeling our cuts and rubbing insect bites, and he did not look very happy. All the noise had disturbed the bird and it had moved much farther into the forest. He politely asked us to be quieter on the next stretch and we tried our best but by the time we had got through the mass of spiky undergrowth to where he was, standing under the tree the bird was in, the damned thing had stopped singing. That was because it had moved and a minute or so later it started singing again, only, to our utter disgust, from all the way back where we had started.

David told us that the next time we had to do it right. We had to be as quiet as humanly possible moving through a thick black forest. If we were too noisy the owl would give up singing and would be impossible to relocate. So, we retraced our foolish steps with the utmost caution, as silently as we could, determined even to not breathe too heavily for fear of missing the bird we were so close to seeing. At last David told us to stop, to remain absolutely silent and to try and stand up straight so that we would be able to raise our binoculars to our eyes if he could find the bird with the light of his torch. One by one we found a break in the thorny tangle of twisted branches surrounding us where we could straighten up our aching backs and hold our binoculars ready to raise them. We stood stock still, the six of us, in that dark thick forest, in the middle of the hot African night, hardly daring to breathe, listening to the bird whistling every couple of seconds. It sounded like it was just above our heads, almost within touching distance, and I thought of it there, that rare and beautiful thing, so close and yet invisible in the black night, and I thought about that for what seemed like a long, long time but it was actually just a minute or so before David whispered, "Ok, I know where the bird is. I am going to switch my torch on now and shine the light by it. Look where I shine the light."

We could not believe he broke the silence when we were so close to the bird let alone his confidence in pin-pointing the thing. How could he know exactly where the bird was? How could he be sure he was going to shine the light straight on it? How could he do it with a toy torch in that blackness? Well, he did, he shone the weak beam of light and there was the bird, and it did not budge it just carried on whistling, just a few paces away not much above head-height, a tiny orange ball of feathers with two burning yellow eyes and silver droplets on its breast. It seemed oblivious to our presence and carried on singing, and there we stood, in the blackest forest of the night, our hearts thumping, sweat running around our wide eyes, staring at that tiny owl, trying desperately to take it all in, yet another moment of wonder. Then, in an instant, it was gone.

*Sokoke Scops Owl, Sokoke, Kenya, 26th January 1988*

The adventure was over for Chief, Tim and The Stid but not for me. I stayed in Malindi while they returned home, back to jobs, careers, houses and security, and I have to admit I was sad, lonely and scared for a few hours. Sad that a great adventure with my friends had come to an end and, suddenly alone with my thoughts, worried that I had made a rash decision to pack it all in, and anxious about how safe I was going to be travelling on my own. I was certainly afraid but I kept telling myself I was in Africa, I had made it that far, and, up to that moment, I had loved it, and, eventually, the feeling that I was going to love the rest of the trip, that so much wonder lay ahead, was so much stronger than the fear.

I slept nine hours straight that night and I stayed in bed for another hour in the morning, thinking about how wonderful it was not to have to jump up and get in the bloody car, and to be able to set off at my own pace, on foot. I took a long walk along the beach and over the raised coral reef down to Vasco de Gama Point and back. The reef was alive with birds, busy foraging in and around the shallow pools. I walked barefoot in a warm sea breeze among Black-headed Herons, Pied Kingfishers, Sooty Gulls, Saunders', Lesser Crested, Greater Crested, Gull-billed and Caspian Terns, Whimbrels, Common, Curlew and Terek Sandpipers, Lesser and Greater Sand Plovers, Sanderlings and White-fronted Plovers, then through trees and patches of scrub along the top of the beach where Yellow-collared Lovebirds, Lilac-breasted Rollers, White-throated Bee-eaters, Golden Orioles, Golden Palm Weavers and Collared Sunbirds lived.

This scene became familiar but always exciting to me during the two weeks I stayed in Malindi and I could still watch the birds while eating breakfast in *The Baobab* listening to M'bilia Bel, a soukous singer from the Congo who the owners loved. Her album *Beyanga* was on a loop all day long and the repetitive sections of the songs were so hypnotic I felt like I could sit there for the rest of the day after a long morning wander, drinking cold beer, eating, writing, reading and raising my binoculars now and again to look at one of the many birds on view on the beach and reef below.

*White-throated Bee-eater, Malindi, Kenya, 30th January 1988*

Malindi 'is for sybarites, bacchanalians and beach lovers' according to Geoff Crowther in *Africa on a shoestring*. I'm all three, if the beach is covered in birds, but the most pleasurable experience to be had in Malindi and one of the main reasons I stayed there was a visit to the coral reef.

Money was tight; it was 100 Shillings (about three British pounds) for a room for the night at the *Travellers Inn*, in the cheap part of town but still at the top of the beach, and the same for a trip to the reef with *Saloni Reef Boats*, the cheapest outfit I could find, so I couldn't go snorkelling every day, but I went every few. On my last visit I persuaded the boatmen, who by then I got on with quite well, to take everyone on board beyond the usual spots, to the best place they knew. It must have been a good part of the reef because they got in the water as well, and as soon as I put my head under the surface I knew I was in a very special place. Bright sunlight floodlit an underwater forest of six-foot-tall stacks of coral, mostly moss-like deep green and pastel blue. After swimming through shoal after shoal of gorgeous black, yellow and white striped and spotted butterflyfish, and purple parrotfish with luminous green lines, one of the boatmen showed me my first Giant Clam. As I examined it I saw a silver-spotted, maroon sea cucumber with a head of waving white tentacles. At the bottom of the shallow sea was a Blue-spotted Stingray, half-hidden in the white coral sand. It bolted off, showing turquoise spots on its grey-brown back and a very long tail. Along the top of an underwater cliff pulsating with life there was a Triggerfish which looked like a brown and orange striped rugby ball, the effect broken only by its busy orange pectoral fins and its powerful-looking stubby mouth, strong enough to crush crustaceans. It retreated into a dark crevice and I swam on, past Blue Demoiselles, thumb-sized fish, bright blue above and golden yellow below, with orange tails, aptly-named Humbugs, swimming sweets, superb Moorish Idols with streamers flowing from their dorsal fins and deep orange bridges at the base of their elongated snouts, long-nosed Bird Wrasses, indigo all over except for long, wavy aquamarine dorsal fins, my personal favourites the Powder-blue Surgeonfish, the most beautiful sky blue with long, glowing orange-yellow dorsal fins and black faces, and a staggering variety of other outrageous creatures.

*Powder-blue Surgeonfish and Threadfin Butterflyfish, Malindi, Kenya, 7th February 1988*

I followed the fish around their watery world until I could hold my breath no longer then I dived again and again before returning to the surface for the final time, gulping in the air before getting back on the boat and desperately trying to remember everything I saw but it was impossible, there was just too much to take in.

Malindi is an old Swahili town, dating back to the 14th century, although as Asian as it is African. The muezzin chants and wails the *adhan*, the Islamic call to prayers, several times each day. Through a loudspeaker it was very loud but once I had got used to it the wailing became strangely calming, even at first call at five o'clock in the morning. After the last call at dusk I would write up my notes of the day, and draw, and think about where to head to next. I thought about Tanzania and Turkana but soon realised I could afford neither and one reason I stayed on after my friends had left was because I knew that visiting all the sites we did in a month was going to be one hell of a rush, and, as well as wanting to explore new terrain, I wanted to return to at least one of the sites we had visited and get to know it a bit better. I couldn't afford to hire a vehicle so all the national parks were out of the question and my favourite place where it was possible to walk around in relative safety was Lake Naivasha so I determined to return there, but first the urge for somewhere new had to be satisfied and since we had seen all possible bee-eaters and rollers but missed one of the kingfishers I decided, having failed to find it around Malindi, and re-read my field guide, and heard marvellous tales about the place, to head north along the Kenyan coast to the island of Lamu, where I might just find the elusive Mangrove Kingfisher.

The Tana River Express bus to Lamu was no express, mainly because a *miraa* dealer was on board and he got out at almost every settlement to sell bundles of the plant which is chewed by many Africans to suppress hunger, stay awake and get mildly high. He laughed a lot, contagiously, and ended up with a bundle of notes bigger than his stash. Between times the bus sped along a dusty track through arid bush, lush bush and pawpaw plantations. After six hours we reached Mokowe, from where a ferry took me and many other people, mostly

Muslim women in their buibuis, the black cloth they use as a shawl, often covering all but their eyes, across a sparkling shallow channel to the island of Lamu, about 50 miles (80 km) south of Somalia. The ferry had to squeeze between several dhows, attractive traditional wooden boats with triangular sails, to get to the waterfront. I had been recommended a place to stay and headed straight there, ignoring the numerous cries from people wanting me to stay at their places. At *Castle Lodge* I was immediately shown to a room on the breezy third floor by a little bundle of happy energy called Kenga. The 'lodge' was a tall white building in the middle of the old stone town with narrow streets barely wide enough for the donkeys, and my shared balcony overlooked a small market where women sat by wooden tables packed with pawpaws, passion fruits, potatoes, mangos, tomatoes and bananas.

I loved Lamu. For a swim I walked south to Shela Beach, miles of pure white sand, and a few times it was just me and a White-fronted Plover there, but mostly I walked north, to a place I called Cemetery Creek, a small, square tidal inlet next to a leafy graveyard where after a week of laid-back birding I found a Mangrove Kingfisher, a bright blue, grey and black beauty with a big red dagger for a bill. It shared the mangroves and graveyard mango and palm trees with Chestnut-bellied, Malachite and Pied Kingfishers, and Carmine, Little and Madagascar Bee-eaters, while out on the mud a fine selection of shorebirds included Crab Plovers, White-fronted Plovers, Spur-winged Plovers, and Curlew and Terek Sandpipers. Sometimes a Caspian Tern or two would fly by town the same day I visited Cemetery Creek and I would fall asleep with a smile on my face because I had seen Crab Plover,

Carmine Bee-eater and Caspian Tern in the same day, more than enough to keep a birder like me happy.

Not a lot happens in a hurry on Lamu; even the birds seemed more relaxed than elsewhere, and after two weeks I thought I had better leave or I might end up spending two years there, so I bought a ticket, got on a boat, crossed the channel to the island of Manda, walked along a boardwalk through the mangroves and got on a plane to Malindi. The *Equator Airlines* forty-minute flight cost me six nights worth of accommodation but it was worth it. I asked the pilot of the eight-seater if I could sit next to him and he said yes. A Carmine Bee-eater flew across the airstrip then we were in the air looking down over Lamu, a sandy, palmy island with the small, flat-roofed town where I had lived a while nestled in palms. Beyond town were the mangrove swamps with muddy winding creeks where I had seen a Mangrove Kingfisher, and long sandy beaches washed by a clear turquoise ocean. To the south we flew over sand spits and reefs then the surprisingly sharp line between the brown silt of the Tana River spilling out of the land and the deep blue of the Indian Ocean, then Malindi came into view and we were soon down on the ground and that was that, another little adventure over.

The next day I took the Tana River Express bus south to Mombasa and booked a room for one night in a dilapidated tower block called the *Cosy Guest House*. It was incredibly hot, in the final build up to the rains, but it was not the heat, nor the humidity which kept me awake, it was the rock provided as a pillow. After a day wandering around the old town where I saw my first Purple-banded Sunbird in the grounds of Fort Jesus at the harbour entrance, I boarded the cream and maroon overnight train to Nairobi. A giant red moon rose and faded to blue as the train climbed away from the coast and I fell asleep to the 'chugg-chugg chak-chak' of metal wheels crossing metal tracks. The next afternoon I boarded another train, west from Nairobi. It took forty minutes to crawl past the Kibera slums on the western edge of the city; mile after mile of a makeshift mass of mud and wooden shacks with rusty corrugated iron roofs crammed tightly together, where people attracted to the big city with all its money and comforts lived in squalor and filth. There is no beauty there. It is all beyond, in the verdant forests clinging to the sides of the Great Rift Valley where deep green Cinnamon-chested Bee-eaters perch, in the acacia savanna that abounds with birds and animals, and on and around the lakes of the valley floor, where there is also an abundance of beautiful life, and where I was bound. Progress was slow down the steep face of the Limuru Escarpment where the train did not so much hug the slope as flirt with it. I shuddered when I heard gravel slipping down into the valley below as the weight of the long train passed over it and was relieved when it reached a cutting, on firm ground but so narrow that my head would have been knocked off had I continued to hold it outside the window. I wanted to look at the wonderful view, out across the African plain.

It was great to be back. I got off the train at Naivasha and crossed the road to *La Belle Inn* at the western edge of the small market town. In no time at all I negotiated what I considered to be a good price for a twelve day stay. The sun hammered down outside but Room 2 was large and cool and had a chair and a desk where I could write and sketch. I ate fresh croissants with my coffee first thing in the mornings and after birding all day dined of an evening on Black Bass or Nile Perch, almost always alone in the spacious restaurant with ten or so large tables laid with starched white tablecloths, shining cutlery and immaculate crockery, while three waiters stood quietly some distance away, gliding over from time to time to offer me another beer or whatever it was I appeared to need. I think I am as hardy as the next man, willing to put up with almost any discomfort, no matter how grim, in pursuit of my dreams, but now and again I like some relative luxury, made all the more pleasurable by hardships recently endured, especially when it costs next to nothing, and so I took it easy in *La Belle Inn*, reading about the birds I had seen during the day with a beer and a cigarette while my fresh fish was grilled in garlic and herbs, the only guest in the spotless twelve-room mansion virtually the whole time I was there. Then, after eating the delicious food, I would retire to my room where fine coffee was served while I finished writing up my notes and diary for the day.

The first night I went to bed early but I couldn't sleep. I was too excited about the morning. After breakfast I walked slowly through the wide belt of acacias that runs along the northeast shore of Lake Naivasha and was busy with birds, and out to the lake itself where birds virtually covered the muddy shoreline and shallows and open water as far as I could see. After a week of hard birding I felt I knew that little bit of Africa quite well but I was always looking for new nooks and crannies, because turning a corner in Kenya can be enough to see new, exciting and unexpected birds. One afternoon, while taking shelter under an acacia from a thundery downpour, I scanned a small ploughed field in a small patch of farmland I had not explored before and there at the far side was a beautiful little bird with a bluish crown, narrow white eyebrows, black face and gorgeous peachy-orange breast. It took a while to sink in but I eventually realized I was looking at my first ever White-throated Robin, a 'shy and skulking' species according to my field guide and one I never expected to see. The beauty was not only the 225th species I had seen in eight days at Lake Naivasha, it was my 500th new bird of the trip.

Day nine was the first day without a cool breeze. By the time I returned from the lake the heat had taken its toll. I woke up with a start at 3 p.m. after an hour of deep sleep. With only a few days left there was no time to waste. I headed for the acacias and some shade from which to watch the White-throated Robin again, and while sitting quietly in a real Acacia Avenue I thought I saw it, or another, until the shy bird in the shadows hopped into view and turned out to be a pretty Robin Chat, yet another new bird for me at Naivasha. Taking another break from my usual route on day ten I *did* see another White-throated Robin and added several more birds to the 'patch list' including Little Rock Thrush. Resting on a rock in that forested ravine in the rift valley wall a mile or so east of town yet another new bird for Naivasha appeared, in a flash. It was a phantom of a flycatcher with a slender ribbon of a silky white tail, four times the length of its body, swishing and swirling behind it as the bird darted and dashed from tree to tree with tremendous zest. Only briefly did it perch and then I saw its black chest, black head with a short crest, and waxy blue spectacles and bill. Then it was off again, in crazy pursuit of flies, flicking around the green ravine before me like something from another world. Even at Naivasha it was hard to believe such natural beauty could have evolved on planet Earth but there it was, plain to see; a fantastic white Paradise Flycatcher.

On day five I saw a staggering 165 different species of bird on my usual eight hour stroll to the lake and back, beating my previous best total for the number of birds seen in a day, 160, by bicycle at Bharatpur, India, a couple of years before, but I missed several species so I decided to try and see even more on day eleven. It began as usual, in the best possible way, with a Lilac-breasted Roller. Although I saw that individual bird every day I was at Naivasha I still stopped to have a good, long look at what may well have been the first one I ever saw, nearly three months before, on the day I arrived in Africa. Before reaching the acacia belt I had to face the kids shouting, "How are you!?!" and "Take a picture!" A few of them followed for a while as usual then I was free to walk alone through the scattered acacias growing out of the thirsty ground. The lovely big wide trees were always alive with birds such as black and white Tropical Boubous. Beyond the acacias there was a strip wispy grass where Crowned Plovers were in residence as usual. The lake was still a long way off, across less and less grass then mud, sun-baked into hexagonal blocks.

When I reached the hut on the shore I sat down on a dug-out with Charlie whose job it was to log the fish caught in the lake, especially the predatory Black Bass which had been introduced from North America and was thought to be depleting the stocks of the other introduced fish, such as Tilapia, a major food source for the local population.

Charlie was more concerned about the water levels. The lake had dried out completely in the past during natural droughts but the unregulated use of water to irrigate the increasing number of flower and vegetable farms around the lake was to the detriment of birds and other wildlife including Charlie's beloved Hippos which, while taking great care, he sometimes swam with. He told me there were still about 3000 of them in the lake and I saw plenty as I left Charlie behind and walked north along the shore in glorious sunshine, stopping constantly to scan the great mass of waterbirds and to make sure I had not strayed too close to the water where the Hippos were snoozing, or too near the bush to my right where some Buffalos had moved in, the two most dangerous large animals in Africa, responsible for more human deaths than any others.

I never failed to marvel at the waterbird spectacle of Lake Naivasha. The muddy shoreline was almost smothered with masses of pecking and probing plovers, sandpipers and stints. Just out from them, wading through the shallows, were many Avocets and Black-winged Stilts, with ibises, herons, egrets, African Spoonbills and Yellow-billed Storks, and, beyond them, flocks of flamingos. Out on the deeper water floated parties of giant Great White and Pink-backed Pelicans, and vast rafts of Fulvous Whistling and other ducks, amongst which dived lots of Little Grebes, while overhead there was a constant flight of foraging gulls, terns, martins, swallows and swifts, the whole lot, in the air, on the water and along the shoreline occasionally disturbed by a passing fish eagle. On the dry mud that particular day there were some Red-capped Larks and six Collared Pratincoles but there was no sign of the 60 Caspian Plovers present a few days before. The pratincoles flew around me, on long wings, gracefully catching flying insects, their chestnut underwings clearly visible against the black, ragged walls of the crater on top of Mount Logonot in the distant background.

It seemed I was in for another marvellous day, especially when I returned to the acacias, walked into a lovely glade and nearly bumped into four Giraffes, an unnerving but incredibly exciting experience on foot. I backed away but the gentle giants seemed at ease with my presence and after a few minutes taking stock of the situation they carried on tearing the leaves off the tops of the trees. I left them in peace - they seemed to exude peace - and carried on and came across a mixed party of Red-cheeked Cordon-bleus, Grey-backed Carmaropteras and a Robin Chat which were all very agitated about something, jumping anxiously from branch to branch and calling loudly and harshly, presumably scolding a predator. I moved forward very carefully because I thought it might be a snake and it was, curled up in some sticks in a small hollow in the dusty ground. It was a thick, black and golden snake about a metre long with a blunt nose and almost certainly a Puff Adder, the snake which kills more people in Africa than any other snake. I shuddered at the thought that I had been wandering about all over the place in those acacias for nearly two weeks in shorts and a threadbare pair of green deck shoes without socks, past snakes that rely on their markings for camouflage and strike when someone steps on them, rather than moving away when approached. Not anymore. After that, and thanks to those little birds, I stuck to the paths the locals used and checked the ground ahead on a regular basis, especially where there was a lot of leaf litter.

Back at the inn, in the early afternoon, I counted up how many species I had seen and after checking and re-checking I could hardly believe it was 154. After a quick coffee and cake I returned to the field, dodging the almost daily late afternoon downpours, to look for the White-throated Robin and I was delighted to find it was still present and therefore such a fine addition to what was already a very special day. On the nearby rugby pitch, sodden after a heavy shower, there were five Black-winged Lapwings with 30 Blacksmith Plovers and 20 Spur-winged Plovers.

I ended the day at the scarp just to the south of town where the cacti-covered rocky slopes and huge fig trees rising from their base supported a completely different avifauna from the acacia woodland a few hundred paces away. The hoped-for flurry of new birds for the day began with the resident Rufous-crowned Roller, a handsome brown and pale purplish bird I always enjoyed seeing, and continued with a Red-fronted Barbet, a striking Chestnut-bellied Kingfisher and a flock of colourful White-fronted Bee-eaters.

I climbed to the top of the scarp so I could look out level with the top of a fruiting fig tree where a flock of ten Green Pigeons had been present for several days. They almost perfectly matched the foliage of the fig tree and were difficult to pick out at first but once my eye was in I watched the gorgeous creatures gorging themselves on the figs, as they did day after day, between long periods of doing nothing, seemingly stupefied. Beyond them was the smooth, pale green sweep of acacias and Lake Naivasha about a mile away, there in the heart of Africa's Great Rift

Valley, where there were more birds than I had ever dreamed of. I sat on the edge of that scarp in the sunshine taking in the view and thinking about how fortunate I was to be where I was for a long while.

When I got up I walked back to the inn as darkness fell, happier than I had ever been in my life. I made straight for my table and after ordering my favourite Nile Perch I began drinking a cold beer, lit a cigarette and counted the birds up. I knew I had missed a few which I had seen on most of the days I had been at Naivasha but was horrified to discover I had not seen a single Pied Crow when all I needed to have done was scan the rooftops of the town. Shaking my head for forgetting I carried on counting and when I got to the end I shook my head again. I couldn't believe it but two more counts confirmed it. In eight and a half hours on foot in a tiny area by Lake Naivasha in Kenya I had seen Hippos and Giraffes, a Puff Adder, such iconic African birds as Lesser Flamingos, Goliath Herons, Crowned Cranes, African Fish Eagles, African Jacanas, Blacksmith Plovers, Lilac-breasted Rollers and Superb Starlings, some less celebrated African birds like Green Pigeons, White-fronted Bee-eaters and Chin-spot Batises, and a great long list of others including Great White and Pink-backed Pelicans, six more egrets and herons, eight more raptors, twenty-four shorebirds, Chestnut-bellied and Pied Kingfishers, African Hoopoes, Green Woodhoopoes, a White-throated Robin, Tropical Boubous, Brubrus and Purple Grenadiers, not forgetting more familiar birds getting ready to depart for more northern climes like myself including Wheatears and singing Willow Warblers, all helping to make a total of 175.

I threw my shoes in the bin the next afternoon sure I was going to stay in for the rest of my last day at Naivasha and pack, ready for the matatu journey to Nairobi in the morning. The canvas shoes were tatty and torn after three months in Africa but with an hour of light left and no rain I took them back out of the bin for one last look at the birds I could have gone on watching for ever.

*Blacksmith Plover, Naivasha, Kenya, 16th March 1988*

*Blue-headed Pitta, Danum, Borneo, 1st January 1991*

7

# MALAYA, BORNEO, SULAWESI and JAVA

After a lazy spring and summer reflecting on Africa I got a job with the London Wildlife Trust again. I was appointed manager of the Thamesmead Wildlife Project and after two years I had enough money to fund a long trip to Malaysia and Indonesia with Chief, the affable ape I had been birding with for ten years, and Al who I had travelled with to see many a rare bird in Britain. Chief is more or less happy to see whatever bird comes his way although there are some birds he loves more than others, especially owls. However, if he doesn't see a particular species like an owl that he really wants to see on a foreign trip then so be it; he shrugs his shoulders and moves on. Al, on the other hand, hates dipping (missing) birds he has made a special effort to see. He wants to see them all and if he doesn't see a special bird he gets angry, upset and despondent, and I feared he was going to do a lot of dipping on this trip, because we would be spending most of our time looking for shy forest birds which may prove impossible to see.

At dusk we walked into an invisible wall of heat and humidity outside Kuala Lumpur airport in Malaya, a truly tropical shock having flown out of England on a cold, grey and grim December day. We were too hot and bothered to haggle for a long time over how many ringgit we should pay for a long-distance taxi, the most reasonably-priced means of transport in Malaysia, so we were soon sitting in an old but air-conditioned *Mercedes*, southbound 90 miles (150 km) to a tiny patch of remnant lowland rainforest in Pasoh Forest Reserve, on a pretty good road which ran through mile after mile of palm plantations where once there was forest full of the birds we could hardly wait a moment more to look for.

It was ten o'clock at night when we arrived at the reserve headquarters. There were several wooden buildings in a clearing but there was not a single light on and not a soul about so we got into our sleeping bags on a veranda and tried to get some sleep before the first dawn. Thanks to the whirling spirals of mosquitoes we had to bury our heads in our bags so it was way too hot and sweaty to sleep and a very uncomfortable couple of hours passed before a park guard turned up and let us into the hostel. It was midnight but Al decided to make some coffee and so we sat there drinking coffee, buzzing with excitement and still trying to come to terms with the incredible racket coming from the cicadas in the surrounding forest. Sleep seemed highly unlikely but once that last mozzie, the one that waits until its victim is just about to drift off into delightful sleep before buzzing around their ears, sounding like a dentist's drill, once it had been located and dealt with, we managed a few fitful hours.

At dawn we were outside in the clearing with our hands on our binoculars, ready. A flock of stunning Scarlet Minivets foraged in the trees and we watched two Greater Racquet-tailed Drongos, glossy dark blue-black birds with very long outer-tail feather shafts ending in twisted pendants, while a pair of White-handed Gibbons yelled out their wonderfully wild hooting duet in the distance. Then we breached the leafy wall around the clearing and entered the tall, thick, damp forest on a narrow trail, brushing through the wet undergrowth and squeezing past slippery tree trunks, with Al out front, Chief behind him and me at the back. We walked very slowly and as quietly as possible, being very careful not to tread on and crack any twigs for fear of scaring off any birds on or near the trail, looking hard for any movement, any sign of birds, but it was an incredibly frustrating morning. Very few birds were calling or singing and when we did stand stock still for ages, waiting for a bird we could hear to break cover it rarely did and if it did the damned thing usually just flashed from sapling to sapling or tree to tree, way too fast for us to focus our binoculars on it. We knew the birding would be tough in such forest but we also knew the best birds were the toughest birds especially the forest floor skulkers and it was those we were concentrating on, notably the colourful Garnet Pitta and the rarely seen Rail Babbler. During the first two days at Pasoh we never saw, never heard, never even thought we would see or hear either, and we even began to think there were none in that damned forest.

There were more leeches than birds. A howl from Al broke the depressing silence of the seemingly bird-less forest the first morning. Chief and I looked at him looking at his socks. White at dawn they were now red, with blood, and his ankles were covered in leeches. We looked around and we could see more coming, looping rapidly toward us from every direction, some on to our boots or gaiters and some beyond there, on our trousers, and one under my shirt on my stomach which I burnt off. They were even in the hostel when we got back and one managed to reach Chief's mug on a shelf at chest height, and, perish the thought, was nearly swallowed in a cup of coffee. Later, some students from the University of Kuala Lumpur turned up and let us use some of their *Baygon*, the local potion, and it was very satisfying to watch the bastard leeches wriggling in disgust as they reached the potent insecticide which we had sprayed on our boots and gaiters.

One morning we saw a gorgeous blue and white male Siberian Blue Robin, a tiny bright green button of a bird with a red bib called a Blue-crowned Hanging Parrot, and a pair of Green Ioras, the male a glorious glowing deep green with two big, bold white bars across the wings. On a late afternoon stroll we bumped into several fantastic birds including a stunning male Scarlet-rumped Trogon, all oranges and reds against the greens and yellows of the forest leaves, a Banded Broadbill with startling yellow centres to the dark wing feathers, another beauty with a blue bill, and a lovely maroon back, that was a male Japanese Paradise Flycatcher, and a beautiful deep green and yellow Blue-winged Leafbird. All wonder stuff but not what we were concentrating on.

We also failed to track down many nightbirds for which Pasoh was renowned. The only owl we heard was a hooting Barred Eagle Owl but we couldn't see it. The main sound at night, and during the day, was the incredible insect din and it took some getting used to. There were thousands of them and close up, some cicadas seemed to be as loud as road drills. When they started up on tree trunks next to the trails at head height it was necessary to move several paces away to protect our ears.

'Tuk-Wee-oo, tuk-Wee-oo' Malaysian Eared Nightjars called as we made our way back into the forest at first light on our third and final day. The babblers were busy and a Rufous-tailed Shama, a long-tailed blue and rufous thrush, was chasing insects on the trail. We also saw an azure blue male Black-naped Monarch, four Black Bazas, small black and white birds of prey, circling over a clearing, and two Chestnut-breasted Malkohas clambering about in a dense vine; large, long-tailed birds, dark green above and dark chestnut below with red featherless faces. Once again, there was no sound nor sight of Garnet Pittas though, and only a few, tantalising, long, drawn-out whistles of a Rail Babbler which produced a sudden flow of adrenalin, soon replaced by increasing amounts of frustration and disappointment as we failed to locate the elusive creature. We would have been very fortunate to have seen the pitta outside its breeding season when it is, on the whole, silent, but, ever the optimists we thought we had a small chance of seeing a Rail Babbler, especially if we came across a calling bird. We were usually fortunate in life but not this time, so we were glad to see the big *Mercedes*, our long-distance taxi, trundle into the clearing, and to clamber in and clear off, to our next destination.

It was a long drive through rubber and palm plantations to Fraser's Hill, a resort surrounded by steep enough slopes to keep loggers at bay. The cool, montane forest spared the axe looked fantastic from The Gap, at the bottom of a steep five mile (8 km) long single track road to the top of the hill, passable uphill one hour, downhill the next. We missed an uphill hour by ten minutes but while waiting for the next hour we were very fortunate to see a pair of Helmeted Hornbills glide along the forested slope above us. The huge birds, over a metre long, were a magnificent sight, their long, mainly white tails trailing behind their broad, mainly black wings. Local birder Nash's house, where many visiting birders stayed, was full and it took us a long time to find a room for the night, a small, dark, damp hovel attached to *The Steakhouse* where it seemed no one else was prepared to stay.

Dawn the next morning was chilly and misty. We were in position at first light on the famous Bishop's Trail hoping to see a Rufous-naped Pitta but we left a few hours later having spent more time removing leeches than watching birds. A flock of fabulous Silver-eared Mesias cheered us up. The small, orange, yellow, crimson, grey-green and black birds looked even brighter than in the painting on Plate 45 of *A Field Guide to the Birds of South-East Asia*, one of the most mouth-watering plates in Ben King's *Magnum opus*. Up at High Pines, the house on top of the hill, we were hoping to find the Cutia, on the aforementioned plate, and we spent a lot of time looking for it, alas without success. We fared better with the Plate 45 on the long walk downhill to the waterfalls, seeing the striking White-browed Shrike Babbler on the way and the very bright yellow and chestnut Black-eared Shrike Babbler on the way back. We did not see the Red-bearded Bee-eater which we had been informed liked to hunt from the forest edge at the bottom of the rubbish tip. There was certainly no shortage of insects for it to catch there, too many for our liking, and the smell in the searing heat was also too much to bear so we began the long haul back uphill, seeing yet another gorgeous bird, a flock of three Fire-tufted Barbets, green above, yellow-green below, with black and red tufts on their foreheads.

After Cutia eluded us again the next morning we watched a male Mugimaki Flycatcher in Nash's garden while he advised us to spend the afternoon walking the Telekom Loop since we were also very keen to see Long-tailed Broadbill, Blue Nuthatch and Sultan Tit. We dipped the lot but we did see some Banded Leaf Monkeys, a pair of Large Niltavas, the male of which was a smashing bird, velvety blue-black with shiny dark blue patches on its head, shoulders and rump, and a male Siberian Thrush, another blue-black beauty which perched perfectly still in the canopy enabling me, through my telescope, to detect some tiny black dots in one of its snow-white eyebrows.

Along the gloomy Bishop's Trail the following morning we confirmed that Rusty-naped Pitta was still on the growing list of rare and or spectacular birds we couldn't find. We did see two Siamangs; big, black gibbons with long hair and very long arms which they extended gracefully to help them move very slowly through the thickest part of the canopy they could find to hide from us. We then made sure Cutia remained on the same list as Rusty-naped Pitta and so on before packing our bags. We had seen some great birds on Fraser's Hill but to tell the truth we were fed up with forest birding and glad to be on our way, with our trusty *Mercedes* driver, this time down to the hot lowlands of the Malay Peninsula and some welcome open country birding. I was sound asleep in the back when a shout from Al woke me. "Bee-eaters!" he yelled and soon we were watching ten Blue-tailed Bee-eaters which were busy chasing bees, close enough to see the yellow and chestnut throats on the gorgeous sleek and green birds with long pale blue tails. The ultimate aim of the trip for me was to see the four new species of bee-eater which were possible so I was particularly pleased to be watching the first.

Before dark, we had one hour around the pools at Kuala Selangor Nature Park on the coast. More Blue-tailed Bee-eaters hunted from some dead trees in a swamp where there was also an absolutely stunning Black-capped Kingfisher with a big, bold, red bill, black cap, white collar, deep blue back and rufous belly. What with lots of other birds and Brahminy Kites and White-bellied Sea Eagles overhead it was a wonderful evening, especially after so many days dipping forest-floor skulkers. When 120 Blue-tailed Bee-eaters flew over our thatched hut on the way to their roost at dusk I was even happier and I went to sleep thinking I would be happy whether I saw a Mangrove Pitta or not the next day, because I knew I would be watching bee-eaters and having become reacquainted with them again after so long I was even more certain they were my favourite birds.

The next day I revelled in the reprieve from forest birding around the open lagoons, marshes and mangroves of the Malacca Strait, lapping up the many colourful, easy-to-see birds, in glorious sunshine. We didn't see Mangrove Pitta of course but there was more than enough wonder to keep me happy; bee-eaters in the flat low morning light, Black-capped, Collared, Common, Smyrna and Stork-billed Kingfishers, egrets, eagles and a surprisingly smart, little, long-tailed bird with striking black and white bands and bars called a Forest Wagtail, not forgetting some Smooth-coated Otters and Silvered Leaf Monkeys.

At dusk we got a taxi to Kuala Lumpur airport where Al charmed us on to an earlier flight. The only trouble was we had to get to the other terminal sharpish so Al insisted we put our rucksacks on and walk, in the debilitating heat and humidity of a South-East Asian night. Once at Terminal 2, a hot and bothered Chief was none too pleased to discover that we could have got a taxi for virtually nothing but he forgave Al when we were at 39,000 feet (11,890 metres) above the South China Sea savouring the prospect of an extra day on Borneo. After a few hours sleep on a pavement outside the terminal at Kota Kinabalu airport we got in the first long-distance taxi to turn up and headed to Mount Kinabalu, the highest peak between the Himalayas and New Guinea, rising to 13,435 feet (4095 metres). The giant slab of rock with a craggy top dominated the scene as we skirted the South China Sea, dotted with islands and cetaceans, before turning east and heading inland to the mountain national park where the staff in charge of accommodation seemed determined to turn us away because we had not booked in advance. While they discussed the situation behind closed doors we looked for birds in the luxuriant headquarters garden and saw an absolutely brilliant male Scarlet Sunbird, iridescent scarlet from head to tail apart from the silky white belly and without doubt one of the most stunning birds we had ever seen.

After a couple of hours we were pleased to be told we could stay in the staff quarters so we dashed down there, threw our rucksacks on our bunks and headed for the Kiau View Trail, then the Silau Silau Trail, in search of Whitehead's Broadbill, Whitehead's Trogon and Whitehead's Spiderhunter, three spectacular Bornean endemics named after the British explorer naturalist John Whitehead who wrote up some of his experiences in *The Exploration of Kina Balu, North Borneo*, which was published in 1893. We were at Kina Balu now but we could not find any of 'his' birds and very few others. It seemed as though Borneo's forests were as bereft of birds as the Malay Peninsula's. It was only at the end of the Silau Silau Trail at the forest edge where there was any avian life. We saw a pair of Blue-and-white Flycatchers followed by a pair of White-crowned Forktails, black-and-white but brilliant birds with pristine, silk-like plumage.

The next morning we set out on the long Liwagu River Trail, a climb of over a thousand feet (300 metres), up through a misty, mossy forested ravine on a narrow trail littered with fallen trees, alongside a small rocky river, which took four hours to traverse. Grey Wagtails, familiar from rivers so many thousands of miles away back home, flitted from rock to rock, but we saw little else until we neared the end of the trail, where a big wave of birds moved through at eye level and contained at least six Fruithunters, soft grey, thrush-sized birds with broad black breast bands, dull yellow throats and black masks, as well as several other endemics, but the best birds were two male White-browed Shrike Babblers, seen from above where we got a rare glimpse of their golden tertial feathers folded across their lower backs.

There was no sign of any of Whitehead's famous birds again the following morning and we saw little else during a dark and dank dawn walk along the Kiau View Trail. It was our last chance because the ambitious itinerary, designed by a naive me, demanded we move on. We hauled our rucksacks up the horrendous hill to the headquarters wondering how many more mega birds we were going to miss. Climbing the final steps there was a tall man at the top, in his forties or fifties, with a pair of binoculars around his neck. A quick chat and we left our rucksacks in the office and, already out of breath, followed his long strides up the hill back to the Kiau View Trail where he had seen a Whitehead's Broadbill a short time before. 'The bird frequents the lower branches of big trees' Whitehead wrote and our first Whitehead's Broadbills, two of them, were sitting quietly in just such a place. John Edge became a firm friend from the moment we set eyes on those resplendent green birds, the first mega we had seen since arriving in South-East Asia eleven days before. John, an Englishman, was on a quick trip to Borneo, a short hop from Hong Kong where he had been living and working for twelve years. He was keen to hook up with three more pairs of eyes and he kindly offered us a lift in his hire car to our and his next destination, Poring Hot Springs. Fortunately for us the car had not arrived on time but John was accustomed to the precise efficiency of a Chinese metropolis not the laid-back Malay way and as precious birding time wasted away he made more and more visits to the office to enquire as to the car's whereabouts. "I'm going to shoot someone in a minute," he said on emerging from the office once again, a phrase which stuck in our minds, probably because after spending a few days with the level-headed lawyer it seemed so out of character. Birding ... it makes normally sane people go a bit crazy.

It was around noon when the car finally turned up, a tiny *Proton*, Malaysia's national car, which the four of us with all our gear took a while to squeeze into. Although John could hardly move for rucksacks we were soon at Poring where we had time for a long wander and we saw a pair of Maroon-breasted Flycatchers, one of only two species in the *Philentoma* genus. I tried to soothe my weary feet in the sulphurous springs but the water was too hot for me.

Our first full day in the lowland rainforest of Borneo began well, with the large Straw-headed Bulbul and a pair of Red-naped Trogons. We then climbed up to the Canopy Walkway, swing-bridges tied between towering tree trunks up to 130 feet (40 metres) above the forest floor. It took some getting used to but then it felt wonderful to be in the rainforest canopy where so many birds spend most of their time, birds like aptly-named, dazzling deep blue and jet black thrush-sized Fairy Bluebirds. As exciting was a huge, almost ethereal, lacy white butterfly which floated oh so slowly by and a flying lizard which glided on to a trunk next to us at some speed, gripping it and closing its 'wings', the extended membranes between its elongated ribs, instantly. Back at ground level we found ourselves in the midst of a big flock of birds that included two cracking Chestnut-backed Scimitar Babblers, a strange Crested Jay and a stunning Black-and-red Broadbill with a massive, wide bill, bright blue above and yellow below. The day came to a fitting end when Al spotted three dinky Black-and-yellow Broadbills, extraordinary creatures, smaller than sparrows, with blue bills, big yellow eyes in black heads, white collars, black upperparts liberally sprinkled with bright yellow streaks, and delicate pink underparts.

The broadbills were so good we went to look at them again first thing the next morning, with the telescope. We then climbed the steep trail up toward the Langganan Waterfall in the faint hope of seeing the endemic Blue-banded Pitta but the blue and red beauty remained silent and hidden in the thick forest. However, just before leaving Poring we did enjoy grilling a pair of colourful Rufous-collared Kingfishers.

We had still not seen a pitta but Borneo seemed to be bursting with birds we had dreamed of seeing for years and we didn't want to leave Poring but we had a flight to catch in Kota Kinabalu the next day and John was heading there so we joined him. He took us to a coastal lagoon he had already been to, not far out of town, where a quick scan revealed our first Grey-tailed Tattler and Long-toed Stints, the latter looking like miniature Wood Sandpipers with their long yellow legs and long necks, and easy to pick out from the more numerous Red-necked Stints with their short black legs, short necks, and pale grey and white plumage. I love shorebirds and I was enjoying myself but John also knew a good place to look for Blue-throated Bee-eaters. He had a flight to catch so he dropped us off at Signal Hill, known locally as Bukit Bendera. On leaving, he refused to accept a single ringgit for all his help but he did receive three long handshakes for his splendid company. Walking downhill past some White-breasted Woodswallows it was not long before we saw the startling blue rump and tail of our first Blue-throated Bee-eater, as it flew gracefully to the top of a dead tree. There it was joined by another and through the telescope we were able to enjoy the birds with pale chocolate hoods, black masks, green bodies and wings, and lovely soft blue throats. Thanks to some music blasting from a nearby shack I was able to dance on the spot to celebrate seeing yet another member of my favourite bird family. After some Nasi Goreng, fried rice, in the quiet backstreets of Kota Kinabalu, we returned to the shore and shorebirds of the South China Sea before heading to the airport where we slept on the restaurant floor once Chief had helped to rid the establishment of guests by looking rather overenthusiastically for a rat he had seen scuttle under the buffet table.

After an early morning one hour flight to Lahad Datu on the east side of Borneo we got a taxi to the Yayasan Sabah office where we obtained our permits and arranged transport for a seven-night stay in Danum Valley. In town we got the supplies in; cooking oil, salt, sugar, coffee, bread, rice, eggs, tins of sardines, beans and Beef Rendang, the spicy local favourite, bananas, oranges, a pineapple, biscuits, chocolate, a long fruitcake and 24 bottles of *Anchor* beer, amounting to one box of food and two of beer. After a long wait we travelled into Danum at speed, along a pot-holed, corrugated track through sheets of rain, in a pick-up driven by a maniac with little regard for the old, rusty, long-nosed, seventy-ton trucks thundering out of the valley with full loads of logs in the opposite direction, although he had no choice to swerve off the track a few times in order to avoid head-on collisions with the monsters. We could make out, through the mud-splattered windows, a lot of felled forest and so it was a rather depressing two hours we spent traversing the 40 miles (70 km) to Danum Valley Field Centre. That, to our great relief, appeared to be surrounded by the most wonderful forest in the world.

Borneo's lowland rainforest is possibly not only the oldest on Earth but the tallest as well, the ancient trees forming a canopy 200 feet (61 metres) above the leaf litter, with some emergent trees rising to a staggering 277 feet (84 metres), and the 169 square miles (438 square kilometres) in the Danum Valley Conservation Area is one of the largest, most important expanses left in South East Asia albeit only part of a 3860 square mile (10,000 square kilometre) logging concession, some of which had already been turned over to palm oil and timber plantations. As well as a wide variety of mammals including Orangutan the astonishing diversity of birds present in the pristine forest is surpassed only in lowland Amazonia and despite our incredibly frustrating experiences with forest birding in Asia up to that point we could not wait to get in there. Unfortunately only an hour of daylight remained so we only had time to walk the short distance to the long swing footbridge over the Segama River, where there was a group of Swedish birders waiting for a Red Giant Flying Squirrel to glide across the river, as it did at dusk most evenings. We didn't see it but some sleek Silver-rumped Swifts zoomed past us low down over the river and when it was nearly dark a crepuscular Bat Hawk drifted over. Back at the Field Centre the rest of the Swedish party were watching a Buffy Fish Owl that was perched on one of the posts holding up the badminton net, waiting to pounce on some of the thousands of beetles, moths and other insects attracted by the court floodlights. The net was covered in the most extraordinary insects including moths the size of our hands, and below the net were a few Rhinoceros Beetles with heavily armoured bodies as big as our thumbs, and two horns, a long one curving back from the head and a shorter one curving forward from the thorax.

Danum Field Centre's main research area is a grid of trails, marked at 100 metre intervals, in primary forest across the Segama swing bridge. At dawn we were in there, searching hard for our first pittas. We saw none but other great birds included a small group of Dusky Broadbills which were not the prettiest of birds, being basically brown, but they did have extraordinarily broad pinkish hooked bills. They were certainly not as attractive as Red Leaf Monkeys, a large troop of which adorned a medium-sized tree. Returning to the forest in the afternoon, with four of the Swedish party, we concentrated on looking for Banded, Garnet and Giant Pittas, all of which had been seen by other members of their party and all of which were not seen by us. Two Garnet Pittas were calling to each other either side of one trail, both very close, but try as we did, from every angle including standing up, crouching down and even lying down, we could not see them. We heard three more but, despondent, didn't look for them for long.

Al and I decided to try the North Trail while Chief headed elsewhere. Near the end of the trail we were standing listening to an unknown bird, possibly a pitta, whistling when another, very brightly-coloured bird hopped out of the gloom into the open on the forest floor and lit the place up like a flash. It jumped up on to a low branch in full view and we were astonished to see that it was a glorious male Blue-headed Pitta. The short-tailed bird, about the size of a small thrush only rounder, was so richly coloured it was hard to believe that such a jewel could live in that forest and yet be seen so rarely. Its azure cap sparkled above a broad black mask and white throat, its back was deep red-brown and its belly shiny dark blue. It was brilliant. Al and I were ecstatic; day one at Danum and we had seen our first pitta, anywhere in the world, and from what I had seen in books, the best pitta of all. Poor Chief; we met him on the bridge and he had not even glimpsed a pitta. Still, we all saw the largest 'flying' squirrel on planet Earth. The dark red creature, which must have been nearly a metre square with the membranes between its legs stretched to maximum, sprung from the trunk of a forest giant and sailed over us, losing several metres in height before landing perfectly on another trunk the other side of the river, about thirty paces away, and it made an astonishing sight.

We spent the whole morning of day two at Danum on the West Trail and could hardly believe our good fortune when we saw a rare and extremely shy male Great Argus, a fancy pheasant with elongated wings and tail. The tail was easily over a metre long and it bounced up and down slightly as the giant bird walked slowly out of the forest on to, along and across the trail. We were also very pleased to see a Chestnut-naped Forktail, a striking black, white and chestnut bird which lives along shaded forest streams. Red-naped and Scarlet-rumped Trogons were also worthy of prolonged stops and, on our return, near the bridge, a female Blue-headed Pitta, deep chestnut-red with a blue tail, hopped across the trail just a few paces in front of us. After a dip in the lovely, cool waters of the gently flowing river in the midday heat, I birded alone for four hours, seeing very little. I arrived at the river when the six o'clock cicada started up, the loudest cicada in the valley, and watched the flying squirrel shimmy up its favoured launching tree but a good half an hour after dark it still had not flown so I carried on back to the hostel where Al and Chief were sound asleep and I had to wake them up for their baked bean curry.

The Swedish party left at half past three in the morning, making a tremendous racket as they did so and then the rain hammered down till dawn so we were not at our peak when we got up. A pair of White-crowned Shamas, long-tailed blue and red beauties, foraging on the garden lawn while we ate two fried eggs for breakfast bucked us up, as did a pair of magnificent Rhinoceros Hornbills which flew along the river, both with eye-catching red and yellow upwardly curved casques on top of their big pale bills. The Swedes were the only other visitors staying at the Field Centre. Now they were gone we knew we would be the first along the West Trail so we tried harder than ever to walk along it quietly, watching where we stood in order to avoid cracking fallen twigs, but the ground was squelchy after the rain and the leeches were out in force so it was difficult to be completely silent. Nevertheless, at regular intervals we scoured the trail ahead very carefully with our binoculars. We didn't see any pittas, and very little else, for a long, long time, and when we stopped for the umpteenth time to scan the trail again, to no avail, we looked at each other, grimaced and shook our heads.

Our spirits were lifted when a slow-moving wave of birds came by. A stunning blue and red male Bornean Blue Flycatcher and two Banded Broadbills held my attention until Al said sharply, "That was a bee-eater!" I searched frantically for it with my binoculars while insisting Al repeated what he saw, where he saw it and what it did, and there it was, my first Red-bearded Bee-eater, perched right out in the open, for the whole world to see including me, the person who wanted to see it more than anyone else in the whole world. The basically pale green bird was perched very upright, its yellow undertail with black trim the first thing to catch the eye, then it was the slightly shaggy, red 'beard' then the rather strange pink forehead in front of its big yellow eyes, making it altogether the strangest-looking bee-eater I had ever seen.

We, me especially, continued happily westward and soon came to a huge fruiting fig tree alive with bright green barbets and leafbirds, blue and black Fairy Bluebirds, and Bornean Gibbons. To ease the pain in my neck I lay on my back on a fallen log and looked up into the broad canopy with my binoculars. There must have been a hundred birds up there, and who knows how many gibbons because they were so difficult to count as they were so shy, although I did watch one walk along a thin branch, well over a

*Black-and-yellow Broadbill, Danum, Borneo, 3rd January 1991*

hundred feet above me, with its long arms hanging down by its sides, with such glorious unconscious confidence.

After a break during the middle of the day we went to a watchtower overlooking a tall tree at the forest edge, seeing a Blue-throated Bee-eater on the way, and to our great delight the afternoon flew by in the company of some incredible birds, most filling the view of the telescope, including a glowing Green Broadbill, some shimmering Fairy Bluebirds, a pair of Ruby-cheeked Sunbirds, a pair of Violet Cuckoos, a White-fronted Falconet and a fabulous Black-and-yellow Broadbill perched a few paces away at eye-level. At dusk there were even more insects at the badminton net than usual, hundreds of them, mostly moths, of all shapes, sizes, colours and Picasso patterns, watched over by the huge yellow eyes of the almost tame Buffy Fish Owl. Standing out amongst even the Rhinoceros Beetles and the silky, black and white moths almost the width of my hand was an even bigger moth, a masterpiece of nature's art with the most beautiful hues of buff and purple, and translucent triangles in its wings, called an Atlas Moth.

On a morning stroll along the forest edge to the watchtower and back I saw a lot more birds than I would have done in the dark depths of the interior, not least two Red-bearded Bee-eaters, as well as a Blue-throated Bee-eater, three Black Hornbills, and three Rhinoceros Hornbills. In the afternoon we undertook the up down up down trek along the East Ridge Trail in search of Orangutan. We had been informed by a park ranger that the great ape builds a 'nest' from branches and foliage to sleep in at night, a bed in effect, and these luxurious platforms were worth looking out for because an Orangutan often stays nearby during the day. We saw no beds and no apes, and very few birds before returning to the steamy grid for the last hour or so of light. Chief still longed to see a pitta and he still did when it got dark.

The drawn-out whistle of the Garnet Pitta was driving us crazy and we were so frustrated by one calling just in from the trail and yet remaining hidden that we crashed into the forest after it and the bird just carried on whistling and we were sure that we were standing right next to it and that we were going to see it any second but we just could not see the bastard! Our first Diard's Trogon and Narcissus

Flycatcher, as well as a large Asian Brown Tortoise and a rare white beetle were some compensation, I suppose.

Four days gone, two to go and Chief still had not seen a single pitta so during a committee meeting with a beer we decided to change our tactics and go it alone, hoping there would be more chance of bumping into pittas on the trails if only one of us was walking quietly along one instead of three. At dawn Al headed to the Rhino Ridge Trail in search of Blue-banded Pitta, Chief wandered aimlessly into the grid, and I determined to lay eyes on a Garnet Pitta if it killed me. At the start of the West Trail I turned north and almost immediately heard a Garnet Pitta. Steeling myself for the fight, telling myself to 'keep calm, remain patient, this time I *will* see it, if I persevere', I listened very carefully until I was sure I had pinpointed exactly where the maddening whistle was coming from. Then I scanned the ground and low branches with my binoculars, from every angle, then I lay down on the ground, despite the leeches, and looked through the undergrowth, then I tried from the standing position again; nothing. There was nothing else for it, I crashed in, only for the bird to stop whistling, and that was that, there was no way I was going to see the bird if it stopped calling.

Frustrated and fuming I moved on, finally getting a decent view of a Fluffy-backed Tit Babbler, a small, rich brown bird with bare blue skin around its eyes, though I never saw the 'fluff', the elongated feather shafts on the flanks and lower back. I also saw a very odd-looking cat-sized animal cross the trail in front of me. It was grey with dark spots and it had two bold black bands across its white throat and chest, and I think it must have been a Malay

Civet. Along the North Trail I heard a very interesting disyllabic whistle coming from the ground, or so it seemed, and so began the wait, and the hope, that the bird might actually pop into view. After fifteen minutes or so - I had no watch - the bird stopped calling and I heard a flutter to my left. Seeing something move on the ground I raised my binoculars as fast as I could, thinking, 'this is it, I'm going to see a pitta!', but what I saw was a very strange-looking bird, a dark-capped, pale-faced, brown-backed, short-tailed bird with bold, broad white streaks on its black underparts. It was a Bornean Wren Babbler, a fine bird and "as good as any pitta!" I said to myself, but I was in denial.

It was so hot in the middle of the day all pittas were fast asleep so I wedged myself in a relatively fast-flowing stretch of the cool Segama River and with just my head above the rippling water looked up at the trees and wallowed in the satisfaction of being there in that rainforest full of birds in Borneo. I may have seen only a few of them but at least I was there, trying, and despite the pittas, the damned pittas, I was actually, loving almost every minute of it. I sat on a hot rock to dry off in the sunshine and returned to the fray. That pitta was heard but not seen and once again that was the story of my afternoon. Al fared much better and was very happy because he had seen Blue-banded Pitta, Garnet Pitta and Bornean Bristlehead. Chief was unhappy, well, as unhappy as Chief ever could be. He still had not seen a pitta and we had one day left.

It is very exciting looking for a new bird in a new place, one that I have dreamed of seeing for years, and I was quite pleased the Garnet Pitta had outwitted and outmanoeuvred me so far, because if I did see it on the last day then it would be all the more thrilling for the chase. That was what I was thinking about in the first light of the next morning, while standing alone on the North Trail. 'This is it, the last chance.' I heard nothing, not even a distant whistle, so I headed for the Rhino Ridge Trail hoping to see Blue-banded Pitta and Bornean Bristlehead, and seeing an extraordinary Greater Mouse Deer instead, a deer the size of a rabbit with very thin and long back legs and a cute triangular face with a tiny black nose.

When I bumped into Chief he told me he had just seen a Bornean Bristlehead and a Dwarf Kingfisher but both birds had flown by the time I took a look. We parted and tired of walking as silently as possible I began clodhopping back to the river only to look up ahead and see a bloody Banded Pitta stood right in the middle of the trail. It was a relatively drab female but it was a pitta! Encouraged and excited I returned to the North Trail instead of heading back to base and I saw quite a few birds, and when I was nearly back at the bridge I heard a Garnet Pitta.

In a last ditch effort I decided to 'go in', to leave the trail, and I followed the bird as it moved slowly away from me, deeper into the forest, with me taking great care to try and remember the exact direction back to the trail, until I was about fifty paces or so in and it seemed like I was about to step on the bloody bird. It was calling so close I could *feel* its presence but I still couldn't see it. The bird then stopped whistling and despite scanning the forest floor and low branches very carefully I had no confidence of seeing it, so I returned, sweating and severely disappointed, to the trail, only for the bird to start calling again.

This time I went in with gusto, crashing through the undergrowth, brushing the lianas aside, and the bird flew up from the ground on to a low branch just a few paces away. I froze, then slowly, very slowly, I crouched down, then I raised my binoculars to my eyes and there it was; a small, deep purple bird with shiny blue eyebrows and wings, and a lovely rich red belly. After a good long look it dropped to the ground and hopped off silently, leaving me to return to the trail and half run half dance all the way back to the hostel, where Al and Chief greeted me with equal joy because Chief too had finally seen a Garnet Pitta.

It was wonderful to stroll slowly along the West Trail during the afternoon listening to Garnet Pittas. We had scoured that square kilometre or so of rainforest for a week and seen 130 species of birds, a remarkable total for such a small area of forest, and yet two more new ones came my way before sunset. A tiger-striped Banded Kingfisher and an endemic Black-throated Wren Babbler, neither of which were a patch on the three Bornean Wren Babblers nearby. I was so calm and quiet and still that I was able to watch them walk nervously across the trail and a fine sight they made, looking like tiny crakes, stretching and twisting their necks to get a good look around while in such an uncustomary exposed position. A big wave of foraging birds came through the trailside trees as well and I was pleased to have the time to enjoy some last looks at the likes of Banded Broadbills and Scarlet-rumped Trogons, before leaving Danum and Borneo.

We then crossed Wallace's Line, the imaginary one drawn by Alfred Russel Wallace in 1859, between the Oriental zoogeographical region and the Australasian one where the birds are almost completely different. For example, unlike on Borneo there are no pheasants, trogons, barbets or broadbills on Sulawesi east of the line, but there are lorikeets and honeyeaters.

From Lahad Datu we flew south on a 19-seater Twin Otter to Tawau in Malaysia then Tarakan in Kalimantan, entering Indonesia through the back door before flying south again, across the equator, to Balikpapan, then east across the Makassar Strait to Palu on the west coast of Sulawesi. There we visited the Directorate General for Forest Protection and Nature Conservation Office (PHPA) to see the very friendly and helpful Rolex Lameanda who arranged our permits to visit Lore Lindu National Park, accommodation at Kamarora and a jeep with driver to transport us there and back. The jeep may have been four-wheel-drive but the suspension was shot and the 30 mile (50 km) journey to Kamarora was a painfully slow and unpleasant two and a half hours on a rocky, pot-holed track that ran by poor but happy people living in palm-thatched huts and working in small corn and paddy fields.

By dusk we were settled in as the only guests at the small PHPA guesthouse, a spacious bungalow overlooking a splendid garden complete with Blue-tailed Bee-eaters. The ranger spoke no English whatsoever and his only Indonesian word seemed to be *Makanan* which has various English interpretations including 'Food', 'Fodder', 'Feeding' and 'Eating', and which he shouted out at frequent and timely intervals during the rest of our stay, much to our delight for his wife produced a never-ending supply of delightful food including satay chicken and grilled fish with fresh vegetables, all of which went down a treat after a week of rice and rendang at Danum.

When I turned the light on at four o'clock in the morning on our first day at Kamarora a rich, reddish-brown, Atlas Moth, wider than my outstretched hand, fluttered around the room and caused quite a stir before I managed to persuade it outside. Coffee and biscuits were soon served and at 5 a.m. we were off, hoping to reach high-altitude forest by dawn. The route up to an old logging camp at Anaso near the summit of Gunung Rorekatimbu was more like a vertical, dry, rocky, river bed than an old logging track so acute was the ascent, and massive the rocky ruts. It was a tortuous 20 mile (35 km) ride, so bad in the end, and getting light fast, that we got out and walked the last couple of miles, seeing some very nice but very shy birds, including an endemic Blue-fronted Flycatcher, a small group of yellow-green Malias, a strange mixture of thrush, babbler and bulbul, and our first pair of Fiery-browed Mynas, slaty blue birds with Waxwing-like plumage and very peculiar eyebrows which appeared to be composed of short, soft orange-red bristles.

Later, lower down the mountain at Dongi-Dongi, we flushed clouds of little blue and black-and-yellow butterflies at rocky stream crossings and saw a lot more birds, virtually everyone of which was a new bird, so many birds in fact that by the end of our first full day at Lore Lindu of the 50 species seen 40 were new, including Purple-winged Rollers, a spectacular male Knobbed Hornbill, which looked like it was wearing a brightly painted mask with pastel blue skin around the eyes, a bulbous blue and black wattle, a big yellow bill with black grooves and red stripes at the base, and a large red casque on top of the bill, and Finch-billed Mynas, smoky-grey birds which like Waxwings have waxy red spines, only on their rumps instead of their wings. I would have given them all up for the one species we didn't see though; Purple-bearded Bee-eater, which was a worrying absentee at the best place for it. We were aching all over from the jeep journey and all the walking by the time we arrived back at the guesthouse so the banana fritters and coffee which appeared almost instantly went down very well.

At 04:30 the next morning we were back in the bone-shaking jeep, on our way up to Anaso again, where we saw several species not seen the day before. Down at Dongi-Dongi rain stopped play so we ended our second day still not having seen any birds with purple beards, or any of the even rarer forest floor skulkers such as Geomalia, which Al was particularly keen to see. After a lie-in until 6 a.m. the next day we were still up in time for a dawn raid in the lowland forest, inside which birds were very shy so we saw very few although it was worth a lengthy wait to obtain prolonged views of the endemic Fiery-billed Malkoha, a long-tailed, grey-brown bird with a bright bicoloured bill, yellow above and red below. Back outside big swifts called Purple Needletails whizzed by and taking to the sunny skies mid-morning were wing-clapping Barred Honey Buzzards and neatly barred Sulawesi Serpent Eagles. We also completed the set of Sulawesi's four endemic mynas with four White-necked Mynas, sleek bluish birds with white bibs and very long tails, and two Sulawesi or Short-crested Mynas, glossy dark blue with whitish epaulettes. This was all before lunch which was a feast of spinach and rice followed by fig pastries and coffee, taken on the shady veranda watching Blue-tailed Bee-eaters swooping and swirling and doing back flips high above the garden.

After two hours of bliss - I was now resigned to having to return another time to look for the purple-beard - we were off again. Chief decided to stick to the forest edge in what turned out to be a successful search for Ivory-backed Woodswallow. Al and I strolled casually back into the gloomy forest, not expecting to see much, but just a few paces in, a dark bird flew across the trail and landed in full view, much to our astonishment since that was such a rare event in the forests of Lore Lindu. It perched on a bare branch to our left. I raised my binoculars to confirm it was what I thought it would be, another drongo, and reeled from shock, because it was not a drongo it was a bee-eater, lit by a shaft of light shining through the canopy, and it was a bee-eater with a slightly shaggy, shiny purple beard. Its head was purple too, fading to brown-purple at the back of the neck, while its back, tail and tail streamers were a beautiful deep dark green. We got a good long look at the beautiful bird before it flew deeper into the forest, where we couldn't relocate it, so Al dashed off to get Chief while I leapt about like crazy in a state of manic euphoria, celebrating the fact that I had seen the bird I had given up on, the bird that completed the trip for me, the fourth possible bee-eater, the Purple-bearded Bee-eater, the one that occurs only on the island of Sulawesi.

I was still buzzing when Al and Chief appeared but we soon got down to the business of trying to find the bird for Chief. There was no sign of it and as the afternoon wore on the forest became increasingly quiet and grim as the cloud cover increased, creating an ominous atmosphere of gloom exacerbated by the continuing absence of the now unmentionable bee-eater. We gave up at dark, with Chief clinging to the remote possibility that the bird might turn up in the same spot at the same time the next day. Back at the guesthouse with a beer in my hand I wallowed in the contentment that comes when a quest is complete. More time with the bee-eater would have been appreciated but despite looking hard on the last day and morning we never saw it again, or another.

From the bus station in Palu we took a bemo, a tiny minibus, to the basic but clean *Pacifik Hotel*, ate chilli fish at a roadside warung, a small, family-owned cafè, and got another bemo to the beach where a stiff sea breeze was blowing and Blue-tailed Bee-eaters were flying low over the white horses. We sat there for a while spitting out custard-like globs of a Durian fruit we had bought because we had been told that it was the most delicious fruit in the world. It smelt like sick and tasted worse. In order to rid ourselves of the taste and say goodbye to Al we retired to *Ebu's Bar* overlooking the bay. Also there were a couple of English road builders, one of whom, having drank rather a lot and procured a prostitute for the night, invited us back to his house where his cook served up lobster and chips, the perfect antidote to Durian.

The wailing mullah woke us up at 4.30 a.m. and not long after Chief and I were in a bemo on our way to the airport. Al would follow later. He had arranged a ten week sabbatical from work and was off to Halmahera and Irian Jaya in search of birds-of-paradise with David Gibbs. The next time I saw him he was in The Hospital for Tropical Diseases in St Pancras, London. Actually, I walked past him in the corridor before realizing it was him. He looked like a ghost and reminded me of 'Mac' McMurphy, played by Jack Nicholson, in the film *One Flew Over the Cuckoo's Nest*; after the character had been subjected to electroconvulsive therapy. His thin, fair hair was all over the place, he appeared to be slightly delirious with a faraway look in his eyes, and he had lost so much weight the hospital smock he was wearing looked like it was hanging on a coat hanger, all hardly surprising because he had cerebral malaria and was lucky to be alive. Malaria symptoms usually kick-in one to four weeks following infection, sometimes later if the unfortunate victim has taken anti-malarials and Al had taken his religiously, with us and in Irian Jaya, one of the worst places in the world for malaria. He still got it and he was very lucky the infection had not taken hold earlier during his travels, in a remote area hundreds of miles from a hospital. When he got home to London he thought he had the flu but he was so ill by the time he went to see his doctor he was sent straight for specialist treatment. Without that he probably would have developed seizures, suffered multiple organ failure, fallen into a coma, and died, in Irian Jaya.

From Palu, Chief and I flew on *Bouraq Airlines*, the 'bus with wings', to Balikpapan then Banjarmasin in Kalimantan, southern Borneo, then south across the Java Sea to Surabaya then west over a giant stained glass window landscape of paddy fields, to Jakarta, arriving after dark. The capital of Indonesia was overwhelming; it seemed like most of the eight million people, a claustrophobic 40,000 per square kilometre, who lived in one of the biggest most sprawling cities on the planet, slept during the heat of the day and were going about their business in the relative cool of the night. Tired and hungry, we struggled to find a room for the night and ended up in a place that cost more than we were normally willing to pay. We asked for a knock on the door at 6.30 a.m. because we never had a watch between us and dutifully got up when we heard it, only to discover that it was 5 a.m. and the knock was for next door. Since we were awake we put our rucksacks on and waved down a taxi to take us to Cililitan bus station where we got on the first available bus, a fancy air-conditioned coach, to Cibodas. It whizzed through the lowlands of Java, a bird-less food production factory where once stood rainforest full of birds and other wildlife including now extinct elephants and tigers. The few adaptable birds which could survive in such a place had been captured by the locals, many of whom prefer birds to be in cages, so we saw no birds, even when we reached the foothills of the island's highland spine. They were covered in equally sterile tea plantations.

As in many places across the planet, due to too many people chopping down too many trees so they can use the cleared land to grow food, and the wood for building and cooking, to see any birds we had to get as high as possible, to the steepest slopes, the ones hard to clear and farm, so we headed to the twin volcanoes of Gunung Gede and Gunung Pangrango, where all but a few of Java's endemic birds just about survive in remote remnant pockets of forest full of tall rasamala trees and tree ferns. After a short bemo ride from Cibodas we arrived at Cibodas Botanic Gardens at the base of Gunung Gede, where, after sorting out a room in the staff quarters at the basic guesthouse, we finally returned to the field, after what seemed like an age, to search for our beloved birds once more.

It was cool, cloudy and damp but the flowering trees and shrubs in the luxuriant gardens and on the forested slopes above were jumping with birds and by employing our umbrellas for the first time on the trip we ended up seeing several endemics and better still a wave of foraging birds which included at least four Blue Nuthatches. At one point there were three of the stunning birds in my binocular view at the same time, acrobatically working a mossy branch with strong legs, probing with white beaks which matched their bold white eye-rings set in black hoods. More eye-catching still were their deep blue-grey backs and exquisite sky-blue, black trimmed, wing feathers.

The next day was even better even though we heard but didn't see a Blue-tailed Trogon, one of Java's most beautiful birds. We were out early and climbed up to the Cibeureum Waterfalls and above, beginning with a male Sunda Blue Robin, all indigo blue except for a black face with a bright white spot above its bill which, at some angles, looked like a light in the dark world of the forest floor. Next up was a male Javan Cochoa, sooty brown-black with a bluish cap, wings and tail, then we saw both endemic fantails, the red-tailed and white-bellied ones, a tiny, almost tail-less Javan Tesia at arm's length, three melodious White-browed Shortwings and a pair of Lesser Forktails. Those were just some of the new birds. Among the many species we had seen before were Black Eagles, a Chestnut-fronted Shrike Babbler, two Siberian Thrushes, Indigo, Little Pied and Snowy-browed Flycatchers, and more Blue Nuthatches. The wonder was not confined to birds either what with some incredible butterflies, a mobile troop of at least ten Ebony Leaf Monkeys, and, at close range, a surprisingly large Javan Gibbon.

*Blue Nuthatch, Gunung Gede, Java, 15th January 1991*

We did not even hear a trogon on the second morning and the afternoon was wet, so wet that for the first time on the trip we had to admit defeat and retreat indoors, using the time to catch up with our notes and sketches, adjust our accoutrements, clean some gear and, in my case, try to ease the pain of my terrible teeth. To my daily intake of anti-malarials *Avloclor* (chloroquine phosphate) and *Paludrine* (proguanil hydrochloride) I added anti-biotic penicillin (in case the source of my toothache was a sinus infection), analgesic *Paracetamol*, and antiseptic and anaesthetic clove oil which was given to me by one of the lecturers accompanying the ecology students from the University of

Brisbane who were staying in the guesthouse. When one of the students put the television on in the evening we could not believe our eyes. The news looked like a science fiction film, because, we were informed, a U.S.-led Coalition, which we did not know existed, had been bombing the hell out of Iraq since we had arrived in Java, and the scenes we were watching were filmed by cameras on board bombers bombing Baghdad at the beginning of Operation Desert Storm. It seemed America thought it was the World Police again. The planet needs a police force but the world is not ready for it yet. Also of concern to us was that there did not seem to be much chance of our flight home stopping in Dubai, as it was scheduled to do, in which case did that mean there would be no flight home?

It was our last day so we tried to forget about any possible problems with our flight and we climbed as high as possible up the volcano to give us our best chance of seeing the trogon. Once again we never heard one but it didn't matter, thanks to a close encounter with a striking White-crowned Forktail, a singing and posturing male White-browed Shortwing, a snowy-browed male Siberian Thrush and two very confiding Red-tailed Fantails, all dusky with white bibs and dazzling outsized orange tails.

Back in Jakarta we were very pleased to find that our flight was due to leave on schedule and that the only change involved stopping at Delhi instead of Dubai, so we still had time for one last bit of birding. In pounding heat at Cilincing paddy fields we saw three superb cerulean and white Small Blue Kingfishers, and a big, black, prehistoric-looking pterosaur of a bird with extremely long, slim and pointed wings, a long tail, a red throat pouch and a white belly turned out to be a Christmas Island Frigatebird, the first frigatebird I had seen anywhere in the world.

A day later I squeezed myself and my rucksack into a tube train in London, looked at the miserable faces of the people going to work and that indescribable feeling of freedom that comes from being on the road far from home in search of fantastic birds and other animals, was gone in an instant. Still, it was nice to be home and to eat my favourite food again. We had not endured anything like Humboldt had when he arrived in Angostura after seventy-five days travelling by pirogue along the rivers of Venezuela but as he wrote in his *Personal Narrative* of his travels in South America between 1799 and 1804, 'Long deprivations make small things pleasurable …', adding, 'I may be wrong in repeating what all travellers feel after long journeys. You enjoy finding yourself back in civilization, though it can be short-lived if you have learned to feel deeply the marvels of tropical nature. The memory of what you endured soon fades … you begin to plan to make another journey …', and so it was that I soon forgot about the leeches and mosquitoes and so on, and started planning the next adventure, and it was not long before I was in Angostura, now known as Ciudad Bolivar.

*Pompadour Cotinga, The Escalera, Venezuela, 7th January 1992*

8

# VENEZUELA and CHILE

At dawn the cloud forest came alive and another dream came true, a blissful dream of ambling through the forests of South America looking at fabulous birds, birds like Green Honeycreepers, Purple Honeycreepers, Golden Tanagers, Blue-winged Mountain Tanagers, Tropical Parulas, shimmering hummingbirds called Long-tailed Sylphs, and bright green Groove-billed Toucanets, every colour imaginable, all while listening to Red Howler Monkeys roaring in the distance. The trees were alive with an incredible variety of birds and while trying to keep up with them I spotted a sloth, so I lay down on my back in the middle of the quiet road to have a good look at it without breaking my neck and the slow-motion shag-pile watched me from its dark mask. There is so much more to birding than the birds but what birds, so many of them that by the end of my first truly fantastic day in South America I had seen an incredible 75 new species in a mind-blowing bombardment of colour and form that also included a black-masked Laughing Falcon, a green and red Collared Trogon, a cartoon-like Common Tody Flycatcher, a small, bold, very active bird with a prominent bill, startling yellow eyes in a black head and bright yellow underparts, and, number 75, a large-headed, thick-necked, hook-billed Russet-throated Puffbird. The day flashed by and at the end of it my mind was whirling with wonder.

I was in Henri Pittier National Park in the Cordillera de la Costa Central on Venezuela's Caribbean coast and at beer o'clock I finally conceded that Al, who had been to Ecuador, was right; South America was brilliant for birds. He was also persistent; it took him four years to convince me to go there, even though there were no bee-eaters. I was reeled in by him, other friends, and plates of paintings, especially those by Guy Tudor, in *A Guide to the Birds of Colombia* by Steve Hilty and William Brown, *A Guide to the Birds of Venezuela* by Rodolphe Meyer de Schauensee and William Phelps, and *The Birds of South America* by Robert Ridgely. The only trouble I had was deciding which country to visit. It couldn't be Colombia because a lot of the best places for birds were controlled by left-wing guerrillas and/or right-wing paramilitaries, funded by cocaine and in conflict with government forces so, swayed some more by the fact that it was one of the few relatively safe countries in South America with a field guide we looked closely at Venezuela and were amazed to discover that so many of the continent's iconic birds occurred there. Convinced that was the place to go, all Al and I had to do was recruit two more team members and Nick Wall and The Stid were soon on board.

I then got to thinking about other classic South American birds like Andean Condor, Inca Tern and Diademed Plover, none of which were possible in Venezuela, and, if we could all wangle five weeks off work over the Christmas and New Year period maybe we could tag another country on to the trip to try and see them as well. So, after some more research I suggested Chile and the others quickly agreed. The main questions that remained were, 'Which sites to visit?', 'How far apart were they?' and 'How long should we spend at each one?', all answered by the birders who had already been to South America and been unselfish enough to write up their experiences for the benefit of others, in often exciting and inspiring trip reports. We grilled some of the authors and their team members at length, on the telephone, in the field or in the pub, and we gleaned much valuable information and made some great friends in the process. We also bought Mary Lou Goodwin's excellent booklet *Birding in Venezuela*. We read that, and the trip reports, again and again, we swotted up on the birds from the field guides and family guides such as *Shorebirds*, we sorted out vaccinations, visas and travellers cheques, we booked the flights, and soon we were ready, and we were very, very excited.

Two weeks before we were due to fly to Caracas *VIASA Airlines'* pilots went on strike. During negotiations the pilots somehow managed to get the airline to agree that the pilots would not have to work on Christmas Eve, the day we were due to fly, so, with the dispute over, we were given an ultimatum; fly out three days earlier or not at all. After almost giving up all hope of actually going there was no way we were not getting on that flight so by some stroke of great good fortune we arrived on the South American continent and in what seemed like no time at all we were in a hired *Toyota Corolla* and on the road to Henri Pittier National Park, named after a botanist from Switzerland who, after arriving in Venezuela in 1917 at the age of 60, classified more than 30,000 plants in the country, including thousands in the park named after him.

There was certainly no shortage of plants surrounding Rancho Grande Biological Station, a jungle 'temple' at the mountain pass of Portachuelo below Pico Guacamaya (The Mountain of the Macaw). Construction of what was to be a grand hotel was abandoned when the workers dropped tools on hearing about the death of the former military dictator Juan Vicente Gomez, in 1935, and the unfinished building soon became part of the forest. From the wide, open, verandas and roof there is a superb panorama of the forest canopy and the forested mountains beyond, where not long after dawn on the second day in South America I saw my first quetzal, the White-tipped variety, one of the first illustrations in the field guides to catch my eye months before. The bulky but beautiful pigeon-sized bird has a short, yellow bill, bronzy green head, metallic green breast and elongated scapular feathers in the wings which wrapped around the sides of the bird like emerald fingers holding the deep red belly. At the summit of the Choroni Road, despite mist and rain, we came across a Golden-breasted Fruiteater, a small, plump, short-tailed, mainly green and yellow bird, often difficult to find because the species likes to sit still in thick cover for long periods, exactly what the bird we watched was doing. We could not find its cousin the Handsome Fruiteater which is endemic to Venezuela but it was time to move on, to the Rio Barragan at the base of the Andes, a 350 mile (560 km) overnight drive away.

After a cramped couple of hours trying but failing to sleep we tumbled groggily out of the car and wearily began looking for birds. The adrenalin kicked in immediately because new birds appeared thick and fast and we were soon shaking our heads at the brilliance of shiny blue Swallow Tanagers, and an elegant Rufous-tailed Jacamar that was as fantastic as I had imagined it to be, probably because it looked like a bee-eater in flight, pursuing airborne insects. However, when it was perched it was perhaps even better than a bee-eater thanks to the metallic golden green upperparts, rich rufous underparts, white throat and very long, very thin, straight bill. After a prolonged search during which Nick and The Stid performed a strange high-stepping dance to rid themselves of some fearsome ants, and a massive, dazzling, turquoise morpho butterfly had jinked along the rocky stream, we saw three Pale-headed Jacamars, the bird the site was famous for but which was not a patch on its relatively common and widespread cousin the Rufous-tailed, the plumage being made up of a variety of browns. Higher up the Santo Domingo Valley the beautiful forest either side of the La Soledad Track came alive when the temperature fell during the late afternoon and a succession of new birds included an almost ridiculously colourful Red-headed Barbet, a small, deep grass green and yellow bird with a big yellow bill and plush red head and breast. Using the last of the light we drove up the steep valley to the *Hotel Moruco* where the prospect of a full night lying flat on a bed seemed almost too good to be true. I thought The Stid was going to suggest, I mean insist, we do some night-birding at any moment but no, he was asleep before me.

The next morning, Christmas Day, before it was light, we nearly left the road a couple of times as Nick drove as fast he could down the almost vertical Santo Domingo Valley to make sure we were on the San Isidro Track for the crack of dawn. His passengers were just glad it was dark and we could not see the drop-offs. Unfortunately it was light when he then had to drive along a narrow shelf at the top of a huge quarry. Band-winged Nightjars flew up from the rough track the other side then we reached a deep forested ravine like a secret hideaway where the male Andean Cock-of-the-rocks were already at their traditional lek, an 'arena' where they gather to display to females. Three glowing orange males, bigger and chunkier than thrushes and brighter than belief, and with crazy curved discs for crests which almost hid their bills, were trying to impress a much drabber female with strange squeals, squawks, grunts and loud 'youii' calls, and exaggerated bows, jumps and flaps, lighting up the otherwise quiet and dark subtropical forest dawn and creating a spectacle the like of which none of us had ever seen before.

It was only when the excited birds calmed down and the surrounding forest burst into life with the calls and songs of a multitude of other, unknown birds that we left the lek and began walking the track along which we soon came across a pair of Golden-winged Manakins, the male tiny and black with a short, bright yellow crest, the feathers of which curled forward over the bill. He stood erect and bobbed from side to side with increasing speed when he began displaying to a female perched right next to him. They were followed by a male Booted Racket-tail, a beautiful little green hummingbird with big blue disks at the end of its elongated outer-tail feather shafts, then a Red-ruffed Fruitcrow, an extraordinary cotinga as big and as black as a crow except for a large, shiny, deep orange-red ruff, and two Emerald Toucanets and many superb butterflies not least large, lime-green swallowtails, even larger blue morphos and a million more we did not know the name of. By mid-morning it was hot and a friendly splash of cold mountain water from a heavily placed boot while crossing a stream turned into a lot of jumping and splashing as our joy overflowed. The good cheer continued while driving very carefully back across the top of the quarry when three Cliff Flycatchers, almost all cinnamon-rufous, including the underwings, flew around like bee-eaters to complete a wonderful morning.

By noon we were back near the town of Santo Domingo where two black, white and silver Swallow-tailed Kites ebbed and flowed overhead, and in a small ravine we saw our first antpitta, a handsome Chestnut-crowned one with large white teardrops on its dark breast. I would like to say 'after lunch' but there was none, only time for a drink according to The Stid, we pulled over to the side of the road a little way up the valley in search of higher-elevation birds, not knowing where to look exactly. Having seen very little after fifteen minutes or so we began to wonder if we should try higher still when, like a tidal wave, came an incredible foraging flock of about a hundred birds which proceeded to do a circuit of the trees and bushes surrounding us for the next two hours, producing a pulsating spell of birding during which all we had to do was raise our binoculars and there would be a brilliant bird in view, sometimes a few and, at the beginning, several new birds. The variety of species was astonishing and virtually all of them were so stunning the world seemed to be illuminated with a riot of gorgeous colours and hues, beginning with Lachrymose Mountain Tanagers, so-called because of the yellow teardrop shapes below their eyes (the lachrymal glands, one for each eye, secrete tears), and continuing with a rufous browed and breasted Brown-backed Chat Tyrant, two green hummingbirds called Merida and Orange-throated Sunangels, the former with a rosy throat shield the latter with a glittering golden orange one, some smaller green 'hummers' called Tyrian Metaltails, bright yellow Black-crested Warblers, ultramarine Masked Flowerpiercers with black masks and bright red eyes, shining cobalt Blue-and-black Tanagers, relatively sombre Blue-capped Tanagers, and, amongst them all, a shocking Orange-eared Tanager, a very rare bird in Venezuela, with dazzling green plumage and burnt orange patches on the sides of the neck.

It was almost all too much to take in. Even a quick glance at the rocky stream far below revealed our first White-capped Dipper and when we looked up into the air for once a Bat Falcon flew over, and still the flock circled us and new birds appeared, including at least four White-throated Tyrannulets, one or two Buff-breasted Mountain

Tanagers, and, finally, in what at first appeared to be a vision it was so gorgeous, a male Chestnut-breasted Chlorophonia, a tiny, plump bird with a lovely green face and throat, blue crown and nape, deep green upperparts and glowing yellow underparts with a rich chestnut breast and line down from there to under the bird's tail.

There were seventeen species in that flock and sixteen of them were new to me. When they moved off we returned in stunned awe to Santo Domingo to search for Torrent Ducks and in no time at all we were watching a pair with two young dicing with death in a torrent, as is their wont, the male's black and white striped head and red bill particularly conspicuous when raised above the rushing water. A walk upstream in the hope of finding the other species associated with the fast-flowing waters of the Andes, the black and grey Torrent Tyrannulet, turned up a pair of the surprisingly smart flycatchers, and even during a late afternoon stroll around the grounds of *Hotel Moruco* we saw three more new birds including a beautiful male Golden-rumped Euphonia with a black face, sky-blue hood, dark blue upperparts and glowing golden-yellow underparts, a fitting end to a phenomenal day, one of the very rare ones when every bird we dreamt of seeing and a whole lot more appeared, from dawn to dusk. Over local smoked trout and a few beers we all agreed that it was our best day birding ever, the best day of our lives in fact.

It was so cold first thing the next morning we had to pour petrol into the carburettor to get the car engine running and it got even colder as we climbed above the Sierra Nevada de Merida tree line up to Pico El Aguila at 13,501 feet (4115 metres) with the highest mountain in Venezuela,

Pico Bolivar at over 16,400 feet (5000 metres), in the distance. We were in the barren *páramo*, the cold, wet 'tundra' of grasses and succulents, tramping over frost-covered ground, because we were hoping to see the Bearded Helmetcrest, an exceptional member of an exceptional family of birds, the hummingbirds, with a dull brownish body and without glitter yes but sporting a long, thin beard of elongated and pointed white throat feathers, and a long, thin crest of elongated black and white crown feathers, which together give the bird a very strange head-on look indeed. It didn't take us long to find one and then another and another, about ten in all, a couple of which were in their full glory. Amongst other *páramo* specialists up there were two Ochre-browed Thistletails, 'little brown jobs' with long, ragged tails. After noon we drove down winding roads through cultivated hillsides to the fine town of Tabay and on to the Pico Humboldt Trail which climbs steeply through subtropical and temperate forests toward two of the three small glaciers in the Merida Andes, forests full of antpittas ... in our dreams. We saw none of the forest-floor skulkers but I was more than happy looking at a much more commonly seen and much more beautifully marked Pearled Treerunner, a sparrow-sized bird bright chestnut above with a cream-coloured throat and brown underparts boldly marked with very neat, black-edged, pearly, teardrop-shaped spots.

Along the trail the next morning we saw four lovely Green-and-black Fruiteaters and some Oleaginous Hemispinguses, possibly South America's most fancifully named but most boring birds, being mostly a dull olive colour. I did not look at them for long though, not when a Plushcap was lighting up the forest. The finch-like bird was bluish grey above with a deep chestnut face and underparts but it was its golden forehead that grabbed the attention; a glowing pin-cushion of short, plush feathers. We did not expect to see that uncommon skulker which made it even more special. We *did* expect to see Collared Incas but they were still a thrill to watch. The large, black-glossed green hummingbirds with big, bold, white breast bands have long needles for bills which they swished about like swords while darting between flowers.

During the middle of the day we cruised along the Valle Grande Road looking for *Datura* flowers, sometimes called Angel's Trumpets, and the bird that might visit them, the Sword-billed Hummingbird, not the most colourful of hummingbirds but the one with the longest bill in relation to body length of any bird in the world. As is the case with so many hummingbirds its bill has evolved to exploit the nectar in particularly-shaped flowers and in the case of the 'sword' it can reach the sugar-rich liquid at the bottom of the long tubular flowers of *Daturas*, plants we were familiar with from the Isles of Scilly in Britain, not that any of us had ever eaten them like some other birders. The plants, especially the flowers, contain alkaloids such as atropine and if eaten the potent combination of neurotransmitter blockers can result in the complete inability to differentiate between what is real and what is fantasy, a symptom displayed by some birders who have never been near *Daturas*. The story goes that at least one of the birders visiting Scilly who decided to 'test the effects' of *Datura* ended up dancing naked on the police station roof. They were lucky, they could have ended up dead, because although some indigenous tribes are known to eat the plant for 'recreational purposes' others, especially in India, have used it as a poison for murder and suicide. Anyway, we could not find any in flower and any Sword-billed Hummingbirds either so we returned to the Pico Humboldt Trail for another attempt at seeing antpittas.

"They're giving me grief!" The Stid said as we stood on the trail hoping one would hop out but it was not to be.

Near dusk we headed south to the pretty Spanish colonial town of Jaji for the night, finding fine places to eat and sleep among the cobbled streets lined with low, white houses with red-tiled roofs. A thick Andean mist rolled down the mountains before we turned in but when we turned out the sky was crisp and starry. By dawn we were in cloud forest along the quiet La Azulita Road where Long-tailed Sylphs and Collared Incas whizzed about the low flowers and shrubs, and Beryl-spangled and Black-capped Tanagers lit up the trees above. In the afternoon we spent four hours wandering about under the exceptionally tall trees in the University of Andes Forest Reserve and saw very few birds until, at the death, we spotted a pair of Crested Quetzals perched quietly in the sub-canopy and enjoyed watching the large metallic green and red birds until it was time to leave.

The Andean forests were cool, damp, lush and beautiful, adorned with bromeliads and draped with long curtains of moss but, as can often be the case, across the world, the more pristine the habitat the harder the birds are to find. These are the birds which cannot adapt to the degradation and destruction of their habitat, cannot survive in open farmland or secondary growth where they would be much easier to see, and are so supremely adapted to live in the habitat they have evolved to live in that they blend into their environment almost perfectly. So, we were very fortunate to have seen the quetzals and I was more than grateful for that as we began the hour-long trudge back to the car, along a muddy trail through bird-less farmland where once there was forest and birds.

As dusk fell we drove back across the Merida Andes, stopped for trout soup in Santo Domingo, paid homage to that astounding valley for birds, and began our descent, back to Rio Barragan where, after a few hours fitful sleep, it was not too difficult to wrench our aching, smelly bodies out of the stuffy, cramped car, for it was with some relief. We were a week into an all-out birding trip now and we were beginning to feel the pace. With The Stid in the crew there is never much time to write up notes let alone sleep.

"I think he's trying to kill us," ex-Royal Marine Al joked as we tottered along the trail. "I'm expecting him to tie me up and put a black hood over my head tonight and interrogate me about my list!"

After the jokes about how interesting that would be I said, "If we carry on like this, we'll have to be stretchered on to the plane home."

The Stid laughed and looked at us as if to say, 'What are you on about?'

A Black-headed Tody Flycatcher woke me up. The tiny bird looked slightly comical at first, with a long, cocked-up tail at one end and a disproportionately large black bill at the other, and on closer inspection proved to be a very striking bird what with a black head, white throat, bright pale green back, yellow-fringed wing feathers and stunning yellow underparts. Back in the car, I saw my first Southern Lapwings and Wattled Jacanas on the drive to Bruzual where there is a suspension bridge over the Rio Apure. From the high bridge we scanned the wide, shallow river for three special birds and we saw them all in three minutes; the small Yellow-billed Tern, the large Large-billed Tern and, best of all, my third new shorebird of the day, the very handsome Pied Plover, a small but tall black and white bird with bright red eye-rings in a broad black mask, on a par if not better than the best African lapwings and plovers. I only stepped back from the telescope to look at the Pink River Dolphins. They really were pink and they had very bulky bodies and long beaks. We knew it was possible to see what are also called Botos or Orinoco River Dolphins, in the Rio Apure because it is a tributary of the Orinoco, flowing down from the Andes and east across Los Llanos to join the Orinoco in central Venezuela.

In order to reach the Rio Apure in the year 1800 it took Humboldt almost two months to cross Los Llanos (The Plains), the vast flat savanna with gallery forest along slow-flowing streams, the size of France. Nearly 200 years later, we drove into the heart of it in about twelve hours, to Hato Pinero, a 270 square mile (700 sq km) working ranch. During the May to October rainy season much of the grassland is flooded, an annual event which limits farming to cattle grazing on huge ranches, some of which have taken up nature conservation and opened up their Hatos (a word from southern Spain that means a large farm for raising cattle) to birders and other people who love wildlife, because the floods attract astounding numbers of birds. We arrived in December when the water-loving species were massing on the few pools left after the floods, arguably the best time even if it was extremely hot. The delightful single-storey ranch house with a low, sweeping, red-tiled roof, white stucco walls, shiny stone floors and old wooden doors, windows, shutters and beams was so airy and cool that for a brief moment we were reluctant to leave it and head out into the 90 degrees of heat but our resistance was futile, there were lots of new and spectacular birds out there. We searched the courtyard first, strolling from the shade of one big mango tree to the next, enjoying our first Burnished-buff Tanagers before reaching the entrance gate, from where we could see a small pool illuminated by seven Scarlet Ibises, shocking scarlet from beak to claw and as amazing as we had imagined them to be.

The hato's owner, Antonio Julio Branger, stopped hunting on the ranch in 1950, having decided in his twenties that he didn't like shooting Jaguars and Pumas anymore. Forty years later the wildlife, apart from big cats, was thriving alongside 15,000 cattle, so we were rather keen to board the back of an open, flat-backed truck and get going on our first 'safari' with Alex, the guide, and Antonio's relatives, Marie and Miguel. After seeing our first Horned Screamers, large, loud waterbirds, and brilliant orange and black Troupials, four Scarlet Macaws flew past and they made a magnificent sight at a metre long with their long pointed tails. They also had a voice to match their outrageousness; a loud, rasping 'raaaaaah' and were still calling as they flew out of view. Before dark we also saw four Yellow-knobbed Curassows, mainly black, thick-legged, chicken-sized birds, at least ten long-necked, long-legged and cock-tailed Grey-necked Wood Rails, some Red

Howler Monkeys and lots of Capybaras. The world's largest rodents have a strange profile thanks to their blunt muzzles, and with their eyes, ears and nostrils all near the top of their heads and their love of water they looked like and behaved like miniature hairy Hippos. After dark we began spotlighting and the powerful lamp soon revealed a pair of orange eyes belonging to a Common Potoo, a large, mottled, streaked and vermiculated greyish brown bird of the night. It was perched bolt upright in full view on a snag and through the telescope we could see that it had a very large mouth surrounded by bristles which help the bird to gather in moths and other insects which it catches in flight. The rather mournful song of this widespread species, five low whistles descending the scale slowly and decreasing in volume, was well described by James Bond in his *Birds of the West Indies* as 'poor-me-all-alone', and it is very evocative of tropical nights in Central and northern South America. We saw four more as the night wore on and between them five Great Potoos, which are a quarter bigger, the size of a crow in fact, and very impressive.

The dawn drive the next day began with a Double-striped Thick-knee, a very long-legged 'shorebird' with striking white eyebrows. The night before, the spotlight had revealed what looked like a million red eyes of Spectacled Caimans along a narrow river so we were a bit surprised when the truck pulled over at the exact same place, ready for our planned boat trip. We were told not to worry about the caimans and settled down to enjoy what turned out to be a slow cruise through a dream, along a river which flowed imperceptibly through the thick riverside gallery forest of South America. Caimans scuttled into the dark water from the dry banks, flushing Grey-necked Wood

Rails in the process. Amazon, Green and Ringed Kingfishers, and blue morphos, flashed past our heads, and a gorgeous dark glossy green and rufous American Pygmy Kingfisher perched almost at arm's length. Surprisingly large Hoatzins, bigger than pigeons with untidy crests, clambered about awkwardly amongst the foliage low down in the riverside trees, close enough to see bare blue skin around their red eyes. Alex fished out a piranha with his bare hand for us to look at, opening its mouth with surprising nonchalance to reveal the razor-sharp triangular teeth, evolved to puncture and shear. He gestured that piranhas were good to eat or that they were good at eating we were not quite sure. The man steering the boat pointed out a large bee's nest slung low enough from the side of an overhanging tree for us to accidentally head-butt it and Alex explained what might happen should we do that and disturb the bees. Since it was a nest of Killer Bees, so-called because they are easily provoked and extremely aggressive in defence of their nests, we were in danger of having to make a very difficult decision; risk being stung to death or dive into the river and take our chances with the caimans and piranhas.

It was a relief to leave the harsh screeching of the Hoatzins behind and glide on, through the smooth water, past Anhingas perched on snags with their wings held out to dry, and Boat-billed Herons hiding in bushes. Two Scarlet Macaws were even louder than the Hoatzins as they flew across a gap in the canopy above. A Rufous-tailed Jacamar sparkled in a riverside tree and then we saw the best bird of all, a Sunbittern, a truly unique beauty which looked a bit like a cross between a small heron and a large rail with a black and white striped head and very ornate, finely vermiculated, black, white, grey and chestnut body, wing and tail feathers. The bird was very happy in our presence and we were able to watch it at close range while it stalked butterflies on riverside rocks with slow, deliberate steps and lightning-fast strikes with its long, thin bill.

The next morning a fantastic Sunbittern flitted along the track in front of the truck, spreading its wings wide and flashing the startling large rufous 'eyes' in them, to warn us off as it would a potential predator. We were returning to the river to look for the bird we couldn't find the day before. This time we walked very slowly alongside it until the heat became unbearable but we could not find an Agami Heron and we had to be and were content with plenty of other birds and a troop of Red Howler Monkeys which were on view for a long time.

Hato Pinero may have been an expensive place to stay, at least for skinflints like us, but it was worth every dollar and more, and I for one would loved to have stayed a while longer but once again it was time to move on and after eating all we could at lunch we set off on the 600 mile (960 km) drive east across Venezuela to the state of Bolivar. It did not begin well. I was driving along the top of a high bund when I stopped and began reversing to have a close look at a dead Crested Caracara but I accidentally reversed over the edge of the bund and down the slope the car went. We came to a shuddering halt near the bottom and after getting carefully out of the car, which was at an angle of 45 degrees, discovered that a knee-high triangular pillar, marking a culvert, had pierced the bottom of the boot and stopped the car from crashing into the ditch below, with us in it. After taking all our gear out of the boot we managed to lift the car off the pillar and get it back to the top of the bund where I was banned from driving for the rest of the trip, although that did not make the remainder of the journey much less traumatic, as three tired drivers took it in turns to speed along the appalling, narrow, potholed, unlit, slippery roads which were almost completely devoid of signs pointing out sharp bends and so on and busy with other vehicles, especially buses and pick-ups, eight out of ten of which would not have been allowed on the road back home, nine out of ten of which had no lights that worked and nearly all of which were driven by lunatics. It was sixteen hours of hell with remarkably just the one puncture and only an hour off, to eat at a lively roadside bar in the outskirts of El Tigre. We all agreed it was best to do the long drives overnight because they saved invaluable birding time, there was no hotel bill or a night trying to sleep in the car, and there was always the chance of seeing nightbirds although that night only a Barn Owl interrupted our serious questioning overnight driving.

The state of Bolivar, named after Simon Bolivar who liberated Venezuela from Spanish rule in 1821, as well as Colombia, Ecuador, Peru and Bolivia (which is also named after him), is one of the top birding areas on the South American continent. The Imataca Forest Reserve for example was a paradise for birds the size of Switzerland at the time we were there, although it was already being exploited for timber, gold, diamonds, copper, bauxite and so on, the way it is in virtually every so-called 'protected area for wildlife' on the planet. That was our first stop and we were keen to get to the *Parador Taguapire* in the small town of El Palmar before dawn so we could book a room and be in the forest, 15 miles (25 km) to the east, for first light but thanks to the horrendous drive we were late. The amiable owner let us book in at 7 a.m. though and suggested we might like breakfast. Since we had missed dawn and could smell coffee we took little persuading and by the time the ham and eggs were on the table half an hour later we had seen six new birds from his garden anyway, including six Black-necked Araçaris, small toucans with large black and ivory bills. The relentless Stid was desperate to get into the forest of course and by 8 a.m. we were on our way but the track was rough and it was mid-morning before we got there and the habitat did not look good, the biggest trees having been felled and logged. Nevertheless, and in spite of the late hour, the place was jumping with birds and in our first hundred paces we saw about twenty new species including two magnificent Red-and-green Macaws and at least ten Turquoise Tanagers. By the end of the day we had also seen Channel-billed and Red-billed Toucans, two more reasons to be glad to be alive. Another new bird was heard frequently but not seen; the shocking, loud, rising then explosive 'wee-wee-YO' whistles of Screaming Pihas drowned out most of the other calls and songs. It was an iconic sound of lowland South American and when there was a chance I tried to take stock of where I was, listening to the real thing in the rainforest instead of a recording back home.

Many more new birds followed the next morning, the best of which were four Purple-throated Fruitcrows and a shimmering pair of Green-tailed Jacamars. I also managed to see another elusive songster, a Musician Wren, a bird with arguably the most enchanting song of any bird, and there are an awful lot to choose from. The Musician Wren lives up to its name because it seems able to play its voice like a musical instrument, composing elaborate melodies of pure whistles that range way up and down in pitch. So lovely was the sound it stopped me in my tracks and when it ended I could still hear the sweet notes in my head, and I could still hear them at midday when I could keep my eyes open no longer and drifted off into a deep happy sleep.

I awoke refreshed and looking round saw Al asleep in the car as well so I woke him up and off we went to bird a trail off the main track, Nick and The Stid having walked off into the midday sun. We soon saw a Reddish Hermit, a hummingbird so tiny we would have dismissed it as a bee had it not suddenly stopped zooming past and perched by the side of the trail. Then we saw a golden-green and bright orange-rufous Great Jacamar, and two Paradise Jacamars, looking very handsome in metallic black with a bronzy gloss to their shoulders, neat white throats and upper breasts, very long, thin, black bills and very long, thin and pointed black tails. I could have watched them all afternoon, sallying out across a clearing from a tall tree to pluck flying insects from the air before returning more sedately to the same tree to juggle their prey down their throats and resume watch, just like bee-eaters. Nick and The Stid returned with tales of White-plumed Antbirds, birds I dreamed of seeing, but I didn't care.

Over breakfast at the parador well before dawn the next day we were introduced to Ramone, a local guide, and four American birders; Roy and Donna Woodall, who were driving their pick-up camper from Oregon to Tierra del Fuego, and Brian from Boston, Massachusetts, who was guiding a quiet lady client. Overnight rain had turned the track into a muddy morass and Ramone advised us to

*Paradise Jacamar, Imataca Forest, Venezuela, 3rd January 1992*

leave our car at the river, at which point Roy and Donna immediately let us hop on their camper and on we went, with Brian, his client and Ramone out front.

Al and I sat on the bonnet until we got to a logging camp deep in Imataca Forest where Ramone told us we would have to leave the vehicles and walk for about forty minutes. Two hours later, two long hours of mud and water on a narrow forest trail, we emerged from another tangle of undergrowth into a small clearing surrounding a huge tree and Ramone gestured for us all to be quiet and to look up at the tree. Through my binoculars I could see a massive stick nest high in what was the tallest tree around. Not long after, a bird rose from the nest, all fluffed up and screaming, and it high-stepped its way along an almost horizontal branch, one of the first branches to leave the trunk, way, way, above us, to where it could keep an eye on us. It was a huge, black, white and grey bird with a massive beak in a face set in a ruff with a crest on top of that, and it had the most enormous yellow feet with long black claws. It was a Harpy Eagle, the largest and heaviest eagle on Earth. Named after the female monster in the form of a bird with a human face in Greek and Roman mythology, female Harpy Eagles, which are larger than males, may reach a height of over a metre and weigh up to 20 lb (9 kg). With so much power and sharp claws as long as fingers the ultimate bird of prey preys on armadillos, peccaries, porcupines, monkeys and sloths, from southern Mexico to northeast Argentina, a large range but one in which the species seems only to inhabit the remotest, most extensive forested areas which are hard to get into, so the chance of seeing a Harpy was one of the main reasons why we were at Imataca, one of the very few relatively accessible places where it may be seen, if a nest is located.

Elated with prolonged views of the awesome eagle we began the long, hot and humid trudge back to the logging camp. It had already started raining by the time we reached there but before we left, the intensity of the rain increased tenfold and by the time we got to our car the red track to El Palmar had turned into a quagmire. So, in the continuing downpour we had no choice but to push, lift and dig the car out of the deepest stretches of mud and long, muddy puddles, with our hands. Still the rain thickened until it was hard to believe how much water was falling out of the sky. It got muddier too, and then we were stuck, truly stuck. No pushing, lifting, digging or swearing could shift the car. As we stood in the rain wondering what to do next Roy and Donna's camper came up slowly behind us. Roy got out of the cab, walked to the back of the camper and emerged with a shovel. We all ran to grab it but he insisted on doing the digging himself and for half an hour we watched the man we thought was about sixty years old dig us out of there with the obvious expertise of someone who had been in far worse scrapes. It was near dusk when the car entered the last major puddle and a great wave of mud and water almost engulfed us as Nick ploughed through it at speed but we emerged the other side and then we all washed the car, and ourselves, as best we could in the rain, before returning to the parador, fourteen hours after setting out.

"Ah, here come the lean, mean birding machines," Brian said as he rose from his table to greet us and we all settled down to the most welcome beers of our lives, and told Brian, who had managed to get out of the forest with little trouble in his four-wheel-drive, all about our journey out.

The next morning we drove west to Vila Lola then headed south on the road to Brazil, seeing two Brown Jacamars by the roadside before reaching the trail at KM67 in time for a couple of hour's birding. The lowland forest was in good shape so birds were hard to see but a superb glossy black male Golden-headed Manakin sat quietly in full view for a long time, and we saw a distant Bearded Bellbird, far too far away to make out the 'beard', the bare pendulous wattles which hang from the species' throat, but within range of its unbelievably loud 'bock' call, repeated every few seconds, one of the loudest of all bird calls, which can be heard over a mile away. Expatriate birder Henry Cleve's guesthouse at KM85 was full so we booked a room in the *Anaconda Lodge* at KM88, a booming mining town sometimes called Las Claritas where, we were warned, it was dangerous to go out at night and mix with the drunken miners, many of whom were, apparently, ex-convicts. We looked aghast at the prices of the beer and food in the lodge and walked into town to one of the wooden shacks called *Restaurant "Don Chin"* and taking care not to meet the eyes of anyone who looked like they had had more than enough to drink, and the ladies of the night, we ordered *quatro cervezas por favor* and *bistec con papas fritas*, both of which were served up speedily and greatly enjoyed. The place was busy, the town was busy and everyone seemed very happy and friendly, and the *cervezas* flowed.

On the way to KM88 it looked like the forest, which formed a wall along both sides of the road for mile after mile, was vast and pristine and that it was going to devour the road with its exuberance but behind what was a façade, just a few km from the road, there were massive scars in the jungle where gold and so on was being extracted. Our gold lay in the untouched blocks of forest that were left and the next day we found enough to make it one of the richest birding days ever. It began at dawn, along the trail at KM70, listening to, then finally seeing, a Screaming Piha, a thrush-sized, drab grey bird but as Al pointed out, "A cotinga!" In stark contrast was my first Black-faced Dacnis, a tiny gem I was particularly keen to see on the trip because the male is bright turquoise blue with a black mask, back and wings, and shining out from its mask are its bright yellow eyes.

Along the trail at KM71 we chanced upon a swarm of army ants. As Henry Walter Bates writes in *The Naturalist on the River Amazons*, 'When the pedestrian falls in with a train of these ants, the first signal given him is a twittering and restless movement of small flocks of plain-coloured birds ... If this be disregarded until he advances a few steps farther, he is sure to fall into trouble, and find himself suddenly attacked by numbers of the ferocious little creatures. They swarm up his legs with incredible rapidity, each one driving his pincer-like jaws into his skin, and with the purchase thus obtained, doubling in its tail, and stinging with all its might. There is no course left but to run for it.' We did not run for it, we tucked our trousers inside our socks and went in after the ants, because the birds we thought we might see were only likely to be seen in the company of ants. We were soon in the midst of about thirty Rufous-throated Antbirds and, as we had hoped, at least ten White-plumed Antbirds, crazy-looking things, dark slate-grey above and chestnut below with striking white plumes on their faces forming short beards and, more amazing still, stiff, vertical tufts rising from the sides of their faces to way above their heads. There were birds everywhere, some just a few paces away, chipping and churring as they leapt and fluttered between vertical sapling stems or dropped quickly to the ground to snap up the insects fleeing a seething mass of ants. 'The errand of the vast ant-armies is plunder ... Wherever they move, the whole animal world is set in commotion' Bates wrote. This is because the main columns of ants, four to six across, seek out, tear into pieces and carry off anything they can handle that cannot escape their path, mostly insects and their grubs, including other species of defenceless ants, but also spiders and even, in rare cases, small mammals. It was great to witness the ants and their attendant antbirds but they soon began moving away from the trail and we were scared to follow them in case we got lost in the forest. At KM73 we did get lost and having refound the old and rarely used trail we had no choice but to retrace our steps, or end up in Guyana.

We spent the last hour or so of light looking across a large area of forest with several emergent trees, most alive, some dead, hoping a cotinga might perch up high at the end of the day, as is the habit of some members of that family of birds. As David W. Snow stated in his fine book *The Cotingas*, 'Though they do not quite approach the birds of paradise in the extravagance of their ornamentation they are, among the passerines, second only to the birds of paradise.' We were in prime cotinga country where 14 species were possible, including several of the very best, so we began scanning hard, only to be distracted almost immediately by a small party of Paradise Tanagers in a tree next to us. They were not cotingas but they were just as exciting thanks to their mad combination of colours; black eyes and surrounds set in brilliant apple green heads on which the feathers were short and scaly and shiny, deep turquoise blue shoulders and underparts, black wings and backs, and flame-coloured lower backs and rumps. The tanagers of paradise would have been a fitting end to such a great day but while enjoying them a sparkling blue bird flew over us and landed in the top of the same tree as the tanagers. We could hardly believe our eyes, because it was a male Spangled Cotinga complete with a purple throat which like the rest of the metallic pale blue plumage lit up when the bird turned and the low light hit it. When the jewel flew off Al, having calmed down a little, checked out a plump-looking bird perched atop a distant dead tree stump with the telescope and then informed the rest of us, with unbelievable uncharacteristic understatement, that he was looking at a male Purple-breasted Cotinga. We rushed to his side and jostled with each other for a look through the telescope, at what, in the low evening light was the fantastic sight of a cobalt-blue bird with a deep purple throat and breast. Al could contain himself no longer. He was ecstatic to say the least and a massive grin and giggle came over him as he danced a little jig in celebration of, "Two *blue* cotingas in a minute!"

It was a thrilling end to a remarkable day, a day during which we also passed 500 species for the trip, in just over two weeks in South America. There were plenty more to look for too. Beyond KM98 on what we were then calling Paradise Road the tarmac suddenly begins to ascend what is known as *La Escalera*. In English this means 'The Staircase', a nod to what seems like a hundred hairpin bends before the top is reached. In the birding world *La Escalera* means birds, lots of birds, colourful and interesting and rare and different birds to the lowlands, many in fast-moving mixed species flocks. Still high from the day before, we drove into the superb tall forest at the base of *La Escalera* at first light, pulled over at KM117, got out of the car and began looking hard at the roadside trees, a stake-out for Guianan Cock-of-the-rock. It was raining but we carried on and a little way up the road we disturbed a large, slinky, black animal which climbed quickly down a tree from what looked like its resting place. It was gone in seconds, leaving us to argue over whether it was a Black Panther or not, while hoping for a flash of orange or to hear a sound resembling rubber ducks being strangled, at least one birder's description of the 'waa-oww' calls of the Guianan Cock-of-the-rock, but there were none. After a couple of hours we moved higher up, where most of the specialities occur and in the first foraging flock of birds we came across was yet another bird we had hardly dared dream of seeing. Perched still and quiet in the low canopy was a pair of Red-banded Fruiteaters, the male an understated beauty in grey and green with a red bill and a bright orange-red band across the breast, the female streaked mossy green. Apart from Guianan Cock-of-the-rock, which we had a few more chances to see, the top birds, not just cotingas, which normally take several days, even a few trips, to track down, seemed to be appearing one after the other. We even had time for lunch, sardine sandwiches, which we ate at the top of *La Escalera* up on *La Gran Sabana*. This is called 'The Great Savanna' in *The Lost World* of Sir Arthur Conan Doyle, in which the author tells the tale of explorers discovering dinosaurs on top of the remote, one-hundred-million-year-old, table-topped blocks of sandstone known as *Tepuis*, which dominate the landscape of southeast Venezuela. We could see a mighty one in the distance, rising with straight sides out of the rolling grasslands, the flat top visible briefly through its almost constant cloud cover.

After a welcome albeit brief rest we got up to look for Giant Snipe, Al with one white leg and one red leg, the sunlight was that raw. The Stid plodged round and round a bog long after the rest of us had given up of course, determined to flush a snipe out, and it was only when we got bored watching him and pretended we were watching something as rare as the snipe that he gave up and came running, as fast as he could through the sticky mud and water. Failing to find a new shorebird was a big blow but we did see two Tepui Goldenthroats, hummingbirds perfectly described by de Schauensee and Phelps in our field guide as 'glittering golden grass green'. We soon got back to seeing the top birds too. There was about an hour of light left and we were looking for the cock-of-the-rock again at KM117 when Brian from Boston came speeding up the road in his 4WD shouting out of the window, "Pompadour at 106.5!" A few minutes and a few hairy hairpin bends later we were looking through the telescope at a male Pompadour Cotinga. The fabulous bird was perched in the top of a dead tree and preening 'its delicate white wings and claret-coloured plumage', in the words of Alfred Russel Wallace in *A Narrative of Travels on the Amazon and Rio Negro*. The bird was indeed a rich, red wine colour, with a sort of gloss or lacquer to its unusual plumage, and equally eye-catching were its big and bright yellow eyes, with large black pupils. They were not on us though and we could relax and take turns with the telescope to cherish the moment, until the light began to fade and we headed for *Don Chin's* and the first of several *cervezas* to celebrate seeing Red-banded Fruiteater, which is a cotinga, and three of the most spectacular cotingas called 'cotinga', in twenty-four hours.

A tough day followed, back in the lowland rainforest on the trails at kilometres 67, 73 and 74 but it didn't matter because we saw the craziest cotingas of all. We heard them first. They were males at a lek and they sounded something like a herd of cows with chainsaws. Once we reached the lek we found the birds easily, four of them perched in the low canopy. Described by Snow as 'grotesque' and by some as 'hunchbacks' to me the Capuchinbirds looked like small night herons with their large bills, long, strong legs and thick, soft plumage, rich pale brown above and cinnamon below, although I suppose their small, bald, blue-grey heads could be seen by some as a little 'grotesque', and the ruff of tightly curled feathers around the back of their heads did give them something of a hunchbacked appearance. They certainly looked like nothing else in the world, especially when they started to display. Before singing, if it can be called that, a male leaned forward and inhaled, making a sort of 'grrrrrrrrrr' noise as he did so. Then he stood bolt upright on his perch, raised and puffed out his ruff, loosened the thick throat and chest feathers, and unfurled the orangey undertail coverts to form what looked like two eggs stuck on to the sides of the bird where its body met its tail, while going 'aaaaaaaa'. The extraordinary noises ended with 'ooo' and the weird display came to a close as the bird leaned back and sank down on to the branch.

It rained from dawn till dusk the following day but we stuck at it until the early afternoon and during a few brief forays from the car with my umbrella I saw a few new birds, the best of which were a very smart, black-hooded Fulvous Shrike Tanager with a large, hooked bill, and an absolutely stunning Black-eared Fairy, an immaculate black-masked dazzling dark green and snow white hummingbird which appeared like a phantom out of the forest flashing the white in its long tail as it flitted and hovered just above my head. Nick and The Stid even managed to see a male Guianan Cock-of-the-rock which put a bit of a damper on the day for me and Al but we only had to wait until dawn the next morning to see the

*Black-eared Fairy, Escalera, Venezuela, 9th January 1992*

big, bright, orange ball with a Mohican crest and long, fine, wavy, orange filaments drooped somewhat untidily over the folded wings. Through the telescope it was a wonderful sight and further proof that cotingas are second only to the birds-of-paradise when it comes to fancy feathers. We then saw two Sharpbills, strange, little known birds with green backs and black spots on the yellowish underparts, considered to be a cotinga by some taxonomists. A pair of Pompadour Cotingas also delayed our return to the upper end of *La Escalera* where we finally found a male Scarlet-horned Manakin, a tiny velvety black bird with a dazzling scarlet head and horns.

I had seen virtually everything I could have dreamed of in Bolivar, not least nine cotingas. For the life of me though I could not make it ten by locating any of the White Bellbirds we heard. The explosive 'klong-klang' that sounded like a giant hammer hitting a huge anvil occasionally rang out across the forested hillsides that were always out of view. We still had cotinga fever and we were faced with a stark choice; stay another day in Bolivar to try and see the White Bellbird or return to Henri Pittier National Park to give Handsome Fruiteater one last shot. Since we had been in bellbird country for days and not been successful and the fruiteater was endemic to Venezuela we decided on the latter. So, we bid a fond farewell to the wild frontier post of KM88 at 14:00 hours and drove, drove, drove, 750 miles (1200 km), along the narrow, pot-holed, slippery, bendy roads of Venezuela for sixteen hours, across the Orinoco and north, arriving at the *Hotel Maracay* at 06:00 and at Rancho Grande, where the trip had begun three weeks ago, at 07:00.

The fruiteater eluded us all day and we only truly stopped thinking about it when we were watching a male Wire-tailed Manakin, an intensely-coloured bird with a scarlet crown and nape, and velvety black back, wings and tail which all contrasted very nicely with the almost blinding yellow of the forehead, face and entire underparts. We had one morning left so we staked out the veranda of Rancho Grande where food is put out for the birds and where, we had been informed, five fruiteaters had appeared the day before. So, while taking our last longing looks at such delights as Long-tailed Sylphs and Blue-winged Mountain Tanagers we waited and hoped for a fruiteater to fly in and with the final minutes racing away a shout went up. By the time I saw what all the fuss was about it was half way across the gardens below but even in flight I could tell it was a male Handsome Fruiteater from above because the bright green and yellow bird had a black head and eye-catching silvery-white tips to the tertial feathers at the base of the wings. We dashed to the tree it looked like it had landed in but a thorough search from every angle and underneath revealed nothing. As one of the Dutch birders present said, "It was eaten by the tree!" I shook my head in frustration and disappointment. It was not the ending I had dreamed of. 'Flight views only' was the last thing I would have wished for had I even thought of that possibility with a fruiteater but there was no denying it the bird was a Handsome Fruiteater, my final and fourteenth cotinga of the 3700 mile (6000 km) tour of Venezuela, although it was not that bird I was thinking of as the half-empty DC10 climbed to a cruising height of 35,000 feet (10,670 metres) on its way to Santiago in Chile, it was the sheer numbers and diversity of birds in South America.

One day we were watching Long-tailed Sylphs in the cloud forests of Venezuela the next we were on the Pacific coast of Chile counting Inca Terns. There were 300 of them roosting on rocks just outside the small town of Arica near the border with Peru and with them were 200 or so Elegant Terns, ten Grey Gulls, thousands of Franklin's Gulls, too many Guanay Cormorants to count, at least a hundred Peruvian Pelicans, over fifty Peruvian Boobies and lots of shorebirds, from Blackish Oystercatchers to Surfbirds and Willets and Whimbrels.

*Diademed Plover, Parinacota, Lauca National Park, Chile, 14th January 1992*

There was a tremendous energy about Arica. The birds were resting but restless. There was much shuffling and toing and froing. Individual birds were moving from place to place amongst the flocks, little parties were breaking off and joining again, and many others were heading out to sea or returning from it, from the Humboldt Current, the cold, nutrient-rich water brought to the surface by upwelling and running along the west coast of middle South America, one of the most productive marine ecosystems on Earth with a vast food chain consisting mostly of anchovies, sardines and jack mackerel. The numbers of birds were testament to the richness of the offshore waters and it seemed like they were struggling to resist the urge to get back out there and reap the inexhaustible harvest.

I didn't know where to look but I settled down to watch the Inca Terns which are not grey above and white below like typical terns such as Elegant but dark slate-grey all over except for their red bills and legs, the tiny yellow wattles at the base of their bills and the thin, white plumes which form what look like rather dashing, drooping moustaches, curling down around their cheeks. Inca Terns eat mainly anchovies, which the agile birds pluck delicately from just below the surface while in flight, using their long and rather broad wings, and forked tails, to great effect. Grey Gulls were worth a long look too, another basically grey but nevertheless good-looking bird with a long, slender, black bill, long wings and long black legs, the deep lead-grey of the body fading softly to a white hood. Grey Gulls breed only in the Atacama Desert of Chile, laying their eggs in a scrape in the sand up to sixty miles (a hundred km) from the Pacific where they feed. They are one of the very few living things that can endure the huge fluctuations in air temperature, surface temperature, humidity and wind speed in the driest desert on Earth where the mean annual rainfall varies from zero to two millimetres and in some places it has not rained for hundreds of years. In this 'absolute desert' there is no vegetation at all and the landscape is similar to the surface of Mars. Even bacteria are few and far between.

To the east of the Atacama rise the Andes, to over 20,000 feet (6000 metres), and the rivers tumbling off the mountains irrigate linear oases that run through the desert to the ocean. Much of the native vegetation in these valleys, especially near the coast, has been replaced with vegetable fields, fruit orchards and olive groves, as well as built development, but what is left still supports small populations of some very specialised birds, and it was these that we went in pursuit of, in the Lluta Valley. The best bird there was what the Chileans call *Pizarrita*; the Slender-billed Finch, which didn't look much like a finch. The long-tailed, plain grey bird had a pointed, bright yellow bill designed for handling insects not the dull, stubby, seed-eating bill normally associated with a finch. No wonder it has been placed in its own *Xenospingus* genus.

Above the valley in the Andean foothills the slopes were very arid and seemingly devoid of life but as we drove higher we noticed a few flowers followed by the odd cactus and shrub, on slopes with a tad more moisture, provided by fog created where the cold Humboldt Current runs close to the hot land and cools the air. Where there is vegetation, even the tiniest scrap, there are birds and it was not long before we saw our first Greyish Miner, a ground-living, lark-like, rather dull bird and nowhere near as exciting to me as male Andean Hillstars, hummingbirds with white breasts and emerald gorgets. We then saw our first Guanacos, the smaller, smarter-looking, wild version of the domesticated Llama, grazing on the most succulent new plant growth they could find.

A few hours above the Lluta Valley we reached the small town of Putre at nearly 11,500 feet (3500 metres), a good place to acclimatize to the altitude before ascending even higher in search of the bird which would make or break the trip; Diademed Plover. The tension over this one bird had been mounting since we had arrived in Arica and it was all we could do to resist heading up to the heights it lives at straight away. The only hotel in Putre was expensive but as usual smooth-tongued Al persuaded the manager to let us book a double room for the four of us, and just to save a few more pesos, he also convinced him to let us eat in the staff canteen instead of the restaurant.

It was freezing at first light and the staff canteen was closed so, for breakfast, we all indulged in a large bowl of hot rice pudding in the local miner's mess that we stumbled upon, being welcomed with open arms. We were already liking Chile very much when we then got to see some more of its fascinating birds during a terrific morning wander around the small green fields and well-vegetated gullies of Putre, not least an aptly-named green hummingbird called a Sparkling Violetear, thrasher-like Straight-billed and White-throated Earthcreepers, and a large, grey-brown flycatcher with a long, hooked bill known as a White-tailed Shrike Tyrant. Another, much smaller, hook-billed bird, black above and chestnut below, was a fine male Black-throated Flowerpiercer. More colour came in the form of Blue-and-yellow Tanagers and some lovely burnt orange, tawny and yellow Black-hooded Sierra Finches while up above in the blue some very smart Andean Swifts, black with white collars, rumps and bellies, whizzed around in pursuit of hardy flying insects.

By midday we could resist no longer. The power of Diademed Plover was too strong. After we had managed to find some fuel, siphoned out of jerry cans, in the almost deserted cobbled streets of Putre, we began heading up the Andes. The tarmac ran out and we continued on a corrugated track up through bird-less, scree-covered slopes to wide, grassy, green flats with pools sprinkled with Andean Geese and Andean Gulls. As we approached the hamlet of Parinacota three Puna Tinamous, stripy-headed birds which looked like 'tumbleweed on legs', scooted across the track. They were merely a distraction. We had arrived in Diademed Plover country and on pulling over and getting out of the jeep we began scanning harder than ever before.

Diademed Plovers live in cushion bogs known as *bofedales* above 13,000 feet (4000 metres) but although there are thousands of such bogs along the wide shoulders of the Andes for some unknown reason the birds do not occur in many of them. They are also only the size of a Dunlin and tend to keep to rivulets with banks just a bit higher than themselves in the deceptively large expanses of bog they do occur in, so they are rare, highly localised and hard to find, especially without a map with an X on it marking where they had been seen before. We concentrated on that X on the map we had and there, just a few paces from the X, was a Diademed Plover! We couldn't believe it. The bird we wanted to see more than any other in South America, at least on the Chile leg of the trip, the small bird we thought would take a day possibly days to track down in the vast, open bogs of the high Andes, took about two minutes to see, and what a crazy-looking bird it was. The Diademed Plover is stocky like a plover but it has a longish, slim bill like a sandpiper, a unique combination. The top of its head was dark, the diadem, or crown, around it, white, the face black, the back of its neck bright rufous, the back grey-brown and below the white bib were the exquisitely very finely barred underparts. We took it in turns to watch it through the telescope as it shuffled along the top of a rivulet but it was soon time to move on, although we thought we could return to watch it as many times as we liked during the next few days.

As far as I was concerned, after the plover everything else would be a bonus and first up, before we got back in the jeep, was an Andean Condor that passed high overhead, its white ruff contrasting with the broad, black, fingered wings. We then drove into Parinacota where less than thirty people live in scattered small houses made of stone, some of which are painted with white lime and thatched with bunchgrass. From some angles the place looked almost exactly like it had been used for scenes in one of Sergio Leone's 'Spaghetti Westerns'. We were surprised any people lived there at all, at over 14,000 feet (4400 metres) above sea level and almost completely surrounded by the *altiplano*, the high plains of dry *puna* where millions of clumps of bunchgrass are separated by bare sandy soil, although dominating the view from the village were the picturesque Parinacota and Ponerape volcanoes, both over 20,000 feet (6000 metres) high. Some geologists think the

Parinacota volcano collapsed about 8000 years ago, creating a massive avalanche which blocked enough rivulets to help form Lake Chungara, claimed by some to be the highest lake in the world at 14,820 feet (4518 metres). It is a shallow, well-vegetated lake chock-full of waterweeds, Giant Coots and Silvery Grebes. Ten thousand or so coots have been counted on the lake at any one time, the largest gathering on Earth of the bird which builds one of the largest nests of any bird, up to ten feet (three metres) long and five feet (one and a half metres) high, with a cup big enough and deep enough for a human to sit in, and where baby coots can shelter from the unrelenting cold winds.

We booked into the dark, draughty hostel in Parinacota then set out on a long trudge across the *puna* in the late afternoon, bumping into some Grey-breasted Seedsnipes, shorebirds according to taxonomists but looking more like doves as they foraged close to the ground on short legs. The name is not so much misleading as plain wrong; the four species in the seedsnipe family of birds feed mainly on the fresh growth of plants not seeds and they have short, stubby bills nothing like the long 'spears' of snipes. We didn't care about avian molecular systematics and shorebird phylogenetic relationships we were just happy to see the first of the two birds on the last plate in *Shorebirds*, a book of dreams, now being fulfilled.

By the time we got back to the hostel I had a thumping headache, felt very tired and cold, and soon afterwards began feeling nauseous. I didn't want anything to eat but Al forced me to sip some hot asparagus soup which I promptly regurgitated. I had altitude sickness. My body could not cope with a 9% drop in the amount of oxygen in the air above 14,000 feet (4200 metres). It seemed a night acclimatizing in Putre had not helped, or perhaps it had because I may have felt a lot worse without that night. One thing was for sure I had to keep a close eye on my condition. Altitude sickness can cause the brain to swell or lead to fluid on the lungs, both of which can kill. I probably felt so bad because I had taken on way too much activity on our first day at Parinacota. I wasn't short of breath which was a good sign, but I was coughing up pink sputum, which was a bad sign, so it was time to be on the lookout for bladder and bowel problems, blurred vision, poor coordination, drowsiness and paralysis. My eyes were not bleeding so at least my brain wasn't about to explode. I was just so tired and cold and all I wanted to do, more than anything else in the whole world, was lie down and huddle up in my sleeping bag and go to sleep.

The next morning The Stid was feeling worse than me. He was still up first as usual and somehow I managed to get out of my sleeping bag and stand upright. Perhaps it was the prospect of seeing three new shorebirds. We were so weary, and our heads felt like they were being crushed, but we struggled half a mile across a spongy cushion bog to reach a shallow, saline lake and suddenly birding in the high Andes was like I imagined it would be; a big blue sky, a huge vista across the *puna* flats to snow-capped peaks and volcanoes, my first grey-headed and green-backed Andean Lapwings flying around, and amongst the more familiar shorebirds sprinkled across the lake such as Wilson's Phalaropes, there were some tiny Puna Plovers with black, white and cinnamon-coloured heads, and about thirty Andean Avocets with crazy, slender, up-curved bills which they were sweeping from side to side through the water, to detect prey such as small crustaceans by touch. With the three new shorebirds were two groups of flamingos; yellow-kneed Andean and red-kneed Chilean. The third flamingo which occurs in Lauca National Park, the smallest, daintiest and rarest, James's, was missing, but the classic Andean scene was completed by a couple of White-fronted Ground Tyrants, one of about ten species of Andean 'wheatears', and two Cordilleran Canasteros, 'small, grey-brown jobs' with some rufous in their long, cocked tails. In Chile, by some strange quirks of evolutionary biology and biogeography, the canastero, cinclodes, earthcreeper and miner bird families are each represented by about six 'small, grey-brown jobs'.

After a breathless walk back across the bog we returned to the hostel where three angels appeared. Seeing the sorry state of The Stid, me, and Nick as well by then, the beautiful Chilean students soon had a brew of coca tea on. The Stid drank tentatively while Nick and I, with zealous belief in the magical powers of a tiny bit of cocaine, got it down our necks as fast as we could. The leaves of the coca plant have been brewed and chewed for thousands of years by the Andeans because the plant contains alkaloids like cocaine which keep fatigue, hunger, thirst and altitude sickness at bay. The effects were remarkable; Nick and I felt a lot better after a couple of hours, more or less normal in fact apart from headaches, but The Stid drank very little and his headache actually intensified, and not long after he was feeling dazed and confused so, very reluctantly, particularly on the part of The Stid, we all agreed, having seen Diademed Plover of course, that we should head back down to sea-level where his lungs needed to be, as soon as possible. When The Stid asked us to stop for a break from the corrugated track, which was bashing his throbbing brain to pulp, a lethargic scan out of the car windows revealed two Puna Rheas, large, flightless birds with long necks, and long, thick legs. That cheered The Stid up, a touch.

Back in Arica we headed straight to the coast for a seawatch, a birding term for scanning the sea with binoculars and telescopes in search of foraging or passing seabirds. At home in Britain there are often few birds to be seen and much of a seawatch is indeed spent 'seawatching', not a bad way to pass the time, but now and again hundreds sometimes thousands of birds may be seen, a wonderful way to pass the time. It all depends on the season, the amount of food available and the weather, onshore winds often resulting in at least some avian action. In just a gentle sea breeze off Chile we saw plenty of birds and The Stid soon began to feel better, especially when our first Pink-footed Shearwater passed by with some Sooty Shearwaters, a bird familiar from home.

The Stid felt even better the next morning when he got a tick as soon as we stepped out of the *Hotel Marcos*; an Oasis Hummingbird that was bathing in the fountain. We were rushing to get to the Azapa Valley to look for that and two other hummers and once there we saw a few Chilean Woodstars and a superb male Peruvian Sheartail, another tiny mite with a tiny bill and an extremely long, whitish tail. We dashed back to the hotel, packed as fast as we could and arrived at Arica airport an hour or so before our midday flight to Santiago, only to discover that there was just one other car in the car-park, and only one person inside the airport, an astonished lady who soon confirmed that we were a day early.

"I'm blaming it on the altitude sickness!" I said in my defence but the others were not having it.

We could not drive to Santiago it was a thousand miles (1600 km) away, so there was nothing for it but to go seawatching, not such a terrible outcome thanks to a stiff southwesterly wind blowing in off the Pacific. Hundreds of Sooty Shearwaters were passing by, flying south, and with them we picked out three Buller's Shearwaters with dark 'm' shapes across their soft grey wings, and a Juan Fernandez Petrel, a slimmer, longer-winged, faster-moving bird.

We celebrated our extra night in Arica with a few more beers than usual, sitting outside and wondering why there were more beautiful women in that sunny town than any other in the world. I woke up to the cooing, soothing, 'Hoopoedoodle hoopoedoodle hoopoedoodle' of White-winged Doves. It is always nice to be reminded by the birds that I am in a foreign place. There were no White-winged Doves in the town of Punta Arenas, nearly 2500 miles (1500 km) to the south, which we reached via Santiago, flying over the glaciers and snow-capped peaks of the southern Andes down almost the entire length of Chile to 53°10'S, farther south than the Subantarctic Islands of New Zealand, far enough south for penguins and in a hired jeep the first place we headed for was a Magellanic Penguin rookery at Seno Otway. We failed to find the colony twice, a frustrating few hours that were saved by a long walk in the sunshine during which we saw a Hog-nosed Skunk with a brown stripe running along its white back, and lots of new birds the best of which were the large and surprisingly handsome silver-grey and buff Black-faced Ibises. Back in town we found the perfect accommodation for us, bed-and-breakfast at *Nena's Hostal* for just over a pound a night.

The first new bird the next morning was a Magellanic Penguin, the first of several on the Strait of Magellan appropriately enough, as we crossed to Porvenir on Tierra del Fuego, but it was the Black-browed Albatrosses I could not take my eyes off, as they glided with great ease and elegance low across the cold water. The first new bird on the 'Land of Fire' was a Great Grebe, an elegant swimming bird with a sleek black head, long, slim, black bill, long, slim, rust-coloured neck and long, slim, dark-backed body lying low in the water and ending with a short, fluffy, buffy, cocked-up tail; another mad variation on the flamboyant grebe theme. The next new bird was a striking twist on the rather more mundane gull clan, a medium-sized, stocky one with a light grey head, neck and body, black back and wings, red legs, pale yellow eyes with red rims and a bulbous, bright red bill called a Dolphin Gull. We were also excited to see our first Magellanic Oystercatchers although they looked almost exactly the same as the everyday oystercatcher at home apart from yellow rings around yellow eyes instead of red around red.

The lack of the shorebird we were especially hoping to see on Tierra del Fuego on the first few pools was a little disconcerting to say the least but when we reached a large lake another scan revealed a dinky, dumpy, dove-like, stone grey and white shorebird with red eyes known as the

Magellanic Plover, a species in a family all of its own because it is so different to all other shorebirds. Suddenly it and many of the other shorebirds around the lake, including what looked like some Two-banded Plovers, rose fast and high into the air, flushed by a Kleinschmidt's Falcon, a rare and magnificent pale morph of the resident race of Peregrine, with washed out head markings, white underparts and glacial grey wings.

We waited for the plovers to return and looked hard for them elsewhere without success and all too soon it was time to think about heading back to the mainland. Having been informed that there was no way back from Porvenir for three days we faced a long drive to the northern tip of Tierra del Fuego to hopefully connect with the other ferry, operating between there and Punta Delgada. Without a useful map and with few road signs to help we nearly ended up in a minefield near the border with Argentina and while lost we saw a Magellanic Snipe, yet another new shorebird, and a surprisingly beautifully marked Chocolate-vented Tyrant, a ground-dwelling, thrush-sized flycatcher with a blue-grey head and breast, rufous belly, and black, white and rufous wings. It was a very welcome distraction from our predicament but difficult to enjoy until we finally connected with Ruta 257 and were back on track.

The queue for the ferry was so long we were not sure we would make it but we did. The only trouble was that nearly a hundred miles (160 km) of gravel track lay between our empty stomachs and Punta Arenas; not much of a problem for people not obsessed by birds but slow going for us because the Patagonian steppe, the overgrazed arid grassland in the rain-shadow of the Andes brushed by dry summer winds and dotted with brackish and saline lakes, was home to a surprising diversity of birds, not least some more Magellanic Plovers, lots of Two-banded Plovers, which looked very smart with two broad black bands across their bold white chests, and our first and what turned out to be only Least Seedsnipe, a very confiding male that we watched from just a couple of paces away, close enough to see the diagnostic line of black feathers running down from its white throat to the black lower breast band. That was the last plate in *Shorebirds*, Plate 88, 'Smaller seedsnipes', complete. It was getting late, Al forced the jeep to go as fast as possible across the dusty plain, the windscreen cracks widening all the time, and fourteen hours after breakfast we finally reached the splendid restaurant called *El Beagle* and rarely has a cold beer tasted so fine. Once again we appeared to be the only customers with our very own happy, efficient waiter and the conger eel dressed with anemones was soon before us and soon dispatched.

We found the Magellanic Penguin colony at Seno Otway at the third attempt although we soon got bored of looking at the penguins standing outside their nesting burrows and wandered off in search of two more possible new shorebirds. It was a windy but splendid wild place in which to look for them; a flat grassy plain next to the sound with a shoreline littered with washed up tree trunks, and low but snow-capped peaks across the wide water, and we succeeded with one shorebird, seeing at least 60 Rufous-chested Dotterels, pretty little plovers with white headbands, grey faces, rufous chests and black breast bands contrasting strongly with their white bellies. Two pale, buffy birds in flight a long way off, showing white wing bars from above, were almost certainly the other shorebird we were after but we did not want to see Tawny-throated Dotterels in flight we wanted to see the straw-striped birds on the ground and study their exquisite markings, so the search continued, although we did switch off shorebirds for a while when we came across a flock of terrific little birds called Thorn-tailed Rayaditos in a small, scrubby thicket. Contrasting with their white throats were three broad stripes flaring across their heads, coloured black, cinnamon and black, two broad and striking cinnamon-coloured bars crossing their dark, folded wings, and large rufous tails, the outer feathers of which had pointy, thorny tips.

There was talk of a 'Red Tide' near Punta Arenas amongst the other guests at *Nena's*, a dense bloom of phytoplankton in the sea which can produce neurotoxins strong enough to paralyze and kill fish, sea turtles, seabirds and marine mammals, and, if ingested via filter-feeding shellfish, humans as well, so we checked as best we could with our poor Spanish that it was safe to tuck into another mountain of seafood in *El Beagle*. We were still alive the next morning, and raring to go with our next quest. The nearest sizeable tract of *Nothofagus* southern beech forest was at Fuerte Bulnes, about forty miles (65 km) south of Punta Arenas. Built in 1843 with a view to establishing a town, the harsh terrain and weather put off settlers and the fort was eventually abandoned. It's not human history that interests us it is natural history, and the reason we went there was to look for one of the largest woodpeckers in the world, the Magellanic Woodpecker, a magnificent bird which lives in unusually large territories and can therefore be very hard to track down. After a long, tough slog through the old, mossy, dark tangle of twisted trees, seeing very little apart from a 'Magellanic' Great Horned Owl, Al, Nick and I were loafing by the jeep cursing The Stid for making us wait before we could head off in search of Tawny-throated Dotterels again, when he came running out of the forest yelling, "Magellanic ... Magellanic ... Magellanic Black Woodpecker!" A short sprint and we were all looking at four surprisingly confiding, very large, black woodpeckers, the male with a shiny scarlet head and Mohican, and the female with a dark red face and stiff, curly, black crest. The other two were probably the young from the previous two years since these woodpeckers usually only have one young each breeding season and they stay with the family group for up to two years. We did not look at them long though because we were drawn to the parents and their crazy crests.

When the woodpeckers moved off so did we, back to Seno Otway in search of Tawny-throated Dotterels. We couldn't find any and we had to be content with 200 of the Rufous-chested variety instead, as well as at least twenty Two-banded Plovers, and plenty of wintering Baird's Sandpipers, Knots and Hudsonian Godwits, all of them 4500 miles (7200 km) or so from their high-arctic nesting grounds. There were so many shorebirds but not the one we wanted to see the most, and we couldn't find any on our last morning in far south Chile either, and we nearly missed our flight to Santiago because Al kicked a tyre on the jeep in frustration and broke the valve, and the jack didn't work so we couldn't get the wheel off to replace the flat. Thankfully, some friendly Chileans in a passing truck came to our rescue.

At Santiago airport we were given a *Subaru* saloon. Finding the road east out of Chile's sprawling capital city to the Andes was not easy and once we succeeded we sustained a double puncture. A local man, passing by on foot, looked us over, and really did mutter, "Crazy gringos." It was ten o'clock at night and getting dark when the first truck that came along stopped to help. The driver took Nick and the flats to San Jose de Maipo, the nearest town, where they somehow managed to find a place to get the tyres fixed at midnight. So, I was rudely awoken from pleasant dreams by the side of the road at half past one in the morning and none too pleased about it. We drove very carefully the rest of the way up the steep road and track that climbed the Yeso Valley. There was not a blade of grass let alone a square inch of flat dust amongst the scree to lie down on, so we had to get back in the car and try to get a few hours kip before dawn.

It was a good job we had seen Diademed Plover before. We walked miles, seeing a lot of birds for such a bleak place, including a Puna Plover with two youngsters and two Grey-breasted Seedsnipes, but we could not find the bird we would have loved another, longer, look at. By late morning the lovely warm early sunshine had turned into a fierce heat so we began making our way down the valley but we soon sustained another puncture. One more would have left us at the mercy of the sun blasting down from the vast blue skies in the shade-less landscape, and with little hope of rescue on the remote track, so we proceeded with great caution to the first garage we could find.

Negotiating one-way-street-Santiago for the second time was as frustrating as the first but we eventually reached

Lago Penuelas where the numerous waterbirds included more new ducks, in a land of ducks, including the cuckoo of the duck world, the long, dark Black-headed Duck.

We decided to make the 'vineyard of the sea', Vina del Mar, our base camp for some coastal birding on the last leg of the lengthy trip. It was day thirty-four of the full-on birding trip and even 'The Leader', alias The Stid, was beginning to crack. He failed to wake the rest of us up before dawn the next morning and only got round to suggesting we find somewhere for breakfast *before* heading into the field when his watched beeped at eight a.m. He was not normally keen on breakfast if it was daylight and birds could be seen. All we could find was coffee and after enjoying that we drove south along the Pacific shoreline, past masses of boobies and pelicans, to the mouth of the Rio Aconcagua near the seaside resort of Concon where along with hundreds of Franklin's Gulls and over 200 Black Skimmers we soon found ten tiny Collared Plovers, the 14th new shorebird species we had seen in Chile and the 19th of the whole trip including Venezuela. We rued the missing Tawny-throated Dotterel but still rejoiced in such a large haul of birds in one of our favourite families.

We also saw a Rufous-tailed Plantcutter, a large finch-like bird with a chestnut cap and under-parts, called a plantcutter because it cuts leaves, shoots, buds and grasses with the serrated edges of its bill, a strange feature for a perching bird and one reason it is in a genus with just two other plantcutters, both of which also occur only in South America, a genus within the cotinga family no less, so Al was particularly pleased. The best bird of the morning for me was a male Spectacled Tyrant, a dinky, plump, black flycatcher with a sharp, pale lemon-yellow bill and similar coloured wattles around its white eyes which looked like small yellow flowers adorning its face. It looked extraordinary in flight too, with flashing white feathers at the ends of its short, rounded, black wings.

Not far away from Concon, in the lovely wooded valley of Zapallar, we saw several Green-backed Firecrowns, tiny hummingbirds dwarfed by an eye-catching, fly-catching Giant Hummingbird, the largest hummingbird in the world, as big as a starling. Just offshore there were hundreds of Humboldt Penguins at a rookery on Isla Cachagua. We could see them from a distance but it was too hot to walk closer, too hot to bird in the middle of the day in fact, and the beach we could see the penguins from was such a nice spot we gave in and relaxed and actually forgot about birds for once, while enjoying an ice cream, a very rare treat indeed, especially during daylight on a birding trip.

We were certainly flagging now, after so many days in the field, and after so many birds, but, of course, The Stid's thoughts soon returned to more serious matters. We were still licking our ice creams when he brought up the possibility of hiring a boat to take us out of Valparaiso, the nearby seaport, to look for seabirds but we all soon agreed that it would be way too expensive. So, we spent the afternoon trying to see a few of the birds we might have seen from a boat, from a headland, at Quintero. All we saw were a few Sooty Shearwaters but the following morning when The Stid had returned to form and made sure we were in position on the same headland by first light, a few more 'Sooties' were joined by two Pink-footed Shearwaters and two Shy Albatrosses gliding south. The albatrosses were bulkier than the 'Black-broweds' we saw in the Strait of Magellan, with pale grey heads and they looked like the next most powerful model in that superior range of seabirds.

There is not much *Matorral,* natural open forest, left in central Chile, even in La Campana National Park, where, in shocking, debilitating dry heat I saw the endemic Crag Chilia, a spiky-billed, white-throated, brown and rufous, long-tailed rock-loving bird, but I missed Moustached Turca, White-throated Tapaculo and White-throated Treerunner, all seen by the others, and I was not happy. I was even less happy when we discovered the marsh where I was hoping to see the pretty patterned Many-coloured Rush Tyrant was bone dry. That was me done. After 35 days birding I was burnt out. I could hardly be bothered to look at my first Rosybill, another duck, in the heat haze at Lago Penuelas, where we stopped off on our way back to Santiago and a night trying to sleep in the airport before the twenty four hour flight home, plenty of time to ponder the statistics; about 600 species seen in Venezuela, a further 200 or so different ones in Chile, around 800 in all, about a quarter of the birds of South America, in not much more than a month.

"Incredible!" I said, "Too many though, too many to take in."

"It's all a blur." Nick added as he nodded off in the seat next to me.

*Spoon-billed Sandpiper, Mai Po, Hong Kong, 23rd April 1993*

## 9

# HONG KONG

The *Boeing 747* I was on appeared to be heading straight for the skyscrapers I could see out of the window. Where else could it be going? There were skyscrapers all around; some so close to the plane people living on the highest floors had their washing out to dry in the rush of air created by the massive machine moving at 200 mph (320 km/h). I could see t-shirts hanging on the lines over the balconies. Then, at a height of about 650 feet (200 metres) the jet suddenly banked 47° right, a manoeuvre known as the 'Kai Tak Heart Attack', and there was the runway, almost directly below, a finger of concrete jutting out into Kowloon Bay, and somehow the pilot got the plane down on to it without ending up in the water.

Landing at Kai Tak airport was a memorable way to start a trip to Hong Kong. I was there because Gary Grant, a friend from my days at the London Wildlife Trust, asked me if I would like to carry out some bird survey work, mostly counting my beloved shorebirds. Nine months had passed since I quit the Thamesmead Wildlife Project where I was manager, due to what I considered to be a lack of necessary funding, and started out as a freelance ecological consultant. Not much survey work was coming my way but I was busy researching and writing a book entitled *Where to watch birds in South America* for Christopher Helm (Publishers) Limited, when Gary called.

From Kai Tak we were chauffeur-driven in a large *Mercedes* to the opulent 33-storey *Furama Hotel* in 'Central', the middle of the skyscraper city on Hong Kong Island, and shown to our large rooms overlooking the harbour. There were no birds amongst the numerous container ships, passenger ferries and assorted other small craft but soaring above the chaos were Black-eared Kites, some hanging in the updrafts outside my window. It turned out that the man who wanted the bird surveys carried out was Mr Fu, the owner of the *Furama*. When Gary had a meeting with him in his office at the top of the hotel the smartly-dressed man with a clean-shaven head barely said a word, merely nodding slightly now and again at which point one of the men standing to his right and left would leave the room sharply to attend to Gary's requests for documents and so on. One evening in our favourite restaurant in the *Furama*,

*The Rotisserie*, Mr Fu stopped to talk to us on the way to his table and suddenly the waiters moved even quicker to fill our glasses and bring our food, and once the word spread through the rest of the hotel that we were working for Mr Fu we were treated like kings.

Mr Fu was part of a consortium exploring the possibility of building a housing complex and golf course on a large area of fishponds at Nam Sang Wai on mainland Hong Kong next to Mai Po Nature Reserve and Deep Bay, a tidal backwater of the Pearl River Delta which is a vitally important wintering and migration stopover site for huge numbers of a great diversity of waterbirds, some very rare. Understandably, the World Wide Fund for Nature Hong Kong (WWF HK), the powerful, local non-governmental nature conservation body and managers of Mai Po were very concerned about what impact such a development might have on the birdlife of Mai Po and the wider Deep Bay area. It was a real hot potato to get involved in. Gary and I were avid conservationists but we were fed up getting nowhere banging on about it. Over a *Tsingtao* or two (Chinese beer, pronounced 'Ching Dow'), not for the first time in our lives we thought maybe it was worth considering working *with* instead of against the 'enemy', the developers, and to see where that would get us, or more importantly, the birds of the Deep Bay area.

Our first visit to Nam Sang Wai was on a sunny but chilly January day. While waiting for the sampan to take us across the narrow, foul-smelling, black channel of filth called the Kam Tin River, I looked around at the makeshift village of old, open, single-storey, grey wooden shelters, standing on stilts along the 'river' and above the fishponds, where people lived surrounded by their own rubbish and shat over a hole in a piece of wood above the ponds or river. Their waste water, food, fat, plastic containers and other rubbish ended up in the river too, where it joined the waste fuel, oil and other chemicals leaking from the adjacent industrial estate, creating a toxic soup probably swimming with pathogens, although it was difficult to imagine anything could live in it. Certainly, no one should have to live next to it. I held my nose while we crossed the sickening stuff and hoped I would not fall out of the tiny sampan into it, while wondering what fresh hell lay ahead. Back on land, over the top of a high, grassy bund, I was delighted to see a complex of small, muddy-watered, reed-fringed fishponds surrounded by tall Red River Gums from Australia and some mangroves, and frequented by a lot of birds, including Chinese Pond Herons, Black-capped and Pied Kingfishers, Long-tailed Shrikes, Olive-backed Pipits, and two Oriental Storks that were standing in the shallows of one of the largest ponds.

The thought of the ponds being turned into a housing complex and golf course did not sit comfortably with us. Although most of the birds could adapt to live on a well-designed golf course with the right water features they would be present in lower numbers. However, the ponds were not working ponds. They had been largely abandoned and become somewhat overgrown. If people were allowed back the ponds would soon be like the active ponds of adjacent Lut Chau, with deep water, steep banks, no vegetation and no birds, in which case a leafy golf course with reed-fringed channels and ponds would be something of an improvement as far as birds were concerned. Lut Chau, it turned out, was also owned by the consortium and

Gary and I thought about that very carefully, and after several more field visits and indoor meetings, and knowing money was virtually no object, we suggested that, in mitigation for the loss of some good habitat at Nam Sang Wai, perhaps the clients would consider turning Lut Chau, about a third of the total area available including Nam Sang Wai, into a state-of-the-art nature reserve and thus form an extension to the protected area of adjacent Deep Bay including Mai Po. We expected some tough negotiations; rarely would such a large chunk of land be given up by developers back home *and* so much money spent on it, but there were hardly any objections and in no time at all, after Mr Fu gave a slight nod, it was agreed, so despite WWF HK still objecting to the project, mainly because they considered the proposed nature reserve insufficient compensation for the loss of the ponds at Nam Sang Wai, we decided to give it a go, to, hopefully, bolster and improve the Mai Po/Deep Bay wetland complex and maybe even set a precedent for future developments in Hong Kong and the rest of the world. If anybody could do it Gary could. He is a very intelligent, knowledgeable and practical human being, able to articulate his innovative ideas far more eloquently than anyone else I know, and implement them. I don't think I would have been comfortable working on a project WWF HK objected to if Gary had not been so enthusiastic and immediately in consummate control of it.

John Edge, who I met in Borneo a couple of years before, lived in Hong Kong. In fact, 'The Edge' lived on the edge. His accommodation, which came with being a government lawyer, was a spacious apartment almost on top of The Peak on Hong Kong Island, at nearly 2000 feet (600 metres) above Central, and my first view from his balcony, a fine glass of red in my hand, was truly spectacular. I don't like cities but I have to admit the sea of skyscrapers below, crammed into a narrow belt of mostly reclaimed land at the bottom of the steep spine of the small island, was an incredible sight. It was dark and the endless towers were lit up like a gigantic still of a firework display. All I could think of was the film *Blade Runner*, but it wasn't a dystopian Los Angeles in 2019 it was Hong Kong in 1993 and as far as I was aware there were no *Blade Runners* down there hunting genetically engineered beings known as replicants although it did look like it probably would not be long before such a thing came to pass.

About 150 years before I visited Hong Kong just 7500 people lived there, mostly charcoal burners and fishermen, in a few coastal hamlets. Standing on The Edge's balcony I was surrounded by six million, yes six million people, living in 400 square miles (1000 sq km), one of the most densely populated places on the planet. We humans are social animals but 6000 people per square kilometre that's crazy. Daniel Boone, the 18th century North American frontiersman, would not have been happy; he thought places were getting overcrowded if he could see another man's fire. He would have felt claustrophobic in Mongolia, where there was just one person per square kilometre in the mid-1990s. Millions more people live on the Chinese mainland past Hong Kong's boundary. From there it is 15 miles (25 km) to Shenzhen, the then rapidly expanding instant city built on levelled hills, just part of the planned Pearl River Delta Mega City, 50 miles (80 km) long and six miles (10 km) wide, designed to accommodate 80 million people, in something reminiscent of the other dystopian future Los Angeles, *Mega-City Two*, the fictional nightmare in the *Judge Dredd* comic book series, which covers much of the west coast of America. Looking down at the skyscrapers below me the thought of them stretching all the way to the Pearl River Delta horizon was suddenly less fantastic, and more apocalyptic.

> I have a Vision of The Future, chum,
> The worker's flats in fields of soya beans
> Tower up like silver pencils, score on score:
>
> *The Planster's Vision by John Betjeman, 1945*

In 1981 Peter Scott visited Deep Bay with a view to the Wildfowl Trust, which he founded, helping the World Wildlife Fund (latterly the World Wide Fund for Nature but still WWF), which he co-founded, to protect an area next to the bay known as Mai Po as a reserve and in 1983 this came to pass. In later life he realized that the WWF, like most conservation organisations, was not very effective against the tide of humanity sweeping the planet, stating that, 'when we first set up WWF, our objective was to save endangered species from extinction. But we have failed completely; we haven't managed to save a single one. If only we had put all that money into condoms, we might have done some good.' He was exaggerating of course; the Wildfowl Trust and WWF are saving many species, albeit mostly in much lower numbers than years ago. However, Peter Scott thought deeply about the future of wildlife, didn't like what he thought, knew there were too many people, and, having the money, decided to conserve as much as he could.

Not enough money alas to save the forests, marshes and paddy fields of the Pearl River Delta. They have almost gone, lost to a staggering tsunami of people and skyscrapers, and yet squeezed in between the sad future of human life there is something else which looks like science fiction, a station where the *Siberian Shorebird Express* stops and the multitude of birds on it take a break to rest and refuel. The birds are migrating from their wintering shores as far south as Australia and New Zealand to their breeding grounds as far north as Siberia, Arctic Russia and even Alaska. They stop off at traditional 'staging' sites and one of these is Deep Bay where in the mid-1990s over 20,000, sometimes 30,000, shorebirds, of over 30 species, paused on their remarkable journeys. The vast majority pass through during April so that is when I needed to be there, to see how many of the birds utilized Nam Sang Wai and Lut Chau, how many might use the site in the future, especially Lut Chau should it become a reserve, and, I admit, to stand my best chance of seeing the rarest of them all, the Spoon-billed Sandpiper.

So it was on our second visit in mid-April when The Edge met Gary and me at Kai Tak and drove us straight to Tai Po Kau Nature Reserve, a small patch of secondary forest. There were a couple of hours of daylight left and The Edge was hoping to show us some of the many migrant landbirds which also pass through Hong Kong during the spring. After an hour and a half walking around the almost silent woods not seeing a single bird for more than a second or two we were rather unimpressed. Then, while we were trying to get a glimpse of a Hainan Blue Flycatcher from part of the trail known as 'flycatcher alley' we heard a high-pitched, chuckling call. The Edge has an amazing ear and instantly recognises the calls of every bird he has heard before. He knew what it was straight away but for once he didn't believe his ears, because the bird he heard was a Bay Woodpecker, the first ever in Hong Kong. The Edge is not a man to leap about when such an extraordinary event happens but his voice did raise an octave or two when we then saw the woodpecker, and again later while we enjoyed a lavish meal in the *Furama*, washed down with fine wine from the cellar chosen by The - very happy - Edge, all expenses paid for of course.

After very little sleep, due to wine, jet-lag and excitement, I was up at four o'clock in the morning ready for The Edge to take me to Mai Po for the first time. We needed to be in a hide at the peak of a high spring tide, ready for when the mudflats in Deep Bay were covered with water and the birds were forced to seek a safe roosting site, a shallow lagoon known as The Scrape. The birds came pouring in, low over the mangroves, in tight flocks which swirled around a couple of times before gliding down to the mud and shallow water in front of us, where the thousands of superb summer-plumaged shorebirds crammed together formed a wonderful spectacle, made up of black Spotted Redshanks, dark, striped Broad-billed Sandpipers, chestnut-red Curlew Sandpipers, black-flecked Marsh Sandpipers, rufous-capped Sharp-tailed Sandpipers, black-masked and orange-breasted Lesser and Greater Sand Plovers, dinky Long-toed and Red-necked Stints, and four Red-necked Phalaropes, amongst which we picked out my first Great Knots with bright chestnut oval markings in their scapular feathers on their backs, and my first deep chestnut-red Asian Dowitchers. After a few incredibly exciting hours the birds became more and more restless, walking about and stretching their wings, seemingly anxious to return to the mudflats to feed up and perhaps continue their journeys northward, and as soon as the tide began to fall small groups lifted off and headed swiftly back out to the bay. That's where we dashed to as well, to a floating hide at the edge of the mangroves where the mud was already being rapidly exposed by the falling tide and flocks of birds were dropping on to it and foraging frantically. Amongst the multitude was my first Nordmann's Greenshank, a short-necked, short-legged, stockier version of an everyday Greenshank. A Hobby zoomed into view and spooked a flock of 2000 Black-tailed Godwits, a magnificent sight as they twisted and turned in colourful motion. A Saunders's Gull and Gull-billed Terns patrolled the mud, sweeping down now and again to grab crabs. Three Chinese Egrets were dashing about with white wings spread, after fish and shrimps at the edge of the mangroves. All very distracting when all I really wanted to do was search through the shorebirds for a Spoon-billed Sandpiper, but when I started again the water retreated so quickly the shorebirds were soon nothing more than distant dots.

Time to move on, inland to some fishponds where there were two Oriental Pratincoles in graceful feeding flight, wheeling around and plucking insects out of the air with casual ease. They were my 33rd shorebird and fourth new one of the day but not as memorable as two summer-plumaged Red-necked Stints foraging with two summer-plumaged Red-throated Pipits on a drained fishpond; the four birds were not only similarly marked they were also all about the same size.

At dawn the following morning Eric, 'my chauffeur', drove me to Nam Sang Wai in the *Merc* and virtually the first bird I saw was a male Siberian Rubythroat, which spent enough time in the open for me to see the beautiful ruby. It was high tide in Deep Bay and the water in a few of the fishponds was very low and amongst the shorebirds sprinkled across the shallows of one were about 250 Wood Sandpipers and 21 Long-toed Stints, the latter looking like dinky versions of the former. More shorebirds and two Ruddy Crakes completed another great day, a working one at that. Being amongst so many shorebirds meant life was good. Then it got better.

A meeting-free morning happened to coincide with another high spring tide so after nut-bread, strawberries, smoked salmon and fine coffee for breakfast Eric picked me up from outside the *Furama* and drove me smoothly to Mai Po for some of the most pulsating birding of my life. Two hours passed by in what seemed like two minutes, at the high tide roost on The Scrape where there were over 2200 shorebirds, 30 species of them, virtually all in superb summer plumage, including, roughly from left to right, 30 Terek Sandpipers, 50 Pacific Golden Plovers, my first Far Eastern Curlew, three regular Curlews, 20 Whimbrels, 500 Black-tailed Godwits, about 1000 Curlew Sandpipers, two Great Knots, 50 Broad-billed Sandpipers, 300 Red-necked Stints, five Long-toed Stints, three finely barred Grey-tailed Tattlers, 20 Spotted Redshanks, 100 Redshanks, ten Asian Dowitchers, a Red-necked Phalarope, 25 Sharp-tailed Sandpipers, three Kentish Plovers, ten Lesser and 50

Greater Sand Plovers, ten Marsh Sandpipers and 30 Greenshanks, with a few Turnstones, Knots, Sanderlings and Grey Plovers mixed in. I scanned the main pack of tightly-packed Red-necked Stints again and again, and there was not one but two Spoon-billed Sandpipers amongst them, one in almost full breeding plumage; a plump 'stint' with a bright white belly, bold dark spots on the sides of its breast and the remarkable bill, very broad at the base and spatulate at the tip. I was able to watch it for some time, walking nervously around a small bay of very shallow water in between naps, and I was ecstatic to say the least. Meetings tore me away but not before a late lunch of delicious leatherjacket, my favourite fish on *The Rotisserie* menu, and, after all the talk and signing off the princely hotel bill, another superb, Japanese, meal, then Gary and I were driven to Kai Tak for our flight home on a Hong Kong high.

I did not return until December when I had to attend way too many meetings but after a poor night's sleep thanks to the chattering Chinese returning from the bars in Wanchai during the early hours of the morning, in a much cheaper hotel, which Gary was paying for, The Edge and his good friend Clive Viney, a chartered surveyor who migrated to Hong Kong from England over 25 years before, and author of the *Birds of Hong Kong and South China* field guide. They picked me up dead early and we headed out on a 'Viney hunch' to the abandoned paddy fields at Yung Shue O in the rarely visited northeast New Territories on the mainland, in search of rare birds on a hot, sunny day, and we struck gold. The little green beauty with a maroon back perched on a roadside wire was a Thick-billed Pigeon, the first one to be seen alive in Hong Kong.

The following spring I enjoyed more wonderful days with shorebirds at Mai Po, and some at Nam Sang Wai where one day I counted 40 Asian Dowitchers roosting amongst about 500 Black-tailed Godwits, 700 Spotted Redshanks, 250 Marsh Sandpipers, 250 Greenshanks, 100 Wood Sandpipers, 20 Red-necked Stints, four Long-toed Stints and eight Red-necked Phalaropes. The birds were flushed a few times by a Peregrine, possibly the reason why the birds were not on The Scrape at Mai Po. The raptor made several high-speed vertical dives into the flocks of shorebirds, causing the terrified birds to explode into the sky and seek safety in the air with some fast, jinking flying of their own but some were not agile enough to escape the raptor's outstretched talons and sought last sanctuary in the water and the Peregrine seemed reluctant to pluck them from there and eventually glided off empty-taloned. Then the birds were disturbed by the border police who mistook me for an 'i-i', an illegal immigrant, hiding behind a bund, and came to arrest me, only to realize, before they reached me, that I was hiding from the birds not them.

The same April I was honoured to be invited to join the renowned Grey Lags team for the annual Hong Kong Big Bird Race, run to raise money for World Wildlife Fund's work at Mai Po. They had won three of the last ten races but finished an embarrassing 11th the last time out. Captained by The Edge the team also included Clive Viney and John Day, an American banker with previous experience of raising considerable sums of money for the International Crane Foundation. Urban Lehner, a journalist with the *Asian Wall Street Journal,* was the driver of the donated *Land Rover Discoverer.* We did not begin well, seeing a Narcissus Flycatcher just before the six p.m. start time but not after. However, a calling Brown Hawk Owl and a spotlighted Collared Scops Owl sent us happily to bed for a few hours.

The long-striding captain then led a forced quick march up the hill in the dark at Tai Po Kau where we heard just one bird, the aptly-named Brainfever Bird or Large Hawk Cuckoo which was going 'brain fe-ver, brain fe-ver, brain fe-ver' faster and faster, the medical result of hearing the birds shout it all day and all night long, which we did. Fortunately there were many distractions, beginning with a Savanna Nightjar, a Barred Owlet and a pair of Bonelli's Eagles at Chau Tau. We were doing well and it was not even 6 a.m. then, around Starling Inlet, we added 37 species in two hours including a tricky Whiskered Tern at Nam Chung, and we were flying. Not for long. Back at Tai Po Kau, where there were more bird race teams than birds, we added just 14 species in two hours. I was pleased a Chestnut-eared Bunting had been joined by another at Fung Lok Wai fishponds, one of my survey sites, and the usual Temminck's Stints were present there, a shorebird not likely to be seen at Mai Po where the race could be won or lost according to how well we did on the shorebird front and we did pretty well, only missing Asian Dowitcher on a fast receding tide in strong sunlight.

With an hour left we headed to Lok Ma Chau and saw a Grey Treepie, taking our total for 24 hours to an encouraging but probably not winning 158, including an incredible 35 shorebirds. More importantly, at 109 Hong Kong dollars per species we had raised over 17,000 dollars, and, with other donations from some of our 136 sponsors, a massive 126,000 dollars (over 11,000 British pounds) in total, 7% of 150,000 British pounds raised by all the teams. We came fourth, behind 159, 162 and 167, but The Edge and Clive were very happy because the old, laid back Grey Lags were back, and we celebrated in style at the traditional dinner at the *Beas River Country Club*. It must have been a very interesting drive back to Hong Kong Island for their friend Bob Ferguson, with three very merry passengers in his car. I don't know, I can't remember.

I do remember the flight home. It took 17 hours because a dispute over airspace forced *Virgin Atlantic* to fly to London via the length of Russia. I was so tired I slept for six straight hours sitting up and when I awoke I could see Siberia, a landscape the like of which I had never set eyes on before, a gigantic maze of melting snow and ice which went on for hundreds of miles. I was back in Hong Kong in early May and got to see Nam Sang Wai and Mai Po as one of the wintering Imperial Eagles might see it, from the air on a magic carpet also known as a *Squirrel* helicopter. The pilot flew very low in the tiny, insect-like, machine, and with the doors open but strapped-in, it was truly an eagle's-eye view.

The clients couldn't buy return economy class flights for a week's work back home in England at short notice so they booked me in upper class on *Virgin Atlantic* instead, a ridiculously expensive and wonderfully luxurious experience complete with an on-board massage and, after a delightful meal, the chance to sit at a bar with a drink and a smoke 35,000 feet (10, 670 metres) above the planet. Back at Heathrow at six in the morning I made full use of the free clubhouse, swimming a few lengths before another massage. What with this, all expenses paid in the *Furama* and drinking a small glass of one of the most expensive and delicious wines in the world, *Chateau Latour 1982*, in our Q.C.'s chambers, Hong Kong birding was a different world from *Wheatley's Waste Not Want Not Tours*, and since I lived within a 75-mile radius of Heathrow airport *Virgin Atlantic* also provided me with a complimentary chauffeur-driven lift home which was worth it just for the look on the driver's face when he dropped me off outside my council flat in Thamesmead near Woolwich, London.

There was so much work to do on Nam Sang Wai and new projects that Gary and his family moved to Hong Kong, into a flat at Discovery Bay on the island of Lantau, and it was on a slim mattress there not the firm deep of the *Furama* where I bedded down each night on my first autumn visit in late September-early October, although I barely noticed it was not the luxury I was used to when in Hong Kong because I spent all but one day of a two week trip doing surveys or birding for fun. Fourteen species in six hours in Tai Po Kau was typical of how frustrating it is looking for forest birds in Asia but they did include two Japanese Paradise Flycatchers and a Pale-legged Leaf Warbler. On my way out a probable King Cobra crossed my path, one of the most dangerous snakes there is. I was not scared I was just happy and glad to *see* a snake, a rarely seen creature anywhere let alone in over-populated Hong Kong where the sight of such a thing usually results in hysteria and someone beating the poor creature to death.

After another hard day's surveying at Ta Tit Yan, a valley adjacent to Tai Po Kau, where the best migrant was a Sooty Flycatcher, I was winding down with a coffee in the plaza at Discovery Bay and while drinking my 'regular

regular' I could hardly believe my eyes when I looked down from my bench and saw a Lanceolated Warbler shuffling out of the knee-high shrubbery, like a streaky mouse. I didn't think I was going to see one of the ultimate skulkers at Mai Po or any other site so it was an unbelievable bonus. There was a bit of a fall in Tai Po Kau the next day and amongst the fine selection of migrants, which now included four Japanese Paradise Flycatchers and two Eastern Crowned Warblers, I saw a bird fly up off the forest floor on to a low branch which it then walked along with its body and tail swaying from side to side. It was an unforgettable Forest Wagtail, a beautifully marked, long-tailed little bird with wide white eyebrows, a greyish brown crown and back, two wide white wing bars, and two black bands across its white breast.

A flock of 18 Black Bazas, small, boldly patterned, black and white hawks, soaring over Tai Long Wan, was the highlight of the next day, followed by an all too brief view of a Pallas's Grasshopper Warbler at Fung Lok Wai. At the same place the next day the spectacular wheeling flocks of Oriental Pratincoles amounted to more than 400 birds. My next destination was Mai Po and more excitement, in the form of a flock of 16 Blue-tailed Bee-eaters that came down from the sky while calling a very pleasant, rolling 'prirrip prirrip prirrip' to catch some bees above the casuarinas before flying high again and rejoining the mass movement of birds south. Travelling with the bee-eaters were two big and yellow Black-naped Orioles and a Pied Harrier, a young bird with deep dark rufous-brown underparts and very rare in Hong Kong. Two days later, on my last day, I was stunned to see a cracking first-winter male Yellow-browed Bunting on a path at Nam Sang Wai.

*Forest Wagtail, Tai Po Kau, Hong Kong, 30th September 1994*

Autumn in Hong Kong proved to be as thrilling as the spring and I could not wait to get back there but it was almost a year later, at the very beginning of September, when the 747 I was on flew into Kai Tak through the remains of Super Typhoon Kent, a tropical cyclone with winds that reached 150 mph (240 km/h) as it brushed past the northern Philippines and southern Taiwan before hitting mainland China 50 miles (95 km) northeast of Hong Kong, leading to flash floods that damaged or destroyed 40,000 homes and killed thirty people. From the plane I saw towering isolated blocks of cloud that looked like giant icebergs in the sky, with the slashes of pale blue cloud running through the middle of them resembling the surface of the imaginary ocean that they floated in.

As soon as it was possible I headed for the West Lamma Channel on the Cheung Chau ferry in search of Aleutian Tern, a species virtually unknown away from the Bering Sea coast between Sakhalin and Alaska where it spends the northern summer. The species' wintering grounds remained unknown but birds had been present in Hong Kong waters during the previous few autumns so I was hopeful. Distant views of up to 14 possibles on the way out were very frustrating but on the return journey one was close enough to clinch the identification.

Another year and a half passed before I was back, this time for the month of May, too late for shorebirds but still in time for plenty of other northbound migrants. It was gruelling work, getting up at stupid o'clock in Gary's new flat in Gold Coast and on to the minibuses with the youngsters who keep Hong Kong going for 24 hours a day. They were on their way home from their night shifts, I was on my way out dead early because I needed to be in position from dawn till dusk to record the movements of egrets and herons to and from their breeding colony in Mai Po village, and to observe their foraging behaviour around the nearby fishponds. I was expecting some long rather boring days but there was rarely a dull moment. The most magical were my first two Black Bitterns which flew north low down enough for me to see their pale, chestnut-streaked necks and amazing spear-like bills, a flock of six Blue-tailed Bee-eaters flying strongly in pursuit of dragonflies before rising toward the clouds and continuing their migration, and best of all, a steady trickle of summer-plumaged White-winged Black Terns, rising to at least 70 on one day and including a phenomenal flock of over 50 twisting and turning over a pond. On a rare day off I saw my first Painted Snipe in Hong Kong.

It was so hot by early June that a thunderstorm broke out one morning and while sheltering from the water falling from the sky under a shack next to a fishpond lightning struck so close I heard it rip through the air. The weather was very different the following winter when I spent weeks shivering in cold northerlies and sometimes very wet conditions. The Grants had moved again, this time to a house on the edge of a small village called Kau Lung Hang, on the mainland. It was a terrific place for birds displaced by even colder weather to the north of Hong Kong in central China, not least an extraordinarily confiding White's Thrush which I was able to watch, from just a few paces away over a garden wall, as it bobbed up and down quite excitedly on legs which worked like springs, and swayed from side to side. Its cryptic plumage, grey-buff above and white below, covered all over in black crescents, giving it a scaly appearance, was poor camouflage at such close range. On one occasion the peculiar creature was accompanied by six Olive-backed Pipits and other garden birds included a couple of Siberian Rubythroats, a few Red-flanked Bluetails and a fabulous male Scarlet-backed Flowerpecker, an exquisite little birdie with what looked like a broad, bright red stripe painted along the top of it, from the crown down to the lower back, contrasting sharply with the blackish sides to the head and breast, glossy blue-black wings and blackish tail. There was a tiny patch of remnant woodland in a pass at the top of the otherwise virtually treeless slopes where, after some tedious days in front of a computer in the house office, I would head for my daily fix with Barry Nicholson, another friend from my London Wildlife Trust days who was a top botanist, expert ecologist, all-round non-nonsense good egg from Yorkshire and Gary's right-hand man. The wood gave up its secretive birds slowly but they included a Mugimaki Flycatcher and a Rufous-tailed Robin. Best of all was the journey back down in the jeep at dusk when we saw the throats of Siberian Rubythroats twinkling in the half-a-million-candle-power spotlight as they ventured out of cover for once to forage along the edge of the track in the gathering darkness.

During that long, cold winter Barry and I spent some time on the slopes of High Junk Peak, a long drive from Kau Lung Hang which had to be negotiated in the dark in Gary's small, rattle-bucket of a second-hand jeep, in order to be on site for dawn. Although much of the survey area consisted of recently burnt grassland I saw six species of thrush one morning: a pair of Blue Rock Thrushes, the male with the rufous underparts of the *philippensis* race; two Violet Whistling Thrushes; four male Grey Thrushes which were very smart birds, dark grey-black above and white below with black spots along the flanks; five Grey-backed Thrushes, two of which were males with lovely orange flanks; an Eye-browed Thrush, told from a male Grey-backed by its less bright orange flanks but striking white eyebrows; and the stars for me, three Dusky Thrushes, one of which was a stonking black and white male complete with rich copper-brown wing panels. Another dawn I flushed a Woodcock, the 46th different species of shorebird I saw in Hong Kong, nearly a quarter of the 200 or so species in the world. It was the last addition to the shorebird list even though I returned for three more visits. One of those was in August when the temperature was around 90°F and the humidity at least 85% every day except one, when it rained all day. In between the showers on the other days I spent most of my time studying dragonflies and damselflies, some of which proved to be equally, if not more, enthralling than the birds, especially the truly beautiful male *Trithemis aurora*, a *Libellulid* dragonfly with such a strong violet hue to the crimson abdomen as to render the popular English name of Crimson Marsh Glider unpopular with me.

The Hong Kong work came to an end after seven years and fifteen visits amounting to over four months in the field. We won the planning inquiries and appeals but the government employed its very best delaying tactics to stop the Nam Sang Wai development, and others, from going ahead, mainly it seemed because of continuing objections from the all-powerful World Wide Fund for Nature Hong Kong, not a bad thing and no doubt the world would be a much better place for wildlife if non-governmental conservation organisations in other countries could hold so much sway. I would have liked to have gone birding at the proposed Lut Chau reserve though. It certainly would have been better for birds than the active fishponds that remained there after all those years.

Instead, I was more than content with a last chance to enjoy a wonderful April day at Mai Po where on The Scrape was a vociferous flock of 150 'gerwicking' Gull-billed Terns. The shorebirds, nearly 4000 and 31 species of them, were already returning to Deep Bay so I dashed to the hide at the edge of the mangroves and welled up with happiness as I watched great whooshing flocks of them swirling around before settling down on the mud, including about 2000 Curlew Sandpipers, 500 each of Marsh Sandpipers and Spotted Redshanks, over a hundred Great Knots, and four Nordmann's Greenshanks, nearly all in their full glory of breeding plumage and at very close range, until the tide fell, more mud became exposed and the birds, like the halcyon days with them in Hong Kong, became distant, hazy dots.

*Inland Dotterel, Strzelecki Desert, Australia, 8th June 1993*

# 10

# AUSTRALIA

Not long after shambling out of Darwin airport at half past four in the morning, thirty hours out of London, I was wading up to my knees in mud.

"Watch out for the big saltie in there," Dave warned me as I waved clouds of sand flies away and plodged through the ooze beside a murky channel in the mangroves of Sadgroves Creek.

"Fifteen-footer," Dave added as I steered away as fast as my bare feet, the mud and the spear-tipped mangrove shoots would allow.

Even small Saltwater Crocodiles are big enough to kill humans. Once in the 'death roll', where the crocodile locks its prey between its jaws and rolls violently over and over, there is no chance of surviving. I very much wanted to see a 'saltie' but not *that* close. Dave was leading me and The Stid on a 'big red chook hunt'. The Chestnut Rail is big, for a rail, and reddish, and looks like a 'chook', a chicken, according to the fishermen of Darwin, who see the bird a lot more than birders.

I was still in shock from meeting Dave at the airport. Months before, I had written to a British expatriate birder living in Darwin called Dave Percival, asking him if he would like to take me and The Stid out birding for the day. I never heard back from him so I was stunned to see a piece of cardboard with our names on it held up by him in the arrivals hall. We didn't see a big red chook, or a saltie, but our first Red-headed Honeyeaters, tiny, busy, black and scarlet birds were superb, and we also saw some Sacred Kingfishers with backs the colour of a shallow tropical sea. The *first* birds we saw on the Australian continent, before the big red chook hunt, were Masked Lapwings. They were walking about on Darwin's lawns, with suburban Straw-necked Ibises, Magpie Larks, and dainty Bar-shouldered and Peaceful Doves. From a shrubbery ventured a pair of Orange-footed Scrubfowls, more like chickens than red rails are, with round, grey bodies and chestnut-brown backs. They were my first megapodes, a family of birds with sturdy legs and feet, 'mega pode' being Greek for 'large feet'. Normally shy, the scrubfowls of Darwin are habituated to humans and they drive people who like tidy gardens crazy with their incessant scattering of soil and leaf litter in search of food, and their mound-building, for the purpose of incubating their eggs. Megapodes don't sit on nests and warm their eggs with body heat like most birds they incubate them in compost heaps which in the case of the Orange-footed Scrubfowl may be higher than a human and the length of a few across. It is the male's job to control the heat and humidity by opening or closing the mound, and turning the eggs, for fifty days or more until the chicks hatch. Baby megapodes are the most *precocial* of any bird; when they emerge from the eggs they burrow out of the mound to make their own way in the world without never knowingly meeting their parents.

There are few things that excite me as much as looking for new birds in a new land. It reminds me of wandering around meadows and woods when I was a boy, seeing birds for the first time, only there are hundreds more fresh wonders in a foreign land. This was certainly the case around Darwin. Some of the birds were beyond my wildest boyhood dreams, birds like aptly-named Rainbow Bee-eaters which were shiny blue-bronzy-green, with red eyes in black masks bordered below by eye-catching azure flashes, fiery orange-yellow throats, burnished orange backs to their heads, and long tail streamers. They looked brilliant perched but in dashing flight they were even more amazing; a superb combination of flashing greens and blues contrasting with black-trimmed bright orange-rufous wings. Still within Darwin city limits Dave showed us a pair of Bush Thick-knees. The long-legged, long-bodied shorebirds lived in a park. They froze when we appeared, relying on their cryptically camouflaged, lined and streaked brown and grey plumage to conceal them amongst the dry scrub but we managed to pick them out and stare into their alert, large yellow eyes, evolved for night work.

At the northern end of Fannie Bay we walked the length of East Point Beach in search of their close relatives the Beach Thick-knee, in a warm wind and the searing heat of a Darwin June, the beginning of the dry season during which nearly every day is sunny. Small Agile Wallabies grazed the open areas above the beach along which we saw our first Pied Oystercatchers amongst lots of other more familiar shorebirds such as Greater Sand Plovers, Terek Sandpipers and Grey-tailed Tattlers but we could not see anything with particularly thick knees. The lack of sleep was beginning to tell when a Manta Ray flew out of the Timor Sea. That's what I assumed the huge airborne black and white triangular being was that landed with a splash offshore. Suddenly I was as keen as The Stid to carry on and I'm glad I did because on reaching the shade of the mangroves at the mouth of Ludmilla Creek I saw an absolutely gorgeous black-headed, golden yellow Mangrove Golden Whistler. Just inland, in the dark undergrowth of a vine thicket, a flash of blue caught my eye and raising my binoculars revealed the azure shoulder of a black and golden green Rainbow Pitta standing on the ground. Nearby were a pair of Red-backed Kingfishers, open-country king insect eaters rather than fishers. They looked very pale blue-green and white as if their colours had been bleached out by the sun beating down relentlessly from almost overhead.

"Now for the shit pits," Dave said.

Darwin Sewage Works was alive with birds. The noisiest were the Galahs, at least fifty of them, and they were making a hell of a racket. The good-looking cockatoos have white caps, soft pink faces and bodies, and soft grey backs, wings and tails, and I particularly like them in flight when they look like a pretty cross between a small hawk and a roller. Sitting, chests out, on the bank of a 'shit pit', were two Australian Pelicans. The planet's eight pelicans are amongst the most extraordinary of birds, thanks mainly to their enormous bills and pouches, and the Australian Pelican has the longest bill of any bird, growing to a length of nearly twenty inches (half a metre). Nearby were at least twenty Pied Herons, lovely birds with deep, dark blue-grey caps, backs, wings and bodies contrasting smartly with silky white necks, yellow eyes and long, slender, pointed yellow bills, but it was not very enjoyable watching them through a high chain-link fence so we asked Dave if we could move on. Next stop was Knuckey's Lagoon where there were lots more waterbirds including three Australian Pratincoles, slender, long-winged, sand-coloured birds with chestnut belly patches, and five fabulous Forest Kingfishers on five fence posts, the most beautiful blue and white birds imaginable with black masks to boot. Near dusk two Red-tailed Black Cockatoos flew over on their way to roost, flying buoyantly with slow, deep beats of their long, rigid, rounded wings, and looking a bit like large, ghostly black Short-eared Owls.

After putting the tent up at Howard Springs Caravan Park it was with some satisfaction that The Stid and I headed to the on-site open-air bar.

"Two beers please, the best you've got," I said to one of the two barmen.

"Give 'em anything, they're *poms*," was our 'Welcome to Australia'.

I had a blinding headache, born of jetlag, sunshine, dehydration and lack of sleep, before I started drinking but by the time I gladly lay flat in the tent I had managed to finish my rough notes on my first day on Australian soil, concluding that it was one of the most wonderful days of my life, and one that had exceeded all expectations, since of the 77 bird species seen over fifty were new to me.

The Earth is alive. The outer rock layer, the crust, is like a round jigsaw puzzle, consisting of seven continent-sized and about a dozen much smaller pieces called tectonic plates. These plates are constantly on the move, conveyed by convection currents in the Earth's mantle, below the crust, and driven by 10,000°F of the primordial heat left in our planet's core after its formation. The mantle is a solid that flows; solid as far as conventional time periods such as days, weeks, years and even decades go, but liquid in geological time, which is measured in many millions of years, liquid that flows like a thick viscous syrup made of magma and solid rocks. Floating on this swirling inferno is the Earth's crust, vast bits of which are drifting about, as they have done for hundreds of millions of years. About 200 million years ago most of the bits or tectonic plates were joined together in a vast landmass we call Pangaea, which stretched from pole to pole. About 20 million years later these plates began to drift apart and during the course of the last 180 million years they have spread out all over the planet, casting New Guinea, Australia and Antarctica adrift on the Australian and Antarctica Plates, and about 50 million years ago the Antarctica Plate broke away from the Australian Plate, leaving two isolated lands above sea level; New Guinea and Australia, which have been isolated from all the other continents long enough for evolution to produce a unique selection of plants and animals. Roughly 85% of the flowering plants, 93% of amphibians, 89% of reptiles, 84% of the mammals and nearly 50% of the birds on the Australian continent occur nowhere else. The extraordinary mammals include the egg-laying monotremes Duck-billed Platypus and Short-beaked Echidna, as well as over 170 marsupials, mammals that raise their young in a pouch (a *marsupium* in Latin) outside the body rather than in a uterus inside the body, including kangaroos, koalas, bandicoots, possums and wombats, and as for birds over 350 species are endemic to the continent and many more live only on the Australian landmass and the nearby island of New Guinea, just a hundred miles (160 km) of shallow sea away.

At Howard Springs Nature Park, a tiny oasis of dense, spring-fed, monsoon forest surrounded by open eucalypt woodland, the day began deep blue and orange with an Azure Kingfisher, followed by two massive kingfishers called Blue-winged Kookaburras, nearly the size of crows with massive shoe-like bills, pale, streaked heads and white eyes. Along the Arnhem Highway to Kakadu we turned off to reach the low, earthen Fogg Dam which was built in the 1960s to flood an area of land in the hope of making it suitable for rice production. The plan failed, partly because the vast flocks of waterbirds attracted to the shallow tropical waters overflowing with food also ate a large portion of the crop. Man and his ridiculous schemes moved on but the birds stayed, so many of them that Fogg Dam became one of the best wetlands in the 'Top End' of Australia. Sometimes we don't destroy nature we help it, albeit in this case by accident. The richly vegetated shallow marsh was chock-a-block full of birds. There were hundreds of Magpie Geese and Wandering Whistling Ducks, along with over 50 Pied Herons and, walking across the beautiful islands of water-lilies, lots of lovely lily-trotters; red-combed, golden-necked, black-breasted, brown-backed birds with extraordinarily long toes which help to spread their already negligible weight and enable them to walk on water-lilies. Amongst the Comb-crested Jacanas was another bird with long toes called a White-browed Crake.

There were plenty of birds in the surrounding paperbark wood too, including a Rainbow Pitta behind a sign saying 'Look out for Rainbow Pittas' and a very pretty Rose-crowned Fruit Dove, a bright green bird with a rosy forehead and orange belly, perched quietly in the low canopy, and completely unafraid of us, standing underneath looking up. At Humpty-Doo Dam a little farther along the Arnhem Highway there was a pair of red-headed, long-legged, grey Brolga Cranes and an equally tall but much more striking Black-necked Stork. Birds, birds, birds, lots of beautiful birds but the temperature was in the nineties and even the wind was warm and we were frazzled. In need of a drink we returned to the campsite shop. Asked if we were having a good day by the owner The Stid answered, "Canny" and after I explained that 'canny' meant pretty good and was in fact a massive understatement The Stid mentioned that we could not find a Great Bowerbird anywhere, to which the owner replied, rather nonchalantly, "You know where your tent is ..." and a few minutes later we were watching a male Great Bowerbird displaying to a female above his bower about a hundred paces from our tent. The rather plain, greyish-brown, thrush-sized bird posed with his head raised and pointed forward, his chest out, back up, wings drooped and tail and legs taut, as he sang a loud, harsh, strangled sort of song with lots of chattering, hissing and mimicry of other birds, and, to cap it all, he then showed off the orange and lilac crest on the back of his neck which had been raised and turned into a sort of rosette. Like all promiscuous male bowerbirds he spends most of the year keeping his bower in tip-top condition in an effort to attract as many females as possible. To a female a well-adorned and well-kept bower means a healthy male with good genes and one she is likely to mate with, although the female present when we were there did not seem as impressed as we were with the bird's elaborate garden which consisted of two parallel rows of interwoven sticks, shin high and curving over and meeting above an 'avenue' down the middle about the same length, the ends of which were adorned with lots of white shells and bits of broken green glass.

With a few minutes to spare before meeting Dave for a few beers we drove to East Point again and on getting out of the car for a casual scan were amazed to see our first Beach Thick-knee roosting on the sand, a big grey-brown shorebird with a massive dark beak and striking black and white striped head pattern. Following Dave's advice, we were at Middle Arm at dawn the next day scanning hard for big red chooks on the mud under the mangroves across the other side of the wide channel. Hours went by without so much as a possible but in the muddy waters were two Irrawaddy Dolphins and, even better, flying by was an unexpected Little Kingfisher, a tiny blue and white jewel that sent us merrily to Darwin airport.

In the arrivals hall at Adelaide airport I was attacked by a giant rucksack, owned by Rob Roberts, my old friend from student days who I travelled to Pakistan, India and Nepal with several years before. Since then he had married Sarah and migrated to Sydney, Australia. The Stid and I were invited to stay with them when we were on that leg of our journey around the continent and although we invited Rob to join us on any of the other legs he said he was too busy to do so. This was not true; he intended to surprise us and he did! Mischievous as ever, he then used his considerable charm to secure a better hire car for a lower price. We then headed for a 'Bottle Shop' and bought a couple of 'slabs' of West End Export, 24-can cartons of beer, as requested by our host for a couple of nights, John Cox. Most of it was gone by midnight, used as lubrication for a long night talking to one of Australia's top birders about what we might see around Adelaide with his help, and about 'Cox's Sandpiper', a mysterious shorebird. Presumed by some to be a full species and named, against his wishes, after its discoverer, the man whose house we were sitting in, the man who thought it was probably a hybrid between Curlew and Pectoral Sandpipers, and who was proved right a few years later when three specimens underwent genetic analysis.

John, an Englishman, had been living in Australia for twenty-five years and in that time he had got to know the avifauna of the Adelaide area rather well. What's more, he was happy to share his knowledge with three complete strangers. He began by pointing out seven new birds to me and The Stid while we drank a soothing cup of tea in his garden at dawn, including the very smart New Holland Honeyeater with a black head, white eyes, dark back, bold black streaks on the white underparts and bright yellow flashes in the wings and tail. Then we were off, to Greenfields Wetlands, a reserve in the suburbs where I saw three new shorebirds in as many minutes; a beautiful Red-necked Avocet, two small, red-billed and red-spectacled Black-fronted Dotterels, and ten Red-kneed Dotterels with neat black caps and broad black breast bands changing to chestnut along the flanks. At Waterloo Road we added eight dark green and white Banded Lapwings.

Our main destination was the Dry Creek Salt Fields which support one of the greatest concentrations of waterbirds in Australia during the austral summer between November and March, when birds which nest as far away as Siberia spend their winters with increased numbers of resident birds in the hot and sunny Adelaide area. During that season it is possible to see over 25 species of shorebird in a day; 34 is the record and over 50 have been recorded in total. Many are also often present in mind-boggling numbers; up to 150,000 stilts have been recorded at any one time. We may have been there in June during the austral winter and seen only ten species of shorebirds but they still included about 25,000 Banded Stilts, a thousand Red-necked Avocets, 200 Red-capped Plovers and 50 Red-kneed Dotterels. One large lagoon was literally covered with Banded Stilts, swimming and pecking delicately like Wilson's Phalaropes, in pursuit of brine shrimps. On other lagoons where they were standing in the shallows or on the muddy margins with Black-winged Stilts and Red-necked Avocets the three species formed pretty patterns of black, white and chestnut. Sharing the lagoons with the shorebirds were pelicans, ibises, Hoary-headed Grebes, square-shaped, zebra-striped, spatulate-billed Pink-eared Ducks, big, dark Musk Ducks, white-eyed Hardheads and black-headed Bluebills. Huge Caspian Terns fished with dainty Fairy Terns and overhead raptors such as White-bellied Sea Eagles and Swamp Harriers passed by, one harrier with a Banded Stilt in its talons.

The saltbush surrounding the lagoons was alive with birds as well. Rather drab Singing Honeyeaters flitted across the bush tops, smart Sacred Kingfishers perched on prominent perches, bright green Red-rumped Parrots dashed by, a flock of 44 paler green Elegant Parrots searched for seeds on the ground, and we regularly came across Superb Fairywrens, a member of another Australian bird family famous for being promiscuous. Males and females pair up for life but both get together with several other individuals. The males are quite romantic though, plucking yellow petals and displaying them to females as part of a courtship display. They are also very good-looking, with shiny blue crowns, ear coverts and backs, narrow black masks, and dark blue-black throats and tails, although they are not as beautiful, to my eye, as male White-winged Fairywrens which were also present. They are bright Cezanne-blue all over except for part of the wings which are a soft white, making the birds, at certain angles, look like they have snow on their backs. The whole place was very birdy and busy and exciting but there was an oasis of tranquility too, where we crouched down between some bushes by a quiet, well-vegetated corner of a lagoon to watch, just a few paces away, a red-eyed and red-spectacled, chocolate-brown and dark slate-grey Spotless Crake, barely bigger than a sparrow, foraging with jerky, exaggerated, wary movements typical of crakes and rails that do not like being out in the open for too long. All these great birds and two Sooty Oystercatchers nearby completed another phenomenal day in Australia, one in which I saw 50 new birds for the second time in four days, and seven of them were shorebirds, one of my favourite families and a major reason for visiting Australia.

After another uncomfortable night on John's lounge floor we were up well before dawn and off with his friend Neil Cheshire over misty hills to some remnant *mallee* near Karoonda where we came across our first 'roos', large Western Grey ones. In the low rainfall belt south of the central deserts of Australia the vegetation used to be dominated by dense, dwarf eucalypts which together form a habitat known as *mallee*, but much of this scrubland, to which many birds are specially adapted, has been cleared since Europeans arrived on the continent to grow wheat. Consequently, the Malleefowl, the bird we concentrated on looking for, was now rare, although males can usually be found in the vicinity of their mounds, so we waited and waited, and wandered around a bit, and waited ... and walked off, and also didn't see any Chestnut Quail Thrushes, or male Splendid Fairywrens, just three females, which were brown with bluish tails, not a patch on the all blue males. We did see a bird much more difficult to see than a Malleefowl, a bird which was even a new one for Australian veteran Neil; a Grey Falcon, a close, pale, relative of the Peregrine, with long, black-tipped wings.

From Karoonda we drove southwest to the northern shores of Lake Alexandrina where we could not find any Cape Barren Geese, and on to Port Elliot on the Fleurieu Peninsula, a lovely little bay where there was a Pacific Gull, a large, black-backed gull with a huge, red-tipped yellow bill, used to smash up shellfish, and a Northern Giant Petrel, a monster of an all dark brown bird also with a massive, red-tipped yellow bill, and long narrow wings like an albatross. Farther southwest, on the wonderful, seemingly endless, white sands of wild Waitpinga Beach, I got down on my stomach on the hard, cold sand, in a gale coming in off the Southern Ocean, to watch a pair of exquisite Hooded Plovers, with waves like waterfalls crashing on to the shore in the background. From afar the birds looked black-headed with pale, sandy-grey backs and white underparts. Crawling closer and closer I could see that they had neat red eye-rings and red bases to their short black beaks. They were so reluctant to fly in the strong wind I was able to crawl right up to the beauties without disturbing their foraging and enjoy one of those rare, magical and precious moments in the close company of wild birds in a wild place. Not just any old birds either but as far as I was concerned the best endemic Australian shorebird that I had seen up to then. We thanked Neil for taking us to see them at such a terrific spot, and we thanked him again when we dropped him off in Adelaide, then we headed north to Port Augusta and beyond, back on to the Stuart Highway which we had left behind in Darwin, nearly 1800 miles (2900 km) away. We were on our way to the Strzelecki Track, into the Australian outback to look for the last endemic shorebird we had not yet seen; the Inland Dotterel. Around midnight we pulled over for some sleep and I was so tired I just lay down on some rocks and slept like a baby.

The Strzelecki Track between Lyndhurst and Innamincka is named after the Polish count, Pawel Edmund Strzelecki (pronounced 'stress-lecky'), a geologist and trailblazer who spent the early 1840s exploring much of southeast Australia, although the track was actually pioneered by Henry Arthur "Harry" Redford who in 1870 stole a thousand cattle from where he was working as a stockman in Queensland and drove them south along the track to Adelaide. Three years later he was tried for the crime but the jury members were so impressed that he had crossed 500 miles (800 km) of such harsh terrain with so many cattle that they found him not guilty. It was an impressive feat. Only ten years earlier the explorers Burke and Wills had set out to cross the continent and died from starvation on their return. The only person to get back to Melbourne alive out of the original party of fourteen was an Irish soldier called John King who managed to find some Yandruwandha Aborigines who fed him until a rescue party arrived.

We only had to travel a few miles in an air-conditioned car along the Strzelecki before we found 16 Inland Dotterels, thus completing the set of Australia's six endemic shorebirds in six days, but I would have walked 500 miles to admire the birds' cryptic colours and patterns, their curious, broad, dark 'teardrops' running down from their eyes, the black Y-shaped breast bands, the rich chestnut bellies of the brightest birds, and their straw-striped backs which when turned to face us made the birds virtually disappear in the tawny grass. They had great camouflage but they were also wary and gradually they moved farther and farther away and our attention turned to a solitary, white-eyed Gibberbird, a small, lark-like, yellowish bird, one of the toughest in the world, capable of surviving where there is virtually no water in a sparsely vegetated desert covered with small shiny stones (the *Gibber*).

Farther along the track the land rose slightly here and there and we pulled over here and there to scour some low shrubland dominated by bluebush and saltbush growing in widely spaced clumps, to allow extensive root-runs for water-gathering, and to walk along dry creeks below long stony ridges with lines of grey-leaved, stunted trees, a habitat known as *mulga*. We were looking for a warbler-sized bird called Chestnut-breasted Whiteface, rarely seen anywhere in Australia away from the Strzelecki. We didn't see it but we did come across some fantastic White-winged Fairywrens, four lovely Cinnamon Quail Thrushes, three pale-streaked, pale brown Thick-billed Grasswrens, running cock-tailed across the bare ground between the bushes at a hundred miles an hour, and some huge Red 'Roos, the largest and most handsome of the 'roos, the largest living marsupials in fact, and the largest land mammals native to Australia. Standing two metres tall the males we saw associating with small groups of females and their young were very impressive with their lovely rich, sandy red coats, very long and powerful hind legs and feet, and long, thick, muscular tails, used as a counterbalance when on the move and those we saw bounding along did so with barely any noticeable effort and surprising grace.

Rob was looking for Inland Taipans, also known as Fierce Snakes, because although they may not grow more than a couple of metres long they are the most venomous land snake on the planet, armed with venom fifty times more deadly than a cobra's, strong enough to kill Rob in forty-five minutes. Worst still, me, so I kept my distance, even when he found a tiny snake under a stone and said it was a Black-headed Snake not a Taipan. The long walk, past abandoned opal mines, continued. Loud 'witt-chee-witt-chee' calls led us to a flock of very smart Chestnut-crowned Babblers, sleek grey-brown birds with long, narrow, white eyebrows, bright white throats and chests, and two neat white wing bars.

Before dark we scouted out a dry creek to camp in, figuring we would be safe from flash floods during the dry season. The outback is a dangerous place. Flash flooding is just one problem to worry about. Lots of people, birders even, have died in the deserts of Australia, where temperatures can exceed 40°C (104°F), mostly from dehydration and hyperthermia, even, in some cases, when they have had an adequate supply of water, because severe heat stroke turns the brain to mush. Meanwhile the sufferer breaths faster to power the heart, which is going like the clappers anyway in an effort to maintain adequate circulation to cool the body down, but it can't cope, organs fail, unconsciousness follows and then death. Most people die because their vehicle breaks down and no one comes along in time to help them so visitors must be self-sufficient and prepared for emergencies, with a high-clearance four-wheel-drive, extra fuel, oil, spare tyres and supplies of food and water, and a radio or some other form of communication. We had none of these things. We drove back to Lyndhurst, a 'roadhouse' with a petrol station, shop and inn, ate a splendid meal, and drank some cans of beer called stubbies while playing pool in *Rowdy and Del's*. Then we drove back to the dry creek to pitch the tents and get some sleep which was not easy; never mind hyperthermia, it was freezing.

No 'bushman's breakfast' for us ('a piss and a good look around'). Rob served up beans under the River Red Gums before we resumed the whiteface search. Still the little tinker eluded us but we did see 36 Inland Dotterels before driving 600 miles (960 km) to Wyperfeld National Park, a small island of *mallee* in a sea of virtually bird-less plains of wheat production. It was our second attempt to see a Malleefowl. We awoke to the shock of rain and the maniacal call of at least two Laughing Kookaburras; 'KOO-koo-koo-koo-koo-ka-ka-ka-KA!-KA!-koo-koo-koo' repeated many times in an incredibly loud chorus well-known from the soundtracks of *'Tarzan'* and other films, mainly based in Africa, where the species does not occur of course, being endemic to Australia. It did not take long to see the largest kingfisher on Earth, a bird with a huge bill, a pale head and body, a touch of pale blue across the wings, and a black-barred, rufous-brown tail. It may be massive but it's not a true 'king fisher', inhabiting open forests and woodlands, even large gardens, rather than wetlands, and feeding not on fish but mostly on insects, worms, lizards and snakes.

Under a ruffled grey blanket of cloud we sorted through hundreds of beautiful Galahs hoping to spot a similar but much rarer Major Mitchell's or Pink Cockatoo but without success. Western Grey 'Roos were everywhere when we set off in search of Malleefowl, Chestnut Quail Thrushes and male Splendid Fairywrens but during a long, wet walk we saw none of them, not that any could have been more amazing than a male Red-capped Robin, a stunning, black and white, round-bellied bird with a bright scarlet forehead and breast, glowing despite the lack of light. We could not take our eyes off it but we had to, Rob had a flight to catch, so we sped back to Adelaide and while Rob flew back to Sydney The Stid and I headed back over the Adelaide Hills in heavy rain, to the Malleefowl mound near Karoonda where the sun came out and after only a few minutes so did a Malleefowl. The surprisingly attractive megapode had a grey body and a cryptically marked back and wings, the whole forming almost perfect camouflage when the bird was seen from behind walking slowly through a thicket. Pleased our persistence had paid off we left the fowl in peace and drove at top speed back to Adelaide airport for our flight, to Melbourne.

Melbourne is a short hop, by air, from Adelaide, about 400 miles (650 km) to the east, but the temperature at midday was way lower at 7°C (45°F) and a Force 7 near gale southerly wind with heavy squalls, some with hailstones, was blowing hard. Great conditions for seawatching but that was not what we were there for. Driving south out of the city was like travelling across Britain in the middle of a dreary winter's day, not being on a foreign birding trip when it always seemed to be hot and sunny, and my gloom deepened as I realized that the 4000 square miles (10,000 square kilometres) of the Melbourne metropolis was strewn across virtually all of the lowlands surrounding Port Phillip Bay and up the slopes and valleys of the Dandenong and Macedon mountain ranges. It all looked too much like home, a once beautiful land ruined by tarmac, concrete, steel and glass, scattered across the landscape like litter, a mess that could never be cleared up. It was a hell of a shock after the wide open spaces of the outback, a sudden return to the built environment of the western world, a world I needed to escape from on an increasingly regular, hopefully permanent, basis.

It was too wet to camp and the accommodation on Phillip Island was too expensive for two skinflints like us so we attempted to sleep in the hire car with rain and hail frequently battering the roof. In Melbourne the locals say, "If you don't like the weather, just wait five minutes" but it was the same in the morning and nearly freezing with a gale and rain ripping in from the Bass Strait. Ten Cape Barren Geese were struggling to stay upright in roadside paddocks along Back Beach Road, a drab juvenile Hooded Plover clung to the sand on Cowrie Beach, and Black-browed and Shy Albatrosses wobbled over the tumultuous seas around 'The Nobbies', a spectacular headland where, offshore, we could just about make out lots of Australian Fur Seals hauled up on rocks out of the white water, although standing up in the wind was difficult. Lighting up the grey scene and our souls were three Flame Robins that were foraging on the ground in a short-cropped paddock. They were being buffeted by the wind but even under the dark grey cloud cover their flame-red throats, breasts and bellies shone ever so brightly. Buoyed by their brilliance we headed for Carrum Sewage Works on the eastern side of Port Phillip Bay where we had arranged to meet Mike Carter, the man who had seen more birds in Australia than anyone else; 750, out of the 800 or so recorded. We were hoping he had lined up a Freckled Duck for us but there were none of the notoriously nomadic and rare waterbirds present. I didn't mind, because there were lots of other birds. None were new but it was just great to be amongst a lot of birds, including hundreds of Hardheads and Pink-eared Ducks, about 50 Black-fronted Dotterels and 40 Red-necked Avocets, some at very close range. Then it was back to Summerland Beach, Phillip Island, for dusk, where under the cover of (floodlit) darkness we watched about 50 Little blue-grey Penguins, tough little birdies the size of Razorbills, bounce on to the hard sand like rubber balls being thrown out of the wild surf, shake themselves off and waddle to their nesting burrows underneath us.

As the sun rose so did we, from our lowered car seats, in successful pursuit of the Rufous Bristlebird, one of three species of bristlebird, all endemic to Australia, which are expert skulkers and much more likely to be heard than seen, at least without the help of Mike Carter who happened to know a place where the rufous variety is a little more obliging. That place was Split Point, just off the Great Ocean Road, southwest of Melbourne, where we saw one on a garden lawn looking a bit like a rufousy, long-tailed, female Blackbird, one of which was foraging next to it. Back nearer Melbourne we arranged to meet up with laid-back local birder Steve Holliday at the world famous, at least amongst birders, Werribee Sewage Works, a shorebird hotspot. Steve led us out to a bay where we saw yet another new and fine-looking shorebird; fifteen Double-banded Plovers, winter visitors from New Zealand, although two were still in summer plumage and sported two bands across their white breasts, a narrow black one above a broader chestnut one. Out on a spit hidden under a bush were three pairs of chest-high waders which we squeezed into before wading across a deep channel to reach Shell Island where we saw six of the 120 or so Orange-bellied Parrots left on planet Earth rise from the samphire flats like electric-green rockets. Once again there were no Freckled Ducks to be seen but there was no time to dwell on that, we had to get to the airport and board a 737 to Brisbane where we hoped the weather would be a little warmer.

We could not find the campsite at Lamington National Park at midnight so we tried to grab a few hours sleep in the car again. When we looked out of the windows at dawn we saw our first Australian Brush Turkeys, more megapodes, with bare red heads and necks like vultures, and Wonga Pigeons, large, slate-grey birds with white flanks neatly marked with two lines of dark grey chevrons. At the edge of the lawn were our first Satin Bowerbirds, a mixed group of green and scaly females and youngsters, and a couple of all satin blue-black males with whitish beaks and blue eyes. Loud chacking 'karrak-karrak' calls turned our heads as a flock of King Parrots whooshed into the edge of a tree next to us, the intense red heads and bodies of the males glowing in the morning gloom. They seemed ridiculously tame for parrots, very shy species in most other parts of the world due to hunting and trapping for the cage-bird trade, but we later learned they were 'garden birds' at O'Reilly's Guesthouse where they even fed out of peoples' hands, along with Crimson Rosellas, slightly smaller but no less colourful parrots.

Although we were over 2000 feet (about 700 metres) above sea level we were hoping the temperature would be higher than around Melbourne as we entered the temperate rainforest but it was shockingly cold, dark and gloomy below the giant trees and birds were few and far between. Miaow calls and loud, ringing whip-cracks gave away the presence of Green Catbirds and Eastern Whipbirds but we could not see them in the thick undergrowth, until, that is, the light, and the temperature, improved a little. Then we glimpsed the beautiful bright green backs of catbirds, and the black crests of whipbirds. The sound of vegetation being ripped apart and falling to the forest floor drew us to a sleek, chestnut-winged, very animated female Paradise Riflebird that was tearing into the base of a stag-horn fern with a long, powerful down-curved beak. The bird was riveting to watch as she moved about with strong taut legs and exaggerated body movements, swaying her head from side to side to get a better look and attacking the fern like a mad woodpecker, in search of insects. We looked hard for a velvety-black male but we knew the chance of seeing one was very slim because they are so shy. The same could be said for Albert's Lyrebird and so it was.

While putting up the tent we saw an exquisite Eastern Spinebill, a small, long-billed honeyeater with a bluish-grey cap, black mask, red eyes, white throat, rufous bib, black half-collar, cinnamon-coloured belly and flashing black-and-white tail. It was busy nectaring, visiting flower after flower, and was so dashing it looked like a hummingbird. Along the Wishing Tree Trail a male Satin Bowerbird was next to his bower, two parallel rows of woven sticks and grass stems decorated at one end with bits of blue drinking straws. A little farther along the same trail there was a flash of blazing yellow. It came from the wings of a male Regent Bowerbird which landed in full view. The startling beauty, the size of a large thrush, was velvety black with yellow eyes, deep yellow wing patches and a bristly golden hood

*Eastern Spinebill, Lamington NP, Australia, 14th June 1993*

that glowed fiery on its forehead. I could still see the intense colour of its forehead in the flames of our camp fire come dusk when the nocturnal marsupials began to appear. First out for the night was a Brush-tailed Phascogale, a grizzled grey carnivore about the size of a large rat with a black 'bottle brush' tail. There were lots of small grey 'roos called Red-necked Pademelons, and a Common Ringtail Possum, about the size of a cat with slightly bulging eyes in a rounded head and a long, coiled-up prehensile tail with a white tip.

The next morning was so cold I put my scarf and gloves on. We made the long trek along the Border Track to one of two relatively accessible places in the world where it is possible to see the Rufous Scrub-bird, one of the most difficult birds to see on Earth and in a family with just one other species, the Noisy Scrub-bird, which is almost as hard to see in a tiny area of south-west Australia. The rufous variety lives on the ground in the dampest, densest, mossiest patches of gloomy undergrowth it can find. We saw a Russet-tailed Thrush, Australia's version of White's Thrush, and two Noisy Pittas briefly but the scrub-bird remained hidden. By late afternoon we were at Python Rock Lookout, overlooking a forested chasm where we saw two hoped-for pigeons; the large, grey, bobble-headed Topknot and the smart White-headed Pigeon, albeit both in dashing flight. Dingoes howled in the distance. We thought they were a long way off but one was in the campsite, lapping up the beans I flung across the grass because my hand nearly caught fire while removing the wobbling pan from the flames and I instinctively threw it into the air. There were just enough left for us to share but the twelve hours to breakfast suddenly seemed a lot longer.

We were back on the Python Rock Lookout Track at dawn the next morning, listening to the extraordinary song of the Albert's Lyrebird. The long passages of loud, jumbled up chomps, shrieks, squeaks, trills and whistles were mixed with mimicry of other species, especially catbirds and whipbirds. We heard the song three times in three hours before one bird seemed close enough to try and see so we left the track and began making our way through the cold undergrowth, expecting a long haul as the bird walked away from all the noise we made but as we moved farther into the forest the song increased in intensity and volume. Then we caught sight of a quivering mass of silvery feathers around a bunch of vertical, rufous feathers. We could not work out which was the head end and which was the tail end, until we changed positions a few times, and then we could see that the rufous fan of feathers was made up of the bird's undertail coverts and that the shimmering veil of filamentous tail feathers was hanging over the bird's head. He was so stirred up and full of passion he appeared to be completely unaware of us watching him but he knew we were there of course and after a while he began to 'chomp' and stamp his feet before lowering and closing the veil, assuming the normal posture of a large, ground-dwelling bird, and walking slowly off into the tangled undergrowth.

Other birds were hard to come by in Australia's cold 'rainforest' so, fed up with the chilly gloom, we drove down Duck Creek Road during our last afternoon at Lamington to spend some time in warmer, open country with eucalyptus and 'pom-pom' trees, where we saw two Varied Sitellas, the birds which fill the nuthatch niche 'down under'. Flocks of yellow-green Bell Miners seemed to be chiming loudly all over. A male Rose Robin, soft grey above with a lovely rose-red breast, flicked his wings and tail like a hyperactive small flycatcher. We watched the delight for a while then headed north, past Brisbane, to the Conondale Range, a splendid land of deep, steep-sided gorges lined with tall woods and forests rising up from the banks of crystal clear, boulder-strewn creeks.

We found a campsite and at dawn the next morning began walking down Booloumba Creek, looking for a thing that sleeps in a hole, swims like a fish, lays eggs like a bird, and suckles its young like a mammal, a creature called a Duck-billed Platypus, possibly the one animal that can be called unique. We had no joy at dawn, nor dusk, when they are usually out and about, but between times we saw lots of birds, including another female Paradise Riflebird tearing a tree apart, Red-backed Fairywrens, all black except for their backs and rumps, and three Glossy Black Cockatoos in slow-motion flight, their tails lit up with two large red panels. For the first time since we had been in Darwin the sun shone hot from the sky and so it was time to have a shower, also for the first time after Darwin, and it was the coldest shower of my life, in water pumped directly from the mountains. I never warmed up until we made fire under the starry sky and ate charcoal-coated sausages and beans, with a Lace Monitor, a rather large lizard, on the lookout for leftovers, of which there were none.

Back at Booloumba at dawn four Yellow-tailed Black Cockatoos, the largest of Australia's and the planet's five black cockatoos, passed overhead with slow, rowing wing-beats, and long black tails with large yellow 'windows'. There was no sign of a platypus again before we broke camp. On our way out of the Conondales we stopped for a very late breakfast at Little Yabba Creek, eaten in the company of 'Honest Des', the owner of the *House-by-the-creek* who took great pleasure in telling us about how badly England were doing in *The Ashes* cricket series in Australia and not telling us where we might see a platypus. He didn't need to tell us where to see a Wompoo; there were three perched quietly in the shade of a tall fig tree above our heads. They are gorgeous, large, long-tailed, fruit doves with red bills and eyes in dove-grey heads, deep, bright, golden green backs, greener wings with golden wing-bars, and a purple stripe running down from their throats and broadening to cover their breasts before giving way to a deep yellow lower belly; "A choice bird," as 'Honest Des' said. He asked us if, "We wanted to see a kookaburra real close," and when we said, "Yea!" we expected him to point to one sitting right under our noses but he started yelling, "Jacko! ... Jacko! ..... Jacko!" and a few minutes later a Laughing Kookaburra was taking strips of raw meat from my fingertips.

We headed south via Esk where I walked into a bar to buy some beers and caused a sudden, shocking silence when the barflies heard my English accent. The only other time I can recall such a reaction in a pub was in far west Wales when I was on my way to Skomer to see my first Puffins many years before; after a long silence the people at the bar there started speaking in Welsh. The Aussies just stopped talking. There was nowhere to camp at Bellbird Grove, not far west of Brisbane, so we had to try and sleep in the car again, only to be disturbed by the police and, later, as they predicted, some 'Yahoos', Australian slang for uncouth louts, in this case full of beer and making a racket. We were still up for dawn, walking across the steep slope of a leaf-littered stony ridge under tall eucalyptus trees, moving as quietly as possible between grassy rocky outcrops, and to our delight we came across a pair of shy Spotted Quail Thrushes, strange, slow-moving, grey-brown birds with dark spots on their backs and flanks, and white spots across their folded wings, helping them to blend in almost perfectly with the background. After a pleasant while we lost them over the ridge and turned our attention to two male Scarlet Honeyeaters. We then drove through the western suburbs of Brisbane where presumably very happy people live in sunlit, wooden houses on stilts, surrounded by open verandas overlooking large, unfenced, luxuriant gardens, full of exotic birds. At Sherwood Forest Park, still in the suburbs, it was good to get out of the car and stand in the warm sunshine watching lots of birds on a richly vegetated lake full of Dusky Moorhens and Purple Swamphens. There were no bitterns and crakes like there had been but two Forest Kingfishers were enough to make me happy before we departed, in time for the next flight, 450 miles (730 km) south to Sydney.

And so, I finally got to visit my old friends Rob and Sarah in their fine house in Balgowlah where it was warm enough to breakfast outside under the vine. By the afternoon The Stid and I were birding again, just up the road at Long Reef, a rocky headland which pokes far enough out into the Tasman Sea to tempt some seawatching and we soon saw several Black-browed Albatrosses, as well as at least ten Fairy Prions which were a very unusual sight so close inshore according to some of Sydney's finest birders who we enjoyed an evening with in the *Duck and Swan* a few days later.

The bliss of my first night's sleep in a bed for three weeks was cut short by The indefatigable Stid waking me up. While Rob was at work, juggling his building projects, we drove south in his 'ute' (utility vehicle) to Royal National Park where cabbage tree palms, lilly-pillies, sassafras, turpentines and tree ferns grow. Virtually the first bird of the day was also 'bird of the day'; a singing male Superb Lyrebird. Many birds are able to mimic the calls and songs of other birds, and other sounds, even man-made ones, and incorporate them into their own symphonies. Some birds' songs are almost all mimicry. Superb Lyrebirds may only mimic about twenty different species, about a quarter of those where they live, but when it comes to imitating other sounds they are arguably the masters. Their medleys of loud and sweet notes, rattles and trills may include a dog barking, a koala growling, a fox squealing, a pig being slaughtered, a child crying, a heavy smoker coughing, a siren, a steam train, a violin, the shutter and motor-drive of an SLR camera, and even the chainsaws chopping down their forests. The pheasant-sized birds are good-looking too. They sing with their train of wispy tail feathers spread in a large fan, the elongated, buff-banded, snake-shaped, outertail feathers spread out wide, and ending in a lyre-shaped curve, a lyre being a similar-shaped stringed instrument popular in Ancient Greece. The fan or veil is then ruffled as the bird 'dances' in small circles on its display mound, meticulously cleared of leaf-litter. The whole performance was quite a sight, and a sound.

The next day we met up with local birder Trevor Quested who The Stid had met in Malaysia. He took us out into the Sydney suburbs where he showed us a Powerful Owl, a big, barred, dark rather ugly brute with a partly-eaten Common Ringtail Possum in its massive claws. In another park a roosting Tawny Frogmouth was wedged between a branch on which it was perched and the trunk of a paperbark tree. The sleepy bird, a bit smaller than a crow, was delicately marked with grey and buff. It had a huge head and a short but wide hooked beak, the tip of a very large mouth, and it inspected us with half-open eyes, appearing rather comical thanks to the quizzical gaze and the short quiff of feathers standing up on its forehead. We left it in peace and walked off in a successful search for three striking Crested Shrike Tits which were about the size of a shrike with a shrike's beak, and boldly marked with crested, black-and-white heads, green backs and bright yellow underparts.

Under Trevor's instructions we headed inland the next day. From a distance, the Blue Mountains really are blue, a hue produced by a fine mist of eucalyptus oil, exuded by the trees which cover the slopes of the Great Dividing Range. We parked the ute at Katoomba where the quiet, cold forest revealed its birds slowly, good birds like Yellow-tailed Black Cockatoos, King Parrots, Satin Bowerbirds, New Holland Honeyeaters, Eastern Spinebills, and three we had not seen before: the Pilotbird, a little reddish-brown job, named after its rarely observed habit of following lyrebirds to catch the insects that they flush; the similar but smaller, pale-throated and rufous-bellied Rock Warbler, the only bird in the *Origma* genus; and the delightful Crescent Honeyeater. We had seen a lot of honeyeaters but few to match the males of this species which are dark grey above and pale grey below with almost black crescents on the sides of the breast and big, bright, yellow wing patches; a lovely combination of bold yellows and smoky greys.

I was unable to raise my wretched self out of bed in time to join The Stid on his return to the Blue Mountains in search of Olive-tailed Thrush with Trevor and wallowed in a luxurious bed till mid-morning. Fretting over how The Stid was getting on I wrote up my notes in the garden accompanied by Magpie Larks and Pied Currawongs before Rob came home with news of a Southern Right

Whale at Long Reef and we were off to join a large crowd watching what turned out to be a mother and calf close inshore, near enough to see the impressive size of the mother. They were still sheltering in the bay the next day when The Stid, flushed with thrush success, joined me although I must admit we spent more time admiring the flying skills of the Black-browed Albatrosses also present.

Rob, The Stid and I picked up Trevor Quested and Gerry Richards at six a.m. the next morning and headed west to the hamlet of Glen Davis in a valley called Capertree which was alive with birds, many of which we saw very well thanks to Trevor and Gerry's local knowledge and Trevor's inimitable, piercing squeaking, done with pursed lips which must have been very sore by the end of the day. The deafening squeaks attracted birds from miles away, especially honeyeaters, curious to see what the hell was going on. The first new bird of the day and one of the best, not lured in by Trevor, was a dashing male Scarlet Robin, a small black-and-white bird with a very bright red breast. It was almost outdone by the Diamond Firetails, 'liddle beaudies' as they say in those parts, named after the white 'diamonds' on the tiny finches' black flanks and the 'fire' at the base of their tails. We also saw Black-chinned Honeyeaters, Turquoise Parrots, Grey-crowned Babblers, a Plum-headed Finch and Wallaroos, a little smaller than kangaroos, but all were left in the shade by Regent Honeyeaters, one of the rarest and most beautiful of Australia's many beautiful birds. We saw at least ten and a couple of them were perfect, every delicately marked feather in pristine condition, from the lemon-fringed black ones of the upperparts to the black-fringed white ones on the underparts, and including the neat, golden-yellow-edged, dark wing and tail feathers. The bright yellow detail was set against a black hood surrounding a pinkish area of bare skin around the eyes. They were stunning.

After six hours of fitful slumber Rob, The Stid and I climbed into the ute again, for the 50 mile (80 km) journey south to Woollongong. The reason I slept so lively was that we were due to board possibly the greatest birding pelagic boat trip on Earth early in the morning. About 90 seabird species, a third of the world total, have been recorded out of Woollongong into the Tasman Sea where the edge of the continental shelf, one of the best places for seabirds, is only about 30 nautical miles from land. We had been warned about the small size of the vessel, the *MV Sandra K*, and she was tiny; a 43 foot (13 metre), 17 tonne timber cruiser licensed to carry 23 passengers.

We untied at seven a.m. and had hardly left the harbour when the first Black-browed Albatrosses materialised at the back of the boat, gobbling up the chopped pilchards and offal being carefully poured overboard. This was the bird bait which is called 'chum' at home but 'berley' on the *Sandra K*. It is usually composed of chopped, mashed and squashed fish and oil, and the more rotten the fish the better because it is the smell which attracts the birds, some from miles away. The fouler the berley the better as long as you don't get a whiff of it, for even those of us fortunate enough not to suffer seasickness reel at the smell of top class chum, while those who do not travel well on water and catch even a hint of it can be seen heading immediately to the side of the boat to add to the mixture already in the sea.

The Black-browed Albatrosses were soon joined by our first Yellow-nosed Albatrosses and from then on these two relatively small albatrosses graced the whole voyage, mostly at almost arm's length off the back of the boat, sometimes sweeping off to swerve around in a circle to reposition themselves, or dropping to the water to scoop up a piece of pilchard, then taking to the air again by running up the big waves and rejoining us with unfathomable ease in the strong wind. It was busy off the stern and sometimes a Shy Albatross would appear amongst the melee, looming larger than the other albatrosses with bulkier bodies and longer wings, but even they were dwarfed by my first Wandering Albatross. It appeared low over the water and almost head on before rising up with its near wing lowered and far wing raised and zooming off, all in one beautiful almost subliminal movement of power, speed and grace. The bird's head and bulky body were white, the wings mainly black, not white like an adult's, but although it was a young bird the wings were still probably over ten feet across, long enough for me, a six-footer, to lie down on one wing with my head on the bird's back and sail with the albatross across the southern oceans, in my dreams.

I took a moment to absorb the moment then got back to watching the other seabirds which were appearing thick and fast, including lots of Fairy Prions, a few Fluttering Shearwaters, very similar to the Manx Shearwaters of home, and a Common Diving Petrel, more auklet than petrel, but I spent most of my time marvelling at the three species of *pterodroma* petrels out there with us, the most dynamic fliers of all seabirds, whizzing and wheeling above the waves; the all dark brown Great-winged Petrels, similar

Providence or Solander's Petrels but with white flashes in the underwings, and dark-winged White-headed Petrels.

It was not a particularly rough trip according to the regulars even though there was a ten foot (3 metre) swell, with larger waves at times, and a stiff wind. The best place to watch the birds from was the cabin roof where there were a few fixed plastic seats, a thigh-high rail around the edge and a bare steel pergola which could be rigged with a tarpaulin to provide some shade. When the boat rolled, which it did all day long, my body would be pulled forward or sideways against my will and my shins would take a blow against the seats as I automatically made a step to stay upright, my thighs would do the same against the rail, or my upper body would be flung into the steel pergola, so it was no wonder that by the end of the day I was bruised and battered, but it could have been worse. At times I was hanging on for dear life and I very nearly went for a swim twice and thought my number was up for a second or two when the cabin roof was pitched from the more or less horizontal to the almost vertical by rogue waves. I could see the ocean heading toward me rapidly but somehow managed to grab hold of the rail and stay on board.

At least I never felt seasick. Poor old Trevor, who only joined us because The Stid was his friend, looked like death was upon him for most of the eight hours we were out there. Nevertheless, after lobster tails for supper lying flat and still at bedtime was very soothing. My thoughts were with the wanderer as I fell into satisfactory slumber and I saw another the next day. It was off Long Reef, where a light southeasterly wind, the best direction for seawatching there, was blowing, good enough for four species of albatross to pass by close inshore; the colossal Wanderer, a Yellow-nosed, at least three Shy, and at least fifty Black-broweds, all accompanied by many Fairy Prions and Fluttering Shearwaters, and twelve Southern Giant Petrels, most of them just off the rocks.

The Stid and I headed south again the next day through the lush pastures alongside the Minnamurra River around Jamberoo and up a steep escarpment to the swamp plateau of Barren Grounds, so-called because it is a well-watered boggy heathland, a world of drizzle and mist and plants, 500 species of them, including many banksias, all of which combine to produce gallons of nectar for birds and insects, insects which, in turn, provide food for even more birds. The lovely landscape looked like the New Forest in England with wide open spaces of knee-high vegetation between stands of bushes and trees, where instead of Dartford Warblers there were even longer-tailed Southern Emuwrens, the males of which were tiny, fine, bright buff birds with pastel blue throats, short wings and six extremely long, filamentous tail feathers. How they kept their plumage in such splendid condition as they moved about in the sopping wet heather was a mystery to us.

The next evening we began the long drive to Deniliquin, a small town on the Riverine Plain either side of the Edward River, 450 miles (725 km) inland from Sydney. At two-thirty in the morning when Rob was too tired to drive anymore, about 300 miles (500 km) out, we pulled over to get some sleep. The Stid and I put up our tent and managed a couple of hours before rain began to pelt the canvas and woke us up. Rob decided to sleep in the back of the ute and tied a tarpaulin over it to keep the rain off but just as The Stid and I thought we might get back to the land of nod he woke us up.

"I couldn't breathe in there!" he shouted, "Let me in."

It was too cramped in the two-man-tent so we all got up and carried on driving, to Turn Back Jimmy Creek and on to Deniliquin where we went to Phil Maher's house at noon, as arranged. A long birding session with the local birdman born in Deniliquin began with hundreds of small white parrots called Long-billed Corellas that were perched in trees in the town, then we visited a rich, rusty, roosting Barking Owl before seeing our first owlet-nightjar, a very strange bird which Phil got to show us by scratching the hollow branch the bird was roosting in. Curious, it came out of its sleeping place, perched lengthways along the large branch and stared at us with its big dark eyes. It was a greyish, finely-barred cross between a small nightjar and a tiny owl, with a long tail and two broad dark stripes across its more brownish face. As dusk fell we watched hundreds of Galahs going to roost at Wannagella. They may be a common bird but Galahs are truly beautiful, especially in big, tight flight flocks when they present a wonderful image in grey and pink.

After sunset we headed out on to the Hay Plains, possibly the flattest place on the Australian continent, maybe even planet Earth, nearly 200 by 125 miles (320 by 200 km), and home to what we had travelled so far to try and see; the Plains-wanderer, a ground-dwelling bird slightly smaller than a starling, the numbers of which have fallen steeply since the natural grasslands have been ploughed up or overgrazed by excessive numbers of sheep. The unique species was originally thought to be a type of buttonquail but it has since been placed with the shorebirds, although still in a family of its own. It runs from danger through the grass rather than flying, using its strong legs, or it crouches close to the ground to make use of its cryptically camouflaged finely scalloped upperparts, and it is crepuscular, foraging for insects, seeds and leaves mainly at dusk and dawn, hence it is extremely difficult to observe during the day and the only real chance of seeing one is at night, with someone who knows where patches of now mainly secondary native grassland have survived the sheep. That someone was Phil Maher, an expert on the Plains-wanderer, and we began searching with him and the landowner, driving slowly in circles over the sparse grassland with lots of bare, red-brown ground, sweeping four mega spotlights from side to side across the ground. We startled lots of cream-streaked Stubble Quails, some tiny, bright buff Little Buttonquails, and a darker Red-chested Buttonquail, all very unnerving when first glimpsed in the spotlight since any of them could have been the rare one.

We were very fortunate according to Phil to locate a wanderer after just an hour, a male, the drabber of the pair but nicely marked with black bars on buff except for a plainer face with prominent large, yellowy eyes. He also had a yellow bill and yellow legs and stood upright on them like a shorebird rather than horizontally like a buttonquail. It was, however, the slightly larger, brighter, more colourful female we really wanted to see so we continued the search in ever widening circles and two hours later we came across one and I lay down on my belly and the beauty walked right up to my nose, so close I could count the white spangles in her black necklace above her rich chestnut breast band. I lay there for a long time, eye to yellow eye with that wonderful, confiding creature under a sky so full of stars I could hardly see the sky.

*Plains-wanderer, Deniliquin, Australia, 1st July 1993*

*Egyptian Plover, Basse, The Gambia, 5th January 1994*

## 11

# THE GAMBIA

The *Basse Express* bus took seven hours to traverse almost the entire length of The Gambia, a distance of nearly 250 miles (400 km). At the beginning of the journey when the bus pulled into the yard at Serrekunda there was a mass scramble because the wily Gambians with loads of luggage amongst the waiting crowd had paid some young boys a few *bututs* to nip on ahead of them and grab the best seats. The packed bus crawled out of Serrekunda half an hour late with me and my girlfriend Georgie seated over a back wheel, the perfect spot to feel the full force of every bump, crack, corrugation and pot-hole in the terrible road while the temperature soared and clouds of dust poured through the open windows, coating everything and filling our eyes, ears, noses and mouths. The bus left too early for breakfast, there was no lunch and the only thing proffered at the stops that looked appetising was peanut brittle, although it was excellent. Fortunately there were also bottles of cold *Coca-Cola*, which I only drink when I am very hot and thirsty, and I drank a few before we reached Basse. About half way there the corrugated-iron roofs of many roadside villages were replaced with thatched round mud huts in hamlets set back from the road. Looking for birds in the flat, grassy savanna with numerous palms and baobabs as the bus rushed along through the dusty air was difficult but I was very excited to see my first Abyssinian Roller, a bright, pale blue bird with long tail streamers, and I counted thirty-two more before gladly getting out of the damned, hot, metal, dust blower of a bus.

Basse Santa Su, a typical, small, rough African town, is situated on the south bank of a big U-shaped bend in the River Gambia. I was in a hurry to get to the river to look for a certain bird but first we went in search of somewhere to stay. We looked at *The Plaza* from the outside but didn't care how cheap it was we were not going inside, and we took a brief look at the black walls of the shared bathroom in *Basse Guesthouse* before leaving sharply, then the two French ladies who had also travelled on the bus and had joined us suggested we take a look at the doubly expensive but relatively clean *Jem Hotel* where we quickly dumped our stuff and headed straight for the river, exhausted, thirsty, hungry and shaky after a long, hot day.

Still, it was not as bad as it was for Mungo Park who in 1795 at the age of twenty-four headed east from Basse into interior West Africa in the hope of being the first European to reach the River Niger and to determine which way it flowed. Over 500 miles (800 km) out he was seized by a Moorish chief and held captive for several months before eventually escaping and reaching the 'majestic Niger, glittering to the morning sun ... and flowing slowly to the eastward.' There, about 200 miles (320 km) from Timbouctou (Timbuctoo), he wrote, in his 'memorandums', 'Worn down by sickness [fever], exhausted with hunger and fatigue, half-naked, and without any article of value by which I might procure provisions, clothes, or lodging, I began to reflect seriously on my situation. I was now convinced, by painful experience, that the obstacles to my farther progress were insurmountable.' Not much later, having made some progress, he was robbed by 'banditti'. 'After they were gone, I sat for some time looking round me within amazement and terror. Whichever way I turned, nothing appeared but danger and difficulty. I saw myself in the midst of a vast wilderness, in the depth of the rainy season, naked and alone; surrounded by savage animals, and men still more savage ... and I confess that my spirits began to fail me. I considered my fate as certain, and that I had no alternative, but to lie down and perish'. Somehow he found the resolve to get up and start walking, and thanks to the initial help of two shepherds he got back to The Gambia in 1797 and eventually back home to Scotland where while working as a country doctor he wrote up his remarkable tale in *Travels in the Interior Districts of Africa*, published in 1799.

My tale was not remarkable but I was enjoying it because at the river I saw that certain bird, a stunning, small shorebird called an Egyptian Plover, looking very exotic with a bold, black-and-white-striped head, a black arrow down the middle of the lovely blue-grey back, and two black lines arcing round the sides of the pale peach breast. Above the fabulous plover was my first Red-throated Bee-eater, although, like the plover, it was too far away to appreciate fully so I hired a metal tub functioning as a boat, which when out on the shallow, slow-flowing, muddy water afforded wonderful views of six Egyptian Plovers and seven Red-throated Bee-eaters. The plovers occasionally flew a little way along the muddy shore, low on bowed wings, flicking them as if to show off the striking black and white pattern. The bee-eaters looked rather dark from a distance but up close in good light they were mainly bright green with black masks, bright red throats and deep, dark, ultramarine blue undertail coverts. They called 'wip wip', 'wip wip', 'wip wip' frequently, especially in dashing flight.

It was difficult to decide what to look at, especially when I spotted a large snake, longer than me, moving swiftly along the riverbank. It was green above and bright yellow below and the very flustered boatman insisted it was a very dangerous and aggressive Black Cobra. It was heading toward the concrete ramp on the other side of the river at the bottom of which several children were playing or helping their mothers do the washing and the boatman yelled out to warn them. We lost sight of it after that and I stopped looking for it because a large, bright blue and black kingfisher flew past, the first of three Blue-breasted Kingfishers to suddenly appear, and they landed close by, allowing my first view of a very beautiful bird with a red dagger sticking out of its pale, blue-grey head, deep black back and shoulders, and an icy-blue wash across the white breast. Suddenly, an hour had gone by, one of the most exciting and wonderful hours of my life.

Next morning there was a confiding Egyptian Plover on the jetty and I got down on my stomach to look it in the eye. You can't say you've seen a bird until you've looked it in the eye. We left the lovely bird to visit the fruit and vegetable market where Red-throated Bee-eaters adorned the trees shading the ladies in brightly-coloured dresses sitting by their glorious produce. It was too hot to eat, too hot to bird. The heat in Basse is legendary; some cold water pipes get so hot the locals make tea straight from them. It was so hot it seemed sensible to board the bus back to the coast, the 'Special Express', which took the same time as the 'Regular Express'.

It was great to be back in the sea breeze, drinking cooling *Julbrew* beers and *Coco Locos* (cocktails of *Bacardi, Malibu* and cream of banana), and eating grilled barracuda, black salmon, red snapper and shrimps. While birding at the coast, before and after the trip to Basse, I saw a second new shorebird, Senegal Thick-knee, a second new bee-eater, Swallow-tailed, and a second new roller, Blue-bellied, all within walking distance of the splendid *Badala Park Hotel*. A small party of green Swallow-tailed Bee-eaters with blue gorgets roamed widely around the *Fajara Golf Course*, where the greens are in fact browns, but I must admit I enjoyed the Blue-bellied Rollers more. They are very different to most other rollers in that they are not mainly pale blue or purplish but half buffy white, half dark ultramarine blue. At times they perched prominently like many rollers but at others they were remarkably inconspicuous, sitting in the shade of their favoured palms until taking flight and revealing themselves with a flash of azure blue in the dark blue wings.

The rollers lived next to Kotu Creek, a little bit of paradise, where, along the wide, shallow, muddy channel, in the patches of mangroves and gallery forest, and around the adjacent paddy fields dotted with baobabs and banana trees, and fan and oil palms, I saw over a hundred species in a day once I had got to know the place. That day, despite another very poor night's sleep due to continuing bouts of sneezing and having to blow my nose almost constantly to remove the stream of thick mucus, resulting from the warm, dry and dusty northeasterly wind blowing in from the Sahara, known as the *Harmattan*, which also laid many locals low, it being my last full day I forced myself upright in bed at dawn, wobbled to the bathroom, washed my face, dragged my clothes on, put my binoculars around my neck and headed for the golf course where for the first time on the trip I failed to find the Swallow-tailed Bee-eaters, not the best start to the 'big day', although the blow was softened by a surprise Pied Hornbill, not an everyday bird at Kotu.

Throaty chuckles drew my attention to a group of fabulous Gonoleks, small birds with golden-yellow crowns, broad black masks, jet black backs, and deep red underparts. At the end of the creek there were four very confiding Blue-bellied Rollers and by the time I returned for a very late breakfast I had also seen a Malachite Kingfisher and two Little Bee-eaters. The heat of the day was spent scanning the sea from a beach bar while drinking tea, watching the usual Caspian and Royal Terns, and seeing two unusual Gannets. Come mid-afternoon I couldn't wait for the temperature to fall slightly so I could set off again and I marched off in the fearsome heat to the sewage works where there was a fine assortment of shorebirds as usual, although I couldn't find the Painted Snipe I had seen there before. An Abyssinian Roller, my first at the coast, made up for that. Along Kotu Creek I was very pleased to find the White-backed Night Heron sound asleep in the thickest part of its usual roosting tree. Then, at the second attempt, I managed to track down the Swallow-tailed Bee-eaters, the one hundredth species of bird seen since dragging myself out of bed. I could not locate the pair of Rufous-crowned Rollers around the paddy fields where they normally resided but while looking for them I flushed a Hoopoe, another first for my temporary patch, and before dusk I made the total for the day 104 with a Red-necked Falcon, a total that also included Pink-backed Pelican, Senegal Thick-knee, Black-headed and Spur-winged Plovers, African Green Pigeon, Giant and Pied Kingfishers, Green Woodhoopoe, and the aptly-named, highly iridescent, purple-headed, green-backed and scarlet-breasted Splendid Sunbird. I love Africa. There are so many beautiful, easy to see, open-country birds.

Two short *tanker-tanker* (bush taxi) rides away were many different birds, in Abuko Nature Reserve, a tiny strip of remnant riverside forest lining Lamin Stream where nine species of egret and heron graced the pools including Black Herons, as well as Hamerkops and Black Crakes. Spotting Red Colobus monkeys in the luxuriant forest was easy. Seeing, identifying and watching birds required patience and persistence, with which I eventually enjoyed a bright green Guinea Turaco, three Violet Turacos with bright crimson wings flashing in flight across a pool, a thrush-sized bird called a Leaflove, one of Africa's notoriously shy, skulking, dull brown, green, grey and/or yellow greenbuls, and, in a small flurry of activity, two Red-bellied Paradise Flycatchers followed by a bluebill and a yellowbill, a Western Bluebill to be exact, a big-headed, glossy black and bright red forest finch with a massive metallic bluish bill.

The Yellowbill, also known as Green Coucal, is a very rare skulker in Abuko and seeing one was completely unexpected. It was a bird I had long wished to see, since spending many a night in the local library after work studying the monumental six-volume, 4859-page *African Handbook of Birds* by Cyril Winthrop Mackworth-Praed and Captain C. H. B. Grant, published over the course of twenty-odd years between 1952 and 1973. I read it and copied paintings from the plates in it into my *Field Guide to the Birds of East Africa* while researching a trip to Kenya several years before and one of the birds that stood out was the Yellowbill, but I never saw one in Kenya so it was very pleasing to catch sight of the mysterious, dark green, long-tailed cuckoo with a big, bright yellow bill in Abuko, although after an all too brief appearance in my world it was gone, back to its world of thick creepers and vines.

*Varied Thrush, San Francisco, California, 8th January 1995*

12

# CALIFORNIA and THE GRAND CANYON

California is a land of extremes. It is only about 80 miles (130 km) from Badwater in Death Valley, one of hottest places on the planet and at nearly 300 feet (90 metres) below sea level the lowest point in North America, to the highest point in the lower 48 United States at over 14,500 feet (4400 metres) on top of Mount Whitney in the Sierra Nevada, the same snowy mountain range where the largest trees on the planet, Giant Sequoias, and the oldest trees in

North America, Bristlecone Pines, grow, and not far away from the stands of Coast Redwoods, the tallest trees on Earth. Some say the most beautiful place in the world is the Yosemite Valley in the Sierra Nevada. Others prefer Pacific beaches, the Mojave Desert with its Joshua Trees, or the orchards and vineyards of the 450 mile (725 km) long Central Valley, one of the seven most fertile regions in the world. Some say 'The sun always shines' on The Golden State and if you like you can swim in the Pacific and go skiing the same day.

It is truly an incredible part of planet Earth. That's why it's the most populous state in America where many millions of people live in vast urban sprawls and move about on hundreds of miles of multi-lane freeways crammed with vehicles, and yet the greatest diversity of terrain on the North American continent still supports a tremendous range of birds, from the deserts through wooded canyons to forested mountains and rich offshore waters. So, not long after dusk one day in December I was driving along the crowded San Gabriel River Freeway in Los Angeles, in a *Buick Regal*, with Georgie in the passenger seat. The eight lanes of heavy traffic was quite a shock for someone who had just got off a very long transatlantic and transcontinental flight, never owned a car in his life and rarely drove one. The vehicle was also an automatic and I kept stalling the damned thing, pushing my foot down on the brake pedal because I thought it was the gear pedal and instinctively trying to change gear, except there were no gears and the lever I could not help moving was changing the instruction to the car from drive to park. I kept parking on that freeway but no one noticed because the traffic was almost at a standstill.

## A MIND-BLOWING BIRDING TRIP TO A PLANET CALLED EARTH

There was no way I was going to leave the freeway. Trying to reach it we had already, accidentally, seen some of the streets in the L.A. suburbs and it looked like we would need bullet-proof vests and an arsenal of large-calibre weapons to survive in them. It seemed like the population of L.A. that didn't belong to a gang was heading for the hills. Was there something we didn't know about? Had the gangs finally taken over the city? Was everyone else escaping? No, it was Friday night and millions of commuters were driving home or away from the city for the weekend. Nevertheless, the shock of it all produced enough adrenalin to keep me awake for the eighty mile (130 km) drive to the *Motel Six* in San Bernardino.

The fifty mile (80 km) drive the next morning up into the mountains was even worse, because there were still an unbelievable number of vehicles on Route 18, all trying to negotiate the steep and winding road in virtually nil visibility, due to thick cloud and rain. We couldn't understand why the route is known as *Rim of the World Drive* until the road emerged above the clouds and ran along a narrow ridge in a beautiful vista of forests and snowy mountains.

"Now there's a damn fine-looking man!" the manageress of the *Bavarian Lodge* at Big Bear Lake said as I enquired about a room.

I had to sit down. Not because of her description of me, because of the price of a room. It was the cheapest in town though, so once the gear had been dumped I set out with binoculars at last and in the pines alongside Big Bear Lake, between sleety squalls, I saw two new nuthatches;

the rather large White-breasted Nuthatch and the much smaller Pygmy Nuthatch, thus completing the plate of illustrations of four species in the *National Geographic Field Guide to the Birds of North America* and the continent's set of one of my favourite families of birds.

There were two inches of fresh snow on the ground Christmas morning and it was still snowing when we set out. There was no way round it: it was the law; if I intended to drive in such conditions I would have to fork out fifty dollars for snow chains. After wrapping them around the tyres I dropped my skiing companion off and headed for Baldwin Lake where 'Mountain Bluebirds and Pinyon Jays can usually be found at any season' according to *A Birder's Guide to Southern California* by James A Lane, two blue birds at the top of the list of fundamental reasons for visiting California, but the snowflakes increased in number and size so I had to retreat before seeing anything blue and return to base where I birded the streets of Big Bear in a blizzard and *did* see some new, mainly blue, birds, called Steller's Jays. Back at the lodge the mad manageress discovered I was a birder and that I had never seen a Bald Eagle. Disgusted, she marched me to her massive four-wheel-drive and we were off, to see, "Several," she said, "that roost in the trees along Eagle Drive, not far away." The residential street was less than a mile from the lodge in fact, but the frozen trees were bare when we got there, and the same was true when I returned later on foot. Then I picked Georgie up from the ski slope and she looked and felt like an icicle.

Worried about the weather we left the mountains while we could. Miles and miles of heavy traffic climbing slowly up them as we descended suggested I had been hasty in my decision but I had back-up plans for blue birds and eagles and by midday we had left the snow behind and were in the warm flatlands around the Salton Sea on the trail of a new shorebird, the Mountain Plover. The sky was blue, the sun was shining and there were birds everywhere; thousands of Snow Geese, 65 Sandhill Cranes, Gila Woodpeckers, and Gambel's Quails, their topknots nodding as they walked between the low bushes, but I couldn't find any plovers.

At more than 200 feet (60 metres) below sea level the Salton Sea is one of the most inhospitable places in North America. Temperatures during the summer are consistently above 100°F and sometimes in the 120s 'in the shade', where there appeared to be no shade. However, fertile sediments surrounding the lake are over 8000 feet (2400 metres) thick hence huge, flat fields without fences or hedges stretch to the horizon. It is these fields, especially the big, brown, bare, earthy ones, which the plovers like and the next day in one such field there were thirty-six of them, some close enough to clearly see their tan crowns and upperparts, glowing white foreheads and buffy breasts. There were no Mountain Bluebirds at Wister Unit though and it was time to move on again, 350 miles (560 km) to the last room in the *Westerner Motel*, Williams, Arizona, via cacti country, the Colorado River, rolling plains with dwarf conifers and, on higher ground, forests of Ponderosa Pines.

From Williams it was a short drive to the south rim of the Grand Canyon, the 220 mile (350 km) long, mile (1.6 km) deep and up to 18 mile (30 km) wide gash in the Earth's surface, carved and sculpted by the planet's most formidable canyon-cutter the Colorado River, which has stripped back successive layers of sedimentary rock full of fossilised ferns, fish, insects, reptiles and trilobites, down down deeper and down to the nearly two billion years old granite and schist at the bottom. From the rim it was difficult to appreciate the scale but the view of vertical, red rock walls and flat-topped buttes and mesas, all rising from the muddy Colorado River far, far below, was truly spectacular. I was just as interested in the local birdlife of course and on a long walk in crisp, cold air I saw my first Western Bluebirds, overshadowed by many, very confiding Pygmy Nuthatches, some of which foraged on the snowy ground so close there was no need for binoculars.

Next day, on our way to Death Valley, we stopped for a break in Searchlight, a gambling hole in Nevada where a coffee was ten cents in a diner full of glum-looking gamblers slumped in front of aptly-named one-armed bandits, their minds permanently polluted by the prospect of a quick buck from the crooked machines. It was a taste of Las Vegas which I insisted on giving a very wide berth. The raining continued to fall as we moved west into California and looked forward to some warm sunshine in the Mojave Desert. Some desert; the Joshua Trees were dusted with snow. We managed to reach Shoshone with two hours of grim daylight left and in continuing rain I headed out in search of some birds, seeing plenty including a pair of exquisite little yellow-headed Verdins.

I drove into Death Valley from the southern end as the morning sun hit the red rocks. The sky was clear and the air winter crisp and we had to imagine how desolate the barren land of rock, sand and caustic saltpans, amid mountain ranges with names like Black, Funeral and Last Chance, must be during the summer when the average temperature is over 100°F and the highest recorded is 134°F. A quick walk around part of Furnace Creek Ranch revealed few birds as expected before we continued, over a snowy Sierra Nevada pass then down through lovely wooded valleys on winding roads to Delano. The next morning I was behind the wheel again, being the only driver, heading north on Highway 99 to Fresno and Merced through 130 miles (200 km) of thick fog, only escaping it when the road climbed up to Mariposa where lo and behold the sun shone all afternoon while I looked for birds around the town. It was a wonderful break from driving in atrocious conditions, looking at the needle-like bills and shimmering red throats of tiny Anna's Hummingbirds, the white eyes of Acorn Woodpeckers, the red heads of Red-breasted Sapsuckers, the red breasts of American Robins and the browns and oranges of my first two Varied Thrushes, once a member of the skulking *Zoothera* genus now in one of its own; *Ixoreus*.

Highway 140 north from Mariposa runs through a beautiful steep-sided valley alongside the rocky Merced River, perfect for American Dippers which were bobbing on the slabs of granite jutting out of the icy water. Round another bend the road narrowed and entered the Yosemite Valley and for several miles the river flowed slowly and silently through snow-covered meadows and tall Incense Cedar and Ponderosa Pine forests with sheer grey granite cliffs shooting straight up from the wide and flat valley floor, over 3000 feet (900 metres) in the case of El Capitan, the tallest unbroken cliff on Earth, with the massive, ice-polished, curve-backed, monolith of grey rock known as Half Dome at the far end of the valley rising nearly 5000 feet (1500 metres) above the river with a sheer rock face of over 2000 feet (600 metres), a vast expanse of grey rock interrupted only by side canyons and frozen waterfalls. Carved by Pleistocene glaciers three million years ago and painted with a fresh coat of ice and snow Yosemite is probably the most beautiful valley in North America and one of the most magnificent in the world, bold claims hard to argue with when standing on that valley floor, even for someone who had already seen the glories of the Pyrenees, Andes, Karakoram and Himalayas.

The most conspicuous birds in Yosemite Valley were Acorn Woodpeckers and Steller's Jays. It was too low for Clark's Nutcrackers according to the rangers, which was a blow, but there's more to birding than the birds, especially in a place like Yosemite. It was far better than I had imagined and I had not allocated enough time to absorb it. I needed to walk it not drive it and vowed to return as I set out on the 150 mile (240 km) drive across California to Monterey on the Pacific coast. Descending the sierra, the road soon reached the foggy farmland of the Central Valley where ninety percent of the grasslands and wetlands had already been ploughed up, drained and tamed, the lovely creeks and rivers replaced by levees, the birds decimated and all but gone outside a few reserves, including Merced and San Luis National Wildlife Refuges where I had high hopes of seeing some Ferruginous Hawks, Lewis's Woodpeckers, Yellow-billed Magpies, Tricoloured Blackbirds and, especially, Mountain Bluebirds, so the thick, cold fog and poor visibility was disappointing. However, even though I could see only fifty paces either side of the narrow roads I did manage to see a fine-looking hawk perched on a fencepost, lots of magpies and some blackbirds.

On Lake El Estero in Dennis-the-Menace Park, Monterey, three new gulls appeared in about three new seconds; the very smart, grey-bodied, white-headed and red-billed Heermann's Gull, slaty-backed Western Gulls and a single young Thayer's Gull, with my first California and Glaucous-winged Gulls also present on the small lake later in the day. Roosting on Coast Guard Pier and the attached floating pontoons in Monterey were Brown Pelicans, Brandt's and Pelagic Cormorants, and over a hundred bickering California Sealions, with Surf Scoters, Pacific Divers and a Sea Otter offshore, the otter floating on its back smashing a crab against a rock on its chest, a much more exciting sight than another new bird even though it was a shorebird. I have to admit the Wandering Tattler's standard appearance and uniform dark grey plumage did not distract me from the otter for long. Having dispatched the crab the pale-headed, be-whiskered beguiling creature took a nap, its dense fur keeping it warm in the cold water.

The sun came out after heavy overnight rain as I watched my first Townsend's Warblers near the lighthouse at Point Pinos, including one very striking black and yellow male. At the point I saw three Black-vented Shearwaters and the last two possible new shorebirds on the trip; Black Oystercatchers, with red rings around their yellow eyes, and broad-chested Black Turnstones, so it was already a great day before we moved on to Point Lobos where there were five Grey Whales close inshore, one of which leapt almost completely out of the ocean before falling back down on its side with a massive splash. A quick walk inland was enough to find a California Thrasher but no Wrentits, another species with a range centred on the state of California.

Big Bear was a whiteout, the Central Valley a 'fog-out' and Monterey a washout. It poured down all day the next day; curtains of water coming in off the Pacific on a Force 7 wind so no whale-watching boats were leaving Fisherman's Wharf and none were likely to for several days, which was a massive disappointment because there were several seabirds I was hoping to see out in Monterey Bay, one of the five most productive marine ecosystems in the world where masses of seabirds and cetaceans feed on huge quantities of krill and vast schools of anchovies, a food web sustained by nutrient-rich waters shaken and stirred by deep-water upwellings from a submarine canyon deeper than the Grand Canyon. There would be no chance of me seeing Fork-tailed Storm Petrels and, worst of all, Black-footed Albatrosses, and possibly a Laysan Albatross, most likely in January, the month it was, unless I did some serious seawatching and Georgie was not keen on that. I did scan the coves, bays and rough sea from the rainswept car for a while, hoping for a windblown bird or two but all I saw apart from some more Sea Otters was a Pigeon Guillemot, a measly crumb that had drifted in from the unreachable feast offshore.

Fed up, we left Monterey and drove north, stopping at Ano Nuevo State Reserve where we walked through a colony of Northern Elephant Seals, not on the beach where they normally resided, in the dunes away from the stormy sea. There were over a hundred blubbery beasts slumbering on the windswept sand including some monstrous bulls up to twelve feet (4 metres) long. They may be huge and extremely heavy but should a rival bull appear on their patch they can shuffle surprisingly quickly over short distances, rapidly enough for the ranger to make sure we gave them a wide berth. Occasionally a big bull arched its thick, wrinkled neck back and with its nose inflated in an ugly bulbous mass trumpeted so loudly we could hear it half a mile away. Farther north we crossed the Golden Gate Bridge then I faced another gruelling stretch of the cliff-clinging Highway 1 as another rain front arrived in off the Pacific and I was very glad to pull into a *Motel Six* in Petaluma for the night.

The woods, marshes, pastures and shores of Point Reyes, a peninsula jutting ten miles out into the Pacific, support a wide range of wildlife, from Bobcats to Wrentits, but it was a duck I was hoping to see the most so I made my way to Chimney Rock at the eastern tip of the hammerhead at the southern end of the peninsula. A fierce wind was whipping across the headland as the bad weather continued but I pushed on and persevered and there below me next to some Northern Elephant Seals amongst the rocks and rough water they love were four Harlequins. Edging as close to the top of the cliff as I dared and trying desperately to hold my binoculars steady in the wind I could make out a duck and three drakes, one of which was in pristine condition. Its fantastically variegated plumage was made up of a crazy pattern of black-framed bright white spots, squares, crescents and stripes set against a gorgeous, dark blue-grey and chestnut background. Returning to the car, glad to be out of the wind, I drove across the 'hammer' to the lighthouse at the western end, where we hoped to see some more Grey Whales but the wind was Force 7 and blowing in over a very rough Pacific so we retreated to Bolinas Lagoon on the more sheltered side of the peninsula in search of another new duck called Barrow's Goldeneye. I couldn't find any but several long scans revealed six Belted Kingfishers.

By the time we got to Muir Woods National Monument it was raining again, appropriately enough given the huge amount of water that falls from the sky along the northern coast of California, which coupled with frequent damp fog helps to grow the tallest trees on Earth. The massive trunks covered in thick, soft, spongy, red-brown bark with deep dark grooves, rose from the damp ground like columns, without branches for well over a hundred feet (30 metres) until, finally, reaching the dark green conical crowns which formed the forest canopy. Deep in that tiny remaining fragment of dark, dank Coast Redwood forest where some trees were 250 feet (76 metres) high, in the continuing downpour, I came across two Varied Thrushes, one of which was my first male, a beautiful creature that is dark slate grey above with orange eyebrows, a broad black mask, deep orange throat, black chest band and orange underparts, a bird that belonged in such a wonderful forest. For a while I forgot about the rain.

It was dry in the car but I would rather have been back in the wet woods watching thrushes than keeping my eyes on six lanes of traffic heading into the streets of San Francisco. 'America's most beautiful city' looked like any other city to me; poor, run-down suburbs, shop-lined streets with more than the usual number of crazy down-and-outs, homeless cranks and poseurs, overpriced tourist shopping malls, and some nicer areas where the rich folk who write the positive blurb about the city live. Most of the people on the bus from Mission to Marina behaved like they had been let out for the day. It was full to bursting but when a squashed passenger suggested to the driver that she shouldn't let anyone else on the driver decided to make more room by braking as hard as possible and therefore throwing everyone on board even closer together, and creating more room. It seemed to me that every freaking weirdo in San Francisco was either driving that bus, on that bus, or visible from it. We should have stuck to the car but I was sick of driving by then. The rain poured forth all the first night we were in town and it was still raining, only more heavily, the next morning when I sought sanctuary in Golden Gate Park. With six Canvasbacks and lots of other ducks on Spreckel's Lake was a Tufted Duck, a very rare visitor from Eurasia, but the best birds by far were five more Varied Thrushes, including another glorious male.

'Thousands flee floods' was the headline on the front page of the *San Francisco Examiner* that I picked up in the airport. High winds and rain lashing against the terminal building windows threatened the flight back home and the next day, when, mercifully, we were home, more than half of the California counties were declared a Federal Disaster Area after the worst storms for nearly ten years continued to cause flooding, landslides, mud flows, more than three hundred million dollars worth of damage, and the loss of several lives.

*Cuban Tody, Guira National Park, Cuba, 21st December 1997*


# 13

# CUBA

The Zapata Rail, a medium-sized brown and blue-grey bird, is known only from a sawgrass swamp on the island of Cuba where just a few people have seen it. In the late 1990s one of them lived in the village of Santo Tomas next to the swamp. His name is Orestes Martinez Garcia although his friends called him *El Chino* ('The Chinaman'). The only times he had seen the bird were after sleeping out in the swamp at night with the mosquitoes and catching a glimpse at dawn, of what is one of the rarest, most secretive and difficult to see birds on the planet, a bird that is so short-winged it probably rarely flies, and is almost certainly crepuscular, searching for insects at dawn and dusk, and possibly strictly nocturnal.

The Stid, Brian Field and I arranged an early morning trip into Zapata Swamp where the rail lives with *El Chino* and his brother Angel, and we were joined by Jean Francois and Helen from Belgium. We travelled into the swamp in two punts, along a deep, narrow channel. When we stopped we were instructed to leave the metal tubs, at which point *El Chino* and Angel were met with open mouths. We were surrounded by water but there was no choice apparently, we had to plunge in. I stepped in, up to my knees, and *El Chino* announced that I was the *primero* birder to plodge into Zapata Swamp barefoot. Neither he nor his brother had warned us that we were expected to wade way into the swamp full of biting beetles and riddled with waist-high sink-holes into which I frequently stepped as I attempted to avoid ripping my feet and legs to shreds on the aptly-named sawgrass. I was not the only one having trouble. Helen, not a mad keen birder like her partner, was not impressed, and after a few hundred plodges she was heard to mutter something about birding, birders and divorces as she swotted away the swarms of mosquitoes, but we still had some way to go before we were told to stop and listen.

None of us expected to see a Zapata Rail, we never even dreamed of hearing one, we were in that swamp because we were hoping to see two other birds; the Zapata Wren, like the rail known only from that swamp, and the Zapata

Sparrow. *El Chino* was listening for wrens. He couldn't hear any so Angel held a speaker above his head out of which poured an almost deafening recording of the wren's warble, loud enough to elicit a response from a bird the other side of Cuba, let alone the swamp. I think we were all very pleased to hear *El Chino* say that the bird would come to us but not so happy to be told it could take forty minutes. While Angel played the infernal racket at full blast he and the rest of us waded on slowly in search of sparrows. After a while we heard one singing and up to four of the rather drab grey and dull yellow birds were soon in view. As we watched them *El Chino* said he would try to get a Zapata Rail to call or sing by doing an impression; there were no recordings of the rail as there was for the wren. Almost immediately we heard a response, a low 'cutucutu-cutucutu-cutucutu' coming from a close clump of sawgrass. *El Chino* was very excited so we began heading in the bird's direction, all thoughts of Zapata Wren, still on its way, put to the back of our minds. As we homed in on the Zapata Rail a Spotted Rail, another bird not easy to see but with a wide range across Central and South America, began singing too.

"Zapata or Spotted?" *El Chino* asked.

"Zapata!" was the unanimous emphatic response.

Just as we were about to encircle the tussock the never-seen rail was still singing from the Zapata Wren arrived. We could hear both rails while we watched the long-tailed brown wren with fine black barring but even though we did not look at it for long by the time we returned to the Zapata Rail hunt the bird had moved to an impenetrable stand of tall sawgrass where it then also fell silent, leaving us back where we started; absolutely no chance of seeing one. We never saw the Spotted Rail either, nor the King and Sora Rails we also heard on the wade back to the punts, and we clambered into them feeling somewhat deflated, despite the fact that we had just seen Zapata Wren and Zapata Sparrow. We would have been elated not frustrated had we known then that the 'cutucutu-cutucutu-cutucutu' sound *El Chino* believed was that of the Zapata Rail was, as has since been proven, the song of the Spotted Rail, and what we had heard was probably a dispute between two of those birds which are relatively common but also rarely seen in sawgrass swamps.

That was only the beginning of what, fortunately, turned out to be a great day, for not long after, in low, wet forest bordering the swamp we saw a shy Grey-headed Quail Dove with a purple sheen across its shoulders. Moving to drier forest with lots of palms, known as *costanera*, *El Chino* strode on, like a clockwork soldier, a passionate man with a purpose in life, his current purpose being to show us *Pajaro mosca*, the endemic bird I most wanted to see on the island of Cuba. He stopped in a clearing and looked up and there, at some flowers high up in a tree, a blurred dot appeared. After hovering in front of the flowers for what seemed like a millisecond it whizzed away with incredible speed. The same happened five or ten minutes later, the dot virtually impossible to spot with binoculars because it moved so fast. The same happened again then *El Chino* worked out where it was perching between its regular visits to the flowers and beckoned us to the other side of the clearing where we could see some thin exposed snags. Telescopes were set up on tripods rapidly and there it was, the smallest bird on this planet humans call Earth; a Bee Hummingbird, just over two inches, about 57 millimetres, smaller than my thumb, from the tip of its needle-like bill to the end of its tail, 30 millimetres minus bill and tail, a body barely more than an inch long. The 'dot' was dark above and white below with a shiny red patch on its chin and pale greenish flanks. Even perched the tiny mite was hyperactive, almost constantly twitching, moving its head from side to side, raising and flattening its crown feathers, shivering its wings and tail, occasionally twittering and making short sallies into the air, flying forwards, backwards, sideways and around before returning to its perch with aplomb. One second it was there, the next it was gone. As quick as a flash it darted from its perch to zap some unseen atom-sized aerial insect, or it dashed in a straight line to the flowers and sipped some nectar before returning to the very same snag on which the telescopes and we were focused. The brilliant little thing just could not sit still. It was absolutely bursting with life!

Back at *El Chino's* house, a tiny, one-storey red brick building with a thatched roof, he marched in and came out with a Bee Hummingbird's nest. The miniature cup of hair and lichens stuck to the top of a twig was little bigger than a thimble and barely big enough for the two tiny white eggs a female lays in it, eggs the size of coffee beans.

Before Brian and The Stid arrived in Cuba I spent a couple of days in Parque Lenin on the southern outskirts of Havana, a noisy but large park with some good woodland and a large shallow lake where I saw some fine birds. There were lots of warblers spending the northern winter there especially Palm Warblers, of which it was easy to see over a hundred a day, and Caribbean specialities included the Great Lizard Cuckoo, or Big Rain Crow, a large, incongruous, long-tailed, brown, buff and white bird. Food and drink were much harder to come by. On my return to the *Motel La Herradura* at 10 a.m. on the first morning, breakfast time in Cuba, I was beckoned to a table and a plate with a bit of cheese on it. After a chat with the chef I managed to secure a one-egg-omelette which was so thin it was almost transparent but I failed miserably as far as coffee was concerned. Food seemed to be a scarce resource in the communist outpost, although the lack of it was not reflected by the size of the inhabitants I saw waddling around the park, which left me wondering what they ate, when they ate it and where they got it from. All I saw were a few baguettes, clutched to the chest like babies. Another mystery to me was the number of people working in the motel. At least ten women seemed to be employed to set the four always empty tables at which no food was likely to be served, and the barman, different every day, seemed to spend the entire day wearing down the empty wooden bar surface by constantly wiping it. Perhaps he had gone mad listening to the thumping bass of the music blaring out constantly in the motel and the whole park.

To save the fifteen dollar taxi fare I decided to walk the couple of miles to the airport to meet Brian and The Stid. This involved following what appeared to be a barely used railway line and I was lucky a train never came along when I was traversing the high single track bridge across a deep ravine near Calabaza. After Brian and The Stid arrived about midnight we hired a *Daewoo* and crashed out, to the boom-boom-boom of the music, at gone one in the morning back at the *Motel La Herradura*.

We were up in time for a promised breakfast at 08:00 but there was none so we got in the car and headed for Guira National Park and had a fine brunch of pork and sweet potatoes at La Palmar, before climbing the limestone hills into the pine woods which were alive with birds. The very best of them was an exquisite Cuban Tody, a small, stubby bird with a large head, red, stick-like beak, bright luminescent green face, back and wings, glowing red bib, blue at the side, and carmine flanks. We were drawn to the beauty by its 'tot-tot-tot-tot' and soft rolling, purring 'pprreeee-pprreeee' calls, the latter the origin of its common local name, 'Pedorrera'. I love the order of birds called Coraciiformes, having seen lots of kingfishers, bee-eaters and rollers, and was glad to add a tody, another bird with the combination of beautiful, often metallic, colours, and the habit of perching prominently. The vast majority of Coraciiformes live in Africa and Asia while the relatively few motmots and todies are confined to Central and South America, and, in the case of the todies, the Caribbean, where there are five very similar species, little bigger than wrens, which catch their food a bit like flycatchers, although todies dart out to glean insects from twigs and leaves rather than plucking prey out of the air.

Almost as amazing as the tody was my first Cuban Trogon, a spectacular bird with a violet-blue crown, black mask, red eyes, metallic green back, black and white chequered wings, white throat and breast, bright red belly and a unique tail with long, winged and pointed feathers, white below, blue-green above. A brown and grey Cuban Solitaire was not much to look at but as is the case with many sombre songbirds it had a beguiling song; a crazy, squeaky mixture of very high-pitched churrs, trills and whistles. Some fruiting palm trees attracted a succession of extraordinary birds, not least a golden-chested Stripe-headed Tanager, a red-chested Cuban Green Woodpecker, a Yellow-throated Warbler and my first male Black-throated Blue Warbler. After a cup of tea we strolled down the hill in search of nightbirds. We were not expecting much but about an hour after dark we were watching a Stygian Owl, a large sooty black owl barred and spotted buff and white. The word stygian is an adjective which means extremely dark, murky, gloomy or forbidding, almost appropriate for such a bird, the loud 'hu!' call of which is seemingly uttered as if to scare someone or something. The bird is considered by some Cubans to be a bad omen and a few even believe a Stygian Owl should be killed if found because the bird has supernatural powers and is able to transform itself into a witch.

The next warm and sunny morning at La Guira was all about todies and trogons. Two todies were engaged in a territorial dispute, calling a lot and puffing out their carmine flanks, and one was so possessed and unaware of me standing almost at arm's length I was able to see its gold lores, the feathers between the beak and eyes. They sent us merrily back to Havana where it took a long time to find some gas for the car and that only with the help of one of many hitchhikers. East of Havana we hit the main *autopista*, the Carretera Central, which spans the complete length of the island; 777 miles (1250 km). We only covered a few hundred, mostly through vast, bird-less, sugar cane plantations and orange orchards where once there was forest full of birds. One place where some original vegetation still existed was the low-lying, coral island of Cayo Coco off the north coast which we reached via a 17 mile (27 km) long causeway as the sun rose into a clear sky above the Caribbean Sea. In thick, dry, xerophytic thorn scrub we saw several grey but surprisingly smart Cuban Gnatcatchers, grey and yellow Oriente Warblers and two Bahama Mockingbirds on a nearby island, Cayo Guillermo, but we did not see any West Indian Whistling Ducks, Thick-billed Vireos or Zapata Sparrows of the *varonai* race. A fine Black 'Crab' Hawk lived up to its name, Magnificent Frigatebirds soared overhead and two Reddish Egrets spear-fished in the shallows. Back in the town called Moron, while drinking a few cervezas, a stream of local lasses pleaded with us to accompany them to a bar and go 'dancing' which, in most if not all cases, we assumed we would be expected to pay for.

We resisted, because we had another early start, and we were back on Cayo Coco for dawn, where once again we failed to find the ducks, vireos and sparrows but a wave of warblers contained Black-and-white, Parula, Prairie, Worm-eating, Oriente, Ovenbird and my first Cape May Warblers. During the heat of the day we drove to Camaguey in the middle of Cuba where we tried to bolster our scant information on the whereabouts of the rare endemics, Cuban Palm Crow and Giant Kingbird, by grilling a local hunter who just happened to be visiting the manager of the *Hotel Camaguey* when we arrived. He knew where to look for the crows but during his twenty years in the surrounding hills he had only ever seen two Giant Kingbirds. I saw my first Northern Jacanas on a roadside pond on our way to Ventientes and near there in a stand of Royal Palms we eventually heard then saw our first Palm Crows which looked just like any other crow.

Our terrible, scribbled map looked like it had been drawn by someone being deliberately vague. On it there were some confusing directions to a site where Giant Kingbird had been seen before. The map appeared to be based on a hillock and during our extensive crow travels we had seen just three hillocks. We decided to try the one which looked like it had the most woodland on it and we were up before dawn but the hillock was nowhere to be seen. It was hidden in mist. After a couple of hours the sun began to burn off the mist and we saw another hillock so we headed for that one, finding our way along farm tracks by trial and error. The people out working in the fields were very friendly, pointing the way when asked, all except for one woman, who gesticulated that we would have our throats cut if we proceeded through one particular gate. At the hillock with no name we saw two kingbirds, both of which looked like the very similar Loggerhead Kingbird to us, but while trying to get better views of them we heard the 'woop-woop-woop' of a Plain Pigeon, another rare and local bird in Cuba, and distracted by three of them we lost the kingbirds.

In 1961 about 1400 exiled Cuban counter-revolutionaries, funded and trained by the CIA, attempted to invade Cuba and overthrow the anti-American Fidel Castro, the dictator who himself overthrew the even more brutal Fulgencio Batista in 1959. They landed in the Bahia de Cochinos (Bay of Pigs) but even with the help of American bombers they were defeated within three days. By the time we reached the Bay of Pigs in the late 1990s there were a few quiet holiday resorts and one of them, Playa Larga, was our base for birding Zapata Swamp and the lowland coastal forest nearby. We were hoping to see most of Cuba's endemic birds during our week in the area and we were very successful, missing only the parakeet, despite the ongoing destruction of the forest, mainly for the production of charcoal, the fuel most Cubans use to cook. Apart from the Bee Hummingbird I was most interested in seeing a Blue-headed Quail Dove, one of four quail doves that lived in the forest. All four are small, shy, quiet ground-dwelling birds and we spent many, mostly surprisingly chilly and wet, hours walking as quietly as possible along narrow trails with our three pairs of eyes fixed laser-like on the forest floor, trying to spot the birds. Our stealth was rewarded with nine Ruddy Quail Doves, eight Grey-headed Quail Doves and two Blue-headed Quail Doves, although the latter were seen too briefly to appreciate their brilliance so I renewed my efforts when Brian and The Stid drove back to Havana to fly home.

I enjoyed three sunny days wandering between Playa Larga and the villages of Los Sabalos, Soplillar and Palpite, watching an exciting variety of birds, from Limpkins, Northern Jacanas and Belted Kingfishers on roadside marshes, to todies, trogons, tanagers and up to fourteen species of warbler per day along the forest trails. On my last full day I awoke before dawn in my cabana to the usual 'Parrot-like squawks and guttural jabbering'. No, it wasn't The Stid talking about the birds not on his list again it was the call of the Cuban Crow, as described by James Bond. No, not that James Bond the one who wrote *A Field Guide to the Birds of the West Indies*, a little gem of a book originally published in 1936. Ian Fleming wrote the James Bond spy novels in his house, called Goldeneye, on the north coast of Jamaica, and used the name of the author of the bird book on his shelf for his fictional secret agent.

Another blazing hot day was under way so I rushed out to a track off the Soplillar road hoping to get my last fix of todies before it got too hot. *Tocororos* were calling - the onomatopoeic local name of Cuban Trogons - and it wasn't long before I was drooling over one of them *and* a tody, at close range as usual. I then heard a hum from the whirring wings of what I thought was a Bee Hummingbird and so it proved, and as I watched the little mite licking up nectar from some flowers high above my head I saw a dove on the track out of the corner of my eye. It walked into the forest but I stood stock still and it came back out again and I could hardly believe I was looking at a fabulous Blue-headed Quail Dove in the open, its jewel-like, blue-black bib shimmering in a ray of sunshine. Through my carefully raised binoculars I examined the striking head pattern; snow white stripes across its face, black lines through its eyes and a sky blue cap, all of which contrasted strongly with the rather sombre earth-coloured body and wings which, when it turned to slip back into the forest with its back to me, merged perfectly with the leaf litter. I walked even more slowly and quietly along the track after that, not easy in such dry forest, and I soon came across two more, also out in the open but even closer, and I watched them for ages before they too walked into the undergrowth and out of sight.

Three more todies and another trogon followed before I cooled down with a swim in the Caribbean. As usual on a birdless beach, I was bored before I was dry, and I couldn't resist one final walk so I headed back to the same track I was on in the morning, hoping for better views of the Bee Hummingbird. It was mid-afternoon and the sun was beating down on my back while waves of oppressive hot air rose from the road so I was glad to reach the shade of the forest, although as usual there were plenty of mozzies and tiny flies which seemed to be composed entirely of biting parts. I heard the hummingbird but could not locate it and I saw very little else apart from a last tody, lit by a shaft of sunlight. Then as I was about to leave, just a few paces still inside the forest from the road, I flushed a quail dove off the ground. Unlike virtually all the others I had flushed in the previous ten days it flicked up just a short distance on to a horizontal branch about six feet off the ground and froze in full view. I was expecting to look through my binoculars at a beautiful Blue-headed Quail Dove but there was no blue to be seen only an eye-catching white streak across the face of a Key West Quail Dove, a fine bird and the fourth and final quail dove in that fine patch of forest.

I had no hire car and there was no public transport so the only way to get from Playa Larga to Havana for the flight home was to hitchhike the hundred miles (160 km). It felt good to be standing there with my thumb in the air again after so many years, enjoying the freedom of being on the road. The only trouble was there were hardly any vehicles on the road. Soon, I was thinking of the many mind-numbing hours waiting for lifts back home when some local hitchhikers turned up. Dennis and his friends were trying to get to Jaguey Grande to buy some papayas. They gave up after half an hour or so, tried farther up the road, gave up there, returned, gave up again and then went back home. This all happened before ten o'clock in the morning, the time I got my first lift, thanks to Dennis's advice which was to hold up a dollar bill instead of my thumb. He also told me not to refuse any lifts, no matter how far the vehicle was going, so I got in the truck that was going to La Boca, just seven miles up the road, and almost as soon as I got out of that truck I climbed into the back of another that was crammed with about fifty people and by eleven o'clock I was at the *autopista*, and only two dollars short. There were hoards of hitchhikers alongside Cuba's main highway, outnumbering vehicles by about a hundred to one, so I stood alone with a dollar bill flapping in the breeze. The attractive young ladies were getting all the lifts in cars so I just ran to the first flat-bed truck that stopped and climbed on the back and settled in amongst the mass of other hitchhikers on their way to the big city, and that was my free transport to Havana, for not a dollar was asked for. Sprawled out in the warm sunshine with my head on my rucksack for two hours I spent the time daydreaming about it being the beginning of the trip not the end, and that Cuba was bigger, much bigger, and that there were greater distances to cover, and lots more new birds to look for, and that weeks no months of exciting travels in search of them lay ahead.

When I had to get off the truck in the outskirts of Havana I had absolutely no idea where I was so I asked the first person who came along if it was possible to get a taxi into the city. For the price of another dollar a boy escorted me to a major junction where he pointed to a beat-up but beautiful old *Chevy*, the owner of which offered me a lift into town for seven dollars. The big shiny car had a shattered windscreen, no other windows, no padding left in the torn leather seats, no flooring, no suspension and four bald tyres. Accompanied by the compulsory incredibly loud music coming from the cassette tape player we crawled along Havana's rough, dusty back roads, weaving around numerous craters because the driver knew the tyres were about to blow and sure enough I soon heard a loud bang and on turning around saw a large puff of dust, blown off the road by a huge puncture. The wheel was quickly replaced with one which looked a lot worse but somehow we reached my intended destination, the *Hotel Lido*, seven hours and ten dollars out of Playa Larga.

In *La Bodeguita del Medio*, the basic backstreet bar Hemingway liked, I raised a glass of cold beer to him for writing *The Old Man and the Sea* before walking in the pleasant evening air to *La Mina* for something to eat. While waiting for my food to be served at an outside table I heard constant pishing noises coming from behind the bushes, the sort of noises birders make to entice birds out of cover, only they were not birders making the noises they were beautiful prostitutes trying to persuade me to part with a few more bucks.

*White-winged Apalis, Zomba Plateau, Malawi, 15th January 1999*

## 14

# MALAWI and ZAMBIA

The cabin crew did the conga up and down the aisles and the free champagne flowed on *Virgin Atlantic's* New Year's Eve flight from London to Johannesburg. When the frivolity ended Nick Wall and I had five hours to wait at Jo'burg airport before our flight back north to Malawi, enough time to watch some extraordinary male Long-tailed Widowbirds displaying between the runways, showing off their bright red shoulders and flowing black tails.

# A MIND-BLOWING BIRDING TRIP TO A PLANET CALLED EARTH

The *Boeing 737* to Lilongwe was almost empty and from my window seat I was able to look down through thunder clouds to the Zambezi River flowing past rosy rocky outcrops in a dark green corner of Mozambique. Soon after, we were in Malawi, a thin, 500 mile (800 km) long country that lies on a very fertile plateau at the southern end of the Great Rift Valley next to Lake Malawi. The rich farmland supports one of the highest human population densities in Africa with more than three quarters of the people living in small villages and growing coffee, tea, sugar and tobacco, on plantations which have replaced a lot of the natural vegetation. However, large areas of good habitats remain and some of them have been 'protected' in reserves and national parks which still support abundant wildlife. One such place is Liwonde National Park and we had pre-arranged a four-night stay there with a local safari company. Our pick-up time at their office in the capital Lilongwe was ten o'clock in the morning. It came and went and it was a Sunday morning and every last Bantu Christian was at church and the city centre was dead, absolutely dead, and Nick and I looked at each other and thought maybe there was something amiss, maybe the company didn't even exist. Not long after, a friendly lady turned up and after a quick coffee and some paperwork we were on our way, with our driver Eric, to the airport first, to meet Chief who arrived bang on time.

Eric then drove quickly but smoothly 150 miles (240 km) south along a quiet road through a deep green land, past cluster after cluster of round huts with overhanging thatched roofs, and the occasional line of low roadside buildings outside which ladies sold bananas, cassava, maize, potatoes, sweet potatoes and rice.

We saw very few birds but that all changed when we boarded a small boat and motored steadily up the wide Shire River, full to its grassy brim, for a wonderful hour in the middle of the African afternoon. After passing a few Nile Crocodiles, and the first of hundreds of Hippos in a stretch of river which is reputed to support the greatest density on the planet, as well as cormorants, darters, egrets and herons, we saw a group of gulls and terns resting on a rare sandbank up ahead and as I said, "Wouldn't it be great if there were a few skimmers amongst them," my first African Skimmer rose into the air on long black wings before settling down again with another seven. With fish eagles and jacanas helping to complete a bountiful scene it felt great to be back in Africa.

We wasted little time getting into the field once at *Mvuu Camp* and exactly seven seconds after leaving our rondavel I saw the bird I most hoped to see at Liwonde; a Böhm's Bee-eater. It, and the many others we saw, was one of those few species which turn out to be better than imagined; lovely deep, dark apple green birds with long tail streamers and orange-rufous heads with black masks and red eyes, swooping down off low, shaded branches to pluck flying insects out of the air and gliding gracefully back to their perches. Everyone was a delight to watch.

At dusk we positioned ourselves by the river to see what might be on the move. Small packs of Squacco Herons, large flocks of White-faced Whistling Ducks, and six skimmers went by before a Bat Hawk glided overhead, a very dark brown and white raptor with long distinctively-shaped wings, broad at the bases, narrower toward the tips, more like a large falcon than a hawk. All this took place to a soothing soundtrack composed by a multitude of insects and amphibians, grunting Hippos and hidden birds called Burchell's Coucals 'pouring water from a bottle' in the riverside reeds and grasses.

Our first full day at Liwonde was fantastic. It began before dawn when we joined guide Ben and guard Zimba, armed with an M16, on a walk to a riverside thicket and the known roosting tree of a Pel's Fishing Owl, one of the world's largest and yet most elusive owls. We had walked about a hundred paces when light rain began to fall and Ben, knowing what was coming, suggested we might like to return to base. It rained hard for the next four hours so we took a long breakfast in the open bar and while doing so spotted a Sedge Warbler, the first one ever seen in the park. Six Elephants playing in the river were far more exciting. We watched them for ages, pushing each other until one rolled over sideways or fell over backwards, and generally seeming to be having a great time, and while watching them I thought long may Elephants play in that cool, secluded river meandering slowly through Malawi.

I could have watched them all day long but our time at Liwonde was short so with the rain a little less heavy we decided to go for a wet walk around the grounds of *Mvuu Camp* where we saw some superb Böhm's Bee-eaters and a bedraggled, long-tailed, black and white Striped Cuckoo. When we returned to the bar at midday the rain stopped. Ben and Zimba soon appeared and we were off again to the thicket but to our utter dismay the owl was not at home. A ruddy-tailed, bright yellow Livingstone's Flycatcher was all we saw until, farther along the riverside in another thicket, Zimba, who was ahead of us should we meet any Elephants, pointed to our left and there was a massive owl. It fluffed up its feathers to make itself look even bigger before flying to the next tree where it felt more comfortable with our presence and we were then able to set up the tripod and telescope and examine the dark wavy bars across the feathers and look into the big black eyes of a Pel's Fishing Owl, a broad-bodied, orange-rufous haystack two feet tall.

Late that afternoon we set off on a long boat trip out on the Shire where the water was calm enough to be able to set up the telescope on the boat and through it we watched in stunned awe a male African Emerald Cuckoo whistling 'hel-lo Geor-gie, hel-lo Geor-gie' from the canopy of a riverside tree. It was a stunner, with a glossy emerald head, throat, back, wings and tail, and deep yellow belly. An equally dazzling pair of Malachite Kingfishers at their nest hole almost right next to us also merited a long look before we slowly slid down river, being very careful to avoid the numerous Hippos, to 'Skimmer Point' where we watched some skimmers skimming next to the boat. The birds flew around buoyantly on long wings before dipping down to fly straight and very low over the water with the tip of the longer lower mandible ploughing the surface, waiting to strike a fish and when it did the birds snapped their bills shut to keep hold of their prey. This was all done with such graceful ease and incredible precision it was truly a wonder to behold, especially at such close quarters.

The amazing day continued with our first Rufous-bellied Heron then, after darkness fell, that and so much else we had seen since dawn was surpassed by a White-backed Night Heron that we spotlighted on its perch in a tree above the boat. The beauty looked at us with a huge reddish eye. Its luxuriantly feathered neck was a rich rufous, its large wings blackish-brown and its sturdy legs yellow. For a while there we forgot about the millions of moths in night flight above the river. They were in our ears, eyes, noses and mouths, and down our shirts. We had to almost swim through them for a while, but they didn't matter, we didn't care, especially when we glided silently into the riverbank with the engine cut to look wide-eyed at some Pied Kingfishers that were roosting on a branch at arm's length. The fantasy of a day still wasn't over. On the way back to our rondavel a beautiful long-tailed, dark-spotted cat-like carnivore called a Large-spotted Genet walked past while out hunting for the night.

We had Sprosser for breakfast; I mean we saw a Thrush Nightingale, a small, brown and grey bird with a faintly russet tail, unspectacular to look at but a true skulker, very rare at home and extremely difficult to see well anywhere. After breakfast we walked around the grounds in rain again and saw a black and white male Puffback, a type of shrike, turn into a snowball by spreading and puffing out its abnormally long, loose, white back feathers, in display. In the early afternoon we climbed into a *Land Cruiser* with Ben, Zimba and Jens Haugaard, a top expatriate birder for a top job; finding the Racquet-tailed Roller, a shy, uncommon roller which lives in tall woodland and does not like to perch in the open like the very similar Lilac-breasted Roller, a very welcome daily sight in Liwonde. Cruising through the *Borassus* palm savanna, open country liberally sprinkled with tall, bare-trunked fan palms, we came across our first all grey Dickinson's Kestrel and a flock of 27 delicate Senegal Lapwings. When we reached some *mopane* woodland, Racquet-tailed Roller country, we got out of the vehicle and began walking through the widely spaced trees between which there was little undergrowth. There were a couple of pairs of striking, black and white 'woodland wheatears' called Arnot's Chats in there but it was a long time before we came across a roller, two in fact, two rather dull and disappointing young Racquet-taileds, without racquets. We searched hard for the adults, right up until dusk but without success, and there was no sign of the Pel's either. It was probably off fishing. While looking for it we heard a down-slurred 'kurrr-kurrr-kurrr' and soon saw an African Barred Owlet, and, while spotlighting on the way back to camp, Ben picked up a Four-toed Elephant Shrew in the beam of light, a mammal the size of a rat with a curious combination of a long nose, large eyes and long legs.

The Pel's was not present again before breakfast the next day but Zimba came to tell us he had found a roosting African Scops Owl so we were off and there the tiny, cryptic beauty was, its mottled and streaked grey-brown plumage almost a perfect match for the lichen-covered trunk it was perched next to. The bird remained so confident in its camouflage we were able to stand just a few paces away, close enough to see a ring of tiny red scales around its huge, bright yellow eyes. How Zimba found it we will never know. If only he had been as good at locating Racquet-tailed Rollers for we failed to find any again during the afternoon when thunder threatened rain and sure enough it arrived at 4 p.m. and continued till dark, leaving us to watch the Hippos in the river from our rondavel and to drift off to sleep to the soporific soundtrack of the African night.

# A MIND-BLOWING BIRDING TRIP TO A PLANET CALLED EARTH

It was raining heavily at dawn when we boarded the boat for the trip out of Liwonde. From underneath my umbrella I saw the skimmers, and lots of Blue-cheeked Bee-eaters swaying on the tops of the riverside reeds. If we had stayed on the Shire River we would have reached the Zambezi but we had to get out of the boat and head north with our new driver, called Everlasting. We asked him to stop so we could wander into Mozambique, seeing a flock of black swallows known as Eastern Saw-wings on that side of the border which ran alongside the road. Next stop was the border with Zambia and by early afternoon we were in the third country of the day, looking out for bee-eaters on roadside wires. Seeing two, silhouetted, I shouted out "Carmine!" in over-enthusiastic optimism, because when we pulled over to look at them in better light they turned out to be European Bee-eaters.

When we arrived at *Wildlife Camp* near Mfuwe on the border of South Luangwa National Park the first question I asked Mark the manager was, "Are there many Southern Carmine Bee-eaters about?" He confirmed what I had read, that the birds were resident in small numbers in the park, nesting in river banks between August and November, but added that they were resident in *very* small numbers and there were *very* few about, and he was reluctant to say we would definitely see some during our three-day stay, which was rather worrying because I had never seen a Southern Carmine Bee-eater and one of the main reasons for travelling to Malawi and Zambia was to see Böhm's and Southern Carmine Bee-eaters.

Dodging the Elephants roaming the dry floodplain of the low Luangwa River outside our hut there was enough time before dark to watch a new shorebird, the grey-headed White-crowned Lapwing, with yellow wattles dangling down from the base of the bill. With at least seven of them along the shallow river a couple of hundred paces from our front door were some Wood Sandpipers, lots of Hippos and some large Nile Crocodiles, while a bee-eater that appeared over the river briefly as a distant silhouette could well have been a Carmine.

It had been a long day and I was tired but after a refreshing sleep I was more than ready for a dawn safari. Mark was our driver and guide for the day. He was a bit of a birder and after a few minutes he said, casually, "Are you guys interested in Dwarf Bittern?" to which the reply was a unanimous, "Yes!" since none of us had seen the rarely observed diminutive heron. He then informed us that during the southern summer one particular bird seemed particularly fond of the narrow ditch alongside the track we were cruising along and a minute or so later a small, dark blue bittern flew out of the ditch and landed on top of a low bush where it adopted the classic camouflage position of a bittern; neck stretched up with its bill pointing to the sky. "Bee-eaters!" was the next shout. They were perched on trackside wires which Mark quickly informed us were some of the most reliable wires to see Carmines on but all 25 were White-fronted, a splendid sight but one I was familiar with from Kenya.

We saw plenty of Warthogs and Zebras, some Elephants and a loose herd of ten Thornicroft's Giraffes, one of several subspecies of Giraffe and the one with irregular-shaped dark patches separated by white that occurs only in the Luangwa Valley. Mark slowed the vehicle down to a gentle stop by a stand of trees on a slight rise called Lupunga Spur so we could take a good long look at another huge area once covered in *mopane* woodland but recently flattened by Elephants which like to eat the young leaves *and* branches. I was looking at the herds of Impala that had moved in when a large bee-eater cut through the air, as only a Carmine can, and glided in to the top of the dead tree right next to us. However, it wasn't carmine-coloured it was orangey-brown with a pale blue crown and edge to its throat. It *was* a Southern Carmine Bee-eater but it was a youngster not a glorious carmine and crimson adult and not what I was hoping for exactly, and so I was ecstatic when it was joined by one of its fabulous parents which perched on a dead snag at close range, bending with the breeze for thirty minutes or so.

Now I could truly relax and thoroughly enjoy the morning drive and the rest of the trip. Ten White-headed Vultures squabbled over a dead Egyptian Goose, the dominant bird puffing out its chest feathers and arching its wings to intimidate its rivals, which included two Tawny Eagles. Damp meadows were dotted with African Fish Eagles, Crowned Cranes, Saddle-billed Storks and African Jacanas. Bateleur Eagles wheeled high above. White-crowned Lapwings walked around the river islands where Pied Kingfishers fished. Big flocks of shocking orange, yellow and green Lilian's Lovebirds flowed to and fro, and there were plenty of Woodland Kingfishers and lovely Lilac-breasted Rollers to enjoy. I love Africa.

During the heat of the day we walked out of camp to try and see the Dwarf Bittern again but we had to retrace our steps very quickly when there was a colossal downpour during which we nearly got struck by lightning, twice. We were not fast enough to avoid a good soaking but we were dry in time for the evening drive, in search of cats and coursers. Chief was not optimistic about seeing any big cats because I had failed to see any Snow Leopards in the Karakoram of northern Pakistan, Tigers in India and Leopards in Kenya. I may have seen a black panther for a few seconds in Venezuela and I did see a Cheetah in Kenya, with Chief, but that was about it for me as far as big cats were concerned so it was no surprise when we failed to see any cats at all for over four damp and dull hours, even though there were supposed to be more Leopards in Luangwa than anywhere else in Africa. "If we don't see one here I'm never going looking for big cats with you again!" Chief joked. There were no Bronze-winged or Heuglin's Coursers either but we did see two Pearl-spotted Owlets, a Spotted Hyaena, some Buffalo, and a bounding Four-toed Elephant Shrew, although the most memorable sight was that of a Dung Beetle repeatedly tumbling off its large ball of Elephant dung.

The following five-hour-long morning drive flew by. The five-hour-long wait for the five-hour-long evening drive didn't. Out again, we were drinking a beer in the bush at dusk when the conversation turned to Leopards once more. After hearing our driver Maxun's tales of the many he had seen we set off, yet again, in pursuit of *Panthera pardus*, on our last chance of the trip, and to our great surprise and delight it was not long before the spotlight fell on a much larger than expected cat. It was sitting upright on a rise overlooking a huge area of destroyed *mopane* woodland where hundreds of Impala spend the night. By the time I got my binoculars on the *Panthera* it was on the move and without doubt a Leopard, a large male at that, a massive, muscular, spotted cat moving in on a herd of nervous Impala. We were then very fortunate to be able to watch the brilliant thing stalking the antelopes for a totally gripping quarter of an hour, before it disappeared into the night, leaving all of us elated.

We left Luangwa shortly after dawn the next morning. There was a slight delay at the border because the lady behind the counter wondered why I didn't look like I did in my passport photograph. With Everlasting's help I explained that the photograph was nine years old and since then I had gone bald. The lady said that that had happened because I was rich; rich compared to her no doubt, but she was not to know that I was not rich in monetary terms, compared to many of my compatriots. Of course, I was exceedingly rich in the wonder of birds and other wildlife.

In Lilongwe we said goodbye to Everlasting, bought some supplies and hired a *Toyota Corolla* for the drive to Dzalanyama Forest Reserve. As the condition of the track deteriorated we began to wonder if we had been wise to hire a low-clearance, two-wheel-drive car in Malawi in the middle of the wet season, and we soon became even more concerned because the track was beginning to look like we might not even make it to Dzalanyama, let alone all the other sites we were hoping to visit. Nick weaved the car around numerous muddy puddles and cruised through the wider ones, and after successfully negotiating a particularly long stretch of water and mud his confidence grew, so he approached another long stretch with more than his usual gusto, only for the car to come to a halt three-quarters of the way through, in deeply rutted, shin-high, mud.

The engine bottomed out on top of a rut leaving the front wheels whirring around in muddy water. We were stuck. As we placed sticks under the wheels to give them something to grip the light rain intensified into a downpour and we were even more stuck. The car would not budge, even with the help of an increasing number of local people who had left their fields to assist us. After another attempt to get it moving failed we began to consider the possibility that we would still be there when it got dark and possibly even the next morning if the rain continued to fall, and, worst of all, that we were probably going to be unable to turn around and get back through the mud we had managed to get through. We were seriously considering heading back because there was surely more of the same down Dzalanyama way.

After an hour or so of trying to shift the car, by which time we looked like mud-covered madmen, two more, local, madmen turned up, laughing at our feeble efforts. Even though they did not speak a word of English it was obvious what they thought needed doing and we did it. Without them we would not have been able to lift the car up and move it sideways so that one of the wheels could get a grip on the side of a rut. Then, with the help of several other people, we pushed the car until the wheel got a grip and started turning. Suddenly the car shot forward and although it slid left and right across the mud it kept going, to the end of the mire. We were then in what Chief calls 'dilemmasville'; should we try and go back through that stretch of mud and water to reach the safety of the main road and the capital Lilongwe or carry on and attempt to reach Dzalanyama where we might see a lot of new birds? While discussing the pros and cons the local people, as far as we could make out, insisted that we had got through the worst and that the road ahead was "pure", and after checking and re-checking that that was actually the case we agreed to push on. It was still raining but to our great relief and whoops of delight the track became sandy, sandy and damp but firm underneath, and our confidence grew again, and not long after, still reveling in gliding smoothly along a drier and drier, flat sandy track, we entered the tall open *miombo* woodland of Dzalanyama. Nick then slowed down so we could listen out for flocks of birds and not far from the rest house we came across one and on getting out of the car we saw some Rufous-bellied Tits, warbler-like Yellow-bellied Hyliotas and a tiny Stierling's Woodpecker, a bird hard to find anywhere else but Dzalanyama.

The government rest house was virtually free of charge but there was no electricity, no generator, no lamps, not even a candle, so it was quite a palaver settling in but we soon had a fire going so we could dry our gear while the caretaker cooked our tinned curry and rice for us, as he insisted. The next day we walked miles through the *miombo* seeing very few birds except those in mixed roaming flocks moving through the trees at walking pace. Amongst these we saw several species endemic or nearly endemic to the habitat including the dull blue and red Miombo Rock Thrush, the lovely little White-tailed Blue Flycatcher, forever bowing, curtseying and stiffly fanning its long blue and white tail, and a green and yellow Olive-headed Weaver.

There were plenty we didn't see and the next morning the only one of those we could find was a Souza's Shrike, which looked like a dull Red-backed Shrike. Fearing the track in would only get worse we gave up on the rest and faced the mud. Fortunately, Chief had a rare brainwave and we had a car full of logs. Thanks mainly to them we progressed surprisingly smoothly and we were soon into the meat of the 250 mile (400 km) drive south to Mount Thyolo where during the last two hours of daylight we tracked down a few beautiful green Livingstone's Turacos, four black, green and yellow White-starred Robins and a black, green and orange Black-fronted Bushshrike.

Amongst the swathes of tea plantations that cover the mountains of southern Malawi evergreen forest birds almost literally cling to the tiny patches of trees spared the axe and that only because they grow on the steepest ridge tops, so we were not surprised to dip several species, notably the rare Thyolo Alethe and the lovely Green-headed Oriole. We would be very fortunate to see a "green-headed whatever it was" or anything else for that matter according to Chip, the owner of Satemwa Tea Estate and Chawani Bungalow, our accommodation for the night. He insisted the local 'savages' would think nothing of chopping someone's head off and that was why the spacious bungalow was equipped with an air-alarm and escape window, and surrounded by night watchmen.

We were still alive the next morning and fit enough to clamber around muddy slopes under tall, dank trees in a wet cloud for five hours although that was not enough to see an alethe or an oriole. During a committee meeting in a tea plantation surrounding Mikundi Forest we decided to move on, to Blantyre from where we descended into the Great Rift Valley and Lengwe National Park. On the way we stopped at Chikwawa to watch five superb Southern

Carmine Bee-eaters bee-catching from roadside wires, and not far past there, to enjoy a loose flock of at least 24 Amur Falcons swooping down from a roadside tree to pounce on insects on the ground. It was hard to leave such a spectacle but we wanted to get to Lengwe before dusk so we pushed on, into a thunderstorm, and as the rain broke we once again found ourselves stuck in mud and water, just a mile from the rest house. Fortunately we were soon joined by some locals who were more than happy to help us out and, passing an abandoned four-wheel-drive that had keeled over at the side of the track into a ditch, we made it to the rundown rest house just before dark.

We began the day in the open country of Lengwe watching an amazing flock of Amur Falcons, Broad-billed and European Rollers, and Blue-cheeked and European Bee-eaters, all swooping around to catch airborne insects. The Broad-billed Rollers were perching up too, allowing us to marvel at their full purple splendour in the early morning light. In a lush thicket we saw a male Narina Trogon, a lovely, glossy bottle green above and shocking deep red below. Much of the park was under water so we returned to base to walk the entrance track in search of Vanga Flycatcher only to discover that much of it was under water as well so, with rain in the air, we decided we had better get out of Lengwe while we could. In no time at all the car was packed but there was no need to panic. Even though the water was a foot deep in places Nick eased the car through comfortably. We were on our way again, back up the rift escarpment to the town of Zomba where we booked into a non-executive room at the *Ndindeya Motel* and indulged in a slow *Ricoffy* (coffee and chicory) on the balcony before spending the last three hours of daylight looking for the rare White-winged Apalis. It rained the whole time and while taking a break in the car and re-reading the scant information we had on where to look for the bird I realized we were in the wrong place and no one was very amused.

The next morning, after fixing a puncture in a record six minutes, we managed to get to the right place and it didn't take too long to find three White-winged Apalises, one of which was a fabulous male, with red eyes set in a glossy black hood, a black back, a long black tail, big snow white wing patches, a silky white throat, a black necklace and bright yellow underparts, glowing orange on the breast. We were able to watch the exquisite little birds foraging low down in a huge tree at close range for nearly an hour, one of the most wonderful hours of my life and another to add to the many already accrued, mostly during trips designed mainly with bee-eaters in mind. When I go on a bee-eater hunt I always discover birds just as beautiful; in the case of the White-winged Apalis, one of the most beautiful birds on planet Earth.

After a relaxing brunch we headed for some *mopane* woodland to try and find an adult Racquet-tailed Roller but it soon started raining so we continued the drive north, a much smoother journey than expected, on a straight, traffic-free road, alongside which there were no birds to stop for in the fields which cover the land between the parks and reserves, so we arrived at Senga Bay, Lake Malawi, in time to look for lily-covered pools where we hoped to see the Lesser Lily-trotter. We soon found such a pool, covered with confiding lily-trotters, all, alas, of the 'Greater' variety also known as the African Jacana.

Following a delicious Lake Perch, known in Malawi as the Sungwa, at *Carolina's* on the Lake Malawi shoreline we were all in the mood for the compulsory trip 'Big Night Out' so we asked the waiter Matthias to escort us to the local hot spots, the first of which was a bar in the nearby village called *Third World*. It was hardly a swinging place, just a couple of barflies and a few other people dancing in a nearby room, so we moved on, to one, two and three more bars, each one a little livelier than the last, and each one with a mainly male mixture of *chamba* (ganja) lovers, beer-drinkers and stupefied people drinking *chibuku*, a lethal, local concoction made from maize. Those that *could* speak asked us about England and Malawi and one of them agreed with us when we said Malawi was a great place by saying, with a slurred voice, "This place is the dog's bollocks!" as he tried to impress us with his best English slang. Full of drink we decided to head for a nightclub in Salima but on reaching the car we discovered it had another puncture. We sobered up a little while fixing it and had enough sense then to agree that the night wasn't the dog's bollocks and that we were better off getting some sleep back at *Carolina's*.

No one stirred until 06:30, well over an hour after the normal start and not the best way to get Chief's last day up and running. After breakfast and lots of coffee we were feeling a little better but birding was delayed again, because we had not one but three punctures to fix. After watching a mechanic do his impressive stuff with rudimentary tools it was great to get back to the pond we found the day before. There was still no sign of the little lily-trotter but there were two Rufous-bellied Herons and an exotic, bluish purple Allen's Gallinule amongst the assortment of other wonder on the beautiful lily pond. We moved on to Mpatsanjoka Marshes but they were too wet to walk through so we returned to *Carolina's* for that great rarity, lunch, somewhat concerned about the lack of little lily-trotters. We were not that hungry but we needed liquid because the temperature seemed like it was in the nineties.

Replenished, we headed south along the lake shore toward what appeared to be another marshy area. It was indeed and we were delighted to discover another even more beautiful pond that was almost covered with blue water-lilies, the absolutely perfect setting for the bird we were after. When, after many long scans, we failed to see any, anticipation turned to consternation. "Surely," I said, "If there are any around here they would be on *this* pond!" More ponds followed, liberally sprinkled with great birds such as the big jacanas, tiny Black Crakes, Purple and Rufous-bellied Herons, a Black Heron turning into an umbrella, Malachite and Pied Kingfishers, and Southern Brown-throated Weavers, possibly the brightest of the many glowing yellow weavers, so much more spectacular than we ever imagined a weaver, a sparrow-like bird, could be and one that constantly demanded attention so dazzling were the males, so amazing in fact that they wouldn't have looked out of place amongst the flocks of tanagers in the Andes or the many richly plumaged birds of New Guinea.

Still the lily-trotter eluded us and the next pond we got to didn't look very good because there were few water-lilies and a lot of open water. So we were very surprised when half way along the side of it Chief flushed something that looked more like a chick than a fully grown bird, but a fully grown adult Lesser Jacana it was, with a rufous crown and bright, rufous-buff patches at the sides of the breast. It was actually more legs than bird, the span of its toes, three forward, one behind, being equal to the length of its body which with the neck, head and beak added on still only amounted to about the width of my outstretched hand. We celebrated with another fish dinner overlooking Lake Malawi where the mysterious huge billowing plumes of what looked like smoke on the water turned out to be 'lake flies', a rainy season phenomenon involving zillions of dancing midges. Known locally as *Nkungo* the giant swarms are occasionally blown to shore where the local women catch them in baskets, dry them, squash them and shape them into a sort of lake fly burger or patty which is then baked or deep fried, making a meal rich in protein but one that tastes, apparently, as one would imagine, like mashed up flies.

After a last look at the Lesser Jacana we stopped at a *dambo*, a very shallow, rushy marsh, on the way to the airport, hoping to see the Locustfinch, a tiny black and red bird that looks like a real dazzler in the field guides. We couldn't find any but it was worth the stop to see the much more common and widespread male Red Bishops which were in full breeding plumage and a glorious sight. They were displaying to the dowdy, camouflaged females, puffing their feathers out and looking like glowing red pom poms. Chief got on the plane home with wet feet while I dried mine out of the car window as Nick drove quickly south to Chongoni Forest Reserve near the town of Dedza where, after beans, tinned pilchards and rice washed down with some bottles of *Manica*, Cervejas de Moçambique Especial de Exportação, I enjoyed a very good night's sleep.

The *miombo* woodland of Chongoni was shrouded in mist all morning but the birds didn't mind and therefore neither did Nick and I. Stimulated by brilliant black and white male Collared Flycatchers we tracked down the bird we most hoped to see at Chongoni, the Spotted Creeper. There were two, one of which flew to and froze against a lichen-covered tree trunk and would have been invisible had I not seen where it landed. I walked up as close as I dared and grilled its cryptic dark brown and buff bars, spots and crescents, until the 'Wallcreeper of the Woods' flew on, to the bottom of the next tree, ready to creep up the trunk of that, leaving me very happy for I had seen one of those few birds which looks great in books and even better in real life. The mist thickened to rain. Reluctantly we withdrew, down the mountain to Dedza and southward to Blantyre again, past brightly-dressed women, drably-dressed men, poorly-dressed children, and numerous villages with round, shaggy-roofed huts, and sacks and sacks of charcoal. By dark we were in *Nyambadwe Guesthouse* with a beer awaiting a fine meal that turned out to be a plate of foul fish heads, ready for another attempt at seeing Thyolo Alethe and Green-headed Oriole.

With evergreen enthusiasm we got up ridiculously early to ensure we were in the remnant forest at the top of Mount Soche for first light but that went out of the window when we drove into low cloud and could not find any signs to aid our poor directions to the invisible mountain. We did make it, eventually, and walking up the lower slopes we heard someone whistling. He came jauntily down the trail, and told us his name was Wisdom and that he was happy that day because he was 'without malaria'. Wisdom showed us the way to the top of the mountain, not the usual way as we discovered later but a better way, through some *miombo* in which we saw lots of birds. The same could not be said of the wet forest at the top where we had to work hard to eke out a few birds, although one of them was a superb Red-capped Robin Chat with a rufous-orange body, and blue-grey back and wings.

On the way down the mountain we met a very serious man who told us his name was Cave Matomba. His next words were, "Do you pray to God?" to which my reply was a hesitant though emphatic, "No." I was caught off guard; I usually do my best to avoid telling someone who believes in a god that I don't. In my experience it is also best to try to avoid a discussion on the subject since virtually every believer I have ever met has not been open to argument about it. I also feel that if I voice my opinion I will offend them, although it never seems to occur to them that they might offend me. However, Nick, another non-believer, was happy to engage Cave Matomba's thoughts and so the man proceeded to talk non-stop about his God as he walked with us, insisting constantly that, "It is what you HAVE to believe!" It was very hard to resist arguing, to try to explain to him that we 'believed' in evolution and that over the course of thousands of million of years evolution and physics and so on, not a god or gods, had produced a wonderful place called Earth, a planet with beautiful landscapes and seas and oceans and skyscapes and the vast array of plants and animals that complete them. I also wanted to tell him that I understood why people found comfort in worshipping something but I also 'believed' that they and the place they lived would be much better off if they worshipped the Earth and/or the Sun and the Moon, something that does exist, something natural, not something that does not exist, something supernatural called a god or gods. I wanted to explain to Cave Matomba that, imagine if all the energy, all the fervour, the zeal, that was used in praying, in worshipping a god or gods, imagine if all that was used to look after the Earth and all the plants and animals which share our home and make it such a fantastic place to live, imagine what an even better place to live it would be! I used up a lot of energy resisting telling him all that and after a while we went our separate ways, always to remain separate I suspected.

In the afternoon we wasted an hour and a half on the wrong road, having to backtrack along what was a very bad road and then battle with the corrugations, pot-holes and puddles along one of the worst roads in Africa, the always-under-repair Thyolo Road. By the time we arrived at the top of Mount Thyolo there were ninety minutes of light left. We were far from optimistic about our chances of seeing a Green-headed Oriole. It seemed like a bird too far. The sky was, for once, sunny though and a pair of broad-winged, bar-bellied Crowned Eagles soared around in it while we scanned the fruiting trees at the edge of the remnant patch of forest, which we thought orioles might visit. Looking through binoculars I saw yellow leaf … yellow leaf … yellow leaf … the ones standing out against the green leaves … then I said, "Hang on a minute … pass me the 'scope … bloody hell … it's … it is … it's a Green-headed Oriole!" We had taken the chance and we had been rewarded, for there in the 'scope was a lovely soft green and yellow oriole with a red eye and bill, basking in the low evening sunshine. It was hard to believe but there it was, for a while anyway, because suddenly it was off, in dashing flight, into the trees.

*Pennant-winged Nightjar, Satemwa, Malawi, 19th January 1999*

Still jubilant, we were making our way merrily back to Blantyre as dusk fell when something even more spectacular, an apparition perhaps, flew across the road. We had never seen one before but there was no mistaking it, it was a bird that looked like it had wings attached to its wings, a male Pennant-winged Nightjar, a fantasy bird with big white flashes across the wings and extraordinarily long black and white primary flight feathers.

At dawn we tackled Mount Soche from a different flank. The *miombo* birds were busy again and this time they included a Spotted Creeper. In the mountain top forest we were surrounded by ants which was good because alethes like ants, and bad because the ants were armed with large and sharp pincers, many of which remained stuck in our socks and trousers after we had brushed those attacking us off. Moving to a safer distance we looked hard for an alethe but it was not to be. We did see another male Black-fronted Bushshrike and some more White-starred Robins before retreating. Then we began the journey back north for the last day of the trip. We had managed to avoid rain for a day and a half so it was a bit disappointing to drive out of the warm sunshine into a wall of the stuff. It was thick enough to obscure the view ahead and slow us down. So, for once, Nick was not going fast enough to fly over the only major broken part of the 180 mile (300 km) long road between Blantyre and Senga Bay. We knew about it, we were looking out for it, but we could not remember where it was exactly and bang, we hit it full on, a huge crack right across the road, hard enough to guarantee a puncture and so it was. Out of the car we got to change the wheel for the bald spare, while it hammered it down.

The last day of the trip was the first truly hot and sunny one. We took a very pleasant early morning stroll south along the shoreline of Lake Malawi to the lily-covered lagoon now graced by large *and* small jacanas, Malachite Kingfishers, a Rufous-bellied Heron and Southern Brown-throated Weavers. After a late breakfast on the shady terrace of *Carolina's* overlooking the lake we set out with the intention of reaching a place on our sketch map called Hippo Pools, in a final attempt to find a Pygmy Goose, another water-lily lover, but found ourselves scrambling up the wooded, rocky slope of Senga Hill, wondering what the hell we were doing. There was a young man up there for some reason and he said he would guide us to a path for ten *kwacha* but after half an hour we were still stumbling through the wood and told the lad we were going back. With "Fook you!" resounding through the trees we climbed down and found an empty campsite which sold ice-cold *Coca-Cola* and while drinking a second bottle of the sweet elixir I spotted the characteristic swoop of a Böhm's Bee-eater. It landed on a low branch of a small tree where the lovely apple-green bird looked a picture. It was our best view of the bird of the trip and it was followed by our first, truly coppery, Copper Sunbird, and our best Lesser Jacana, so the first cold beer of the evening went down very well indeed and the Lake Perch tasted better than ever while we wrote up our notes and watched the almost continual lightning turn the night over Lake Malawi pale blue.

Two Lilac-breasted Rollers and two European Bee-eaters lit up the telegraph wires on the way to Lilongwe Airport. Having checked in I was summoned on the intercom and taken by the Chief Security Officer to an x-ray machine behind the check-in counter where he showed me what looked like a bomb in my rucksack. It did not look good: a square black box connected to a smaller black box by what looked like some thick wires; the battery holder, light and straps of my headlamp.

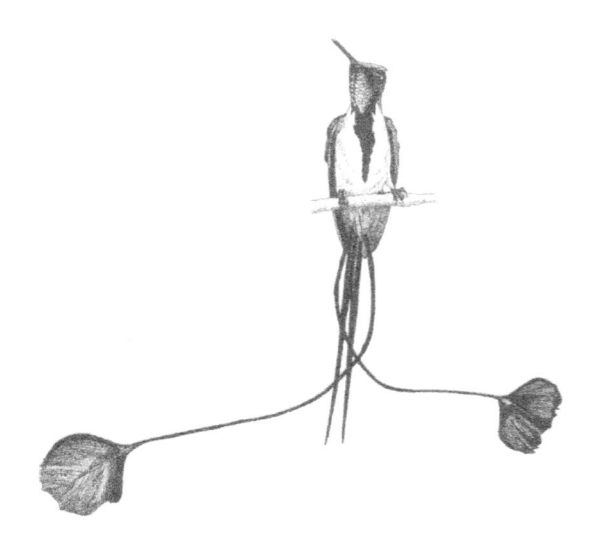

*Marvellous Spatuletail, Rio Chido, Peru, 23rd November 2002*

## 15

# PERU

In June 1990 my friend Mike Entwistle, aged 30, and his friend Tim Andrews, aged 32, were walking along a river near the city of Tingo Maria in central Peru looking for birds when they were shot dead by guerrillas belonging to the *Sendero Luminosa*, the Shining Path. The ruthless drug trafficking terrorists conducted a violent campaign throughout Peru during the 1980s, assassinating leading opponents, slaughtering peasants and bombing the country's cities because they wanted to restore a communist government. According to one of Peru's newspapers, *La Republica*, quoting Tingo Maria residents, a group of armed men appeared suddenly and attempted to lead Mike and Tim away at gunpoint. Apparently, the taller of the two, which would have been Tim, tried to make a run for it, was gunned down, fell in the river and floated away. Mike, it is presumed, was then taken to a camp where he too was killed. No bodies were ever recovered.

The Shining Path controlled large areas of Peru, with Tingo Maria at the centre of their operations. Mike and Tim were probably aware of that. They certainly knew that the city was the gateway to one the richest areas for birds in the world. It seems their passion for birds got the better of them and they were unable to resist going there despite the dangers. What they didn't know was that the guerrillas almost certainly suspected they were U.S. Drug Enforcement Administration (DEA) agents because such agents, it was rumoured, would sometimes disguise themselves as birdwatchers, hence their field guides, notebooks and even English accents counted for little when it came to pleading for their lives.

Even though the leader of the Shining Path, Abimael Guzman, was captured just two years later, the organization fell apart into splinter groups, guerrilla activity diminished and peace returned to most areas where the Shining Path had been active, Mike's death put me off going birding in Peru for years. However, when I heard Al, Chief and another friend, Simon 'Foggy' Fogg, were planning a trip there, albeit an 'organized' one with a 'leader' loaded with playback equipment to lure out skulking antpittas and the like, and an expedition bus to get around in, I was severely tempted to join them because I had long dreamed of watching a little wonder called a Marvellous Spatuletail, one of the most spectacular birds in the fabulous family of hummingbirds. With many other iconic South America birds possible, twelve years after what happened in Tingo Maria I caved in, and another friend, Paul 'The Colonel' Macklam, signed up too.

It took four hours at 500 mph (800 km/h) to fly across the Amazon, all of which, on the line the plane was on, appeared to be covered in forest, with only the occasional black or brown river meandering through the green. We were up at 03:30 for the early flight back north from Lima, over the snowy peaks of the Andes, to Cajamarca where the evil Spanish conquistador Francisco Pizarro captured the Inca King Atahualpa in 1532. Atahualpa presented his captors with a room filled with silver and gold for his freedom but the Spaniards still killed him and shared the spoils. Sitting on the same *Antonov* with me and my friends were Colin Bushell, a Peru birding veteran leading the trip, and Don Sykes and Rob Thatcher, two other British birders who had joined up via Colin. At Cajamarca airport we met our cook Romero, his assistant Guillermo, and the two drivers of a 20-seater, high-clearance bus in which was stowed the required camping equipment.

From the sprawling, low-rise city we drove past short, brightly-dressed peasants with high hats tending their small plots of land by the side of a rough track that lead to the valley of the Rio Chonta. In an arid gully there we got the trip off to a magnificent start with a successful search for one of the world's rarest birds, a Grey-bellied Comet, quite a large hummingbird with a short, straight needle-like bill, chrome-green crown and back, blue spangled throat, very long, dark wings and a very long and pointed bronzy-green tail which helped to make the bird look a bit like a jacamar, especially when it perched prominently on the spikes at the top of giant yucca leaves in between stiff-winged glides across the gully. It was great to be in hummingbird country again, although it was depressingly deforested. In the bus we climbed the treeless hills to another *quebrada*, a Spanish word for a usually dry ravine, where there were some ravaged remnants of tree cover, enough to support seven species of 'hummers'. There is no need to describe in detail all of the tiny, multicoloured, glittering little dazzlers, buzzing softly up and down, forwards and even backwards, with unbelievable speed and precision, before hovering in front of flowers to lick up nectar, then whirring off in an instant. Their names say it all; Speckled Hummingbird, Black and Tyrian Metaltails, Chestnut-breasted Coronet, Purple-throated Sunangel, Shining Sunbeam and Mountain Velvetbreast.

Up at 03:30 and off along more barren hillsides, the few trees present being imported, quick-growing eucalypts; good for fuel useless for most South American birds and other wildlife. The rich natural forests have gone because there are so many people needing wood for cooking and warmth and building, and if the Quechua farmers have enough wood they clear the land anyway, so they can grow potatoes, chilli peppers, maize and tomatoes, mostly on tiny plots of land and often on steep terraced hillsides because fertile land is in such short supply and every scrap of soil has to be used. They also grow *Coca* and have chewed the leaves or drank coca tea (*Mate de Coca*) for thousands of years, believing it suppresses fatigue, hunger, pain and thirst, and helps relieve altitude sickness by reducing the amount of oxygen needed by the body. The leaves contain alkaloids such as cocaine but the amount of cocaine in a cup of coca tea prepared from one gram of leaves contains about four milligrams of cocaine compared to 20-30 in a line of chemically concentrated cocaine rapidly absorbed through the nostril. So, although *Coca* in its natural form is a mild stimulant the tiny amount of cocaine which is absorbed very slowly from the leaves does not produce the same high associated with Charlie, coke, crack, call it what you will, there are hundreds of names on the street for cocaine. *Coca* bushes thrive in the poor soil of northern Peru, need far less attention than most other crops, and the end product is far more profitable so the temptation to grow *Coca* for the cocaine trade is very hard to resist. Plenty succumb.

Our drug of choice is birds so off we went, to an area of remnant, arid, acacia and cacti scrub where we saw a pair of endemic and endangered, of course, Great Spinetails, grey-brown, dirty white, long-tailed birds belonging to a large group of very similar-looking small skulking species with long spiky tails, many of which we were to see during the coming weeks.

A lie-in until 04:30 then up through rolling hills to the wide, heavily cultivated valleys of the Peruvian Andes where there were few birds, even in the remnant patches of *Polylepis*, the low gnarly woods above the treeline. However, the small selection did include the first Tit-like

Dacnis ever seen on the 'North Peru Circuit', a superb, tiny, all deep blue bird. Moving higher, to bushy slopes above Cruz Conga at 11,800 feet (3597 metres) we arrived in 'The Land of the Tyrants', seeing a pair of brilliant, black and white barred and streaked Black-crested Tit Tyrants, Black-billed and White-tailed Shrike Tyrants, a small brown and grey Jelski's Chat Tyrant, and three mainly grey Rufous-webbed Tyrants, named after the cinnamon-rufous undersides to the wing and tail feathers, a very attractive feature when the wings and tail were spread in flight.

After a night in the delightful *Hostal Celendin* we were up at 04:30 and off to a tiny patch of cloud forest where a red-billed, red-legged, dark and light grey Slaty-backed Nightingale Thrush called like a cat and sang like a squeaky gate. Then we climbed to a high pass which we crossed to enter the Marañón Canyon where the headwaters of the Amazon run northwest along the eastern base of the Andes through a deeply eroded arid mountain valley for over 300 miles (480 km), a valley nearly 10,000 feet (3000 metres) deep, over twice the depth of the Grand Canyon. At the northern end of it the Rio Marañón turns northeast and flows through forest to where it meets the Rio Ucayali, after which it is known as the Amazon.

On the cactus-covered western slopes of the canyon we saw a pair of black-faced, yellow-billed, Grey-winged Inca Finches, our first of five members of the *Incaspiza* genus of birds, all of which are endemic to the Peruvian Andes. Lower down where the vegetation was thicker we saw a Marañón Thrush, brown above with white underparts boldly spotted with darker brown, and a Buff-bellied

Tanager, the buff breast of which intensified to orange around the neck and on the crown. Carrying on down the canyon on a narrow switchback track we passed some stomach-churning, virtually vertical drop-offs, all the more terrifying from the window of a high-clearance bus swinging from side to side. I was glad to get out and walk down to the river, stopping to watch pairs of Buff-bridled Inca Finches and a very pretty Yellow-faced Parrotlet. When we reached the tiny settlement of Balsas, having descended about 7000 feet in 25 miles (2134 metres in 40 km), the crew set up camp by the river as we watched six Peruvian Pigeons, the colour of a good claret, which I could have done with a glass of to celebrate another day.

At 05:30 I took a long look at a Spotted Sandpiper bobbing along the Marañón then we were off again, slowly climbing the steep, rocky, scrubby slopes of the eastern wall of the canyon on a rough track with countless hairpin bends and colossal drop-offs, up and up and up, around the sharp ridges of the Andes, to patches of cloud forest which had yet to be chopped down. They were alive with birds including five types of flowerpiercers, small birds with upturned and hooked bills used to pierce the base of flowers in order to get at the nectar; the orange-eyed Bluish Flowerpiercer, black and red Black-throated, all black White-sided, ultramarine blue Masked, and my first Moustached, a handsome black bird with a white moustache and a broad rufous and buff band across the breast. The best forest was at 12,000 feet (3658 metres) at the legendary Abra Barro Negro (Black Mud Pass) between the Marañón and Utcubamba Canyons. Among the gnarled elfin trees was a large and varied foraging flock of birds amongst which I particularly remember picking out a brown and rufous Streaked Tuftedcheek with long white feathers on the sides of its neck forming prominent tufts, two bright chestnut Pearled Treerunners, three black, blue and yellow Hooded Mountain Tanagers, and a lovely Ochraceous-breasted Flycatcher, dark green with an orangey face, throat and upper breast. There were plenty of hummers too; a Sword-billed which was too fast for me to see more than a blur, a more obliging Coppery Metaltail, and best of all a male Rainbow Starfrontlet lapping up nectar a couple of paces away. When seen head-on in the right light the incredible bird did indeed appear to have a yellow star of feathers shining out of the rainbow of feathers on its forehead. Near dusk we headed down to the small town of Leymebamba where there was another delightful little *hostal*.

Up at 03:30, in time for Abra Barro Negro at dawn and by 07:00 we had seen the little-known endemic called Russet-mantled Softtail, a relatively dull, thrush-like bird. I was far more excited about two Grey-breasted Mountain Toucans that were plucking fruits from a trackside tree. The first thing I always notice about a toucan is the large bill and the birds I was looking at had particularly crazy ones that were yellow and black at the base, and red and black at the tip. Mizzle turned to rain but the birds remained busy. I looked in the red eye of a Hooded Mountain Tanager then the blue eye of a Mountain Cacique. I couldn't make up my mind which was the best; a Violet-throated Starfrontlet or an Amethyst-throated Sunangel. Two black-masked otherwise all deep blue White-collared Jays provided yet more colour and variety. In drier conditions during the afternoon along a mule trail leading down from the pass I was very disappointed to miss another fast-moving Sword-billed Hummingbird but a stunning Yellow-scarfed Tanager almost made up for it, being a bright, deep blue bird with a black head and a golden yellow band running down over the top of the head to behind the eyes.

Up at 03:30 for the second dawn raid at Abra Barra Negro but we were confined to the bus in heavy rain until past 06:00 when we could stand the frustration no longer, retreated down the slope a little and ventured out on to the mule trail again. A mixed flock of Yellow-scarfed Tanagers, Scarlet-bellied Mountain Tanagers and green and yellow Cloudforest Brush Finches brightened up the dull morning, followed by my first Grass-green Tanager, an extraordinary, bright garish green bird with a chestnut red face, and red bill and legs, and a pair of Barred Fruiteaters, which looked like beefy green and yellow thrushes, the male with a black hood and red bill.

Our travels continued mid-morning, on the pot-holed road to Pomacochas, north along the Utcubamba Canyon, a very narrow crack in the side of the Andes, so tight in places the track had been cut into the canyon wall. At times the brown water in the boulder-strewn river, which was in a hell of a hurry, ran through beautiful stretches of open woodland, but there was no time to stop until we saw the first of two Fasciated Tiger Herons; black-capped, finely-banded (fasciated) river birds. It was also nice to get out of the bus to watch a pair of mad Torrent Ducks teaching their youngster to tackle some rapids. There was so much water in the river that in places it lapped the side of the track which had also taken a battering from rain and landslides since a solid start to the wet season, so it was no wonder that it took eight hours, twice as long as normal, to reach Pomacochas, so long in fact that there was no time to look for the Marvellous Spatuletail.

Yes, we were finally in Marvellous Spatuletail territory, a very small area above 7000 feet (2134 metres) on the eastern slopes of the Utcubamba Valley of northern Peru. However, before looking for the bird that would make or break the trip for me the leader deemed it necessary to look for Pale-billed Antpitta at the top of the Rio Chido Trail. So, we were up at 05:00 in order to start the climb at dawn, up a very muddy and very steep mule trail which eventually reached a bare sloping shelf among remnant patches of cloud forest where our camp, taken up by four mules, was set up. After seeing two distant and therefore rather dull-looking Chestnut-crested Cotingas and a pair of Lulu's Tody Tyrants, the male a tiny green and yellow bird with a bright rufous head, we began the ascent to the *Chusquea* bamboo patches, home of the rare antpitta. Alas, the hunt for the antpitta was delayed, not that I minded because when we reached a small clearing full of flowering bushes our young local guide caught a glimpse of *'el colibri con los corazones'*, 'the hummingbird with the little hearts', a rare sight along the Rio Chido Trail and not one we were expecting to see.

We must have disturbed it from some flowers so we stood back a little and waited to see if the *colibri* would return. After a few minutes it did but it was so small and fast, dashing about from bush to bush, that it took a few more return visits, over the course of about an hour, for us all to finally line up the phantom in our binoculars for more than a few seconds. The tiny hummer had a shining purple-blue crown, a long, thin glinting green beard, and extremely long and bare and wire-like outer tail feathers that ended in large blue spatules or 'hearts' which bobbed about behind the bird as it hovered in front of the white flowers. The bare shafts of the tail feathers were so long, about six inches, say fifteen centimetres, that they looked like insect legs to me, and the bird's body was so small that while watching it fly this way and that I was reminded of a crane fly or daddy longlegs zooming around a light in a room in a house it had accidentally flown into.

We didn't see the antpitta but there were plenty of other wonders; shimmering green Long-tailed Sylphs, green-black Collared Incas with big white bibs and white tails flashing in the dark forest as they delicately positioned themselves with their supreme flying skills underneath long-petalled pendant flowers, three more Grey-breasted Mountain Toucans, my first Flame-faced Tanagers, and a very impressive Crimson-mantled Woodpecker. So, having seen all those birds *and* the surprise spatuletail, the potential bird-of-the-trip, I was very content when I wrote up my notes while sitting at the entrance to my tent before dinner was served.

The leader broke out the rum to celebrate seeing the special hummingbird. I'm not sure if it was the alcohol, the spatuletail or nine hours sleeping on a slope that resulted in many strange dreams, mostly forgotten when I rose at 05:00 ready for what turned out to be a long, rather boring morning mostly stood in silence hoping calling antpittas would hop into view next to the playback machine. It was not my cup of tea but I did see a pair of dinky Rusty-breasted Antpittas perched together like two big brown and orange eggs, and a larger, dark-capped Rusty-tinged

Antpitta. The pale-billed variety didn't even tease us with a glimpse so some members of the team were very reluctant to leave the valley but leave we did. It was a tricky descent, with shin-high mud in places, enlivened by hearing the loud, piercing shrieks of a distant flock of White-capped Tanagers then, after a long wait, seeing the longed-for beauties albeit briefly before they were flushed by an over-excited Al. The tanager is the sole species in the *Sericossypha* genus, a Latin word for 'silken blackbird' and at first that is what the White-capped Tanager appears to be, except for what looks like a blob of fresh snow on the top of the head and visible at close range, a dark red throat and chest.

Back by the road to Pomacochas we sat amongst some flowers on a steep hillside hoping a male spatuletail would appear and one or two did, and one even perched by me with its 'little hearts' held high and parallel with its tiny body. Back at the *Puerto Pumas Hotel* we played pool on a bald table in a large, high room surrounded by huge paintings of deformed women. We were the only guests and our cooks prepared our food in an empty kitchen, in what was a rather lavish establishment for a remote part of the Andes, one, it was rumoured, that was otherwise used only by people with an interest in a certain local 'crop'.

Up at 04:00 for a short drive, on the first smooth surface of the trip, to Abra Patricia, an Andean pass from where there was the rare and phenomenal sight of almost unbroken forest, ridge after ridge of it, as far as the horizon, and what made the vista even more exciting was that we knew that the tall, moss-draped cloud forest and stunted, elfin forest, on the eastern slopes of the Andes, were two of the richest habitats for birds on Earth.

On the highest ridge we could easily reach we saw an all midnight-blue male Royal Sunangel and a pair of Bar-winged Wood Wrens. Then we walked downhill through a grand parade of fabulous birds. Amongst nearly a hundred species seen, an amazing total for a day of forest birding, were Swallow-tailed Kites, Masked Trogons, Green-and-black Fruiteaters, Inca Jays, a small, large-headed, bristly-faced and black-streaked puffbird called a Lanceolated Monklet, and twenty birds with tanager in their name including Blue-browed, Flame-faced, Golden, Orange-eared, Paradise and Vermilion. There were so many birds in one flock that it took my brain hours to work out that the large, uniform green one I got a very good view of must have been an Olivaceous Piha. When I brought this up, as delicately as I could, at the log it didn't go down very well since I didn't mention it at the time and it was a cotinga, not the most colourful cotinga but a cotinga and most of the party were mad about cotingas, arguably and Olivaceous Piha aside, the most spectacular family of birds in the Americas.

Up at 04:30 to work our way up to Abra Patricia, seeing another fine selection of birds not least a male Andean Cock-of-the-rock, two more Grey-breasted Mountain Toucans, a glamorous Versicoloured Barbet, and a pair of gorgeous blue Yellow-throated Tanagers, not forgetting a superb morpho butterfly which was pale blue above and orangey below. After the first fireflies appeared we heard the fast bubbling call of a Cinnamon Screech Owl and an hour later we were watching the beauty, clinging to the side of a thin silver trunk, in the spotlight, at one of the few known places in the world where that was possible.

Up at 04:30 in time to walk a muddy trail through misty cloud forest first thing, in the faint hope of hearing and maybe, just maybe, being the first visiting birders to see the endemic Ochre-fronted Antpitta in the field, only to join the short list of those who had tried and failed. I was glad we tried though because between pulses of rain we watched a pair of Emerald-bellied Pufflegs courting, the feathers that looked like emerald enamel plating on the tiny male hummingbird's belly glowing in the gloom. Back at the road the rain turned torrential, forcing Chief to crawl out of the gutter he was catching up on some sleep in. We escaped the cloud we were in by heading a little lower. Four Swallow-tailed Kites glided around below eye-level, shafts of sunlight lighting up their slaty upperwings in sharp contrast to the green slopes beyond, and they gracefully swooped down to pluck prey from the tree tops. A male Golden-headed Quetzal perched up in full sunlight, its head glowing. I was still the butt of playful jokes about the Olivaceous Piha and even though we all saw what was almost certainly the same bird at the same place in the same flock the quips continued. Pig-like squeals led us to a party of Andean Cock-of-the-rocks in a fruiting tree, including three bright orange-red males and an orange-brown female. In the late afternoon a pair of Black-mandibled Toucans duetted in an open tree-top, their yellow throats puffed out and their heads and massive black and yellow bills thrown back as their loud yelps carried far across the forested slopes. A morpho was still on the wing. It flew very slowly past me at knee-height, its pale blue upperwings glistening. I got to thinking some of the local 'crop' must have been added to my lunch because my mind was spinning with all the wonder.

We were up at the now usual time of 04:30 for an eggy bread breakfast. Not long after, we were listening to growling cock-of-the-rocks and gurgling oropendolas while trying to see the rare, canopy-dwelling Ash-throated Antwren again but failing. A pair of Scaled Fruiteaters perched in the open canopy of a tree level with the roadside, were far more exciting to me. Through the telescope the green-eyed, black-capped, white-throated male looked like nothing I had ever seen before. He sat there for ages, turning his head from side to side ever so slowly as if in some kind of trance, occasionally uttering a downward-inflected whistle, and was in view long enough for me to marvel at the details of every neatly marked feather, especially the neat, bright olive trims to the black ones on the back, and the dark olive edges to the pale yellow ones on the breast and belly, all of which presented a scaly effect, hence the bird's name.

Our first stop in the afternoon involved getting out of the bus, looking up and seeing a rare Black-and-chestnut Eagle circling low overhead with an even rarer Orange-breasted Falcon. It took a while for that moment to sink in and we were still reeling from it while looking at a male Royal Sunangel in the telescope then a superb singing male Chestnut Antpitta. At dusk we entered the forest, fireflies everywhere, frogs clicking and croaking, in a rather half-arsed and hence failed attempt to see one of the world's least known birds, the tiny Long-whiskered Owlet, which was not discovered until 1976 when two were caught in a mist-net near where we were. Despite considerable effort another was not caught again until 2002, three months before we were there, and another five years passed before the bird was seen in the wild for the first time.

The cockerel started crowing at 04:07, seven minutes late. Not long after, there was the sound of zips being unzipped as eight weary travellers dragged themselves out of their tents ready for another attempt at Ochre-fronted Antpitta. It rained in the night and it was still raining as we walked along the muddy trail through the gloomy, sodden forest as quietly as we could. There were few birds up and about and plenty of mud which Colin, The Colonel, Al and I had to face again because when we got back to the bus Colin, the esteemed leader, discovered that he had dropped his radio in the forest. Once we had recovered it we headed downhill in search of drier weather but all we found was rain and it did not stop until early afternoon when the birds went crazy and it was fantastic to watch the swirling flocks of flycatchers and tanagers until beer o'clock.

Up at 04:30, breakfast at 05:00 and on the road at 06:00, in the rain up and over the pass to Pomacochas, down to the corrugated-iron roofs of Pedro Ruiz then through a narrow gorge into increasingly hot and arid country with dense desert scrub before reaching the broad Utcubamba Canyon bottom where there was a handsome Pied Plover on a shingle bar in the river. At noon we stopped in some scrub west of the hot and dusty town of Bagua Grande and soon found the often elusive Little Inca Finch. By the end of the day we were in the *Hotel El Bosque* in Jaén and after spending a while in wild Peru I felt shocked and disappointed to arrive in such a large, modern, busy city.

Up at 04:00 and along the road north toward Ecuador, into heavily degraded arid acacia scrub at Tamborapa in search of some little brown jobs which to me were just slightly different versions of a more widespread antshrike, sparrow, spinetail and thornbird, all rare endemics and ticks on the world lists of some in the crew. Most of their required results were heard but not seen, at least by me, despite the leader playing the calls and songs of the birds endlessly, a very trying part of the trip for me. I almost hate it actually, that kind of birding, if it is actually birding. Yes, I was seeing birds I probably would not have seen without an experienced leader armed with bird recordings, and a lot more birds in general thanks to the ground crew enabling the maximum amount of time birding, and it was great to be fed and watered regularly, but being driven to a site, standing about listening to a recording of a bird's call or song, waiting for a wild bird to respond to it, to be lured into view, long enough for the listers to tick it off, then moving on to the next one and it all beginning again, that is not my kind of birding.

I also did not like the speed at which we moved from site to site and the rigid itinerary which meant it was not possible to stay at a site that was good or move on from one that was bad. It was all so well organized there were few opportunities to experience the thrill of finding and identifying birds on my own, something that is also often all the better for a long wait and some hard fieldcraft. There was just so little room for any unpredictability, one of the most exciting twists of birding, and therefore little chance of the deep lows and soaring highs of much less organized trips, the ones I was used to and loved. In short, my first 'organized' trip did not feel like much of an adventure.

Back to Tamborapa where even the possible birds that were not rare included two of the most boring birds in the world; the aptly-named Dull-coloured Grassquit and Drab Seedeater. Only the chance of seeing the colourful Maranon Crescentchest kept me going in the increasing heat and we didn't even hear that, even in response to playing its song incessantly, so I was glad to move on, albeit to a different patch of equally poor habitat which was even more unyielding all afternoon.

We drove out of Jaén shortly after 04:00 and I promptly fell asleep, awaking with a start to see a lovely, wide, high-walled valley called the Chamaya Canyon, with bare and scrub-covered cliffs, and a rocky river flowing through paddy fields. When we reached the lowest pass in the Peruvian Andes, the Abra Porculla, which at 7000 feet (2134 metres) was still high enough to be above the clouds, we got out of the bus into the sunshine and wandered slowly between shrubby gullies in a successful search for the localised Piura Chat Tyrant, a small long-tailed bird, dark brown above and grey below with bright white eyebrows, a white throat and three rufous bars across its wings. Outside Olmos we stopped at some roadside paddy fields where the rice was being threshed by hand alongside Pale-legged Horneros; upright, chunky, thrush-sized birds with grey caps, bold white eyebrows, long slender bills, orange-rufous upperparts, pale underparts, short tails and long, pale, stout legs. Strutting along boldly with high steps, holding their heads back and thrusting their breasts forward, they looked like cartoon birds.

The very hot afternoon was spent bouncing around on the bus as it traversed a dry, rocky river bed in a wide wadi for hour after hour, in order to reach the remote Quebrada Frejolillo, an impressive canyon come ravine where during a couple of hours birding before dark we saw an Elegant Crescentchest, a small black-headed bird with long buffy white eyebrows and throat, and a black crescent across its breast, above the chestnut underparts. We camped on bare ground in arid acacia scrub and a long night's sleep produced more strange dreams, two of which I remembered for once. One involved walking along a street having fun arm in arm with a famous actress I considered to be very attractive who then turned out to have club feet covered in blood. This dream, I recalled, seemed to be mixed in with the other, in which I was living in a big house with my mother (my parents, both alive at that time, had always lived together and never in a big house) while the soil outside rose steadily up the sides of the house, compressing it as it did so, until I woke up, still alive but feeling rather perturbed.

I was out of my tent at 04:30 when it was still dark and the three-quarter crescent of Venus was rising above the high canyon wall in a very starry sky. It was already warm when we set off at dawn with a local guide who led us up to dry wooded slopes where we enjoyed an almost constant flurry of fine birds before mid-morning when the heat became too much for them, and us, and we beat a sweaty retreat. Noisy flocks of tiny, short-tailed, green Pacific Parrotlets and long-tailed, green Red-masked Parakeets zoomed back and forth, in between low-flying silver-rumped Tumbes Swifts. Tiny, almost tail-less, green and violet Short-tailed Woodstars darted here and there. Blue and yellow Tropical Parulas and black and yellow White-edged Orioles coloured the sun-bleached woods where a male Black-tailed Trogon perched upright in full view, its iridescent green head and upper breast shining above the deep, bright red lower breast and belly. A yellow-eyed Peruvian Screech Owl roosted in the open. White-tailed Jays perched briefly while flying through the trees, long enough to marvel at their gorgeous blue backs. And there were at least four White-winged Guans, the main reason for being there, because the rare, large dark brown-black birds survive only in a few quebradas in the west Andean foothills of Peru.

We left Frejolillo mid-morning and by midday we were birding the El Tocto Track in 100°F and almost blinding sunshine. The heat from the cloudless sky was bouncing off the bare baked ground. It was uncomfortable and exhausting but worth putting up with for the blackmasked, bright lemon yellow Tumbes Tyrant Al tracked down before common sense prevailed and we hit the road again, moving on to our final base-camp in north Peru, the city of Chiclayo, just inland from the Pacific.

Up at 04:00 and off to Batan Grande where in a heavily overgrazed remnant patch of natural arid thorn scrub and woodland we were pleased to see some very rare birds, including a pair of small, mainly grey Peruvian Plantcutters, not much to look at, and a Rufous Flycatcher, a lot to look at, for the large tyrant flycatcher had a dark grey-brown crown and back, rich cinnamon throat, breast and belly, and bright rufescent wings and tail. While looking for the birds struggling to cope with the widespread clearance of their habitat for sugar plantations and paddy fields, and the degradation of what is left by charcoal burners, firewood gatherers and goats turning the land to dust, I managed to enjoy some last long looks at the likes of glittering green and rufous-bellied Amazilia

Hummingbirds, surprisingly small nuthatch-sized Scarlet-backed Woodpeckers, and White-tailed Jays, while listening to a desert soundscape dominated by the three coos of Pacific Doves and the loud, kookaburra-like cackles of Pale-legged Horneros. What a contrast to the hovel that was the outskirts of that human habitat called a city. I was glad to get in the *Fokker* at Chiclayo airport but it wasn't long before I was in the outskirts of an even bigger city of six million people called Lima, in the hell we call traffic. Somehow our new driver Rafael managed to keep our new, much smaller bus moving through the mayhem and we were soon ascending arid hills and the narrow Rimac Valley to reach the lovely *La Quinta Hotel* in the Santa Eulalia Canyon.

Up at 03:30 and in the bus to climb what is more of a chasm than a canyon, on a track hewn from massive, almost vertical walls of rock, above shocking drop-offs, to over 10,000 feet (3000 metres) where the Mate de Coca was very welcome. It was therefore with renewed enthusiasm that I clambered up and down the ridiculously steep edges of potato fields in an unsuccessful search for a small bird called a Rufous-breasted Warbling Finch. While I was panting the others were casually strolling down the valley and watching a warbling finch from the track. It was gone by the time I arrived and to cap it all I walked into a spike of a giant yucca and sliced my face. Marian, cook and fixer for the southern leg of the trip, dressed the wound with alcohol while holding the back of my neck and blowing gently on to my cheek. "Stop" I whispered in a tone suggesting it was all a bit too exciting, which made Al, Chief and The Colonel roll their eyes and laugh, at a man who had been single for far too long.

It was chilly until the sun rose above the surrounding walls of rock then it was down to rolled-up shirt-sleeves as we searched for the fourth *Incaspiza* of the trip, the Great Inca Finch, seeing five of the black-faced birds. Shortly afterwards we saw another endemic, a Thick-billed Miner, a small ground-dwelling bird which waved the orange bands in its blackish wings as it sang its whirring song from a bare rock atop a vertical drop-off. There were plenty of hummingbirds about as well including the one we hoped to see in Santa Eulalia, a dark glossy green gem with a red throat called a Bronze-tailed Comet.

The almost military sleep-deprivation exercise took on a new twist when, for a change, we got up for the day's birding, not in the small hours, but the day before, and boarded the midnight bus to Marcapomacocha. I was hoping to nod off and catch up with a bit of sleep but I had the misfortune to be in the front passenger seat, prime position to imagine the potential carnage as other buses and trucks hurtled up and down the steep narrow road which winds through the Rimac Valley. One double-decker bus sped past us on the way up then proceeded to overtake every truck in front of us, usually on blind bends. Meanwhile, petrol-tankers which looked like they had been used for the film *Duel*, so big and old and rusty and covered in dust were they that it was hard to picture what they once looked like, came rumbling and swaying down the opposite carriageway at crazy speeds.

Seven hours after leaving Santa Eulalia we reached Milloc at 16,000 feet (4877 metres) where we drove along a rough track that led to a patch of *Polylepis* forest, one of the few known sites for the rare White-cheeked Cotinga. Two miles from the forest the vehicle we had been given for the southern leg of the trip proved, as suspected, to be unsuitable for the task, and was felled by a double puncture. This meant we had to walk the rest of the way, pleasant enough in the high Andes where a narrow white water river ran through a cultivated valley below soaring slopes of scree and towering crags and ridges, above which soared two very high Andean Condors, but we arrived at the *Polylepis* way too long after dawn, the best time for the cotingas.

After a very successful time in northern Peru this came as a massive blow to those obsessed by rare endemics, especially cotingas. Some were upset, annoyed even, especially Al, but Chief, The Colonel and I were not that bothered. Many of the cotingas are fantastic as far as looks go but I thought White-cheeked was one of the drabbest members of the family and arguably one of the dullest birds in South America. I was more interested in seeing Diademed Plover again and so I was happy to get back on the bus, which had been fixed, and to be on our way to the bogs where we might see the plover. However, by the time we reached the Milloc-Marcapomacocha junction we had sustained two more punctures and a battered exhaust, and the team decision was to return to the Central Highway as soon as possible, for repairs, much to my consternation since that meant driving right past Diademed Plover country with several hours of daylight left.

It felt like the trip was beginning to fall apart, and all because of the stupid bus. When it pulled up outside the cafe we had been sitting in for several hours it was obvious the driver had failed to get all of the punctured tyres replaced with new tyres, which led to another team meeting and, based on the bus not being up to the tasks, the decisions were made not only to cancel a return to the cotinga site but to abandon the planned excursion to Lake Junin. I was almost as annoyed as an even more furious Al, since having failed to see the unique and colourful Many-coloured Rush Tyrant in Chile ten years before I was particularly keen to visit Lake Junin, where I stood a good chance of seeing that as well as the grebe endemic to that lake. Al became so incensed about missing the cotinga he wanted to be taken to Lima airport immediately so he could go home. I don't think he calmed down for a day or two. I was calmer by bedtime, because at least we were going to look for Diademed Plovers the next day.

Glorious sunshine lit up the beautiful scene at Marcapomacocha. The vast arena of spongy bogs surrounded by bushy slopes, great swathes of scree, massive rock walls, high ridges and higher mountains, the mightiest of which had a pyramidal peak surrounded by snow, was magnificent, and a wonderful setting for a wonderful bird. How fitting it was that The Colonel, the only member of the crew who had not seen the bird before, was the one who pinned down the first plover, a very confiding bird that we were able to watch for a long time as it foraged along the edge of a rivulet, close enough to examine the very finely-barred grey and white underparts, and the peculiar, long, thin, slightly drooping bill, more like that of a sandpiper than a plover.

Andean Geese and Andean Lapwings helped complete the scene, along with a pair of White-bellied Cinclodes, a rare, striking rufous and white thrush-sized bird, and my first

Puna Snipes but on a long walk, during which I saw two more Diademed Plovers, I failed to find any Rufous-bellied Seedsnipes, which would have been another new shorebird. I overdid it of course, not a good idea so high up, and altitude sickness struck me down, but despite a crushing headache and terrible lethargy I dragged myself out of the bus and up a steep stony slope to watch a Stripe-headed Antpitta bounding higher up the slope like a miniature kangaroo with wings. Then it was time for the longed-for descent and all too soon we returned to the Rimac Valley and that crazy road and then the heat, dust, people and blaring horns of low-rise Lima.

Up at 04:30 in time to board the *MV Alondza* at 06:00 for the long-awaited, eagerly anticipated and much-talked-about pelagic boat trip out into the Humboldt Current in the Pacific off Peru. As the small boat chugged out of Callao, Peru's main port and, allegedly, cocaine smuggling capital of the world, we were accompanied by hundreds of Inca Terns, Franklin's Gulls and Peruvian Boobies, with smaller numbers of Elegant Terns. Once out on the smooth ocean the first small pack of Sabine's Gulls rose from below the bow revealing the striking triangles of white, grey and black in their upperwings. They were followed by hundreds more, yes, hundreds of Sabine's Gulls, and lots of Pomarine Skuas. Farther out there were birds and dolphins everywhere; thousands of birds and hundreds of Dusky Dolphins. One bird we hoped to see was much bigger than the many birds on view and it wasn't long before we noticed a very large bird coming toward us. It was our first Waved Albatross and one or two of the large gliders were on view for the rest of the day, and a few were close enough to see the very fine, wavy vermiculations of grey and white on the birds' backs and bellies, after which they have been named. More eye-catching were their white heads and breasts with a hint of buffy-yellow, huge dull yellow bills and very long wings, brown above and mainly white below. Waved Albatrosses build their nests, lay their eggs and raise their young on just two rocks in the whole world; nearly all of them on the island of Española in the Galapagos with a few on Isla de la Plata off Ecuador. In November, when we were there, they have young to feed and those from the Galapagos travel about 620 miles (1000 km) southeast to the Humboldt Current off Peru in search of crustaceans, fish and squid, all of which turn to an oily liquid during their return journey to Española where they regurgitate it into the ravenous chicks' open bills.

A black and white chequered Cape Petrel came into view before the first Sooty Shearwater and slightly larger and paler Pink-footed Shearwaters of the day, then suddenly, Elliot's, Markham's and Wilson's Storm Petrels were over the silky sea and I began scanning hard for the second dream bird possible on the pelagic. A very distant and brief sighting went down as a probable but there was never a definite which was a massive blow because Hornby's Storm Petrels are arguably the world's most striking storm-petrels and they rarely stray from the Humboldt Current so are only likely to be seen on such a pelagic off Peru.

There was also no sign of the third possible 'mega' after hours of searching, and the amount of energy being put into seeing it had fallen to almost zero when the time came to turn back, forty miles (60 km) out into the Pacific. On hearing we were heading in, I for one renewed my efforts and began scanning hard again, and not long after I spotted a distant group of four birds sitting on the smooth ocean which appeared to have dark heads. We steamed toward them, they rose, and they *did* have dark grey hoods, and paler, smoky grey backs, and very distinctive wings with triangles of grey, white and black, and deeply forked white tails. They were Swallow-tailed Gulls, beautiful birds which like Waved Albatrosses are virtually confined to the Galapagos Islands when nesting, although they also occur on Malpelo Island, a long way off the coast of Colombia.

On the way back in to port a faulty engine cut out and we drifted a mile back out to sea before it cut in again, then some marine litter got wrapped around the 'prop' and left us drifting in the Pacific once more but I didn't care, not after one of the best boat trips of my life, and I still didn't care when fourteen hours after setting out, three hours later than expected, we finally climbed on to the jetty back in Callao. True, I was hungry, and desperate for a beer, but it wasn't long before we got to celebrate a sensational day with grilled sea bass shish kebabs washed down with cold beers and pisco sours, Peruvian cocktails containing *pisco*, the brandy-like base liquor, lime juice, syrup, egg white and Angostura bitters. Back at Marcapomacocha when we drove past the Diademed Plovers it looked like the trip might come to a disappointing end. There was no danger of that now, not having seen the plovers and so many brilliant seabirds on the pelagic.

Somehow we were up at 05:30 and away by 06:00 when Lima was already wide awake. It was our last day of the trip and we travelled north along the Pan-American Highway through the sand and rocks of the Atacama

Desert to Lomas de Lachay where the desert fog resulting from the cold current offshore licks the slopes of the hills, just enough to sustain some scant vegetation, home to the likes of Least Seedsnipes and plain grey lark-like Coastal Miners while a swathe of yellow flowers was literally humming with hummers, zigzagging from flower to flower almost at arm's-length. They were mostly Purple-collared Woodstars and Oasis Hummingbirds but there were also a few Sparkling Violetears. The male woodstars, barely bigger than my thumb, were adorned with iridescent aquamarine gorgets with a purple band below, outshining even the slightly larger, magenta-throated Oasis Hummingbirds and larger metallic green violetears.

Farther north along the coast, in a bare field, was the final member of a bird family for me, a Peruvian Thick-knee, which was almost the same colour as the grey-brown dust it was standing on, apart from its big yellow eyes and the black stripes running back from them. Now I could enjoy the final few hours which we had planned to spend at some coastal lagoons and a beach watching a wide variety of waterbirds and maybe even a Many-coloured Rush Tyrant, a bit of birding I had been looking forward to for a long time, but it was not to be. The radiator in the damned bus boiled over and we were left stranded under the blazing sun in the Atacama Desert.

*Black-headed Bee-eater, Loango National Park, Gabon,
14th November 2003*

## 16

# GABON, SÃO TOMÉ and PRÍNCIPE

In 1999 Roy Baker, a 70-year-old birder originally from Luton, England but then living in Canada, was one of a group of fourteen Canadian, American and British birders on an organized tour to Gabon in West Africa. They were being guided by two leaders from a bird tour company based in America, as well as Patrice Christy, the local birdman, and pygmy trackers, and the day had come to look for one of the rarest and most spectacular birds they hoped to see. The pale crow-like bird with a colourful head called Red-headed Picathartes or Rockfowl lives in primary West African rainforest where, for a nest, it sticks a half cup made out of dried mud to a rock wall, often in a cave. The cave with a small nesting colony the tour group intended to visit was a hard two to three hour slog through thick forest on narrow trails normally used only by a few pygmies from the village of Bokaboka, a three hour drive northeast of Makokou in remote northern Gabon. The group was split into two, those who could walk fast and those who wished to go slowly. Roy joined the 'fast' group but he couldn't keep up and had to stop for a rest at which point one of the tour leaders told him to stay exactly where he was on a narrow trail and to link up with the 'slow' group when they came along. When the 'slow' group reached the cave, having not seen nor expected to see Roy on the trail, the leader of the first group was horrified to see that Roy wasn't with them. It has since been surmised that Roy didn't wait for the 'slow' group, started out on his own to catch up with the 'fast' group and took a wrong fork in the trail. He was never seen again, despite Patrice, pygmy trackers and a Gabonese army helicopter scouring the area for days. They found his rucksack but no other signs and were left to assume that he ended up stuck in some nearby swamp forest with no food, no water and no shelter, his cries for help unheard.

For a short while in Petit Loango National Park I got a taste of what Roy may have gone through when he first realised he was lost. I had just seen a bird as rare and spectacular as a rockfowl but I had little time to enjoy it becasue there was a plane to catch. However, determined to watch the beauty for as long as possible while the others in my party walked on, I made the sometimes fatal decision to leave the trail and while being careful to check my surroundings and not go too far from the trail, in my excitement I became disorientated almost immediately. Leaving a forest trail is dangerous. Unable to curb my enthusiasm I had done it before, in Borneo, 'going in' for pittas, and got away with it. In Gabon I made a mental note of tree trunks and fallen trees before leaving the trail, I even broke a couple of saplings like the pygmies do as I stepped carefully through the undergrowth, and I only walked in about twenty paces but after I had turned around a couple of times while looking for the bird, which I couldn't see, every way through the forest looked like the same tangle of trunks, branches and leaves. I had no idea which way the trail was. If I walked the wrong way I could be in serious trouble.

I tried to remain calm but I soon felt my heart beating hard in my chest and my breaths getting shorter so I sat down on a fallen tree trunk for a smoke and said to myself there was no need to panic because if I stayed put the others would surely find me as long as I stayed close enough to the trail for them to hear me shouting when they came looking. Ed, our South African guide at Loango, had told us he would hoot like an owl if one of us did get lost and we were to hoot back. I thought I would hear a hoot soon because there was not much time before we had to leave to catch a plane but I didn't hear any hoots for what seemed like an age. I was scared. I even started thinking about how I would walk in ever increasing circles until I hit the trail, when the hoot sounded. I hooted back and a few minutes later I was back on the trail with Ed and the others. Suddenly, in what was no time at all really, everything was back to normal and I began walking back along the trail, thinking of Roy and what might have been.

For years I had dreamed of going to Gabon, ever since Dave Sargeant who lived there for five years produced his monumental *Birder's Guide to Gabon* in 1993. It revealed the presence of so many beautiful birds which were very difficult to see elsewhere, and I was particularly interested in Black-headed and Rosy Bee-eaters, as well the more widespread Black and Blue-breasted Bee-eaters, because, still convinced three bee-eaters I saw at Bharatpur in India were Chestnut-headed, albeit beyond the species' normal range, I only needed to see the aforementioned four to have seen all 26 members, as it was then, of my favourite family of birds. Naturally, I wrote to Patrice Christy, who helped Dave Sargeant with his guide, twice, asking if he was able to help guide me but due to the eccentricities of the Gabonese and/or British postal services I never received the replies he was to tell me in person that he sent. So, when I heard that Jon Hornbuckle, a leading world bird lister with a list already in excess of 7500, was planning a trip there, I, in a state of barely containable excitement, contacted him immediately, hoping he would let me join him. He said he needed to consult the other members of the crew and when I heard that it consisted of Simon Colenutt, Martin Hunnybun, and two other fanatical world listers, Neil 'The Batis' Bostock, who was to become the first person to pass 10,000 species, and Philip Rostron, I began to have my reservations. Although Jon reckoned his trip would cost half the price of the tours offered by major bird tour companies it was still, in effect, an 'organized tour' and the last trip I had been on, to Peru, was my first 'organized tour' with a leader using playback and serious listers wanting to tick off every possible bird, and there were times when I regretted joining that, even though most of the people in the group were my friends. All of the people going to Gabon were listing strangers! However, it was a rare chance to visit Gabon at such low cost and possibly the only chance I might get to see the final four bee-eaters so when the crew agreed I could join them I was dancing.

At dawn the view from the *Boeing 767* flying over the coast of Gabon was of thick rain clouds and, where there were breaks in the cloud, plenty of water on the ground, which did not bode well. Although it was the best time to track down some birds we knew we were taking a risk visiting Gabon during the wet season. A few hours after landing we were drifting with the tide in a long dugout called a pirogue on the wide Moka River near the capital Libreville, the outboard engine having spluttered to a halt. It seemed we wouldn't make it to the river mouth where we hoped to see the rare White-crested Tiger Heron and Loango Weaver. There was a hardly a bird to be seen from our precarious position mid-river under a thick blanket of heavy grey cloud and to make matters worse a bee-eater drifted too high overhead to be identified but was, Patrice Christy, still the best bird guide in Gabon, said, almost certainly a Rosy. The outboard did start again and it ran, intermittently, until we reached the entrance to the creek where the tiger heron had been seen before, and then it cut out again and we were adrift once more. The pirogue owner poled us back out to the main river where he tied up to a mangrove in sight of other passing pirogues which might be able to help but traffic was light on the Moka on a Sunday. If no one came along soon, he told Patrice in French, the widely-spoken language of the former colony, there was no need for us to worry because he knew a friend of his would be passing in two to three hours. We could only sit there and wonder if 'two to three hours' in Gabon was the same as 'two to three hours' in the rest of Africa; that is, any number of hours, usually a lot more than stated. All hopes of tiger herons, weavers and bee-eaters seemed to be drifting away like the tide.

An hour or so passed before another pirogue appeared and Patrice persuaded the owner of that to take us all onboard. Just before we reached the best section of tiger heron creek his outboard slowed and stopped. We drifted around for a while before he got it going again but, unsurprisingly, we saw no tiger heron before reaching the village of Moka, a ramshackle mess of wood and corrugated iron, home to Nigerian refugees. After a short walk we reached the Atlantic coast where seven skimmers were skimming; a sight beautiful enough to cheer the most miserable of birders, well me anyway. Over a hundred more went by and back near the village a pair of Loango Weavers cheered up the listers. The pirogue we reached the village in was long gone, the original one didn't turn up for our return journey as arranged, the daily equatorial downpour had begun and while we took shelter under a dry porch with our first beers of the trip Patrice went off to try to procure a third pirogue. An hour later we were off, speeding along in the lashing rain, me huddled up underneath my tightly-held umbrella, pointing dead ahead. We stopped twice, to pick up the owner of pirogue number one, and to refuel, which involved shifting a huge drum of petrol from bow to stern alongside the violently rocking pirogue. Then we were off, on the final push back to the outskirts of Libreville.

The next morning we flew south along the wild, west coast of central Africa, a wonderful sight from the air, for someone who loves planet Earth, of long sandy beaches with barely a human footprint, undisturbed, unpolluted lagoons and rivers, and great swathes of rainforest. It was too good to be true and didn't last long of course. All too soon we were touching down on the tarmac at Port-Gentil, the centre of Gabon's petroleum and timber industries, and second largest city in the country. While waiting for the next flight another high-flying, unidentifiable bee-eater was probably a Rosy, and exactly the same happened farther south at Gamba, a town built by *Shell Oil* to house up to 7000 people, mainly their employees involved in extracting the offshore reserves.

Yet another short flight and we were at Omboue where on a gloriously sunny morning we boarded an open-top *Land Cruiser* for the drive on a solid dirt track to Loango National Park. There were so many birds it took three hours to cover thirty miles (50 km). We soon came across some more airborne bee-eaters, low enough at last to see the vivid rosy-red underparts and dark slate-grey upperparts of my first Rosy Bee-eaters, a rare colour combination and yet another perfect quirk of nature's art. There were about fifty of the lovely bee-eaters, sweeping and swooping and dashing and darting low over the ground and high in the air all around us. Some landed in a bush by the side of the track and I could see their red eyes and black masks bordered below with white cheek lines. So it went on for the rest of the day, the *journée fantastique*, *'The Day of the Rosy Bee-eaters'* for we saw many more and with them, at one point perched in the same tree, was my second new bee-eater of the day, the smaller, bull-necked Blue-breasted, also black-masked but bright grass-green beauties with yellow throats bordered below with deep dark blue and cinnamon bands. In the air with the Rosies were at least thirty African River Martins, catching aerial insects and taking them to their colony in the sandy ground a short distance away. For once the word unique was appropriate because this species belongs to a subfamily of swallows and martins that since the extinction of Thailand's White-eyed River Martin in 1978 has only one member. They have larger heads and stouter bills than other swallows and martins but what is more striking about them is their uniform velvety blue-black plumage which is very different to the majority of the family, most of which are blue above and white below. River martins are strong fliers as well and some sailed close enough to see that they had bright red eyes and bills.

Roberta welcomed us to the brand new *Loango Lodge*, with a bar, restaurant and ten thatched bungalows shaded by palm trees alongside Iguela Lagoon, where extreme anglers hope to reel in a huge Tarpon. Across the long lagoon lies the park, a mosaic of rolling savanna and forest, or *plaine* as the locals call it, beside white sand beaches where Elephants and Buffalo stroll, and Hippos surf! I enjoyed a delicious lunch of Red Snapper before a splendid afternoon's birding during which I saw a new shorebird and a new roller, two other major reasons for dreaming of Gabon for so many years. The black-capped Forbes's

Plover, with two chicks, had red eye-rings in a grey-brown face and throat, below which there were two black bands across its white breast. The Blue-throated Roller looked rather plain in comparison, nearly all cinnamon-chestnut with a hint of purple below although the broad bill was bright yellow and there was a rather obscure pale blue centre to its throat. We were welcomed back to the lodge by the 'You!' calls of a Nkulenga Rail but, alas, like the Buff-spotted Flufftail we heard whoooooooooing like a distant foghorn on a night-drive, we did not so much as catch a glimpse of either of the rarely seen skulkers.

The Red-chested Cuckoo sings 'It will rain' all day long but rain stopped play just for a while the next morning, delaying our first foray into the nearby swamp forest where the great birds came slowly but steadily. A black White-crested Hornbill with very long tail feathers tipped with white, and a brown Red-billed Dwarf Hornbill were with at least ten Pied Hornbills. A shocking black and red finch-like bird was a Western Bluebill. A Fire-crested Alethe is a small brown and white forest-floor job. After lunch we spent a long hot afternoon looking hard for Black-headed Bee-eater. Ed Truter, our guide at Loango, was made fully aware how much we all thought of this bird, which it is possible to see at only a few safe locations in West Africa, and he took us straight to the spot where he saw 'a few' a couple of weeks before. There, we scoured the edges of the gallery forest, running in wide strips through the savanna grassland grazed by Buffalos, Elephants and Red River Hogs.

We saw no bee-eaters with black heads but we did see lots with rosy bellies, at a breeding colony of about a hundred pairs that made a magnificent spectacle. At one moment the air was full of Rosy Bee-eaters calling 'krrrp krrrp' and 'wik wik', the next the ground was lit up by their glorious colours as they landed on the sand before taking food down to their young hidden in burrows. Wandering alone later, as is my wont, I had a face-off with a hefty-looking Red River Hog with his long-bushy white whiskers held horizontal to his black brow and muzzle as he tried to decide, like me, between fight-or-flight. We both chose flight, then thunder then rain then the African night and a cold beer to celebrate the existence of Rosy Bee-eaters.

We were ready for breakfast at 05:30 but Pamela, the chef, was nowhere to be seen. Still, had she not been late we may not have noticed the Shining-blue Kingfisher perched underneath the restaurant decking. By mid-morning we were working some forest when we heard the hoots, grunts, screeches and screams of a troop of Chimpanzees. They did not seem to be too far in from the track so Ed said he, Martin and I, lagging behind the others, should go in so we did, down a slope into a small heavily forested valley where we followed the stream as best we could, stopping only to listen and work out where the apes were. Farther in than Ed had anticipated the first ones came crashing down the tall trees in order to get to the ground as fast as possible for their escape, then they all came down in a mad rush. One shocked and inexperienced youngster dropped fifty feet or so straight to the ground, its fall broken only by a liana it grabbed on the way down. A large female came walking toward us on all fours about twenty paces away and looked as shocked as us when she saw us and she quickly turned and ran. It was all tremendously exciting.

After it had been quiet for a few minutes we walked up the other side of the small valley and another large female dropped down a tall trunk, her feet thumping the ground as she scampered off. We waited for more but the forest fell silent again so we moved on a little and after we thought they had all gone two more which had been hiding high above came hurtling down in a blur behind us and hit the ground running. We stayed where we were, on high alert for more, scanning the canopy and listening hard but there was no sound for some time. It was over and there was time to think about what had just happened. The excitement of hearing them, the thrilling chase, the shock of actually seeing some truly wild Chimpanzees, close up, was an incredible, literally breathtaking, experience. To be walking through the same wild forest as those big, brutish, scrawny-looking, rather ugly animals, clearly our closest relatives, was something I will never forget.

Back on the track, in the tall wall of trees alongside it, there was a large mixed troop of monkeys, composed of brown, tufted Grey-cheeked Mangabeys and blue-faced, grey-brown Moustached Guenons. A party of strange birds called Rufous-bellied Helmetshrikes came by, close enough to see their red bills, red 'spectacles', white heads and black backs. Then, from the back of the moving vehicle, I saw my first Black Bee-eater, a virtually all dark and dusky juvenile which was perched on the outer branches of a fallen tree and was soon joined by its parents, which were superb, delicate, black, scarlet-throated birds with shimmering turquoise spangles sprinkled across their breasts and bellies. They pulsated with life, swishing their tails and turning their heads constantly, the spangles catching the light as they did so, always on the lookout for prey flying by and ever ready to pursue it in fast flight before returning to their perches in more leisurely fashion to de-sting and devour.

I didn't want to leave them but we had to, in order to board a *Boston Whaler*, the 'unsinkable legend', a lightweight foam core boat with not one but two outboards, ready for what turned out to be a wonderful afternoon and evening cruise along the M'Pivie, a black-water river. At about fifty paces wide it looked like a channel of black ink flowing through the tall, thick, green forest. A couple of small Slender-snouted Crocodiles lurked under the overhanging vegetation. Grey and black Cassin's Flycatchers flicked out from low snags above. A pair of brilliant, glossy dark blue birds perched on another snag were not sunbirds as one might expect, they were swallows, White-throated Blue Swallows to be exact. Shining-blue Kingfishers shot by, lighting up the dark scene, and low overhead was a mixed flock of swifts, containing tiny black and white Sabine's Spinetails, larger, very short-tailed Cassin's Spinetails, and a single, back-flipping Black Spinetail, a rare bird we were very fortunate to see. The main reason for cruising along the M'Pivie was to look for fishing owls and Martin soon spotted one. It was a Pel's perched in full view and the first of four of the giant gingery owls. The rare one, seen by very few people, came next; a Vermiculated Fishing Owl, smaller and darker than Pel's with boldly streaked underparts, although Ed was just as excited to spotlight a Beecroft's Anomalure, a grey and buff flying squirrel.

An early morning search for forest-edge species turned up some spectacular deep forest birds that are usually very difficult to see, including a grey and vinous Long-tailed

Hawk with what looked more like a pennant trailing behind it than a tail, and a brilliant little blue and orange White-bellied Kingfisher, filling the lens of a telescope minutes after Patrice said, "This bird is very difficult to see perched". It started raining in the afternoon and we saw not a single bird from then until dusk and even beyond when we visited a small island in the lagoon hoping to see the rare Olive Ibis or perhaps even a Spot-breasted Ibis.

Over dinner we met Mike Fay, an ecologist famous for walking 2000 miles (3200 km) across the Congo including the length of Gabon, then helping to convince President El Hadj Omar Bongo of Gabon to create a network of thirteen national parks covering over ten percent of the country's surface area. With offshore oil reserves running out and the country heavily reliant on timber exports to make money the President was persuaded that thanks to the wildlife which survived in Gabon's forests he could make money out of ecotourism as well as wood. Personally, I doubted it. Not the President's integrity the possibility of ecotourism taking off in Gabon. When I was there in the early 2000s Gabon was the least densely populated country in central Africa with an estimated million people living in a country twice the size of England, and three quarters of the land was covered with lowland tropical rainforest still full of charismatic Chimpanzees and Gorillas, as well as Forest Buffalos, Forest Elephants and stunning birds galore. However, Gabon was not an easy country to get around, there was little if any accommodation at the best sites, and perhaps more significantly there was not a wide variety of easily-seen 'plains mammals' or a Maasai Mara or Serengeti to watch them in, so I was not convinced it could compete for tourists with the well-established safari destinations of East and Southern Africa. Millions of people had been visiting those places for decades, compared to about a thousand per year in Gabon, and ecotourism was a major source of income in countries like Kenya and Tanzania which both had a superb tourist infrastructure complete with professionally trained guides, and a wide variety of accommodations and safaris.

Mike Fay described a bird he had seen that afternoon just across the lagoon, while trying to track down a Black-headed Bee-eater for us (everyone was on the case now). It sounded like the bird Mike saw could have been a White-crested Tiger Heron so although we had a plane to catch early the next morning we decided a quick look was in order. We were almost near where the bird had been seen when Ed called us back to look at a bird under the canopy of the tree he was pointing at. Expecting it to be the paradise flycatcher Patrice had heard moments before we were shocked to see a large but sleek, deep grass-green bee-eater with a black head and burnt orange breast. Still desperate to find the bird I most wanted to see at Loango, Ed had spotted what could so easily have been overlooked at the last possible moment, and Jon Hornbuckle and I had now seen every bee-eater on Earth.

I fell in love with bee-eaters in the Camargue and after my first ones there most of my travels had revolved around the other 25 members of what became my favourite family of birds. My celebrations were restrained in the company of so many strangers; I threw my cap in the air and danced around a little bit under that superb Black-headed Bee-eater but inside I was exploding with pure happiness. Of course, it would take a while to sink in; the eighteen years, twelve countries and many adventures it took to fulfil one of my most outrageous fantasies but I had done it, I had seen all the bee-eaters. In my excitement I left the trail to get better views of the superb bird and as aforementioned I got lost in the forest. Not for long, thankfully. Ed found me, but he didn't find a tiger heron.

When we got back to the lodge there was a very grumpy American fisherman sitting in the back of the *Land Cruiser*. He was even grumpier, "really pissed" in his own words, after the breakneck drive along the pot-holed track to Omboue. "I could'a been killed!" he complained, a slight exaggeration but we were travelling too fast to bird, which was a shame because it would have been nice to stop and watch the African River Martins and Rosy Bee-eaters again. If we missed our flight we would have had plenty of time; the next one was not for three days. Of course, on arrival at Omboue we were informed the flight was delayed. There was not enough time to go back to the river martin colony but in the hour available I got to see a new shorebird instead; at least a hundred Grey Pratincoles, at the nearby lagoon. Normally most active at dusk, many of those we saw were gliding around fly-catching in the middle of the day, the small birds showing their striking black and white wing patterns as they wheeled around with great grace, plucking tiny insects out of the air.

Back near Libreville we squeezed in a couple of hours birding in a large scrubby forest clearing at Bolokoboue, seeing a brilliant male Black-bellied Seedcracker, a small, bright red and black bird with white crescents above and below its eyes, and a bill a Hawfinch would be proud of.

Cheered by more great birds and the West African beats blasting out of the bars on our way back through Libreville I went crazy and bought everyone a beer to celebrate seeing all the bee-eaters.

At four o'clock in the morning I was pacing the platform of *la gare de Ayem* waiting for the Transgabonais train to get going again. It was already three hours behind schedule, though not as late as usual. I didn't mind it stopping actually, because it was much warmer outside than inside the train where the air-conditioning was too cold for me to sleep. I could hardly complain about a chilly train in Gabon when Mary Kingsley, a Victorian spinster in her early thirties, was a member of a party travelling through the 'Great Forest' of Gabon in 1895 that 'were two hours and a quarter passing [a] swamp ... only going in right over head and all twice ... One and all, we got horribly infested with leeches, having a frill of them round our necks like astrakhan collars.' Her classic account of her journey through Congo Français was published in *Travels in West Africa* in 1897.

Once we reached Lope, 180 miles (290 km) down the line from Libreville, I enjoyed a coffee on the terrace of the hotel overlooking the landscaped grounds above the Ogooue River where we could see some distant White-crowned Lapwings and Rock Pratincoles. Closer to, in eye-level flowering trees were two little gems called Superb and Violet-tailed Sunbirds. We headed down to the full, fast-flowing Ogooue for better views of the shorebirds and a nice cool paddle in one of central Africa's great waterways, on its way to the Atlantic. The Ogooue forms the northern boundary of Lope National Park, a fine swathe of savanna, gallery forest and patches of lowland rainforest known as *bosquets*, where I counted a surprising flock of 27 Forbes's Plovers on our way to a bridge across a small creek running through a patch of forest where we spent most of the morning hoping to see but only hearing Fiery-breasted Bushshrike. Patrice then took us to a small swamp where he discovered the very rare Dja River Scrub Warbler in Lope nearly a decade before, one of the handful of known sites for the notoriously shy and skulking little brown job. Patrice predicted that the one we were about to look for, on hearing the sound of its own voice from his machine would almost certainly rise out of the reeds at speed, fly around briefly and perch out in the open for a second before diving back into the swamp for the rest of the day. It did exactly as he said until it landed near the top of a largely leafless bush and sang its head off in full view for what must have been nearly a minute, more than enough time to see the grey face, lightly streaked throat and long tail. It dropped down into the reeds but came out again, a couple of times, and poor Patrice didn't know where to look. He did say, after lunch, that the afternoon plan was "to watch the birds go to bed" back at the bridge over the creek, a plan foiled because virtually all of the birds had already gone to bed by the time we got there, although a female African Finfoot showed well ... for a finfoot.

I slept like a baby for a solid six hours, waking at 04:15, which meant I got a technical lie-in, a great rarity on a birding trip, because breakfast was at 06:00. I saw my first Johanna's Sunbird half way through an omelette then we got on our way to Mikongo, stopping only to look at a tiny, round, short-tailed brownish bird on the track that turned out to be a Small Buttonquail, a bird that very rarely ventures out into the open. I was particularly pleased because I had just seen that almost mythical bird portrayed in old European field guides with the evocative name of Andalusian Hemipode, Andalusia being one region in Spain where the secretive bird may now be extinct.

The *Mikongo Conservation Centre* is a forest research camp run by the Zoological Society of London, with a particular interest in habituating Gorillas to human presence so that visitors may see them in the wild, as is the case in other parts of Central Africa. In a forest clearing there were six thatched wooden huts with verandas, and a communal hut in which meals were served. As soon as we had dumped our bags we split into two; Jon, Phil and Patrice went one way while The Batis, Simon, Martin and I were led into the forest by Aime and Ghislain, Bongo-Mbenga pygmies who glided smoothly and silently through the forest along the maze of narrow elephant trails with us slipping, stumbling and sweating behind them, for two hours, stopping only to watch a Blue Cuckooshrike, all deep dark blue except for a blackish face. It was two precious hours to appreciate where I was and what I was doing, fulfilling a long held dream to walk in the West African rainforest in search of some very special birds.

When we came to a relatively open area amongst the dense forest, where there was a rock nearly as high and wide as a two-storey house Aime and Ghislain gestured for us to settle down quickly and they soon erected a screen between us and the rock made from some loose-leaved shoots. On one side of the rock was a nest with an egg in it belonging to a pair of birds we were hoping to see. Shortly after sitting down we had to get up and run. Aime thought there was an elephant nearby, a dangerous animal when surprised in the thick forest, but it was a female Chimpanzee which looked back at us somewhat perplexed before moving off. When we returned to our look-out my happy life soon became very uncomfortable. In the forest at Lope there are ticks, sand flies, tsetse flies and filarial flies, the ones that look like orange hover-flies and are known locally as *mouche rouge* and carry *Loa loa*, a nematode worm which the victim of a fly bite can see crawling across the outside of their eyes. However, Lope is most famous for its sweat bees, so numerous in one area that it is known as the *Forêt des Abeilles* - the Forest of Bees. They found us almost immediately and soon we were all surrounded by our individual swarms, except Aime and Ghislain, who had placed some leaves behind their ears, and did not have a bee near them. We placed the same leaves behind our ears but they made no difference. The difference was Aime and Ghislain had walked through the forest for two hours without breaking a sweat whereas we all had shirts soaked with the salt the bees were after. The constant thrum was terrible but at least they are only the size of grains of rice. They are also stingless but they or whatever else was trapped under our shirts inflicted some painful bites, bad enough to keep us moving about, far from ideal behaviour when trying to see the shy forest bird we were looking for.

Nevertheless, after a very tiresome hour or so, Aime and then Martin glimpsed one of the pair of birds. It was another hour before I got a brief view of the head and back of one hopping immediately out of view along the ground, and another long hour with the bees passed with only Aime seeing one. 16:00 hours, time to return to base, was rapidly approaching when Aime spotted one again and

*Red-headed Picathartes, Mikongo, Lope National Park, Gabon, 16th November 2003*

this time Martin, Simon and I got on the extraordinary bird that was perched in a spindly tree near the nest, almost completely in the open. The Batis was standing next to Aime but couldn't understand his directions and just missed the bird as it dropped to the ground. He was not happy. Ten to fifteen minutes later though, Aime somehow spotted one through a labyrinth of leaves, perched up and preening in full view at eye level, and once everyone was on the right line we were all able to enjoy prolonged views of a superb Red-headed Picathartes, the bird the unfortunate Roy Baker was after, and it was close enough for us to see a narrow black band of tiny bristle-like feathers between the bright blue skin of the forehead and the bright red skin of the back of the head. As astonishing as the bird's head was the immaculate plumage. The steel-grey upperparts looked like they had been polished while the pale grey neck and breast, and pale, yellow-buff belly, seemed to be made of silk.

It was well past four o'clock in the afternoon and we not only had to go we wanted to go and it was a joy to get moving along a trail again and leave the bees behind, the bird under-the-belt, but just as we started to enjoy the freedom from the terrible thrum what the approaching thunder had threatened arrived. The rain poured from the unseen sky, then it fell in waterfalls from the trees, instantly turning the trail into a muddy stream, and despite employing my much-maligned umbrella I arrived back at base camp as wet as everyone else. Rarely has beer o'clock been so appreciated and enjoyed. Dry again, I sat back with a smoke and quickly came to the conclusion that it had been worth the effort and would have been worth a hell of a lot more to see a picathartes.

The next day, during nine hours inside the forest, home to hundreds of different bird species, I saw a mere nineteen of them. Most memorable was a singing male Forest Robin, a tiny bird with a black head, white spots before its eyes and a lovely deep orange throat belting out a sweet stream of high-pitched whistles. We heard but did not see plenty of birds of course, notably a Chocolate-backed Kingfisher which eluded even Aime's phenomenal eyes. Enough was enough so we spent the last hour or so of decent light outside the forest, scanning the edge as almost black clouds tumbled in. I turned away from three Black Bee-eaters to watch a pair of Vanga Flycatchers at their nest, a ridiculous affair, being a small, neat, silvery-grey cup moulded onto a thin horizontal branch and fully exposed in a small bare tree. Patrice assured us this was not a problem for a very aggressive little bird as the male flew in and perched nearby before flitting to the nest and settling down to incubate the eggs. The small, stocky bird has a glossy black head, chest and back, and white belly, with a spiky crest, a slightly hooked bill, eye-catching yellow eyes, short tail and broad, very rounded wings. She was different altogether with a shorter crest, greyish head, rufous back and dirty white underparts.

The next morning we had a chat with the 'Gorilla Girls' who were trying to habituate the local Gorillas, something that can take several years with animals that have been hunted for centuries. They told us that we might bump into a family group of them while birding. I would much rather have seen some Gorillas than Latham's Forest Francolin and Black Guineafowl, the two birds most wanted by the listers that we didn't see, although two Grey-headed Kingfishers flying around a green clearing, the low early morning light catching their icy blue wings, made the morning session memorable. A large, noisy troop of Grey-cheeked Mangabeys, and Crowned and Putty-nosed Monkeys accompanied us for a long time although rarely did I see a single animal out in the open in the thick canopy, so shy were they. A calling Fiery-breasted Bushshrike was even more elusive. The low whoops of the colourful skulker were tantalisingly close but the beauty failed to grace the lenses of my underused binoculars.

Arriving at Lope railway station a train with wagon after wagon of huge tree trunks passed by for a depressingly long time. There would no longer be Gorillas, Chimpanzees, Elephants, picathartes, a multitude of other birds and millions of other animals where they had come from. Only an hour behind schedule we boarded the train to Franceville and slowly trundled south alongside the Ogooue River, a huge wild mass of water rushing past black shiny rocks through a thickly forested wild land in heavy rain. Over 400 miles (640 km) out of Libreville we reached the end of the line and two hours later, near midnight, I was shown to my spartan room in the *Hotel de Leconi*. There before my delighted eyes was a double-bed. The only trouble was I had just five hours to enjoy it.

Not long after dawn we were on the edge of the Bateke Plateau, named after the local tribe, in far southeast Gabon near the border with the Republic of the Congo, scanning the bushy savanna, seeking out and seeing several birds which have very restricted ranges, including the very smart Black-collared Bulbul and a warbler called a Salvadori's Eremomela, adding, after a short siesta during the heat of the day, a pair of Angola Batises and the large, mottled grey-brown Congo Moor Chat. European, Little, Rosy and White-throated Bee-eaters, and Long-tailed and Swamp Nightjars completed a fine day. We were back the next morning, walking miles across the short-grass savanna in the big wide open under cloudy skies, seeing partridge-like Coqui and Finsch's Francolins, Black-bellied and White-bellied Bustards, Black-rumped Buttonquails and Temminck's Coursers, a fine bunch of birds that would have been even more exciting had they not all been seen in flight only. The same was true of the White-throated Bee-eaters although they look just as good on the wing as perched, gliding over the golden grass on stiffly-held, similar-coloured, black-trimmed wings. They kept those of us primarily interested in nature's art happy. The species, subspecies and potential species of larks, pipits and cisticolas satisfied the listers.

Moving on to Lake Lekoni we all saw a Great Snipe, in flight only of course, and Simon and I flushed two tiny birds which were up and away into the bright light too fast to identify or enjoy and were probably what we were after; the very pretty and elusive Locustfinch. To cap it all, the very moment we arrived at the Black-headed Bee-eater back-up site near Bongoville the leaden skies poured forth an inevitable deluge and ended the day's birding. There may have been plenty of water falling from the sky but there was none coming out of the showers in *Hotel de Leconi* or any food on its way. We appeared to be the only guests but, as Patrice explained, the members of staff were far from helpful because hotels in Gabon are obliged to employ local people who would much rather be tending their cassava plots than waiting on impatient tourists. It therefore seemed rather odd that the hotel walls were covered in fantastic murals depicting the simple life. I was hungry but I could wait. The most important thing was that there was plenty of cold *Regab Biere* to drink while trying to come to terms with a rather disappointing day.

With only a morning left in Gabon we were out and about at the crack and I had a brilliant start to the new birding day thanks to a European Bee-eater perched in the same tree as three Rosy Bee-eaters in perfect low early morning light. We then heard the distinctive, jerky, liquid, whistling song of a Gorgeous Bushshrike and to our amazement the yellow-browed, black-masked, crimson-throated, black-chested, deep green skulker leapt out into the open and moved closer and closer while almost constantly on view. My last Blue-breasted Bee-eaters were a couple with a youngster. Back at Bongoville we had three hours left to winkle out one or more Black-headed Bee-eaters. A Black Bee-eater, several White-fronted and three Littles made an incredible seven species of bee-eater in six hours but we could not, to Patrice's astonishment, find the eighth, there at one of the most reliable sites for the species on the planet. Fortunately, while sitting in Franceville airport, I could only imagine what a disaster it would have been if Ed had not spotted the one at Loango, for our time in Gabon was up and we were about to fly to Libreville and on to the Gulf of Guinea island of São Tomé.

I didn't want to go to São Tomé and Príncipe, I wanted to stay in Gabon and wander through the forests and savannas forever, in search of more bee-eaters and other birds and Gorillas and Nature's innumerable other wonders, birding and travelling in wild places, living the life I love. I didn't want to spend my time and money looking for versions of mainland birds which happen to be endemic species because they have been isolated on islands for what some taxonomists consider to be enough time to make them different enough, mainly in the way they call and sing, to be full species, and therefore precious as ticks on a list to some members of the crew, for they presented them with a chance to get closer to their 'holy grail' of 8000, maybe 9000, even 10,000 species, or, in the case of a few of them, nearer being the world's leading lister. Jon Hornbuckle reluctantly admitted his major aim in life was to see more bird species than anyone else and that when he sees a new bird he sometimes smiles but usually just thinks, 'I'm glad I've got that one down.' (Fourteen years later, in July 2017, having seen over 9500 species and achieved his goal of being number one Jon was badly injured in a car accident in the south of France and, tragically, lost his memory of all the birds he had seen and all the places he had been, which was more than most, a truly terrible end to a remarkable life for he never recovered and, aged 74, passed away in February 2018.)

The avian aesthetics I live for are not high on the list of most listers. However, I had signed up for the whole trip and could not change my plans, and, anyway, some of the 25 birds endemic to the two islands promised to be interesting, and, more importantly, there was a good chance of seeing my first tropicbird.

We had ten minutes exactly to grab our bags and board the *Dash 8* to São Tomé, a small plane which certainly dashed, enough to make me feel like I was actually in a jet, and the pilot didn't even seem to slow down to land as we plopped down on to the tarmac runway. Soon we were eating Barracuda washed down with Portuguese beer. No people were living on São Tomé when the Portuguese first landed on the island in about 1470. They shipped slaves there from the mainland to work in now largely abandoned cocoa, coffee and sugar plantations. By 2003 the people were growing crops such as bananas and cassava below steep slopes, some of which were still covered in dense forest, watered by some of the most impressive rainfall on the planet, the average annual amount being a prodigious 16 feet (5 metres).

The next day I was awake early. I walked out of the hotel, looked down the dirty street of dilapidated, pastel-coloured buildings and saw my first tropicbird. It was distant, as was another at the airport later, so I was hoping I would see one closer on the island of Príncipe which we reached on a *Twin Otter*. I had never seen such a place; a small, verdant tropical island, ten miles by five (16 km by 8 km), with huge, bare black basalt volcanic plugs rising from the forested slopes into the clouds. Before and after an excellent seafood lunch washed down with the smoothest pineapple juice I have ever tasted at our *Pensao*, the *Residencial Palhota*, we saw, with the help of local guide Pedro, the five birds deemed to be endemic to the island; a dull olive sunbird, a dull, dirty-white warbler-like speirops, a dull golden weaver, even a dull glossy starling, and a much more interesting bird called Dohrn's Thrush Babbler, an oddity because it could be a thrush, a babbler, a flycatcher, a warbler, or something else entirely.

The managers of the lavish *Bom Bom Resort* which caters mainly for rich fishing folk who dream of reels screaming with marlins and sailfish agreed to take us out on their boat. We wanted to visit the Tinhosas Islands where there was a huge colony of Sooty Terns and a chance of a few frigatebirds, probably Ascension Frigatebirds wandering from Ascension Island, 1500 miles (2400 km) away, but at the last minute we were told that we would not make it there and back in time for our flight to São Tomé so we had to make do with a relatively short excursion to some small offshore rocks where some panting Brown Boobies and Brown Noddies were resting in the dense humid heat, and on to a massive offshore volcanic pinnacle known as Ilhéu Caroço around which glided at least ten White-tailed

Tropicbirds. Too high to look in the eye, their tails were actually more of a pale apricot colour than white and they trailed behind them like ribbons as they sailed past the almost vertical grey crags and dense green palm forest, making a wonderful, strangely primeval scene. A few flying-fish flung themselves out of the Gulf of Guinea on the way back to land, in time for an octopus for lunch.

During nearly twelve hours on a narrow slippery trail up to a crater lake called Lagoa Amelia in the high centre of São Tomé we saw eleven of the fifteen island endemics, the best of which was a male paradise-flycatcher, a beautiful, shiny blue-black bird with a bluish bill, bluish 'spectacles' and an extremely long tail. I saw eighteen species of bird all day; the island's avifauna may be highly endemic but it is also depressingly depauperate. The next morning we headed along the east coast in two jeeps past small bays with big surf, and plantation after plantation. It was at one such palm plantation that we turned off the road and headed inland to the Rio Io Grande from where we walked along an overgrown ride through the long-neglected palms before reaching the forested slopes where there were no trails so the going was hard, walking on small loose rocks up a steep ridgeline through thick forest. Then it started raining then it started pouring, stair-rods pelting through the trees, so much water everywhere my umbrella was of no use. Some superb paradise-flycatchers lit up the gloom and four Dwarf Olive Ibises which flew up off the forest floor to perch on large horizontal branches in the trees almost above our heads kept our minds off the rain for a while but by the time we arrived at a clearing deemed fit enough to camp in by our local guides we were all soaked.

It looked like being a wet afternoon's birding too but mercifully real rain fizzled out and we were able to look for São Tomé's great rarities without too much discomfort. We saw very little. A Black Cobra, introduced from India to take out the rats which were eating the cocoa pods, was the most exciting. This very venomous snake is usually killed on sight by the locals, who when bitten have been known to chop limbs off for fear of not making a hospital in time for the anti-venom, having between thirty minutes and two hours to save their other limbs and their lives. Less exciting was a São Tomé Short-tail, a dark brown and light brown wren-like warbler deemed by taxonomists to be, of all things, a wagtail! Near dusk when we were almost back at camp we heard and then spotted not one but two São Tomé Scops Owls, one a grey morph the other a bright rufous bird, which cheered everyone up, even me, who thinks one scops-owl looks like any other scops-owl.

Ten hours lying in a hot tent on a mattress composed of uneven mud and tree roots was not conducive to sleep so I was feeling pretty groggy and grumpy while I drank the most disgusting coffee I had ever tasted the next morning, and I was not the only one, hence there were no dissenters when Jon outlined the day's plan which went something like, "All we need is the fiscal and the grosbeak then we can get out of this shit-hole before it rains again." Lucio led us up a ridge where it didn't take long to find one of the rarest birds in the world, a São Tomé Fiscal, a black, white and yellow shrike with a very long tail and a fine song composed of clear, repeated fluty whistles. There were no grosbeaks though and it didn't take long for the whole team, even the most hardened listers, to vote to give up looking for the hardest endemic to see, a pretty pathetic effort I thought, considering we had experienced just one night of serious discomfort on a trip to equatorial Africa, although I was more than happy to give up looking for a brown bird with a big beak, and hopefully see some more tropicbirds. Anyway, we broke camp and walked back down to the jeeps, past the green-with-moss old plantation house where Kurtz, the ivory trader who went mad and turned himself into a Congo demigod in Conrad's *Heart of Darkness*, and was reprised by Marlon Brando in the film *Apocalypse Now*, would not have looked out of place.

After a long, thundery, wet, stuffy, sweaty night in a tent, zipped up to keep the mozzies at bay, I was first up, tropicbirds on my mind. I walked twenty paces under some palms to an almost orange beach where there was a Common Sandpiper bobbing about, a long way from its summer home in Europe, like me. As if to jolt my still sleepy brain and remind me where I was a Straw-coloured Fruit Bat flew by. I seawatched for nearly an hour, enjoying three Brown Boobies gliding gracefully by, but there still seemed to be no tropicbirds on São Tomé. It started raining heavily as we drove along the coast in search of breakfast, somewhere close we hoped, but on and on and on we drove, our stomachs empty and aching, and our bloodstreams screaming out for caffeine. When we finally stopped it stopped raining and as we waited and waited for breakfast to appear at the *Pousada Roca Sao Joao* seven White-tailed Tropicbirds, one about every ten minutes, came in off the sea and sailed over the forest, and one of them circled a few times before dropping down into a gulley where its nesting burrow was below the balcony we were scanning from, enabling me to finally look a tropicbird in the eye.

Money matters dominated the end of the trip as we all settled up with Jon. I was left with a few coins in my pocket and a couple of IOUs to pay on my return home, bad news considering the already beleaguered state of my bank balance. Still, I expected an overdraft when the crew said I could join them and I am so glad I did because Gabon was fantastic. Grounded due to my impecunious condition I missed a night out in Libreville so it was even easier to get up early on the last morning of the trip to say farewell to that top man Patrice over coffee and croissants under the palm trees.

Blessed with a window seat on the 767 I looked at the African landscape for hours. It became increasingly arid north of Cameroon and Nigeria. Large rivers with huge sandbanks disappeared from view, cultivation ended abruptly, then came the Sahel, then the Sahara which was surprisingly varied at first but eventually all I could see were long lines of sunlit red dunes with the odd patch of flat ground and then just regularly spaced dunes as far as the horizon, a far cry from the overcrowded grey and grim suburbs of London where there was so little beauty, so little joy; a world away from the sparsely populated, bird-filled verdant forests and savannas of Gabon.

*Turquoise-browed Motmot, Chichen Itza, Mexico,*
*16th January 2005*

# 17

# MEXICO

Many hundreds of years ago the Mayan people built cities with huge stone pyramids in the tropical forests of Central America. One of the largest was Chichen Itza on the Yucatan Peninsula in Mexico, where the Temple of Kukulkan overlooks the Great Ball Court where players tried to hit a rubber ball through stone hoops on the court walls and legend has it that the losing *Capitan* would decapitate the willing winning *Capitan*, thereby bestowing upon him the ultimate honour, a direct route to heavenly paradise. The Mayans may have been bloodthirsty - the hearts of prisoners, slaves, orphans and illegitimate children were regularly presented to their gods - but they were more advanced in mathematics and science than European people at the time when Chichen Itza was a thriving city, from about 600 to 1200. For example, the Temple of Kukulkan, which survives to this day, is a pyramid with 365 steps, 91 in each of the staircases on the four sides plus the top platform, representing the days of a year; that is, the time it takes for the Earth to travel around the sun. More incredible is that the Mayans built a staircase down which wriggles what appears to be a giant serpent - Kukulkan was an important serpent god - when the sun sets on the spring and autumn equinoxes, an effect created by the shadow cast by the sinking late afternoon sun. Why the city was abandoned during the 1400s no one knows but the people may have fled due to problems growing food, cocoa and tobacco. There was no chance of them returning either; the Mayan empire, like the Aztec to the north, was destroyed by the Spanish invaders in the 1500s.

I have never been much interested in history; I was on my way to Chichen Itza, with The Colonel, Nick Wall and Simon Colenutt, to look for nature's art not Mayan art, and one bird in particular, the all dazzling blue wings and tail that's a Turquoise-browed Motmot. I saw one before we got there, another alongside the entrance road and a third in the forest surrounding the ruins, through Simon's technicolour dreamscope. Perched quietly under the low canopy the bright medium-sized bird was surprisingly well camouflaged in the shades of green and brown around it but betrayed by a glimpse of glistening blue from its swinging tail. Once located we could see the green crown and nape blending into a rich brown back, shiny pale turquoise eyebrows, a black mask ending in sharp points below the eyes and edged, under the eyes, with feathers like sparkling turquoise darts, a large, dark, slightly decurved bill, a shaggy black stripe edged with large turquoise darts down the centre of the green throat and chest, cinnamon belly, very bright, blue wings edged black, and an extraordinary tail, bright blue tipped black with two elongated central tail feathers, bare shafts for more than half their length but ending in large, black-tipped, turquoise racquets. I had never seen anything like it. My first motmot was as good as, if not better than, any of the bee-eaters, better than I had dared to imagine.

I had seen all the bee-eaters and one of the five species of virtually identical todies; now it was time for the motmots, named after an American Spanish imitation of the birds' low hoots. Six out of the nine species known at the time lived in Mexico. A couple were very difficult to see but I had seen two of a possible four before breakfast on my first day in the country because with a Turquoise-browed along the entrance road were two Blue-crowned Motmots, more uniform green and less startling but still stunning birds. Nevertheless, they were almost surpassed by my first Yucatan Jays with deep black heads, necks and underparts, conspicuous yellow legs, and pure, bright turquoise-blue upperparts including the wings and tail, all with a superb sheen. Mexico appeared to be all turquoise. I liked it.

## A MIND-BLOWING BIRDING TRIP TO A PLANET CALLED EARTH

During the heat of the middle of the day we drove across the low-lying limestone plain known as the Yucatan to the small town of Felipe Carrillo Puerto along 'Kingbird Highway', a road lit with many lemon-bellied Tropical Kingbirds perched on roadside wires. After securing a couple of rooms in the *Restaurant Bar y Hotel El Faisan y el Venado* (The Pheasant and the Deer) and some superb shrimp fajitas we dashed to the nearby forest but we saw very few birds during a hot afternoon.

We drove back into the forest at first light, flushing lots of Ovenbirds off the track before we reached the entrance to Sian Ka'an Biosphere Reserve. We were hoping an Ocellated Turkey might stroll across the lawns between the reserve buildings. Instead, there were two crazy-looking, chicken-sized birds called Grey-necked Wood Rails, with short, black tails cocked-up. We were the only four human beings walking the track through the overhanging forest that morning and we saw, in quick succession, a yellow-bellied Black-headed Trogon, a rail-like rich brown Mexican Black-faced Ant-thrush, and a lovely male Rose-throated Tanager. Birding was less heady but steady afterwards as we added Ivory-billed Woodcreepers, Black Catbirds, Blue Buntings and both motmots.

There are few if any better places to be at dawn than in a forest clearing as the first rays of the sun light up one side and the birds come alive. A superb Collared Forest Falcon, a retiring, rarely seen raptor, perched up just long enough for us to see the white collar contrasting with the blackish crown, sideburns, back and wings, and the bird's very long tail and yellow legs. Nearby there was a brilliant Blue-crowned Motmot and a male Grey-throated Chat, actually a 'New World Warbler' and the first of a possible eighteen new such birds on the trip, birds almost as attractive to my eyes as bee-eaters, todies and motmots, and another of the major reasons for being in Mexico. Along the track was yet another, my first Keel-billed Toucan, a truly extraordinary bird which, seen as briefly as it was, appeared to be composed merely of a large black tail, a black and white body and a giant multicoloured bill. There followed a 300 mile (480 km) drive through increasingly fragmented forest and more and more fenced pastures to the Usumacinta Marshes, actually more ditches, pools and paddies than marshes, and only visible from the busy Route 186 but in the two hours of light left we saw lots of waterbirds, although none were the hoped-for Bare-throated Tiger Heron or Pinnated Bittern.

At dawn the next morning we headed up the hairpin bends of the first hills to rise up from the wide coastal plain, on our way to Palenque, another Mayan city. We were keen to get on the trail by the Temple of Inscriptions before any other tourists could disturb the birds. The temple is a stepped pyramid where the tomb of K'inich Janaab' Pakal, who ruled from 615 to 683, was hidden. Surrounded by rainforest his kingdom must have been a lovely place to live but like other Mayan cities it was abandoned for unknown reasons around the 9th century. On the forest floor were Wood Thrushes, with striking black spots on their white underparts, but above them we could not find any Tody Motmots and we fared little better along the Cascada Trail, at least as far as birds were concerned, for a troop of about seven Black Howler Monkeys were foraging in the trees above. The day had begun with a big Keel-billed Toucan and it ended with some smaller, black, yellow and red toucans called Collared Araçaris. Some young ladies who came over to see what we were so excited about were also appreciative, their eyes and smiles wide as they said, quietly, "Oh! Tucanos!"

We returned to Palenque the following dawn and I took time out from the bird search for once to listen to a rainforest waking up; the deep, guttural growls and roars of howler monkeys, ear-piercing screeching and squawking parrots, clucking, gurgling and popping oropendolas, rollicking wrens, humming hummingbirds, and the squeaks and whistles of a multitude of unknown unseen birds and animals. When there was enough light amongst the giant buttresses, strangler figs and leaves of all shapes and sizes and every shade of green, it was possible to see a movement here and there and the first birds became visible; a toucan and some araçaris high above, a Kentucky Warbler down below, and with it and the Wood Thrushes on the rocky forest floor there was what I hoped for but never really believed I would see; an almost tail-less bright brown ball of a bird with black-tipped blue-grey feathers lying overlapped on its smoothly curved back, called a Scaled Antpitta, a very shy and reclusive bird.

Montezuma, the Aztec emperor murdered by the Spanish conquistador Hernán Cortés, was taking revenge on *me*, fellow European bastard. I was emptying my foul-smelling, uncontrollable bowels on a regular basis while searching the Usumacinta Marshes for Pinnated Bitterns and Bare-throated Tiger Herons, succeeding in the case of the former. Fork-tailed and Scissor-tailed Flycatchers adorned the low wire fences beside the highway which was busy with a long military convoy, presumably on its way between local politico-religious conflicts or to another Zapatista uprising. In the mad midday heat, with Montezuma's Revenge still on my mind, I saw an odd bird fly past me and lethargically tracked it down to a bush and was amazed to see a grey-brown and buff cuckoo with a black mask which could only be a Mangrove Cuckoo, a rather long way from any mangroves.

Then it was time to move on again, into the largely deforested Chiapas-Guatemala Highlands where the tree-lined ridges were sharp, the valleys deep and the short red-skinned people lived in wooden shacks topped with corrugated-iron sheets reflecting the strong sunlight. Some were selling maize at *topes*, man-made bumps in the roads designed to slow traffic down in the villages, to a standstill a cynic might argue, so that selling vegetables is easier. We had read warnings not to slow down too much because some *topes* make a bandit's life easy and we had also read there were plenty of them in Mexico. The road up to San Cristobal de las Casas was long and winding, not conducive to the sleep I needed, not that sleeping was possible for long because I had to leave the vehicle at regular intervals in order to empty my bowels of air and liquid. Blessed relief came only when we settled in the splendid blue and terracotta *Hotel el Cerrillo* where I lay in a double bed with lots of blankets to keep me from the mountain chill, with a toilet close by.

After no dinner and no beer and a good night's sleep I was feeling much better the next morning, especially after seeing my first Olive Warblers. The 'pine runners' have rich tawny-orange heads, throats and breasts, neat black masks, soft grey, slightly olive, backs, and two bold white wing bars. They are in a family of their own, the *Peucedramidae*, from the Greek *peuke* for pine and *dromos* for runner. The forested hills of San Cristobal were litter-strewn by the roadside, bird-strewn within. The Olive Warblers were in waves of dainty, boldly-marked and colourful New World Warblers which roamed the oaks and pines. Frequent flocks were dominated by lots of yellow-faced Hermit Warblers and black and yellow striped and streaked Townsend's Warblers, while in the largest flock, which we spent a long and very exciting time with, were my first Crescent-chested Warblers and, best of all, a Pink-headed Warbler, a strangely coloured and marked bird that is reddish brown above with faint rosy red wing bars and dark reddish below with a silvery pink head, neck and chest. We were lifting our binoculars all day long to look at the beautiful little birds which also included two Red-faced Warblers and a superb male Golden-cheeked Warbler. Curiously, there were few other birds, apart from a predator, a 'White-breasted' Sharp-shinned Hawk, and some striking Rufous-collared Thrushes.

I had lots of dreams again overnight, alas unremembered. Nick recalled one of his from a couple of nights ago when I was ill. I died, from dysentery, and he and the rest of the crew could not decide whether to carry on with the trip or not, and, if they did continue, on how to dispose of my body. They decided to go on, thinking, correctly, that that was what I would have wanted but, alas, the dream ended before the juicy bit, my disposal. San Cristobal was frosty and enshrouded in freezing fog first thing in the morning but glorious sunshine lit the hills above where once again there were warblers everywhere we looked, including two more new ones; a stunning Golden-browed Warbler with wide eyebrows glowing between a rich chestnut crown and face, and my first of the three *Oporornis* warblers on Plate 18 of that wonderful book *New World Warblers* so beautifully illustrated by David Quinn and David Beadle. It was a grey-headed and yellow-bellied MacGillivray's Warbler, named by American birdman John James Audubon after William MacGillivray, a Scottish friend of his who wrote a large part of Audubon's *Ornithological Biographies* published between 1827 and 1839 along with the classic *Birds of America*.

In the 1990s the Mexican government adopted neo-liberalism, switching the economy from the public sector to the private sector. This was not popular with economically marginalized indigenous groups, especially in the San Cristobal region. The local peoples' grievances were taken up by a small, revolutionary, leftist guerrilla group, led by a man known only as *Subcomandante Marcos* and known as the Zapatista Army of National Liberation. They declared war against the Mexican state and the conflict flares up now and again. With the Mexican army conspicuous in the region and rumours circulating about Zapatistas hiding out in and around the Cerro Huitepec Reserve we decided against birding there, relinquishing our only real chance of seeing the localized Blue-throated Motmot. Instead, we hit the busy, narrow, winding, dangerous mountain road to Tuxtla Gutiérrez. Numerous roadside shrines above almost vertical drop-offs marked where those who had pushed their luck or swerved to avoid someone else pushing theirs, had fallen to their deaths, but no one seemed to care, mad drivers just tore along as fast as they possibly could, thinking nothing of overtaking on blind bends, even the drivers of the long, big-nosed *Kenmex* trucks, some towing two petrol tanks. All very worrying when they were travelling in the same direction but nowhere near as scary as when they came hurtling around a bend from the opposite direction.

Had the Tuxtla Valley still been forested the scenery would have been a welcome distraction but it has been trashed by too many people. Then we saw Tuxtla Gutiérrez, a vast horrible low-rise messy sprawl of a city covering almost the entire width of the valley. A tiny scrap of forest remained in and around the Zoológico Miguél Álvarez del Toro, a small zoo named after one of Mexico's most distinguished ornithologists, where we *did* see a new motmot, the gorgeous Russet-crowned which was various shades of green with an almost orange crown. Good views revealed spiky metallic feathers below its eyes which were a deep, deep blue with a hint of lilac, and its shining blue tail was complete with perfect, black-tipped racquets. Running around the grounds of the zoo almost like chickens were Great Curassows and Highland Guans, normally very shy, wild forest birds but allegedly 'wild' there. They are good to eat and have been hunted almost to extinction in Mexico so it was great to get good views of such rare and retiring birds, wild or not.

On its way north from the Chiapas Highlands to the Gulf of Mexico the Rio Grijalva is carving a canyon called *El Sumidero* ('The Sump'). The road to it from Tuxtla took some finding but we still appeared to be the first along the El Roblar Mirador Trail because we flushed a female Great Curassow. We also saw our first two Rufous-capped Warblers but we didn't see most of what we were looking for, notably the highly localized Belted Flycatcher. The spectacular setting almost made up for the missing birds, for the narrow canyon's 3000 foot (900 metre) high terraced walls rise almost vertically from the river far, far below. Way, way above Black Vultures scored 9.8 for their synchronised flying displays on the thermals.

West and south we drove, down toward the Pacific through tree-dotted ranch land, reaching the coastal plain via a series of hairpin bends through a lovely wooded pass. At the coast it took a long time to find a Giant Wren in one of the thickets between the orchards and pastures. At over eight inches (20 cm) long it really is a giant, for a wren, with a bill to match, and it's a big bird with a tiny range, being endemic to a short stretch of the southern Mexican coast. It was very hot and we needed food and shelter, and beer. The sleepy one street town on the Pacific popular with *chiapanecas* and *chiapanecos*, girls and boys, from the whole state of Chiapas at weekends was called Puerto Arista. We settled on a small basic hotel within earshot of the Pacific rollers and ate a whole *Mojarra* each, fine fish washed down with cold *Corona*.

A coastal lagoon full of avocets, godwits, whimbrels, willets, sandpipers, stilts and yellowlegs was the perfect place to begin a new day. While a red moon fell below the Pacific a red sun rose above the mountains. Cormorants, egrets, herons, ibises, spoonbills and pelicans poured in along the river from their roosts, flying low over our heads before landing in the lagoon where there were already plenty. Belted and Green Kingfishers perched prominently in the lovely low light. A Reddish Egret 'danced' after fish alongside more sedate Snowy Egrets, their aigrettes bouncing as they appeared to walk on water across the shallows. Six Magnificent Frigatebirds sailed around overhead. There may have been no tiger herons but it was still great to be alive on planet Earth.

When the sun was high in the sky we moved on, to the thorn woods on the Tapanatepec Foothills where a male Orange-breasted Bunting blew us away with its beauty. The bird, the size of a sparrow, is bright shiny blue above apart from a mossy green crown and upper back, and deep, deep yellow below going on golden-orange on the chest. After a long hot search we saw one of its sister species, another of Mexico's endemic wonders, a bird as, if not even more, beautiful, a virtually all blue bird, a blue I had never seen before, not even in a Cézanne, a shocking electric blue perhaps, across the whole bird except for the white eye crescents and its lower belly which was not pink as the books say but a lovely lilac colour. The bird is called a Rose-bellied or Rosita's Bunting, Rosita being the wife of Adrien Jean Louis François de Sumichrast, a Swiss naturalist who when he discovered the male bird named it after his wife because they were the two most beautiful creatures he had ever seen. The Rosita's Bunting we were watching was soon joined by an Orange-breasted Bunting and two of the most beautiful birds in the world were perched side by side in the same fantastic field of view.

Back on new and smooth tarmac we had to negotiate several military checkpoints. The soldiers were after drug and gun runners not bird runners and were very friendly once they realized we were on our way to Tehuantepec to look for Adrien Sumichrast's Sparrows, another Mexican endemic although rather more sombre than the three male Orange-breasted Buntings also present in the litter-strewn roadside scrub. We left there at 17:00 hours hoping to make the city of Oaxaca (pronounced O-tha-ca or, if you prefer, Wa-haka!) not too long after dark but even with The Colonel at the wheel, upping the pace a little, chasing the light and terrifying Simon, it took three and a half hours to negotiate the busy road which wound through convoluted hills covered in scrub and more and more cacti, and it had been dark for a long time before we reached the rather grand, for us, *Hotel las Rosas.*

We had just four hours sleep but free coffee first thing meant we were ready as ever for our first full day on the flanks of Cerro San Felipe which rises over 10,000 feet (3000 metres) not far east of Oaxaca. After reading about the bird-filled thorn scrub and pine-oak forests so many times at home it was great to be there at last and even though we struggled to find many birds in the scrub we did see the one I most hoped to see, an odd-coloured but terrific little bird with a lime green crown, soft grey face, back and underparts, striking white eyes and bright lime-coloured wings and tail, called a Slaty, not a more appropriate 'Limey', Vireo. Higher up in the forest there were plenty of birds, mainly multicoloured and patterned little warblers again although they now included our first Red Warblers, all amazing red except for white sides to their faces. Everyone except me saw the rare endemic, Dwarf Jay, at one of the few known locations on Earth, but none of us saw any Bumblebee Hummingbirds, Aztec Thrushes or Chestnut-sided Shrike Vireos so we were pleased we had planned a second day on the mountain, although we failed to find all three again, *and* the jay. I could live without the jay and we had another chance to see the rest so we decided to move on.

First stop the next day was the scrub-covered slopes below the ruins of the ancient Zapotec city of Monte Alban where I saw my first Virginia's Warbler, not the most striking New World Warbler being almost all grey-brown but no less fascinating close up when I could see white rings around the large dark eyes and subtle shades of yellow on the chest and at the base of the tail. It was followed by my best view yet of a male Black-throated Grey Warbler, the tiny yellow tufts of feathers in front of the eyes visible at last, and also present was an impressive Boucard's Wren, which replaces the Cactus Wren in southwest Mexico, two Blue Mockingbirds and two male Ocellated Thrashers, good to look at but better to listen to, their song being a rich and varied jerky warble.

It was a terrific start to an otherwise torrid day during which it took twelve hours to travel 330 miles (530 km) from Oaxaca to Toluca, 40 miles (64 km) west of Mexico City, a long way short of our intended destination, Angangueo. The journey was smooth to begin with, on a quiet toll road through red-rock canyons and desert with tall Saguaros. Then we reached the outskirts of a place where a wandering tribe called the Aztecs settled during the 13th Century. During the next 200 years they built a city called Tenochtitlan and a mighty empire of some twelve million people who believed that they lived in the world of the 'Fifth Sun' and that one day that world would be destroyed. To postpone the end of their world they fed their gods daily, with 'chalchiuhuatl', a precious form of 'nectar' found in human blood. To provide a continual flow of 'nectar' warriors wearing jaguar pelts and eagle feathers constantly attacked neighbouring tribes, enabling priests to sacrifice up to a thousand people a week, and

20,000 a day after major battles. This all came to an end when the Spanish conquistadors, possessed with a hunger for gold, silver and land, arrived at the beginning of the 16th Century. When the Aztec emperor Montezuma met Hernán Cortés in 1519 he thought Cortés was the Aztec feathered serpent god of wind and learning, Quetzalcoatl, and welcomed him with gifts, but Cortés took Montezuma prisoner and slaughtered hundreds of the Aztec nobility. Those left organized a revolt but were defeated, Montezuma was killed and many of the rest of the Aztecs were killed or tortured or put to work in gold mines, and Tenochtitlan was destroyed to make way for what is known today as Mexico City. By 2005 the Mexican capital was one of the world's largest and most overcrowded metropolises with about 20 million human beings crammed into a shallow high altitude valley ringed by mountains and volcanoes where the pollution from their homes, vehicles and work places disperses so slowly they have to live in air contaminated with a cocktail of carbon monoxide, nitrogen dioxide, sulphur dioxide, suspended particles and ozone, causing headaches, sore eyes, breathlessness, lethargy and insomnia. The so-called savages of Tenochtitlan, Chichen Itza and so on lived in beautiful cities surrounded by forest. The so-called civilized inhabitants of Mexico and numerous other cities across the world today live in the complete ugly opposite where even the air is not fit to breathe.

With the car population approaching five million Mexico City had a *Hoy No Circula* policy (today [your car] does not circulate) in 2005, an attempt to cut down on smog, as well as the unbelievable traffic. Cars were prohibited from within the city limits on certain days of the week according to the last digit of the license plate. I was alone in suggesting we avoid the place like the plague but oh no the rest insisted we stick to the main roads and save a few miles. So, after checking and double-checking our license plate was good for a Thursday, in we went, like sitting ducks. Minutes later a policeman on a motorbike waved us over. He said the days that we were allowed inside the city had changed, that we would have to pay a 5000 peso fine (£65 British pounds each), and then take the car to a police station until the next day. We said we would turn around and leave, "Pronto!" He walked off, talked to colleague, came back and said if we paid him 3000 pesos (£40 each) there and then he would escort us out of the city. *Still* in the city, our escort and extortionist swept away down a side street leaving us on a main road, and not long after we were pulled over at the next police roadblock. After a lengthy debate - we had no proof of what we had paid - two policemen accepted our story and allowed us to proceed. We were still in the Federal District though and there were police everywhere so a very stressful couple of hours followed as we tried to navigate our way through the traffic and endless unsigned suburbs of the vast sprawl of Mexico City, so desperate to avoid being stopped again that The Colonel drove as close as he could to the back of any truck he could find in the hope that none of the numerous police would be able to see the car's plates.

Seeing a sign, at last, that said we were leaving the city limits, was as joyful a moment as seeing any rare foreign bird but the relief was brief because all roads seemed to lead back into the dreaded hell we had just escaped from. Then we saw Xinantecatl, the massive 15,000 foot (4500 metres) high, snow-capped extinct volcano, rising above the smog, then a sign for Toluca which meant that we were definitely heading out of Mexico City, never to return.

We left Toluca one minute behind schedule at 06:01 when the temperature was 2°C. It fell to zero before we climbed to Angangueo and the Santuario de la Mariposa Monarca el Rosario, the sanctuary of Monarch butterflies which we were the first to enter when it opened at 09:00, and to climb the numerous steps, hard going at 10,000 feet (3000 metres). Forty minutes later, having seen just one Monarch, we were standing under the roosting trees which looked like they were made out of Monarchs, so many were there covering them. Thirteen million we were told, in an area the size of a few football pitches, clinging, several deep, to the needles on the drooping boughs of Oyamel Firs. Even some trunks were sprinkled with them and in places dead ones formed a layer of 'butterfly litter' on the forest floor. It was an unbelievable sight, even before the first rays of the morning sun began to penetrate the forest and strike the boughs of butterflies. Slowly, their wings began to vibrate then they took to the air, singly at first then in small groups of five to ten, then in great swathes. The masses of Monarchs swooped out to glide between the trees and soon the forest was thick with them, thousands of them, then ten thousands, then hundreds of thousands, so many we could hear the quiet murmur of millions of fluttering wings amongst the trees.

The golden butterflies, the size of the palms of my hands, were heading out of the forest to the flowers in the sunlit valleys below, so I stood in one of the flyways and watched in awe as an endless stream of black and gold wings jinked slowly past me, some below my knees, some by my waist and many past my face, almost touching me.

Come the northern spring the Monarchs will head out of the trees and migrate north. Some might go as far as Texas before laying their eggs on Milkweed plants. The caterpillars will feed on these plants and pupate and emerge as new adults and continue north. The next generation then carries on northwards and so forth until, toward the end of the northern summer, in September and October, millions of new adult Monarchs will migrate south from Canada and the United States. Those to the west of the Rocky Mountains don't go far, mostly to California, but virtually all the Monarchs to the east of the Rockies - 250 to 600 million of them - fly up to 3000 miles (4800 km) to a few mountain fir forests in the Central Highlands of Mexico where they arrive around November, eight months and about five generations after leaving. No one knows how the genetic material presumably vital for navigation is passed from generation to generation during metamorphosis when most of the tissues and cells of a caterpillar are broken down inside the pupa before being reformed as an adult. It simply beggars belief how they do it, as did the sight of them in that Mexican forest.

From Angangueo it was 400 miles (640 km) and ten more hours on the road, to Colima, mostly along a virtually empty *autopista*. Next morning we managed to get the hire-car ten miles (16 km) up a rough, rocky, rutted track on the slopes of the smouldering, glowing cone of Volcán de Fuego. Steam rose from around the rim a couple of ridges away, smoke out of the vent, one side of which glowed pale red from the heat inside, and the leaves around us were covered in a fine layer of volcanic ash. According to the only other people we saw all day, some volcanologists heading to the top, the 'Volcano of Fire' was the most active volcano in Mexico and exploded, on average, ten times a day. They did add that we were almost certainly safe to continue looking for Aztec Thrushes, Chestnut-sided Shrike Vireos and so on, so, reassured that we were far enough away to make our escape should there be an eruption followed by lava flows and waves of hot ash, we carried on climbing, on foot, for a couple of hours. We saw very little apart from some speedy hummingbirds which, as had been the case most of the trip, whizzed past us without stopping, until, at last, there was a male Magnificent Hummingbird head-on, its green gorget glowing. My first Colima Warbler was less sensational; a drab grey-brown bird and skulker to boot but at least I had finally seen one after somehow not seeing one in Texas nearly twenty years before. Higher up, the track levelled out, affording brilliant eye-level views of a huge, busy foraging flock of warblers which looked especially beautiful in the low late afternoon light, particularly two Red-faced Warblers, and with more wonder like Red Warblers was my first Grace's Warbler, a lovely, delicate, black-streaked, blue-grey and white bird with yellow eyebrows and throat.

Our second day on the volcano began with stunning views of some Grey Silkies. We had seen a few before, at Cerro San Felipe, but they were distant and like many things in life they were something else altogether when seen close-up. The males were particularly attractive with their blue-grey heads, chests and backs, short grey crests, white eye-crescents, ochre-yellow lower bellies and long slender tails, all softly and sleekly feathered like their close relatives the waxwings. After watching a cracking black, white and red Painted Whitestart we yomped up to where all the action was the day before and in the beautiful, tall pine-oak forest I was very happy watching the same species as the day before when I noticed two different birds high up under the canopy. It took a long time to get a decent view of the shy and retiring birds but with patience and persistence, two virtues birders need to be very friendly with, I worked out that the mottled dark brown and white birds were Aztec Thrushes. Simon also managed to see them but the view of the birds, far above and from below, was poor, and so a longed-for moment became a very frustrating experience. Nick and The Colonel missed them altogether. They were higher up the volcano watching, of all things, a Chestnut-sided Shrike Vireo, but when we reached them it had gone and they said they would gladly swop it for the thrush. So, a committee meeting was convened under the great plume of ash billowing out of Volcán de Fuego and the motion carried to return to the fire for a third day.

The decision paid off. By mid-morning I was watching a pair of Chestnut-sided Shrike Vireos. They were in a huge varied flock of birds foraging at eye-level along the opposite side of a narrow oaky canyon, looking for insects low down, almost at ground level. I had not seen birds like them before. They were about the size of a small thrush with a very large head and powerful hooked bill. The brighter male has a blue-grey crown extending down the back of the neck and merging smoothly with the green to golden-green back and wings, wide, bright lemon eyebrows, white eyes in a narrow black mask, black whiskers, and a narrow chestnut breast band spreading and

*Chestnut-sided Shrike-Vireo, Volcan de Fuego, Mexico,*
*31ˢᵗ January 2005*

broadening along the white flanks. Endemic to the highlands of southern Mexico and Guatemala which we would be leaving the next day it was very relaxing for me to see that dream bird so early and to not have to fret about it for the rest of the day, so I enjoyed my last walk up the volcano immensely and especially two Russet Nightingale Thrushes, a stunning black and yellow male Dickey's Oriole, and Olive and sixteen species of New World Warbler including Red and Red-faced. It was all so relaxing I even found time to lie down on my back and rest my weary legs while looking up at the lofty canopy and blue sky, and, after a croaking Raven had sailed over, even slip into a pleasurable semi-snooze with the sun shining on my face and a light breeze. Refreshed, I reached the highest point I managed to climb up to, where Nick had found a fruiting tree full of White-throated Thrushes and with them was a pair of Aztec Thrushes. The female was a disappointingly dull and lifeless bird perched on a bunch of white berries but the male was more active and attractive, with the bright black and white wings we had dreamed of laying our eyes on for so long.

The next morning we went looking for Red-breasted Chats, actually New World Warblers, on a scrub-covered hill known as La Cumbre, and we saw one but alas it was dowdy female not a brilliant male. We also saw a Lucy's Warbler, one we expected to be rather dull but which turned out to be a little bit brilliant thanks to its silvery grey plumage and the scarlet glitter on its crown. It was disappointing to find hardly any water at the Manzanillo Marshes, leaving us little chance of finally getting to see a Bare-throated Tiger Heron, and we ended the day walking down the quiet cobbled road through thorn forest to the beach at Playa de Oro seeing very little. Between times however, there were two lovely smoky grey Heermann's Gulls in Manzanillo Harbour, Mexico's main Pacific coast port, where we tracked down a boat and negotiated what seemed a fair price for a pelagic trip the next day.

Our boat for the morning was the sport-fishing lancha *MV Nereida* captained by Miguel Fregoso. After leaving port on schedule at 7 a.m. we motored steadily across smooth water for two hours to *Piedra Blanca*, a huge guano-splattered rock sticking out of the Pacific, where amongst the massed ranks of Brown Boobies I saw an odd one out and yelled, "Hey, that booby's got blue feet!" and sure enough there was a Blue-footed Booby, a new bird I was not expecting to see. What I was expecting to see were my first Red-billed Tropicbirds and there was no problem with that because about thirty of them were commuting to and from their nesting crevices, their white streamer tails making them look so elegant, and their black masks and deep red bills so handsome. They were struggling to land due to the pirates, the much larger Magnificent Frigatebirds, that were after the food the tropicbirds had in their gullets, but most made it in safely and got to feed the next generation of beauty. I was more than happy to celebrate with a rare long lunch of superb seafood soup overlooking the Laguna de Barra de Navidad where we were shocked to see another Blue-footed Booby fly past before a Royal Tern caught a fish and was immediately pursued by a frigatebird which stooped from on high. The tern flew about like crazy in an attempt to avoid giving up its catch and the pair nearly ended up in the restaurant with us before zooming off and out of sight.

When the heat of the day began to subside we headed to the Barranca el Choncho, a short canyon that cuts through the coastal hills with a narrow tongue of forest in it. There, a pretty Fan-tailed Warbler became the 44th New World Warbler I had seen in 20 days and the final one of the 18 new ones I had hoped to see on the trip. Its long, white-tipped, slate-grey tail was constantly fanned as it foraged on or near the rocky ground close enough to see the glowing orange-yellow throat and breast. The barranca was alive with birds, including five bright blue and black San Blas Jays in a bare fruiting tree, two Tropical Parulas, dusky Red-crowned Ant Tanagers and two more splashes of colour called Painted Buntings. I also saw a Coati

Mundi, a male with a long, bushy, banded tail held straight up, and a long, slender brown body led by a long mobile snout.

El Choncho did not give up all of its treasures though, so with one day left on our lightning three and a half thousand mile (5600 km) tour of Mexico we were back at dawn. However, it was not until the afternoon that we saw our first Citreoline Trogon, a superb male with a dark grey head and breast, golden green back and bright lemon yellow (citreoline) belly. Rosy Thrush Tanager and a male Red-breasted Chat remained good reasons for another trip. This one had been fantastic enough and all the merrier for not being 'organized' like my previous two trips, to Gabon and Peru. So, after a couple of *Pacifico* beers we went mad and celebrated another wonderful time hunting down and seeing so many new, exciting and beautiful birds in new terrain with a lobster each, in our favourite breezy outdoor restaurant overlooking the Laguna de Barra de Navidad, and carried on drinking until the *Tequila* ran out.

I don't remember returning to the *Hotel Caribe*. I do remember waking up the next morning when the alarm went off but being unable to move. It went off twice more before I managed to get to my feet and then only because Nick and Simon were banging on the door. I let them in and invited them to wake up The Colonel who was still asleep on top of his bed, in the foetal position, fully-clothed. There were still birds to see but we didn't see them along the Playa de Oro Road before heading north, and rain put paid to any hopes of seeing Military Macaws at El Tuito so we pushed on to Puerto Vallarta.

The next day we began the long drag home. From 35,000 feet (10,670 metres) up in the air I could see the rectangular fields of the mid-eastern United States of America stretching all the way to the horizon. American Airlines 580 was full of loud, grumpy, ugly Americans who never said please or thank you. How handsome and pretty those Indians were, who used to live down there, with such freedom and joy. How wild, rich and vibrant the land they lived happily on was. How empty and sad it looked to me that day. As we approached Chicago that night I counted 35 lines of blinding lights, along the main routes radiating out from the shore of Lake Michigan, with millions more in between. In the words of Neil Young from his song *Pocahontas*, 'Paddles cut the water, In a long and hurried flight, From the white man. They killed us in our teepees, And they cut our women down, They might have left some babies, Cryin' on the ground ... They massacred the buffalo ...', and all so the white man could live his miserable life cooped up in a '... little box at the top of the stairs.'

Too many people have wrecked much of Mexico as well, but where some relatively untouched habitats remained, especially the swathes of oak and pine forests on the hazy blue hills and smoking volcanoes, there still lived lots of beautiful birds, and in one place, millions of Monarch butterflies, which, when in flight, formed one of the finest spectacles imaginable, even on planet Earth where there are still so many. That is what I remembered the most when we were out over the Atlantic.

A MIND-BLOWING BIRDING TRIP TO A PLANET CALLED EARTH

*Shoebill, Lake Albert-Nile Delta, Murchison Falls National Park, Uganda, 5th December 2005*

## 18

## KENYA, UGANDA and TANZANIA

In May I met Alice. In July we fell in love. Birding can be thrilling and wondrous but rarely is it as extreme, exciting, stirring and joyful as falling in love with someone falling in love with you. In November we flew to Kenya, for Alice wanted to go on an adventure. She said she had always dreamed of going to Africa. I said, "Let's go then."

We arrived late on a Saturday night. Maurice, from the *Orchid Hotel*, met us with the words, "You need to leave Nairobi as soon as possible. On Monday Kenya is going to be having a referendum and some people have already died."

So, Sunday morning, Maurice took us to a crazy busy open-air bus station where Alice stood aghast, trying to take in her first experience of Africa while I helped lash our rucksacks to the roof of a small bus. There were an awful lot of people crowded around numerous buses and minibuses called *matatus*, seemingly parked at random amongst the masses, and many of the people were not trying to get on a bus or a *matatu*, they were hawking their wares or up to no good. Alice had never seen anything like it. I had, but not for some time, so I tried my best to look and act confident and in control, like we had caught a bus in Nairobi a million times before. Once on the move a preacher stood up at the front of the crowded bus and shouted at everyone until we reached a checkpoint where a policeman got on and began walking down the aisle. Every passenger scrambled to put their seatbelts on but Alice's wouldn't work and by the time she struggled to clip it together everyone around us, including the policeman, were staring at her. Once the belt worked the policeman seemed satisfied that the bus was safe and allowed it to carry on to Naivasha.

One fine day seventeen years before, I saw 175 different species of bird by Lake Naivasha on foot, a phenomenal total for such a small area, even in the African bush. I spent two weeks covering more or less the same ground on walks from Naivasha town and saw 235 species in all. One morning I walked into an acacia glade and almost bumped into three Giraffes. Agatha Christie was right when she wrote, 'Never go back to a place where you have been happy. Until you do it remains alive for you. If you go back it will be destroyed'. There was no chance of seeing any Giraffes or anywhere near as many birds this time around, for instead of a wide belt of acacias and small fields the lakeside was lined with monstrous greenhouses as big as factories. Inside them were some of the 150,000 migrant workers attracted to the area where not long ago less than 10,000 people lived. They earned a pittance producing cheap flowers for the European market, and beside the giant domes of plastic were the hovels in the unplanned shanty towns they lived in. There was no proper waste control so their shit flowed into the lake, along with the toxic pesticides used to produce perfect flowers, and the once clear waters of Lake Naivasha, teeming with birds and other wildlife, had turned a quiet, murky brown, not that there was much water left, because one rose needs seven to thirteen litres of water to grow. And all so Europeans who have lost touch with nature can put the beauty of nature inside their houses, when so much lies outside, and brighten up their dull lives with dying flowers. I saw the horror from the window of a *matatu* speeding along the track to *Fisherman's Camp*, where Chief, The Stid, Tim and I pitched our tents in paradise all those years ago.

Alice was still dazed and confused, not to mention scared out of her wits, when we leapt off the *matatu* but all her cares, and mine, mainly about her, were blown gently away as we strolled down into the lush lakeside campsite, still, I was so glad to see, shaded by giant yellow-barked Fever Trees. A tiny metallic green and yellow Variable Sunbird dashed past us, fearless, iridescent blue and green Superb Starlings waddled over the grass, and on the way to our pitch a flock of African Hoopoes flitted out of our way. Once the tent was up we wandered through the extensive campsite grounds, marvelling at many birds, not least a beautiful Lilac-breasted Roller and a colourful flock of green and orange Fischer's Lovebirds, and we stopped to watch the foraging antics of a troop of small grey Vervet Monkeys. At the lake there were many more birds, from tiny Black Crakes with yellow bills and red legs to huge Great White Pelicans. Yelping African Fish Eagles soared above hovering Pied Kingfishers and the only thing scaring Alice now was the first Hippo she saw. It was almost totally submerged in vegetation about twenty paces from the boardwalk and it was so still Alice thought it might be dead, until it rolled over to remove an African Jacana from its head.

At night the Hippos leave the lake to graze the grass in the campsite and when I was last there we had to be very careful getting into the tents at night and wait for the Hippos to return to the lake before getting out of them in the morning. Since then an electric fence had been installed, to keep the Hippo's pastures separate from the campers. They may look slightly amusing but Hippos are massive, aggressive and surprisingly nimble, with a giant mouth and teeth like tusks, and they kill more people in Africa every year than any other wild animal; hundreds of people. A mother will fight anything that comes between her and her calf, and all adults will attack most things between them and water, where they feel safe. No one should take a chance with Hippos but eight months before we arrived at *Fisherman's Camp* an Australian tourist, a mother of two, climbed over the electric fence to get a closer look at a Hippo in the dark and ended up dead. The regional police chief was quoted as saying, "The hippo attacked the woman, flipping her into the air before tossing her on the ground and trampling her."

It was nice to bed down for the night knowing we need not worry about them, even though we could hear some munching away a few paces from our tent. There was not much chance of any sleep though, for the sounds of the African night were not the braying of zebras, the laughs of hyaenas or the hoots of owls but vehicles, voices and thumping bass till three o'clock in the morning.

It was not what Alice had dreamed of for so long. Nor was the local 'village', where we walked along a busy, litter-strewn, pot-holed track past streets of basic shacks where the flower pickers slept, looking for the local shop where we stocked up on water and biscuits. A long afternoon stroll around the campsite was more like it, watching the numerous, mostly spectacular, birds, like a dazzling blue and orange Malachite Kingfisher. There were so many birds Alice was having trouble remembering their names but she was spot-on when she said the 'Megakite Kingfisher' had a wrapping-paper head; the bird was so close she could see its long, shiny blue-green crest feathers barred with black. Near our tent was a troop of lovely Black-and-white Colobus Monkeys, black with white brows and beards, silky white shawls and frilly white tail tufts, one of which was dozing on its back with its legs in the air, on a horizontal branch high above.

At dawn the next day we climbed on to our hired bicycles and were at Hell's Gate National Park, a few miles away, by seven. The reason we were allowed to cycle through Hell's Gate was because there were no Lions but we were somewhat surprised the park authorities considered it safe for us to ride past herds of Buffalos, not far behind Hippos on the list of the most dangerous large animals on the continent. They may look like big cows but Buffalos, especially lone males, are highly unpredictable and quite capable of killing just about anything, including Lions. We frequently made sure they were at what we considered to be a safe distance, about a mile, as we made our way slowly through the grassy plain below the vertical red crags of the wide gorge where rabbit-like Rock Hyraxes and Rüppell's Vultures lived. A Giraffe looked down at us from the top of the cliffs and two more, a mother and a calf, were amongst the bushes below. Plenty of 'Tommies' (Thomson's Gazelles) and Zebras were grazing the land where people were not allowed to live. We saw some Warthogs trotting in line with their skinny tufted tails held erect behind them, and small herds of tan-coloured Coke's Hartebeests or Kongonis, large antelopes that had high eyes and long faces which made them appear as if they were looking down their noses at us, in more ways than one. In amongst the animals were Ostriches and with them a Kori Bustard, while lots of green and red White-fronted Bee-eaters hunted from large stones strewn across the ground with other rocks being used as lookouts by black and white Schalow's Wheatears and brownish-black Anteater Chats. Perched on a larger more distant rock and reluctant to leave its prey was a Verreaux's Eagle, one of the largest eagles in the world, looking all black except for a bit of white on its back.

*Fisherman's Camp* was so lovely we stayed another day then it was dawn at Lake Naivasha dusk at Lake Baringo. We took a *matatu* to Naivasha town then got into another, which was full of people dressed head to toe in pure white. They were *vaPostori*, or Apostles in Shona, from the Gospel of God Church. Nearly a hundred miles later we were in Nakuru where we waited a long time in the high heat of the day for the next *matatu* to fill up with people and provisions. From there it was three hours north along the mainly flat and dusty, overfarmed and overgrazed, Great Rift Valley floor, to *Roberts Camp* on the shore of Lake Baringo where we were the only campers. There were two other visitors, an elderly German couple looking for dragonflies, but they were staying in one of the cottages.

We had just enough time to see a few birdies before dusk, and some Hippos, none of which prevented us from retiring safely to the tent where the number of mosquitoes was lower than outside but the heat and humidity higher, and so we baked and sweated for nine fitful hours before it was light. There was no electric Hippo fence at *Roberts Camp* and we heard a few in the night, which was surprising considering the parched campsite grounds were mostly composed of rock and dust, not the favourite food of voracious herbivores, or the perfect mattress.

A new day began the best possible way, with bee-eaters, Blue-cheeked ones by the lakeside. In the well-watered green grounds of the grand *Lake Baringo Club* next to the campsite we saw some superb Red-and-yellow Barbets, the bird, of the hundreds possible, chosen to adorn the cover of our *Field Guide to the Birds of East Africa*, probably because they are so colourful and striking with their red bills, reddish faces, orange-yellow underparts and brownish-black upperparts dotted with numerous neat round white spots, well over a hundred of them not including the long spotted tail. Back in the campsite we checked out the garden of a large pyramid-shaped wooden house named after the Hamerkop, an all-brown heron-like bird with a hammer-shaped head which builds a giant pyramid-shaped nest strong enough for a man or woman to stand on. In the garden we were very excited to see a white African Paradise Flycatcher with a black crest, head and throat, and an extremely long streamer-like tail. A fine lunch was taken alfresco at the *The Thirsty Goat*, the campsite cafe, where, in a magic fruiting bush next to us, appeared a procession of lovely birds; a black and white Red-fronted Barbet, a female Black Cuckooshrike, that is a very delicately marked olive and yellowish-white bird with dusky crescents all over and has beautiful bright yellow trims to the wing feathers, a Violet-backed Sunbird with a metallic dark blue tail, a yellow Icterine Warbler, and a normally shy but shocking Sulphur-breasted Bushshrike, pale grey and green above with an intense yellow forehead and underparts which glowed orange across the breast.

When I was last at Baringo I spent a very hot day with a hangover failing to find a Heuglin's Courser, a small cryptically camouflaged crepuscular bird which hides in the shade during the harsh sunshine of daylight hours. Nearly two decades later I decided to engage the help of local birders Joseph and Wilson from the village of Kampi ya Samaki just across the way, in order to try and see said courser. They led us into the thorn scrub alongside the lake and after about ten minutes Wilson pointed at the ground several paces in front of us. Neither Alice nor I could see anything resembling a bird then, like a *Magic Eye* picture, it came into focus. A Heuglin's Courser had turned to face us when it detected our presence and froze, relying on its superb camouflage to hide, even when we were so close. Hardly able to believe it was there and that it seemed happy to allow us to approach even closer we crouched down to look at the beauty at eye-level on the ground and from just a few paces away we could examine it feather by feather. The bird had more neckwear than Alice; below its whitish throat was a chestnut pendant, below that a broad buffy necklace with vertical black streaks, then a narrow black necklace, a broader whitish one and, finally, another, narrow chestnut necklace. Together with a striking head pattern and buff-fringed dark brown upperpart feathers it almost matched its background perfectly and refused to move even when we shuffled a little closer and settled down to enjoy an all too rare moment in the company of a rarely-seen bird. We also saw two tall Spotted Thick-knees and a colourful Yellow-winged Bat, and all the while European Bee-eaters called and dashed through the hot air overhead to complete a truly memorable day.

The next morning Alice did not stop talking for two hours after she said she would stop talking. The fear, the wonder, the sheer excitement of being in Africa for the first time, was all too much. Like me she was so happy to be there, together, and all her emotions poured out of her. We were still beaming at the end of the day when once again we were the only customers at *The Thirsty Goat* where, on arrival, there was one large round table laid with silver cutlery on a pure white cloth, just for us, and unlike the night before we were able to enjoy a delicious meal at our leisure without having to beat a hasty retreat, because there was enough of a breeze to keep the mosquitoes at bay and us relatively cool as we also wrote up the day's events. It had been a lazier day, at Alice's request, eating a slow breakfast and a long lunch, between swimming and showering and a bit of birding, enough to wallow in the wonder of a pair of Klaas's Cuckoos, the male iridescent dark green above and snow white below, the female bronze-brown above with green bars and white below with fine russet bars, as well as black and white Jackson's Hornbills, the male orange-billed the female black-billed, Grey-headed Kingfishers with deep chestnut bellies and stunning, bright cobalt-blue wings and tails, gorgeous, sleek green Blue-cheeked Bee-eaters, and Lilac-breasted Rollers, Red-and-yellow Barbets and Superb Starlings.

It was a wrench to leave Lake Baringo, as it was Lake Naivasha, but, as usual, time and money determined the pace of travel so we were soon in a *matatu* on our way to the market town of Marigat. One of the passengers, a man called Rane who said he was a detective with the Kenya Police Service (KPS), offered us a lift from Marigat, where he had a vehicle waiting, to Eldoret. I accepted his offer all too readily and soon began to agonise over my hastiness, especially while we waited to be picked up. I was thinking most people are good, especially poor people who use *matatus*. Bad people, intent on robbing tourists don't target *matatus* because tourists don't use them. However, I seriously questioned if detectives with the KPS travelled in *matatus*. When Rane turned up he was alone, which was a relief because another thought racing around my mind, apart from him not being a policeman and having a gun or another weapon, was what if there were two or three other men with him, enough to overpower us, rob us and do what I tried not to think about to Alice. Then we were off, along smooth tarmac, up and over the Tugen Hills and down into the Kerio Valley then up again, up and up the western side of the Great Rift Valley, a massive ragged wall of rock, and there was no trouble, only a very friendly guy at the wheel who was presumably glad of the company on a long drive. In fact, Rane was such a good man that when we got to Eldoret he took us to the bus station and helped us buy our tickets for the night bus to Uganda.

We had a long wait at Akamba bus station, into the night when, with only a few other people about, we attracted the attention of a couple of very shady characters, two young men chewing *miraa*, also known as *khat*, which suppresses hunger and increases excitement. They appeared to be eyeing us and our rucksacks up and down for some time and even after I deliberately started up a conversation with them to relieve some tension I felt very uncomfortable in their presence. They seemed to know that the bus we were waiting for was always late and we thought they might be waiting until we were the only people left at the bus station before they tried to rob us so I readied myself and released the blade of the *Swiss Army Knife* in my pocket. The bus was due to arrive from Nairobi at one o'clock in the morning. That came and went and most of the few other people around went as well, and it was a long anxious hour and a half before that bus pulled in and it felt so good to look at them out of the window of that bus and to be on our way again, on the road in the African night, so good we were soon sound asleep.

We awoke to the shout of, "Immigration!" After our passports had been stamped we had to walk across the eerie no man's land between Kenya and Uganda while lightning blazed constantly in the Ugandan sky. In Kampala a few hours later we got into a taxi driven by a crazy man called Iga who after knocking someone off a moped dropped us off at *Red Chilli Hideaway*. Ragged, hot, dusty, filthy, longing for a bed, we were unable to resist the offer of a cheap bungalow instead of another night in the tent. One day, we hoped, we might live in such a spacious place back home but the garden wildlife would not include Vervet Monkeys, fruit bats and such fabulous birds as the deep purple Ross's Turacos with short, flicking, flashing crimson wings, the 'garden pigeons' confiding enough when perched to see the individual crimson bristles of their mad *Mohicans*, or Black-headed Gonoleks, the 'garden thrushes', actually bushshrikes jet satin black above with cream-coloured eyes and deep scarlet below, or the 'garden starlings', that in Kampala's case are brilliant glossy green, blue and purple Splendid Starlings.

Staff at the Ugandan Wildlife Authority (UWA) assured us it was safe to visit Murchison Falls National Park even though Steve Willis, who with his wife Debbie set up the *Red Chilli Hideaway* we were staying at, was murdered in the park three weeks before we arrived. He went to help four people who were attempting to be the first to ascend the River Nile by raft but had got stuck at a set of rapids. As they all left the river in his *Land Rover* two Lord's Resistance Army (LRA) fighters opened fire on the vehicle and Steve was killed. The other three in the vehicle ran into the bush to hide but one could not escape because of his injuries and he was brought back to the vehicle as the fighters looted it then set it alight. He thought he was going to be shot but he was left alive and eventually rescued, with the others.

The LRA had been waging a war in northern Uganda and southern Sudan for nigh on twenty years. Why, nobody seemed to know. The mysterious leader, self-declared prophet Joseph Kony, may have set out to cleanse the Acholi people, using biblical references to explain why he killed what were his own people, or perhaps he and his senior commanders liked their lifestyle which included taking the pick of the girls they captured. Most of the 20,000 children they had abducted so far were used as expendable troops and often sent into battle without weapons. Many were even forced to kill their own parents, leaving them with little reason to leave the LRA. The ongoing presence of the murderous bastards meant that the UK Government Foreign Office advised against travelling to northern Uganda but we were convinced by the UWA and more importantly the staff at *Red Chilli Hideaway* that Steve's killers were rogue fighters operating way beyond the normal area of LRA influence so, also encouraged by the likelihood of security in the park being stepped up, we agreed to carry on as planned.

Murchison Falls National Park was a tricky place to get to on public transport, there being none beyond Masindi, over 50 miles (80 km) to the south, and even that place was only accessible on the post bus, the view from which was, initially, of a verdant green, leafy country, albeit heavily populated. Farther north the road reached increasingly arid bush overgrazed by long-horned *Ankole* cattle. The bus was so popular with the Ugandans two large ladies and another with a baby wiggled their bottoms down to the floor and wedged their bodies into the aisle where they looked far more comfortable than we were on our tiny, hard, bouncy seats with virtually no leg room. At Masindi we headed straight to the UWA office where Thomas advised us to hire a taxi to get to Murchison, for a ridiculous price of 120,000 *shilingi*, soon reduced to 80,000 when he saw how high my eyebrows were raised. They were still half way up my forehead a few moments later, 80,000 being well above our budget, when he said, "Or ..." and proceeded to explain that we could wait until the next day when we might be able to travel in a park vehicle free of charge. So, the long wait began, in a banda barely big enough to swing a sparrow in at the *New Court View Hotel*.

Next morning we were told to return to the UWA office at noon for an update. At noon we were told the vehicle would leave at 2 p.m. so we took lunch in the large *Masindi Hotel* where the only guests appeared to be Piapiacs, all-black magpie-like members of the crow family. At 2 p.m. we were told there were two park vehicles in town and they would probably leave at 4 p.m. so we parked ourselves on the porch of the UWA office and I amused Alice by knocking down some mangoes from a tree knowing full well that 'Africa time' could be anytime and so 4 p.m. came and went, and so did 5, 6 and 7. At half past seven a large open-backed truck pulled in, full of happy, loud, larking, mostly drunk workers from the park that had spent the day boozing in Masindi. It was a free ride and a novelty at first bumbling along listening to the laughter but it soon became rather uncomfortable trying to stand up amongst a mass of overflowing bags of bananas, flour and other goods, clinging on to metal bars for dear life as the truck tore along the heavily corrugated and pot-holed track, making a tremendous clatter. Sitting down wasn't an option, there was nothing to hold on to and the track was so bad the truck was like a bucking bronco, so standing upright without being flung over the side and dodging branches of overhanging trees soon became extremely tiresome. For fifty miles that truck took a hell of a battering, and so did we.

"What do you think of Wheatley's Waste Not Want Not Tours now?" I asked Alice with a grimace.

In a much chirpier mood, she just laughed, but she was as relieved as I was when, after three gruelling hours, we saw the lights of the village of Paraa up ahead and soon we were enjoying the extreme pleasure of lying flat and still in a hut at the *Red Chilli Camp*.

It was worth every minute of the truck ride, every hour of the wait, to cruise up the Nile to Murchison Falls past Nile Crocodiles basking on the shore, hundreds of Hippos, lots of Elephants, Olive Baboons and Waterbucks, Goliath Herons, and over a hundred glorious Red-throated Bee-eaters. The falls are only 130 feet (40 metres) high but the rushing Nile explodes with such force as it squeezes through a 23 foot (seven metre) gap the rock either side actually shakes. The sight was impressive, even from a considerable, safe distance but what I really hoped to see on the boat trip was a Shoebill, a unique stork-like bird which lives in the remotest swamps of central Africa, from southern Sudan to Zambia. It has a massive, hooked, clog of a beak literally the size of a shoe, used to catch baby crocodiles and large fish, especially Lungfish. The tall bulky bird looks stately when fishing, standing stock still, but it has been known to strike with such force and speed that the bird has ended up falling over and collapsing in an almost comical splash. They may be big but they are rare and shy, and they spend a lot of time in papyrus stands or other vegetation higher than a human, and they are therefore one of the hardest birds to see in the world. One of the most easily accessible places where there is a good chance of seeing one is Murchison Falls National Park, sometimes along the Nile upstream from Paraa, plied by the daily boat to the falls which we boarded but more often downstream. The trouble was we would have to hire a boat to go that way and that would be very expensive.

During a long lunch break the next day when we were avoiding the heat, we struck gold, when we were told that a party of Dutch tourists had hired a boat to travel downriver the next day and we were more than welcome to join them. Overjoyed at the chance to see a Shoebill we lay down on our backs on a bench each by the river and sang *Heaven* by Talking Heads before watching a Common Sandpiper bob along the back of a yawning Hippo, a Goliath Heron float downstream on a magic carpet of vegetation and, across the river, a big tusker come to take a long drink. Life was great.

Early the next day we boarded a small boat called *Mamba* with our new Dutch friends and headed down the Nile toward the Lake Albert Delta, scanning hard for a Shoebill, a proverbial needle in a papyrus stack miles and miles long. Hippos seemed to fill the river, Elephants splashed in it, long Nile Crocodiles basked beside it, Black-and-white Colobus Monkeys adorned the riverside trees and there were birds galore; darters, fish eagles, jacanas, Goliath Herons, a flock of about 200 tern-like Collared Pratincoles, hundreds of real terns, five species of kingfishers including three Giants, and Blue-breasted, Blue-cheeked and Red-throated Bee-eaters, to mention a few.

After about three hours, near the delta, Captain Nero, yes that is what he said his name was, pulled up by the bank of the river and we scrambled on to some dry land. After walking through some trees we came to a swamp with what looked like a blue stone statue stuck in the middle. Apart from its impressive size and that extraordinary bill what struck us most about the Shoebill was the side-on view of its huge head with the massive horn-coloured bill, a tiny pale eye and a short almost silly tuft at the back of its crown. It did not move a muscle while we watched it although we were not in its company for long because, to my horror, the overzealous Nero flushed it and the massive bird flew off on big wings into an inaccessible corner of the swamp. Alice and I had seen the bird called a Shoebill and that felt fantastic, although we couldn't find another one, despite scanning hard all the way back.

We spent a lot of time by the river the next day, thinking mostly about how fortunate we were to have met the Shoebill while watching Red-throated Bee-eaters and Elephants. The day came to a shocking end after dark when a thunderstorm moved in with booms and cracks so loud they made me wince, lightning that was almost continual and rain so heavy I feared the shelf the camp was built on would be washed away down to the river about half a mile below. Wearily I wandered to the toilets the next morning only to find three Warthogs sheltering in there. I made a swift exit and they scuttled out after me. After breakfast we lugged our rucksacks down to the park gate and began hitchhiking, hoping for a lift to Masindi, and, maybe, with a massive stroke of luck, even Kampala, and we waited and waited. Some Silverbirds, superb flycatchers, silvery satin grey above and rufous-orange below, helped pass the time until, after two and a half hours, we were invited into a battered *matatu* which had been hired, with a driver, by Nancy from Atlanta, Georgia, and Royce from Uganda, to take them and four children on a trip to Murchison Falls.

We didn't get very far. A full petrol tanker with a broken axle was stuck right in the middle of the red dust track. A long wait seemed inevitable but a convoy of Indians and Hare Krishnas, the chanters seeking 'the highest eternal pleasure' without eggs, fish, meat, tea, coffee, tobacco, alcohol, drugs or sex without the purpose of procreation, were determined to get by and so we stood there, in the middle of Africa, with our mouths open in astonishment as we watched lots of Indians arguing loudly over the many possible courses of action while orange-robed Hare Krishnas rushed about trying to fill up a big ditch at the side of the track with sticks and stones. They had been at a conference in the park and their leader, it seemed, was in a hurry to leave. By the time part of their convoy had been pushed past the petrol tanker it had been fixed and after it had been reversed to one side there was room for the rest of us to get through.

It was good to be on the move again but the *matatu* soon turned off the main route, into a forest clearing where Nancy announced that they were going Chimpanzee tracking and asked if we would like to join them, to which the response was an emphatic, "Yes please!" I then saw that we were at Kaniyo Pabidi in Budongo Forest Reserve, the only known site in East Africa where there was a chance of seeing Puvel's Illadopsis, so I was on the lookout for a party of the secretive dull brown and grey birds as we began walking through the beautiful rainforest, remarkable for the size of the fig, ironwood and mahogany trees, untouched by an axe or saw. Soon we heard the loud hoots, screams and screeches of Chimpanzees and not long after we were amongst a large troop of at least twenty, some rapidly ascending and descending the massive trees with ease, some sitting and lying on lofty branches scoffing figs. One large male with huge muscular arms and legs squatted on a horizontal branch not far above our heads and apart from his tiny pink penis looked very menacing. Occasionally a cacophony of screams and screeches would break out and at one point some Chimpanzees ran past us, thumping the wide buttresses of trees as they made their way along the ground; young males wooing a female apparently. An arresting moment occurred when a dark face appeared through the undergrowth, looking straight at us just like another human being. Then there was a crashing of branches and leaves and falling debris and they were gone and we were left wondering if that incredibly exhilarating hour of our lives could ever be bettered.

Back on the road Nancy told us they were going all the way to Kampala and that completed a great day for us. In the *Backpackers Hostel* on a leafy hill overlooking the large city we took it easy for a couple of days. 'It's ok having a break from birding' I tried to convince myself as I watched a singing male Scarlet-chested Sunbird in the grounds, after all, as Alice kept reminding me, "this is *not* a birding trip!" Down in the city there were more *matatus* than ants. We dodged and weaved through them and the almost as numerous motorcars, motorcycles, men and women and children, in order to book a bus to Bwindi Impenetrable National Park, down in far southwest Uganda on the border with the Democratic Republic of Congo, and at 05:30 the following morning we boarded one.

We will never forget *'The Bus to Butogota'*. For five or six hours we hurtled along smooth tarmac past roadside stalls overflowing with bananas, mangoes, tomatoes, pineapples and water melons then we reached Ntungamo, a long way from Kampala and not far from Bwindi, where we turned off the main highway on to a badly eroded red dust track and went round all the villages in some heavily populated, deforested, rounded hills, drifting in and out of some sort of sleep as the bus just went on and on, much, much longer than we had been led to believe, and somehow, at every stop, more people managed to cram into the already extremely overcrowded bus. When I was awake I was on the lookout for roadsigns to try and work out where the hell we were and boy was I glad to see one with 'Buhoma 32 km' on it, for that meant it was only another 15 km (about ten miles) to Butogota where we would at last be able to get off that damned bus to see if our legs still worked, and what joy it was to walk again after nine hours crammed into a tiny double seat next to an aisle packed with people and their goods, to stretch our long legs ... for about five paces, because we were quickly shown to a pick-up truck, the only transport available for the final leg to Buhoma. Somehow, Alice ended up inside on the front seat while I swayed around while trying to stand up outside in the back, with about twenty other people and our luggage for seventeen terrible kilometres along a horrendous winding track, the racing driver at the wheel seemingly having forgotten we were there.

As usual it was all worth it, to sit on the veranda of a banda with a cold beer overlooking a richly forested valley and mountain side where there were no mosquitoes and no rain, and to lie down, stretched out and flat, on a bed, and listen to the cicadas instead of Kampala's barking dogs and boom-boom-boom. From the same veranda the next day, after blissful sleep, we watched an aptly-named Great Blue Turaco, a spectacular creature, 'Great' in size *and* looks with a short, stubby, red-tipped yellow bill, a stiff, small black brush for a crest, a verditer-blue head and upperparts, apple-green, greenish-yellow and chestnut underparts, and a very long blue and greenish-yellow tail. Also in the 'garden' at the forest edge were paradise flycatchers, orange-breasted Lühder's Bushshrikes, blue-black male and dusky-barred, yellowish female Petit's Cuckooshrikes, and Cinnamon-chested Bee-eaters, gloriously green birds with yellow throats bordered black, and deep cinnamon chests and bellies. Later, we saw three dust-bathing in a powdery hollow on a dry track, spreading and fanning their wings to their sides and looking so shiny green as they cleaned their feathers and skin. We were staying at the *Buhoma Community Rest Camp* for 15 U.S. dollars a night and we could not have been in a better spot if we were paying the 400 U.S. dollars for the fancy lodge up the track, and what's more the little we *were* paying was going to the local Buhoma Mukono community not an international conglomerate who owned the private, ridiculously luxurious, lodge.

Six years had passed at Buhoma since March 1999 when 100-150 former Rwandan Interahamwe Hutu death squad members, responsible for the massacre of over 500,000 moderate Hutus and Tutsis in the Rwandan Genocide of 1994, crossed the border from the Democratic Republic of the Congo, less than an hour's walk away, and attacked a group of 31 people in Bwindi, killing four Ugandans, and kidnapping 14 tourists and their Ugandan guide who, on a forced march to the Congo, was doused with gasoline and set alight. After the women were raped eight tourists considered to be moving too slowly were bludgeoned and hacked to death with machetes. The remaining six were sent off to tell the Ugandan authorities that the Interahamwe would continue to rape and murder tourists in Bwindi because the park was a major source of foreign income for Uganda and they wanted to destabilize the country and let the world know there was a war going on in the region. Bwindi was closed for several months but gorilla-trekking had been back to normal for some years when we arrived, even though up to 15,000 Hutu rebels were still thought to be hiding out in the Congo, raping, looting, murdering, evading incursions by the then Tutsi-led Rwandan armed forces, and waiting for the next opportunity to re-take Rwanda.

We took a long walk the next morning, to the small but beautiful Munyaga Waterfall, with a guide up front and an armed guard at the rear. Giant tree ferns flourished in the shade alongside rocky clear-water streams and waterfalls, in a wonderland of every shade of green, the water flowing slowly through a luxuriance of young trees and shrubs growing rapidly in the dappled light below branchless towers of wood well over a hundred feet (30 metres) high with lofty canopies decorated with bunches of spreading epiphytes and draped with hanging mosses. It was a beautiful rainforest but the birds, many of which were heard, were hard to see and the only one we got any sort of view of during the two hour walk to the waterfall was a Mountain Masked Apalis, a long-tailed dark green bird with a black head. However, 'by fortune' as our seed-collecting guide pointed out, we fared better on the return, seeing, amongst others, a deep green Black-billed Turaco and a Bar-tailed Trogon, a brightly-coloured medium-sized bird with vivid green upperparts, a scarlet belly and a long tail which from below was white with fine dark bars.

During a long lazy afternoon on the veranda a handsome dark grey L'Hoest's Monkey, with a splendid white ruff, sat in the open on a low branch at the edge of our 'garden' for a while then, with an early beer on the go, I saw a pair of

Black-throated Apalises, a tiny, canopy bird making a rare excursion almost down to head height where I could see the black mask, broad white moustache and bright yellow belly of the splendid male. After that stroke of amazing good fortune I wandered merrily with Alice amongst the fireflies twinkling over the camp grounds.

In the morning we went down to the river in search of Short-tailed Warbler. The stripe-headed mite eluded us, as it did when we returned during the afternoon. Between times, on the veranda, Alice watched a Great Blue Turaco fly down on to a branch but the branch was too light for the bird and it kept going down with the turaco clinging to it and the big bird disappeared into a bush before fluttering back up into view and looking rather flustered and Alice couldn't stop laughing. There were plenty of other birds around the banda and there were birds galore in the park's large tracts of rainforest but the most well-known inhabitants of Bwindi are the Gorillas. After three days in the fairy tale forest we headed off in search of them with overflowing adrenalin and anticipation, climbing the steep forested slope opposite our banda on a muddy and sometimes slippery switchback trail. Up and up we went, through some gloom, through some glades, up to the head of a gully where we met the trackers who had been out since dawn. They said the Gorillas were on their way. The Gorillas were not on their way, they were there! Out of the rustling giant nettles five paces away to our right emerged the enormous silverback. He walked slowly on all fours to where a tree had fallen in a storm and the saplings had yet to get going and he sat down in the sunshine. He was truly magnificent, with massive shoulders and arms, a great bare chest and a head which was so big that it looked like he had two heads. There, ten paces away, he stared straight ahead, seemingly oblivious to us and lost in thought it seemed, as he waited for his troop to come down the slope behind and join him. His presence was awesome and all-consuming and it was very difficult not to make the forbidden eye-contact with him when he did once flick his eyes in our direction but this we had been told to avoid so as not to unsettle him. Even if he did become alarmed about the safety of his family it was impossible to imagine him attacking us, so completely comfortable did we feel in his company.

I found it very hard to take my eyes off him, even when his troop of twelve arrived, but I watched the ones bold enough to break cover. They were a few of the much smaller females, and some youngsters who bundled quickly down the slope through the thick vegetation and playfully out into the glade. Some stopped to eat nettle stems while others carried on, down into the bowl at the head of the gully which was overflowing with giant nettles, a favourite food of Bwindi Gorillas. There, most of them disappeared into the forest of nettles while a few, mostly the very young, climbed up the larger plants until the stems bent and they were left hanging by their hands before falling joyfully back to the ground. There was much swishing and swaying of nettles as the youngsters played and while they did so the silverback, the superb silverback, got up and joined them, walking sedately into the swathe of nettles and disappearing from view. Ivi, one of the trackers, found him, half-hidden, grooming a female before gently grabbing a nettle stem, slowly bending it down to his mouth, delicately stripping the bark off and then chewing the pulp with his terrible teeth, most of which appeared to be in poor, blackened condition. And then our allotted hour with the Gorillas was over. It was the shortest hour of our lives and it was with great sadness that we turned to leave them, as Dian Fossey so eloquently put it in *Gorillas in the Mist*, to 'peacefully meander ... their contented, harmonious days ... replete with sunning, playing and feeding'. So, we made our way back down the mountain to our banda where we sat, later in the afternoon, looking up at the dip in the forested slope high above us where, earlier, we had spent the best time of our lives.

I asked Ivi to keep a look-out for Black Bee-eaters on the way down from the Gorillas and he pointed out three of the little gems which I was keen for Alice to see. They swooped up from snags with their chestnut wings then landed again and we could just about make out the turquoise spangles running down their breasts. Back at the banda we sat watching the 'garden' in the afternoon and saw a Great Blue Turaco gurgling and whirling as it glided by, a pair of Vanga Flycatchers, three Ross's Turacos, four Black-and-white-casqued Hornbills flapping hard across the slope, several White-throated Bee-eaters flying out fast to catch bees from their favoured tall tree, and, near dusk, there was another moment of excitement as a Crowned Eagle with a monkey in its talons sailed across the forest to a huge tree where it settled down to eat.

The Gorillas were still on our minds at the end of the day though. Thinking about them brought a lump to my throat. There are not many left in the mountains of Central Africa. Too many people live on the fertile slopes of Bwindi and the other volcanic mountains in the Virungas where the Hutu Interhamwe are on the run, the Tutsi army after them, and Congolese soldiers and other paramilitary outfits are also up to mostly no good, and as the number of people increases and tribal warfare rumbles on and on in a never-ending circle of horrific violence even the so-called protected areas for Gorillas at the very top of the mountains come under more and more pressure as the tide of humanity rises ever more up the mountain sides.

We all need somewhere to live. We need to build nests like birds and other animals, somewhere safe to raise our young. We need the materials to build them, we need land to grow food and we need water. Trees need to be cut down to clear land on which to grow food, and to provide wood to build with and to cook with. This has very little impact on the environment and plants and animals if there are a few of us but there are not a few of us there are billions of us. Throughout the highlands of the world where people live in large numbers what little remains of the original natural forest is virtually restricted to remnants on the steepest slopes where it is difficult to clear the trees and level the land. Such pockets are sometimes and usually grudgingly declared parks or reserves but many governments do little to stop the inevitable encroachment of more and more people into such areas.

Thoreau was right when he wrote, 'There can be no very black melancholy to him who lives in the midst of nature' but it is a bittersweet business being a birder, loving nature, not being detached from it like so many folk, watching with terrible despair as the tide of people comes in and covers the land and never goes out again. To a birder like me it is simple; more people means less habitat means less birds, and other wildlife, the same as it ever was and same as it always will be because there ain't a politician on the planet prepared to do anything about it.

Politicians and world leaders shudder at the thought of being asked, "Are there too many people?" because if they say, "Yes." they will be accused of being anti-human but the main reason they refuse to confront overpopulation as an issue is because they cannot think of a way of running a country without a growing economy, and as far as they are concerned a growing economy means more people making more stuff for more people to buy. One day they will have to deal with it but stemming population growth will require some radical changes in the way the world works, and governments are not in power long enough to do anything radical. For example, in a four-year political cycle they spend a couple of years tinkering then a couple more trying to get back into power. The time governments are in power needs to be increased so that they can put in place often radical long-term rather than short-term measures, and carry them through, for the sake of the planet, the people who are going to be living on it, and its mind-blowing wildlife.

Arguing that there are too many people is not anti-human anyway. It's pro-human, because the lower the number of people the higher the quality of life of those people. They will have more water, more food and more wildlife. Most politicians believe people want higher standards of living, better medical care, longer lives and so on, because they think these things make people happier but while the human race as a whole is healthier, safer and richer than we have ever been survey after survey reveals we are not any happier. I think this is because most people are increasingly disconnected from nature. Most people have a very low quality of life because they live in a world which is over-populated, over-farmed, over-sprayed, over-tarmaced and over-concreted, not a world of marshes, meadows and woods alive with a profusion of flowers, butterflies and birds.

We are wrecking our home, the beautiful planet we call Earth, and we are wrecking our well-being, because we continue to chop down what woods and forests are left, drain wetlands, dam and pollute rivers, plough and poison grasslands, and loot and litter oceans. We even contaminate the air we breathe. A few are trying to do something about it but individuals, numerous non-governmental organizations and a few government bodies are all, in the words of E. O. Wilson, the Pulitzer Prize winning biologist, "just piddling around with efforts here and there, the aggregate of which is not even close to what we need". As Emerson, the transcendentalist philosopher who wrote a famous essay called *Nature*, pointed out a long, long time ago, 'goodness must have some edge to it - else it is none.' The conservation organizations are as scared as politicians to say that the edge is that they are fighting a losing battle so long as there are too many people. They fear losing too many members, politicians fear losing voters. They all would do well to remember what Thoreau wrote in *Walden*; 'There are a thousand hacking at the branches of evil to one who is striking at the root.' Conservationists and politicians are pruning the branches while the root, too many people, grows stronger.

Most of the problems the planet faces come down to the same cause; there are too many of us. This is the reason for the degradation and destruction of our home, planet Earth, our beautiful home, because to support too many of us, to build us all nests, heat our nests, and feed and water us, we have to drain too many wetlands, plough too many meadows and chop down too many forests. Eventually, if we do nothing about it there will be so many of us nature will be extinct and the end of nature is the end of the world. At the absolute minimum it will only survive with a gracefully declining human population. If we do nothing about it future generations will live in an unimaginable world without trees, flowers, butterflies, birds and so on. And yet nature is so good for our well-being. Nature makes us happy. So, selfish animals that we are, we need to start doing something about there being too many people and save nature, if only because it will save us.

By 2020 there were more than eight million people to one Mountain Gorilla. To never see an ash tray made out of a gorilla's hand again they and the forests they live in must be properly protected, not just on paper, but that doesn't look like it's going to happen so their days seem numbered, especially taking into account Central Africa's preponderance for political turmoil, tribal conflicts, civil wars and so on. It's a terribly sad situation and for anyone who has spent an hour with a silverback and his family in the forest, like Alice and I, simply devastating.

While we packed our rucksacks we heard Chimpanzees screaming in the forest across the valley. We were both feeling lethargic, a bit flat after the high with the Gorillas perhaps, or maybe it was the thought of moving on and leaving Bwindi, or four weeks taking doxycycline, our malaria prophylactic. However, we managed to muster enough energy for a sluggish stroll along the river during which we saw two Black Bee-eaters perched just above the water, a Yellow-spotted Barbet in a rare wave of birds, and an Equatorial Akalat, similar to a European Robin, attending an ant swarm. Then we humped our rucksacks up the 55 steps to the track and slumped under a tree to wait for Babas, the guy who drove us to Buhoma and promised to take us back to Butogota. We were amazed when he not only turned up but on time. He drove fast to Butogota, thinking nothing of overtaking on blind bends in a cloud of dust, and dropped us off at the *Green Tree Lodge* where we were served a small pile of rice and two very skinny, long dead, rancid fish which looked like they had been buried for some time and dug up again.

There was no need for the wake-up knock on the door; the bus to Kampala drove up and down Butogota's only street blasting its horn at half past four in the morning. God, that's what he said his name was, still knocked on our door as requested, and at 05:00 we began nine and half hours of drifting in and out of sleep, disturbed only by the cockerel at the front of the bus occasionally crowing, the hawkers at each stop, selling everything from grasshoppers to watches, and thoughts about too many people, brought on by the scene outside the window; farmland where once was forest, humans where once was Gorillas, Chimpanzees and so on, living in, even still building, mud huts, surrounded by filth and eating very little while their cattle and goats ate everything that dared to rear its head out of the soil under the eucalypts, the fucking eucalypts, foreign fast-growing wood of no use at all to the vast majority of the thousands of insects, birds and other animals evolved to thrive in African rainforest.

Our first night back in a city for a while was such a comedown thanks to loud music and a hundred dogs barking. I preferred the zing of insects, the tinkling frogs and the hoots of owls I was already missing. After another night we were glad to be on the road again, heading back to Nairobi on *Akamba's* 'Royal' bus service which meant bigger seats, no people or luggage in the aisles, a semblance of air-conditioning and free eggy-bread and sausage for breakfast. Unfortunately *Akamba* were not in charge of road repairs so it was still a bone-shaking twelve hours on the pot-holed piece of slim tarmac that is East Africa's main highway. The view wasn't up to much either and in Kenya it was even worse than in Uganda, for any infertile land in or out of the so-called protected areas was all but litter-strewn desert, overpopulated and overgrazed by biblical numbers of people and their cattle and goats. From Nairobi we took the Riverside Shuttle bus south to Arusha in Tanzania where we booked a room in the very clean *Hotel Flamingo*. Dodging annoying, persistent young men working for the many local tour companies offering safaris we headed for the office of one of them recommended to us by two fellow travellers in Nairobi and arranged a trip to the Serengeti with a vehicle, driver and cook, briefly becoming shilingi millionaires after a visit to the bank to withdraw enough money to pay for it.

After so little wonder for what seemed so long - a week had passed since we left Bwindi - it was fantastic to be in the Africa Alice had imagined. In Tarangire National Park we cruised through semi-arid tawny savanna with bulbous Baobabs, pom-pom-like Doum Palms, wispy acacias and many bare termite hills, a fine landscape complete and replete with ostriches, partridge-like spurfowl, pigeon-like sandgrouse, Blacksmith Plovers, lovebirds, Little Bee-eaters, Lilac-breasted Rollers, black-and-white shrikes, Ashy and Superb Starlings, and lots of animals. Elephants stood in circles in the shade under acacias, all facing outward with their ears flapping to keep cool. Thirsty Giraffes were visiting waterholes where a youngster drank with its legs splayed and straight, while mother watched. There were also plenty of Olive Baboons, Zebras, Wildebeests, Waterbucks, Impalas and tiny antelopes with large eyes called Kirk's Dik-Diks. Alice's first Lion was a lioness stalking a family of Warthogs, which ran for their lives, in all directions, but the lioness sprinted at them and emerged from a melee with a young one hanging limp in her mouth, blood dripping on to the dry ground.

Alice said it was like arriving in Africa again. Tarangire was certainly what we had dreamed our trip to Africa would be like but our late evening contentment was shattered when we checked the contents of our money belts before going to sleep and discovered we were both exactly 80,000 *shilingi* short, about £40 British pounds. We kept our money belts around our waists but they got damp from sweat sitting in the back of the *Land Rover* on our way to Tarangire so on arrival at the campsite, in our excitement to get back into the field in Africa, we tucked them into our day-sacks and left them in the vehicle while taking a long walk, during which time our driver, cook and a couple of campsite staff set up camp. Questions whizzed around our heads. We thought that since an exact number of notes had been taken, and our credit cards and passports left alone, it must have meant that the robbers thought that we were rich enough not to notice the missing 80,000, especially when we had paid over a million each for the safari, and that they who had committed the crime had probably done so before and got away with it. Would the local people working at the campsite be so devious? If so, were our driver and/or cook in on it? Did they turn a blind eye? We were not convinced the local people would do such a thing off their own backs, without our driver and/or cook knowing, so surely the whole 'gang' was responsible. We were furious and got up and dressed and went to look for our driver and cook but it was 10:30 p.m. and they were sound asleep in their tent, and while wondering whether to wake them or not we got to thinking it could have been a lot worse and that by causing a massive fuss then we might jeopardise our chance to see the Serengeti so we decided to back away and to try and sleep on it.

In the morning we agreed to confront the tour company at the end of our safari but it was impossible not to think about the robbery and who did it as we drove along the best road we had travelled on in East Africa, up to the rim of the Ngorongoro Crater, the largest unbroken crater on the planet which was formed about two and a half million years before when a volcano erupted and the top of the cone collapsed, leaving a round hole about 2000 feet (600 metres) deep and over twelve miles (20 km) across. From the rim, the view was amazing. It was a bit hazy but we could make out Elephants and Buffalos roaming across the savanna between groves of acacias. We wanted to head down there for a closer look but we had arranged to visit the Serengeti first so we carried on west, through fertile farmland and rolling hills with small acacias down to 'the place where the land goes on forever', the Siringitu in Maasai. The vast rolling plains of golden grasses and wooded acacia savanna in the Serengeti, and the contiguous Ngorongoro area and Maasai Mara across the border in Kenya, support the greatest numbers and most diverse selection of land mammals on Earth; about three million animals including over a million Blue Wildebeest. It sure is big country, very big country, where a vast plain reaches the horizon, dotted with acacia stands, wooded hillocks, rocky outcrops called kopjes and the thickly wooded Seronera River. Life abounds; amongst the many Buffalos, Grant's and Thomson's Gazelles, and Wildebeest and Zebras was a herd of about fifty Elephants, three Giraffes, and several Lions including a Lioness half asleep in a tree and a male which sat up showing his massive head and mane before yawning and flopping back to the ground. For a few hours there we forgot all about the robbery, so absorbing was the wild African scene.

Dawn in the Serengeti; a bit chilly, red lines of cloud across the wide sky, and Lions and Spotted Hyaenas heading for shade after a night hunting. The abundance of herbivores means there is plenty of food on the hoof for predators and we saw lots of Lions during the first full day. Two Lionesses appeared to be hunting a herd of Zebras, hiding in long grass ready to pounce on the last Zebra to go by but when it walked almost past their noses the Lionesses ignored it. They hunt mainly at night of course, when it's much cooler, but maybe they just can't help themselves, can't curb their instincts, even when resting up during the day. The Leopard we saw the afternoon before was back draped over its favourite branch after its night out hunting, dozing with its legs and tail hanging down. A Cheetah, a superb, long, sleek, spotted cat, rested in the pale shade of thin acacia branches. There were so many animals the birds were background for once although we did spend a long time watching a Martial Eagle mantling its prey on the ground with its wings, to hide it from a potential thief in the form of a Steppe Eagle perched in a tree above. Later, we saw another bloated and bloodstained Martial perched atop a trackside tree. Two Secretary Birds landed with a short run and just about managed not to fall over. Montagu's Harriers, mostly males, floated over the grasslands. Temminck's Coursers panted under the burning sun out on the short-grass plains. A flock of Yellow-throated Sandgrouse drank warily at a waterhole. Lilac-breasted Rollers adorned the acacias. Dust spouts whizzed by, tsetse flies bit, one almost piercing my jugular, and gradually the heat subsided and as the sun neared the far horizon a Leopard walked along a dry creek, its mustard eyes scanning for potential prey. It stopped to sharpen its claws on a tree trunk before hiding in the grass, ready to pounce. We drifted off to sleep with so many wonderful images in our heads.

The next day was Lion day. The Lionesses are the most impressive. They do virtually all of the hunting, working together to skillfully stalk, charge and bring down virtually anything on four legs including Zebras, Wildebeests, young Elephants, Hippos, Buffalos and even Rhinos. They are very strong, with jaws and teeth powerful enough to suffocate an animal when they bite its throat, to crunch bones and to tear muscles apart. Watching them lolling about during the heat of the day with their short white beards, footsore paws turned upwards and pestered by flies they look anything but terrifying but when they are hunting it is easy to see why most animals don't stand a chance. We lost count of how many we saw in the Serengeti but perhaps the most memorable sight was a pride of eleven walking out from the shade of the riverside trees on to the open plain in the late afternoon, as they prepared to hunt in the dry grass which went on and on and on and in parts, large parts, was carpeted with Thomson's Gazelles, Wildebeests and Zebras, as far as our binoculars could see.

By the river earlier in the day we saw two Spotted Hyaenas tearing into the bowels of a dead Zebra. One emerged with a bloody face and neck, a macabre sight. Two Black-backed Jackals and some vultures looked on; what with so much killing there were plenty of vultures. Not far from the hyaenas a Lioness was finishing off the back half of another Zebra. The front half was in the river waiting to be despatched by the crocs. They seemed in no hurry. They must have been gorged already. Elsewhere, we watched a huge mother Elephant trumpeting in alarm and smelling the air with her trunk raised high as she nervously circled her invisible newborn, worried about it being taken by Lions, and out on the plains we saw three Cheetahs lying down together in the shade of a bush, waiting for their chance to eat. The Serengeti is not serene; it's dramatic and gruesome.

The Serengeti Africa was the Africa we dreamed of though, at least until the evenings. Back home, we talked of sitting around our own campfire of an evening with a cold beer before eating something delicious and drifting off to sleep listening to hyaenas and night birds. Instead we had to eat in a giant cage, safe from the Lions, with what must have been well over a hundred other people, many not particularly interested in wildlife, only 'ticking off' the Serengeti it seemed, before lying in our cots in our tent listening to numerous self-absorbed inconsiderate bastards, completely unaware and utterly devoid of respect for where they were, drinking, laughing, joking and shouting. Finally, late into the African night, the sound of zips being zipped up ceased, the buffoons shut the fuck up and I could lie there and listen, and one night I did hear a distant hyaena 'laughing'.

Without the sightseers the Serengeti is how I imagine much of East Africa looked like three and a half million years ago, when the earliest known hominids or apes walked on two feet across the plains near Olduvai Gorge, between the Serengeti and Ngorongoro, where all those years of erosion had exposed their footsteps, a replica cast of which lies in the museum there. After looking at their prints and thinking about what the three of them might have been doing it was back to the modern world and a long line of vehicles parked at the side of the road. A *Landcruiser* had rolled over, two tourists had been seriously injured and their guide was waiting for the flying doctors from Arusha to arrive. We saw the plane before we reached the *Simba Campsite* on the rim of the Ngorongoro Crater where after a long look at the fantastic view we took great care to pitch our tent as far away from everyone else as possible but hopes of a quiet night were dashed by an inebriated Indian repeating the few English phrases he knew over and over and louder and louder while a drunk Finn barked out his national anthem.

I was much happier watching an iridescent bronze, copper, green and purple Tacazze Sunbird under a pink sky at dawn. After climbing into the *Land Rover* we descended a bumpy dusty track into the hazy, parched, magnificent amphitheatre of life called the Ngorongoro where there were many Zebras and about a thousand Wildebeest in one long line heading for water across the crater floor. The line water left in Lake Magadi looked like a mirage complete with a picturesque party of Lesser Flamingos reflected in the silver sliver. Nearby, a beautifully lit flock of Yellow-throated Sandgrouse flew off with a chorus of comical 'a-eg-ur-ur-ura' calls. A Kori Bustard flew past, a rare sight in flight, and it was quickly followed by an even more astonishing Saddle-billed Stork, its long black and white wings whooshing, its black neck and black-banded red spear of a bill stretched out before it. There wasn't much water in the swamp either and masses of Hippos were rolling, snorting, sparring and tumbling over each other in a shallow crowded pool, accompanied by a couple of hundred Cattle Egrets.

Out on the plain a Lioness and three of her youngsters walked by so close we could hear mother panting. It seemed they had been forced off a kill by a pack of Spotted Hyaenas, one of which was brave or foolish enough to walk between the mother and her cubs. Six European Bee-eaters called, caught bees and landed close enough for us to hear them bashing the venom out of their prey before tossing them up into the air and gulping them down their open bills. A huge old bull Elephant dusted itself, throwing clouds of dry dirt over its body with its trunk to help prevent its sensitive skin becoming sunburnt. Two more were on a long tramp to water, the one in front with very long curved tusks. A handsome moustached Lanner Falcon with a dark grey back and white breast and belly with black darts and spots, perched on the ground right next to a track. On the short-grass savanna a curve-bellied mother Rhino grazed close to her pale grey youngster. Ngorongoro is a spectacular wonderland.

All too soon we were back in Arusha where we carefully explained to our driver and cook what had happened at Tarangire and that we only had enough money left to last us to the end of our trip, which was the truth, and therefore we were unable to tip them. We were very careful not to say that the amount of cash stolen from us was almost the amount we had been advised to tip them, and because Alice and I were not convinced that they were not involved and at the very least they were too casual about keeping our belongings safe, we felt that they should not get a tip anyway.

All this was assuming we had some money left of course, since whoever the robbers were they could have written down the details of our credit cards and passports and somehow bled our accounts dry while we were on safari. So we approached the ATM in Arusha with extreme trepidation. We couldn't find out what the balances of our accounts were but the machine went chugg ... chugg ... chugg and some notes slid out so we presumed there must be at least some money left. Moving on to the tour company office they blamed the local people at Tarangire, as expected, and described several, far worse, incidents so, assuming our money was still in our accounts, we felt we had got off lightly. We thought long and hard about our driver and cook that night. They had looked after us very well so we called them up and they came to the hotel and we gave them a small tip and they seemed very pleased, particularly the driver who was very glad to hear that the money we had left for the rest of our trip appeared to be in our bank accounts. He then apologised profusely for what had happened and shook our hands many times during a somewhat sad and strange goodbye.

After two lazy days in Arusha we got a bus to Moshi, a large town on the lower slopes of Mount Kilimanjaro which we were happy to see briefly at dawn one morning before it was obscured by cloud, as is the case most days. Our *Lonely Planet* guidebook stated that Moshi's bus station was 'chaotic and full of touts and disreputable types'. We found it very relaxing. Maybe we were getting used to African bus stations after six weeks on the road. We were not getting used to African buses; the *Raqib Classic Coach* to Mombasa appeared to be an old school bus, not designed for two six-footers like us or the excess number of other passengers and their luggage jammed into it for eight hours on a rocky track through Tsavo West National Park and a bad road from Voi, the main road between Nairobi and Mombasa.

The world of wildlife on land is brilliant; flowers, trees, butterflies, birds, mammals, to mention a few, not least on the plains of East Africa, but it is matched if not exceeded by what Jacques Cousteau called *The Silent World*, his classic book published in 1953, for beneath the sea is another world altogether, especially where there are coral reefs, where hundreds of different fish species and other animals live, often in close proximity. I loved my visits to the silent underwater world the last time I was on the Kenyan coast and was determined to return to it with Alice, so we wiped on the 'goop and goo' (suntan lotion and mask cleaner), squeezed a snorkel and mask over our heads, pulled on some flippers and swam back and forth over and through the coral forest where living amongst the multicoloured stacks of 'trees' were a multitude of crazy wonderful fishes, too many to remember, too amazing to describe, too varied to name, in a mind-blowing explosion of brilliant colours and fantastic patterns.

After each snorkelling trip I closed my eyes and I saw fish, a kaleidoscope of fish. For hours I flicked through one of my favourite books, *A Field Guide to the Coral Reef Fishes of the Indian and West Pacific Oceans* written and beautifully illustrated by Doctor Robert Herbert Carcasson and published in 1977. Only after studying it very carefully was I able to attempt to put names to the some of the many marvels. The most striking, to my eyes, were the Powder-blue Surgeonfish that are sky-blue with black faces, golden eyes, incredibly bright yellow dorsal fins and black and white tails. There were many square-shaped butterflyfish with protruding snouts and steep foreheads, such as the deep mustard-yellow Raccoon Butterflyfish with striking black and white masks, and the black, white and orange Threadfin Butterflyfish, named after its very thin dorsal filament. Shoals of almost luminous yellow, black-spotted Sweetlips liked to float under the crests of coral columns. A large grouper with tiny, black-trimmed blue spangles all over its orange-red body is called a Coral Trout or Hind. Many parrotfishes have only Latin names, for example *Scarops rubroviolaceus*, an orange-pink phenomenon fading into lemon-yellow with very pretty luminescent green lips and 'eyebrows'. Graceful, long-beaked, long blue bodied and green-finned fish go by the name of Bird-wrasses. Moon Wrasses have long, red-flecked green bodies, frilly golden tails, purple-striped fins with blue trims and radiant strips of green and purple across their faces.

Amongst such astounding variety it is hard for a fish to stand out but a small school of Moorish Idols drifting by with their 'sails' aloft always catches the eye. Sometimes it is their white dorsal fins rising high above them and ending in long white streamers which grab the attention, sometimes their orange-saddled, white tubular snouts, and sometimes the wavy black, white and yellow stripes running from the top to the bottom of the extraordinary disk-shaped fishes.

It was a magical week to end our trip but it did not start well. The small town of Watamu was not for us; there was too much *wazungu* flesh on show ('people with white skin', burnt brown by the sun) so we set out on our first morning at the coast in determined pursuit of a better base for our last week in Africa. To conduct our search we would have to march in the heat along the strip of burning, crumbling tarmac running south along the coast, checking places out on the way. We had not walked far though when we were offered a lift by an Italian man called Giovanni who took us to his lovely, open, shaded house overlooking the entrance to Mida Creek where we were soon supplied with a very welcome cold drink and his wife Nikki told us about a place called Mwamba.

It was about a mile back toward Watamu so we walked there along the blinding white sand beach with a cool ocean breeze in our faces, warm water lapping our bare feet and Crab Plovers towering above many other shorebirds. Being atheists we were somewhat reluctant to stay at a place run by a Christian conservation organization called *A Rocha* spouting a mission 'to make God's love for His world known by demonstrating how to practically care for it' although the world certainly needed caring for and we also agreed with their aims 'to achieve the long-term conservation of threatened habitats and species through the involvement of local communities' so we were soon converted, not to God but to the cheap and basic but lovely, airy, clean white-washed room at the top of the beach where Alice, whose eyes lit up when she walked through the flowering bushes of the garden, and I could fall asleep to the swoosh of the Indian Ocean and the zing of cicadas after a day full of birds and fishes.

If there was no trip to the reef we tried to get to Mida Creek, a broad tidal expanse of mud and sand crawling with crabs and Crab Plovers. At the end of the boardwalk through the mangroves surrounding what is more of a bay than a creek there was a viewing platform in front of which, at the edge of a high tide, we counted hundreds of roosting shorebirds. The small ones were to the left the large ones to the right, the small ones being Curlew and Terek Sandpipers, Lesser and Greater Sand Plovers, and Greenshanks, the large ones taking the form of Grey Plovers, Curlews and Whimbrels. Plenty of Gull-billed, Lesser Crested and Saunders's Terns were also present but the stars were the Crab Plovers, an incredible 726 of them.

On a visit at low tide I stuck to the mangroves and struck gold with White-throated Bee-eaters, a Carmine Bee-eater, a Purple-banded Sunbird, a pair of small, cute, neat, short-tailed and boldly patterned grey, black and white flycatchers called Pale Batises, and, following a flock of Golden Orioles, I came across a mixed foraging flock of birds containing Chestnut-fronted and Retz's Helmetshrikes, both so approachable I could see the bristly blue wattles surrounding the yellow eyes of the grey-brown Chestnut-fronteds and the bristly red wattles around the yellow eyes of the almost black Retz's.

If we could not get to the creek or the reef there was not much to do. It was way too hot to leave the room for long, and anyway there were very few birds living in the sun-baked bone dry scrub inland; some tiny, hyperactive, glossy green and yellow Collared Sunbirds, a few very shy, stripe-headed, brown and buff Eastern Bearded Scrub Robins which were mostly heard only, whistling away, and some Zanzibar Sombre Greenbuls, one of the most boring birds in the world. However, on our last day we faced the sun and walked the white sand beach south to the entrance of Mida Creek where the shallows, shores and sand between rock pools full of miniature colourful fish were strewn with shorebirds. After the fish were egrets, herons, ospreys, fish eagles and Pied Kingfishers. Inland, seven Carmine Bee-eaters floated over the scrub and one landed close by; a shock of carmine and crimson with an almost iridescent beryl-green head and throat, black mask, vivid carmine-pink body, deep crimson wings and bright turquoise-blue lower belly, one of the most fabulous creatures to have evolved on planet Earth.

The price of paradise? Listening to prayers before meals and then talking to deluded do-gooders piddling with the world's problems. They *were* doing some good but Mwamba was a bubble. Outside was a place called Mombasa where a mob wielding sticks ran alongside the bus we were on, after an alleged thief who, judging by some stories in the national newspaper probably ended up being lynched. The taxi from the bus station to the hotel was driven by a man in a fez boasting about his nine children and the fact that he never slept because he was either driving or doing 'jiggy jiggy', to make more children. Walking to a cafe along Moi Avenue we watched a wretched dirty tramp in rags kneel down to drink the rank black water out of the litter-clogged gutter along the filthy, dusty, noisy, overcrowded road.

Our cabin on the night train to Nairobi was tiny, neglected and without water but we had a bunk each and we could stretch out gloriously flat so it was a million times better than a bus and it certainly beat drinking out of a gutter. Clatter, clatter, clatter, clack, clack, clack soon sent us to sleep even though the soundtrack was occasionally interrupted by the long screech of metal wheels sliding instead of rolling along a metal track. We got up early to watch the sun rise over the African plains. It was cloudy. The plains were bare. The land was broken. Desperately poor, barely-fed barely-clothed people who looked like they had just survived a nuclear war were hiding out in barely habitable mud huts surrounded by litter blowing across once fertile now overgrazed tree-less and pasture-less plains dotted with skinny and dead cows.

Here and there some natural habitat had somehow escaped destruction. Scattered patches of small flat-topped acacias, for some bizarre reason no doubt, had been spared the axe, for now. They helped to hold the soil together and stop it blowing away and there was just enough grass growing in it to support a few Grant's and Thomson's Gazelles, and Impalas and Zebras, and enough insects to feed some bustards and ostriches. We even saw three Giraffes where the railway skirted Nairobi National Park, a last tantalising, tainted taste of wonder before we trundled into the grim suburbs, overcrowded city centre and black billowing fumes of traffic in Nairobi, our final resting place on that once beautiful continent, much of which has been spoiled beyond belief by our fellow human beings.

One day at Mwamba when there was no trip to the creek or the reef my spirits sank like a stone. Alice blamed the lack of my daily fix; birds and fish, but I think there was more to it. It wasn't just the desecration of Africa and the beautiful planet Earth as a whole it was that our trip was coming to an end. It suddenly hit me hard that I was going to miss the creek and the reef, and walking along Ghost Crab beach, and the ocean breeze through the window on our naked bodies, and the cicada zing, and the deep satisfied sleep that comes at the end of perfect days, and the freedom of being on the road, and all that was Africa.

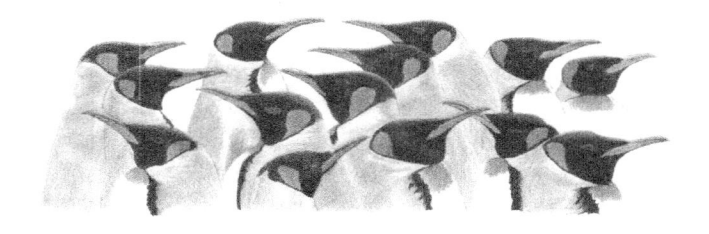

*King Penguins, South Georgia, 26th November 2006*

# 19

# THE FALKLAND ISLANDS, SOUTH GEORGIA and ANTARCTICA

When Alice and I got back from Africa we didn't have any money or jobs, but not for long. My friend Simon Colenutt said I could do some survey work for his ecological consultancy company so we moved into a small place on an old farm in Hampshire. It was quiet, the rent was cheap, Alice soon found work as a waitress in Romsey and just ten months after Africa we were off again, to Antarctica, the final continent for me.

We very nearly didn't make it. After spending an unscheduled night with just a few hours sleep in Madrid due to an eight hour delay to our flight to Argentina caused by what the captain described as "a poor engine." Alice, me, Al, Chief, Foggy, Nick and The Colonel eventually reached Buenos Aires, only to be told that we had missed our connection to Ushuaia where our ship would sail from the following evening, with or without us. To make matters worse, all six scheduled flights to Ushuaia the next day were fully booked so we would have to rely on stand-by to get to the ship on time. After a second unscheduled night with just a few hours sleep we arrived back at Buenos Aires airport at half past three in the morning. We were two days from home but still three hours from the ship. Ragged from a lack of sleep, things were looking grim, very grim indeed.

Al and Nick parked themselves at the check-in desk, determined to glean the tiniest bits of information they could about seat availability on *Aerolineas Argentinas* flights to Ushuaia. At 05:20, ten minutes before the first flight of the day was due to depart, Al told the rest of us that three seats were available. Alice overheard someone say, "Should we let Alice and Nigel go?" We couldn't look anyone in the eye and I was nearly in tears thinking about whether to accept the offer or not, should it be made, and if we accepted, about getting on the ship and sailing to Antarctica without some of my best friends. The thought of going on a trip we had all dreamed of going on together for so long without them was unbearable. When the offer was made, as we knew in our hearts it would be, it was a terrible decision to have to make. We refused of course but my true friends persuaded us to go and so, with great reluctance, we shuffled our way to the check-in desk.

While our passports were being looked over Chief and Nick were also offered seats, which cheered us up a little but not much. Al, Foggy and The Colonel were still stuck. Soon the four of us were airborne, flying south over the vast, flat fertile plains of northern Argentina known as the Pampas then, after a long doze, the very sparsely populated, cold, windswept steppe, desert and snowy mountains of the southern Andes in Patagonia. The plane descended in tight circles over the last, snow-flecked, stark, dark grey mountains, down to Ushuaia, the 'end of the world beginning of everything' as the sign said, the most southerly town in the world, where no two of the wooden houses were the same size, shape or colour.

In no time at all we were on our way to Tierra del Fuego National Park. It would all have been tremendously exciting, a little bit of birding before we got on the boat, but all we could think about were Al, Foggy and The Colonel, then Chief received a text message saying they were on their way too and should make it in time and suddenly all the tension, all the worries ebbed rapidly away. It looked like we would all be going to Antarctica together, as we always wanted to, after all.

The birding was suddenly much more enjoyable and got even better when I caught sight of a Spectacled Duck, a scarce bird I didn't expect to see, and striking thanks to the large, white oval spots between the eyes and the bill. There was a man standing next to us who was travelling on the same cruise, with a major bird tour company, and I said to him, "That must be a tick for you!"

"I've no idea," he said, "You'll have to ask *Birdquest*."

The poor man didn't hunt down his own birds. He had been shown so many he didn't know what he'd seen and what he hadn't. I shook my head and we carried on and saw some more fine birds, not least Great Grebes, Black-chested Buzzard Eagles and Thorn-tailed Rayaditos, although the best bird was the one I hoped to see the most, the one I missed in Chile. It was a White-throated Treerunner, which behaved like a rather large nuthatch but looked very different, being a rich brown above and white below with a dark mask and beautiful, black-fringed, teardrop-shaped white feathers running along the dark chestnut flanks. Rarely have I enjoyed a break from birding for a long lunch so much, a traditional *asado* lunch of barbecued beef, chicken and lamb, with Alice and my friends. After two days of trouble life was great again. The morning's birding had been so much more pleasurable for the news that we would all probably make it, and after facing the possibility of not making it how much sweeter the voyage ahead would be.

The 17-day voyage from Ushuaia to the Falkland Islands, South Georgia and Antarctica, and back via the Drake Passage, is probably the best boat trip anyone can take in their lives. Our boat was built in Finland in the early 1980s. The *Professor Multanovskiy*, a nimble white ship just 213 feet (65 metres) long and with a passenger limit of 48, was designed for polar and oceanographic research, and equipped with anti-roll stabilisers and an ice-strengthened hull. It was clear and sunny as the lines were cast off at 17:30 and the Russian Captain Sergey Nesterov eased the *Multanovskiy* out of Ushuaia. International law required us to participate in a mandatory emergency exercise before we got properly underway and so, having located our life vests in our basic but cosy cabin and noted our designated lifeboat and muster station, the alarms duly went off and we soon found ourselves crammed into a cold, hard, totally enclosed capsule which we soon decided we wouldn't want to end up in during a real emergency let alone spend any time in, especially in rough seas, and so we were very glad to clamber out and get on deck.

As the *Multanovskiy* sailed east along the Beagle Channel past high, dark forested slopes of drowned mountains with evocative place names like Cape Deceit, Fury Island, Last Hope Bay and Mount Misery, we were on the lookout for Magellanic Diving Petrel, the channel being about the best place on the planet to see the tiny black and white seabird, and we saw one before the Andes sunk beneath the waves at Punta Pájaro (Bird Point). At the end of the day we entered the open ocean, the deep, cold and tempestuous South Atlantic where storms travel eastwards with some of the strongest winds and highest waves on Earth.

I needed a long night's sleep but I was so excited at the prospect of seawatching the next day I was awake by 04:30. My bleary eyes registered two Sooty Shearwaters sweeping past the porthole as I quickly got dressed and when I got on deck I could see thousands of the dark brown, stiff-winged 'Sooties'. I was soon wide awake and watching the first of the day's Southern Giant Petrels following the ship. The huge birds, sporting a variety of shades of brown and grey with bulky yellowish bills and wings nearly as long as the Black-browed Albatrosses, arced back and forth effortlessly all day long. They were a wonderful sight but not as stirring as the big albatrosses. The first was an adult Wandering Albatross gliding low over the ocean with its wings spanning eleven feet or three metres or so, longer than any other bird, and what a truly magnificent sight it was, 'more majestic, more supreme in its element, than my imagination had pictured' as the scientist Robert Cushman Murphy wrote in his journal when he was on the whaling brig *Daisy* in 1912, also on his way to South Georgia. Although I had seen a wanderer before it was a brief view of an immature bird off Woollongong, Australia. Off Tierra del Fuego I got to watch an adult for as long as I wanted as it glided alongside and so I finally felt that I now belonged, as Murphy put it when he saw his first one, 'to a higher cult of mortals'.

Only the meanest of mortals could fail to admire a Wandering Albatross riding the wind or come to that its close relatives the royal albatrosses which we also saw several of during the rest of that first day at sea. The Wanderer may have been from South Georgia, just a few hundred nautical miles away, but the royals had flown around the globe, from the islands they nested on, south and east of New Zealand, no mean feat and yet relatively easy with their long narrow wings evolved for travelling vast distances with hardly a flap. I spent most of the day admiring albatrosses but I did occasionally turn my attention to other birds, such as the much smaller, clean, crisp, pied Pintado or Cape Petrels which accompanied us for virtually the whole voyage, often hanging in the wind almost at arm's length off the stern or to port or starboard, all dark White-chinned Petrels, big for petrels, larger even than Sooty Shearwaters, and amongst the many dark birds there were lots of small blue-grey petrels with dark M patterns on the upperwings and crisp white undersides, called prions, distant and relatively dull at first, close and beguiling as time moved on. Smaller still were the Common Diving Petrels and hundreds of Wilson's Storm Petrels, and with them were a few speedy Grey-backed Storm Petrels, with mostly white underparts. Unlike half of the poor passengers, laid low with seasickness due to a heavy swell and a big roll, I seawatched the whole fantastic day and at the end of it I was very tired and a little emotional, with being there and all the wonder there, and when I finally lay flat in my bunk and shut my stinging eyes I could still see seabirds gliding over the ocean.

Eight Striated Caracaras, long-winged and long-tailed scavengers, were soaring together over a hilly, heathy island in the Falklands as we sailed slowly into the archipelago. After dropping anchor we took our first ride in one of the ship's black rigid inflatable boats (RIBs) known as *Zodiacs*. Accompanying us to New Island there were some porpoising Gentoo Penguins, also on the way to shore. It was a beautiful day as we walked past banks of yellow gorse and grazed fields dotted with Austral Thrushes, smaller Dark-fronted Ground Tyrants, larger more colourful male Long-tailed Meadowlarks with bright crimson chins and chests, families of Upland Geese, and a daintier, more finely barred, pair of Ruddy-headed Geese.

At the top of a very high cliff we sat in total rapture amongst a mixed breeding colony of yellow-crested Rockhopper Penguins, which were snoozing in the warm morning sunshine or gurgling loudly or pecking the neighbours, black and white Imperial Shags with yellowish caruncles in front of their eyes which are encircled by the most beautiful blue rings, and hundreds and hundreds of Black-browed Albatrosses. A lot of the albatrosses were sitting on single eggs in deep nests of mud bound with vegetation, looking very handsome with their exquisite dark eyebrows, while others made us laugh as they made their way to the flight-pad at the cliff edge with their large flesh-coloured webbed feet slapping the ground. Then we were in awe as they leapt off the cliff into the wind and floated in mid-air right next to us, heads lower than tails, wings buffeted by the updraught, the tips of the feathers along the trailing edge flickering, and tails vertical and fanned. Then with a barely noticeable flick of a feather and an indistinct twist of the tail they were off, sailing down to the ocean to begin the next foraging trip.

In the afternoon we took to the *Zodiacs* again and after negotiating a floating kelp forest we were dropped off on sunlit Carcass Island, free from introduced predators such as cats, rats and mice and therefore full of birds. On the flotsam and jetsam at the top of the beach we saw our first Cobb's Wren, a larger darker brown version of the everyday wren not named after Chief whose real name is Nick Cobb but after Arthur Cobb who, in 1908, shot a wren on that very island. The specimen was sent to the Natural History Museum in London where it was described as a new species, *Troglodytes cobbi,* one of the two endemic birds on the archipelago along with a steamerduck which we saw soon afterwards. Also foraging amongst the seaweed were a few Blackish Cinclodes, dull thrush-like birds virtually impossible to see anywhere else in the world. On the shimmering sand at the water's edge was a splendid pair of Magellanic Oystercatchers with yellow eyes. Walking through the dunes I almost stepped on a ridiculously tame South American Snipe. Inland from there, on some 'rough', we watched two pairs of Canarywinged or White-bridled or Black-throated Finches, the female finely streaked dark on brown the male a lovely subtle blend of greens and greys and yellows contrasting with a small black mask and throat bordered with white. Beyond them we could see some classic black and white Magellanic Penguins standing outside their nesting burrows. On the way back to the ship four Peale's Dolphins rode the bow of the *Zodiac* and later, from the bow of the ship, I saw a Commerson's Dolphin, a much more striking animal with a mainly white body contrasting with the black head, dorsal fin and rear end. It had been another wonderful day and I was so tired and bleary-eyed by the end of it I could hardly stay awake to write and there was so much to write about.

The next morning we took the *Zodiacs* into the islands' capital Stanley, a tiny town of mainly white houses with mostly green and red roofs. Those interested in such places walked the streets. We, the birders, headed out to the disappointingly degraded countryside around the town where we still managed to track down some Rufous-chested Dotterels and Two-banded Plovers. Some of the lovely shorebirds were sitting on nests, and some had chicks which were no more than balls of fluff with beaks and outsized legs. We also saw some more Black-throated Finches and a pair of Silvery Grebes building a nest. The beautiful buoyant birds have golden fans behind their bright red eyes. After a splendid lunch the *Multanovskiy* sailed east at a cruising speed of 12 knots, back out into the South Atlantic which was flat calm, so calm the Black-browed Albatrosses, Sooty Shearwaters, and Black-bellied and Wilson's Storm Petrels only just managed to stay airborne, there being virtually no wind to provide them with lift. By the evening the ocean they so gloriously graced was so unbelievably still it looked like it was made out of molten blue glass infused with shades of pink and purple, a fantastic scene completed by an orange sunset and so beautiful I almost cried from the sheer joy of being alive in such a place.

A fourteen-hour seawatch, interrupted by the occasional doze and meals, began at 05:00. Above the ocean arced, banked, glided and swept albatrosses, petrels, prions and Pintados. I watched them all day - I could watch them forever - as cloud filled the sky, the swell built, the temperature fell and, toward the end of the day, light snow began to fall. It was then that I became an even higher class of mortal for the most southerly and most elegant of all the albatrosses appeared. The soft, silky, sooty brown birds with silvery bodies and backs, very long, slender wings and long pointed tails go by the name of Light-mantled Albatrosses. Two sailed gracefully around in unison above the water before one peeled off and came into the stern, so close we could see the pale blue sulcus, the fleshy lateral line or groove along the lower mandible of the otherwise dark grey, delicately hooked, bill.

There were five off the stern the next morning and they followed the *Multanovskiy* for hours, using the minimum of effort to stay aloft and looking so handsome with their dark heads and white eye-rings, and so at ease with their element, the cold wind, down at the southern end of the seas. They are wonderful, although I also fell in love at first sight with Blue Petrels, beautiful birds with neat black caps, white foreheads and throats and underparts, and a bluish hue to the grey back and tail, the end of which has a narrow, black subterminal band and a diagnostic, broad, bold white tip. Wandering Albatrosses were with us again and some adult Grey-headed Albatrosses, another globetrotter which circles the southern end of the planet, covering up to 7500 miles (12,000 km) in search of food for themselves and their young on each foraging trip. In the afternoon we sailed into a blizzard, a wall of pinkish-grey cloud and snow out of which materialized six more visions from paradise known as Snow Petrels, pure white birds, every feather on them, although their bills and eyes are black. They flew, with a slightly stiff-winged action, up and down to port for ages, delighting everyone who was on deck and those who rushed up to see them. Snow Petrels live where there is ice so as soon as they drifted off we were on full alert for that significant entry in the logbooks of ships heading south; 'First Ice'. An iceberg, no matter how big, is free-floating, like a piece of driftwood or a message in a bottle, and once cast off from the main bodies of ice at the poles it travels wherever the winds and currents take it and it was not long before we saw our first, hundreds of miles north of Antarctica, a massive chunk of white higher than the nearby Shag Rocks which rise up to 230 feet (70 metres) out of the South Atlantic Ocean.

The next day began like a dream; Snow Petrels, Blue Petrels, Light-mantled Albatrosses and, visible off the bow, some snowy mountains rising steeply out of the ocean, the backbone of a remote island called South Georgia, with pyramidal peaks nearly 10,000 feet (3000 metres) high, glaciers, snowy slopes, black cliffs, and black beaches sprinkled with the white breasts of millions of penguins. "One of the world's most glorious spectacles - like the Alps in mid-ocean," Robert Cushman Murphy called it.

The Antarctic outpost is about a hundred miles long (160 km) and 25 miles wide (40 km), so rugged, cold and windswept the vegetation is composed almost entirely of columns of tussock grass, and some herbs and mosses, "not wood enough to make a toothpick," as Captain James Cook put it. The sky is rarely blue even during the short summers when fog, rain, snow and high winds are the norm. It looks bleak from some angles and yet South Georgia is home to possibly the greatest concentration of life on Earth, an abundance of mammals and birds which in the mid-2000s included about three million fur seals, 400,000 elephant seals and an estimated 60 million seabirds including about 22 million pairs of Antarctic Prions, two million pairs of Macaroni Penguins, 400,000 pairs of King Penguins and 4000 pairs of Wandering Albatrosses. There is no airport nor airfield; the only way to get there is by ship, boat, yacht, whatever you can lay your hands on that floats, because, if you are truly excited by wildlife, the ultimate one-off experience is a trip to South Georgia and Antarctica.

We arrived on a rare day when the waters were calm and the sky *was* blue. We took our first *Zodiac* excursion into a beautiful small cove called Elsehul where groups of King Penguins stood behind a line of aggressive fur seals, so many of them we were unable to land, so we set foot on South Georgia a little way along the coast in Right Whale Bay. Then we still had to tackle the fur seals, which are not 'true' seals, related to otters, but 'eared' seals like sealions, with an ancestry closer to dogs and bears; Captain Cook called them 'sea bears'. Adult males, up to six feet (two metres) long, are strongly territorial and when their patch of beach comes under threat they rear up high on their strong fore-flippers, raise their heavy heads and thick bull-necks, and with their hind flippers turned to function like feet they shuffle along fast enough to catch rivals or humans when, without hesitation, they lurch rapidly forward and bite with long canine teeth. Since about 1910 when there appeared to be none left to hunt they have been so successful the aptly-named beachmasters (or bastards if you prefer) line virtually every beach on South Georgia and so every landing has to be organised very carefully. The tetchy, snarling barrier of flippers, fur and teeth is only possible to penetrate with the help of expedition team members armed with sticks although striking the intimidating beasts roaring and growling with teeth bared is not allowed so the team are reduced to waving said sticks while roaring and mock-charging themselves, in order to force a gap in the line of seal defence and enable the ship's passengers to get through.

Beyond the fur seals in the mountainous arena of Right Whale Bay was a flat plain almost covered in a great swathe of silver, white, yellow and gold, the colours of thousands of adult King Penguins, and patches of brown, the crèches where the youngsters hang out, their dark beaks and short-feathered heads poking out of what look like downy brown overcoats way too big for them. King Penguins are curious birds and after Alice and I sat down and kept still for a while several youngsters came over to investigate us, presumably to see or smell if anything was edible. They get hungry waiting up to three months for their parents to return with food from foraging trips. When the adults do return they announce themselves by standing with their legs taut, gleaming white chests out, necks stretched to the full, heads thrown back and bills pointing at the sky to send their wail as far as possible. Somehow, their youngster recognises the somewhat sad, trumpet-like call amongst the great cacophony that is going on constantly all around, and calls back. Sitting by the 'penguin highway', between the beach and the colony, where the adults were passing in both directions, a few of them took a little time out to inspect me. They were so tall we ended up beak to beak as it were and so another fantastic day in my life came to pass.

The next day was even better. It began at 05:00, with the now usual palaver; try to keep 'seawatcher's eyes' open while waking up, roll out of bed, stand up, put on thermal long johns and first layer of clothes, shuffle along the corridor to the restaurant for a quick coffee and croissants, return to cabin to don wellington boots, waterproof trousers, fleeces, bright yellow parkas (so we would be easily spotted if lost), life-jackets, thermal beanies, binoculars, cameras, sun-block, lip-salve and sunglasses (so we would not get snow blindness), walk back along the corridor to turn our tags (to let the ship's staff know we have left the ship), climb up the stairs to get on deck and while gasping at the latest spectacular scenery wait to climb down the outside of the ship into the first *Zodiac* to be launched at 06:00.

Off we went, skimming across the water to an exposed black sand beach ruled by fur seals. Beyond the teeth in The Bay of Isles was one of South Georgia's largest King Penguin colonies which almost completely covered a flat expanse of gravel beds crossed by shallow melt-water streams, a glacial delta called Salisbury Plain, the place where in 1912-13 Robert Cushman Murphy collected many of his specimens. The delta lies between two massive glaciers. The one to the east Murphy named after Frederic Augustus Lucas, Director of the American Museum of Natural History at that time. The one to the west he named Grace, after his wife whom he married just before his year at sea and on South Georgia. Three decades later, using his journal and the letters he sent to his wife, he wrote a book called *Logbook for Grace* which is absorbing when he writes about wildlife, harrowing when he describes the massacre of countless whales and seals.

The thousands of Kings swept left and right and up the lower slopes of the mountains beyond. There were plenty on the beach too, some coming in some going out and I watched squads of them torpedoing out of the ocean and bouncing on to the black sand. With their bellies full they got to their feet and after a while, to steady themselves after so long away in the water it seemed, they joined the procession on the long waddle across the slippery slime of guano to their young, somewhere among the long, wide stretch of brown furry feathered birds that ran through the wavy lines of the silver, black, white and orange of the adults. After the magnificent sight, smell is the next sense to be bombarded, with the slightly acrid odour of penguin shit, which has a hint of ammonia. Then the ears tune into the din; the whistles of the young and the wails of the old. Up close I could hear the thumping of flippers too, as the adults whacked each other while squabbling and jostling for position. Everywhere there was a great toing and froing, something going on, a tremendous bustle, relieved here and there by pairs meeting up again and greeting one another serenely with slow-motion synchronised head waving. There was time too to examine some birds in detail, to marvel at the tiny dense feathers on their heads which form a kind of velvet that looks black at a distance but has a greenish hue close up. It is the orange lower mandibles of the beaks and deep golden 'ear-muffs' and upper breasts that turn the eye though, fading to bright yellow on the chest then the satin ivory of the belly which contrasts beautifully with the tiny, bristly, silvery feathers down the back. It was so thrilling to be amongst them, to be 'a penguin' for a while, amongst the throng, no matter how many colonies we visited.

Back at the beach a Snowy Sheathbill was perched on a *Zodiac*, a strange bird the size and look of a small chicken, and completely at ease in the presence of humans. All of its feathers were white but its stubby beak was dirty yellow and its face bare and pink, a characteristic of carrion-feeders like vultures and appropriate for a bird which eats carcasses, seal placentas, eggs and chicks. We were on the last *Zodiac* back and on one of the first to leave for the next destination, Prion Island, where amongst the tussocks at the top we watched a few young Wandering Albatrosses dozing or stretching their ridiculously long wings. They were waiting for one of their parents to return from their lengthy foraging trips with some seafood soup. When adults did arrive back the huge birds made several low passes, some just above our heads, before spreading their wings, tails and huge webbed feet to act as brakes and bundling to the ground very ungracefully, for an albatross. One nearly completed a somersault on landing and took an age to get itself together before waddling over to its youngster to regurgitate some liquid fish. The same bird's partner came in as well, a rare event, and there was a great ceremony as the pair greeted each other with their great

*Light-mantled Albatrosses, South Georgia, 27th November 2006*

long wings spread and tails cocked, and a lot of head bowing and waving, and bill clapping. Sitting surprisingly snugly amongst the tussocks I looked up after another snow flurry and saw two pairs of Light-mantled Albatrosses sailing back and forth in superb synchronized flight along the nearby cliff-top. A beak's length apart one pair traced long sweeps and curves with consummate ease, against a backdrop of sea and snowy mountains, until they flew straight out from the cliff in formation, level and parallel, and split apart with matching graceful arcs to the left and the right, the perfect end to one of the most magical sights of my life.

We were the last back for lunch, then, after a welcome siesta to rest my stinging eyes, there was time for a third excursion, into the wide beach of Fortuna Bay, backed with mossy slopes below massive slabs of rock, yet more snowfields, glaciers and colossal pyramidal peaks which disappeared now and then in wispy, grey, snow-laden clouds, all still on a scale I struggled to comprehend. Big birds like Light-mantled Albatrosses with wingspans of about six feet (two metres) looked like specks against the blue face of a glacier, seen at what seemed like close range from a *Zodiac*. We were in search of nesting Light-mantled Albatrosses so we strode purposefully along the beach, taking great care to avoid the fur seals but stopping to look at the bull Elephant Seals. The mild-mannered masses of blubber sprawled on the sand looked like they had been dropped from a great height and landed with a splat. Named after the male's large, inflatable, trunk-like proboscis not their size, the behemoths may live long enough to reach a length of twenty feet (six metres) with a girth of nearly ten feet (over three metres) and a weight in the region of 9000 lb (4000 kg), five to six times the bulk of the relatively dainty females.

While the bulls are ashore, usually for several weeks, they fight rivals by rising up to bite each other's necks, often leaving both bleeding badly. The strongest get to mate with a harem of females one of which, as Alice observed, looked slightly alarmed when a massive bull put a suggestive flipper around her. Most of the females in Fortuna Bay were looking after shiny black, rubbery pups with disproportionately large, black, lustrous, marble-like eyes. It was the huge males which demanded attention though. Although they may rear up their small heads and open their pink mouths to sigh or yawn or protest, with a moan, groan, bark or snarl, about a rival or one of us being too close, they are like Gorillas; gentle, peaceful animals.

At the end of the long broad beach there was a deep creek between us and a tussock-topped cliff where we could see a few nesting pairs of Light-mantled Albatrosses so we summoned a *Zodiac* and leaping quickly out of it we climbed up to watch a pair of the beauties, one sitting on a nest the other standing above it, calling with its bill open skywards. We watched and listened to the wild wavering 'pee-ow' for so long we were the last back to the ship.

The next morning we visited the largest King Penguin colony on South Georgia, in St Andrews Bay, where about 100,000 birds raise their young below a huge semi-circle of steep snowy mountain slopes and bare, dark grey pyramidal peaks rising into swirling clouds of snow. We then sailed back northwest to Grytviken, which I was not keen on seeing. Why the people who worked out the cruise schedule thought a walk around the decrepit, wind-ravaged, rusty-roofed factories of an old whaling station where so many horrors took place was appropriate on a trip to one of the world's last wild wonderlands was beyond me. I went ashore though, because I wanted to visit Ernest Shackleton's grave. He was tough. In 1901 he reached 85°15' S with Captain Scott and Edward Wilson, the farthest south any human beings had ever been but still 300 miles (480 km) short of the South Pole. On his own expedition in 1907-1909 he led a party of four to a new 'Farthest South' at 88°23' S, just 112 miles (180 km) from the pole, before being driven back by five consecutive days of 'blinding, shrieking' blizzards, '60 to 70 of frost', exhaustion and insufficient food. In December 1914 he set sail on the three-masted *Endurance* from Grytviken for the Antarctic continent again, despite dire warnings from the whalers that the ship might be trapped in ice should she venture too far south. They were right. The *Endurance* was beset by pack ice in January 1915 and drifted nearly 573 miles (922 km) within the ice, driven by the clockwise current in the Weddell Sea, for ten months before the crew had to abandon ship when she was finally crushed. For five months they camped on the ice, slowly drifting north until it began to break up underneath them and they were then forced to take to the lifeboats they had taken off the *Endurance*. The weak, cold men managed to row forty miles (64 km) in six days, to Elephant Island but despite their enormous relief on reaching land it was uninhabited and nobody knew they had been shipwrecked or where they were so there was virtually no chance of being rescued.

In order to save their lives Shackleton decided that he, Frank Worsley, Tom Crean and three others would try to sail one of the lifeboats, the 22 foot (6.7 metre) long and less than seven foot (2.1 metre) wide *James Caird*, to South Georgia, where they could get help from the whalers. Somehow, they crossed 800 miles (1287 km) of the roughest waters on the planet, through gales and snowstorms, and thanks to Worsley's exceptional navigation skills reached South Georgia, after a fortnight.

They then had no choice but to land on the dark, desolate, uninhabited, windward southern side of the island, when the whaling stations were on the north side. No one had ever done it before, even attempted it, but, barely alive, Shackleton, Worsley and Crean climbed over the unexplored mountains of South Georgia to the Stromness whaling station where they arrived in rags in May 1916.

Shackleton had but one thought at that time; how to rescue the 22 men left on Elephant Island. First of all, Worsley, with a boat and crew from the whaling station, recovered McCarty, McNish and Vincent on the south side of the island. Shackleton then chartered a boat to get to Elephant Island, only to find heavy pack ice barring the way. He went on to the Falklands, from where another boat made a second attempt to reach the island, again without success due to the pack. So Shackleton went to Punta Arenas in Chile where a small pilot ship *Yelcho* was placed at his disposal and on the third attempt, with Worsley also aboard, in August 1916, twenty months since the *Endurance* sailed from South Georgia, they finally reached the island. "All well?" Shackleton shouted as he approached the men in a small boat. They were.

Five and a half years later, on the morning of the 5th of January 1922, Shackleton died of heart failure aged 48 aboard the *Quest*, lying off Grytviken. He was leading another expedition, to circumnavigate the Antarctic continent. According to the instructions of his wife Emily he was laid to rest with a cairn and cross to mark his grave but these were later replaced with a granite headstone bearing a nine-pointed star, a personal motif that he used throughout his life as a guide and inspiration.

Some think Shackleton's tale or Scott's terrible, fatal haul to the South Pole and back in 1911-1912 was *The Worst Journey in the World* but the book of that title describes what may well have been just that. It was written by Apsley Cherry-Garrard and refers to a five-week sledging trip taken on the same Antarctic expedition of 1910-1913 during which Scott died. Cherry-Garrard, Henry 'Birdie' Bowers and Edward 'Bill' Wilson, the same man who reached 'Farthest South' with Shackleton, travelled from Cape Evans to Cape Crozier and back on what Wilson described as, "the weirdest bird's-nesting expedition that has ever been or ever will be." No one had undertaken such a journey during the middle of the dark Antarctic winter but that was, Wilson believed, when Emperor Penguins started incubating their eggs. It was the embryos inside them that he was after because he thought they may shed some light on a possible evolutionary link between birds and dinosaurs. Most scientists at the time thought that 'ontogeny recapitulated phylogeny', that is the stages in the development of an animal embryo (ontogeny) resemble or represent the stages in the evolution of the animal's remote ancestors (phylogeny), and it was thought that the young embryos of Emperor Penguins, believed to be primitive birds in the early 1900s, may have vestiges of teeth and even features linking bird feathers to reptilian scales. The embryos collected on the weirdest bird's-nesting expedition turned out to be too old to investigate the bird-dinosaur link, and ontogeny was subsequently discovered not to recapitulate phylogeny, as my A Level Biology teacher Mr Lowis told me, but in the 1990s, eight decades after what turned out to be Wilson's futile adventure, the link between birds and dinosaurs was made.

Wilson, Bowers and Cherry-Garrard set out in late June 1911, man-hauling two sledges 130 miles (200 km) across ice pressure ridges and crevasses, more often than not in gale force sometimes hurricane force winds and blizzards with temperatures averaging minus 60°F and falling to 77°F below. It was so cold that Cherry's chattering teeth shattered. At night, to get into their sleeping bags they had to thaw the granite-like ice in them with their 'warm' feet from their boots. At Cape Crozier they built a camp consisting of their tent and a small stone 'igloo', to create some shelter against the unrelenting wind. From there they climbed down to the Emperor Penguin colony and collected five eggs but returned with just three because two burst in Cherry's mitts during a fall. He wrote, 'All day it had been blowing a nasty cold wind with a temperature between -20 and -30 ... Now it began to get worse ... Such extremity of suffering cannot be measured: madness or death may give relief. But this I know: we on this journey were already beginning to think of death as a friend.' The next morning the tent, next to the igloo, was blown away by 'solid walls of black snow'. Without their tent they were dead men. There was no way back to base without the shelter it provided from the storms. The next day the blizzard hurricane ripped the canvas roof off the igloo. Huddled against a wall in their wet sleeping bags under the drifting snow they occasionally checked if the others were still alive. Cherry prepared to die and wrote, 'Men do not fear death, they fear the pain of dying.'

After two days and two nights without a meal there was finally enough of a lull in the wind to cook some pemmican (a high-energy tinned mixture of powdered meat, fat and sometimes dried fruits), then, in a little glow of light, they went to look for the tent and were astonished when Bowers found it half a mile away. He tied himself to it every night they camped on the way back. Over a month after setting out they staggered into base camp as much dead as alive, having survived some of the continuously lowest temperatures ever endured by human beings. Their frozen clothes had to be cut from their bodies and the looks on their faces haunted the expedition photographer, Herbert Ponting, for days.

The *Multanovskiy* repositioned while we slept and early morning found us in another glorious setting called Royal Bay where Alice and I climbed a crag and sat amongst some tussocks high above thousands of King Penguins so we could watch Light-mantled Albatrosses sail to and fro along the edge of their nesting cliff. They were opposite us at eye level, across a deep, narrow gulley and below a magnificent mountain slope. Light hail and sleet washed our backs but we could have sat there all day watching the ultimate gliders and listening to their 'pee-ow' calls. We counted fourteen nests, neat mounds of mud and vegetation with a cup for the single egg, and watched a couple swaying heads and rubbing open bills together before taking to the air for a spot of synchronized flying, wheeling around together, tightening the bond, just like us. A White-chinned Petrel came in and disappeared down its burrow, and Antarctic Terns, Brown Skuas and a Snow Petrel passed by, completing another fantastic morning.

On the way back to the ship in a snow storm we visited the face of the Weddell Glacier, a cliff made out of ice. Then we sailed south alongside the snowy mountains of the sea to Cooper Bay where three shallow coves lie below more towering peaks at the southeast end of the island. Grumpy fur seals were very tightly-packed below a hard, slippery snow slope which we clambered up carefully. We were accompanied by some Gentoo Penguins but we were trying to reach a small colony of Macaroni Penguins. Macaronis are by far the most numerous nesting penguins on South Georgia but almost all of them nest on inaccessible steep headlands on the windward coasts so Cooper Bay is one of few places where it is possible to get a good look at the small, red-billed and orange-crested birds.

Sleet and snow swirled around us as we made our way back to the ship and then we were surrounded by birds as we sailed south through hundreds of Black-browed Albatrosses, White-chinned Petrels and Blue Petrels, and hundreds of thousands of prions. There were birds as far as our worn-out eyes could see, over what was a sea of seabirds in a seabird lover's dream. More and more icebergs included a distant low block which looked as big as a country and another of the chocolate-ripple variety, a rare and sensational sight because it looked like a block of ice cream twice the size and height of the ship, the dark brown streaks being made up of sediment from when the iceberg was still part of a slow-moving glacier or even volcanic dust. As the number of prions fell away Blue Petrel numbers rose and a Light-mantled and several Wandering Albatrosses appeared. We even saw a couple of South Georgia Diving Petrels, and what a place to see so many birds gliding over the ocean against a backdrop of exploding white surf, black headlands and a great long line of glaciers and snow and mountains, the highest peak a gigantic dollop of snow at the end of South Georgia.

The scenery got better and better during our all too brief time cruising along the coast of South Georgia. One wonderful vista was followed by an even more spectacular one, right to the southern end at Cape Disappointment, given that name by Captain Cook when he saw a rugged coast leading back northwest and realized that South Georgia was an island and not part of the as yet undiscovered 'Anti-Arctic', as he had hoped. A Snow Petrel saw us off south into the grey, lumpy, misty Scotia Sea where the next morning an icy wind was blowing, straight out of Antarctica. There were icebergs, crazy icebergs, everywhere, of every imaginable shape and size, ranging from elephant-seal-sized 'growlers', small but still a serious danger to ships without ice-strengthened hulls, through tumbling wind-and-water-sculpted 'bergy bits' the size of small houses, to some as big as the ship to one best described as an ice island, possibly up to 300 feet (100 metres) high, ten miles (16 km) across and forty miles (64 km) long according to the ship's radar, so big it looked like the edge of the Antarctic ice shelf and so long we had to sail around it. Freshwater melting from the bergs into the sea helps the growth of phytoplankton which provides food for zooplankton which birds eat and there were birds everywhere amongst the ice; Black-browed Albatrosses, Blue Petrels, Pintado Petrels, prions and several Light-mantled Albatrosses, one of which came by at head height, pretty eye to bleary eye.

It was all so beautiful I was up at four in the morning. There was snow on deck and even more ice on view, especially to port where a mass of brash and pack blocked our way to the South Orkneys, rising high and mainly snowy out of the Scotia Sea in the misty distance. The awesome icebergs included one with blue holes. Though the surface of icebergs is white the ice deep within is transparent blue, as in glaciers, and when the blue is seen, the pristine blue of untainted ice, it usually means a berg has rolled over. Seabirds wheeled and whirled along and above the cliffs of white ice of the massive tabular blocks floating in a deep blue sea. All this, in a light as clear and crisp as it is possible to be. It was a pristine, truly wonderful world of water, ice, sky and light, completed by so many birds and whales. In days gone by almost all the whales of the Scotia Sea were harpooned and butchered in order to, in the words of Herman Melville in *Moby-Dick*, 'illuminate the solemn churches that preach unconditional inoffensiveness by all to all'. There are still nowhere near as many as there once were but we saw a lot of 'blows' (whales surfacing for air in the distance) and two schools of Fin Whales, but even they were surpassed by our first Antarctic Petrels. The dark cold brown birds have broad white bars along the rear of the upperwings, almost all white underwings, and white tails with dark terminal bands, and they are very striking, even in the dazzling world they glide through.

Antarctic Petrels raise their young on the Antarctic continent, some in the most southerly bird colony on Earth, which is over 300 miles (480 km) inland and within ten degrees of the South Pole, farther south than the places Emperor Penguins raise their young. The petrels sit on their single white egg in depressions lined with gravel on steep slopes and cliffs alongside the only other two bird species to reach so far south; Snow Petrels and the predatory South Polar Skuas.

Birds are everywhere on Earth. The petrels and skuas have been seen at the South Pole. Northern Fulmars, Kittiwakes and Snow Buntings have been observed at or near the North Pole. Alpine Choughs soar over cliffs at over 27,000 feet (8235 metres), just a couple of thousand feet below the summit of Everest, and other birds such as cranes and geese migrate over the Himalayas each spring and autumn. African Skimmers nest on the shores of Lake Turkana in northern Kenya where the ground air temperature rises above 100°F (40°C). Life is everywhere on Earth. Microscopic organisms live underneath ice floes, on the deepest seabeds, in volcanoes, in pools of sulphuric acid, even on the surfaces of high-altitude clouds. Over 200 species of bacteria live in and on every human being, about ten million of them per square centimetre of skin, with more inside. Even large animals live in what we consider to be extreme places. Polar Bear footprints have been seen within two degrees of the North Pole, presumably in pursuit of Ringed Seals which have been recorded there. Emperor Penguins endure temperatures down to -76°F (-60°C) and hurricane-force winds while incubating their eggs during the Antarctic winter. The Siberian Salamander can survive winter temperatures as low as -69°F (-56°C). In mountain regions Snow Leopards are occasionally seen as high as 18,000 feet (5500 metres), a Wolf has been spotted at 19,000 feet (5791 metres), Yaks probably forage as high as 20,000 feet (6100 metres) where Large-eared Pikas also occur, Jumping Spiders, which probably eat wind-blown waifs, live under stones frozen to the ground nearly 22,000 feet (6700 metres) up the slopes of Everest, and a Common Toad has been found at over 26,000 feet (8000 metres).

Lower down, in Africa, some of the Great Rift Valley lakes are caustic enough to burn human flesh and yet support a broth of brine shrimps and blue-green algae which in turn feed flamingos with legs protected by specialized scales. In the Sahara, Desert Silver Ants hunt at midday, eating insects which have died in the heat of 115°F (46°C). Way down in the oceans there are eyeless shrimps, giant clams, crabs, squat lobsters, giant tube worms, octopuses and fish, a whole community of animals, living in the dark, surviving on bacteria which feed on sulphur in the super-hot water gushing from deep-sea vents at 662°F (350°C). Deeper down, a red shrimp has been recorded at a depth of 35,802 feet (10,913 metres) in the Marianas Trench. Even some large animals enter the abyss. Sperm Whales have been recorded diving as deep as 6560 feet (2000 metres) and they probably reach 10,000 feet (3048 metres) in pursuit of Giant Squid. And above the surface of the oceans and seas fly a multitude of birds, including the hundreds of prions, Pintado Petrels and Southern Fulmars we saw when we reached the Southern Ocean, the deep cold waters encircling Antarctica south of 60°S and subject to intense storms, high winds and huge waves.

We were far enough south for the wind to be noticeably colder, and for there to be monstrous icicles hanging from the icebergs. At the northern edge of the Weddell Sea Alice and I stood on the sunlit bow of the *Multanovskiy* and tried to take in the scene, dominated by ice in myriad forms; brash, bergy bits, growlers, bergs, floes and mostly floating plateaux. Anchoring off Paulet Island a high fin cut through the water. It was a male Killer Whale, followed by two more. Beyond them we could see the massive snow-covered ice-cap dome of Dundee Island and the snow-free extinct volcanic cone of Paulet. We landed on a pebble beach on Paulet that was littered with ice-sculptures, football-sized works of nature's art made by wind and water. A sharp smell of ammonia drifted over from the nearby colony of a hundred thousand pairs of lovely little Adélie Penguins, with black heads and backs, white bellies, stubby pink and black beaks, and white rings around their eyes. The silky little beauties were everywhere. Some were porpoising in from the sea, popping out of the water, and waddling up the scree to the colony. Especially memorable were a group of nine tobogganing across the frozen lake, using their stout legs to push and wing tips to steer, and moving much more rapidly than on foot. Above the fantastic black and white mass of penguins Snow Petrels scooted across the high, steep slopes of scree where Wilson's Storm Petrels came in and entered their burrows in broad daylight, the bright yellow webs between their tiny toes visible with our naked eyes as they braked before disappearing amongst the loose small rocks.

Late in the night we sailed through the Antarctic Sound, between the tip of the Antarctic Peninsula and the Joinville Island group, but we were too tired to stay on deck and watch yet more wonder and too tired to think of words worthy of it all. By morning we were in the South Shetlands, not at Elephant Island as hoped, because there was too much of a swell to land, but at Half Moon Island, a small crescent-shaped islet with a small colony of Chinstrap Penguins, where there was also quite a swell, and ice, glaciers, snowy mountains and light cloud all around. Alice and I sheltered from a wicked wind on a pebble beach while watching some Chinstrap Penguins, below a high, grey basaltic column splattered with bright orange lichen. There were many more Chinstraps at Baily Head on Deception Island, a volcano jutting out of the ocean shaped like a horseshoe which we were fortunate to land on in some chop which made getting in and out of the *Zodiacs* more interesting than usual. It was not the first time Chief mistimed his step up on to the rim of a bouncing rubber boat and took a tumble into the cold water with his camera gear in a rucksack on his back.

We were being lashed by sleet and snow showers by then and back at sea the ship rocked and rolled its way south down the west side of the Antarctic Peninsula. By morning we were in the wonderland of the Gerlache Strait sailing past coastal cliffs of ice and smooth sweeping curves of snowfields sculpted perfectly by the wind. That was nothing compared to the Lemaire Channel, a seven mile (11 km) long canyon of black rock, ice, snow and Snow Petrels, narrowing to less than half a mile (700 m) in places and with walls rising almost sheer into a shroud of mist at over 3000 feet (1000 m), too steep in many places for much snow to lie, but there was plenty of snow on the shallower slopes and in the air, and lots of ice, in the side valleys clogged up with glacier calves and in the main channel where they spilled into. The ship zigzagged through the bergs and crashed through the brash as we looked at the fantasy scenery of cold white ice, glacier blue ice, sweeping snowfields, black rock pinnacles, sea mist, snow flurries and Snow Petrels.

There was not another ship in sight, no sign that any human had ever set foot there. An hour later we were playing pool at Vernadsky, the Ukranian Antarctic Base. Alice and I won the mandatory match against Chief and

The Colonel, both mean pool players, on a bald table with big heavy balls, in a very cosy bar where a couple of stiff vodkas went down very well indeed.

That was 'Farthest South' for us; 65°15'S. We sailed back north, through the Lemaire Channel again, where, as I had planned, when there was no one else on the bow, I persuaded Alice to join me there, in the most beautiful place on Earth, so I could propose ... that Alice and I spend the rest of our lives together ... and presented her with a small dark green box in which was a specially commissioned silver ring with ten emeralds; her favourite metal, gemstone, number and colour. She was stunned and completely lost for words, and all she could do was laugh nervously, but, eventually, and more importantly, she said, "Yes!"

At the evening meal I ordered a bottle of champagne for the first time in my life and the seven of us drank a toast to me and Alice. After dinner we carried on celebrating, Alice and I getting together in the first place, and life in general, especially life at that particular time, with a few *Tequilas* and Alice was asleep before her head hit the pillow. We were both a bit groggy the next morning so we were particularly pleased to come across a smooth boulder to sit on at the edge of Useful Island, from where we watched some Gentoos dive into the water, flippers tucked in tight to their sides, with blue and pink candy floss clouds overhead. We had to high-step through deep snow to reach that comfortable seat in Antarctica, and on our way back to the *Zodiac*, leaving deep blue holes in the snowfield big enough to swallow a Gentoo or two.

The *Multanovskiy* continued north, to Neko Harbour in Andvord Bay at 64°51'S where I set foot on Antarctica, the seventh and last continent for me. Alice and I made our way up through a broad snowfield at the base of the mountains and while Alice tobogganed down a snow slope on her behind for fun I watched and listened to the adjacent glacier, seeing a beautiful new colour I called crevasse blue, and hearing, as hoped, a few ripping cracks as the tongue of the glacier broke up. Although the chance was slim I was also hoping to see the glacier calve; the spectacular event where a giant slab of ice breaks off and crashes into the water. I had about an hour. It was in vain but I enjoyed the wait, watching Antarctic Terns and Snow Petrels fly past the icy blue crevasses in the glacier face. Back in a *Zodiac* with Alice we did get to see a small section of ice fall into the steely grey bay, a bit too close for comfort actually and the driver got a good telling off when we reached the ship, for had there been a massive calving we would have been overturned by the resulting wave and thrown into the freezing water where due to hypothermia life expectancy is less than an hour.

On we sailed, through the wonderland of blues and whites and blacks and greys of seas and ice and glaciers and snowy mountains, for the last time, and our Antarctic dream came to an end cruising quietly, almost reverentially, through the magical, snow-capped glittering islets and ice-lined channels of the Melchior Islands in a *Zodiac*, a good place to look for Humpback Whales and Leopard Seals apparently. We saw neither and very little else alive but it mattered not one jot because the scenery was more than enough.

Next morning we were in the Drake Passage, the 500 mile (800 km) stretch of open ocean between Antarctica and South America, famous for rough weather, high seas and birds, so it was a compulsory all hands on deck day, except it was only me, Foggy and Nick up there at 04:30. The rest joined us somewhat later, and we only took the odd break for the rest of the day, including the usual one following someone mentioning, "Cake down below!" We saw plenty of birds, at least at first, including the last of the Light-mantled Albatrosses, and lots of whales, well, lots of blows, so many blows but barely a glimpse of an actual animal until, way out in the passage, we came across three Humpback Whales; two adults and a youngster. They surfaced many times right next to the ship, mostly just off or even under the bow. Take any drugs you like you'll never see anything like a rainbow in the blow of a Humpback Whale but even more memorable was the moment the largest of the three glided by the bow, from right to left, just under the surface, just under me, so close I heard the roar at the end of the blow when the magnificent creature surfaced for air and smelt its fishy breath. It was a deeply enriching and emotional experience that came to a sad end when they dived deep and away, leaving the lasting image of their tail flukes outspread above the surface.

The palaver required to get on deck to seawatch reached new heights on the last day of our voyage for it was by far the roughest. A gale force 8 nor'westerly that got going overnight had whipped up a 30 foot (9 metre) swell and the odd 50 foot (15 metre) wave, providing a mere taste of what the Drake Passage is like in really bad weather. I loved it. The wind and sea provided the ideal conditions in which to round off the wonderful seawatching, bringing out the best in the aerial acrobatics of albatrosses, mainly the handsome Black-browed but also several majestic Wanderers, gliding through cavernous troughs between waves, across the faces of the huge slabs of water and up and over the top of them, where they changed position with a tiny tweak of a wing or tail feather to catch the wind again. It was hard graft seawatching all day though, standing on deck for hours, constantly shuffling feet to stay upright and lifting binoculars to admire the birds, banging into stairs and rails and at times clinging on for dear life as the ship rolled with the swell, so severely one time that Chief went over and did the luge down an inclined gangway and would have ended up in the Drake Passage but for the rail at the end.

I was incredibly tired but it being the last day I persevered until seven in the evening, leaving the deck only for some sustenance and to comfort poor Alice who like many of the others on board was suffering from the swell. Due to the weather Captain Nesterov steered the *Multanovskiy* well clear of Cape Horn and I saw it only from afar before I retired to my bed, completely knackered and a little sad after the voyage of over 3000 nautical miles, over 5500 kilometres, had come to an end when a Black-browed Albatross rocked to one side to crest a wave and turned away, leaving me almost in tears.

*King-of-Saxony Bird-of-paradise, Tari Valley, Papua New Guinea, 27th August 2008*

## 20

# NEW GUINEA

It took four days to get to New Guinea. It's a long way from near Land's End, England, via Brunei on the island of Borneo and Brisbane in Australia, to the capital of Papua New Guinea, Port Moresby. Once there, I boarded a *Dash 8* to Kiunga, a town on the Fly River nearly 500 miles (800 km) inland, and the gateway to the third largest expanse of lowland rainforest left on Earth, after the Amazon and the Congo, home to some of the most incredible birds on the planet. I was with Chief, Foggy,

Nick, The Colonel and his wife Lou, as well as three others; Mark Harper and his parents, and Sam Woods, the requisite leader of the organized tour, the unavoidable way to travel in search of birds in a country where during the short lowland dry season all, absolutely essential, local guides, are booked up by international bird and wildlife tour companies. Our man on the spot was Samuel Kepuknai, a former aircraft maintenance engineer and outboard motor mechanic who had been showing birders the best birds around Kiunga for twenty years.

Samuel was crucial because birds-of-paradise, especially males, are extremely shy. They, like many birds on New Guinea, are very wary because their species have been hunted for thousands of years. There are few large mammals on the island so big birds such as cassowaries and pigeons, and even smaller birds such as birds-of-paradise, have long been important sources of protein. Many birds have also been, and still are, captured and killed for their plumes, which men use in the wigs they wear while dancing in ritualized warfare and traditional ceremonies called *sing-sings*. They use the fancy feathers of birds such as parrots and lorikeets but the main sources of decoration are birds-of-paradise. The birds' fabulous ornaments are also exchanged in the 'bride wealth' payments when daughters are married, and they are treasured and traded, so much so that one of the reasons men and women live separately in tribes such as the Huli in the Tari Valley is that the men are afraid that if they get into an argument with their wife or wives the women will damage or destroy their precious feathers and the wigs they make with them, so the men live with their feathers and the women live with their pigs.

On seeing a *sing-sing* for the first time in 1955 David Attenborough wrote, 'It was one of the most spectacular and barbaric sights I have ever seen. I made a rough calculation. There were over five hundred beplumed dancers. Between them, they must have killed at least ten thousand birds-of-paradise to adorn themselves for this ceremony.' Fortunately, for the birds, traditions have given way to modern influences, communities have become slightly more westernized, hunting birds-of-paradise for plumes has declined, and since much of New Guinea is composed of rugged mountainous terrain numerous birds-of-paradise still live in peace far from human settlements and, for now, logging and mining companies.

Due to the terrain there are few roads so travelling beyond human settlements is very difficult. Even Port Moresby is essentially an island within an island, unconnected by road to the highlands inland where the canyons, mountains and massive river basins are prone to earthquakes, landslides, volcanic eruptions and extreme rainfall, all of which make road construction and maintenance extremely hazardous. Therefore, the best way to get around is by plane, although the air service is notoriously unreliable, partly due to the high-altitude weather which can make piloting planes very dangerous. Once off a plane visitors have to look for birds near towns and the only way to see the birds most visitors want to see, male birds-of-paradise, for any length of time, is to visit their display courts and trees, known only to a few local guides. In addition, since all the land, even what at first sight appears to be untouched trackless rainforest, is in fact private property, a local guide is essential, not only for maximising the chances of seeing male birds-of-paradise and many others but also for seeing them safely.

## A MIND-BLOWING BIRDING TRIP TO A PLANET CALLED EARTH

It's simply not possible to just get off a plane, hire a vehicle and go birding in New Guinea. Apart from the lack of public spaces in which to look for birds there is also the Papua New Guinea custom of *Payback* to worry about, whereby the relatives and fellow tribesmen of a victim of an offence whether it be theft, assault, rape or murder are obliged to pay back the perpetrator or any fellow family or tribe members, for the wrong-doing. In many areas it is considered an insult to the victim's family, clan and tribe if the police and the courts arrest and punish the offender first; retribution must come from the tribe itself. For a visitor the main problem is driving. For example, if a motorist accidentally hits and injures or kills someone, or a dog or a pig for that matter, they and all of their passengers risk being badly beaten or killed as *Payback*, a practice which also applies to those on public transport. Worse still, some local people believe all white people belong to the same 'tribe'.

Papua New Guinea has long been regarded as a risky place to visit, something usually taken on only by missionaries, mercenaries and miners, and even though cannibalism and headhunting were made illegal in the 1960s continuing tribal warfare and roaming violent gangs meant many parts of the country were still strictly off-limits to tourists when we arrived fifty years later. Papua was still listed as one of the most dangerous destinations to visit and Port Moresby rated the worst city in the world in which to live, not surprising given the gangs of 'raskols' blamed for a high number of rapes and murders in what the Australian Department of Foreign Affairs and Trade described as a, 'general atmosphere of lawlessness'. I believed that so long as we were with local guides we would be safe.

Samuel turned up before first light, with a long narrow dugout which the ten of us, plus Samuel and his assistant, just about squeezed into. At dawn we pushed the dugout off the bank and began motoring slowly along the wide Fly River. After a while it was good to hear the outboard stop. We glided into shore, clambered on to land and walked a short way to a large clearing in some swamp forest where we could see three tall, thin, bare trunks of broken palm trees, the dancing poles of a male Twelve-wired Bird-of-paradise. Almost immediately a large bird flew across the clearing with a floppy undulating action and landed on one of the dead palms and we all got very excited but it was only a less impressive bird-of-paradise, a decidedly more sombre cross between a crow and a starling called a Glossy-mantled Manucode. However, the next bird that came bounding in and perched on all three poles was the male Twelve-wired. He was shouting, 'haw haw haw' 'kaw kaw kaw' to let any females that might be in the vicinity know he was at home and asking if they fancied a dance and who knows what else. He was close enough to marvel at his velvet black body and deep, fluffy, yellow, candy-floss-like flank plumes, from which led, and I counted very carefully, eleven long bent-back 'wires'. It was a bird the like of which I had never set eyes on before, full of energy, bouncing up and down the top of a stump with strong legs but it was extremely wary and was not prepared to stay in the open for long. After he flew off I desperately wanted to wait for him to return and maybe even see a female appear and watch the display. When a female lands by a male he pulsates his round black breast shield edged with luminescent green and 'dances' up and down the pole with exaggerated movements, in order to best expose his pink thighs. If the female is impressed with them and stays he then perches above her, sways from side to side, hops from foot to foot and sweeps her face with his 'wires', after which she may let him mate with her, but not always. Samuel sensed that was not going to happen the morning we were there and he said we should move on, so we were soon ploughing along the Fly again.

Not long later, Samuel gently steered the dugout to the right and we arrowed into the smaller Elevala River where, while gliding slowly through the pristine lowland forest of New Guinea, giant bats called Great Flying Foxes flew lazily overhead on their way to their roosts while small parties of squawking Eclectus Parrots set out for the day from theirs, the females red and royal blue, the males emerald green. Also airborne were flocks of Collared Imperial Pigeons and a few Channel-billed Cuckoos, the largest of the cuckoos. Brahminy Kites were up too. Sacred Kingfishers dashed by, the colour of a shallow tropical sea. Dark rollers called Dollarbirds perched up. Then I saw my first Palm Cockatoo, a massive dark grey parrot, flying along the forest edge at the side of the river. It was a truly awesome sight as it flew with majestic slow beats of its huge, broad, immaculate, shiny grey wings, before landing in full view where I could see its huge hooked bill and crazy crest, the long swept-back feathers raised in alarm at the sight of people. It was followed by a small party of even larger and almost as spectacular Blyth's Hornbills, New Guinea's only hornbill species with huge, black, whooshing wings, white tails and, in the case of the males, rich silky buff ruffs. Lowland New Guinea was as wild as the world could be and I was already falling in love with it.

For a long time I forgot about how uncomfortable it was wedged into the dugout but I was still glad to get out and on to a muddy trail which led to a thick twisted tangle of vines under the canopy of the tall forest where according to Samuel a male King Bird-of-paradise liked to display every day. We stared in vain at those vines with our necks aching for hours waiting for the King to appear, distracted only by a Little Paradise Kingfisher, a blue and white but inconspicuous bird which I located in the dark understorey by the swinging white spatules at the end of its long tail. I was alone in seeing the whole bird and the same happened at the same time with a whistling Hooded Pitta which I managed to locate on the forest floor thanks to the silvery blue blaze on its shoulder glistening in the gloom.

Back on the Elevala there were few birds active in the heat of the afternoon as expected so I enjoyed watching the large dazzling blue Ulysses Swallowtail butterflies jinking and twinkling along the forest edge. The birds I was hoping to see were most likely to be seen just before dusk anyway, when they leave the ground to go to roost. They seemed to be eluding us until near dark when Samuel casually swung the dugout around, brought it to a silent halt and calmly pointed to a tree on the riverbank where the world's largest pigeon, the Southern Crowned Pigeon, was perched. At twice the size of a Band-tailed or Wood Pigeon with a much rounder belly it was certainly an impressive bird, beautifully marked too with a deep maroon breast contrasting with the grey head and dark grey back, wings and tail. Its large grey filigree crest made it look even bigger while it bobbed up and down on its thick pink legs, flashing its large white wing patches at us and glaring down with its bright red right eye. We left it in peace and returned to Kiunga, to the accompaniment of the low, slow, booming hoots of Greater Black Coucals skulking in the riverside thickets, and a magical first day on the island of New Guinea came to an end.

Lowland rainforest birds, be they in New Guinea, Asia, Africa or the Amazon, are perhaps the hardest birds of all to see. There may be more species of them than in other habitats but they usually occur in much lower numbers in much thicker vegetation. Under the 130 foot (40 metre) high canopy of dipterocarps, figs, laurels and mahoganies above us in New Guinea was a mass of creepers, lianas, ferns, palms, rattans and saplings reducing the light and visibility even more so it was easy to hear the loud nasal 'kyer-kyer-kyer-kyer' or 'qua-qua-qua' calls of male King Birds-of-paradise but much harder to see the birds. Their plumage may be amongst the brightest of any birds but they are smaller than starlings and shyer than a Sumatran Rhinoceros. Coming across one quietly searching for fruit and insects is virtually impossible so we were glad Samuel had a back-up display site. Unfortunately, like the first one, it was unoccupied. A bit flustered, he had to resort to a third, top secret stake-out normally reserved for filthy rich film-makers.

While we watched the lower than usual vine tangle it displayed in a Black-sided Robin perched low down on a vertical stem and a noisy mob of Rufous Babblers passed by but I barely looked at them. My eyes were on the vines and a long wait in the dripping forest of the Trans-Fly came to an end when there it was, 'in the 'scope', a fantastic male King Bird-of-paradise, the 'blood-and-snow bird' as The Colonel aptly put it, a bird difficult to do justice to in words. Alfred Russel Wallace got the closest I think. He was very moved when a dead one was brought to him on the Aru Islands in 1857, describing it as, 'a specimen which repaid me for months of delay and expectation. It was a small bird, a little less than a thrush. The greater part of its plumage was of an intense cinnabar red, with a gloss as of spun glass. On the head the feathers became short and velvety, and shaded into rich orange. Beneath, from the breast downward, was pure white, with the softness and gloss of silk, and across the breast a band of deep metallic green separated this colour from the red of the throat. Above each eye was a round spot of the same metallic green; the bill was yellow, and the feet and legs were of a fine cobalt blue, strikingly contrasting with all the other parts of the body. Merely in arrangement of colours and texture of plumage this little bird was a gem of the first water.' What Wallace did not mention were the two long 'wires' tipped with emerald discs hanging down from the very short tail, which the bird raises above its head and waves when displaying, or the two emerald-tipped fans which are spread from the sides of the bird's breast at the same time.

Nothing could compare to the king, except perhaps a male Flame Bowerbird so some of us spent over an hour and a half inside a cramped sweltering dome made out of palm fronds, humming with mosquitoes and crawling with leeches, overlooking his bower, a small stick-lined avenue, before the roar of approaching afternoon rain ended our chances. Having failed, we were left with a stark choice the following morning; make a second attempt to see Greater Birds-of-paradise displaying or try for the bowerbird somewhere else. The team decided to head for the famous 'grassy knoll' or 'Manucode Mound' along Boystown Road where it was possible to look over quite a bit of logged forest where the bowerbirds were known to make mid-morning flights between fruiting trees. Samuel did not appear to be keen on the idea. He must have known the state of the 'road' which was actually a deeply rutted and very muddy track made worse by recent unseasonal rainfall. The advance party in the 4WD saw a male Flame Bowerbird fly over as soon as they arrived but the gallant; me, Nick, The Colonel and Lou, who arrived later, were even more fortuitous, especially me for I was standing next to Mark when a second male flew by and landed in full view high in a tree and Mark was on it like a flash with his telescope and kind enough to let me have several seconds of the soft warm glow of deep yellow and orange, from bill-tip to tail-tip. Even in flight, with a black trim to the broad, rounded, bright yellow wings, the Flame Bowerbird looked fabulous.

Along Boystown Road there was time too to enjoy the long, loose, thin white feathers forming what looked like fancy moustaches, and long thin white feathers looking like wayward eyebrows, of some Moustached Treeswifts perched high up at the forest edge, as well as a Palm Cockatoo which flapped powerfully in and landed on a huge drooping frond of a massive palm tree. I was admiring its long crest feathers waving in the breeze when the rest of the team decided to dash to the Greater Bird-of-paradise site to try to see them, as well as a Blue Jewel Babbler. We saw neither, because it was too late in the morning. I thought we should have tried for the babbler where we were so it was a rather grumpy me sitting in a mini-bus travelling into the foothills of the Star Mountains.

*Palm Cockatoo, Trans-Fly, Papua New Guinea,
20th August 2008*

We were off to look for a completely different set of birds that live in the mid-montane forests surrounding the town of Tabubil, planned and built solely to serve the monstrous Ok Tedi mine, one of the largest open-pit copper and gold mines to scar the face of planet Earth. For the most part the road north from Kiunga runs parallel with the Ok Tedi (Ok means river), a wide, fast-flowing muddy river rushing past islands of grey gravel. During the wet season the river fills up and often damages the road. We got along no problem and there was enough light left to visit Ok Menga, a tributary of the Ok Tedi, where a Torrent

Flycatcher, a silvery-white bird with a bold black cap, black wings and a bobbing black tail, whistled while catching flying insects above the massive boulders in the tumbling water, the virtual convergent evolution twin of the Torrent Tyrannulet which inhabits Central and South America's wild rivers. And we also saw New Guinea's equivalent of South America's Torrent Ducks, the less striking brown-headed and barred-bodied but still thrilling Salvadori's Teals. Two bobbed downstream followed by a third, an interloper it seemed for it caused quite a scuffle, the three of them disappearing rapidly down the river in a slightly disturbing brutal flurry of flailing wings and jabbing bills.

We moved into the *Cloudlands Hotel* where there was another fight taking place, between some 'sparked' locals, the New Guinea term for drunk. It was all over in a minute or so and we sat down with the miners and engineers and ate pizza. Tabubil is known as 'Umbrella Town' because it lies in one of the wettest places on Earth where the average annual rainfall is over seven, sometimes eight, even ten, metres. It rains nearly every day but it didn't the day we visited Dablin Creek, a long hot day mostly 'standing about looking at nowt', hours of frustration barely relieved by a distant black speck with white flank plumes which was a bird-of-paradise called a Carola's Parotia, and a slightly larger speck, jet black one moment gold the next, which was a male Magnificent Bird-of-paradise. I wanted to see them well not like that, watch them at close range for a while, but the only way to see such birds like that is to visit their display courts on the forest floor and Samuel knew of none. We did get good views of a few birds. A small, black, white and red Mountain Peltops perched upright on a high snag, looking out for flying insects. Two close but fleeting, bright warbler-sized birds had shiny blue-grey upperparts edged black and glowing yellow underparts, most intense on the front of the head, hence the species name; Goldenface. Best of all were a pair of Red-breasted Pygmy Parrots which I could hardly be bothered to look at through my binoculars so high up in the massive tree above us were they and so indifferent was I due to the hours of lack of excitement but when Sam got them in his telescope I was immediately blown away by their diminutiveness. Barely longer than my middle finger they are one of the smallest parrots in the world and even in the 'scope they looked like deep green beans. They were far, far better than the bird preferred by the tickers amongst the team, the small, dowdy, grey-green Obscure Berrypecker, thee bird to see at Tabubil because it is very rarely seen anywhere else.

We stood about even longer the next day, nearly twelve hours in fact, down at Ok Ma, and, as was the case the day before, due to not having permission to enter the forest, we were only allowed to walk up and down a short section of track, by the side of which there was not a single log to sit on, so for the second day on the trot the only respite from walking up and down up and down or standing still on the hard gravel, in very uncomfortable wellington boots, came when I plonked my bony arse down on the stony track, and it was as, if not even more, frustrating than the previous day because there were even less birds to look at. To be fair the day *did* start very well, for just before dawn when we were watching a Papuan Boobook, a small chocolate-coloured owl, several Shovel-billed Kingfishers began calling and the race was on, to locate one before they fell silent again, as the species normally does when it gets lighter. A bird soon piped up with the far-carrying, monotonous, ringing, plaintive whistles close to the track and it was swiftly pinned down by Sam who caught sight of its rich buff breast in the shadows. It's a brute of a kingfisher that is also notable for its rarity and elusiveness, not its beauty, and the basically brown bird's most striking feature is the remarkable short broad bill, like a smaller version of a Shoebill's bill, used mainly for digging up worms, grubs and so on from the forest floor.

After that rush of excitement birding became extremely difficult. I knew we could forget Greater Melampitta, a long-legged black ground bird. Nearly everyone hears one, no one ever sees one, probably because it roosts and possibly lives underground, in limestone sinkholes, the only bird known to do so. Jewel babblers are not much easier to see and when one of the Chestnut-backed variety showed for a millisecond I missed it. It *was* exciting to listen to the loud upsweeping 'wow-wow!' whistles of male Magnificent Riflebirds most of the day but how I longed for one to perch where we could see one of the bloody things. For several hours we heard the multifarious calls and songs of lots of birds but saw very few, because most of them had the uncanny neck-breaking knack of foraging behind the leaves in the highest trees or when they did show for a second or two they did so at the back of the canopy, against the light. It was all extremely frustrating. I *did* see the usually inconspicuous but hulking form of a bluish Stout-billed Cuckooshrike and when there was nothing else to look for or at which was most of the time I got to know the two Moustached Treeswifts which were on view all day very well indeed.

With half an hour to spare before our flight the next morning we opted to check out a vast forested slope where Samuel thought we might see the unusual Pesquet's or Vulturine Parrot, a rare bird near human habitation because its brilliant red feathers are prized by the locals. Just as the tension with the time began to mount Samuel quietly announced that the terrible growling screams we could hear in the far distance were those of our quarry and before we had time to pinpoint the birds a group of five were in the air, flapping and gliding across the slope high above us, the red wing patches flashing, before landing in a lofty tree where, through the telescope, we could just about make out the vulture-like hooked bills and bare faces of the slaty, blackish brown birds.

After two gruelling days around Tabubil I was desperate to move on, to the Central Highlands where there were not only lots more birds-of-paradise and other birds, most of them were reputedly relatively easy to see. We flew in another *Dash 8* to Kagamuga airstrip, Mount Hagen, got into a mini-bus and sped east along the Highlands Highway to *Kumul Lodge*, the local word for bird-of-paradise. Situated up in the moss forests at over 8500 feet (2860 m) the rustic lodge, built, owned and managed by local people, looked lovely but there was no time to enjoy it as usual for not long after arriving we were taken to a fruiting tree frequented by a male Crested Bird-of-paradise, long thought to be a bird-of-paradise but subsequently considered to be one of just three satinbirds which live only in the central ranges of New Guinea. We didn't have to wait long for a tantalising flash of deep orange, the colour of the fruit eater's plush crown, nape, back, rump, tail and wing feathers, which contrasts with the deep, velvet black chin, throat, breast and belly. A glimpse was enough for the tickers but not for me, Chief and Nick who stayed under the otherwise lifeless tree, standing stock still so as not to deter the bird from returning and sure enough he came blazing back in, slowly, slowly, lower and lower until we watched in open-mouthed awe as he stopped bounding around the tree to preen his unbelievably bright plumes for fifteen minutes in full view.

When we returned to the lodge the others were standing on the veranda overlooking the biggest bird table in the world, a wide shelf on stilts sprinkled with tropical fruits beloved of honeyeaters, parrots and birds-of-paradise, some of which are rarely observed anywhere else. We were looking forward to gripping the others off with tales of the satinbird only to be gripped back by their sighting of a male Brown Sicklebill. There was a female on the bird table, a long-tailed curve-billed bird-of-paradise with a chestnut cap, olive-brown upperparts and boldly barred underparts. Not bad but not as spectacular as the male. Fortunately, possibly the most extraordinary bird I have ever seen returned, to the lawn by the bird table where it foraged on the ground like a thrush, except it looked nothing like a thrush. It was bigger for starters, with a long, very slim, strongly down-curved bill, shimmering blue head, metallic blue back, soft brown breast, purple and fine white flank plumes, and an extremely long, shimmering blue, down-curved, pointed tail. It looked like a cross between an exotic pheasant and a huge hummingbird. Add a bright yellow gape, icy blue eyes and the machine-gun call, at a volume similar to the real thing, one of the most remarkable sounds made by a bird or any other animal, and even the satinbird suddenly seemed relatively plain.

One of the birds apart from birds-of-paradise I dreamed of seeing after I first flicked through the exceptional illustrations by Dale A. Zimmerman and James Coe in the *Birds of New Guinea* field guide published in 1986 was the one which dominates Plate 43, the striking Crested Berrypecker. It is an elusive high mountain endemic, away from the *Kumul Lodge* garden that is, where I saw two close enough to enjoy the lovely, waxwing-like, silky soft blue, bright green and yellow plumage. However, they were not as exciting as the surprisingly good-looking male Fan-tailed Berrypecker dashing about the garden like a frantic flycatcher, the dazzling metallic blue-black upperparts and tail, and white bases to the long, fanned, graduated tail, flashing in the sunshine. Also in the grounds was my first black, yellow and white Black-breasted Boatbill, while back at the bird table were a few black-barred, deep green Brehm's Tiger Parrots, and underneath the table, looking for spilt seeds, were a pair of tiny Bronze Ground Doves.

We had to be up early the next morning for a long drive downhill to Kama in the Minamba Valley where there was a Lesser Bird-of-paradise lek in a casuarina grove by the sweet potato fields surrounding a small village. The three males present were rather subdued but they still looked ravishing with their rich yellow and white flank plumes fluffed out. Had there been more than one female about for more than a few seconds they may have gone into full display, bouncing around the branches with their plumes raised and waving about but it was not to be, so with the heat rising and the chances of seeing male birds-of-paradise in full display falling, we moved on. At the wide, shallow, rocky Lai River, after a long search under the midday sun, I spotted a distant Torrent-lark, and strode after it at speed because as I suspected it proved to be yet another truly exceptional bird of New Guinea, with immaculate, thick, ink black and silky white plumage. I was very happy watching it bobbing up and down like a similar-sized sandpiper as it foraged amongst the riverside rocks, before I was dragged away.

Returning to the lodge we passed small hamlets of thatched, wood and rattan huts nestled in a narrow heavily cultivated valley between high forested ridges. The only excitement during a long afternoon, apart from the simple thrill of walking a forest trail in the highlands of New Guinea, was a small wave of birds containing a fine black and yellow male Regent Whistler and a Blue-capped Ifrita, a small, chunky, busy, buffy-brown bird with a black-edged blue crown. After dark I was writing up my notes in the lodge when Sam appeared with news of a Mountain Owlet Nightjar, a finely barred, flecked, mottled, spotted and streaked grey and white bird of the night, more owl than nightjar, with long whiskers curving back over the head and a call like a squeaky toy.

I was nervous the next morning. The big day had come, the one on which we were to visit Tonga, a steep-sided valley frequented by the Blue Bird-of-paradise. After a short drive downhill we faced a long hard climb on foot to a fruiting tree at the edge of the forest near the ridge top. I arrived breathless and shaking and hardly able to hold my binoculars steady but there was plenty of time to calm down before a few Superb Birds-of-paradise appeared, including an adult male with a complete metallic blue-green breast shield. While trying to keep track of them two bulkier-looking birds came in from a different direction and both showed a lot of blue as they landed in the fruiting tree. They were an immature male and female Blue Birds-of-paradise and they were not as shy as the Superbs and were happy to pluck the fruits half out in the open and it was relatively easy to see their pale bills, striking white crescents above and below the eyes, and the beautiful blue wings but neither were the full adult male I had dreamed of seeing for so long. A male did appear, for a few seconds and at long range on the forested slope behind us, but it was merely a tantalizing taste of the bird I most wanted to see on the trip so when I had to leave with the rest of the team, most of whom were happy with the tick next to the species on their world lists, I was severely disappointed and already trying to arrange a second attempt.

In the afternoon we headed into high mossy forest again, on a trail which was steep at first then levelled out along a contour. It was along there that we heard one of the characteristic sounds of New Guinea cloud forest, described in the field guide as 'a spluttered jumble of notes poured out at a machine-gun pace'. To me the song sounded like an electronic pulse. Max, our local guide, soon pointed out the singer, a male King-of-Saxony Bird-of-paradise, perched on a dead snag. At first glance it did not look like a bird-of-paradise, being small and relatively dowdy although closer prolonged views revealed a satin black cape and yellow underparts, quite bright on the breast, and there was no doubt left in my mind that it was a bird-of-paradise when I turned my attention to its adornments. The bird has two very long pearly pennants, one attached to each side of the head, and which the bird is able to manoeuvre independently or in unison, in any direction, using muscles in the skin of the head like the ones we use to move our eyebrows, so that one pennant may be pushed forward and the other back, both may be held in a parallel curve and so on. The remarkable plumes, twice as long as the bird itself, are unlike any other feathers known to exist, and to me they resembled insect antennae at a distance and a line of little plastic tiles close up, pale blue on one side pale gold on the other. We waited to see if the bird would fly down to a looping vine and display to a passing female by bouncing up and down on the vine while calling and waving the pennants but he stayed put on his lookout post. It didn't matter though, because I could see what he was about and that he was truly one of the most amazing birds I had ever seen, so good in fact that I forgot all about Blue Birds-of-paradise, for a while anyway.

The next morning Chief, Nick, The Colonel, a somewhat reluctant Foggy and I returned to Tonga hoping to get better views of the full adult male Blue Bird-of-paradise but we never even saw the young male or female. While looking, we spoke to some kids who were on their four mile walk from the village where they lived to the school down in the valley. One 16-year-old happy girl called Pauline spoke very good English and said she wanted to be a lawyer when she was older because she would make lots of money.

In what may have been a lighthearted moment she said, "You are wasting *your* money, coming all the way to Papua New Guinea to look at birds!"

I laughed and said, in a slightly more serious tone, "When you've got lots of money ask yourself if you are any happier then than you are now."

I was not very happy at that particular time. We had seen a male Loria's Bird-of-paradise, now Satinbird, on our way to Tonga, a chubby black bird with an iridescent blue forehead and strange yellow gape like a baby bird, and there were plenty of Superb Birds-of-paradise in and around the fruiting tree again, one a good-looking male, but with reports from our next destination and last chance suggesting that no male Blue Birds-of-paradise had been seen recently a worried man returned to *Kumul Lodge*.

Our next destination was the wide fertile Tari Valley in the Central Highlands where hundreds of Huli people and their large umbrellas made a colourful sight as we landed on the airstrip. From there we took a mini-bus up to *Ambua Lodge*, an extremely expensive establishment at the edge of superb upper montane forests festooned with ferns and epiphytes at nearly 7000 feet (2100 metres), high enough to warrant a welcome electric-blanket at night. *Ambua* is the Huli word for yellow clay which along with red ochre is used to paint the faces of the Huli Wigmen who wear the flamboyant wigs made of bird-of-paradise feathers along with bones of cassowaries, hornbills and pigs, during their ceremonial sing-sings, fashioned on the displays of birds-of-paradise. People travel from all over the world and pay a lot of money to see these dances but I had flown to the other side of the planet and spent an awful lot of money to see the birds they celebrated and after so many years yearning to be in the highlands of New Guinea I was finally there, standing on the long, snaking, sloping lawn amongst the carefully manicured curving shrubberies of *Ambua's* grounds, overlooking the Tari Valley and the rugged forested mountains surrounding it, where lived so many rare and spectacular birds.

*Ambua* is worth whatever the cost. It is so well-situated many birds-of-paradise visit the grounds and there were no less than five different species in the fruiting tree next to the thatched round bungalow Nick and I had been allocated the first day we were there: two Superb Birds-of-paradise, a pair of Loria's Satinbirds and three species which were new to us; a very short-tailed rather plain black Short-tailed Paradigalla, two black-headed brown and buff female Lawes's Parotias and, much more exciting, a few female and a full adult male Princess Stephanie's Astrapias, the black male with what resembled a ruff, so thick was its shimmering blue-green collar of feathers, and a giant, broad, stiff, gracefully down-curved tail.

We were up at 04:00 hours and not long after we were standing silently in the black forest hoping to hear and see a rarely-seen Feline Owlet Nightjar. All we heard was the crazy chorus of cicadas and two trucks struggling up the nearby road. Moving quickly down the road we went in search of Black Sicklebill, listening for the sharp far-carrying 'Quink! Quink!' song notes which usually blare out from the valley sides around dawn. We heard none. However, Joseph Tano, our jowled and moustached local guide, knew a dead snag a male liked and sure enough there was the bird, only the large long black shape was miles away across the forested slopes and only visible for a couple of minutes before the sea of cloud below us rose up the valley and hid him. A Mountain Kingfisher 'blew a referee's whistle' a couple of times but was gone before we could lay our eyes on it, as was the case with that species for the remainder of the trip, and the rising clouds then put paid to a third and final attempt to try and see a full adult male Blue Bird-of-paradise.

I shook my head in despair as we climbed back up the road in the mini-bus, out of the cloud, then plodded along a narrow trail through the dank, dark, thick gloomy forest where, for a change and thanks to Joseph, we were treated to some unprecedented success in seeing several of the world's best skulkers. An Ashy or Black-capped Robin was seen very well for a very shy olive-brown bird with a bold black and white head, as was a chestnut male Forbes's Forest Rail despite the fact it frequented a particularly impenetrable patch of undergrowth. Then we heard the insect-like trill of a Lesser Melampitta and saw the reclusive little black bird with red eyes and long legs. I, at the back of the forest trail line as usual, saw another rarely encountered ground-dweller, a Papuan Logrunner which scuttled across a side-trail. And to cap it all word passed quietly down the line that Joseph had heard the squeaky contact calls of a bird virtually no one ever comes across. After ten minutes ducking and weaving all of us had seen not one but two Papuan Whipbirds, moss green-grey birds, the male with a black throat and white moustache. Joseph couldn't believe it. He said that it was the first time a whole group of visitors had ever seen the whipbird and that they were the best views he had ever had, in over twenty years. All this while listening to the ethereal high-pitched whistling song of Lesser Ground Robins, invisible even at a few paces, the machine-gun volleys of a hidden Brown Sicklebill, and the constant King-of-Saxony static, a male of which was at the roadside when we got back there twirling his antennae all over while we were still shaking our heads in disbelief at our good fortune.

I was very tense the next morning. I had persuaded Sam to arrange one last chance to see the bird I thought would make or break the trip for me. First of all though we headed up to Bailey's Bridge to try and find a New Guinea Harpy Eagle seen by the driver of our mini-bus while we were in the forest the day before. The first bird of the day was a King-of-Saxony Bird-of-paradise twitching his pennants. Then we were shocked to hear the repeated low 'uumpph' of a calling eagle. We raced downhill and Mark spotted the bird while the mini-bus was still moving, causing quite a scramble as we tried to get out and into a position where we could all see the bird through the trees by the road. The massive grey-brown eagle was perched up high in the trees on the slope before us calling constantly and through the telescope we were able to see the short wings, long tail and long legs of a predator evolved to catch small mammals in thick forest, especially possums.

For me the eagle was a mere distraction. The time had come to look for the blue bird. With me were Nick, The Colonel and Lou. The others considered the possibility of a few more ticks more tempting, even, to my astonishment, Chief who is not a lister. They went up the hill while we headed down it, to a track which led us to a very large 'garden' owned by a man who has to remain anonymous. The Blue Bird-of-paradise is a relatively rare bird-of-paradise with a limited distribution in the mid-mountain oak forests of Papua New Guinea. Where humans have lived for a long time in these mountains their need for housing materials, firewood and land to grow food has led to a lot of forest being chopped down but one of the few birds that seems able to tolerate some such habitat degradation, to an extent, and can apparently survive in secondary growth and even be seen in and around the Papuans' 'gardens', is the Blue Bird-of-paradise.

However, garden owners blessed with the birds are rather reluctant to let visiting birders into their gardens because neighbours jealous of the money the owners receive for doing so have been known to kill the birds or at the very least chop down the trees they sing from or display in, so we were extremely fortunate to have been invited to a garden, albeit surreptitiously. When the sincere thank yous were over the owner turned and led us into his leafy plot of land where tall trees shaded a wide variety of fruits and vegetables, and as soon as we could see right across the garden there was the bird I had dreamed of seeing for a long, long time. It was perched in the open at the top of a tree, calling 'wahr, wahr, wahr, wahr, wahr, wahr, wahr' with its striking white bill wide open and pointing skyward. The male Blue Bird-of-paradise has a black head, neck and body with bold white eye crescents but the most striking feature is the beautiful blue wings, a blue the like of which I had never seen before, in any other bird, or anywhere else, a sort of bone china blue, so pure it has to be seen to be believed.

During the following hour the bird moved around the whole plot getting closer and closer and at one point it jumped down a tall open tree with exaggerated bouncing leaps, clinging briefly to the branches with its strong feet, until it was out of view behind the thick understorey close to the ground which was a great shame because I am almost certain the bird performed its courtship display there. As normally happens, the bird had arrived early morning, alighted high in the canopy and called to announce his forthcoming display then, after moving around from song post to song post, he descended to a horizontal or sloping branch near the ground. There,

# A MIND-BLOWING BIRDING TRIP TO A PLANET CALLED EARTH

*Blue Bird-of-paradise, Tari Valley, Papua New Guinea, 31st August 2008*

unseen by us and almost everyone else who has ever attempted to see the display, he slowly swung backwards until he was upside down then he expanded his beautiful blue elongated flank feathers across the front of his body to form a shimmering fan with a red-trimmed black ovoid in the middle, the two blue 'eyes' at the end of his very long tail 'wires' falling in an arc on either side of him. While he then made the fan ripple and the ovoid throb the bird made an otherworldly noise perhaps best described as a pulsating electric-like buzz which sounds like it has been made by a machine, a future machine, not one we are familiar with today. This 'song' is uttered at a frequency barely detectable with a human ear but we were so close I was sure I could just about hear it. Suddenly the bird reappeared at eye-level less than twenty paces away and there was the view I had dreamed of, a male Blue Bird-of-paradise perched with its back toward me showing the full extent of the gorgeous blue wings. He moved up and above us and there he stopped to preen and as he did so he opened the fan he spreads in display and I saw it sparkle for a second.

The brilliant day got even better in the afternoon when we came across our first and as it turned out only fully-tailed adult male Ribbon-tailed Astrapia, a medium-sized black-looking bird which actually flashed green, blue and purple about the head and neck according to the angle of light on the silken feathers, but it's the incredible tail that grabs the attention, the two white ribbon-like central tail feathers extending for at least three times the length of the bird's body and curving down below it in a beautiful sweeping arc. Despite such an extravagant adornment the aptly-named Ribbon-tailed Astrapia was unknown to the world outside New Guinea until 1939 when a visiting naturalist noticed the tail feathers in a warrior's wig, since when it has been discovered that the bird lives only in the cloud forests of a small wild region of the highlands of western Papua New Guinea, a wonderful world it shares with Princess Stephanie's Astrapias, a male of which we saw in the lodge grounds the same afternoon. The day wasn't all about birds-of-paradise though. Heading uphill late afternoon we stopped to watch a superb Black-mantled

Goshawk glaring down at us, a male with a slaty black head, back and tail, and rich chestnut underparts. Higher up, in the stunted trees of the elfin forest was a silky smooth, blue and green Crested Berrypecker. When we breached the tree line and reached the pass known as Tari Gap at nearly 10,000 feet (3000 metres) a covey of Brown Quails walked through the ferns. We couldn't find any Archbold's Bowerbirds nor did a Rufous Woodcock emerge from the forest edge to display at dusk as hoped but a pair of Australasian Grass Owls, darker backed than Barn Owls, cruised up and down above the alpine grassland to bring one of the greatest days to a close.

The next morning I headed to the lodge kitchen with a picture of a Hercules Moth, a species with a wingspan wider than my outspread hand and the largest surface area of wings of any flying insect. I had heard they were sometimes attracted to the lights at *Ambua* and I was soon escorted to the back of the lodge where I was shown two clinging to the rattan wall. One, in much better condition than the other, was a beautiful massive moth in lovely reddish shades of brown sprinkled with silver dust and with crescent-shaped 'windows' in the middle of each of the four wings. The elongated tips of the fore wings were shaped like snakes' heads and complete with slit red eyes, evolved to put potential predators off, and the hind wings had long, broad twisted tails. The silky body was almost the size of my thumb and at the head end were two large feather-like antennae. When I held the moth in my hand it felt weightless and gripped my finger so tightly it was quite a struggle to get it back on to the lodge wall, safe from the Great Woodswallows which would swoop down and eat the moth should it take to the wing during daylight.

It was sad to have to leave *Ambua* and the Tari Valley and its birds-of-paradise. It already seemed like it had been a dream as I boarded the flight to Port Moresby. From there we drove to a small quay called Tahira Marina in the mangroves around Bootless Bay to catch a boat to *Loloata Island Resort*. The southeast trade winds were blowing hard which meant a much anticipated snorkelling trip to the rich coral reefs was cancelled but left some rare time to relax and reflect, with a cold bottle of *South Pacific* beer, before dinner, which was a delicious mixture of pumpkin and squid. Then we retired to our spacious cabins on stilts with a view across the bay to the forested mountains of mainland New Guinea and what a wonderful feeling it was to lie back in bed, the ocean breeze wafting through the open windows, in the knowledge that I had been to those mountains and seen the Blue Bird-of-paradise.

And there was time for more birds-of-paradise and so it was no problem getting up at stupid o'clock again in order to reach Varirata National Park in time for the dawn when the forested ravines resound with the raucous cawing of male Raggiana Birds-of-paradise. Alas, we arrived a little too late to see the colourful birds displaying, according to our local guide Daniel Wakra. He had a fine long beard and was wearing a pair of loafers which looked far from appropriate for a hard day's birding in New Guinea but Daniel knew the forest trails were dry and, more importantly, where and how to find some terrific birds. After hearing the loud whistling trill of a Yellow-billed Kingfisher he had the beauty lined up for us all in seconds. Against a bright background the classic kingfisher bill looked partly translucent. At its base the bird's eye was almost encircled by a black crescent which made the eye look almost comically huge in its crested ginger head. The lovely bird's back was black, grading into dark green, and its wings were blue. Entering the forest on a narrow trail we bumped into a wave, yes a foraging flock of birds, the second but first slow-moving one of the trip, and in it were several new birds, including Black-faced, Spot-winged and striking black and white Frilled Monarchs, as well as some Hooded Pitohuis, smart thrush-sized birds with black heads, wings and tails, and chestnut brown bodies, famous for being one of few poisonous bird species. The Papuans knew for a long time - it is one of the few birds they refuse to eat - but it was not until the 1990s that the research student Jack Dumbacher discovered potent neurotoxins in the skin and feathers, ingested when the birds eat tiny Melyrid beetles which themselves probably pick up the toxins from fungi.

As the flock began to move away a Black-billed Brush Turkey walked out in front of me and those that chased after what is a very difficult bird to 'tick' saw a Painted Quail Thrush, an even harder bird to track down, which I did not find very amusing since I would swop a turkey for a quail thrush any day. The flurry of activity continued with no less than three poorly-named Brown-headed Paradise Kingfishers calling in the understorey, their deep dark blue shoulders catching what light there was and their long, narrow, white-tipped royal blue tails pumping up and down as their slow descending trills rang out around us. It's true, their heads are brown, but they could just as easily have been named Orange-breasted or Orange-rumped Paradise Kingfishers. A Barred Owlet Nightjar that Daniel had staked out beforehand was not at its usual roosting site inside a hollow dead tree stump but Daniel being Daniel had a back-up stump which one popped out of when he scratched it and glared back at us with red eyes. With the heat of the day approaching and bird activity almost at a standstill Daniel refused to let the excitement wane and showed us his next trick, a bulky stick nest with a Doria's Hawk perched on the edge of it, a large long-tailed heavily barred rare endemic goshawk not disposed to soaring outside the thick forest in full view and so poorly known that the nest we were looking at may well have been the first ever recorded.

That was that in the forest for the day because we wanted to look for a rare, nomadic open-country bird on the way back to *Loloata*. Now, I am not a lister, a ticker, call them what you will, those people to whom birds are merely ticks on a list. One such list is the 'World List', kept by most widely travelled birders, including me, although I am not obsessed with ensuring that one day it will reach 8000, 9000 or even 10,000. Such 'birders' are collectors. I'm more into the aesthetics; what I call nature's art. I love to travel to see certain birds not lots of birds which are little more than versions of other birds, and I like to watch those certain birds in beautiful places. I do keep a rough list though and I worked out before travelling to New Guinea that I might reach the region of 4000 species while I was there so I kept tabs on where my list more or less was and as we pulled up at a swampy rank field I decided the next new bird I saw would be number 4000. I considered the Pheasant Coucal, a large black ungainly bird in view to my left unworthy of my milestone and turned away until it was out of sight. Then I concentrated on looking for the little bright chestnut and black finch with an outsized blue bill known to be in the area and with the help of the others I was soon looking at two Grand Munias. Back at *Loloata* I celebrated the event alone, watching the sun set with a beer and a smoke, and thinking about how fortunate I was to have discovered birds as a boy and to have travelled so far to see so many since.

There is so much more to birding than the birds of course and the next wonder up was a Banded Sea Krait which slid across the path as I made my way to my cabin for the night. Named after the broad black bands along its silvery-white body the snake also has a laterally-compressed flat tail to aid swimming. It was heading for the sea to hunt mainly conger and moray eels which it paralyzes with powerful neurotoxins. Kraits rest up on land and the next day there was a bigger, two metre long specimen coiled up outside my cabin.

The wonder on the last day in New Guinea was avian and it began with my first sight of displaying birds-of-paradise. We made absolutely sure we were in position at the display trees in Varirata at first light second time around and soon after, the two male Raggiana Birds-of-paradise we could see began calling, 'Wa wa wa WAH WAH WAH WAU WAU WAU WAU ... WAU ... WAU'. They attracted a female and when she appeared the males bowed before throwing their thick spray of salmon-red flank plumes high over their backs, the flare of colour contrasting starkly with the greens and greys of the surrounding forest and looking like something from another world, as the birds also quivered and beat their short, rounded, fanned wings, and pranced on their chosen display branches. When the female, who seemed nowhere near as impressed as us, flew off the males calmed down immediately, folded away their

*Raggiana Bird-of-paradise, Varirata National Park,
Papua New Guinea, 2nd September 2008*


plumes, resumed their normal posture, and returned to preening their marvellous feathers, calling out every now and again. Females came in a couple of more times and the males turned themselves into gorgeous flaming flares again, a truly phenomenal sight that together with the loud calls ringing out through the forest finally made me feel like I was truly in the land of the birds-of-paradise.

The next astonishing bird was a Rufous-bellied Kookaburra, not the first one we had seen but still a stunner with a broad white collar separating the black head and back, bright, shiny azure blue wings, deep cinnamon-rufous underparts, and a beak like a white dagger. It is a fairly large kingfisher but not as big as the Blue-winged Kookaburra, one of which was nearby. When there were no mobile birds to look at, to keep things ticking along, as Daniel liked to do, he showed us something at roost and that morning it was three Marbled Frogmouths, which he could easily have shown us the day before. Whatever his methods, the birds' complex camouflaged plumage which made them look like branches meant we would never have seen them without his unbelievable hunting skills. Like the day before, I saw three superb Brown-headed Paradise Kingfishers and three species of monarch flycatchers along the forest trails, except this time around they were Spot-winged, Black-winged and Golden instead of Spot-winged, Black-faced and Frilled, although we saw a pair of the fancy Frilled later on, both with large blue wattles around their eyes and the male with a snowy white ruff.

Back in the forest in the afternoon all I saw during the first hour was a blur whizzing past me which I was told was a Chestnut-backed Jewel Babbler. It could have been anything as far as I could tell so it looked like the day, like many in Papua, which started with fireworks, would die a slow death, but for once it didn't, for although we saw just a few birds in a few hours they were all spectacular. First up was a shiny blue-breasted Red-bellied Pitta that was just about visible standing on the forest floor through a maze of undergrowth. Then we saw a perched, yes a perched, male Growling once Magnificent Riflebird, an otherwise terribly shy velvety black bird-of-paradise with a flexible metallic throat shield which I saw, through the telescope no less, shine blue, green and purple. Then, at the death of a dazzling last day, after a very long and frustrating wait, a legendary skulker walked along a patch of forest floor that I was scanning with my binoculars. After listening to its drawn-out high-pitched whistles for what must have been nearly an hour and with little hope left of seeing the damned thing to then see a silky smooth male Painted Quail Thrush walk into my field of view was one of the sweetest moments of my life. The beauty really did look like it had been painted very carefully by a skilled artist, who used rusty-brown along the top, orange for the eyes, in a broad black mask, snow white for a stripe between that and the black chin and upper breast, and to finish off the masterpiece, a rich cinnamon wash along the flanks.

Looking back over the trip on the long way home it was the birds-of-paradise that I remembered the most though. I could hardly believe that I had enjoyed fantastic views of male Blue, King, King-of-Saxony, Twelve-wired, Superb, Raggiana and Lesser Birds-of-paradise, Brown Sicklebill, Ribbon-tailed and Princess Stephanie's Astrapias, Short-tailed Paradigalla and Growling Riflebird, not forgetting three manucodes and the former birds-of-paradise, Loria's and Crested Satinbirds. I had tasted paradise and I wanted more and that's why, six years later, I was back. I had been nowhere else. All available funds had been put in the New Guinea pot, only this time I was heading for the western half of the island not the eastern, to West Papua, the Indonesian province formerly known as Irian Jaya.

# A MIND-BLOWING BIRDING TRIP TO A PLANET CALLED EARTH

*Wilson's Bird-of-paradise, Orobiai River, Waigeo, West Papua,*
*7th October 2014*

It was great to be back in the hot chaos of a small airport terminal building in the tropics, full of people speaking a different language. I love the excitement of being in a new, strange place at the beginning of yet another adventure, in a land I have dreamed of visiting for many years, especially somewhere remote where there are still great forests where some of the planet's most amazing birds survive.

A young lady approached us as we emerged from the crowd. She knew we were birders, she had seen them before. Her name was Like, pronounced Leeka, Wijaya.

She was from the Raja Ampat Islands off the west coast of New Guinea and the founder and managing director of *Papua Expeditions* who I had contacted months in advance to guide me, Chief, Foggy, Nick, The Colonel and Lou around West Papua. She worked with her husband Iwein Mauro, an intrepid birder from Belgium, who met us at the *Meridien Hotel* in Sorong.

After a rapid change of clothes we were off, through the hot, dusty, humid sprawl of shacks, shops, scooters, small yellow buses called bemos, and people of New Guinea, along a terrible pot-holed road out into the sticks where we pulled over to walk a forest trail with Iwein and a local guide called Maurits, in search of the first dream bird. We heard the long trilling whistle of one almost immediately and then it was in view, a spectacular Red-breasted Paradise Kingfisher, the salmon-red of its breast, belly and puffed-up rump feathers so deep and bright. The kingfisher's short, stocky, straight beak was also red, its cap dark blue, the broad mask black like the back and wings except for the shining azure-blue shoulders, and the long central tail feathers were also blue with white spatules at their tips. I couldn't believe how quickly we had seen such a little-known bird. I was also astonished that all the illustrations I had seen of the species so utterly failed to capture its brilliance and I was still reeling from the shock later in the day when we saw an even shyer and more elusive kingfisher. The loud 'tuuu-tu-tu' whistles followed by a short descending trill of the Hook-billed Kingfisher is a familiar sound throughout the lowland and hill forests of New Guinea at dawn and dusk but the bird is rarely seen, being at least a crepuscular and probably a nocturnal hunter, and perching silently in dense tree cover during the day. We were extremely lucky to come across one which became active before dusk and even more fortunate to have Maurits with us, a man with well-honed hunting skills and phenomenal eyesight. It was he who spotted the calling creature of the night perched deep in the forest. It was a male with a large boldly striped head, giant eyes evolved for night work, a heavy, flattened, hooked bill thought to be used for digging for invertebrates, a dark back and pale breast. The rather primitive-looking bird was so close we could make out its scaly pale blue crown. I was in a daze; we had been in West Papua one day and already seen Hook-billed and Red-breasted Paradise Kingfishers.

Next morning we were up at 04:30 in order to board a motor launch for the trip across the Dampier Strait before the wind got up and made the waters dangerously choppy. The skipper pushed the boat to its limits, which made for a bumpy ride as we skimmed the tops of the small waves, so it was a welcome relief to finally slow down in the calmer, smoother waters off the island I had longed to visit since reading Alfred Russell Wallace's *The Malay Archipelago*, the rugged, limestone, heavily forested Waigeo, largest of the four main islands of the Raja Ampat archipelago, the others, to the south, being Batanta, Salawati and Misool. We landed at a place where there were a few wooden shacks on stilts, about twenty miles (32 km) from Muka where Wallace washed up 154 years before in 1860. Like then there were still no roads, not even tracks, and the people still got about in outrigger canoes, and rarely ventured inland. After checking in with them, the landowners, we stepped down into in a larger open boat and followed an outrigger paddled by father and young daughter up the Orobiai River. Soon, we ran out of water and began walking along the grey gravel islands exposed during the dry season, heading inland up the river valley with thickly forested steep slopes. It was the stuff of dreams, well my dreams, almost like an expedition to a little-visited land, with proper pristine forests, not remnant patches, where I was going to look for some incredible birds, birds-of-paradise no less. And then it got better. After wading the shallow channel of the river we walked along a trail to the most beautiful campsite in the world, a small clearing from where we could see massive Blyth's Hornbills whooshing across the forested slopes above and listen to the cicada din which was almost deafening and nearly drowned out the calls and songs of the as yet unknown tropical birds surrounding us.

Iwein, Maurits and a couple of local people put up some wooden poles, shinned up them and tied two very large tarpaulins between them. Their purpose was to keep the rain off the two raised gravel beds on which we set up our camping mats and mosquito nets, mandatory on an island with Chikungunya, Dengue Fever and the sometimes fatal *falciparum* strain of malaria which Iwein contracted only a year before. In the afternoon we began hiking up a steep slope on a narrow stony trail but we soon had to stop because walking on the trail ahead of us was a Western Crowned Pigeon. The massive pigeon is rare near human settlements where they are hunted but rather tame where let be, so we got a good view of the mainly grey bird with a maroon back and shoulders, a white wing patch and a beautiful crest that seemed to be made out of lacy frost.

It was hot, humid and hard going and The Colonel and Lou, nearly crippled with arthritis and still recovering from recent heart surgery, decided to turn back, leaving me, Chief, Foggy and Nick to complete the ascent with Iwein. He led us to a hide in the forest made out of sticks and palm fronds. It was narrow and a few paces long with just enough room for a collective bench for four or five people, made out of sticks tied together. Once seated, following Iwein's instructions (he had now retreated), we carefully brushed aside the palm leaves placed across the long narrow opening at the front of the hide to make our own windows into the otherwise secretive world of one of New Guinea's and planet Earth's most fabulous birds. There, right in front of us, was the display court of a male Wilson's Bird-of-paradise.

We tried to stay as quiet as possible, to resist the urge to wave the mosquitoes away or to move an aching limb, and searched and searched with wide eyes for the bird, but it didn't seem to be there. We waited and waited, and then, as if by magic, he was there. How he got there without us noticing we didn't know but suddenly he was perched a little above head height directly in front of us, facing left. The dazzling male Wilson's Bird-of-paradise began preening its finery and then occasionally shouting out a rolling, 'dyu-dyu-dyu-dyu-dyu-dyu-dyu' to let any females in the vicinity know that he was at his court and ready to display, his bare blue skin skull-cap glowing, his green velvety breast cushion shimmering, his stiff shiny yellow cape of feathers stretched taut, and the glistening scarlet pad on his back puffed up. The bird was a riot of colour. Even the shoulders and wings which looked relatively dull brown from some angles had a bronze sheen at others, and when the bird opened his mouth to call out he revealed a beautiful bright yellow gape. And the colours were so intense. We had all seen birds-of-paradise before but we had never seen anything like a male Wilson's Bird-of-paradise.

Suddenly the stunner leapt down to the ground in his court to do a bit of energetic gardening, snapping off new leaves at the base of saplings and flinging them, as well as dead and fallen leaves, and the odd stone, aside, in order to keep his display ground perfectly neat and tidy. He was hoping that if any of the females touring six such courts in the area were to stop at his immaculate arena they would stay to watch him perform in it but none came. As he moved around his court with exaggerated hops or leaps from sapling stem to sapling stem with sturdy, deep purple-blue legs and feet we could see his skull-cap from above and it was so bright it looked like it was lit from the inside, and indeed it is even visible at night. We could also see his two elongated, tightly curled, metallic central tail feathers, which took on a silver-violet hue when they caught the light. The bird had so many adornments it was impossible to take them all in, even while he perched quietly very low down for a while.

He could not sit still for long however and suddenly he jumped on to a vertical sapling stem and, seemingly unable to contain his fervour, practised a bit of his display, uttering a strange, subdued, strangled sound while raising his black epaulettes, transforming the shimmering green breast cushion into an almost complete iridescent green disc, waving the curly tail feathers and quivering with apparent uncontrollable ardour. I just couldn't take my eyes off him and watched intensely as he switched between more gardening, perching up and calling, and practising his display, for three hours, which went by in what seemed like three seconds, during which time I nearly shed a tear or two, so emotional was the experience of getting to know the Wilson's Bird-of-paradise.

I was awake at 04:00 and not long after I was walking a trail with Chief, Foggy, Nick and Maurits who led us up through the black forest without a torch, to the narrow top of a ridge where we stood listening to the dawn chorus dominated by the loud harsh yodelling of friarbirds. When they calmed down we could hear the nasal 'wark-wark-wark' squawks and yowels of the birds we were hoping to see. They were making their way to their display tree and announcing their imminent arrival to any females within hearing range. The tree was the tallest one on the ridge of course and the birds liked to show off their gorgeous red feathers in the canopy so a neck-breaking hour followed, watching four of the very excitable beauties dashing around from branch to branch with characteristic big, exaggerated, bird-of-paradise leaps, calling all the while and stopping dead now and again to swing down and perch upside down while fanning and fluttering their short rounded wings and rocking their bodies from side to side as the two very long twisted central tail feathers which look like thick wires fell down to surround the birds in perfect heart-shaped frames.

I was very glad good old Nick lugged his telescope up the steep trail for through it I was able to see a Red Bird-of-paradise in all its glory; the bright yellow pointed bill, iridescent emerald green throat, bright yellow neck and shoulders, and the chestnut body with the rich, elongated, stiff red flank plumes held in a beautiful curve. None of the birds perched still for long though. Like the Wilson's Bird-of-paradise they seemed possessed with passion. Well, for an hour or so and then their excitement waned, presumably because there were no females left to try and impress. After calming down they dispersed into the forest where there was virtually no chance of seeing them. So it was time to move on, only before we did Maurits spotted a Waigeo Cuscus in the open canopy of a large emergent tree that was rooted down the ridge so that the marsupial with thick, woolly, grey fur about the size of a medium-sized monkey was almost at eye-level. The shy and rarely seen normally nocturnal creature was watching us with its big orangey eyes, bulging under wrinkled eyebrows, in an orange-red face. It moved extremely slowly, like a sloth, turning its head from side to side and unfurling its long, thick, creamy, prehensile tail, furry for the most part but bare and scaly at the tip.

After leaving the cuscus in peace we saw another Western Crowned Pigeon which flew up noisily from the forest floor to a large limb under the canopy enabling us to look it in the red eye and study its long, sturdy, pale and scaly legs. Back on the main trail we met Lou and The Colonel coming down from the Wilson's Bird-of-paradise court. They were deliriously happy because they had been watching the bird for hours. We were all happy to then indulge in a long lunch and siesta during the intense heat of the middle of the day. Returning to the field mid-afternoon, I almost immediately saw a brilliant deep blue and bright orange Papuan Dwarf Kingfisher, with a very long dark bill. Alas, I was also the only one to clap eyes, albeit very briefly, on a very shy Red-bellied Pitta, so everyone else experienced a totally bird-less two hours.

"That's birding in New Guinea," Iwein said, barely lifting his eyebrows.

Back near camp we did see the large hump-backed bill and blue eyes of one of six very scarce Brown-headed Crows, and down at the river a superb Brahminy Kite distracted me from the Common Sandpipers as it circled down to pluck a fish with its outstretched yellow talons from near the surface with nonchalant ease.

Up at 04:00 again and after honey and palm sugar parathas Chief, Foggy, Nick and I began the hike up to the Wilson's court for first light. Once again Maurits was out front walking casually up the narrow trail in the darkest dark imaginable. He had a torch but didn't bother using it so we were very surprised when he turned it on, not to see where he was going, but, even more astonishing, to point it straight at a Common Paradise Kingfisher roosting on the bend of a looping liana several paces from the trail, a dazzling blue and white phantom in the black forest, its azure blue cap and shoulders reflecting what little light there was shining from Maurits's torch, enough actually for us to also see the silky white underparts and very long pale blue central tail feathers with white spatula-shaped tips. We couldn't believe it; all those hours looking for one in daylight, in West Papua *and* Papua New Guinea, without success and Maurits spots one in the dark, dark night. How did it do it? How did he know it was there? How did he know where to point the torch?

I quietly asked myself and the others these questions while we got to know the Wilson's Bird-of-paradise a bit more. He was at his court virtually the whole four hours we were in the hide, the bird that has got everything; a clickety-click of wings every time he flies, tiny pompoms of black feathers above and below the short black bill and above the eyes, a banana milkshake-coloured gape, six patches of glowing bare blue skin separated by narrow lines of tiny black feathers on the top of his head, a velvety metallic green breast cushion come shield, yellow and red pads on his back, and another red band formed by the folded wings, all stretched and preened and constantly attended to with the utmost care. Even the bird's legs and feet are a beautiful pale silvery purple from one angle, deep purple-blue from another, and then there are the perfectly curled tail wires which look like they have been made from metal, black one second, silver the next. And when he wasn't checking his attire he was calling out to the local females or attending his garden, leaving it only very briefly, presumably to gulp down some fruit nearby as quickly as possible so as not to miss a passing female. The bird was a true wonder, and so it was Nick and I returned for another few hours during the late afternoon.

Planet Earth is a gallery, where a live exhibition of nature's art is being held. The Wilson's Bird-of-paradise is one of the star exhibits although there are many more among the millions of works on show and each and every one of them is more subtle, more intricate, more beautiful, more enchanting, more fascinating, more exciting, more entertaining and more inspiring than any other exhibit that is or has been on display in any other exhibition. As far as is known it is the only exhibition like it in the universe. It is also the only one that is open all day and all night, all year round. And it is completely free.

I love travelling around the gallery. Just the prospect of a trip is so energising it transforms my life. I dive into the planning I enjoy it so much, then comes that first day in the field in a new distant land surrounded by unknown birds. Such days have been some of the happiest of my life. Then there is the freedom that goes with travelling, the freedom from the tedious tasks of everyday life, the cares and worries, and the routine. Travel also makes it so much easier to live in the moment and to not think about the past and the future, because everything is shiny and new. The many reasons to stay at home, to not go, sometimes to places many consider dangerous, are soon forgotten, and while it is tempting to play it safe, the more I am willing to risk the more alive I feel. At times I find it frightening to contemplate getting to and around certain countries, and how to look for the birds there, especially in what may seem like the most out-of-the-way places, but more often than not the actual travelling turns out to be surprisingly easy and pleasant. Travelling also heightens the senses and the joys of being alive, and it can be so exhilarating that the longer I am on the road the better, and when I was on Waigeo I wished I could stay longer, much longer, and explore the island properly, and the other islands in the Raja Ampat archipelago, and then mainland New Guinea, on an extensive trip through a magical world with beautiful birds. Fortunately, I had the health and the strength to do it but unfortunately I didn't have the time and the money, and so it was that I was already feeling sad about having to leave in the morning.

Back in camp my ankles and lower legs were itching like mad. I hardly noticed when I was with the Wilson's but the chiggers had already got me. Hundreds perhaps thousands of the near-microscopic skin-eating larval mites had crawled on to me, injected their digestive enzymes and started sucking up my liquid skin, leaving a mess of incredibly irritating red welts which I desperately tried not to scratch for fear of a secondary infection and from there that jungle rot known as tropical ulcers, very common in New Guinea and very difficult to get rid of because the large open wounds are perfect for other bacteria to colonise. The tour leader gave me the magic potion she carried; a traditional natural oil known in Indonesia as *minyak tawon* and I applied it rigorously every night for the rest of the trip. It provided only light relief but I dreaded to think what the itching would be like without it. I might have felt better with a cold beer in my hand but we were not allowed any when we were camping, even on our last night on Waigeo, because Like did not think it was fair on the locals who were prohibited from alcohol in a country where a drunk wielding a machete - nearly everyone carried a machete - could cause a lot of trouble.

Before breaking camp the next morning we went for a night walk and spotlighted a wide-eyed and wide-beaked Marbled Frogmouth. Then, way too soon, it was time to leave Waigeo. Half way across the bumpy Dampier Strait we should have stopped at an atoll to watch Beach Kingfishers and snorkel over a coral reef but a dispute over which local owned the land some international company wanted to buy and build a dive resort on meant it was in our best interests to stay away, especially considering that one group of local people burnt down the last resort built there. Instead we ended up rocking and rolling along a terrible hot dusty road for forty minutes north out of Sorong, the last stretch of which was spent nodding off due to some lunchtime *Bintang* pilsner to celebrate the Wilson's. I woke up when we arrived at a remnant stretch of mangroves and shortly afterwards I was watching three massive blue and white Beach Kingfishers with their huge dark bills agape in the shocking heat. The crab-catchers were a long way off but perched prominently and it was easy to make out their white heads and underparts, and lovely blue backs, wings and tails.

In 1858 Alfred Russell Wallace sailed into Dorey Harbour, a small village on the north coast of the island of New Guinea. When we arrived on a *Bombardier* aircraft from Sorong it was a big town known as Manokwari. We flew east across the Bird's Head or Vogelkop Peninsula, over the Tamrau Mountains where sharp ridges with side-ridges were mostly forested and interrupted only by braided gravelly rivers, then along the flat coastal plain where most of the lowland forest was gone, replaced by oil palm plantations. Wallace was unable to travel far inland due to the rugged terrain but after just a couple of hours ascending a very rough track in a four-wheel-drive we reached a community guesthouse near the village of Kwau, not far from Mokwam, at over 5000 feet (1500 metres) in the Arfak Mountains, famous in the birding world for some of the toughest birding there is; looking for rare birds-of-paradise on remote, steep, muddy, forested mountain slopes in the one of wettest places on the planet.

In the old days visitors had to camp. We luxuriated in a large wooden building on stilts, with a tiny kitchen and three bedrooms. There was no electricity or water but we *had* beds *and* mattresses. Better still, the guesthouse was surrounded by a beautiful garden full of banana trees and flowering shrubs, and illuminated by a stunning male Tithonus Birdwing, a very large butterfly with wide black forewings with two bright greenish-yellow stripes, and round hindwings which were a deep greenish-yellow with black spots, while on its black thorax it wore a thick bunch of red silky hairs. I was almost bursting to get out there, birding, in the mythical Arfak Mountains. After four very disappointing and frustrating hours I was left wondering what all the fuss was about. I saw nine species well enough to identify but mostly briefly and against the light, and not including Spotted Jewel Babbler, a pair of which lived along the Loop Trail five minutes flat walk from the guesthouse, or a Vogelkop Bowerbird which lived in the same place.

As well as birds-of-paradise New Guinea is home to 11 of the 17 bower-building birds, the other six species being confined to Australia. Male bowerbirds are expert architects, landscape gardeners, collectors and artists, constructing complex bowers out of sticks and other materials on the ground, sometimes in a display court decorated with usually colourful items. The bower and the 'garden' it is in is also the conjugal bed, although once mated the female builds the nest and raises the young alone. Each species builds a unique bower although there are two main types: *Avenue bowers* with two or more walls of upright sticks with a passageway between them, and *Maypole bowers* with a central pole, usually the straight trunk of a sapling. The Vogelkop Bowerbird belongs to the *Maypole* group and builds the largest and most elaborate bower in New Guinea. It looks like an extravagant giant straw wig that has been placed carefully on a flat area of the forest floor. Made of slender sticks, it is supported by a central sapling with the untidy peak of the roof up to a metre high. The whole construction is wider still, with a large entrance and front lawn both decorated with discrete piles and spreads of flowers, fruit and fungi, as well beetle wing cases, berries, leaves and nuts, or, near human habitation, metal and plastic rubbish such as bags, bottle tops and even beer cans. It takes about a year to make the bower and decorate it and the area in front. Different birds have different collections and attend to them daily although, unfortunately, the one on the Loop Trail at Kwau looked unkempt with only an untidy spread of blue-black leaves outside it. Iwein thought the bird had abandoned it and was building a new bower, he knew not where, so seeing the bird, away from an active bower, would be very hard.

After banana fritters at 04:30 Iwein led me, Chief, Foggy and Nick up a steep but thankfully dry trail in the dark. On our way to another display court of another bird-of-paradise we heard the rather hoarse 'warh warhh warhhh' of a Feline Owlet Nightjar, a bird we very much wanted to see but Iwein took the opportunity to point out one of the great problems with birding in New Guinea. The trail marked the boundary between neighbouring villages and we were only allowed on the land of the village of Kwau and if we crossed the border to look for birds and the neighbours found out they would demand anything up to 10,000 U.S. dollars as 'compensation' and if that was not paid they may decide to kill any 'trespassers' as, what they considered, retribution. The area of the Arfak Mountains we were in had the highest homicide rate in the region. People were regularly being killed for the craziest reasons. For example, if someone was related to someone deemed to be possessed by evil spirits they would be for the chop and the people doing the chopping would be attending church that very morning, it being a Sunday. So, even though there was a chance we might not be spotted or leave the slightest trace of our trespassing it simply was not worth crossing the boundary to where we could hear the owlet nightjar.

We carried on up the trail to a small hide which we settled into before first light, in time to listen to the wonderful dawn chorus of zinging cicadas, whistling robins and the deep far-carrying 'oo's of various doves and pigeons. As soon as there was a smidgen of light we watched the court before us intently and not long after a Wattled Brush Turkey, black with grey bare skin on its face and neck, a small red comb and a red wattle, walked across the court, and soon after that, at five minutes past six, a male Western Parotia appeared, in typical bird-of paradise style, as if out of thin air, and perched on a branch above his court. It was still almost dark, there was hardly a glimmer of light to reflect off anything but the bird's triangular white forehead shield glowed like a beacon, as if it were made from something unknown to man, some precious metal mined from a planet in another galaxy, another universe, when in fact it was composed of earthly feathers evolved to glow brilliant white.

When he dropped down to the ground to tend to his display ground he looked larger than expected, between a blackbird and a crow in size, with a bulky black body, narrow tail and beautiful blue eyes. The body looked big because he had a 'tutu' come 'cloak' come 'cape' that surrounded him from the neck down to the belly, which is composed of specialized thick velvety black upper breast and flank feathers. This he fanned a little now and then as he hopped around his dance floor clearing it of dead leaves so that the area of open ground stood out starkly from the otherwise chaotic forest-floor cover. When he finished 'gardening' he leapt up to a head-high branch and stayed there for an hour or so, preening and calling out every so often with an almost explosive, parrot-like shriek. While we waited in eager anticipation for a female to visit and stimulate him to display a small brown Lesser Ground Robin hopped out of the shadows for a few seconds, a plain Blue-grey Robin made a slightly longer appearance, and a Green-backed Robin with a grey head, white face, white eyes and yellowish breast perched right in front of us for long periods; three extremely shy birds which were highly unlikely to be seen so well walking the trails.

At half past seven the parotia suddenly dropped to the ground and soon after a female appeared. He seemed to ignore her until she landed on a specific branch, one above the middle of the court which he had earlier wiped with grey lichen. Her perching in that very particular spot was the trigger for him to start displaying immediately. After raising his six stiff spatula-tipped head 'wires', nearly half the length of his body, high above his head, he fanned out his black-speckled, green and gold upper breast shield. Then he raised his 'cloak' so that he looked a bit like a black lampshade on legs and 'danced' a full circle under the female with his legs taut and moving in a blur, and his head and head-wires waving from side-to-side at a thousand miles an hour, the whole bird pulsating with so much passion it seemed about to burst. Then she was gone and he suddenly stopped, shook his feathers back into place, lowered his head-wires and flew off at great speed. None of us spoke. None of us knew what to say. No words seemed appropriate. We were mesmerized by what we had seen; a male Western Parotia 'dancing' in the Arfak Mountains, a dream come true and a dream so much better than anything our puny brains could have possibly come up with, for the intensity, the excitement, the sight of that bird 'dancing' just a few paces away were all so far in excess of that portrayed on a screen. What we saw was real and we were blown away by the brilliance of it.

*Western Parotia, Kwau, Arfak Mountains, West Papua, 12th October 2014*

Still stunned, we returned to the tussle with the forest, trying to see some birds without display courts or trees, birds like the Long-tailed Paradigalla, one of the rarest and least-known birds-of-paradise, and endemic to the Arfaks. We didn't see any because, Iwein explained, some local hunters had recently started acquiring guns and had shot all the rather tame paradigallas within reasonable walking distance of Kwau and other villages in the area. We *did* see a bird-of-paradise, two young males of the isolated Arfak subspecies of Superb but it was another very disappointing afternoon. The day ended well though, when the cooks served up sweet and sour Red Snapper for supper.

Up at 04:00 and off on a long steep descent through the forest to two display courts of Magnificent Birds-of-paradise. They were a couple of hundred paces apart and both, typically, on a rather steep slope where some trees had fallen and the birds had cleared the surrounding ground of vegetation. One court had a hide placed especially for photographers, Chief and The Colonel in our case, where the male did not show very well, while Nick and I revelled in over three almost uninterrupted hours in the company of a glorious male in front of the other hide. He looked very different to a Wilson's Bird-of-paradise but his behaviour was very similar. Adorned with a golden mantle he perched up calling 'cheer-cheer-cheer-cheer-cheer' louder and louder, puffing up his feathers and preening, or dropped down to keep his court clean. No females came by to inspect his garden or his glory so he practised his display a few times instead, clinging tightly to the base of a favourite vertical stem with his bright violet blue legs and feet while leaning back to best show off his pale lime-coloured gape, huge, pulsing, soft velvety, blue-trimmed glistening green breast cushion come shield, the golden nape-cape which was flipped up to form a halo encircling the back of his head, the deep carmine patch between his golden wings, and the long, thin, stiff, curled tail wires, held at the best angle to catch the light and turn them blue. A visiting female would see all this from above, as we did, for he liked to perform at the bottom of his court, slightly below the hide. When he was higher up the court at eye-level, preening and sometimes calling out, his head looked a bit scrawny until I focused the telescope on it and could see it was actually like a pin-cushion with velvety bobbles at the base of the ever so pale blue bill, tiny round pale spots between the bill and the eyes on the soft black face, very thin pale flecks behind the eyes, and a soft chestnut cap ruffled up buff at the rear.

We could have watched him all day but our time was up. Maurits collected us and we began making our way back uphill, listening out for birds of course. There was not much point *looking* for birds but, after hearing them clucking, we did see, to my astonishment, a pair of White-striped Forest Rails, one of the hardest of the hardest forest-floor skulkers to see. They were scampering through a jumble of fallen trees, branches, ferns, mosses and other thick vegetation on the slope below us but by some stroke of good fortune I pointed my binoculars in the right place at the right time just as the male darted from cover to cover, seeing a small rich chestnut bird with narrow white stripes on darker wings.

Farther up the trail Iwein and Maurits went off-piste up a steep slope where the forest had a preponderance of tree-ferns, in search of roosting Feline Owlet Nightjars. I must admit I didn't hold out much hope of success because it is such a little known species and yet it was not long before we heard a "whoop!" A mad scramble followed as Maurits led us up the slope to a small tree. Perched bolt upright next to the trunk staring straight at us from a vine tangle a few paces away at head-height was the most extraordinary creature. I was told it was a bird but it didn't look like any bird I had ever seen. It had thick fluffy white eyebrows, long stiff whiskers around its beak which were pointing in all directions but mostly straight up in front of its big brown owl-like eyes, and the beak was wide, convex and strongly hooked which together with a whitish moustache gave it an almost comically grumpy expression. Being small-headed, a bit pot-bellied and long-tailed it was more Meerkat than cat and its plumage was equally bizarre, the variety of rich browns being strikingly flecked and mottled with black, white and buff, and including broad white stripes down its chin and throat, and along the flanks. They may not be as glamorous as the birds-of-paradise or as clever as the bowerbirds but like those families owlet-nightjars are basically New Guinean, and a little bit crazy.

The strange bird certainly helped to make it an exceptional day and I loved being in that forest, despite the flies that liked eyes. Alas, the cloud thickened and darkened and rain was in the fresh wind so, having seen just seven species of bird by two p.m., we headed as quickly as we could back up the steep slope to the guesthouse which I am very glad to say we reached just as the light rain turned into Arfak rain. It came down in torrents accompanied by thunder and lightning, and so much was pouring off the roof of the guesthouse that The Colonel took a shower in it.

It's not difficult to get up at four or five in the morning when bedtime is eight or nine at night, even if sleep is disturbed by some swamp monster snoring in the next room, occupied by Chief and Foggy, or chiggers, which caused one of my ankles to burn like fire. After honey and palm sugar pancakes we were off; me, Chief, Foggy and Nick, up and up through wonderful forest full of tree-ferns and massive trees draped with moss, to a ridge at over 6500 feet (2000 metres) where we looked hard for but failed to see any Black or Black-billed Sicklebills. We did find the hardest bird to see though, another bird-of-paradise almost hunted out in the area; an Arfak Astrapia. Alas it was a female which looked a bit like a slim, dull, black magpie. Five Regent Whistlers were also rare birds in the Arfaks, in that they were boldly patterned, brightly coloured and not shy or skulking! A black-headed, white-throated, black-breasted, yellow-bellied male out in the open was a most welcome sight in the gloom of the forest.

While standing in the best place to look for Black Sicklebills, on a trail along the top of a narrow ridge overlooking a thickly forested ravine with huge trees the canopies of which, favoured by the sicklebills, were almost at eye-level, I was very surprised to see a Vogelkop Bowerbird working its way past. Its name makes it sound exciting but in life it is just a rather large, uniformly drab brown bird. Much more interesting and exciting, to me, was a Narrow-striped Dasyure which I saw crossing an opening on the forest floor. The small, dark chocolate-brown-coloured marsupial had a longish tail and a long nose which made it look like a giant shrew. On the way back down Maurits saw a Spotted Jewel Babbler. None of the rest of us even glimpsed it of course. Twelve hours after setting off we returned wearily to the guesthouse and some very welcome coffee and cake, followed not long after by a delicious pumpkin and potato stew.

We returned to the parotia court the following dawn where the extraordinary creature danced again, and a Wattled Brush Turkey peered from behind a tree, decided something was up, and turned back. The final, midday, hour, in the Arfaks was spent on the Loop Trail where once again we did not hear nor see a jewel babbler. In fact we did not see a single bird. On the way back down the rough track to Manokwari we stopped at the village of Maibri where, once permission had been granted by the chief, Iwein and Maurits rapidly constructed a screen out of tree fern fronds which we hid behind for an hour hoping a truly spectacular, intense orange and yellow male Masked Bowerbird would visit his bower, a very small avenue of sticks decorated with bluish fruits. He didn't, so we retreated to the track hoping he and others would perch up in the tall trees toward evening, as is their wont. They didn't that particular evening so we carried on down the badly eroded track, torn apart by Arfak rain, across the bottom of steep ridge sides covered in forests full of beautiful birds impossible to see, down to the *Aston Hotel* in Manokwari, a rather lavish 4-star establishment with no beer! Iwein 'forgot' to mention that it was not only a dry hotel, but it was in a dry town.

After a rare lie-in until 06:30 we were driven to Manokwari airport past millions of mopeds on one of which dad was taking his three children to school, him with helmet them without. The departure lounge overlooked the single runway and the short grass areas surrounding it so my binoculars were out straight away. I wanted to scan for Little Whimbrels and Oriental Plovers, two of the few of the two hundred odd species of shorebirds in the world that I had never seen, two short grass specialists there was a slim chance of catching up with this time around. I could just about make out three fuzzy shorebird shapes at the far end of the runway to the right which we all assumed were probably Pacific Golden Plovers, a much more common species, but after Mr Fogg joked sarcastically that the next plane would flush them and they would land right in front of us so we could identify them for sure, a *Sriwijaya Air* jet appeared from nowhere, taxied to the very spot the birds were in and, on taking off, flushed them and to our disbelief they flew in our direction and landed right in front of us. When I saw their long necks, plain backs and the shocking length of their long legs I knew they were definitely not Pacific Golden Plovers. When one then walked down a taxiway toward us and close enough to see that its legs were yellow we were all sure we were looking at three Oriental Plovers.

Having seen so many shorebirds I rarely encountered a new one so those plovers were a wonderful bonus, a terrific pick-me-up after a long streak of missing birds, and a moment of great excitement on what was otherwise a dull day travelling between sites. So it was that I boarded the *Bombardier* to Jayapura in high spirits. On the way from there to Lake Sentani I saw a new record number of people on a moped; a teenage girl and four presumed younger siblings, all with the wind in their hair. By the lake there were some bee-eaters, of the Blue-tailed variety, gliding around and perching up and purring, always a welcome sight, celebrated with a *Bintang* at last.

A fiery sun rose over Lake Sentani as we drove along the winding road to Nimbokrang, a sprawling town where we stopped to pick up some equipment. While waiting to continue I remarked that one of the drivers looked like he had been up all night. He had. When he dropped us off at the trailhead he was informed by mobile phone that his one-year-old daughter had died of malaria. Porters walked off with our rucksacks and we followed them along an old, wide logging track known as Jalan Korea, through secondary forest, before switching to a narrow trail through primary lowland forest full of palms, where virtually the first bird I saw was a chunky-looking kingfisher that flew across the trail up ahead. Maurits found it perched of course although it took him a long time to get us all on what was a rare, little-known forest bird called a Blue-black Kingfisher, deep blue and black with a white throat and rufous belly. Walking on, Maurits then surpassed even his supernatural self when he spotted, with his naked eyes while laden with bags and clearing the trail with his machete, a Rufous-bellied Kookaburra perched under the canopy a long way off the trail. It was an incredible feat and the bird, a male with a blue tail, was a brilliant sight through the telescope. He then turned his hand to building bridges when we came to a couple of deep creeks. With Iwein's help he felled two medium-sized trees and laid them across the creeks, completing the job with hand-rails fashioned out of the branches.

After about five miles we reached a clearing where big blue tarpaulins were soon rigged up over wooden platforms about waist height off the ground, our billet for the next three nights. Iwein explained why we had to sleep so high off the ground. The main reason was the leeches although he also almost casually mentioned that we were surrounded by Death Adders, striped masters of disguise that lie coiled in ambush beneath loose leaf litter, a deep ring of which lay all around us once the ground had been swept clear. There they lurked, wriggling their grub-like tails to lure in passing lizards, frogs, small mammals and birds, before striking with their highly toxic neurotoxin, powerful enough to kill a birder in six hours. Iwein said we should be especially careful if we had to get up in the night to empty our bladders.

I also remembered that it was at the same campsite a year before that Iwein and Like were confronted by a very angry man and his pack of dogs. He stormed into the clearing yelling and waving a machete and slashing at poles, very upset about his snares being removed from the forest, and he ran at Iwein and Like who, with their lives seemingly in danger, managed to calm him down. It is not unknown in West Papua for a man so aggrieved to attack and even murder others as retaliation for what westerners might consider a trivial offence and even though the man appeared to come to his senses a village elder had to be called in to solve the matter, after which the man with the machete apologised profusely to all concerned. When I mentioned this to Iwein he played it down and reminded us that it was just as dangerous, if not more so, in many other parts of New Guinea, not just West Papua. Only a year before, a gang of violent robbers had attacked a group of walkers including seven Australians and a New Zealander, on the popular Black Cat Track in Papua New Guinea. The hikers had just set up camp when the men appeared at dusk, wielding machetes, bush knives, spears and guns. They set about the seven porters first because they were from a coastal village not a local village and deemed to be trespassing, so they swung their machetes at the porters' legs and chopped some off completely, to stop, in their eyes, the porters from carrying on walking on their land, and then they hacked two of them to death, before robbing the walkers, injuring four of them, and disappearing into the jungle.

I concluded there was more chance of being killed by a Death Adder where we were. Add the incredible heat and humidity, leeches, trees covered in ants, swarms of sweat bees and mosquitoes, and *Muaib Jungle Camp* might not sound very attractive but I loved it. A short walk away, through the 'Ring of Death', was the River Muaib where during a couple of late afternoon hours we saw two Azure Kingfishers, a female Lesser Bird-of-paradise, some high-flying flying-foxes, and a Papuan Nightjar.

It was thanks to Martince, pronounced Martin-ja, that we were able to enjoy the most productive morning of the trip so far, in terms of numbers and species of birds seen. The wise old lady owner of the land we were camping and birding on didn't sell up to an oil palm company who would clear this mad wonder and plant miles and miles of monotonous palm trees for profit. Unlike most landowners along the north coast of West Papua she turned down what would have been a huge one-off payment for her community and opted for a steady, long-term income from ecotourism instead. The 21 different species of bird we saw didn't include a male King Bird-of-paradise who wasn't at home, and the male Twelve-wired Bird-of-paradise which visited his display stump very briefly was moulting, but we did see two new birds-of-paradise; the purplish black Jobi Manucode and a female Pale-billed Sicklebill, an odd-looking creature with a long, slim, strongly hooked, ivory-coloured bill, dark cap, bare lavender-coloured skin around its dark eyes, plain olive-brown upperparts and richly barred brown and buff underparts. She was, like other birds-of-paradise, full of life, energetically probing, prodding and stripping bark, and tearing at epiphytes growing on large branches. For some reason the patch of forest the sicklebill was in was alive with birds. A Yellow-billed Kingfisher was followed by a Blue-black Kingfisher then an even more unbelievably blue beauty called an Emperor Fairywren, a male, which was intense dark sparkly blue all over except for a paler blue crown, and a black mask and wings. Even the female was boldly-patterned with a blue crown and black mask, rich chestnut back, wings and flanks, and white underparts. The pair were both extremely difficult to see as they furtively flitted about with their tails cocked and fanned in a dense thicket also occupied by a family of White-eared Catbirds which were even more skilled in the art of skulking although I was fortunate to see the beautiful shiny grassy green back and wings of one of them when it glided low down between bushes.

After a quick nap we were off again, on a long hike to a patch of swamp forest with palms held up by skirts of stilts, past fresh cassowary footprints; large three-pronged imprints in shallow wet mud about half the size of my boots. There was not much chance of seeing the actual bird or any New Guinea Flightless Rails, Victoria Crowned Pigeons or Blue Jewel Babblers thanks to the amount of noise Iwein and Maurits made clearing the trail although we probably wouldn't have seen any birds at all without

Maurits whose star turn during the latest walk was another blue beauty, a Papuan Dwarf Kingfisher. After two hours we reached a Lesser Bird-of-paradise display tree. It was a long way off and partly obscured, and the small viewing area was a mosquito-infested pool, so me, Chief, Foggy and Nick, all of whom immediately knew the views of the birds, if any, were not going to be anywhere near as good as the ones we had had in Papua New Guinea, soon began wondering if we should be looking for birds we had not seen before. After a couple of rather glum hours the birds showed briefly but didn't look like they were going to display so we headed off on the long walk back to camp and about half way there we flushed two Victoria Crowned Pigeons. They flew up into the thick canopy high overhead and we thought we had lost them but that man Maurits located one behind the thickest screen of branches, leaves and vines imaginable and we took it in turns to look at the superb bird through the telescope. The huge dark grey and maroon pigeon had red eyes in a small black mask and a beautiful, large, bushy, star-spangled array of delicate dark and light grey feathers for a crest, far larger than its head. Too soon it was time to move on and complete the walk back to camp before dark, and about half an hour later I detected the smell of woodsmoke, the smell of foreign birding adventures, and then we were back in camp after a real hard day's birding, and life was good.

In the blackness before dawn in New Guinea's northern lowland forest I lay awake on my mat under my mosquito net and took the time to take in the atmosphere, dominated by the loud, low-pitched, slowly descending booming hoots of never seen Greater Black Coucals, a sound like that of water falling out of a large upside down bottle, a fantastical tropical sound and a marvellous one to listen to while waking up. A little light and we were on the trail, walking over leaf litter and leeches, waving mosquitoes out of our faces, moving slowly, quietly, in a line, past massive buttressed trees rising far above, stilted palms, palm fronds and strangler figs, through dappled sunlight, small clouds of little yellow butterflies, twinkling blue butterflies and big white butterflies with four large 'eyes' called Silky Owls. The most amazing flying insect was not a butterfly but a day-flying moth, one without an English name but a scientific Latin name of *Cocythia durvillii*. Its clear wings looked like stained glass windows with black veins and trims, bright red where the forewings met the electric blue head, thorax and abdomen. When we lost the marvel we carried on, under a shower of leaves released from above by a waft of wind, then we heard the steam train whooshes of huge Blyth's Hornbills' wings flying overhead, above the canopy and out of sight. Lizards called blue-tailed skinks shuffled out of our way as we went on, and now and again we glimpsed birds, and on the odd occasion we even saw a bird, sometimes well enough to enjoy, the best of which was a lovely female Ochre-collared Monarch with a luxuriantly feathered ochre collar, throat and upper breast plus blue eye-rings and a blue bill. By the time we were back at camp five more wonderful hours had been added to my life.

We were off again at 3 p.m., without Lou and The Colonel because Lou was throwing up her breakfast. The rest of us headed out alongside the River Muaib which was littered with branches, trunks and whole trees brought down by wet season storms and flung this way and that by floods. It was a long shot but we were hoping to see a cassowary, one of the planet's biggest birds and yet one of the hardest to see, on an island where so many birds are so hard to see. It was hot and humid but there were a lot of mosquitoes so I pulled the collar of my dark green shirt up, buttoned the long sleeves up and even put my gloves on, in an effort to leave no skin exposed. The bastards didn't give up of course; they turned their attention to where my clothing was tight against my skin, around my shoulders, elbows and knees, and attempted to bite me there, with some success. What with leeches as well it sounds unpleasant but it wasn't, because I was birding New Guinea, fulfilling a dream, and more specifically that afternoon, there was a slight chance I might see a cassowary.

Not far along the trail we came across a small flock of birds. I only saw one of them properly but it was a female King Bird-of-paradise. The rest were hidden behind leaves in the tallest trees as usual. They moved on and so did we, and Iwein spotted a Great-billed Heron perched near the top of a riverside tree and I just managed to see the very large, gangly, uniform grey-brown bird as it flew off. Iwein then spotted a Spotted Cuscus atop another tree, a surprisingly large and beautiful animal with thick fur. Apart from the large dark round eyes it was all orange, even its bare face. When it sensed our presence it moved very slowly, using its large claws and long prehensile tail to cling to the flimsy branches, and as we watched it a Palm Cockatoo flew in with heavily swishing wings and took a look at us while hanging upside down with its crazy long-feathered crest spread.

Moving on, we came across the fresh footprints and fresh droppings of a cassowary, and then we heard the long 'roar' of one, pretty close, and I started to dare to think that we might actually see the bird I never expected to see. It may be a large flightless prehistoric dino-bird, the third largest living bird after the Ostrich and Emu, but on the island of New Guinea where it has been hunted for meat and feathers for thousands of years the species has become extremely wary. In northeast Australia where cassowaries are considered, by some people, to be the most dangerous birds in the world, they are not so shy, and being in possession of a vicious kick and long razor-sharp claws they are best given a wide berth because there are old reports of them killing people by slashing them.

Iwein told us that the shaggy black birds with bare blue and red faces and necks, high helmet-like casques on the top of their heads, and massive legs and feet, appeared to be present in good numbers around our camp at Muaib and that there may actually have been a cassowary within a couple of hundred paces of us all the time we were there, hidden by the thickness of the forest. That was about all we could expect though, for they rarely allowed themselves to venture any closer, although a few previous visitors had been fortunate enough to see one with the help of Iwein and Maurits who quickly erected temporary palm screens overlooking the birds' favourite fruit which had fallen from a tree. Cassowaries kick fruiting trees to see if the fruit is ripe; if it is the fruit will fall, if it isn't the birds will go and kick another tree, and it is possible to hear cassowaries kicking trees from miles away. We never heard any kicks, or a roar again, despite waiting some time. Iwein walked on and we followed him. He said the bird we heard must have thought we were too close for comfort and also walked on, in the opposite direction. Maurits thought we should have stayed put, stayed quiet and stayed dead still, in case it was walking toward us when it roared. We will never know.

The next morning Chief, Foggy, Nick and I set out again with Iwein and Maurits in a last-ditch attempt to set eyes on a cassowary while Lou and The Colonel began the five mile slog to the trailhead. Lou was very ill with stuff coming out of both ends but she made it out, and to the airport, and on to the first leg home, the flight to the island of Biak, but while waiting on the runway tarmac there the stewardesses called a doctor. He soon came on board and spoke to Lou when her head was not in a sick-bag. With raised eyebrows he then examined the container she kept her twenty-pills-a-day in. Looking at her again, he deemed her unfit to fly and ordered her to leave the aircraft. She was taken straight to the hospital where she and The Colonel were very relieved to hear the tests for malaria were negative. The airline *Garuda Indonesia* then put Lou and The Colonel up in the best hotel on Biak and when her condition, presumably the result of a nasty gastrointestinal infection, improved the next day, they let them fly to Jakarta, from where they made it home two days after the rest of us.

Back at Muaib the rest of us walked a long way, to the River Grime, pronounced Grim-ey. We didn't see many birds and the feeling we might see a cassowary was not there, unlike the day before. We did hear a lot of Blyth's Hornbills whooshing overhead, saw one flying lower through the forest than any before, and a nice male with a thickly-feathered rich orange-tawny head and neck perched in the open. We also came across the remains of a hornbill by a small fire that had been made by two or three hunters working the riverbanks, and also amongst the ashes were feathers that once adorned a Victoria Crowned Pigeon. Iwein was disgusted and very disheartened as he and Maurits set about looking for snares set to catch the birds and they soon found and removed some, an extremely disappointing experience for them, on land where there was a signed agreement with all the local clans saying there would be no hunting. That said, hunting on a small scale has a negligible impact on the bird populations of Papuan forests and is hardly worth worrying about when the surrounding clans are selling up their land to companies who will clear the forest completely and plant vast oil palm plantations. What a lot of local people don't seem to be able to get their heads around is that there will be no point them setting any snares then.

Back on the trail we came to a tall fruiting tree which was almost overflowing with Orange-bellied and Pink-spotted Fruit Doves, not that we got very good views of them so secretive were they. Some Sulphur-crested Cockatoos were more conspicuous. They were making an ear-splitting racket and I watched two of them erect their forward-curving crests and spread their wings, showing the beautiful lemon-yellow wash on the undersides, while they carried on screaming and screeching. By ten o'clock in the morning we were back at camp and after packing up we set off on the midday march out, a trudge interrupted by two Victoria Crowned Pigeons walking along the trail ahead of us before flying up with loud claps of their wings, as well as our last Rufous-bellied Kookaburra, which, like all the others we had seen and every Lilac-breasted Roller I had come across in Africa, merited a long reverential look.

The last birds we saw were seven more crowned pigeons. They were in the secondary forest alongside the old logging track, a rare sight, of a bird usually found only in primary forest, and possibly a result of a temporary lack of suitable fruits there. After three hours we reached the trailhead, and, after a short drive, Nimbokrang, where we were very relieved and happy to see that Lou and The Colonel had made it and were enjoying a cold drink. Then it was a long drive back to the *Travellers Hotel* in Sentani where it was a delight to remove my boots, see no leeches and head down to the restaurant for a cold beer or two.

There was plenty of time to reflect on the trip on the long journey home, especially birds-of-paradise, and one thing I thought about was that if I ever bumped into Phil Hurrell again I would apologise. I met him in the late 1980s to talk about a trip Al and I were planning to Indonesia. He had travelled extensively in that part of the world and rediscovered Schneider's Pitta, endemic to Sumatra, in 1988, over 70 years after it was last recorded. Phil was mad about pittas and fanatical about birds-of-paradise but I didn't get it. I thought birds-of-paradise were a bit gaudy and over-the-top and not like birds as I knew them at all. I had never seen one in the flesh at that time, only illustrations and poor photographs in books, so I didn't know what I was talking about but I've seen a lot now and it's time to tell Phil that he was right and I was wrong. I may love bee-eaters even more but there is no doubt, in my mind, that birds-of-paradise are the world's most amazing birds.

What images, be they in a book or on a screen, cannot portray and what Phil was doing his best to get across to me, is the richness of the colours, the fantastic variety of feathers, the intensity of the displays and, more especially, the birds' dynamism. Everything they do is done with such extraordinary verve. They just cannot sit still. Even males which appear to be taking a break from displaying or almost continually tidying their display courts or trees are always preening their plumage to perfection or calling loudly to let any passing females know that they are at home and ready to strut their stuff. They are constantly on full alert, ready to spring into immediate action should any members of the opposite sex appear and when they do the males fly with unbelievable speed to the exact spot in their court or tree they feel they must perform in, even the wings in many cases making some sort of noise, as if to let the females know they are moving into position, and then they show off whatever it is in the incredible variety of modified feathers they possess to the absolute best of their ability, for only the number one male will get to mate. They are so wound up in the presence of a female they look like they are going to burst with passion.

Male birds-of-paradise have to eat as well and when they do, as is the case with the young males and females, they go about foraging with equal gusto, not just hopping from branch to branch but positively leaping and bounding with tremendous zest, almost strangling the moss-covered branches with their strong feet and legs, stopping briefly to pluck fruit or shuffling and bounding their way along trunks, boughs and branches while peering rapidly from side to side, over and under branches and leaves, gleaning arthropods and other insects as they go, or tearing epiphytes, moss, bark and rotting timber apart with their powerful bills and digging out prey hiding in them, showering the forest with debris. The males do this all with such vigour and speed it seems they cannot bear to be away from their display court or tree for too long, in case they miss some passing females. It is mesmerising to watch them, to behold their extraordinary, unrelenting energy. In Papua New Guinea I had seen something of what Phil was trying to convey to me but it was the times I spent in West Papua, especially those hours with the male Wilson's Bird-of-paradise on Waigeo and the Western Parotia in the Arfak Mountains, that finally convinced me that birds-of-paradise really are something else.

*Bee-eaters, Bryher, Isles of Scilly, England, 16th May 2004*

## 21

# THE LOCAL PATCH

I have been fortunate enough to have travelled all around planet Earth, to all seven continents, some several times, and seen thousands of species of birds and lots of other wildlife, in some of the most spectacular places. I have seen nearly all the birds and other animals in the photographs which were plastered across my bedroom wall when I was a teenager, and all those red dots on the map of the world on my wall now are not the places I dream of going to, they are the places I have been to. I have written six *Where to watch birds* books covering six continents and I have designed a website from scratch called *Where to Watch Birds and Other Wildlife in the World*, all extolling the virtues of travelling the world in search of wild birds in wild places, and each devoted to encouraging and helping others to organize successful and enjoyable trips abroad, but the first and most important destination for a birder like me is a local patch. That is, a place, preferably a short walk from the front door, where it is possible to see a wide range of birds and other wildlife any day of the year. Travelling the world and seeing new birds in new terrain is tremendously exciting but it's not necessary to fly to the ends of the Earth to enjoy the wonder of birds and other wildlife, and spending years getting to know a local patch is an adventure in itself. There are fresh and exciting experiences to be had at home too. After all, seeing a Sabine's Gull is as thrilling as seeing a Swallow-tailed Gull, and a Stoat is as exciting as a Sloth, it just depends where they are.

My first local patch was Robinswood Hill, an outlier of The Cotswolds near Gloucester in England. That is where, with patience and persistence, I got to know the birds of inland Britain, beautiful birds like Long-tailed Tits, Blue Tits, Bullfinches, Goldfinches, Green and Great Spotted Woodpeckers, Jays, Nuthatches and Yellowhammers. That hill is where I learnt their calls and songs, different plumages, and behaviour, and figured out which species were resident, summer visitors, winter visitors, or migrants passing through during the spring and autumn. Particularly exciting regular migrants included Redstarts and Ring Ouzels, and one spring morning I saw my first Tree Pipit and Pied Flycatcher, a male no less, in the same hedge in a couple of minutes. In cold weather a Woodcock sometimes made me jump for joy, and every now and again I would see a real patch rarity like a Hawfinch.

When I moved to the south coast of England to study for a degree in Biology I still visited the hill during holidays but my new local patch was the seafront from Southsea, where I lived, to Eastney at the entrance to Langstone Harbour in Hampshire, although I actually spent more time birding at the other end of the harbour at Farlington Marshes, a half hour bus ride away. The mudflats and wet pastures were a complete contrast to Robinswood Hill and I got to know a totally different set of birds, especially shorebirds which soon became my favourites. So, when I moved back to Gloucester after graduating I began birding the wet fields and pools in a bend in the River Severn at a place called Sudmeadow next to Gloucester Rubbish Tip, introduced to me by legendary local birder Gordon Avery, known in some circles as 'Gordon Ivory', a reference to an extremely rare gull he saw at Frampton-on-Severn and kept to himself and a few others. The best bird I saw at Sudmeadow wasn't a shorebird though it was a Short-eared Owl, that, since the patch wasn't within walking distance, I saw after being knocked off my bicycle. I was still visiting the hill as well of course and when I headed there after spending some time in the winter desolation of the Karakoram in north Pakistan where it was hard to see more than ten species a day, it was an absolute revelation to walk around a vibrant green landscape lit up by birds like Blue Tits and Bullfinches, and see over thirty species.

After a couple of years back in Gloucester where I worked at the Gloucester Centre for Environmental Education I became a Field Officer for the London Wildlife Trust. I was very busy and slept on a friend's sofa in a flat in Shepherd's Bush for several months and I didn't have a local patch in what was a low point in my life. True, there were parks nearby but they didn't inspire me, so I was very pleased when a couple living in the same flat said I could rent a room in a flat they bought in Tottenham, because it was within walking distance of the ten Walthamstow Reservoirs. During a year and a half living there I saw a fine variety of waterbirds, the best of which were drake Goldeneyes and Goosanders, resplendent on calm sunny winter days, but that oasis in a concrete desert always felt like a temporary patch, because deep down inside I knew I had to leave my job, my room and the reservoirs to fulfill a teenage dream to travel to Africa.

When I returned from Kenya I lived with my friend Chief in Reading for five months and was without a proper patch again, although I did learn a lot about Green Sandpipers at nearby Dinton Pastures. Then I landed another job with the London Wildlife Trust, as manager of the Thamesmead Wildlife Project. Thamesmead was a flat expanse of what was once salt then grazing marsh, on the southern bank of the River Thames less than ten miles (16 km) east of the centre of the London metropolis. The draining of the marshes began in the 1500s with the development of the old Royal Woolwich Arsenal at the west end. During the 1800s the arsenal expanded rapidly and by the First World War 73,000 people were employed there, in a secret city within a city, a maze of firing ranges and munitions stores called 'tumps' (round islands surrounded by moats) connected by a canal and miles of railways. However, the place was abandoned after the Second World War, and in 1967 the Greater London Council (GLC) began building a 'new town' there, on top of the old arsenal and across the remaining marshes to the east. The architect Robert Rigg was influenced by housing complexes in Sweden where it was believed that lakes and canals reduced vandalism and other crime so he incorporated narrow canals, five lakes and large green spaces in his design. It was all very 'modern' in the 1960s, but the mix of 'calming' spaces, houses, medium-rise buildings and 12-storey blocks of flats almost all built entirely of concrete became more famous for the brutalist style of the more built-up areas that featured in various films including Stanley Kubrick's *A Clockwork Orange*, in which Alex, a sociopathic juvenile delinquent, leads a small gang of thugs on an horrific crime spree in a dystopian, near-future Britain. When I moved there in 1988 Rigg's canals and lakes, as well as the old tump moats, were littered with stolen motorbikes and shopping trolleys discarded by disgruntled youths, and arson was rife.

With the job of attempting to inspire some respect for the wild tumps and water bodies, as well as lobbying planning officers and landscape architects to save as much as possible of the remaining marshes, came a one-bedroom second-floor flat in Whinchat Road, in the new town. I had sold virtually everything I owned eight months before so that I could spend as much time as possible in Africa, including nearly all my vinyl records and the turntable, amplifier and speakers I played them on. I returned from Africa happier but poorer than ever and when I moved to Thamesmead I had nothing; no cooker, fridge, chairs, tables, bookshelves or music, but the rent was peanuts and for the first time in my life I had a place of my own and it felt great. In what seemed like no time at all I had all those things *and* a large desk in my bedroom, made out of the kitchen door, and what's more, five minutes from my front door was a new and exciting local patch.

Thanks to a munitions inspector at the arsenal called Richard Ruegg there was a fairly good record of the birds present in Thamesmead during the early 1800s. He was often out on the marshes with his gun and he wrote up some of his experiences in a little book entitled *Summer's Evening Rambles Round Woolwich*, published in 1847. 'With an anxious brow and heavy heart have I escaped from the throng of humanity, with its gloom, and anger, and sadness, with its cares, and sorrows, and anxieties - its meshes of folly and its vortices of crime, to revel in green fields, and to spend one hour at least, with Nature. No bird, let loose from the gin of the fowler, ever soared into its pure blue home more joyously'. Time had changed nothing. I felt exactly the same nearly 150 years later even though I had far less birds to 'hunt'. Ruegg watched wild swans and geese, Corn Crakes, 'common' Red Kites, the 'occasional' Little Bittern and he summed up the status of Wryneck as 'tolerably abundant'.

Between 1945 and the late 1960s John Burton, who worked for the BBC Natural History Unit, recorded large numbers of breeding Lapwings, Redshanks and Snipes but a huge reed-bed which he thought supported up to 150 pairs of Reed Warblers was turned into Southmere during the construction of the new town in the early 1970s, a boating lake surrounded on three sides by concrete towers.

Meanwhile the badly polluted River Thames had been cleaned up and huge numbers of waterbirds returned, mostly to Woolwich Bay along the northern border of Thamesmead, and during the early 1970s there were peak mid-winter counts of 4000 Pochards, 1720 Teals, 1600 Shelducks, 800 Tufted Ducks and 485 Pintails, as well as 2000 Dunlins. What the birder Peter Grant described in his book *The Thames Transformed* as 'the single most important site for wildfowl on the Inner Thames' was soon gone though. A new river wall enclosed the tidal bay so that it could be in-filled and used for housing.

By the time I arrived in the late 1980s there were just 237 acres (1sq km) of grazing marsh left, about 15% of the original expanse, and it was all at Erith Marshes next to Crossness Sewage Pumping Station at the eastern end of Thamesmead. Teal, Shoveler, Snipe and Yellowhammer were all extinct as breeding birds and there were not many Skylarks, Meadow Pipits, Yellow Wagtails, Little Grebes, Lapwings, Redshanks and Reed Warblers left, although other resident birds and breeding summer visitors did include Cuckoos, Kingfishers, Turtle Doves, Stonechats, Reed Buntings and a pair of Black Redstarts that nested on Belvedere Power Station next to Erith Marshes, not a bad list for somewhere so close to the middle of London.

During the seven and a half years I lived in Thamesmead I learnt that the narrow mudflats left along the river, the occasionally exposed lake edges and the few shallow pools sitting on the deep sandy soil used to cap the old arsenal and destined to be built on, attracted a wide variety of shorebirds. During the autumn up to twenty Common Sandpipers could be seen, mostly along the river, and I was surprised to discover that five or six usually remained throughout the winter months, along with a few Green Sandpipers, and one winter they were joined by a Wood Sandpiper, a very rare event in Britain. Also during the autumn, in favourable weather, especially southeasterly winds, a prolonged riverwatch often revealed passing gulls and terns, and during one August-September period I was thrilled to see up to 70 Black Terns, 60 Common Terns and eight Sandwich Terns, accompanied by the odd adult Little Gull and young Arctic Tern, and a Little Tern.

Winter birding could be spectacular when the tide was rising and the shorebirds rose from the mudflats and flew to their roosting site on the banks of Great Breach Creek at Erith Marshes. Over 2000 shorebirds and ducks were sometimes present including a thousand Dunlins wheeling around in clouds of bird smoke, with 400 Lapwings, 150 Redshanks and up to twelve Ruffs. A few Pintails swam in the river, 600 Teal whistled softly in the reedy channels, and nearly a hundred Snipes hid in the marshes where a flock of over a hundred Stock Doves and small numbers of Corn Buntings helped make a day list of over 50 species a regular event. With Water Voles present too, what remained of Erith Marshes needed to be saved so I submitted a design and management plan and a few years later the site did become a 63 acre Local Nature Reserve.

I may have lived in one of the largest cities on the planet but I had a great local patch. It wasn't Erith Marshes though. I lived at the west end of Thamesmead, where a hole in a fence let me into another world, a large area of undeveloped private land that I usually had to myself, apart from the security guards with very poor eyesight. I enjoyed

*Jack Snipe, Thamesmead, England, 31ˢᵗ January 1994*

many a wander there, and even a few local rarities, such as a singing Nightingale, a November Woodlark, and a Dartford Warbler two weeks later. Perhaps even more surprising was an astonishing build up of Jack Snipes in a tiny patch of flooded grassland, the numbers of which rose from two in mid-November to twelve on the last day of January the following year, and there was still one left on the first day of March when I also saw a 'Common' Snipe and a Woodcock. The first Rook I saw, after over seven years without one, was the perfect example of the unpredictability of even patch birding, and a bird so 'common' elsewhere but so rare where I lived that it got me whooping and dancing. One of the biggest whoops of all was for a Waxwing which landed in a rowan tree visible from my desk during my last January in Thamesmead, followed by a flock of six nearby in early March. In a winter which had seen thousands arrive in Britain I still felt very fortunate indeed to see some of the beauties on my local patch, and even the country's twitchers who were watching a Cedar Waxwing from North America in Nottingham were nowhere near as excited as I was when I saw the 'Bohemian' Waxwing from my window.

I saw over 100 species of bird every year I lived in Thamesmead, 118 once, 50 on most long walks, and 142 in total but as the years passed I felt more and more like I was winkling out the wonder in an increasingly ugly setting. I was fed up living in a big city. I had had enough of the concrete, traffic, foul air, litter, noise and crazy numbers of people, and their depression and aggression. We may be the only living things that can appreciate the beauty of our surroundings yet the majority of us seem content to live in ugly cities, while many animals, presumably oblivious to the visual quality of their surroundings, live in beautiful places. Our ancestors had better views from their caves than we have from our cafes. We evolved, over the course of 150 million years, in beautiful wild places, more than long enough to feel at home in them, not in cities, which have not been around for long. We are plains animals; hunter-gatherers who need wide open spaces in which to wander, under big skies. We need the soil beneath our feet, between our fingers, fresh air in our faces, and the peace and beauty of wild places. They excite and refresh us. Cities are artificial, alien, even brutal places, infinitely disconnected from the world we evolved in, a beautiful world with trees, flowers, butterflies and birds. Most people don't live surrounded by this beauty anymore. Many don't wander about wild places. This is why they are unhappy.

I wasn't unhappy. I could always take solace in nature. I was very fortunate to live next to an oasis in a desert of concrete, tarmac, steel and glass, where I could see a wide range of flowers, butterflies and birds, but that oasis was getting smaller and smaller as more and more houses were built for more and more people. I wanted to live somewhere that couldn't happen. I was single again and could live where I wanted to, and I wanted to live by the sea, where I could walk and write, and fall in love with someone who would fall in love with me.

I had also resigned as Thamesmead Wildlife Project Manager, partly because I felt I had achieved most of my goals and partly because I thought the new project budget was way too small to be effective. I became a freelance ecological consultant and started writing *Where to watch birds* books. I didn't have to live in London. I could live almost anywhere my meagre funds allowed. My favourite place in the world was the small island of St Agnes in the Isles of Scilly, so I wrote a letter to the post office there asking the people who managed it if there was any accommodation on the island I could rent all year round. I doubted it. As far as I could ascertain from my visits in the 1980s there were about seventy residents living on the island, nearly all in accommodation attached to farms, guesthouses, a pub, a cafe and a post office, and all other properties were holiday lets. It was certainly a long shot but the potential prize would be a dream come true.

*Nighthawk, St Agnes, Isles of Scilly, England, 9th September 1998*

'Two thousand drunks clinging to some rocks' was how someone once described the Isles of Scilly, a low-lying archipelago of granite islands, islets, reefs and rocks sprinkled across about ten miles (16 km) of shallow water in the northeast Atlantic 28 miles (45 km) southwest of Land's End, England. The five largest islands are inhabited by people and most of them live on the island of St Mary's, where in the space of a few hundred wobbly steps at the top of the quay there are, at times, five places to get a drink; the *Mermaid Inn*, the *Atlantic Inn*, *The Bishop & Wolf* public house, the *Scillonian Club* and the *Porthcressa Inn*, not to mention several hotel bars and restaurants, and there is even a hotel and an inn in the 'country' should anyone needing a drink find themselves in the 2.5 square miles (6.5 sq km) of land. The four off-islands are well-served too.

The Isles of Scilly are also well-known for mild winters, clean sea air, long white sand beaches, peace and quiet, and, amongst birders, their seemingly magnetic attraction to rare birds. When the St Agnes Bird Observatory operated for a decade from 1957 several birds from North America were seen for the first time in Britain and Ireland, including Northern Waterthrush (St Agnes, 1958), Bobolink (St Agnes, 1962), Red-eyed Vireo (the first one found alive was on St Agnes in 1962), Parula Warbler (Tresco, 1966) and Blackpoll Warbler (St Agnes, 1968). The possibility of seeing such birds and a wealth of other lost migrants, including some from the opposite direction of Siberia, enticed more and more birders to the islands and by late September 1975 a few hundred saw Britain and Ireland's first Yellow-bellied Sapsucker, first living Black-and-white Warbler and third Scarlet Tanager. By the 1980s nearer 500 birders were holidaying on the islands in September-October, with the numbers peaking in 1987 when 800 to a thousand were ferried across to Tresco to see Britain and Ireland's second Philadelphia Vireo.

For various reasons including fewer rarities and increases in travel and accommodation costs the number of visiting birders fell sharply during the early 1990s. However, the combination of wonderful scenery and birds from all points of the compass on a sparsely populated small island was still a description of paradise to me, so when the managers of the post office on St Agnes replied to my letter inquiring about accommodation saying it just so happened that an elderly lady who had been living in an old holiday let for many years was planning to move to the mainland and that I could move into said let if I wanted to it didn't take me long to say yes, I wanted to!

About a year after reading that letter my few belongings arrived on St Agnes in a shipping container which was transferred on to the quay by a small crane aboard the *Lyonesse Lady*, the Isles of Scilly's small cargo ship. Once unloaded, my bird books, desk and so on were taken to my new home on two trailers pulled by tractors, along St Agnes's main 'road', a concrete-covered track barely half a mile long. My shack by the sea was tiny; a main room a few paces long and even less wide, a bathroom barely able to accommodate a shower, a kitchen just wide enough for a gap between the sink on one side and my *Baby Belling* cooker and fridge on the other, and a bedroom just the right size to wedge my small double-bed into. It would have been hard to swing a Goldcrest in there but I didn't care. Outside was St Agnes, my dream island; a mile long, half mile wide, low-lying slab of granite with a very convoluted coastline, part rocky, part sandy. My home was right in the middle, where there were many small fields, most of which were used to grow early daffodils, sheltered by tall hedges of introduced evergreens. My desk, in the main room, overlooked a small garden thick with shrubs and an old twisted tamarisk tree frequented by flycatchers in the autumn. Wintering Water Rails and Firecrests liked to bathe in my leaky pond. Song Thrushes patrolled the tiny lawn for worms, and my floor for crumbs. At dusk Hummingbird Hawkmoths and sometimes much larger Convolvulus Hawkmoths hummed at the honeysuckle wrapped around the pillars of the porch roof.

At the bottom of the short garden is Barnaby Lane which a White's Thrush flew along one day. I loved walking along that lane, lined with lovely elms, and out into the big wide open of the rocky heath of Wingletang, and down past the white sand beach of Beady Pool to Horse Point out in the Atlantic Ocean, to seawatch. Back along the main track is the eye-catching lighthouse, a broad, round, white, 74 feet (23 metre) high tower overlooking the elm copse, orchard and mature garden of what was once The Parsonage but was then a large family home. Down past the lighthouse the track leads to a chamomile meadow where I once got down on my stomach to watch five freshly-feathered young Curlew Sandpipers with icy orange breast-sides pulling grubs out of the ground just a few paces away. Next to the meadow is an almost perfectly round brackish pond called Big Pool surrounded by concentric rings of rushes. Just to the east is the rocky bay called Per or Porth Killier, to the north a smaller bay known as Per or Porth Coose and to the west one of the sweetest spots in all the world, a shallow cove called Periglis where a long curve of seaweed-strewn white sand is often alive with shorebirds during the autumn and winter.

Autumn on St Agnes usually gets under way with the arrival of the shorebirds, although the first to arrive usually do so in summer. They come from the north, some to stay for the winter some bound for the mud and sand of Africa. Curlews and Redshanks may turn up in early July, followed by a Greenshank or two, Dunlins and Common Sandpipers, then, in late July to early August, Sanderlings, Turnstones, Knots and Bar-tailed Godwits. Adult birds turn up first, then the young and it is juvenile Sanderlings I loved best. The islanders call them, like most small shorebirds, 'twillies', but I like to call them 'spangles' after the tiny white spots on the black feathers on their upperparts. From mid-August the variety of lost and passing landbirds normally begins to increase, especially if the wind is in the southeast, and by the end of the month the island can be liberally sprinkled with Wheatears, Whinchats, Yellow Wagtails, Pied and Spotted Flycatchers, Robins and a fine assortment of warblers, often including Icterine and Melodious. With them are Wrynecks. After mid-September come Goldcrests and Firecrests, and Meadow Pipits, with the first Yellow-browed Warblers from near the end of the month. Amongst these regular visitors are regular rarities, sharing the island in October with thrushes and finches.

After the end of autumn passage, around about mid-November, my favourite way to start the day and one of my fondest memories of living on the island was to walk the beaches at dawn, especially when the wind went northwest and cleared the air and made it sheer joy to walk and watch the birds in the fresh air and fantastic crisp clear light, sometimes with a cloud scene painted a beautiful mixture of pink, lilac and lead, the latter illustrating the thick shower clouds steaming in. I liked to watch the sun rise into such clouds, lighting the rain sometimes and producing scenes resembling rock concert lightshows, except of course they were far more spectacular.

During the winter the Sanderlings in Periglis are joined by Purple Sandpipers, while Golden Plovers grace Wingletang and a Merlin hunts the few small birds left, mostly Meadow Pipits and Rock Pipits. More interesting than the winter birdlife was the weather, which was more often than not rough to very rough if a southwesterly airstream was in full flow. A survey once carried out to grade areas of the British coast according to how rough the seas were rated areas on a scale of one to ten, ten being the roughest, but when the surveyors reached Scilly they had to give it a score of eleven. Sometimes St Agnes, the most southwesterly and exposed island in the archipelago, seemed to be surrounded by white water, so wild was the weather. There was only one way to start the day then, at Horse Point, the southern tip of the island and islands, and one December spell of seawatching stands out. I was up before first light five days on the trot, sipping a sleepy coffee and eating a cookie as the light behind the tamarisk at the end of the garden began to bloom. Then I put my waterproofs, boots and binoculars on before a brisk walk down Barnaby Lane. I could just about hear Song Thrushes singing above the rush of wind. On Wingletang I got my first view of the ocean and boy it looked rough, which was good, and the wind was strong, which was even better. I had to lean against it to stay upright as I crossed the top of the tiny bay called Beady Pool, which was being bombarded by the breakers booming in. Walking over the low ridge between there and the point I had to bend low to make any headway against the force of the wind then it was swiftly down the short slope to snuggle down in my favourite place, sheltered from the worst of the wind and rain and spray by the side of a big rock.

The seawatch begins. Water shoots up above 'the rock' just offshore. Most of the water between there and me is a mass of white foam and spray. Beyond there huge Atlantic rollers, as far as the horizon, are coming in, relentlessly. The massive waves crash and splash and explode on the rocks just below me, making a tremendous thunder and sometimes causing the ground to shake. I keep an eye on the danger but mostly look out to sea. There are plenty of seabirds heading west, into that wind, over the big old, rough old, sea. Gannets catch the eye first, their black-tipped white wings contrasting strongly with the grey water. Razorbills race by in small groups low over the sea, accompanied by the odd whirring Little Auk, so small some are merely a blurred black and white speck. It was a good early winter for this scarce visitor to Scilly and I enjoyed quite a run from late November to mid-December with up to eight birds on a seawatch.

They were great to see but it's the Kittiwakes I like the most. A few hundred of them come from the east and move west past the point before and just after first light. When the weather is grey they look so pristine with their brilliant white underparts and, in the case of the adults, lovely grey upperwings with triangular black tips which make the long tapering wings look like they have been dipped in ink. The young birds in what is called their first-winter plumage are even more striking. For some reason unknown to me they look even brighter white below than the adults while the upperwings are also mainly white with a strongly contrasting black zigzag across them. They are small birds and one moment they look brittle the next supreme, as they fly into that wind, which is almost strong enough to blow me over. In fact, the rougher the weather the more the Kittiwakes seem to like it, probably because the wind and waves whip up more small fish, invertebrates and plankton to the surface, and that's where they were heading those five dawns in December, the wild waters just west of Horse Point.

On the last day of the five, still content just to watch the Kittiwakes, I thought I spotted a smaller bird amongst them but I lost it in one of the great troughs between the rollers. Then it was up again cresting a wave, closer in, close enough for me to see the black underwings of what was a beautiful adult Little Gull, which I was then able to follow with my binoculars as it joined a foraging flock of fifty or so Kittiwakes. They were dipping to the surface of the sea just beyond the surf and while watching them I saw one of the two Balearic Shearwaters that had glided by earlier. It was dip-diving in an ocean so clean and clear that I could see it swimming with half-folded wings below the surface and there in the next waterfall of a wave coming in were two Porpoises body-surfing. Another hour of wonder had passed all too quickly, the sun had cleared the clouds on the horizon, and the sea was molten red for a moment before I got up and turned for home.

The weather usually calmed down by March, the start of spring, when Pied and White Wagtails normally arrived, with a Hoopoe or two. I once saw three in one field, nothing compared to the 17 that Francis Hicks, long-time island resident farmer and birder, saw together, way before my time in 1965. My other favourites amongst the long list of regular spring passage migrants were the Wheatears, which lit up even the island's lichen-lavished rocks, although it was also great to live on an island where Woodchat Shrikes, Golden Orioles and the odd rarity were also to be expected.

With spring migration coming to an end in mid-June and 'autumn' migration beginning in early July there is not much summer on St Agnes, at least as far as birds are concerned, and, fortunately, it was my least favourite time of the year anyway, the island being too overcrowded with human visitors for my liking. There are, relative to mainland Britain, few breeding bird species on the Isles of Scilly; between fifty and sixty in an average year, although less than forty actually on St Agnes. There are no owls, woodpeckers, Jays, Magpies, Rooks, Coal and Long-tailed Tits, Nuthatches, Treecreepers, Bullfinches or buntings for example. However, there are high numbers of Wrens, Robins, Dunnocks and Song Thrushes, and some seabirds, including Guillemots, Razorbills and Puffins but they can only be seen on boat trips to the uninhabited and undisturbed outlying islands and rocks. I couldn't wait for the tourists to go home and autumn to take off on the bird front, for amongst the usual but exciting array of passing shorebirds and landbirds there was always the chance of rare birds, very rare birds.

I also looked forward to the autumn because the rare birds attracted, in turn, birders, and there was a fine bunch of them on St Agnes from late September to late October, fifty or so in total and enough characters to write another book this long. Some of them were old friends like Al, Ando and Chief, and some were new friends they brought with them, including the gentle birding maniac Paul Hindess better known as The Fiend, and Paul Macklam also known as The Colonel. They all loved a day in the field and big nights out, and sometimes we liked to celebrate life back at mine where they slept on the floor. It was rather cramped when they were all on the island at the same time. One night, back from *The Turks Head*, the island pub, there were all of us and several guests squeezed in there, making quite a racket, none more so than a large and jovial chap from The Midlands called Steve but known to the St Agnes regulars as Tawny Frogmouth, an Australian bird with a rather large gape. I know nobody who can drink like Ando and The Colonel but Frogmouth always insisted on trying and, as usual, as the night wore on the rest of us, also rather worse for wear, began to see the effects of his foolishness, so much so that we suggested that perhaps it was time for him to leave. This he eventually did, only to reappear at my door about half an hour later, saying, rather slowly and not very clearly, "Nigel, I appear to be unable to find my way out of your garden," an admittedly leafy but rather small affair about twenty paces long and seven paces wide with a narrow but obvious path along one side. It never occurred to me that anyone could get lost in my garden, drunk or sober, day or night, but somehow Frogmouth did, or maybe he just had a little sleep in the shrubbery. Whatever happened - he never remembered, that night, the next morning or years later - whatever happened, while he was escorted out of the garden and back to his holiday let, the rest of us laughed so much discussing the various theories put forward to explain what he may have been up to that some of us ended up in stitches on our hands and knees.

Apart from a small flock of Pallas's Sandgrouse which reached St Agnes during the famous 1863 irruption the first very rare bird to be seen on the island was in 1951. Following the death of her mother in 1951 Hilda Quick moved to Priglis Cottage (her preferred spelling of Periglis) where she lived until her death in 1978 aged 83. While living there she produced many bold and attractive wood engravings, some of which appeared in her fine book, *Birds of the Scilly Isles*, published in 1964. In that book is a chapter entitled 'Jam Over The Years', rare birds being 'jam on the daily bread of normal observation', in which she wrote, 'So, without further excuses, I will tell a few tales of the birds that I have met here from time to time' and she began with one that took place on the 22nd of June 1951.

'Within three months of my coming to S. Agnes to live, Ludwig Koch came to stay (for convenience in getting to Annet to record Shearwater voices). We were at breakfast when a neighbour popped in to say, all in one breath, "A-press-photographer-is-arriving-on-the-launch-and-there-is-a-very-strange-bird-in-the-lane!" (I had a glimpse of something unusual when fetching the milk). So out we went in a hurry, and the strange bird was kind and sat on a telephone wire where it could be watched from close quarters; it was obviously a Bee-eater ... the underwing showing copper-coloured. At rest, we could admire the lovely green colours, with russet throat patch. On looking up Bee-eaters, all this turned out to be the wrong colour for the Common bird, and eventually it was identified as a Blue-cheeked Bee-eater.' At the time it was believed to be 'a first for Britain' but about ten years later, in 1962, John Parslow examined a stuffed 'Bee-eater' that had been shot on St Mary's on the 13th of July 1921 and which was in the bird collection of the Isles of Scilly Museum, and he re-identified that as a Blue-cheeked Bee-eater so it became the first, although the two remained the only ones known to have reached Britain until 1982.

Now, like Miss Quick, I would like to tell a few tales of the birds that I met on St Agnes when I was living there, beginning with the 6th of September 1998 when during eight and half hours glued to the side of my favourite rock at Horse Point I watched in awe as 245 Cory's Shearwaters and 11 Great Shearwaters passed me by, in what seemed like a beautiful dream, one I will always remember for 'big

*Cory's and Great Shearwaters, St Agnes, Isles of Scilly, England*

shear's' shearing over a big sea. They came after a deep low pressure system had sped across the Atlantic and it or the one right behind it carried a very rare bird to my island. Late at night on the 8th of September I was told that a visitor to the island had seen a Nightjar while walking home (relatively sober) from *The Turks Head*. I was there before dawn the next morning, looking over the bracken-covered slope between the pub and Gugh Bar, the sand bar between St Agnes and Gugh, because, taking into account the recent weather, I was convinced the bird was going to be a Nighthawk not a Nightjar, from America not Europe. I saw nothing resembling either and returned home disappointed. Then I tried desperately hard to forget about fast-moving Atlantic depressions and Nighthawks while failing to write anything any good until about one o'clock in the afternoon when my phone rang.

A minute later I was sprinting past The Parsonage when I came across Francis Hicks.

"Fran! There's a Nighthawk down on your farm!" I yelled out loud in between panting.

"Yes, I know ... would you like me to show you where it is?" he calmly replied, having seen a couple on St Agnes before, although none for sixteen years.

Fran led me, slowly, oh so slowly, down through a grassy field, along a hedge and into a ploughed field where he pointed to a Nighthawk that his farmhand, Mark Sedgman, had spotted resting on top of a furrow. I was shaking with excitement then, when it flew for no apparent reason, floating in ecstasy, as the bird rose gracefully into the air and with a couple of lazy flaps flipped over a tall hedge, its snow-white wing patches and tail spots flashing as they caught the sunlight. It was nowhere to be seen the other side of the hedge though, so I ran home to let the world know there was a Nighthawk on St Agnes, the first one in Britain and Ireland for nine years, the last one being on the nearby island of Tresco in 1989. I spent the rest of the day looking for it but it was not until dusk when I saw it again, flying over *The Turks Head* to where the 'nightjar' was seen the previous night, the slope I scanned so hard at dawn, where I watched it hunting moths with great agility.

That day and the next four were a brilliant blur. During the second day the very welcome rare visitor roosted in a ploughed field near Porth Killier and I had the pleasure of escorting fifty or so twitchers over from the mainland to see it. There were just few of them left when, with dusk approaching, the bird stretched out a wing, took to the air and returned to its favoured slope where it flew to and fro with supreme elegance just in front of a very appreciative audience who whooped with delight every time it passed close by, almost under our noses at times. During the next three days it roosted in a field above Covean and was seen very briefly at dusk each evening in increasingly inclement conditions due to a strengthening northwesterly wind. On the morning of the 14th, presumably the Nighthawk's sixth morning on the island, the bird that had brought so much joy to me and so many others was roosting in the same field but people watching it thought something about the bird wasn't quite right and they walked up to it and picked it up. The Nighthawk was dead. It weighed 44 grams, half of what it should have weighed. The windy nights meant there were few insects airborne after dark and the bird was unable to find enough food. I was devastated and with a lump in my throat I had to fight hard to hold back the tears when I was shown the poor bird in *The Turks Head*.

Eleven days later the twitchers were back. When I reached the fruit cage, a small field down by Lower Town Farm, near the end of my morning rounds, Doug Page, a regular birding visitor to the island, was there. Not long after, a large grey warbler appeared and I said, "Look at the conk on that!" It had a very prominent pointy-looking beak and it dipped its tail downwards when it called 'chack'.

"What do you think it is Nigel?"

"It must be an Olivaceous Warbler!"

It turned out that the *British Birds Rarities Committee* member had been looking for the bird all morning. He had been told about an interesting 'grey Icterine Warbler' seen by

Renton Righelato, another regular visitor to the island, the evening before but declined to tell me. He also thought it was an Olivaceous Warbler, an even rarer bird in Britain than a Nighthawk, and much harder to identify, and because it was about the eighth for Britain and Ireland and potentially the first twitchable one since a two-day bird in Suffolk three years before and one on St Mary's ten years previous to that, I wanted to make sure I was sure before walking briskly home to put the news out, and even then, after the bird's name had appeared on the pagers of birders all over the country, I experienced more than the usual amount of post-identification panic. For a few minutes there and several times after, I thought a better birder might come along and say, "Hang on a minute, I think it's a so-and-so warbler" but none of the many who twitched it did during its two-week stay.

The Olivaceous Warbler's last day on the island was the 8th of October and it was by far the star bird of a very disappointing month for rare birds until a big low swept in from the Atlantic with the wind gusting a wild Force 10 westsouthwest on the 24th, the last or last but one Saturday in the month when most of the birders who spend a week or two or three on the island usually head for home. They departed on the first passenger boat to St Mary's, the *Spirit of St Agnes*, the one I was crew on. The paltry wages from working on the *Spirit*, my small retained firefighter allowance, the meagre rewards from writing bird books and some lucrative but sporadic ecological consultancy work paid the rent in paradise. Somehow we managed to get the birders to St Mary's in that ferocious wind, from where they headed to the mainland and home, waved off with the usual jokes about what they were going to miss.

The Olivaceous Warbler had departed before most of them had arrived and there had been very few scarce let alone rare birds for nearly three weeks, on any island in Scilly not just St Agnes, despite favourable weather conditions for the transport of American birds across the Atlantic, so most of the departing birders were not worried about something turning up after they had left. However, it had happened before and it happened again; two mornings later, after over a month without a major rarity arriving during the best time of the year, an American Robin landed on the lawn on Gugh. The bright, handsome specimen soon flew across the narrow channel to St Agnes and began feeding in the same field above Covean in which the Nighthawk had roosted. Soon the twitchers were back again, for it was the first twitchable American Robin in Britain and Ireland for ten years.

1999 was one of the most remarkable years for rare birds in Britain ever, especially during the autumn on the Isles of Scilly, and particularly on St Agnes. In April I nearly fell of the back of Mark Sedgman's tractor when an adult Night Heron flew by, the first of at least six to reach the islands. It was even more exciting to come across a male Subalpine Warbler in May. At the end of June 'big shear's' arrived in large numbers during unseasonal strong southwesterly winds. Two Cory's Shearwaters on the evening of the 28th suggested I should return at dawn, which I did, despite the rain. The sight of a Cory's going slowly by on my first scan hinted I might be in for something special. Twenty minutes later, a second came into view. It was heading a group of five and then came group after group, every five minutes or so, and then a rush of over 50 in ten minutes, accompanied by at least ten Common Dolphins, some of which leapt clean out of the ocean to join the shearwaters in the air. After that wonderful sight the numbers of shearwaters fell away until another 30 went by in ten minutes. All too soon it was time to leave for crewing on the *Spirit*, 170 Cory's Shearwaters having passed by in what seemed like two seconds but was in fact two hours.

At 11 minutes past 11 a.m. on the 11th of August 1999 the sun was eclipsed by the moon. Purple flames flared out from the edge of the sun before the 'diamond ring' shone so bright I had to look away. The birds didn't seem to take much notice. On the 17th of September a low pressure system developed to the northwest of Ireland and intensified during the night, winding up the speed of the southerly wind in Scilly to a Strong Gale Force 9 on the Beaufort scale by midday on the 18th when I was trying to tie the *Spirit* up to the quay on Tresco in lashing rain, the skipper David Peacock having rashly promised to ferry two St Agnes residents there. We also had to drop some people off on St Mary's where during my lunch break I saw a Buff-breasted and two Pectoral Sandpipers on the airfield. I didn't want to be crewing though I wanted to be seawatching and I only managed to squeeze in two two-hour shifts, at the beginning and the end of the day, still enough to see over 400 Great, over 50 Cory's, 41 Manx, 21 Sooty and three Balearic Shearwaters, as well as seven European Storm Petrels, and a Leach's Storm Petrel along the surf, and ending with a flock of over 250 Great Shearwaters wheeling over the water straight out.

More Monarch butterflies than ever arrived, from America, by the end of September and I saw up to five a day including two together in my garden. With them came a Baltimore Oriole. I was unable to get to Bryher where it was but I did manage to see my first Bee-eater in Britain, a bright young bird on St Mary's.

October was staggering even by Scilly's extraordinary standards, and the 5th, 6th and 7th of October 1999 may have been the most amazing three consecutive days for rare birds in Britain ever.

When I returned to St Agnes after a morning crewing at 12:45 on the 5th Rick Hicks, island farmer, said to me, "Have you seen the thrush then?"

"What thrush?"

"The Siberian one."

The Bradshaw family, who had been visiting St Agnes in October for many years, had seen a Siberian Thrush on Gugh, the seventh for Britain and Ireland and first twitchable one since a one-day-bird in Norfolk five years before. Once I had ascertained that, I ran there, only to be informed that the bird, one of the most skulking known to mankind, had originally been seen eating blackberries on the top of a bramble bush, but had since gone to ground. So, I dragged myself back to the quay for an afternoon at work on the Spirit, desperately hoping I would see the bird in the evening. Back on Gugh by five o'clock, I saw the thrush very briefly in flight before it went into hiding again. Then I started getting a little teasy, as they say on Scilly, because the chances of looking the bird in the eye before dark seemed very slim, and the last one in Britain was gone the next day. A long, worried, wait ensued and I began to think about dipping. That seemed a strong

*Siberian Thrush, Gugh, Isles of Scilly, England, 5th October 1999*

possibility when the bird flew along a hedge straight toward me and perched up on top of it for a good minute or so in that last lovely low light of the day. I couldn't help but yell, "It's blue!" after it flew off. It certainly was. It may have been a young male but it was a beautiful deep dark blue above and down its flanks, and it had a striking white eyebrow.

A long night in *The Turks Head* followed and the next morning James Siddle and Ren Hathway, who had slept on my floor, kept me busy making cups of tea as we discussed what to do. Ren was keen to return to Gugh for better views of the Siberian Thrush since he was working on a painting of one for the cover of a forthcoming book called

*Thrushes*. James and I were not so keen on the prospect of joining what would no doubt be vastly increased numbers of twitchy twitchers there, so the three of us decided to wait for news on whether the thrush was still present or not while attempting to relocate a Subalpine Warbler seen the day before down at Troytown Farm. Arriving at the small fields of the farm, I said I would walk around the field on the right while suggesting that James could do the one on the left and Ren might as well continue down the track between them.

When James and I returned to the track Ren came wobbling up it weak-kneed from shock and in a voice wavering into the high octaves said something like, "I think I've ... I've ... just seen a ... I've just flushed a ... White's Thrush!"

He told us he had seen a thrush fly out of the bottom of a hedge a few paces in front of him, along the hedge and into the corner of a field, a large dark thrush with a striking black and white tail. We thought he must be joking, because White's Thrush was the other species he was painting for the cover of *Thrushes*. A brief conversation based on, "Are you sure?!?" then unfolded with me adding something like, "It's not possible! There can't be a White's Thrush on St Agnes *and* a Sibe' Thrush on Gugh!"

Ren couldn't believe it either and he began to doubt himself, especially after James put the news out. He was actually shaking but James and I didn't doubt him for a second. We took him home for another cup of tea and asked him to describe the bird again before showing him Ian Lewington's plate in *A Field Guide to the Rare Birds of*

*Britain and Europe* comparing the tails of White's and Mistle Thrushes. Covering up the names, I asked him to pick the one he saw. It was true; there was a Siberian Thrush on Gugh *and* a White's Thrush on St Agnes. It could take a lifetime to see one of them in Britain but now it was possible to see both in the same day, less than a mile apart.

The thought of masses of manic twitchers trying to see a White's Thrush, even more notorious for skulking than Siberian Thrush, in Tim Hick's fields was horrible. We quickly considered every way we could think of to avoid the cretinous one percent trampling all over the place and decided, with Tim's permission, to carry out what is known in birding circles as an organized flush, whereby James, Ren and I would walk along the back of the hedge the bird appeared to land at the bottom of and try to flush it out for the masses to see, thereby keeping any idiots out of the fields. The time was set and relayed via pagers, phones and CB radios. James, Ren and I started walking the hedge and disappeared behind it, out of sight of the hundreds gathered at the top of the field the hedge was at the bottom of. We had not gone far when we heard a hushed cheer. The organized flush had worked. The bird did exactly what we hoped it would. It flew out in front of the crowd. We couldn't see them but we could hear them and they had obviously seen the bird. The only trouble was Ren and hundreds of other people had seen the bird, much to Ren's relief, but James and I hadn't.

We trudged gloomily back to the joyous line of birders and all the way along it, acknowledging the thanks of many happy people with bowed heads, handshakes and jokes as we went, right to the other end of the line, to see if Bryan

*White's Thrush, St Agnes, Isles of Scilly, England,
6th October 1999*

Thomas from St Mary's had managed to photograph the bird. When we reached him he told us that it had flown by too fast for him and when he pointed to the bottom corner of the field where it had dived into it the White's Thrush flew out and back to where we had flushed it from, far enough for James and I to see the bird very well, albeit in flight only. Then, we were as happy as everybody else.

After seeing the Siberian Thrush and a superb Radde's Warbler just up the road from where the White's Thrush was, a second organized flush for an even bigger crowd was equally successful but on the third and final attempt on that first day the black and gold beauty flew out of the hedge on our side and around the small field we were in, banking in one of the corners with its black and white tail spread, and no one else saw it. The second flush was the last time the White's Thrush did what was expected of it. After visiting virtually everywhere on the island it settled down in the fields next to the main track opposite the end of Barnaby Lane and yet it was not until nearly two weeks after Ren first saw it, that I saw the super-skulker on the ground there, when the strange creature was bobbing up and down like a Jack Snipe. It remained in those fields for over a week but one of the shyest birds on the planet was rarely on view and talking to many of the tightly-packed mass of mostly miserable birders clogging up the island's main drag during that time it seemed it took an average of four days to see the beautiful but damned thing.

Mainland twitchers who had not dropped everything for the Siberian Thrush now faced missing two megas. Most buckled under the pressure and headed for St Agnes which from the 7th of October 1999 was under siege. The 6th ended with a Red-breasted Flycatcher so I had seen that, a White's Thrush, a Siberian Thrush, a Radde's Warbler, and two Monarch butterflies, one in my garden, in a day, on St Agnes and Gugh, the sort of list I used to make up when I daydreamed about a walk around Fair Isle. That day the 6th of October 1999 such a daydream came true where I lived, in my favourite place in the world. Then the daydream became a fantasy.

After watching a splendid Siberian Stonechat during the morning of the 7th I headed to *The Turks Head* to meet Al, Ando, The Colonel and The Fiend, who had already arrived for their annual stay on St Agnes. They were on Gugh and were probably going to be late for our arranged meeting in the pub if they had not seen the Siberian Thrush so, since it was such a lovely sunny day I sat

# A MIND-BLOWING BIRDING TRIP TO A PLANET CALLED EARTH

*Short-toed Eagle, St Agnes, Isles of Scilly, England,*
*7th October 1999*

outside in the empty garden with a pint, a very rare treat for me, especially in the middle of the day. From where I was sitting I could see the crowds on Gugh and I tried to pick out my friends amongst them with my binoculars. I couldn't recognize any of them so I scanned around rather casually looking for birds. I didn't see much but after a while something caught my eye and on raising my binoculars I saw a massive bird-of-prey flying past the pub on its way to St Mary's, massive that is in the eyes of a birder used to seeing nothing bigger than an Osprey. In that first millisecond I thought it must be an Osprey, a good year tick on St Agnes, but it was too big and too broad-winged and I found myself saying out loud to no one, "It's an eagle!" It was an eagle. Just after 1 p.m. on the 7th of October 1999 a Short-toed Eagle flew in off the sea over St Agnes and on to St Mary's, the first Short-toed Eagle ever seen in the British Isles.

The crowds waiting for the White's Thrush to reappear may not have seen that but they did see a first for Britain fly over their heads. Amongst them was Britain's leading lister Ron Johns who had the rare pleasure of adding a bird to his lengthy British List without having to move a muscle, let alone drive across the country or fly to a remote island. Meanwhile, on Gugh, my friends and other St Agnes regulars who had just arrived for their annual birding holiday, plus a hundred or so ecstatic twitchers, who had all just seen the Siberian Thrush, heard someone shout out the immortal words, "Large eagle over the Parsonage!" A mad scramble ensued as the dazed and confused crowd ran here and there as they tried to get to a spot where they could see the 'large eagle'. Some, including Al, stumbled and fell, into the bracken and brambles, and he arrived at *The Turks Head*, shortly after seeing a Siberian Thrush and a Short-toed Eagle, covered in scratches but he didn't care, and with Ando, The Colonel, The Fiend and assorted others we sat in *The Turks Head* garden celebrating our good fortune most of the afternoon, evening and night, into the early hours.

It was all so incredible we celebrated every night for a week, joined for some of it by Chief, Foggy and John 'Spotter' Mason, another old friend. I'm not sure how we managed to get up in time for the boat to St Mary's on the morning of the 14th when they all had to leave but I do remember walking up the slope to the airfield with them to see two Upland Sandpipers, the first time two had been seen together in Britain. As we approached the people watching the birds they began to disperse rapidly and we were told by someone leaping down the slope past us that there was a Blue Rock Thrush on Porthloo Beach. After a quick look at the delightful sandpipers I left my poor friends to catch their flights to the mainland and began walking very briskly to Porthloo where I was very quickly joined by about 700 other delirious birders who had gathered to watch only the third ever and first twitchable Blue Rock Thrush in Britain, a rather handsome male.

The next day I finally got to see the Yellow-billed Cuckoo that turned up on Tresco on the 12th. It was the 15th of October, or 'Radde's Friday' as it became known because there were at least seven Radde's Warblers on the islands that day. I didn't see a single one but I did see the next rare bird, a Rustic Bunting at Troytown Farm on the 20th. The birders who regularly visited the Isles of Scilly during October had enjoyed one of the best if not thee best spell of birding of their lives and as the last full day for most, Friday the 22nd of October, dawned, many were content to spend it glowing with the satisfaction of having seen so many sensational birds, with perhaps a little thought at the back of their minds that wouldn't it be nice to round it all off with one more mega. Well, it was 1999 and even that year's satiated birders were in for one last treat, thanks to the remains of Hurricane Irene which brought with it a Chimney Swift. This time it was St Mary's turn again and on the same island was a beautiful crisp juvenile White-rumped Sandpiper, on the same beach as the Blue Rock

Thrush was a week before. It was the first of at least seven such sandpipers to reach Scilly in late October 1999, the largest number ever seen in one place in Britain.

In the storm's wake came a juvenile Long-tailed Skua off Horse Point, my first on St Agnes, on the day the autumn's second Nighthawk was found on Bryher, and the day most of the regular mid-October visitors departed of course. As they did so, brilliant bird artist Martin Elliott arrived to stay on my floor, hoping to see the White's Thrush but we couldn't find it in three days and to cap it all we probably glimpsed another Nighthawk one dawn. When I heard that the Chimney Swift had moved from the north end of St Mary's to Peninnis Head at the south end I thought it might be on its way to St Agnes so I left Martin to the doomed search for the thrush and headed for that famous watchpoint *The Turks Head* to scan the skies and, hopefully, add the swift to my St Agnes list. I couldn't see it though, so when hunger arrived instead, I returned home for lunch which I decided to eat in my sunlit garden, just in case. Halfway through a coffee and a smoke I heard a shout of "Chimney Swift!" from the main track where the horde was still lined up hoping to see the White's Thrush, and on looking up there it was, sweeping around overhead and joining Pallid Swift on my garden list.

The autumn was not over yet. That day and the next saw yet another mass arrival of rare birds, this time involving ducks, in the form of a Surf Scoter, a Blue-winged Teal, two Green-winged Teals and one or two Lesser Scaups. A dejected Mr Elliott departed and Pete Clement, appropriately enough the author of the forthcoming book on *Thrushes*, the book Ren was illustrating, arrived, and when he looked over a wall at Lower Town Farm he saw, almost below him, the White's Thrush. It remained there until the 9th of November, foraging on the large lawn when undisturbed but even after an extremely stealthy approach, via two tall thick hedges, fine-tuned over days, every time I sneaked a look through a tiny hole in the nearest hedge it flew up into the hedge nearest it and disappeared. I tried everything to see that bird out in the open on that lawn for more than a few seconds but failed miserably.

In between my futile attempts to see the White's Thrush well I did stumble upon a male Subalpine Warbler down Barnaby Lane and the next morning when I was watching it again a male Yellowhammer, a much rarer bird on St Agnes, dropped in to the next field for a few minutes. And still the incredible autumn was not over. On November the 12th a 'tacker' down Troytown Farm turned out to be a noisy Dusky Warbler which was dashing around the very fields which had already hosted White's Thrush, Radde's Warbler and Rustic Bunting that autumn, one of the best ever on the Isles of Scilly and especially St Agnes, my home. The wild island of wonder was a truly great place for a birder to live although when I had to leave a year and a half later it was not so much the rare birds I missed as the big shear's over big seas, big skies, fantastic light, and the shorebirds sprinkled across Periglis Beach.

*Fea's Petrel, 7.5 miles (12 km) south of the Isles of Scilly, England, 8th July 2001*

When I lived on St Agnes I rented an old holiday let. It belonged to a couple who also owned the adjacent house. When they retired and left the island the new owners' daughter decided she wanted to live in my shack by the sea and because there was nowhere else on the island for rent I had to face the dreaded prospect of leaving the place I loved. At least the shocking news stirred me into action. I spent my final winter on the island writing the damned book that I had been putting together for years, something

I had promised myself I would do while I was on St Agnes and, indeed, one of the main reasons for moving to a quiet place by the sea. It was a tale about how nature illuminates life, based on an imaginary birding trip to Kenya, and it was terrible so it went in the bin, with lots of other stuff when I started packing. I didn't want to pack I wanted to be birding on my last few days in my favourite place in the world, but I had such a bad back I could hardly stand up to walk let alone finish packing my few belongings, mostly heavy books. And to cap it all, the new owner was drilling holes in the other side of the wall next to my bed, where I lay in pain. I didn't know whether to cry, scream or laugh. My head hurt more than my back thinking about it all.

I was offered a room for the summer at *The Turks Head* if I worked there, and there were other kind offers with summer but not winter accommodation including crewing on the passenger boats based on Bryher. However, I decided to move to St Mary's and a job as a porter at *Tregarthen's Hotel* where I was provided with room and board for seven months of the year, and a wage which if I was frugal enough with during the summer would enable me to rent a place for the winter and fund the odd birding trip abroad. To add to my misery at leaving St Agnes my publishers Helm dropped the seventh and final book in my *Where to watch birds in the World* series covering North America due to declining sales of the other titles, resulting from the instant information available on the internet.

I thought the job 'hotel porter' would involve carrying luggage to and from the thirty rooms in the hotel. I was right but I actually spent more time doing hotel maintenance, and transporting the food and other essentials that are needed for running a Three Star Hotel, from the quay where everything arrived from the mainland, to the hotel. It was a massive change compared to my easy life on St Agnes, but, in order to carry out all these and more tasks I was supplied with a mini 'bread loaf' van which came in very useful during the quieter moments of the six-day working week because I could dash off in it to look for birds, sometimes with several birders inside, and once with some hanging out of the back as we passed, at speed, the hotel manager and his wife out for bike ride.

One of the few advantages of living on St Mary's was that it was so much easier to board the evening 'pelagics'; boat trips several miles offshore, catering mainly for anglers hoping to catch Blue Sharks but which birders also join because they offer the chance to see seabirds close up, notably Wilson's Storm Petrels, a very hard bird to see in Britain any other way. So it was that in early July of my first summer on the main island that I embarked on only my sixth 'pelagic'. About seven and half miles south of the islands on the *Kingfisher* I picked up an unusual-looking bird coming in low and head-on straight toward the boat. It looked about the size of a Manx Shearwater but it was flying with deep powerful wing beats and it appeared to have a dark mask. In no time it was with us and it banked sharply off to the right just off the starboard beam showing dark underwings and the shout went up, "It's a Fea's!"

The quiet lapping of waves against the boat was shattered as the seven birders on board scrambled to get a good view because the last two Fea's Petrels which had been seen off Scilly, two and five years before, had flown straight past. This one looked like it was going to do the same as it shot by the stern and we thought that was that but no, the bird turned back with a wonderful lazy-looking loop and passed the boat again, and again and again, ending with one more memorable sweep past the starboard side.

Never before had birders in Britain and Ireland had the chance to see this fantastic seabird at such close range and for so long, and I for one was buzzing for weeks, first and foremost because I had been fortunate enough to watch a *Pterodroma* petrel, a 'winged runner', one of the most graceful of all birds, close up on a boat trip from the island I lived on, in Britain, and secondly because it so happened to be close enough to be identified as the first definite Fea's Petrel recorded in Britain. There had been several probables and I had even seen one of them, a bird which flew past Porthgwarra in Cornwall over a decade before.

A pelagic in mid-August the same summer was a classic for another reason. There were no large shearwaters, no Wilson's Storm Petrels, no *Pterodromas*, or other rarities, I was just gloriously happy watching European Storm Petrels hanging over the white crests next to the boat, and some Common Dolphins, leaping clear as they made their way to the front of the boat where I was able to lie down on the bow and watch them at almost arm's length as they sailed through the sea just below the surface, swimming with no effort whatsoever it seemed, over and under each other and upside down, and occasionally bursting out of the water, close enough to look them in the eye. They were an incredibly exhilarating sight, as good as any Wilson's or

*Sabine's Gulls, Isles of Scilly, England, 14th September 2003*

Fea's, and so it was that I returned happily home while watching waves of phosphorescent dinoflagellates glowing green in the deep dark blue.

One mid-July pelagic a couple of years later we spent two hours with a feeding frenzy of over a hundred Common Dolphins, and a hundred Gannets. Circling and criss-crossing the melee we came across two Cory's Shearwaters as well, and we followed them for the rest of the evening as they weaved their way in and out of the surging, surfing and leaping dolphins, and diving and cackling gannets, a spellbinding night of nature's art which ended with a fire in the eastern sky at dusk. There were no more large shearwaters that summer but a fantastic, unprecedented, flock of four adult Sabine's Gulls spent an hour with us one evening in mid-September. The restless migrants bound for the South Atlantic made pretty patterns with the black, white and blue-grey triangles of their eight wings when they flew around the boat - Sabine's Gulls seem to be all wings - and once they rose high above the sea and seemed ready to move off, only to zigzag round and back down while squealing loudly.

It was the relaxing, enchanting and uplifting evenings at sea, always with European and often Wilson's Storm Petrels, regularly with beautifully-coloured Blue Sharks, sometimes Cory's and Great Shearwaters, usually gliding gracefully around the boat at extremely close range, occasionally something rare like a Fea's, and the phosphorescence on the way home, that softened the blow of the St Agnes dream being shattered and kept me sane during the five crazy summers I dashed everywhere but nowhere in that little van on St Mary's.

Getting to the off-islands was also much easier from the hub, a great advantage during periods when lots of scarce and rare birds turned up. One particularly crazy week was at the end of March 2002. On the 22nd I arrived at one end of St Agnes as a Little Bustard flew from the other, never to be seen again. Two days later I watched an Alpine Swift at whooshing distance on Tresco for ages. The next day I was looking at a Little Bunting on St Mary's when John 'Higgo' Higginson, my birding companion on Scilly, phoned me to say he was watching the Alpine Swift *and* a Pallid Swift, on Bryher. I looked the latter in the eye the next day. Three days later I drove like the wind, with five birders in the back of the van, to Deep Point on St Mary's hoping but failing to intercept a Red-billed Tropicbird which it turned out had only briefly followed the *Scillonian III* on its way to Scilly, about four miles (six km) to the east. It was only the second for Britain, the first having been seen from a yacht 20 miles (32 km) southsoutheast of Scilly the previous June. That morning a male Sardinian Warbler landed on St Agnes and on the 31st I watched the superb silverback singing on Wingletang.

Four great birds in eight days was nothing compared to four in forty minutes one mid-May day when Al, Foggy and his friend Dan came to St Mary's on a twitch. They had already seen a Citrine Wagtail at Marazion and a Basking Shark from the plane that turned back to the mainland because of fog by the time they finally landed on St Mary's in the early afternoon. I picked them up in the van and drove down to Old Town to scan Peninnis Head for the Lesser Kestrel which had been present for a few days but had not been seen for hours. After a few minutes a shout went up from some other birders that there was a Little Swift overhead, a first for Scilly, and while we locked on to that a ringtail Montagu's Harrier flew past. We were still in shock when news broke that the kestrel was at Carn Morval. We piled into the van we saw a Woodchat Shrike while walking out to where the kestrel was hanging in the wind, disturbed only by a passing Hobby. It was incredible birding, even for Scilly.

On Sundays, my days off, I liked to visit Bryher during the spring and autumn migration seasons, usually with Higgo. Like St Agnes it was possible to cover most of the mile long, half mile wide island in a day although we usually concentrated on the arable fields at the southern end and the rough fields east of Great Popplestone Bay below Shipman Head Down at the northern end. Higgo didn't accompany me one September Sunday when the island was alive with migrants including a juvenile Red-backed

Shrike. I was exhausted on my return to St Mary's and just about to sit down to a welcome cup of tea in my room back at the hotel when my phone rang. There was a first for Scilly on the uninhabited island of Annet. Ten minutes later I was in a full RIB bouncing across the water at top speed. After walking across the island I saw what appeared at first to be a uniformly dark brown little mite of a bird. It was more mouse than bird actually, and it scuttled under a boulder before emerging around the other side where I could see the heavily streaked head and body of a Lanceolated Warbler, which Renton Righelato had stumbled across earlier.

In early November the same year, a strong westerly airflow across the Atlantic got Higgo and I all excited about a Killdeer, an American plover prone to vagrancy to Britain in late autumn. We thought one might be blown to St Agnes. It was a remote possibility and became a bit of a joke between us but the first chance we had we got on a boat there. On arriving on the magic island we split up in an effort to cover as much ground as possible. Higgo headed to Periglis, me to Covean and Wingletang, and that is where I was when I received a text message from Higgo on my mobile phone which read, 'Killdeer Periglis now'. I laughed and texted back, 'Very droll!' not believing it for a second. I then stopped to eat my lunch before carrying on with a lovely walk, slowly progressing toward Periglis as planned. When another text came through, this time from our birding friend Spider on St Mary's, saying there was a Killdeer on Periglis I still wasn't convinced but, admittedly, a little worried that there might be one. So, now with a phone signal strong enough to call Higgo I did, and he then watched me pick up pace past the campsite then trot then run to his side whereupon he pointed to a Killdeer standing on sandy Periglis Beach, the first on Scilly for over a decade and the first twitchable one in Britain for several years.

Another time Higgo didn't visit Bryher with me was in mid-May 2004. He decided to take a chance and join a rare trip to the untrodden turf of Annet. The day did not start well for me. There was a very low tide so I didn't reach land until 11:30, 45 minutes later than expected. With time so short I strode quickly up to Shipman Head Down hoping a summer-plumaged Snow Bunting which had been on Bryher and Tresco during the week and out of reach due to work might still be present. It wasn't and neither was anything else so by midday I was leaning on a gate at the northern edge of Popplestone Fields thinking about what to do next when my mobile phone rang. There was a Coal Tit on St Mary's, a shocking piece of news because while the Coal Tit is a scarce autumn stray to the islands it is very rare in spring. When the call was over I looked up and saw an odd-looking small bird flying toward me from the north, quite high up like a migrant not low down like a local, so I quickly raised my binoculars and was amazed to see that it was a Coal Tit. The bird landed in a tall hedge to my left so after phoning the news out I walked along it hoping to see the bird perched and if possible check if it was one of the *ater* subspecies from the continent.

Then I heard the 'magic sound' and all thoughts of the Coal Tit left my mind. Hearing the unmistakeable rolling, purring 'prrrup' was a longed-for moment that had taken eight springs on Scilly to come along. All I thought about was seeing what I could hear calling high above me. Listening carefully, trying to pinpoint the sound in the sky, I was sure I could hear more than one. 'They're up there somewhere, high up' I said to myself, 'just a quick look, just a decent view of one of them, just the colours, that'll do, just come low enough so I can see one of you, please!' I tried to forget how many had been heard but never seen on Scilly as I frantically scanned the sky above. It was torturous looking for them because those that are seen in the spring usually pass straight over and the last time a flock was seen by more than a fortunate few was over twenty years before when seven spent a week on St Agnes. There were lots of House Martins and Swallows foraging low enough to see their colours but nothing larger, more colourful, so I ran around the hedge to a place where I could see more sky. I could still hear them but all I could see were the martins and swallows, for a while, then I thought I could see a larger bird above them and raising my binoculars like lightning I locked on to the sleek body, long, stiff, triangular wings and long tail of what I consider to be the best bird on the planet but it was still high in the sky, too high in the hazy sunshine to make out any colours. Then I saw another one and another one. There were at least three, all too high to see their colours but, "Yea, definitely three of them!" I yelled it to myself and finished it off with, "Three Bee-eaters!!!"

Then my mobile phone rang. I could see the word HIGGO on the screen and before he had time to ask me about the Coal Tit, a bird he had never seen on his local patch, his beloved island of Bryher, I screamed, "Bee-eaters! Three Bee-eaters! Now! High over Popplestone!" After a brief silence, after the shock had subsided a little,

Higgo, back on St Mary's from Annet, said something like, "The bastard's got three Bee-eaters as well!" to the birders next to him. After a few more expletives he added, "We're on our way matey! Keep us updated!"

I ran through the fields toward where I thought the Bee-eaters were moving to, hoping, hoping so much, that they would come down out of the sky and stick around, at least long enough for Higgo and the others to see them. When I stopped to scan I saw that they were a little lower, low enough to make out the pale blue underparts. My view was partly obscured by the slope of Watch Hill though so I ran up and around the side of it terrified of losing the birds while they were out of sight but when I got to where I thought I needed to be, to my utter relief there they were, sweeping and swooping low over a fallow field full of Cow Parsley and swarming with winged insects in the warm sunshine. They were calling continuously and their glorious colours glowed in the sunlight pouring over my shoulders, illuminating their golden backs, black-trimmed, shining turquoise outer wings, frosty foreheads, and yellow throats. I had seen hundreds of Bee-eaters abroad but I had never seen any in the spring, when their plumage is at its peak, and there they were, the best birds on Earth, in all their glory, on Bryher, my favourite place to be on a Sunday. And the gorgeous things hunted with such style, casually flying around one minute, flying fast and direct the next, to pluck bees with ease from the air before gliding gracefully to the top of a tamarisk to de-sting and devour them.

There were moments while watching them when I realized that another dream had come true; I had finally come across a flock of Bee-eaters on Scilly, but it was still difficult to enjoy the moment fully while waiting for the others to arrive. The birds were migrating. I could see it in them. I could feel it; their zest and their desire to push on. They looked so vibrant, so alive and so edgy. They looked as if they wanted to be somewhere else, and soon. They made me anxious. I wanted them to stay. I wanted the others to see the stunners. Ages seemed to pass before Higgo and the rest arrived, and twenty minutes after, twenty blissful minutes, enjoying the birds even more and enjoying my friends enjoying them, the birds could contain themselves no longer. After being on the island for an hour and a half they took to the air and headed off toward Tresco, leaving me fighting back a tear or two after one of the most deeply emotional experiences of my life.

Another bird that stirs me so is the beautiful Buff-breasted Sandpiper, in my view the best of the bunch of North American shorebirds which reach Scilly every autumn, and in the September after the Bee-eaters I spent my most moving hour ever with an incredibly tame threesome that walked right up to and past my nose while I led on my stomach, lifting their feet high and bobbing their small round heads like pigeons as they scoured the short grass for insects. That close to the exquisite creatures, I could see the dark brown spots which look like freckles on their shoulders, the neat white edges to every feather on their backs, and the feathers near the neck that are so small the pale edges look like perfectly-formed, sparkling, silvery drops of water .

That same September very few other scarce or rare birds reached the islands, most unusual for Scilly, and when the westerlies finally subsided after over two weeks some drizzle and mizzle made the visiting birders with underused binoculars even more miserable. They and the locals who were hoping and hunting for rarities as well, clung to the mantra, 'The biggy travels alone'.

The last Tuesday of that September dawned bright and sunny. Rarity hunters renewed their efforts. Not me, I was at work, sitting in the van in the town square waiting for more hotel guests to arrive by bus from the airport, when Mick Turton came over for a quick chat before he boarded a boat to one of the off-islands. "What's your prediction today then Nige?" he asked. I had looked at the weather charts and seen a long southerly airflow so in outrageous hope rather than belief I said, "Cream-coloured Courser!" He laughed as he left and like many others his head began to sink a little again around midday, by which time most rare birds are found, because there was no news from anywhere of any unusual birds. It looked like being another very quiet day, right up to nearly half past two in the afternoon when the world changed.

Higgo called me with the incredible news, so shocking it took a long time to sink in. Then it all came flooding back; that evening twenty years before almost to the day spent scanning empty fields near Leigh-on-Sea in Essex for the last Cream-coloured Courser to reach Britain, present the previous four days but absent the day I got there. It was a terrible experience so, despite being at work, there was no way I was going to miss the chance to see the latest one. After hastily arranging some sort of cover I climbed down the quay steps on to the first RIB available and ten minutes later I was on St Agnes. Tristan Hick, island resident and fellow firefighter when I lived there, was about to leave the quay in his golf-buggy and he was good enough to tell me to get in, and brave enough to take it right to the end of the narrow, bumpy and rutted Barnaby Lane, so I was the first person from St Mary's to arrive on the scene. I ran over to where Fran Hicks and a few other birders on St Agnes for the day were standing and there it was, a crazy courser dashing about on long white legs in one of Mike Hicks's fields. It looked rather incongruous; a tall desert-coloured desert bird on close-cropped green grass but it was an extraordinary and thrilling sight made all the more remarkable for the bird having possibly arrived from North Africa that very afternoon. Amongst the fast-growing crowd was Martin Goodey, a Scillonian, who pointed out that he was watching the courser from the same spot he had seen a Wood Thrush and near enough the same place he had seen a Caspian Plover. Nigel Hudson said to Paul Dukes, who found said thrush, "You must have seen the Essex one," referring to the courser I had *not* seen two decades ago. Paul's reply left even Nigel Hudson speechless.

"No, I missed that," adding, with a well-timed pause, "but I did see the one at Blakeney," which was in 1969, fifteen years before the Essex individual.

"St Agnes does it again!" was what I said, as usual, once I had calmed down a bit, referring to the thrush, the plover, the courser and many more very rare birds which had somehow reached that tiny island after travelling thousands of miles from all points of the compass. After half an hour or so the courser was flushed by a cow and took to the air with fast, flicky, rising flight, the black underwings making it look even more exotic.

Over 200 twitchers arrived the next day. Nearly all of them dipped, their agony at not seeing the bird compounded by news of its rediscovery on St Martin's as they made their weary way home. Back they came and I joined them for another, longer look. The courser then moved to St Mary's airfield, in time for the middle two weeks of October when the majority of birders stay on the islands, so they were very pleased. However, there were few other rare birds to excite them during most of that October. It was so quiet some thought it was the worst ever October for rare birds on the islands. Successive low pressure systems sweeping swiftly across the Atlantic raised hopes of North American strays, only for them to be dashed again and again, and to make matters worse when one did turn up it was, not for the first time, on the Monday after the third Saturday of the month when most of the birders return home.

Like the day the courser turned up almost a month before, it dawned bright and clear, and I, having finished work for the season, headed to St Agnes where I saw, as hoped, three Waxwings on what was once my local patch. Then the shuddering news broke. As with the courser it took some time to sink in. Birders looked at their pagers again and again. No one could believe it. There had only ever been five in Britain and Ireland, only three of them were alive and only one of them was twitchable and that was for one day only, in Ireland. What the news amounted to was; the first chance for virtually every British birder to see a dream bird in Britain. Inundated with phone calls from birders sprinkled across the off-islands the boats on St Mary's were mustered, and, from every island, every point on St Mary's, and every corner of mainland Britain, the long, nervy trek to Trenoweth began.

When an Olive-backed Pipit, a similar-looking bird, flew out some people began to doubt the reliability of the remarkable sighting but it was true because not long after I was looking at an Ovenbird, something I thought would never happen in Britain. The pipit-like New World warbler was walking across a pine belt floor a few paces away with its head bobbing and tail flicking up in characteristic fashion, and it made a quite extraordinary sight.

Alas, the bird was not well. It lived long enough for Higgo to get back in time from the mainland to see it but the bird was on its last legs by then and, like that other long-distance traveller the Cream-coloured Courser, it was eventually taken into care, and the two star birds of the autumn died within hours of each other, a terribly sad but presumably common fate of tired, lost and starved birds, a long, long way from where they should be.

A month after the Ovenbird two more birds arrived from America; a Black Duck and a Surf Scoter, and at the same time Mike Hicks got a brief view of a coot in a field on St Agnes, a very odd place for a coot to be. It was extremely shy and it took nearly a week for him to see that it had white undertail coverts and was therefore almost certainly an American Coot. He kindly invited the St Mary's birders over to have a look for it but I only managed a brief view of the bird silhouetted in flight and I was left with a scarcely believable line in my notebook; 'untickable views of American Coot, shooting out of a high hedge'.

Taking into account regular avian visitors to the islands such as American shorebirds, Purple Herons, Hoopoes, Bee-eaters, Golden Orioles, Red-rumped Swallows, Red-breasted Flycatchers, Red-throated and Olive-backed Pipits, Rosy Starlings and rarities, which in my four and a half years on St Mary's included Cream-coloured Courser, Killdeer, Sora Rail, Chimney, Little and Pallid Swifts, Black-throated Thrush, Pied Wheatear, Blackpoll, Lanceolated and Sardinian Warblers, Bobolink and Ovenbird, the Isles of Scilly are one of the most exciting places for a birder to live in Britain but, as with St Agnes, it was not all about the rarities and scarce migrants for me, it was also about watching birds in a wonderful place.

The trouble was I was driving everywhere and nowhere, becoming more and more discontent with a frequently crazy busy job and the knowledge that I would never have enough money to buy a house on Scilly and therefore be free to chose what to do for a living. The only accommodation available during the spring and autumn seasons, the best for birds, came with jobs, mostly jobs that took up five or six days a week, leaving little time for birding and to really enjoy living on Scilly. I had had enough of that frustration, so much so that I was actually thinking of leaving, when, one weekend in May 2005, I was introduced to Alice.

She was a lost soul living in Cornwall who wanted to love and to be loved. She liked birds, she liked butterflies, she liked the outdoors, and best of all she liked me, and I liked her so we met up again, in Cornwall and on Scilly, and our relationship was sealed in September while sitting at the top of Porthloo Beach with a glass of wine each enjoying seventeen superb young shorebirds foraging at high tide; five Bar-tailed Godwits, seven silver-spangled Sanderlings, two Curlew Sandpipers, two Dunlins and a lovely Knot.

Alice thought they were as magical as I did. She knew nature was magical. She got it. She saw its beauty, felt its power, knew its worth, and that was it for me, for us. We were in love. So my time on Scilly came to happy end with three windy late-October days camping on St Agnes. We saw two Short-eared Owls on Gugh but the best sight was Saturn through Mike Hicks's powerful telescope. Then we boarded the *Scillonian III* and, accompanied by Common Dolphins leaping into the rain, we sailed to a new life.

*Bee-eaters, Cot Valley, Cornwall, England, 27th April 2008*

After two years living in Hampshire enough was enough. Alice and I had Nightingales for neighbours but we missed the sea. We booked a holiday let bungalow in Marazion, Cornwall for two weeks and from there, with Ned our six-month-old son in tow, we headed out in search of somewhere to rent, and soon I had a new local patch; Cape Cornwall, for seawatching, and Cot, Kenidjack and Nanquidno Valleys, leafy gaps in the rugged coast of the Land's End or Penwith Peninsula famous in the birding world for providing shelter to passing birds including plenty of rare ones, all within easy walking distance of our front door in St Just, the most westerly town on mainland Britain, about eight miles (13 km) west of Penzance.

My first day birding on the new patch was the 23rd of March, the very same date I headed out with a notebook and binoculars to look for birds for the first time in my life, on my original patch, Robinswood Hill in Gloucestershire. In and around Cot Valley I saw 33 species by lunchtime on what was my 33rd birding anniversary. By the end of the day I had seen 40 species, including Goldcrest, a bird I always like to see on my anniversary because it was the best bird I saw on that first day. Along the coast were a few pairs of Stonechats, Ravens riding the wind, and a Peregrine, with Gannets offshore and, best of all, a male Wheatear, a spring passage migrant. It was all very exciting especially when I thought about the prospect of a wide variety of more migrant birds passing through during the spring and autumn, perhaps including a rarity or two, all in a relatively wild and scenic part of Britain.

A month later, on a quiet sunny Sunday afternoon, Alice, Ned and I were sitting on what became known as 'The Magic Bench' when three Sparrowhawks flew by, one after the other, up Cot Valley and out of sight. After a minute or so a bird briefly swooped up above the trees the hawks had disappeared behind but it didn't look like a hawk and I was sure I saw a millisecond flash of bright colours as it turned and fell behind the trees again. I put it down to 'bee-eater fever'; being constantly on high alert for the calls or sight of bee-eaters overhead, which I contracted for several weeks every spring for the nine years I lived on the Isles of Scilly, and since. On that day in Cot Valley the fever was particularly acute because three Bee-eaters had flown over Land's End, a few miles to the south, the day before. Alice persuaded me to check the bird out so we walked up the track a little to where we could scan more of the upper valley and there perched on a telegraph wire was the unmistakeable form of a silhouetted Bee-eater. I was off, using a short-cut unsuitable for the buggy Ned was in, and soon I was under said Bee-eater and there on the same wire were two more.

By the time I had contacted some local birders Alice and Ned joined me and one of the Bee-eaters darted out, caught a bee and returned to the wire just twenty paces away in full sunlight. It was perfect; the elegant pose of the sleek, long-bodied, long-winged, long-tailed bird, perched almost upright as it de-stinged and devoured its prey, the glorious not gaudy colours, and the sound of purring bee-eater calls. I could even see the fine needle-thin tip to the long slightly down-curved black bill. I had seen hundreds of Bee-eaters in Europe and Africa and even three in spring before but that was the best view I had ever had, the closest I had ever been to a Bee-eater, the bird that was in my opinion the best bird on Earth, and there it was on my new local patch. All three were dashing after bees, swooping closer and closer while their calls combined to form a loud, very excitable, ripple of purring trills. It was a truly beautiful sight and sound, and although the birds were often silhouetted against the bright blue sky sometimes they swept low enough for us to look down on their dazzling combination of red-browns, golden yellows and blue-greens, against the backdrop of the valley. Later, after some other birders had arrived, the birds began drifting slowly inland, using higher wires to sail out and hunt from, and we left for home as happy as could be.

Less than a year later Tom, the fourth member of the family, arrived, since when, come rain or shine, more or less, we have all gone for a Sunday morning family stroll. One such early April morning as we neared town on our way home from Cot Valley a white Gyr Falcon flew across the lane in front of us. It was low down, gliding slowly and powerfully into an east wind, and a tremendous shock in black and white. However, it was a brilliant but all too brief sight, for the bird was soon gone, past St Just and inland. I immediately contacted everyone who I thought might be interested. Long-time local birder John Ryan had a great idea; he headed for a B-road which runs north-south alongside Woon Gumpus Common a couple of miles due east of St Just, hoping to intercept it, and when he got there a quick scan revealed the bird perched on a distant fence post. It soon flew but remained in the area all afternoon during which time a handful of other people managed to see a rare white Gyr, although not everyone present, including Alice, the boys and me.

The next morning I was up early, anxious to get into the field to look for the falcon which I thought could be commuting between Cape Cornwall and Woon Gumpus Common. First of all though, as usual, I looked out of a window at the back of our house, this time in case the falcon flew past. I had just got out of bed and was still half asleep but I saw two or three Herring Gulls diving down at something on a stone wall. The local gulls mob the resident Buzzards if they fly low over town and any unfamiliar raptors in the vicinity but I had never seen them mobbing something perched before. They were most upset though, and, as I soon saw through the window binoculars, with something white. For a moment I thought it might be the Gyr but even while this thought formed in my weary head there was a doubt in my mind because if the white thing on the wall *was* a bird and I was pretty sure it was, it seemed too big and too white for the Gyr. I moved to a different window, in the boy's room, and through the binoculars I saw something I could hardly believe. Partly obscured by a bare bramble it was definitely a bird and it definitely wasn't a Gyr. It was too broad and too white, all white by the looks of it. I refused to believe it but my brain kept telling me it was a Snowy Owl. Then the bird swivelled its huge round head and looked up at one of the Herring Gulls; it *was* a Snowy Owl.

Getting the telescope set up was a massive palaver with me shaking with shock, two very excited children at my feet and not a lot of room for three more legs belonging to the tripod at the top of the stairs but with Alice's help I managed it and the bird was still 'in the 'scope' when fellow local patcher Phil and his wife Jane arrived from their house fifty paces away, a few minutes later. They were just in time because the bird then flew and quickly dropped low and out of sight. It may have been very tired, possibly after a sea crossing, because Phil soon discovered that it had landed on another stone wall two fields away, and it spent the next twelve and a half hours on that wall, until dusk when it was seen flying off. There was no sign of it the next morning and it was ten days later when someone stumbled across it at nearby Carn Kenidjack. Two days after that the owl moved to Bartinney, a bit farther away, where, just after dusk, Spider, a friend over from the Isles of Scilly, and I watched it fly strongly southwest. I joked, "It's off to bloody Scilly!" and the next day that's where it was, and where it stayed until mid-May.

Two years later another Snowy Owl landed near Jean Lawman who was seawatching from Carn Gloose, ten minutes walk from our front door, and the huge black-barred snow-white beauty was happy to sit on a stone wall just twenty paces away, close enough for us to marvel at the cleanest, purest, whitest feathers and whiskers imaginable, on and around her beak. She was very alert, often opening wide her wonderful luminous yellow eyes, constantly preening, yawning, looking up and around, and when a local Kestrel dived at her she raised her feathers and wings and puffed herself up to look even bigger.

About a month after the Gyr Falcon and Snowy Owl the family consensus was to take our Sunday stroll down Cot again because the boys liked to play on the small beach at the bottom. We left there before noon and returned home for the rest of the day completely oblivious to the fact that there was a pelican on the sea just to the north of the beach for a while, possibly within view of where we were. I knew nothing about it until the following day by which time it had been identified as a Dalmatian Pelican, a bird, it was subsequently discovered, that had been tracked from Belarus to France just before it crossed the Channel to Cornwall and which some people thought might be a wild bird and therefore potentially a first for Britain.

The next morning it was spotted flying inland over Land's End and I managed to catch up with it near Sennen. The next day, Alice and I dashed down there again and, following Cornish birders Royston Wilkins and his son Leon, we pulled up behind their van and watched the magnificent bird soaring low down by Trevorian Common. It made an astonishing sight in flight, especially because it was so much bigger than the Buzzards mobbing it and causing it to dive a couple of times to avoid them. The pelican liked to soar; one fine day it soared over and around Drift Reservoir for over four hours.

Later that May a Lammergeier, a bird as rare as the pelican if wild, was spotted by the Severn Estuary before moving to Dartmoor then the Bodmin Moor area in north Cornwall. Penwith birders started to get very excited because we thought the bird could be heading south in an attempt to get back to mainland Europe where it had presumably flown from in the first place, and it might end up at the end of the land in the southwest. So, Pete Fraser headed to Morvah, a good vantage point about three miles (5 km) northeast of St Just, and while scanning for the 'lammer' he picked up the pelican. He phoned me because he thought it was in the air near St Just and I dashed to the windows at the back of the house and there it was, circling over the north side of town. It drifted slowly south almost over the house, low enough to see the bright orange pouch of its massive bill and the curly feathers on its face, so low I looked it in the eye through my binoculars before it passed over and away in the direction of Cot Valley. I carried on scanning for it and half an hour later a Red Kite drifted over and two hours after that a flock of ten appeared, a tiny fraction of the spectacular annual late spring influx into west Cornwall. The following day nine more made it to my end of the coast and with them was an eye-level Black Kite.

In thirteen springs on the patch I have seen five Black Kites, including two together soaring with 31 Red Kites, five Bee-eaters including the three together, five Hoopoes, three Wrynecks, six Woodchat Shrikes, six Golden Orioles, four Rosy Starlings, a Dalmatian Pelican, a Night Heron, a high-flying Crane, a Gyr Falcon, a Snowy Owl, an Alpine Swift that nearly took our chimney off, a Tawny Pipit, a Subalpine Warbler, a male Red-backed Shrike, thanks to fellow Boscregan watcher, the indefatigable 77-year-old Colin Moore, a summer-plumaged Lapland Bunting and a singing male Cirl Bunting, and yet few if any of these scarce and rare birds are as colourful, vibrant and exciting as the first male Wheatears of the year to arrive from Africa. The fresh-in, black as black, blue-grey, peach and white birds are a truly uplifting sight after such a long, relatively dreary, time, lighting up the patch suddenly with their resplendent fresh and sleek plumage. One spring in late May I saw a very large Wheatear, a 'Greenlander', so big and bright it looked like a colourful thrush with an especially rich grey-blue nape and mantle.

Having started birding proper on the 23rd of March 1975 it is always a joy to mark the anniversaries with the first male Wheatear of the year and that was just about the case to celebrate 45 years birding in 2020 when, after a long fruitless walk around the patch with the boys during the morning, a quick look at the Cape in the evening revealed three Wheatears including two superb males. That was my 6193rd birding day, 5535th in Britain, more or less, so I reckon since I started birding at the age of fourteen I have spent 37% of the days of my life in the field watching birds for at least one hour, usually a few hours, and many times many more. That is a third of my life! That is my 'success'.

Spring in the far west starts a long time before Wheatears and Swallows arrive. Guillemots and Razorbills, already in summer plumage, may make their first visit to The Brisons in February. These twin stacks, nearly 90 feet (27 metres) high three quarters of a mile (one km) off Cape Cornwall, look like the ex-president of France Charles de Gaulle lying on his back in a bath, due to the southern crag bearing a resemblance to his rather *grande nez* and the northern the rather large belly he developed later in life. The name 'The Brisons' is from the French 'brisant' meaning 'reef breaker' in English. The Cornish name, Enys Vordardh, means 'Breaker Island'. By the end of March or in early April the auks on the general's *embonpoint* are usually joined by a few Puffins. By mid-July they and their young are gone, out to sea where they spend the rest of the year although in stormy winter weather hundreds sometimes many thousands of auks (Guillemots and Razorbills, never Puffins) can be seen passing the Cape.

The Swallows that stay to raise young on the patch arrive a little later than the first migrants of late March, usually after the first week of April when the Blackthorn blossom may be so thick it looks like snow. As April warms up there is suddenly a noticeable increase in shades of green and the first Whitethroats arrive. By mid-May Cot Valley is so thick with green it is transformed into an almost tropical forest which resounds with the lovely loud whistles of singing male Blackcaps. Life is good when there is an Orange-tip butterfly flitting around a leafy, sunny dell while a Blackcap sings.

The second half of May and early June is usually the time for Red Kites, a Hobby or two and perhaps something unusual. On the first day of June 2020 I got up, looked out of the back window, saw an odd-looking bird amongst the

Starlings on the playing field, grabbed the binoculars, looked through them and saw a Rosy Pastor. I like the old English name for this starling now in a genus, *Pastor*, of its own. It comes from the Latin *pastor* which means shepherd, a reference to the bird's habit of following grazing animals in search of the insects disturbed by them. The first one I saw on the patch in spring, two years before, was in a field of sheep. Like that year there was an influx into Britain in 2020 but it was still a great surprise to see one. By then, our 11-year-old son Tom was starting to get very keen on birds and from that day on he checked every starling he saw. Then, twelve days later, his dream came true. There, in exactly the same place, was a different, pinker Rosy Starling. He was ecstatic and insisted that that day was the best day of his life. When he got equally excited when I spotted a third and even pinker bird, a fabulous adult male, on a TV aerial from the front windows of the house and we were then able to watch it at close range in a garden five houses down the road, I started to dare to think that he might just be on the brink of a brilliant life; one long, flowing dream full of birds and birding adventures.

By the end of May into early June there are usually several species of butterfly on the wing including the first brood of intricately-marked Small Pearl-bordered Fritillaries. One late May was memorable for hundreds of Painted Ladies which brushed past Alice and I, sometimes alone sometimes in delicate little flurries sometimes in thick clouds, a tiny fraction of millions which had flown across Europe to Britain from the Atlas Mountains of Morocco. The day after the bulk of them arrived, the extensive bed of the large umbellifer which lines the stream in the lower

Cot Valley, the extremely poisonous Hemlock Water Dropwort, was covered in a giant blanket of the pretty black, white and orange butterflies.

One June, on part of the outer patch I rarely visited, I stumbled upon a small colony of Silver-studded Blues, beautiful but strange, tiny creatures that rarely flutter above ankle height and almost never venture more than a few human paces during their four or five days of adult life on the wing. Butterflies need to warm up before they can fly. They usually do this by basking in the sun so the best days to be out and about looking for them are long hot summer ones. Alas, such days are rare in far west Cornwall. When it's sunny it's usually windy and normally very windy from the east; good for stray birds in spring and autumn but bad for birding, until the wind drops. When sunny and still days do come along I like to linger by the hawthorns and smell the soft sweet blossom which takes me back to my younger days wandering around Robinswood Hill when there seemed to be many more blazing hot still summer days, and many more days when I lived in the moment, without thoughts of days gone by or days to come. Those were times when I had far less expectations, virtually nil responsibilities and no need for useless money. I have been much poorer, lonelier, less travelled and many happy memories shorter than I am now but I don't think I am any happier than I was in those younger carefree days when I had all the time in the world to wander through the fresh wonder of the woods and meadows.

I am happy walking along the Cot Valley stream during the summer if the sun is out, for it is illuminated by Beautiful Demoiselles and Golden-ringed Dragonflies. The bright metallic blue veins in the four flickering wings of the demoiselles and the bright yellow bands on the long black bodies of the dragonflies would not look out of place in a tropical rainforest. I watched a female Golden-ringed Dragonfly ovipositing under an overhang once, 'bouncing' up and down with fantastic flight control as she stabbed the tip of her abdomen into the base of the shallow stream and posited her eggs there. Perhaps the most exciting sunny day insects of all are Hummingbird Hawkmoths which hover and hum exactly like hummingbirds, often at honeysuckles, occasionally in our garden, sucking up nectar from the flowers with a tube nearly as long as their body called a proboscis.

When we moved to St Just we saw lots of Basking Sharks but the tall narrow black fins Alice and I spotted by The Brisons one late September day didn't belong to Baskers. They were Killer Whales, presumably a large male and two companions, and they appeared to be hunting, turning this way and that, and a few minutes later we saw what they may have been after, at least two Risso's Dolphins that were hurrying north. That is the only time we have seen either cetacean in our waters and it was such a rare sight, here or anywhere, and over so quickly, Alice and I often wonder if we witnessed it at all. We must have done; we can still remember being so excited. Common Dolphins and Porpoises are a frequent sight and occasionally the pod of Bottlenose Dolphins which live around southwest Britain pass by close inshore. On one occasion a long Minke Whale was feeding with some Common Dolphins.

During our second summer in St Just we saw up to ten Baskers a day, one of which breached five times like a

Humpback Whale close in to the Cape. The Basking Sharks have gone but Bluefin Tuna have returned, although they are harder to spot than Mola molas or Sunfish which I sometimes see off the Cape, where they give themselves away by flapping their long fins, possibly to attract gulls which eat parasites living on the body of the fish. One calm August day while scanning for Sunfish and so on I was amazed to see a shark, a grey one, which from my position above it at the Cape looked too bulky for a Blue, the shark I am familiar with. It was about six feet long, maybe more, with a small dorsal fin, and settled in one spot just below the surface for ages. After a good long look at it and some research at home I thought it was either a Porbeagle or more likely a Mako, which is, as far as is known, a rare summer visitor to Cornish waters.

It would be a strange day if we didn't see any Grey Seals, watching the boys play on Cot Beach or gathering in Porth Ledden, the rough rocky cove north of the Cape where sometimes they can be heard moaning loudly. Large land mammals include a few Foxes that haven't been shot, and Badgers. I once came across a Badger in broad daylight on a sunny day in May. It was making its way through a field of long grass, proceeding with gusto and loud snuffling and snorting sounds, pushing its face into tufts of grass with some force. After a while it seemed to detect my presence, probably my smell, and stopped dead with its head buried in some buttercups. Then it looked up and scampered off toward the nearby sett, leaving me stunned and smiling for days.

Equally surprising and exciting was what happened when I arrived at one of the two tiny pools in Nanquidno Valley on the last day of one year. I was in full view and there was no cover to hide behind but three Otters, the first I had seen for many years anywhere in Britain, carried on swimming around the pool and diving to catch fish, and they didn't detect me for twenty minutes even though all I could do to avoid being seen was duck down below the horizon. Otters have such superb eyesight, hearing and sense of smell I think I got away without being noticed because I just happened to be downwind. I was also as quiet as I could possibly be of course, and I dared not move a muscle, even slide my binoculars from my eyes, as I watched all three of the surprisingly large animals catch a fish during that precious time which only came to an end when two surfaced about five paces from me with their heads raised high on the lookout. One saw me and made a noise like a bark and they both turned and swam away, and I never saw any of them surface again.

I had never seen Otters so close and for so long hence I was back at first light the first day of the New Year and I stayed with Ned while Alice went off to have a look for herself, returning with a big smile on her face. The Otters were still there the next dawn when I watched them fishing for half an hour. During their extensive travels underwater one of them swam under the bush overhanging the pool which I was hiding behind, so close I saw bubbles of air hitting the surface when it was underwater. It was an incredible three days made all the more remarkable by the fact that I haven't seen an Otter on the patch during the twelve years since! They are here, studies have proved it, but they are almost strictly nocturnal, partly because they are avoiding humans who have persecuted them for so long and partly because Otters don't like dogs and there's no shortage of them. I see very few people out for a walk without one, and often wonder why.

It is always very exciting when a Stoat appears. The low-slung animal with big paws grabs the attention immediately, possibly because it's so full of energy it's hard to imagine it living very long before its heart bursts, or maybe because at close range it's possible to see the beautiful, silky, shiny, smoky wispiness of the animal's coat. If I am very fortunate I see one two or three times a year. Twice I've come across one high up a tree, where the Stoat is as agile as a squirrel amongst the branches but not so graceful when it comes to descending the trunk, and a few times I've seen one leaping, somersaulting and squealing while attacking Rabbits, behaviour believed to bamboozle the rodents which seem to freeze from fright whenever the deadly predator appears.

Summer starts and ends with Swifts. It is heart-warming to see them wheeling around over town in early May after so many months away, flying through Europe and touring Africa. It 'means the globe's still working' in the words of Ted Hughes, in his excellent poem about them. One early June day five birds dropped down out of reach of a cool northwesterly to catch the flies along the stream where it meets the beach at the bottom of Cot. Alice, Ned, Tom and I stood on the rocks in the rushing water and watched the birds whoosh past our heads at terrific speed before snapping up a fly, banking, turning and lining up to do it all over again, for what was an absolutely awesome half an hour. Near the end of their short stay, on still sunny evenings in late July to early August, ten to twenty whizz and scream over town, as if committing the place to memory before they depart. Then, just like that, it seems, the three months they are with us are up and they are gone, and it is seawatching time, and I love seawatching.

When I say 'seawatching' I don't actually mean watching the sea although I do a lot of that. No, what I actually do is watch the sea *and* the birds flying over it. When I lived on St Agnes I got away with seawatching without a telescope because the birds passed so close. Unlike virtually every other birder in Britain I didn't have a 'scope for many years and this earned me the nickname 'Scopeless', which was bestowed upon me by Mush, Mashuq Ahmad, who seems to have a nickname for every birder he knows, most of which are far more derogatory than mine. Like me, several birders living in far west Cornwall could be described as birding bums, in that they love birds and birding and everything that goes with it so much that they do their level best to live outside the long death march of steady employment and suburban life, and to avoid many other ridiculous, unwritten laws of normal society, in order to arrange their lives so that they can spend as much time birding as possible.

Not long after I moved to Cornwall some of them very kindly held one of their regular outings to a public house for a good chat at the *Kings Arms* in St Just, a five minute walk from my place. When I arrived Brian Field bought me a pint. Not long later someone else bought me another. I didn't buy a drink all night and when the subject of my nickname came up Colin Moore, who I had just met, said he had an old telescope I could have, and Brian Field added that he had a tripod he didn't use anymore, so by the end of the night I had not spent a penny, made a few new friends, and gained a *Manfrotto* tripod, one of the best there is, and an iconic, top quality *Leica Apo-Televid* telescope in a waterproof case, which, a few days later, I retrieved from a log basket by the side of Colin's fireplace where it had been left unused for a couple of years. I still go by the moniker of Scopeless, since the 'scope is technically on a long loan, but I don't care because the *Apo* has made seawatching from Cape Cornwall so much more enjoyable. Ten years after that rare night out in St Just Brian Field died of a heart attack while seawatching at nearby Porthgwarra. The last two lines he wrote in his notebook were, '5 Cory's, Bonxie.' If I can go the same way, with the same birds, that will be fine with me.

When I'm seawatching I especially like to watch a sea with shearwaters over it, birds so named because they glide very low over the water with their wings held out straight, raising them regularly, like sails, to catch the wind and fly, fly for miles and miles, with hardly any effort, only slight tilts of the body from side to side to change the wing position, when the tip of the lower wing may shear the water. By far the most numerous off the Cape are Manx Shearwaters. They are present all year round, although there are only a few during the winter when most of the British and world breeding population has migrated 6000-7000 miles (9000-11,000 km) across the Atlantic to the rich waters off Brazil and Argentina. The first ones usually arrive back off the Cape in late March and then the numbers build up steadily and by summer there may be thousands out there. I have seen at least 10,000 birds, sometimes more than 20,000, in a few hours several times, when the birds pass by at over a hundred a minute in a mesmerising, non-stop, all-action flow of black and white birds moving from right to left, with the flow rising up and down in and out of the troughs as they use the wind to make their way south. When there is little wind there may still be thousands out there, sitting on the sea in large rafts or gliding by slowly and, in the right conditions, looking like a mass of twinkling white stars over a silvery sea as their bellies catch the light against a cloudy horizon.

With them, in much smaller numbers, usually when the winds are in the west or northwest during the late summer and autumn, there may be some Sooty Shearwaters, on their 17,000 mile (27,000 km) circuit of the Atlantic Ocean up the east side of North America and across to Britain and Norway before returning south to their nesting islands in the South Atlantic. They are spectacular fliers, especially when tacking south past the Cape across a northwesterly gale, moving much faster than Manx Shearwaters on long, narrow, pointed wings, sooty above silvery below, and I could watch them all day. Happiness is Sooty Shearwaters at the end of the road, and it only takes twenty minutes to walk to the Cape, which is at the end of the road our house is on.

'Dusky Shearwaters', as I like to call Balearic Shearwaters, from the Mediterranean, are usually around from June right through to January, normally in small numbers, although I saw over a hundred one rough day in early October. Over fifty also passed during one of my greatest seawatches. It was late October, the wind was a near-gale westerly, the swell 25 feet (7-8 metres) and in four hours I saw far more (at the time) 'Dusky Shearwaters', Bonxies or Great Skuas, and Gannets than I had ever seen. The Gannets went by in what resembled a blizzard all morning, a constant stream of at least 12,000 of them at about 50 per minute for the whole four hours, and I counted 200 skuas, made up of a Pomarine Skua, 17 Arctic Skuas and an incredible 182 Great Skuas.

On two occasions one August I saw five species of shearwater on single seawatches, thanks to a few Cory's and Great Shearwaters. To master the art of seawatching one has to learn how to spot and identify the two 'big shear's' when they are going by a long way out, especially the wave-hugging Cory's that glides so close to the surface. This takes years, and I still haven't perfected it.

The same summer there were a lot of Wilson's Storm Petrels off Scilly, Ireland and even the Cornish coast, but most were, like Cory's and Greats, at the Porthgwarra end so I held out little hope of one passing the Cape, and yet, in a light westerly wind on a late July morning not ten minutes after my first scan I picked up a storm petrel which glided a long way then a long, long way, and it wasn't flapping a lot and rocking from side to side like a bat, like a European Storm Petrel, a more familiar sight off the Cape, and it didn't have that clipped-wing action, it was more relaxed, and what's more, on looking hard through the 'scope, there were no white bars on the underwings just a smoky silvery sheen, and across the upperwings there were two bold pale grey panels, two of the distinctive characteristics of a Wilson's Storm Petrel.

Taking stock later, trying to absorb the moment, I couldn't believe how fortunate I had been, to have decided to go seawatching that day, at that time, when conditions were not particularly good for seawatching, to have been there when that black speck flew over a miniscule part of the vast amount of sea, for the bird to have flown by close enough for me to have spotted it, identified it and enjoyed the sight of it, gliding, gliding, gliding, past the end of my road. It may be one of the commonest birds on the planet, I may have seen many when I lived on Scilly and many more abroad but that one bird happened to fly past my seawatching spot when I was there, probably the only one to fly past in who knows how many years. I sat outside with a smoke and a glass of red later that day and a rare moment of mellowness unfolded. Since then the more I think about it the more incredible it seems, that a bird with a wingspan of 16 inches (40 cm) that I have seen entering a nesting burrow on Paulet Island in Antarctica, that may travel 18,000 miles (30,000 km) up and around the Atlantic in a huge loop between breeding seasons at the other end of the world, should fly past the Cape when I was there.

It's almost impossible to describe to someone who has never been seawatching, the anticipation, excitement and drama of a 'big seawatch' when the time of year and weather conditions combine to produce a mass movement of birds. This happens rarely but there is always a chance, especially in September when the great prizes, if the wind is strong enough from the northwest, are Leach's Storm Petrels and Sabine's Gulls. It took me ten years to see my first 'Leach's' off the Cape and two came along on the same day as four 'Sab's', as well as ten Grey Phalaropes, Arctic, Great and Pomarine Skuas, and several rainbows, in what was a seawatching classic.

There are not so many birds off the Cape during October but one autumn there were so few migrant landbirds

*Black-browed Albatross, Cape Cornwall, England,
18th October 2016*

passing through I was glad to head there in a northwesterly wind. I was in position for first light, hoping for a late Sabine's Gull. Half an hour later I began my next scan from the right with my binoculars and I couldn't believe what I saw. There was a 'black stick' coming my way.

I had seen the sight thousands of times before, mainly between South America and South Georgia, so I knew what it was instantly. That first sight though was still tremendously exciting. Somehow I managed to remain sufficiently calm, at least at first, to get the telescope on the bird immediately and, with the adrenalin levels increasing rapidly, I watched the mega sail slowly by without so much as a flap, just beyond the Vyneck, the rock only about a third of a mile out, close enough to see the short, dark, handsome brow of a Black-browed Albatross, a seawatcher's dream for anyone on a British headland and that minute with that albatross was one of the most fantastic moments of my life.

There are few dull days at the Cape. Even when there are no Manx Shearwaters, usually during the winter, there are always the master gliders called Fulmars and now and then a 'bombardment' of Gannets, sometimes a few hundred of them, with ten, twenty, even more at a time, raining down into the sea to catch fish. A flock of Oystercatchers may fly past below me, on their way to or from their roosting rock in nearby Porth Ledden, making pretty black and white patterns against the sea or surf. I always feel a warm glow when Ravens glide by at eye-level as they round the Cape, just a few paces in front of me, and they nearly always utter a deep 'krark' when they see me. Some days a chattering of Choughs may play in the wind above me. And if it isn't birds there may be Bottlenose or Common Dolphins out there.

And there is always the sea to watch, and the scene to appreciate, for apart from the occasional ship or trawler or local crab or lobster boat there is no evidence of man or anything to suggest humans ever existed. From the Cape the world looks like it once did, a wild world untamed and untainted by man, the world our ancestors lived in, the world we evolved in, long enough to feel at home there.

That is why wild places still feel like home, why we feel rested and relaxed in them, and why they are so refreshing and invigorating. We evolved outdoors and that is why we need to be outdoors. We have not evolved to live happily in towns and cities. They are still a strain on our nerves. They make us anxious, aggressive and depressed. This is why we need at least some respite from so-called civilization on a regular basis, in wild places which are as essential to our mental and physical health as food and water.

Across much of the planet we live on, the planet that is our home, not least the terribly overcrowded island of Britain, the wild places that are good for wildlife and us are being degraded and destroyed. The sea, at least on the surface, is about all that is left of what the world looked like when we were born. Across the world the number of people continues to grow and the land they live on is covered with ever more sterile fields of food, houses, roads, motorways, shopping centres, supermarkets, warehouses, industrial estates, towns, cities, telegraph wires, electricity pylons and so on. The land is all but ruined. The sea still looks wild. That is why I have to live by it. Every time I go to the Cape the hours pass by in what seem like minutes. I always see something interesting, often something exciting and now and again something amazing. The time never fails to take me higher and I am always loath to leave.

On my way to or from the Cape during the late summer and early autumn I usually walk down to Porth Ledden, hoping to watch a Common Sandpiper or two bobbing on the boulders. Very few shorebirds grace the rocky shores of the patch but some pass the Cape on migration, especially Whimbrels, sometimes in large numbers. Down in a gulley by the Cape there have been a few Wrynecks although the best place for that regular autumn migrant is above Polpry Cove which is on my circuit from home when I am not seawatching. I stroll down to and up out of Cot Valley, then to Boscregan, either through the arable, pasture and wild fields or along the coastal path through the scrub, heather and gorse at the top of the cliffs, sometimes all the way to the bottom of Nanquidno Valley, before returning the opposite way, to Cot again and home.

I don't usually linger long in Cot Valley; it's too leafy and therefore hard to find unusual small birds, but I did stay there a while one September day when, after hearing the repeated short, sharp, piercing, high-pitched whistles of an excited Kingfisher, I quickly repositioned where I was going to have a coffee and there it was right in front of me, before flying a little to perch in exactly the place I had always dreamed of one being perched, a few feet above the stream in an overhanging sycamore, where it looked like a greenish-blue and orange jewel in a thick tropical forest. The beauty sat there for ages, allowing prolonged views of what was only the fifth one I had seen on the patch. Then, for no apparent reason, the bird leapt off the branch and shot past me, low down through the wood, and disappeared upstream. It was truly a very rare encounter and it left me smiling for a long, long time.

When the first Goldcrests and Firecrests arrive, usually in late September and early October, it really starts to feel like there is a chance of a rarity, raising hopes exponentially, but the higher the hopes the bigger the disappointment and October, traditionally the best for rare birds in west Cornwall, is usually a very quiet and frustrating month when almost every day in Cot Valley can seem the same. Some days, particularly damp foggy ones, it is eerily quiet in what resembles an Andean cloud forest, where amongst the impressive stands of *Gunnera* or Giant Rhubarb, verdant ferns and dripping trees there are few birds to get excited about. No fruiteaters (except Blackcaps), hummers, quetzals, toucans or tanagers, although the latter are here replaced by colourful Chaffinches and there may be a female Blackbird without a tail pretending to be an 'antpitta'. Such days certainly stir the imagination and are vivid reminders of times spent in forests high on the mountain slopes of the world especially in the Andes of Venezuela and Peru, where there are also lots of 'no-see-ums', 'tik-ing', 'tsee-ing', 'zee-ing' and 'zitt-ing' like the Robins, Goldcrests, Song Thrushes, and Blue and Great Tits, all getting very wet as they forage for food amongst the wet leaves of Cot Valley.

One October day was very different. True, it started with fog but that soon backed off and the wind had been in the east so I was hoping to see my first Yellow-browed Warblers of the autumn. After three hours scouring the valley I was leaning on my favourite gate, a little frustrated at having seen but only briefly, one of two Yellow-browed Warblers I had heard. Ten minutes later I turned to head for home and saw a long-tailed, golden olive brown and black thrush, bigger than a Blackbird, fly out from behind a sycamore and around me in an almost complete wide circle, high enough at first for me to see bold black and white bands flash on the underside of the nearest wing before the bird dropped down very low to swoop across the field in front of me then flip over a hedge to my right and disappear from view. "White's Thrush!" I said to myself in sudden realization when I saw the underwing, and when it passed me very low down and I could see the pale gold bars across the upperwings there was no doubting it.

I ran up the lane to try and get a signal so I could phone the news out. A crowd of thirty or so soon gathered but there was no sign of the bird in the large garden I thought it might have flown into, or anywhere else during the rest of that and the next four days during which I did just about everything, short of getting shot, looking for that damned bird. I say 'damned' because I saw the 'ten year bird' for ten seconds, the great rarity I think one can reasonably expect to come across if one works a patch in a good area for such birds on a regular basis for so long. All that time, and I saw the 'mega' for just ten seconds. I had been extremely fortunate to see the bird at all of course but it was still incredibly frustrating to have seen it for such a short time. Fellow patch birder Phil thought he may have glimpsed it, flying away low down into thick cover two days later, near where it had come out of that first day, but apart from that the ultimate skulker, only the second one to have been seen in Cornwall for over a hundred years, and the first for fifty years, was never seen again.

The best place for landbirds on the patch is Boscregan where there are low stone hedges and fields full of seeds of swathes of Corn Marigolds, Purple Viper's Bugloss and so on, left to grow wild. Walking along the edge of a field there on a mid-October morning a Corn Crake rose from my feet and flew low across the whole field allowing me an excellent, prolonged view of its rich red-brown inner wings and sending me home very happy. The Corn Crake is a very rare bird in Cornwall, one of the few that has escaped the eyes of Royston Wilkins, the man who has seen over 400 species in the county, and more than anyone else.

I like to come across rare birds. It's exciting. Sometimes, in the right conditions, I proceed through the patch a bit like a robot, scanning left and right and above, hunting down my prey like the cyborg assassin in the film *The Terminator* but I have not had a lot of luck 'finding' rare birds and in my opinion luck is the main factor involved. Not many take much 'finding' actually; they just appear in front of people. One birder may walk along a track and hear and see nothing. The next may hear the distinctive 'tak' of a Dusky Warbler or catch a glimpse of shiny red and 'find' a Siberian Rubythroat. Most birders fortunate enough to come across rare birds stumble across them rather than 'find' them. And isn't the word 'find' just another in a long list illustrating the arrogance of the human race? I didn't 'find' the White's Thrush, it just happened to fly out and around me. That pesky bird was on my mind for weeks afterwards and it wasn't until early November that I got to think about a different bird, a Waxwing, a minute's walk from our front door. Alice, I and the boys, then aged three and five, who were remarkably still and quiet, watched the beauty a few paces away. A month later three more turned up in town, a wonderful 'schtrilling' threesome, which were even more confiding.

The same November I grabbed my binoculars off my desk, ran down the stairs, put my shoes on, ran to Phil's house fifty paces away, took my shoes off, ran up his stairs and there out of a little back window I saw the elusive 'funny warbler' he had been seeing briefly in his garden for a few days. The sandy-coloured bird finally foraged out in the open long enough to conclude that it was a Subalpine Warbler and it turned out to be the first to overwinter in the county, and possibly the country. It was a rather good 'garden tick' for Phil and, exactly a week later, for me, as it finally made it across the road.

As I have said before, the first three weeks of October are usually so quiet I cannot wait for the end of the month when the sometimes spectacular visible migration season really gets going and usually lasts until at least mid-November. It is three weeks or so of the year I love almost as much as seawatching. Some birds such as crests, flycatchers, robins, thrushes, wheatears and warblers migrate at night. Others, mostly species that flock together, including pigeons, pipits, larks, buntings and finches, move during the early part of the day. Some mornings the sky seems full of these birds and every time I raise my binoculars I can see small flocks going over, making for some very exciting birding. Chaffinches are the most numerous, amounting to hundreds sometimes, and with them I hope to pick up the nasal calls of Bramblings. Some birds rest and feed in the fields before moving on again and if I am very fortunate I might come across a male Brambling and see the blaze of orange across the bird's breast and shoulders.

One early November Sunday morning family stroll was a bit special thanks to a patch record of seven Bramblings, including three lovely males, in a big Chaffinch flock at Boscregan. The Bramblings were so good I returned for more the following morning and I was watching two superb males perched in the top of a sallow when a white bird landed next to them, a really white bird; a white redpoll! And while watching that, a small streaky thing appeared below, a bird so dingy it could only be a Serin and so it proved when it flew down to the ground and I saw the conspicuous bright yellow rump. When the redpoll flew down to some burdocks it too had a striking rump, a great broad white one, as well as almost unstreaked clean white flanks and undertail coverts, a big white wing-bar and general overall frosty background colour. It was an Arctic Redpoll, only the second for Cornwall and that only by two days. Once again I was left thinking about how fortunate I am to have such a brilliant local patch where it seems just about anything is possible.

Birds usually carry on moving until around mid-November and occasionally the sky explodes with massive flocks of hundreds of Wood Pigeons and Starlings, and, less often, Redwings and Fieldfares. Migrant Blackbirds and Song Thrushes don't like flying during the day and usually hide in the hedges, four or five bursting out here and there when I walk along them. When there are so many birds it can be exhausting but exhilarating counting them all, and I always feel sad when the great flight ends because that is usually the last great birding excitement of the year over.

I am, to my shame, rarely if ever out at dawn during the summer so when I am out and about as the sun rises above the cliffs from inland, and turns the still water in the exposed rock pools to molten gold, I know winter has arrived. Many similar days lie ahead, until that first male Wheatear of spring, unless ... the weather turns very cold, as it did one winter when most of Britain and Eastern Europe endured the longest cold spell for nearly thirty years. Then there was an influx of birds into slightly milder far west Cornwall, as worm-eaters sought soft unfrozen ground to probe into. By the end of the first week of January 2010 it was impossible to count the Golden Plovers, Lapwings, Snipes, Redwings and Fieldfares around Cot Valley. The hungry birds filled the fields while many more flew around looking for somewhere to land and feed. Many were weak; normally shy Snipes foraged out in the open on short grass with Golden Plovers and Lapwings which walked about very slowly just a few paces away, too tired to fly it seemed. After being around for a couple of days the thrushes entered the town, where they tore up the leaf litter in the gutters along the edges of the roads and streets, leaving tell-tale lines of tossed matter all over the place. There had never been a thrush not even a Blackbird in our tiny front garden but that morning I looked out of the window and saw four Redwings and a Fieldfare, and in the afternoon 48 Fieldfares, a few Redwings and a Mistle Thrush swarmed over the tiny sprig of cotoneaster in the backyard and stripped it bare of berries in fifteen minutes. The next day the thrushes had moved on and after that there were less Lapwings, Golden Plovers and Snipes in the fields roamed by three fat Foxes.

At the end of the same year I was very keen to get out there on a December day because we awoke to snow, a few inches of it, and it carried on snowing and when I ventured out the following morning there was another fresh dusting, and a blizzard to boot. Ten minutes later the sun was out and the amazing light bouncing off the snow on the ground turned a Red Kite into a silver kite as it flapped lazily north low down over white fields. Red Kites are rarer than snow in West Penwith during the winter. The raptors I normally expect to see at that time of the year are the resident Buzzards, Kestrels and Sparrowhawks while a nearby pair of Peregrines pay an occasional visit and sometimes the missiles with wings are joined by a Merlin, and if I am very fortunate it will be a tiny, orangey and glacial blue jack male. Hen Harriers graced the fields during the first few winters but they are a rare sight now.

Four inches of snow fell in four hours on the last day of February one year, enough to make a snowman in the garden behind which a Firecrest foraged on the ground. The next day, when it snowed for another four hours, the Cape was covered with thrushes, mainly Redwings with a few Fieldfares and Song Thrushes, trying to find food where the snow was less thick. Lapwings and Golden Plovers flew around but the most marvellous sight was a Black-headed Gull which took on a brilliant white as it flew past against the steel-grey sea and clouds.

It snowed on the 1st of March 2001 when I lived on St Agnes, a very rare event on Scilly, so I extended my morning walk to include the leeward side of the island because that's where the snow settled, and I was amazed to flush a Chough. It was quite a shock, because apart from a bird seen briefly in October 1992 it was the first to reach the islands since 1899. Unknown to me one had already been seen in far west Cornwall and it was soon joined by a second then a third which was believed to be the St Agnes bird. The following year two became a pair and they bred and raised young for the first time in Cornwall since 1947. By 2020 there were fourteen breeding pairs in Cornwall and they raised 43 young. Not surprisingly then, the Chough is an 'everyday bird' on the patch and a very welcome one too, especially after the breeding season when families get together and form large noisy flocks, the biggest yet on the patch comprising 26 individuals.

The deep Cot Valley provides winter shelter and food for beautiful Blue, bold Great and exquisite Long-tailed Tits, a few Goldcrests and usually an elusive Firecrest, often a male, sometimes with fire alight, the silky flame lighting up the dull, damp, often windy days, and my life. One mid-November the very centre of the valley, the most sheltered spot in rain and wind, was illuminated by a bright striped sprite called a Pallas's Warbler, all the way from far Siberia.

If it is calm and sunny during the winter it feels great to be alive while walking the fields, for I love the low winter light that makes all the birds look so much brighter and crisper, birds such as Lapwings with their beautiful green backs. There are always lots of Chaffinches and Linnets, and some Meadow Pipits and Skylarks, and in some winters up to fifteen Woodlarks, very difficult birds to see on the ground so well camouflaged are they. Woodcocks are more autumn birds but one winter I was treated to my best ever view of one. It froze when it saw me and stood stock still on the damp leaf litter under a sallow at Boscregan Bog, and I was able to enjoy examining the intricately patterned and very richly coloured reddish-brown plumage, and look it in the massive eye, eyeing me.

The Black-headed Gulls which spend the winter along the shore are usually joined by a few Common and Mediterranean Gulls, and around New Year ones or twos of Iceland and Glaucous Gulls. After one mid-January blow three Grey Phalaropes rode the rollers at the bottom of Cot Valley, flitting over the breakers and delicately picking food from amongst the froth, their heads rocking rapidly. Two were still present when it snowed and it was so cold that long icicles formed on the cliffs above them. One remained into February when in continuing windy conditions it was joined by two lovely adult Little Gulls dipping down feet-first to pluck morsels from the surf, their black underwings flashing, a scene which was yet another reminder of how glad we were to have taken that risk to find somewhere to live by the sea.

When the weather turns windy in the winter and it often does I usually head for the Cape not Cot. It's so rough at sea sometimes that we can hear the Atlantic Ocean crashing against the cliffs with a deep roar from our front door, a mile away. The swell one January was 20-30 feet (6-9 metres) and the waves even bigger so I decided against seawatching from my usual spot, a wise decision given the scene I was greeted with when I did manage to get there a few days later, for the slope was littered with small rocks, stones and vegetation torn from the cliff above. The whole of Porth Ledden was white, as was most of the sea between the Cape and The Brisons, and hundreds of crisp Kittiwakes floated above the froth over the maddest part of the maelstrom, in storm force winds.

That storm was followed by a run of four more big blows. In Porth Ledden the sea looked like milk washing in on to the rocky beach hidden by foam and froth, and off the Cape the Atlantic looked like it had had enough and was about to explode. Large gulls were heading north into the gale close in past the Cape one morning so, hoping to see a Glaucous or an Iceland Gull, I stood watching from behind a wall so that just my head and shoulders felt the full push of the relentless wind, and a juvenile Glaucous Gull almost sneaked past under my nose.

Another February day I had to half-crawl to my seawatching spot in an arctic blast approaching a strong gale. Guillemots and Razorbills normally rush by in flocks of around ten to fifty low over the water but it was so windy they were arcing past like shearwaters. Three quarters of a mile out over the wildest water hundreds of Kittiwakes were foraging in the wing-cracking wind and as if that was not enough to contend with a Peregrine appeared amongst them in full attack mode. The biggest sea I have ever seen, anywhere in the world, even the Drake Passage which I have experienced in a gale, was off the Cape another February, when in a westsouthwesterly Storm Force 9-10 the Sea State was officially declared as 'occasionally phenomenal' for the first time in the eight years we had been living in St Just. There was a 30-35 foot (9-11 metres) swell and some waves were like mountain sides. When they met the land they exploded white and the water blew up into the blizzard of foam and froth already whirling all around, and yet riding the wind over the crazy ocean and making light of it all were the usual Gannets and Kittiwakes, and five Bonxies.

I still head to the Cape when all is calm sometimes, good conditions in which to look for porpoises, passing dolphins and birds fishing from the surface. One such day in late February I was hoping to see a Red-throated Diver, a species which moves north early on spring passage. I don't see many Red-throats and they usually fly by a long way out, whereas Great Northern Divers are more regular and the odd one stays to fish for a while, so when I arrived at the Cape that day and saw a big diver between the Cape and The Brisons I assumed it would be a Great Northern. However, when I got the bird in the 'scope I was shocked to see albeit a long way off in hazy sunshine that the bird's bill looked mainly white with a hint of yellow, and what's more, it was pale at the tip and pointing skyward. I tried to talk myself out of it, repeating the mantra that 'rare birds are rare' in my head, but there off the Cape was a White-billed Diver, a very rare bird in Cornwall and around southern Britain. There was something going on that day, because I saw at least ten Porpoises and eight Red-throated Divers including an unprecedented party of five on the sea, one of which was in summer plumage!

The White-billed Diver stayed five days, long enough for me to enjoy the bird completely, for I was not only thrilled to come across it and see it so many times but even more pleased that a bird, passing through British waters on its way north to its breeding grounds on the Arctic coast of Russia, landed on the sea off the Cape when it could have settled anywhere around the coast of Britain. Four years later, give or take a couple of days, the last bird I picked up while scanning was the same or another White-billed Diver, in exactly the same place as the last one.

Another good thing about sitting on a headland looking out to sea, when there are not too many birds passing, is that there is time to think. I try not to fill my life with things to do, to make myself so busy that I don't have time to stop and think, to ponder life, to ask myself if I am living the life I want to live. I don't want to sleepwalk through life. It's so short I think it's very important to ask ourselves how we would like to spend it. Nearly all of us just want to be happy or content. Surveys always say most people believe they are happier when they think they have high status in society but I don't think being busy or feeling important is the best way to achieve happiness or contentment, at least in the long term. Some philosophers say the secret of happiness is to live in the moment but when it's quiet on the bird front at the Cape I cannot help thinking about the past and the future, where I have been and what I have done with my life, and where it looks like I am heading and what I might be doing. Sometimes I think about how I will look back on my life when it comes to an end for I have long believed it of immense importance that when I come to die I will know in my heart that I did my best to live my life to the full, that I was not too tentative, that I took a few risks, that I lived not merely existed, because the first rule of life is to live it.

Somehow, during the course of nearly 14 billion years, via the chance combination of countless physical, chemical and biological factors, and innumerable strokes of cosmic good fortune a planet called Earth formed from stardust, just the right distance from a star called the Sun, and during the last 3.6 billion years single-celled organisms came to be and evolved into sea plants, jellyfish, trilobites, winged insects, dinosaurs, birds and mammals, including very complex multi-celled organisms made up of trillions of atoms, or stardust, called human beings. In that barely comprehensible vast expanse of time we have not only come to the grossly under-appreciated state known as existence, we have also evolved the brain and senses which enable us to enjoy the beauty of the planet we live on. We are not the programmed product of evolution. We are not the culmination of anything. Life on Earth will continue to evolve whether we are on it or not. There is no purpose to life, to the Universe. We just are. It just is. We are here by chance, against all odds, but any minute now your heart could stop beating. Soon, without oxygen, your brain will stop working. You will be dead, and when you're dead, you're dead. There is no heaven. There is no hell. There is no afterlife just life, and I think the only thing that matters, the only way to be happy and content, is to find, build and pursue your own way, to be true to yourself, to try and live the life you imagine, to try to fulfil your dreams, and to not end up regretting not living boldly enough. It doesn't matter if you fail so long as you grow old content in the knowledge that you tried.

I have had a great time on planet Earth. Perhaps that is why I am not scared of dying. Stardust; that's all we are, and perhaps, when I die, some of my atoms will travel through 'the bloodstream of the land' like the one Aldo Leopold describes in his beautiful book *A Sand County Almanac*, an atom that lodged 'in a leaf that rode the green billows of the prairie June, sharing the … uncommon task' of 'flicking shadows across a plover's eggs'. My life has been a wonder-filled life, full of the beauty of planet Earth. Nature helps to makes me happy and content. I love to walk amongst it. There is always something interesting and exciting, be it a good view of this, a better view of that, perhaps a bird never seen before, maybe a dream come true, anything is possible, even on the patch. Tomorrow I am going there again and already I am wishing it was morning.

# BIBLIOGRAPHY

**Abbey E.** Desert Solitaire. McGraw-Hill, 1968.
**Alden P and Gooders J.** Finding Birds Around the World. Andre Deutsch, 1981.
**Allen B.** (Editor) The Faber Book of Exploration. Faber and Faber, 2002.
**Baker J A.** The Peregrine. Collins, 1967.
**Bakewell S.** How to Live: A Life of Montaigne. Chatto & Windus, 2010.
**Bates H W.** The Naturalist on the River Amazons (Two volumes). Murray, London, 1863.
**Beebe W.** Pheasant Jungles. G P Putnam's Sons, 1927. (World Pheasant Association, 1994)
**Beston H.** The Outermost House: A Year of Life on the Great Beach of Cape Cod. Doubleday, 1928.
**Brown L and Amadon D.** Eagles, Hawks and Falcons of the World (Two volumes). Country Life Books, 1968. Published in one volume by The Wellfleet Press in 1989.
**Brown L.** British Birds of Prey. Collins (New Naturalist), 1976.
**Brown L.** Encounters with Nature. Oxford University Press, 1979.
**Brynildson I and Haage W.** Birds in Art: The Masters. Konecky & Konecky, 1990.

**Bryson B.** A Short History of Nearly Everything. Doubleday, 2003.
**Byrd R E.** Alone: The Classic Polar Adventure. G. P. Putnam's Sons, 1938. (Kodansha America, Inc., 1995)
**Cade T.** The Falcons of the World. Collins, 1982.
**Campbell B.** Birdwatcher at Large. J M Dent & Sons, 1979.
**Cherry-Garrard A.** The Worst Journey in the World. Constable, 1922.
**Condry W.** Pathway to the Wild. Faber & Faber, 1975.
**Cousteau J.** The Silent World. Hamish Hamilton, 1953.
**Cramp S. *et al* 'BWP'** or Handbook of the Birds of Europe, the Middle East and North Africa (Nine volumes), 1977-1994.
**Darwin C.** Voyage of the Beagle. Henry Colburn, 1839.
**de Montaigne M.** Essays. Penguin Classics, 1958. First published in France in 1580.
**de Saint-Exupéry A.** Wind, Sand and Stars. Penguin, 1995. First published as Terre des homes, 1939.
**del Hoyo J.** (Editor) All the Birds of the World. Lynx Edicions, 2020.
**Dodwell C.** Travels with Fortune. W H Allen, 1979.
**Dodwell C.** In Papua New Guinea. Oxford Illustrated Press, 1983.
**Ennion E A R.** The House on the Shore. Routledge & Kegan Paul, 1960 dated 1959.
**Ennion E A R.** The Living Birds of Eric Ennion. Victor Gollancz, 1982.
**Fisher J & Peterson R T.** Wild America. Collins, 1956.
**Fjeldså J and Krabbbe N.** Birds of the High Andes. Zoological Museum, University of Copenhagen and Apollo Books, 1990.
**Fossey D.** Gorillas in the Mist. Houghton Mifflin, 1983.
**Harrison P.** Seabirds: an identification guide. Christopher Helm, 1983.
**Hemingway E.** The Old Man and the Sea. Jonathan Cape, 1952.

**Heyerdahl T.** The Kon-Tiki Expedition. Gyldendal Norsk Forlag, 1948 (Norwegian edition). George Allen & Unwin, 1950 (English edition).
**Hilty S L and Brown W L.** A Guide to the Birds of Colombia. Princeton University Press, 1986.
**Hilty S L.** Birds of Venezuela. Christopher Helm, 2003.
**Hose C.** The Field-Book of a Jungle-Wallah. Witherby, 1929. (Oxford University Press, 1985)
**Hosking E.** An Eye for a Bird. Hutchinson, 1970.
**Hughes T.** Ted Hughes: Collected Poems. Faber and Faber, 2003.
**Humboldt A V.** Personal Narrative of a Journey to the Equinoctial Regions of the New Continent. Penguin Classics, 1995. First published in French, in seven volumes, 1814-1825.
**Jonsson L.** Bird Island: Pictures from a Shoal of Sand. Croom Helm, 1984. First published in Sweden by Atlantis Publishers.
**Jonsson L.** Birds and Light. Christopher Helm, 2002.
**Jonsson L.** Lars Jonsson's Birds: Paintings from a Near Horizon. Christopher Helm, 2008.
**Jonsson L.** Winter Birds. Bloomsbury, 2017. First published in Sweden by Bonnier Fakta, 2015.
**Junger S.** The Perfect Storm. W. W. Norton & Company, 1997.
**Kaufman K.** Kingbird Highway. Houghton Mifflin, 1997.
**Kerouac J.** On the Road. Viking Press, 1957.
**Kingsley M.** Travels in West Africa. Macmillan, 1897.
**Kirwan G & Green G.** Cotingas and Manakins. Christopher Helm, 2011.
**Lansing A.** Endurance. The Story of Shackleton's incredible voyage to the Antarctic. Hodder & Stoughton, 1959.
**Leopold A.** A Sand County Almanac. Oxford University Press, 1949.
**Lockley R.** The Way to an Island. J M Dent & Sons, 1941.

**Lockwood W.B.** The Oxford Book of British Bird Names. Oxford University Press, 1984.

**McKibben B.** (Editor) American Earth: Environmental Writing Since Thoreau. Literary Classics of the United States, 2008.

**Marchant J, Prater T and Hayman P.** Shorebirds. Croom Helm, 1986.

**Matthiessen P.** Under the Mountain Wall: A Chronicle of Two Seasons in Stone Age Guinea. Viking, 1962.

**Matthiessen P.** The Wind Birds: Shorebirds of North America. The Viking Press, 1973. The text was originally published in The Shorebirds of North America, Gardner D. Stout (Editor). The Viking Press, 1967.

**Matthiessen P.** The Snow Leopard. Chatto & Windus, 1979.

**Matthiessen P.** Indian Country. Collins/Harvill, 1985.

**Mearns B & R.** Biographies for Birdwatchers. Academic Press, 1988.

**Mearns B & R.** Audubon to Xantus. Academic Press, 1992.

**Mearns B & R.** The Bird Collectors. Academic Press, 1998.

**Melville H.** Moby-Dick. Penguin Classics, 1992. First published (in three volumes) as *The Whale* in 1851.

**Moitessier B.** The Long Way. Sheridan House, 1995. (La Longue Route. Editions Arthaud, 1971)

**Mountfort G.** Portrait of a Wilderness. Hutchinson, 1958.

**Mountfort G.** Portrait of a River. Hutchinson, 1962.

**Mountfort G.** Portrait of a Desert. Hutchinson, 1965.

**Mountfort G.** The Vanishing Jungle. Hutchinson, 1969.

**Muir J.** The Eight Wilderness Discovery Books. Diadem Books, 1992.

**Murphy D.** Where the Indus is Young. John Murray, 1977.

**Murphy R C.** Logbook for Grace. Macmillan, 1947. (Time Life Books, 1965)

**Newby E.** A Short Walk in the Hindu Kush. Secker & Warburg, 1958.

**Newton I.** Bird Migration. Collins (New Naturalist), 2010.

**O'Hanlon R.** Into the Heart of Borneo. The Salamander Press, 1984.

**O'Hanlon R.** In Trouble Again: A Journey Between the Orinoco and the Amazon. Hamish Hamilton, 1988.

**Park M.** Travels in the Interior Districts of Africa. W. Bulmer and Company, 1799.

**Peacock F.** Chamberlain's Waders: The Definitive Guide to Southern Africa's Shorebirds. Pavo Publishing, 2016.

**Raby P.** Bright Paradise: Victorian Scientific Travellers. Chatto & Windus, 1996.

**Raby P.** Alfred Russel Wallace: A Life. Chatto & Windus, 2001.

**Ridgely R S and Tudor G.** The Birds of South America (Two volumes). Oxford University Press, 1989 and 1994.

**Ripley D.** Trail of the Moneybird. Longmans, 1947.

**Robertson D.** Survive the Savage Sea. Elek Books, 1973.

**Seebohm H.** Siberia in Europe. John Murray, 1880. Siberia in Asia. John Murray, 1882. Reprinted as The Birds of Siberia (One volume), 1901.

**Severin T.** The Spice Islands Voyage: In Search of Wallace. Little, Brown and Co., 1997.

**Shepherd N.** The Living Mountain. Aberdeen University Press, 1977.

**Shipton E.** That Untravelled World. Hodder & Stoughton, 1969.

**Shipton E.** The Six Mountain-Travel Books. Diadem Books, 1985.

**Slocum J.** Sailing Alone Around the World. The Century Company, 1900.

**Smith S B.** Wild Wings to the Northlands. Witherby, 1970.

**Smythies B E.** The Birds of Borneo. Oliver & Boyd, 1960. Second Edition, 1968. Third Edition, 1981.

**Snow D.** The Cotingas. British Museum (Natural History)/Cornell University Press, 1982.

**Steinbeck J.** The Log from the *Sea of Cortez*. Penguin, 1995. First published as Sea of Cortez, Viking Press, 1941.

**Summers-Smith D.** In Search of Sparrows. T & A D Poyser, 1992.

**Thomas J & Lewington R.** The Butterflies of Britain & Ireland. Dorling Kindersley Ltd, 1991. Revised editions by British Wildlife Publishing, 2010 and 2014.

**Thoreau H D.** Walden. Ticknor and Fields, 1854.

**Tilman H.W.** The Seven Mountain-Travel Books. Diadem Books, 1983.

**Tilman H.W.** The Eight Sailing/Mountain-Exploration Books. Diadem Books, 1987.

**Tunnicliffe C F.** Shorelands Summer Diary. Collins, 1952.

**Turgenev I.** Sketches from a Hunter's Album. Penguin Classics, 1990. Originally published in the Russian Journal *The Contemporary* between 1847 and 1851.

**Voous K H and Cameron A.** Owls of the Northern Hemisphere. Collins, 1988.

**Wallace A R.** A Narrative of Travels on the Amazon and Rio Negro. Reeve & Co., 1853.

**Wallace A R.** The Malay Archipelago: The Land of the Orang–utan, and the Bird of Paradise (Two volumes). Macmillan & Co., 1869.

**White G.** The Natural History of Selborne. Penguin Classics, 1977. Originally published by Gilbert White's brother, Benjamin, in 1789.

**Worsley F A.** Shackleton's Boat Journey. Hodder & Stoughton, 1940.

**Wulf A.** The Invention of Nature: The Adventures of Alexander von Humboldt, the Lost Hero of Science. John Murray, 2015.

# A MIND-BLOWING BIRDING TRIP TO A PLANET CALLED EARTH

Printed in Great Britain
by Amazon